MW00355730

Methods
and Materials
for teaching the gifted

Fourth Edition

Methods
and Materials
for teaching the gifted

Edited by
Frances A. Karnes, Ph.D.,
and Suzanne M. Bean, Ph.D.

PRUFROCK PRESS INC.
WACO, TEXAS

Library of Congress Cataloging-in-Publication Data

Methods and materials for teaching the gifted / edited by Frances A. Karnes, Ph.D. and
Suzanne M. Bean, Ph.D. -- Fourth edition.
     pages cm
  ISBN 978-1-61821-267-2 (pbk.)
  1. Gifted children--Education. 2. Gifted children--Identification. I. Karnes, Frances A. II.
Bean, Suzanne M., 1957-
  LC3993.M48 2014
  371.95--dc23
                              2014017524

Copyright ©2015 Prufrock Press Inc.

Edited by Lacy Compton

Cover and layout design by Allegra Denbo

ISBN-13: 978-1-61821-267-2

No part of this book may be reproduced, translated, stored in a retrieval system, or transmitted,
in any form or by any means, electronic, mechanical, photocopying, microfilming, recording, or
otherwise, without written permission from the publisher.

Printed in the United States of America.

At the time of this book's publication, all facts and figures cited are the most current available.
All telephone numbers, addresses, and websites URLs are accurate and active. All publications,
organizations, websites, and other resources exist as described in the book, and all have been
verified. The authors and Prufrock Press Inc. make no warranty or guarantee concerning the
information and materials given out by organizations or content found at websites, and we are
not responsible for any changes that occur after this book's publication. If you find an error,
please contact Prufrock Press Inc.

Prufrock Press Inc.
P.O. Box 8813
Waco, TX 76714-8813
Phone: (800) 998-2208
Fax: (800) 240-0333
http://www.prufrock.com

DEDICATION

We dedicate this book to our families for their support and love:

» Ray, Christopher, John, Leighanne, Mary Ryan, Mo, Emma, Brooks, Betsy Karnes, and Jack Sullivan, and
» Mark, Meriweather, and Hudson Bean.

This book also is dedicated to all gifted students and the teachers who help them realize their potential.

TABLE OF CONTENTS

SECTION IV: STRATEGIES FOR BEST PRACTICE

SECTION V: SUPPORTING AND ENHANCING GIFTED PROGRAMS

ACKNOWLEDGEMENTS

We thank the chapter authors who have given their time and expertise to contribute to this book and to the field of gifted education. To Joel McIntosh and the staff at Prufrock Press, we extend sincere gratitude for the opportunity to work on this book. For supporting this book and other professional accomplishments, we offer deep appreciation to our colleagues and administrators at The University of Southern Mississippi and Mississippi University for Women.

INTRODUCTION TO THE FOURTH EDITION

BY FRANCES A. KARNES AND SUZANNE M. BEAN

The fourth edition of *Methods and Materials for Teaching the Gifted* gives readers a current look at the best strategies and practices in the field of gifted education. The revised text offers a fresh approach to differentiating instruction for gifted learners. Many of the leading experts in gifted education have contributed their findings about what works best for gifted learners in the 21st century. The newly revised edition is an excellent introduction to gifted education with rigorous, relevant, real-world learning.

A special focus is given to using the Gifted Education Programming Standards and the Common Core State Standards. All chapters of this comprehensive textbook are written by respected leaders in the field of gifted education. The authors review the unique needs of gifted learners and give current information on instructional planning and evaluation, strategies for best practices, and ongoing enhancement and support of gifted programs.

Section I offers information related to the importance of standards to ensure that gifted and talented students receive the quality and type of educational services they need. The Gifted

Programming Standards identify the characteristics of effective programs and services in gifted education and ensure a degree of consistency across schools and school districts so that all students receive a quality education. Educators of gifted learners also must examine the Common Core State Standards to determine the degree to which they respond to the varying needs of gifted students.

Section II offers a synopsis of the unique characteristics of many types of gifted learners, followed by Section III, which offers many chapters for instructional planning, focusing on differentiating content, processes, products, learning environments, and assessments for gifted learners. Section IV features the current best instructional practices for innovative thinking and leadership, problem-based learning, technology literacy, independent study, simulation and gaming, and more. Finally, Section V offers the latest information on finding external funding sources for gifted programs as well as important public relations strategies for building and maintaining support for gifted programs. Each chapter in the fourth edition gives updated resources including new books, teaching materials, and websites for teaching gifted learners.

Preservice and in-service teachers who work with gifted students in the general education classroom and in specialized programs will find the fourth edition useful for rigorous and relevant instructional planning. The fourth edition will also help school principals, curriculum coordinators, and other administrators who oversee gifted programs and services, ensuring that they are current on the best strategies and curricula for learners in kindergarten through grade 12. Parents of gifted learners may also use the text as a guide for home instruction or as a supplement to the instruction their children receive in school.

CHANGING FORCES
IN EDUCATION

GIFTED EDUCATION PROGRAMMING STANDARDS

1 Chapter

BY SUSAN K. JOHNSEN

Since 1957, when the Soviet Union launched Sputnik, there has been a call for standards for both students and teachers. This national standards movement gained impetus with the publication of *A Nation at Risk* (National Commission on Excellence in Education, 1983). In this report, the National Commission on Excellence in Education recommended that schools, colleges, and universities set higher expectations and develop a nationwide system of state and local standardized tests. Over the past 30 years, all of the states have adopted some form of standards-based education system and professional associations have approved teacher practice standards and content standards in most subject areas. The No Child Left Behind Act has required states to certify highly qualified teachers and to test students annually in mathematics and reading in grades 3–8 and once in high school (U.S. Department of Education, 2008). More recently, the Council of Chief State School Officers (CCSSO) and the National Governors Association (NGA) Center for Best Practices initiated professional committees to develop professional standards for teachers and the Common Core State

Standards (CCSS) in core content areas. This work culminated in the development of the Interstate Teacher Assessment and Support Consortium (InTASC) model core teaching standards (CCSSO, 2011) and national standards in English/language arts and mathematics (NGA & CCSSO, 2010a, 2010b, 2010c). Currently, assessments are being designed to measure students' performance (see Partnership for Assessment of Readiness for College and Careers [PARCC] Assessment, n.d., and Smarter Balanced Assessment Consortium, n.d.) and teachers' performance on these standards (see Teacher Performance Assessment, 2011).

Gifted educators have become involved in this standards movement to ensure that gifted and talented students will receive the quality and type of educational services they need. They have developed books for using the CCSS with gifted and talented students (see Johnsen & Sheffield, 2013; VanTassel-Baska, 2013), developed professional teaching preparation standards (see Johnsen, VanTassel-Baska, & Robinson, 2008; Kitano, Montgomery, VanTassel-Baska, & Johnsen, 2008), and developed program standards (see Johnsen, 2012; National Association for Gifted Children [NAGC], 2010). Although all of these standards work together in forming a comprehensive and cohesive approach for developing teachers and curriculum that is effective with gifted and talented students, this chapter will address primarily the NAGC Pre-K–Grade 12 Gifted Programming Standards (Gifted Programming Standards)—their purpose, history and development, description, and use.

Purpose of the Gifted Programming Standards

Standards are important to professional fields and provide benefits to all educators (Johnsen, 2011a; 2012). Given the lack of a federal mandate to identify and serve students with gifts and talents, coupled with the great variations in services across states, the Gifted Programming Standards can identify the characteristics of effective programs and services in gifted education and ensure a degree of consistency across schools and school districts so that all students receive a quality education (Johnsen et al., 2008). They provide coherence, structure, and guidance for establishing quality gifted education programs.

They ensure that gifted and talented students are adequately recognized and served at school, in the community, and at home. Because they describe quality program characteristics, they enable educators to establish critical benchmarks for improvement, which leads to more effective program evaluation. Along with evaluation, they provide a structure for developing policies and rules at the local, state, and national levels. With the Gifted Programming Standards, policymakers and legislators can focus on what is important in gifted education and advocate for rules and new legislation.

The Gifted Programming Standards also build consensus and help differentiate gifted education from the broader field of education. These differentiating characteristics then help gifted educators build respect toward and promote programming for gifted students. Others outside the field of gifted education are able to understand the importance that the field of gifted education places on serving underrepresented populations. The Gifted Programming Standards reinforce the idea that diversity exists in our society and in each individual's expression of gifts and talents (Johnsen, 2006).

The standards can be used as a guide for professional development of individual teachers and for entire school districts, informing others about evidence-based classroom practices that are essential to improving outcomes for gifted and talented students. They can also help faculty in teacher preparation institutions identify relevant theory, research, and pedagogy in designing courses. Moreover, they can provide points for discussion and collaboration among educators, families, and other community stakeholders (Johnsen, 2011a). Without standards, services to gifted and talented students are left to the discretion of decision makers who may or may not have a background or even an interest in gifted education.

History and Development of the Gifted Programming Standards

The first set of standards developed in the field of gifted education were competencies for teachers in the early 1980s when the NAGC Professional Training Institutes involved university faculty and practitioners in discussions of professional development issues and training guidelines (Kitano et al., 2008; Robinson & Kolloff, 2006). During the same time period, The Association for the Gifted, a division of the Council for Exceptional Children (CEC-TAG), established standards in 1989 to address professional development of teachers, including coursework for initial teacher preparation programs. The NAGC Professional Development Division continued this early work by conducting a series of symposia, which eventually resulted in the NAGC Standards for Graduate Programs in Gifted Education (Parker, 1996). NAGC and CEC-TAG (2006, 2011) next collaborated in developing initial and advanced standards for the preparation of teachers. The initial teacher preparation standards were approved and adopted by the National Council for Accreditation of Teacher Education in 2006; the advanced standards, in 2011. The initial standards are for those programs that are directed toward educators who are seeking their first certificate in gifted education, whether it is at the undergraduate or graduate level. The advanced standards are for those educators who already have an initial certificate.

Paralleling this work in teacher preparation, gifted educators developed the first Gifted Program Standards in 1998, which were designed to assist school districts in developing and implementing programs (Landrum & Shaklee, 1998). These standards were organized within seven areas (e.g., Program Design, Program Administration and Management, Socio-Emotional Guidance and Counseling, Student Identification, Curriculum and Instruction, Professional Development, Program Evaluation) and included minimum and exemplary performance levels. Each standard also provided a description, rationale, benefits, potential barriers, and sample outcomes (Landrum, Callahan, & Shaklee, 2001).

The effort for revising the 1998 Gifted Program Standards took more than 10 years and involved NAGC, CEC-TAG, and others who sought to improve the education of gifted and talented students. NAGC created a Professional Standards Committee that oversaw the revision work. Initially, the committee aligned each of the 1998 Gifted Program Standards to the teacher preparation standards and identified research support for each standard. The research support included literature/theory-based, research-based, and practice-based research as defined below (CEC, 2010).

1. *Theory/literature-based.* Knowledge or skills are based on theories or philosophical reasoning. They include knowledge and skills derived from sources such as position papers, policy analyses, and descriptive reviews of the literature.

2. *Research-based.* Knowledge or skills are based on peer-reviewed studies that use appropriate research methodologies to address questions of cause and effect and that researchers have independently replicated and found to be effective.

3. *Practice-based.* Knowledge and skills are derived from a number of sources. Practices based on a small number of studies or nomination procedures, such as promising practices, are usually practice-based. Practice-based knowledge or skills also include those derived primarily from model and lighthouse programs. Practice-based knowledge and skills include professional wisdom. These practices have been used so widely with practical evidence of effectiveness that there is an implicit professional assumption that the practice is effective. Practice-based knowledge and skills also include "emerging practice," practices that arise from teachers' classroom experiences validated through some degree of action research. (pp. 9–10)

Following this alignment and identification of research support, the Professional Standards Committee made recommendations to the NAGC Board for updating the standards. A smaller workgroup was then appointed to make the revision. The revision needed to (a) reflect the current research in the field; (b) align to the teacher preparation standards so that they shared common themes (e.g., diversity, twice-exceptional learners, technology, differentiation); (c) integrate special education and recent special education regulations into the standards; (d) provide more specificity within all of the program standards; and (e) consider the variations among state policy, rules, and regulations that influences the standards' language. The workgroup surveyed NAGC and CEC-TAG members to identify their use of the standards and other areas for revision and then developed these principles in revising the standards (Johnsen, 2012; NAGC, 2010):

1. *Giftedness is dynamic and is constantly developing.* Within the Gifted Programming Standards, students are defined as those having gifts and talents rather than those with stable traits. This definition is in line with current understandings of giftedness. Instead of a static definition of giftedness (e.g., a student is either gifted or not), more researchers have acknowledged the developmental nature of giftedness, which includes a set of interacting components such as general intelligence, domain-related skills, creativity, and nonintellective factors (Cattell, 1971; Gagné, 1999; Renzulli, 1978; Tannenbaum, 1991). This developmental perspective strongly influences identification and programming practices because educators are aware that a point-in-time test or a once-a-week program may not recognize or develop giftedness that takes time and supports.

2. *Giftedness is found among students from a variety of backgrounds.* The workgroup made a deliberate effort to ensure that diversity was included across all standards. Diversity was defined as differences among groups of people and individuals based on ethnicity, race, socioeconomic status, gender, exceptionalities, language, religion, sexual orientation, and geographical area. Because the underrepresentation of diverse students in gifted education programs is well documented (Daniels, 1998; Ford, 2011b; Ford & Harris, 1999; Morris, 2002), specific evidence-based practices needed to be incorporated to ensure that identification procedures were equitable (Ford & Harmon, 2001; Frasier, Garcia, & Passow, 1995; Harris, Plucker, Rapp, & Martinez, 2009), curriculum was culturally responsive (Ford, 2011a; Ford, Tyson, Howard, & Harris, 2000; Kitano & Pedersen, 2002a, 2002b), and learning environments fostered cultural understanding for success in a diverse society (Harper & Antonio, 2008; Zirkel, 2008).

3. *Standards should focus on student outcomes rather than practices.* The workgroup decided not to identify separate acceptable versus exemplary practices as in the previous 1998 Gifted Program Standards but to focus on the practices' effects on students. This emphasis is in agreement with the national movement toward accountability. Rather than counting the number of practices used, it's more important to examine the effect of the

practices on gifted and talented students' social, emotional, and cognitive development.

4. *All educators are responsible for the education of students with gifts and talents.* Educators were defined as administrators, teachers, counselors, and other instructional support staff from a variety of professional backgrounds (e.g., general education, special education, and gifted education). Research suggests that collaboration enhances talent development (Gentry & Ferriss, 1999; Landrum, 2002; Purcell & Leppien, 1998) and improves the likelihood that gifted students with disabilities receive services in gifted education programs (Coleman & Johnsen, 2011).

5. *Students with gifts and talents should receive services throughout the day and in all environments that are based on their abilities, needs, and interests.* The workgroup decided to use the word "programming" rather than the word "program," which might connote a unidimensional approach (e.g., a once-a-week type of program option). This emphasis is critical given the patchwork of programs and services that are currently provided to gifted and talented students, which vary from state to state and from school to school (NAGC & Council of State Directors of Programs for the Gifted [CSDPG], 2010–11).

Based on the principles, the Gifted Programming Standards were therefore quite different from the 1998 Program Standards because they (a) focused on student outcomes, (b) included only those practices that had research support, (c) were aligned with the NAGC/CEC-TAG teacher preparation standards, (d) included more standards that emphasized diversity, and (e) emphasized stronger relationships between gifted education, general education, and special education.

Following the development of a draft set of Gifted Programming Standards, the workgroup presented them at the NAGC University Network meeting and at special sessions at the NAGC annual convention. Comments were collected and used in revisions. A final draft was presented to the NAGC and CEC-TAG Boards in 2010.

Both boards unanimously approved the new standards and they were released at the 2010 NAGC annual fall convention.

Description of Gifted Programming Standards

The final set of standards contains six areas for programming: Learning and Development, Assessment, Curriculum Planning and Instruction, Learning Environments, Programming, and Professional Development (see Appendix A). Within each of these standards are listed student outcomes and evidence-based practices. For example, within the Learning and Development Standard, one of the outcomes is, "Students with gifts and talents demonstrate self-knowledge with respect to their interests, strengths, identities, and needs in social emotional development and in intellectual, academic, creative, leadership, and artistic domains" (Student Outcome 1.1). One of the two evidence-based practices that might influence the outcome is, "Educators engage students with gifts and talents in identifying interests, strengths, and gifts" (Evidence-Based Practice 1.1.1). The Gifted Programming Standards therefore describe not only what practices need to be implemented in meeting the standard but also how the practice might affect the gifted and talented student's development.

Each of the six standards represents an important emphasis in developing and implementing effective programming for students with gifts and talents and are described below:

1. *Learning and Development.* Educators, recognizing the learning and developmental differences of students with gifts and talents, promote ongoing self-understanding, awareness of their needs, and cognitive and affective growth of these students in school, home, and community settings to ensure specific student outcomes (NAGC, 2010, p. 8).

This first standard is foundational to the remaining standards because educators must first understand the population's characteristics and needs before providing services. The student outcomes recognize learning and developmental differences of gifted and talented students and stress each student's self-understanding, awareness of needs, and cognitive and affective growth. To achieve these outcomes, educators (a) help students identify interests, strengths, and gifts (Lee & Olszewski-Kubilius, 2006; Simonton, 2000; VanTassel-Baska, 2009); (b) develop activities that match each student's developmental level and culture-based learning needs (Ford, 2011b; Hébert, 1991; Shade, Kelly, & Oberg, 1997); (c) use research-based grouping practices that allow them to interact with individuals of various gifts, talents, abilities, and strengths (Gentry & Owen, 1999; Kulik & Kulik, 1992; Rogers, 1991); (d) provide role models, mentors, and identify out-of-school learning opportunities (Bloom & Sosniak, 1981; Hébert & Speirs Neumeister, 2000; VanTassel-Baska, 2006); (e) collaborate with families (Moon, Jurich, & Feldhusen, 1998; Williams & Baber, 2007); (f) design interventions to develop cognitive and affective growth (Kerr & Kurpius, 2004; Kettler, Shiu, & Johnsen, 2006); and (g) provide students with college and career guidance (Greene, 2003; Maxwell, 2007).

2. *Assessment.* Assessments provide information about identification, learning progress and outcomes, and evaluation of programming for students with gifts and talents in all domains (NAGC, 2010, p. 9).

The student outcomes in this standard relate to each student's (a) equal access, ability to show talents and gifts in different domains, and express diversity during the identification process; (b) demonstration of advanced and complex learning on assessments; and (c) ability to show significant learning progress as a result of evaluation. To achieve these outcomes, educators use evidence-based practices to (a) develop environments and instructional activities where students can express diverse gifts and talents (Borland & Wright, 1994; Grantham, 2003; Hertzog, 2005); (b) use comprehensive, cohesive, ongoing, and technically adequate procedures during the identification process that do not discriminate against any student with potential (Ford & Trotman, 2000; Johnsen, 2011b; Ryser, 2011); (c) use various types of qualitative and quantitative assessments such as performances, products, off-level tests, and other types of pre-/postmeasures to assess students' progress (Baker & Schacter, 1996; Baum, Owen, & Oreck, 1996; Reis, Burns, & Renzulli, 1992; VanTassel-Baska, 2007) and (d) implement an evaluation that has sufficient resources and is purposeful, reliable, and valid for examining the effectiveness of practices on student learning (Avery, VanTassel-Baska, & O'Neill, 1997; Callahan & Reis, 2004; Moon, 1996).

3. *Curriculum Planning and Instruction.* Educators apply the theory and research-based models of curriculum and instruction related to students with gifts and talents and respond to their needs by planning, selecting, adapting, and creating culturally relevant curriculum and by using a repertoire of evidence-based instructional strategies to ensure specific student outcomes (NAGC, 2010, p. 10).

This standard addresses not only curriculum but also talent development, multicultural strategies, and materials and resources. Desired student outcomes include students' (a) demonstration of growth commensurate with their aptitude, (b) development of their abilities in their domain of talent or area of interest, (c) use of independent investigations, and (d) use of knowledge and skills for being productive in a multicultural diverse and global society. To achieve these outcomes, educators (a) develop comprehensive, cohesive programming for students with a variety of gifts and talents that is based on standards, incorporates differentiated curricula in all domains, uses a balanced assessment system, and paces instruction according to each student's rate of learning (Kitano et al., 2008; Stiggins, 2008; Tomlinson, 2004; VanTassel-Baska, 2004); (b) use specific strategies such as critical and creative thinking, metacognitive, problem solving, and inquiry models (Anderson & Krathwohl, 2001; Elder & Paul, 2004; Hartman, 2001); (c) develop and use culturally responsive curriculum that integrates career exploration (Ford, 2006; Ford et al., 2000); and (d) use high-quality resources (Pyryt, 2003; Siegle, 2004).

4. *Learning Environments*. Safe learning environments foster personal and social responsibility, multicultural competence, and interpersonal and technical communication skills for leadership in the 21st Century to ensure specific student outcomes (NAGC, 2010, p. 11).

Specific student outcomes within the broader area of personal competence include the development of self-awareness, self-advocacy, self-efficacy, confidence, motivation, resilience, independence, curiosity, and risk taking. Within social competence, students develop positive peer relationships and social interactions; within leadership, personal and social responsibility; within cultural competence, skills in communicating, teaming, and collaborating with diverse individuals; and within communication competence, interpersonal and technical communication skills. To achieve these outcomes, educators create environments that (a) have high expectations, provide opportunities for self-exploration, support diverse learners, and view mistakes as learning opportunities (Cross, Stewart, & Coleman, 2003; Dweck & Kamins, 1999; McKown & Weinstein, 2008; Neihart, 2002); (b) provide opportunities for social interaction and solitude (Norris, 2003; Nugent, 2005; VanTassel-Baska, Cross, & Olenchak, 2008); (c) provide opportunities for development of personal responsibility and leadership (Pleasants, Stephens, Selph, & Pfeiffer, 2004; Ross & Smyth, 1995; Smyth & Ross, 1999); (d) promote positive interactions with artistic/creative and chronological-age peers (Enersen, 1993; Olszewski-Kubilius & Grant, 1994); (e) model appreciation for diversity and support structured opportunities for collaboration among diverse learners (Cline & Schwartz, 2000; den Brok, Levy, Rodriguez, & Wubbels, 2002); and (f) teach a variety of forms of communication, including the use of assistive technologies (Berger, 2003; Kitano & Lewis, 2005; Kolesinski & Leroux, 1992).

5. *Programming*. Educators are aware of empirical evidence regarding (a) the cognitive, creative, and affective development of learners with gifts and talents, and (b) programming that meets their concomitant needs. Educators use this expertise systematically and collaboratively to develop, implement, and effectively manage comprehensive services for students with a variety of gifts and talents to ensure specific student outcomes (NAGC, 2010, p. 12).

In this standard, educators use a variety of programming options that are implemented by teams of educators who have adequate resources and policies and procedures to implement comprehensive services. Outcomes include each student participating in a variety of coordinated and comprehensive programming options, which are guided by clear policies and procedures that enhance their progress and performance and address future career goals. To achieve these outcomes, educators (a) develop and implement a comprehensive set of services such as acceleration, enrichment, grouping, individualized learning, mentorships, internships, and technology that develop relevant student talent areas (Berger, 2003; Colangelo, Assouline, & Gross, 2004; Johnsen & Johnson, 2007; Kulik & Kulik, 1992; Renzulli & Reis, 2003; Siegle & McCoach, 2005); (b) coordinate services and collaborate with families and other professionals from general education, special education, and related professional services (Campbell & Verna, 2007; Coleman & Johnsen, 2011); (c) provide sufficient funding to meet programming goals (Baker & Friedman-Nimz, 2003; NAGC & CSDPG, 2010–2011); (d) create clear policies and procedures that address advanced learning (Ford & Trotman, 2000; Zeidner & Schleyer, 1999); and (e) provide professional guidance to students regarding career options (Greene, 2003; Maxwell, 2007; Wessel, 1999).

> 6. *Professional Development.* All educators (administrators, teachers, counselors, and other instructional support staff) build their knowledge and skills using the NAGC/CEC-TAG Teacher Standards for Gifted and Talented Education and the National Staff Development Standards. They formally assess professional development needs related to the standards, develop and monitor plans, systematically engage in training to meet the identified needs, and demonstrate mastery of standards. They access resources to provide for release time, funding for continuing education, and substitute support. These practices are judged through the assessment of relevant student outcomes (NAGC, 2010, p. 13).

This standard addresses high-quality educator development that creates lifelong learners who are ethical in their practices. Student outcomes include the development of talents in the social and emotional areas as a result of educators' professional learning. To achieve these outcomes, educators (a) participate in ongoing, research-supported, and multiple forms of professional development that models how to develop environments and instructional activities for students with gifts and talents (Garet, Porter, Desimone, Birman, & Yoon, 2001; Kitano et al., 2008); (b) provide sufficient human and material resources for professional development (Guskey, 2000; Johnsen, Haensly, Ryser, & Ford, 2002); (c) become involved in professional organizations and read publications related to gifted education (Callahan, Cooper, & Glascock, 2003; Landrum et al., 2001); (d) assess their practices, identify areas for personal growth, and participate in ongoing professional development that addresses these areas (Bain, Bourgeois, & Pappas, 2003; Gubbins et al., 2002); (e) respond to cultural and personal frames of reference (Ford & Trotman, 2001; Frasier et al., 1995); and (f) comply with rules, policies, and standards of ethical practice (Copenhaver, 2002; Klein & Lugg, 2002).

Using the Gifted Programming Standards

How might educators use the Gifted Programming Standards? The Gifted Programming Standards may be used in a variety of ways such as self-assessment, identifying student outcomes and assessments, selecting teachers, professional development, program evaluation, and advocacy. All of these uses are important to the development, implementation, and improvement of programs and services for gifted and talented students.

Self-Assessment

The Gifted Programming Standards can be used for self-assessment in determining whether or not a teacher, a school, a school district, or even a state is implementing best practices and addressing important student outcomes. For example, teachers might want to consider which evidence-based practices are already being implemented in their classrooms, which ones are effective with students, and which ones might need to be implemented. At the school or district level, educators might self-assess by aligning the standards with local and state programs and identifying which standards are and are not being covered. Following this review, educators then might identify one or more standards to implement school- or districtwide, which would also entail the specification of student outcomes, professional development activities, and implementation supports. At the state level, educators might identify which standards are included in the state plan and identify standards that may be missing or less emphasized. At this level, the self-assessment might lead to new rules and regulations.

Identification of Student Outcomes and Assessments

Using the standards, educators might want to review the student outcomes as a whole. The outcomes can be clustered into three categories: personal, social, and academic (see Table 1.1). Is the school addressing all three of the categories? If not, which ones might be important to address immediately and which ones might be considered at a later time? What assessments might be used to measure the

TABLE 1.1

Summary of Student Outcomes

Personal Student Outcomes	▸ Demonstrate self-knowledge. ▸ Understand how they learn and grow. ▸ Recognize preferred approaches to learning. ▸ Demonstrate understanding of differences. ▸ Develop knowledge and skills for a diverse society. ▸ Value their own and other's language, heritage, and circumstance. ▸ Demonstrate growth in personal competence and dispositions for academic and creative productivity.
Social Student Outcomes	▸ Possess skills in communicating, teaming, and collaborating with diverse individuals and across diverse groups. ▸ Develop social competence manifested in positive peer relationships and social interactions. ▸ Use positive strategies to address social issues, including discrimination and stereotyping. ▸ Demonstrate personal and social responsibility and leadership skills. ▸ Develop competence in interpersonal and technical communication skills.
Academic Student Outcomes	▸ Demonstrate growth commensurate with ability. ▸ Become more competent in multiple talent areas. ▸ Demonstrate advanced oral and written skills, balanced biliteracy or multiliteracy, and create expressions. ▸ Become an independent investigator. ▸ Identify career goals and pathways for developing talents. ▸ Access resources to develop talents.

student outcomes? How might assessments be used to monitor learning progress over time? How might the results from the assessments be linked to gifted education programming and services? Assessments to measure student outcomes might include off-level standardized achievement measures, end-of-course or AP exams, rubrics for assessing complex products and performance, critical or creative thinking measures to assess process skills, pre-/postassessments, portfolio assessments, or student self-assessments such as journals, written products, or surveys. More free and available assessments that measure all categories of student outcomes might be found in the resources section of this chapter and in Appendix B of the *NAGC Pre-K–Grade 12 Gifted Education Programming Standards: A Guide to Planning and Implementing High-Quality Services* (Sulak & Johnsen, 2012).

Selection of Gifted Teachers

The Gifted Programming Standards and the NAGC CEC-TAG teacher preparation standards are excellent tools for selecting gifted teachers and coordinators of gifted education programs. Specific classroom practices can be selected for developing hiring criteria. For example: Does the teacher know how to design differentiated curricula that incorporate advanced, conceptually challenging, in-depth, distinctive, and complex content (see standard 3.1.4)? Does he or she use preassessments and pace instruction based on the learning rates of students and accelerate and compact learning (see standard 3.1.6)? Does he or she use inquiry models (see standard 3.4.4)? Does he or she collaborate with other educators in planning programs for students with gifts and talents (see standard 5.2.1)? Does he or she help students in identifying interests, strengths, and gifts (see standard 1.1.1)? These practices and many others within the standards are observable and helpful in identifying teachers who would provide quality instruction to gifted and talented students.

Professional Development

Following self-assessment, educators can target specific evidence-based practices for professional development at the classroom, school, or school district level. For example, educators across grade levels might want to learn more about how to implement different problem-solving models (see standard 3.4.3). The school district would then provide specific learning opportunities, perhaps related to designing problem-based curriculum and assessments to measure student progress in problem solving. Follow up and curricular resources would be provided to help teachers implement the new curricular and instructional practices. The newly designed assessments would be used to examine the effect of the practice on increasing students' problem-solving knowledge and skills. These assessments might then be used to drive more professional development in the specific practice or to new practices that the school and teachers might wish to implement.

Program Evaluation

The standards can help educators establish school- or districtwide benchmarks to monitor the progress of implementing specific evidence-based practices and their effects on student outcomes. Some example evaluation questions might include: To what degree are students demonstrating self understanding (Student Outcomes 1.1, 1.2, and 1.3), demonstrating advanced and complex learning (Student Outcome 2.3), developing abilities in their domain of talent (Student Outcome 3.3), demonstrating leadership skills (Student Outcome 4.3); and demonstrating progress in cognitive and affective areas (Student Outcome 5.1)? Collecting assessment data on student outcomes will help identify which practices are most effective and areas that need to be addressed to improve the overall program.

These data might also be used to develop an action plan (Cotabish & Krisel, 2012; NAGC, 2010). Questions that might be addressed in the plan would include:

» To what extent do we use this practice?
» What do we do to support this practice?
» What are the desired student outcomes?
» What are the gaps between what we do and what is desired?
» What information needs to be collected or action needs to be implemented?
» Who will be responsible?
» What is the timeline?

All of the evaluation data will be helpful in showing the value added by having specialized programming for gifted and talented students, in sustaining the services, and in requesting needed human and material resources.

Advocacy

All educators can use the standards to advocate for gifted education programs because they describe best practices and important student outcomes. They can be included in presentations to inform educators, policymakers, and the community about the characteristics of effective programming. Involving grassroots and administrative-level individuals can assist in policy development at the district and state level, which ultimately builds a foundation for gifted education programming that will not disappear during lean economic times (Johnsen, 2012).

Summary

The Gifted Programming Standards are part of a larger network of standards that are intended to improve the quality and type of educational services for gifted and talented students. Standards serve multiple purposes including the delineation of gifted education as a field, recognition of gifted and talented students, the identification of evidence-based practices and critical program characteristics, the specification of desired student outcomes, consistency of programming across schools, the evaluation of programs, and advocacy.

The Gifted Programming Standards were developed over a 10-year period and involved multiple stakeholders including teachers, administrators, parents, university faculty, state directors, and professional organizations (e.g., the NAGC and CEC-TAG). The standards were based on the 1998 NAGC Program Standards and the NAGC-CEC teacher preparation standards. The revision reflected the current research in the field, the national movement toward accountability, and the diversity within schools. This work culminated in the publication of the Gifted Programming Standards in 2010.

The final set of standards contains six areas for programming: Learning and Development, Assessment, Curriculum Planning and Instruction, Learning Environments, Programming, and Professional Development. All of the standards interrelate and need to be considered as a whole in implementing effective programming for gifted and talented students. Within each standard, student outcomes and evidence-based practices are identified. The practices are based on three types of research: theory and literature, peer-reviewed studies, and practice or model programs. Student outcomes address personal, social, and academic development of gifted and talented students.

Educators will find the Gifted Programming Standards useful in self-assessment, identifying student outcomes and assessments, selecting qualified gifted teachers, professional development, program evaluation, and advocacy. The main purpose for the standards in gifted education is to ensure that each and every gifted student receives the type of programming and services that will develop his or her talents and help him or her reach his or her goals.

Teacher Statement

How many times have you heard, or possibly even said, "The one thing you can always count on is change?" Change is a part of our everyday lives. Change is certainly a part of the world of education. As a teacher of elementary gifted students I have been involved in and witnessed the ever-revolving "wheel of change" over the years. Change is inevitable. Change is good. Change is progress. Yet, even as I visualize this spinning wheel of change in education, I am able to see its center. For the wheel is anchored, stable, and I also realize that some things will never change. For me, this is where my understanding of the Gifted Education Programming Standards comes into play. These gifted standards provide gifted education programs across the nation with a stable foundation on which to build. They were created to ensure that every gifted student receives appropriate programming and services that allow him or her to reach their individual goals. This reminds me of the role I play and the responsibilities I have as a gifted education teacher.

In my classroom, standards provide me with a road map that I use to guide and direct my teaching. I use them to help identify best practices and to help me create quality gifted educational experiences for my students. Understanding my students' interests and strengths helps me to better plan appropriate activities for them. These activities help better prepare them for the 21st century and incorporate the specific student outcomes and skills deemed appropriate for an elementary gifted student. I use an interdisciplinary approach in my planning and teaching, where my students are encouraged to assume personal responsibility and leadership roles through service learning projects, career exploration, and interest-based units of study using the most current technological resources and a wide variety of other materials. I am constantly seeking out and searching for the very best opportunities, resources, and experiences for my students. The standards allow me to self-assess, on an ongoing basis, as to whether or not I am addressing the whole child—socially, emotionally, and cognitively—and whether or not I am using best practices to do so. I reflect frequently to ensure that I am indeed addressing the unique needs of every student I teach. The standards also provide guidance as to specific professional development opportunities I should seek out in order to improve my skills as a teacher of the gifted. I am able to search for specific learning opportunities that will enhance my teaching and drive my instruction since I have a clearer understanding of what my students should know and be able to do. Finally, I use the standards to help me solicit support for my students and our gifted program. It is a program I thoroughly support and believe in myself, and I understand I am my students' voice. I must advocate for them and their unique needs. To not do so would be an injustice to my students. Change will happen, but if I can use the gifted programming standards as they were intended to be used, I can be that stable and secure anchor that my students desperately need.

—Dawn Dawkins, Teacher of the Gifted, Mississippi

DISCUSSION QUESTIONS

1. In examining the gifted education standards, how do your school district's standards compare? Your state's standards?

2. In assessing your implementation of these standards, what are your strengths? Your weaknesses? Develop a professional development plan for yourself.

3. How might you use the standards in advocating for gifted education services?

4. Which student outcomes does your gifted education program currently address the most? What are the gaps in the program?

5. What would you use in assessing student outcomes in the personal, social, and academic areas?

6. Create a form for observing teachers' best practices based on the standards. What did you include? Why?

7. If you were planning professional learning for the teachers in your school or in your school district about the standards, what would you include in your presentation?

Resources

Publications

Farkas, S., Duffett, A., & Loveless, T. (2008, June). *High-achieving students in the era of No Child Left Behind*. Washington, DC: Thomas B. Fordham Institute. Retrieved from http://www.edexcellence.net/publications/high-achieving-students-in.html

This report describes how the bottom 10% of students have shown progress in reading and math but those at the 90th percentile have made minimal gains. The authors concluded that this pattern is associated with the introduction of accountability systems in general.

Johnsen, S. K., & Sheffield, L. J. (Eds.). (2013). *Using the Common Core State Standards for mathematics with gifted and advanced learners*. Waco, TX: Prufrock Press.

This book describes how the CCSS for mathematics can be used with gifted and advanced learners. It includes an alignment of the CCSS standards with the gifted education programming standards, differentiated learning experiences and assessments, and ideas for implementing the standards.

Johnsen, S. K. (Ed.). (2012). *Using the NAGC pre-K–grade 12 gifted education programming standards*. Waco, TX: Prufrock Press.

Each of the Gifted Education Programming Standards is described in this 312-page book. Chapters focus on creating environments for social and emotional development, creating programs and services for culturally and linguistically different gifted students, identifying gifted students, curriculum planning and instruction, instructional strategies, programming models, professional development, evaluation, state models, designing action plans, and advocacy. Appendix B describes assessments that might be used in measuring student outcomes.

Johnsen, S., VanTassel-Baska, J., & Robinson, A. (2008). *Using the national gifted education standards for university teacher preparation programs*. Thousand Oaks, CA: Corwin Press.

This book describes the 10 content standards that educators in teacher preparation institutions can use to develop coursework for initial gifted education programs at the undergraduate or graduate levels. Specific suggestions are made for course and assessment design.

Kitano, M., Montgomery, D., VanTassel-Baska, J., & Johnsen, S. (2008). *Using the national gifted education standards for PreK–12 professional development*. Thousand Oaks, CA: Corwin Press.

The authors show how the teacher preparation standards might be used by pre-K to grade 12 practitioners in assessing teacher needs, identifying expected outcomes for professional development, building a standards-based professional development model, assessing professional development activities, and infusing the diversity standards within professional development models. Appendices include classroom observation instruments and needs assessments.

National Association for Gifted Children. (2010). *NAGC pre-K–grade 12 gifted programming standards: A blueprint for quality gifted education programs.* Washington, DC:
Author. Retrieved from http://www.nagc.org/ProgrammingStandards.aspx

    This publication contains the Gifted Programming Standards and a brief over-
view describing how the standards might be used, how they were developed, how
they relate to other professional standards, and how they are supported by research.

Plucker, J. A., Burroughs, N., & Song, R. (2010, February). *Mind the (other) gap! The
growing excellence gap in K–12 education.* Bloomington: Indiana University, School of
Education, Center for Evaluation and Education Policy. Retrieved from https://www.
iub.edu/~ceep/Gap/excellence/ExcellenceGapBrief.pdf

    Although the majority of states describe how the percentage of students per-
forming at advanced levels on state assessments has increased, these authors suggested that it is difficult to determine if these increases reflect actual improvement
in advanced performance. This report described how the majority of states have
experienced worsening excellence gaps among different subgroups of students. They
concluded that focusing on minimum competency gaps is not a sound strategy for
reducing excellence gaps.

VanTassel-Baska, J. (Ed.). (2013). *Using the common core state standards for English language arts with gifted and advanced learners.* Waco, TX: Prufrock Press.

    This book describes how the CCSS for English/language arts can be used with
gifted and advanced learners. It includes an alignment of the CCSS standards with
the gifted education programming standards, differentiated learning experiences and
assessments, and ideas for implementing the standards.

Websites

Advanced Standards in Gifted Education Teacher Preparation—http://www.nagc.org/
advancedstandards.aspx

    These are the standards for preparing teachers who already have an initial certif-
icate in gifted education. They focus on assessment; curricular content knowledge;
program, services, and outcomes; research and inquiry; leadership and policy; professional and ethical practice; and collaboration.

Common Core State Standards Initiative—http://www.corestandards.org

    The CCSS in mathematics and in English/language arts can be accessed at this
website. Along with the books that show how to differentiate the CCSS (see Johnsen
& Sheffield, 2013, and VanTassel-Baska, 2013), these standards provide a curricular
framework aligned to 21st-century skills.

InTASC Model Core Teaching Standards: A Resource for State Dialogue—http://www.ccsso.
org/Documents/2011/InTASC_Model_Core_Teaching_Standards_2011.pdf

    The InTASC model core teaching standards can be accessed from this website.
The 10 standards address the learner and learning, content knowledge, instructional
practices, and professional responsibility.

NCATE Program Standards and Report Forms—http://www.ncate.org/Standards/ProgramStandardsandReportForms/tabid/676/Default.aspx

The initial standards in teacher preparation can be retrieved at this website. These standards contain the knowledge and skills that every gifted educator should know and be able to do.

References

Anderson, L. W., & Krathwohl, D. R. (Eds.). (2001). *A taxonomy for learning, teaching, and assessing: A revision of Bloom's taxonomy of educational objectives.* New York, NY: Longman.

Avery, L. D., VanTassel-Baska, J., & O'Neill, B. (1997). Making evaluation work: One school district's experience. *Gifted Child Quarterly, 41,* 124–132.

Baker, B. D., & Friedman-Nimz, R. (2003). Gifted children, vertical equity, and state school finance policies and practices. *Journal of Education Finance, 28*(4), 523–555.

Baker, E. L., & Schacter, J. (1996). Expert benchmarks for student academic performance: The case for gifted children. *Gifted Child Quarterly, 40,* 61–65.

Bain, S., Bourgeois, S., & Pappas, D. (2003). Linking theoretical models to actual practices: A survey of teachers in gifted education. *Roeper Review, 25,* 166–172.

Baum, S. M., Owen, S. V., & Oreck, B. A. (1996). Talent beyond words: Identification of potential talent in dance and music in elementary students. *Gifted Child Quarterly, 40,* 93–101.

Berger, S. (2003). Technology and gifted learners. In W. A. Owings & L. S. Kaplan (Eds.), *Best practices, best thinking, and emerging issues in school leadership* (pp. 177–190). Thousand Oaks, CA: Corwin Press.

Bloom, B. S., & Sosniak, L. A. (1981). Talent development vs. schooling. *Educational Leadership, 39,* 86–94.

Borland, J. H., & Wright, L. (1994). Identifying young, potentially gifted, economically disadvantaged students. *Gifted Child Quarterly, 38,* 164–171.

Callahan, C., Cooper, C., & Glascock, R. (2003). *Preparing teachers to develop and enhance talent: The position of national education organizations.* Reston, VA: ERIC Clearinghouse on Disabilities and Gifted Education. (ERIC Document Reproduction Service No. ED477882)

Callahan, C., & Reis, S. (2004). *Program evaluation in gifted education: Essential readings in gifted education series.* Thousand Oaks, CA: Corwin Press.

Campbell, J. R., & Verna, M. A. (2007). Effective parental influence: Academic home climate linked to children's achievement. *Educational Research and Evaluation, 13,* 501–519.

Cattell, R. B. (1971). *Abilities: Their structure, growth, and action.* Boston, MA: Houghton Mifflin.

Cline, S., & Schwartz, D. (2000). *Diverse populations of gifted children: Meeting their needs in the regular classroom and beyond.* Columbus, OH: Prentice-Hall.

Colangelo, N., Assouline, S. G., & Gross, M. U. M. (2004). *A nation deceived: How schools hold back America's brightest students.* Iowa City: The University of Iowa, The Connie Belin & Jacqueline N. Blank International Center for Gifted Education and Talent Development.

Coleman, M. R., & Johnsen, S. K. (Eds.). (2011). *RtI for gifted students.* Waco, TX: Prufrock Press.

Copenhaver, J. (2002). *Primer for maintaining accurate special education records and meeting confidentiality requirements when serving children with disabilities—Family Educational Rights and Privacy Act (FERPA).* Logan, UT: Utah State University, Mountain Plains Regional Resource Center.

Cotabish, A., & Krisel, S. (2012). Action plans: Bringing the programming standards to life. In S. K. Johnsen (Ed.), *NAGC Pre-K–Grade 12 Gifted Education Programming*

Standards: A guide to planning and implementing high-quality services (pp. 231–254). Waco, TX: Prufrock Press.

Council for Exceptional Children. (2010). *Validation study resource manual.* Arlington, VA: Author.

Council of Chief State School Officers. (2011, April). *InTASC model core teaching standards: A resource for state dialogue.* Retrieved from http://www.ccsso.org/Documents/2011/InTASC_Model_Core_Teaching_Standards_2011.pdf

Cross, T., Stewart, R. A., & Coleman, L. (2003). Phenomenology and its implications for gifted studies research: Investigating the lebenswelt of academically gifted students attending an elementary magnet school. *Journal for the Education of the Gifted, 26,* 201–220.

Daniels, V. I. (1998). Minority students in gifted and special education programs: The case for educational equity. *Journal of Special Education, 32,* 41–44.

den Brok, P., Levy, J., Rodriguez, R., & Wubbels, T. (2002). Perceptions of Asian-American and Hispanic American teachers and their students on teacher interpersonal communication style. *Teaching and Teacher Education, 18,* 447–467.

Dweck, C. S., & Kamins, M. L. (1999). Person versus process praise and criticism: Implications for contingent self-worth and coping. *Developmental Psychology, 35,* 835–847.

Elder, L., & Paul, R. (2004). *The art of asking essential questions.* Dillon Beach, CA: The Foundation for Critical Thinking.

Enersen, D. L. (1993). Summer residential programs: Academics and beyond. *Gifted Child Quarterly, 37,* 169–176.

Ford, D. Y. (2006). Creating culturally responsive classrooms for gifted students. *Understanding Our Gifted, 19*(1), 10–14.

Ford, D. Y. (2011a). *Multicultural gifted education* (2nd ed.). Waco, TX: Prufrock Press.

Ford, D. Y. (2011b). *Reversing underachievement among gifted Black students: Theory, research, and practice* (2nd ed.). Waco, TX: Prufrock Press.

Ford, D. Y., & Harmon, D. A. (2001). Equity and excellence: Providing access to gifted education for culturally diverse students. *Journal of Secondary Gifted Education, 12,* 141–148.

Ford, D. Y., & Harris, J. J., III. (1999). *Multicultural gifted education.* New York, NY: Teachers College Press.

Ford, D. Y., & Trotman, M. F. (2000). The Office for Civil Rights and non-discriminatory testing, policies, and procedures: Implications for gifted education. *Roeper Review, 23,* 109–112.

Ford, D. Y., & Trotman, M. F. (2001). Teachers of gifted students: Suggested multicultural characteristics and competencies. *Roeper Review, 23,* 235–239.

Ford, D., Tyson, C., Howard, T., & Harris, J. J. (2000). Multicultural literature and gifted black students: Promoting self-understanding, awareness, and pride. *Roeper Review, 22,* 235–240.

Frasier, M. M., Garcia, J. H., & Passow, A. H. (1995). *A review of assessment issues in gifted education and their implications for identifying gifted minority students.* Storrs: University of Connecticut, The National Research Center on the Gifted and Talented.

Gagné, F. (1999). My convictions about the nature of abilities, gifts, and talents. *Journal for the Education of the Gifted, 22,* 109–136.

Garet, M. S., Porter, A. C., Desimone, L., Birman, B. F., & Yoon, K. S. (2001). What makes professional development effective? Results from a national sample of teachers. *American Educational Research Journal, 38,* 915–945.

Gentry, M., & Ferriss, S. (1999). StATS: A model of collaboration to develop science talent among rural students. *Roeper Review, 21,* 316–320.

Gentry, M., & Owen, S. V. (1999). An investigation of the effects of total school flexible cluster grouping on identification, achievement, and classroom practices. *Gifted Child Quarterly, 43,* 224–243.

Grantham, T. C. (2003). Increasing Black student enrollment in gifted programs: An exploration of the Pulaski County special school district's advocacy efforts. *Gifted Child Quarterly, 47,* 46–65.

Greene, M. J. (2003). Career adrift? Career counseling for the gifted and talented. *Roeper Review, 25,* 66–72.

Gubbins, E. J., Westberg, K. L., Reis, S. M., Dinnocenti, S. T., Tieso, C. L., & Muller, L. M. . . . Burns, D. E. (2002). *Implementing a professional development model using gifted education strategies with all students* (Report RM02172). Storrs: University of Connecticut, The National Research Center on the Gifted and Talented.

Guskey, T. R. (2000). *Evaluating professional development.* Thousand Oaks, CA: Corwin Press.

Harper, S. R., & Antonio, A. (2008). Not by accident: Intentionality in diversity, learning and engagement. In S. R. Harper (Ed.), *Creating inclusive campus environments for cross-cultural learning and student engagement* (pp. 1–18). Washington, DC: National Association of Student Personnel Administrators.

Harris, B., Plucker, J. A., Rapp, K. E., & Martinez, R. S. (2009). Identifying gifted and talented English language learners: A case study. *Journal for the Education of the Gifted, 32,* 368–393.

Hartman, H. J. (2001). *Metacognition in learning and instruction: Theory, research and practice.* Dordrecht, The Netherlands: Kluwer Academic Publishers.

Hébert, T. P. (1991). Meeting the affective needs of bright boys through bibliotherapy. *Roeper Review, 13,* 207–212.

Hébert, T. P., & Speirs Neumeister, K. L. (2000). University mentors in the elementary classroom: Supporting the intellectual, motivational, and emotional needs of high-ability students. *Journal for the Education of the Gifted, 24,* 122–148.

Hertzog, N. B. (2005). Equity and access: Creating general education classrooms responsive to potential giftedness. *Journal for the Education of the Gifted, 29,* 213–257.

Johnsen, S. K. (2006). *New national standards for teachers of gifted and talented students. Tempo, 26*(3), 26–31.

Johnsen, S. K. (2011a). A comparison of the Texas State Plan for the Education of Gifted/Talented Students and the 2010 NAGC Pre-K–Grade 12 Gifted Programming Standards. *Tempo, 31*(1), 10–28.

Johnsen, S. K. (2011b). Making decisions about placement. In S. K. Johnsen (Ed.), *Identifying gifted students: A practical guide* (pp. 119–149). Waco, TX: Prufrock Press.

Johnsen, S. K. (Ed.). (2012). *NAGC Pre-K–Grade 12 Gifted Education Programming Standards: A guide to planning and implementing high-quality services.* Waco, TX: Prufrock Press.

Johnsen, S. K., Haensly, P. A., Ryser, G. R., & Ford, R. F. (2002). Changing general education classroom practices to adapt for gifted students. *Gifted Child Quarterly, 46,* 45–63.

Johnsen, S. K., & Johnson, K. (2007). *Independent study program* (2nd ed.). Waco, TX: Prufrock Press.

Johnsen, S. K., & Sheffield, L. J. (Eds.). (2013). *Using the Common Core State Standards for mathematics with gifted and advanced learners.* Waco, TX: Prufrock Press.

Johnsen, S., VanTassel-Baska, J., & Robinson, A. (2008). *Using the national gifted education standards for university teacher preparation programs.* Thousand Oaks, CA: Corwin Press.

Kerr, B., & Kurpius, S. (2004). Encouraging talented girls in math and science: Effects of a guidance intervention. *High Ability Studies, 15,* 85–102.

Kettler, T., Shiu, A., & Johnsen, S. K. (2006). AP as an intervention for middle school Hispanic students. *Gifted Child Today, 29*(1), 39–46.

Kitano, M. K., & Lewis, R. B. (2005). Resilience and coping: Implications for gifted children and youth at risk. *Roeper Review, 27,* 200–205.

Kitano, M., Montgomery, D., VanTassel-Baska, J., & Johnsen, S. (2008). *Using the national gifted education standards for PreK–12 professional development.* Thousand Oaks, CA: Corwin Press.

Kitano, M. K., & Pedersen, K. S. (2002a). Action research and practical inquiry: Multicultural-content integration in gifted education: Lessons from the field. *Journal for the Education of the Gifted, 26,* 269–289.

Kitano, M. K., & Pedersen, K. S. (2002b). Action research and practical inquiry: Teaching gifted English learners. *Journal for the Education of the Gifted, 26,* 132–147.

Klein, J. P., & Lugg, E. T. (2002). Nurturing young adolescents legally and ethically. *Middle School Journal, 34*(1), 13–20.

Kolesinski, M. T., & Leroux, J. A. (1992). The bilingual education experience, French-English, Spanish-English: From a perspective of gifted students. *Roeper Review, 14,* 221–224.

Kulik, J. A., & Kulik, C. C. (1992). Meta-analytic findings on grouping programs. *Gifted Child Quarterly, 36,* 73–77.

Landrum, M. S. (2002). *Resource consultation and collaboration in gifted education.* Mansfield Center, CT: Creative Learning Press.

Landrum, M. S., Callahan, C. M., & Shaklee, B. D. (2001). *Aiming for excellence: Gifted program standards: Annotations to the NAGC Pre-K–Grade 12 Gifted Program Standards.* Waco, TX: Prufrock Press.

Landrum, M. S., & Shaklee, B. (Eds.). (1998). *Pre-K–grade 12 gifted program standards.* Washington, DC: National Association for Gifted Children.

Lee, S.-Y., & Olszewski-Kubilius, P. (2006). The emotional intelligence, moral judgment, and leadership of academically gifted adolescents. *Journal for the Education of the Gifted, 30,* 29–67.

Maxwell, M. (2007). Career counseling is personal counseling: A constructivist approach to nurturing the development of gifted female adolescents. *The Career Development Quarterly, 55,* 206–224.

McKown, C., & Weinstein, R. S. (2008). Teacher expectations, classroom context, and the achievement gap. *Journal of School Psychology, 46,* 235–261.

Moon, S. M. (1996). Using the Purdue three-stage model to facilitate local program evaluation. *Gifted Child Quarterly, 40,* 121–128.

Moon, S. M., Jurich, J. A., & Feldhusen, J. F. (1998). Families of gifted children: Cradles of development. In R. C. Friedman & K. Rogers (Eds.), *Talent in context: Historical and social perspectives on giftedness* (pp. 81–99). Washington, DC: American Psychological Association.

Morris, J. E. (2002). African American students and gifted education. *Roeper Review, 24,* 59–53.

National Association for Gifted Children. (2010). *NAGC Pre-K–Grade 12 Gifted Programming Standards: A blueprint for quality gifted education programs.* Retrieved from http://www.nagc.org/ProgrammingStandards.aspx

National Association for Gifted Children, & Council for Exceptional Children, The Association for the Gifted. (2006). *NAGC-CEC teacher knowledge and skill standards for gifted and talented education.* Retrieved from http://www.ncate.org/Standards/ProgramStandardsandReportForms/tabid/676/Default.aspx

National Association for Gifted Children, & Council for Exceptional Children, The Association for the Gifted. (2011). *Advanced standards in gifted education teacher preparation.* Retrieved from http://www.nagc.org/advancedstandards.aspx

National Association for Gifted Children, & Council of State Directors of Programs for the Gifted. (2010–2011). *2010–2011 State of the states in gifted education: National policy and practice data.* Washington, DC: Authors.

National Commission on Excellence in Education. (1983). *A nation at risk: The imperatives for educational reform.* Washington, DC: U. S. Department of Education.

National Governors Association Center for Best Practices, & Council of Chief State School Officers. (2010a). *Common Core State Standards for English language arts.* Retrieved from http://www.corestandards.org/ELA-Literacy

National Governors Association Center for Best Practices, & Council of Chief State School Officers. (2010b). *Common Core State Standards for mathematics.* Retrieved from http://www.corestandards.org/math

National Governors Association Center for Best Practices, & Council of Chief State School Officers. (2010c). *Common Core State Standards for mathematics, Appendix A: Designing high school mathematics courses based on the Common Core State Standards.* Retrieved from http://www.corestandards.org/assets/CCSSI_Mathematics_Appendix_A.pdf

Neihart, M. (2002). Risk and resilience in gifted children: A conceptual framework. In M. Neihart, S. M. Reis, N. M. Robinson, & S. M. Moon (Eds.), *The social and emotional development of gifted children: What do we know?* (pp. 113–122). Waco, TX: Prufrock Press.

Norris, J. A. (2003). Looking at classroom management through a social and emotional learning lens. *Theory Into Practice, 42,* 313–318.

Nugent, S. A. (2005). Affective education: Addressing the social and emotional needs of gifted students in the classroom. In F. Karnes & S. Bean (Eds.), *Methods and materials for teaching the gifted* (2nd ed., pp. 409–438). Waco, TX: Prufrock Press.

Olszewski-Kubilius, P., & Grant, B. (1994). Social support systems and the disadvantaged gifted: A framework for developing programs and services. *Roeper Review, 17,* 20–25.

Parker, J. (1996). NAGC standards for personnel preparation in gifted education: A brief history. *Gifted Child Quarterly, 40,* 158–164.

Partnership for Assessment of Readiness for College and Careers. (n.d.). *The PARCC Assessment.* Retrieved from http://www.parcconline.org/parcc-assessment

Pleasants, R., Stephens, K. R., Selph, H., & Pfeiffer, S. (2004). Incorporating service learning into leadership education: Duke TIP's Leadership Institute. *Gifted Child Today, 27*(1), 16–21.

Purcell, J. H., & Leppien, J. H. (1998). Building bridges between general practitioners and educators of the gifted: A study of collaboration. *Gifted Child Quarterly, 42,* 172–181.

Pyryt, M. C. (2003). Technology and the gifted. In N. Colangelo & G. A. Davis (Eds.), *Handbook of gifted education* (3rd ed., pp. 582–589). Boston, MA: Allyn & Bacon.

Reis, S. M., Burns, D. E., & Renzulli, J. S. (1992). *Curriculum compacting: The complete guide to modifying the regular curriculum for high ability students.* Waco, TX: Prufrock Press.

Renzulli, J. (1978). What makes giftedness? Reexamining a definition. *Phi Delta Kappan, 60,* 180–184.

Renzulli, J. S., & Reis, S. M. (2003). The Schoolwide Enrichment Model: Developing creative and productive giftedness. In N. Colangelo & G. A. Davis (Eds.), *Handbook of gifted education* (3rd ed., pp. 184–203). Boston, MA: Allyn & Bacon.

Robinson, A., & Kolloff, P. B. (2006). Preparing teachers to work with high-ability youth at the secondary level: Issues and implications for licensure. In F. A. Dixon & S. M. Moon (Eds.), *The handbook of secondary gifted education* (pp. 581–610). Waco, TX: Prufrock Press.

Rogers, K. B. (1991). *The relationship of grouping practices to the education of the gifted and talented learner: Research-based decision making series.* Storrs: University of Connecticut, The National Research Center on the Gifted and Talented.

Ross, J., & Smyth, E. (1995). Differentiating cooperative learning to meet the needs of gifted learners: A case for transformational leadership. *Journal for the Education of the Gifted, 19,* 63–82.

Ryser, G. R. (2011). Fairness in testing and nonbiased assessment. In S. K. Johnsen (Ed.), *Identifying gifted students: A practical guide* (pp. 63–74). Waco, TX: Prufrock.

Shade, B. J., Kelly, C., & Oberg, M. (1997). *Creating culturally responsive classrooms.* Washington, DC: American Psychological Association.

Siegle, D. (2004). *Using media and technology with gifted learners.* Waco, TX: Prufrock Press.

Siegle, D., & McCoach, D. B. (2005). Extending learning through mentorships. In F. A. Karnes & S. M. Bean (Eds.), *Methods and materials for teaching the gifted* (2nd ed., pp. 473–518). Waco, TX: Prufrock Press.

Simonton, D. K. (2000). Cognitive, personal, developmental, and social aspects. *American Psychologist, 55,* 151–158.

Smarter Balanced Assessment Consortium. (n.d.). *Smarter balanced assessments.* Retrieved from http://www.smarterbalanced.org/smarter-balanced-assessments

Smyth, E., & Ross, J. (1999). Developing leadership skills of pre-adolescent gifted learners in small group settings. *Gifted Child Quarterly, 43,* 204–211.

Stiggins, R. (2008). *Assessment manifesto: A call for the development of balanced assessment systems.* Portland, OR: ETS Assessment Training Institute.

Sulak, T. N., & Johnsen, S. K. (2012). Assessments for measuring student outcomes: Appendix B. In S. K. Johnsen (Ed.), *NAGC Pre-K–Grade 12 Gifted Education Programming Standards: A guide to planning and implementing high-quality services* (pp. 283–306). Waco, TX: Prufrock Press.

Tannenbaum, A. (1991). The social psychology of giftedness. In N. Colangelo & G. A. Davis (Eds.), *Handbook of gifted education* (pp. 27–44). Boston, MA: Allyn & Bacon.

Teacher Performance Assessment. (2011). *Stanford University and Pearson collaborate to deliver the Teacher Performance Assessment (TPA).* Retrieved from http://www.pearsonassessments.com/pai/ea/teacher/about/news/newsrelease031711.htm

Tomlinson, C. A. (Ed.). (2004). *Differentiation for gifted and talented students.* Thousand Oaks, CA: Corwin Press.

U. S. Department of Education. (2008). *A nation accountable: Twenty-five years after A Nation at Risk.* Washington, DC: U. S. Department of Education. Retrieved from http://www2.ed.gov/rschstat/research/pubs/accountable/accountable.pdf/

VanTassel-Baska, J. (2004). *Curriculum for gifted and talented students.* Thousand Oaks, CA: Corwin Press.

VanTassel-Baska, J. (Ed.). (2006). *Serving gifted learners beyond the traditional classroom.* Waco, TX: Prufrock Press.

VanTassel-Baska, J. (Ed.). (2007). *Alternative assessments with gifted and talented students.* Waco, TX: Prufrock Press.

VanTassel-Baska, J. (Ed.). (2009). *Patterns and profiles of promising learners from poverty.* Waco, TX: Prufrock Press.

VanTassel-Baska, J. (Ed.). (2013). *Using the Common Core State Standards for English language arts with gifted and advanced learners.* Waco, TX: Prufrock Press.

VanTassel-Baska, J., Cross, T., & Olenchak, R. (Eds.). (2008). *Social emotional curriculum for the gifted.* Waco, TX: Prufrock Press.

Wessel, L. E. (1999). *Career counseling for gifted students: Literature review and critique.* Retrieved from ERIC database. (ERIC Document Reproduction Service No. ED427267)

Williams, E. R., & Baber, C. R. (2007). Building trust through culturally reciprocal home-school-community collaboration from the perspective of African-American parents. *Multicultural Perspectives, 9*(2), 3–9.

Zeidner, M., & Schleyer, E. J. (1999). Evaluating the effects of full-time vs. part-time educational programs for the gifted: Affective outcomes and policy considerations. *Evaluation and Program Planning, 22,* 413–427.

Zirkel, S. (2008). The influence of multicultural educational practices on student outcomes and intergroup relations. *Teachers College Record, 110,* 1147–1181.

Appendix A
NAGC PreK–Grade 12 Gifted Education Programming Standards

Gifted Education Programming Standard 1:
Learning and Development

Introduction

To be effective in working with learners with gifts and talents, teachers and other educators in PreK–12 settings must understand the characteristics and needs of the population for whom they are planning curriculum, instruction, assessment, programs, and services. These characteristics provide the rationale for differentiation in programs, grouping, and services for this population and are translated into appropriate differentiation choices made at curricular and program levels in schools and school districts. While cognitive growth is important in such programs, affective development is also necessary. Thus many of the characteristics addressed in this standard emphasize affective development linked to self-understanding and social awareness.

Standard 1: Learning and Development

Description: Educators, recognizing the learning and developmental differences of students with gifts and talents, promote ongoing self-understanding, awareness of their needs, and cognitive and affective growth of these students in school, home, and community settings to ensure specific student outcomes.

Student Outcomes	Evidence-Based Practices
1.1. Self-Understanding. Students with gifts and talents demonstrate self-knowledge with respect to their interests, strengths, identities, and needs in socio-emotional development and in intellectual, academic, creative, leadership, and artistic domains.	1.1.1. Educators engage students with gifts and talents in identifying interests, strengths, and gifts. 1.1.2. Educators assist students with gifts and talents in developing identities supportive of achievement.
1.2. Self-Understanding. Students with gifts and talents possess a developmentally appropriate understanding of how they learn and grow; they recognize the influences of their beliefs, traditions, and values on their learning and behavior.	1.2.1. Educators develop activities that match each student's developmental level and culture-based learning needs.
1.3. Self-Understanding. Students with gifts and talents demonstrate understanding of and respect for similarities and differences between themselves and their peer group and others in the general population.	1.3.1. Educators provide a variety of research-based grouping practices for students with gifts and talents that allow them to interact with individuals of various gifts, talents, abilities, and strengths. 1.3.2. Educators model respect for individuals with diverse abilities, strengths, and goals.

Student Outcomes	Evidence-Based Practices
1.4. Awareness of Needs. Students with gifts and talents access resources from the community to support cognitive and affective needs, including social interactions with others having similar interests and abilities or experiences, including same-age peers and mentors or experts.	1.4.1. Educators provide role models (e.g., through mentors, bibliotherapy) for students with gifts and talents that match their abilities and interests. 1.4.2. Educators identify out-of-school learning opportunities that match students' abilities and interests.
1.5. Awareness of Needs. Students' families and communities understand similarities and differences with respect to the development and characteristics of advanced and typical learners and support students with gifts and talents' needs.	1.5.1. Educators collaborate with families in accessing resources to develop their child's talents.
1.6. Cognitive and Affective Growth. Students with gifts and talents benefit from meaningful and challenging learning activities addressing their unique characteristics and needs.	1.6.1. Educators design interventions for students to develop cognitive and affective growth that is based on research of effective practices. 1.6.2. Educators develop specialized intervention services for students with gifts and talents who are underachieving and are now learning and developing their talents.
1.7. Cognitive and Affective Growth. Students with gifts and talents recognize their preferred approaches to learning and expand their repertoire.	1.7.1. Teachers enable students to identify their preferred approaches to learning, accommodate these preferences, and expand them.
1.8. Cognitive and Affective Growth. Students with gifts and talents identify future career goals that match their talents and abilities and resources needed to meet those goals (e.g., higher education opportunities, mentors, financial support).	1.8.1. Educators provide students with college and career guidance that is consistent with their strengths. 1.8.2. Teachers and counselors implement a curriculum scope and sequence that contains person/social awareness and adjustment, academic planning, and vocational and career awareness.

Gifted Education Programming Standard 2: Assessment

Introduction

Knowledge about all forms of assessment is essential for educators of students with gifts and talents. It is integral to identification, assessing each student's learning progress, and evaluation of programming. Educators need to establish a challenging environment and collect multiple types of assessment information so that all students are able to demonstrate their gifts and talents. Educators' understanding of non-biased, technically adequate, and equitable approaches enables them to identify students who represent diverse backgrounds. They also differentiate their curriculum and instruction by using pre- and post-, performance-based, product-based, and out-of-level assessments. As a result of each educator's use of ongoing assessments, students with gifts and talents demonstrate advanced and complex learning. Using these student progress data, educators then evaluate services and make adjustments to one or more of the school's programming components so that student performance is improved.

Standard 2: Assessment
Description: Assessments provide information about identification, learning progress and outcomes, and evaluation of programming for students with gifts and talents in all domains.

Student Outcomes	Evidence-Based Practices
2.1. Identification. All students in grades PK–12 have equal access to a comprehensive assessment system that allows them to demonstrate diverse characteristics and behaviors that are associated with giftedness.	2.1.1. Educators develop environments and instructional activities that encourage students to express diverse characteristics and behaviors that are associated with giftedness. 2.1.2. Educators provide parents/guardians with information regarding diverse characteristics and behaviors that are associated with giftedness.
2.2. Identification. Each student reveals his or her exceptionalities or potential through assessment evidence so that appropriate instructional accommodations and modifications can be provided.	2.2.1. Educators establish comprehensive, cohesive, and ongoing procedures for identifying and serving students with gifts and talents. These provisions include informed consent, committee review, student retention, student reassessment, student exiting, and appeals procedures for both entry and exit from gifted program services.
	2.2.2. Educators select and use multiple assessments that measure diverse abilities, talents, and strengths that are based on current theories, models, and research. 2.2.3 Assessments provide qualitative and quantitative information from a variety of sources, including off-level testing, are nonbiased and equitable, and are technically adequate for the purpose. 2.2.4. Educators have knowledge of student exceptionalities and collect assessment data while adjusting curriculum and instruction to learn about each student's developmental level and aptitude for learning. 2.2.5. Educators interpret multiple assessments in different domains and understand the uses and limitations of the assessments in identifying the needs of students with gifts and talents. 2.2.6. Educators inform all parents/guardians about the identification process. Teachers obtain parental/guardian permission for assessments, use culturally sensitive checklists, and elicit evidence regarding the child's interests and potential outside of the classroom setting.

Student Outcomes	Evidence-Based Practices
2.3. Identification. Students with identified needs represent diverse backgrounds and reflect the total student population of the district.	2.3.1. Educators select and use non-biased and equitable approaches for identifying students with gifts and talents, which may include using locally developed norms or assessment tools in the child's native language or in nonverbal formats. 2.3.2. Educators understand and implement district and state policies designed to foster equity in gifted programming and services. 2.3.3. Educators provide parents/guardians with information in their native language regarding diverse behaviors and characteristics that are associated with giftedness and with information that explains the nature and purpose of gifted programming options.
2.4. Learning Progress and Outcomes. Students with gifts and talents demonstrate advanced and complex learning as a result of using multiple, appropriate, and ongoing assessments.	2.4.1. Educators use differentiated pre- and post- performance-based assessments to measure the progress of students with gifts and talents. 2.4.2. Educators use differentiated product-based assessments to measure the progress of students with gifts and talents.
	2.4.3. Educators use off-level standardized assessments to measure the progress of students with gifts and talents. 2.4.4. Educators use and interpret qualitative and quantitative assessment information to develop a profile of the strengths and weaknesses of each student with gifts and talents to plan appropriate intervention. 2.4.5. Educators communicate and interpret assessment information to students with gifts and talents and their parents/guardians.
2.5. Evaluation of Programming. Students identified with gifts and talents demonstrate important learning progress as a result of programming and services.	2.5.1. Educators ensure that the assessments used in the identification and evaluation processes are reliable and valid for each instrument's purpose, allow for above-grade-level performance, and allow for diverse perspectives. 2.5.2. Educators ensure that the assessment of the progress of students with gifts and talents uses multiple indicators that measure mastery of content, higher level thinking skills, achievement in specific program areas, and affective growth. 2.5.3. Educators assess the quantity, quality, and appropriateness of the programming and services provided for students with gifts and talents by disaggregating assessment data and yearly progress data and making the results public.

Student Outcomes	Evidence-Based Practices
2.6. Evaluation of Programming. Students identified with gifts and talents have increased access and they show significant learning progress as a result of improving components of gifted education programming.	2.6.1. Administrators provide the necessary time and resources to implement an annual evaluation plan developed by persons with expertise in program evaluation and gifted education. 2.6.2. The evaluation plan is purposeful and evaluates how student-level outcomes are influenced by one or more of the following components of gifted education programming: (a) identification, (b) curriculum, (c) instructional programming and services, (d) ongoing assessment of student learning, (e) counseling and guidance programs, (f) teacher qualifications and professional development, (g) parent/guardian and community involvement, (h) programming resources, and (i) programming design, management, and delivery. 2.6.3. Educators disseminate the results of the evaluation, orally and in written form, and explain how they will use the results.

Gifted Education Programming Standard 3: Curriculum Planning and Instruction

Introduction

Assessment is an integral component of the curriculum planning process. The information obtained from multiple types of assessments informs decisions about curriculum content, instructional strategies, and resources that will support the growth of students with gifts and talents. Educators develop and use a comprehensive and sequenced core curriculum that is aligned with local, state, and national standards, then differentiate and expand it. In order to meet the unique needs of students with gifts and talents, this curriculum must emphasize advanced, conceptually challenging, in-depth, distinctive, and complex content within cognitive, affective, aesthetic, social, and leadership domains. Educators must possess a repertoire of evidence-based instructional strategies in delivering the curriculum (a) to develop talent, enhance learning, and provide students with the knowledge and skills to become independent, self-aware learners, and (b) to give students the tools to contribute to a multicultural, diverse society. The curriculum, instructional strategies, and materials and resources must engage a variety of learners using culturally responsive practices.

Standard 3: Curriculum Planning and Instruction

Description: Educators apply the theory and research-based models of curriculum and instruction related to students with gifts and talents and respond to their needs by planning, selecting, adapting, and creating culturally relevant curriculum and by using a repertoire of evidence-based instructional strategies to ensure specific student outcomes.

Student Outcomes	Evidence-Based Practices
3.1. Curriculum Planning. Students with gifts and talents demonstrate growth commensurate with aptitude during the school year.	3.1.1. Educators use local, state, and national standards to align and expand curriculum and instructional plans. 3.1.2. Educators design and use a comprehensive and continuous scope and sequence to develop differentiated plans for PK–12 students with gifts and talents. 3.1.3. Educators adapt, modify, or replace the core or standard curriculum to meet the needs of students with gifts and talents and those with special needs such as twice-exceptional, highly gifted, and English language learners.
	3.1.4. Educators design differentiated curricula that incorporate advanced, conceptually challenging, in-depth, distinctive, and complex content for students with gifts and talents. 3.1.5. Educators use a balanced assessment system, including pre-assessment and formative assessment, to identify students' needs, develop differentiated education plans, and adjust plans based on continual progress monitoring. 3.1.6. Educators use pre-assessments and pace instruction based on the learning rates of students with gifts and talents and accelerate and compact learning as appropriate. 3.1.7. Educators use information and technologies, including assistive technologies, to individualize for students with gifts and talents, including those who are twice-exceptional.
3.2. Talent Development. Students with gifts and talents become more competent in multiple talent areas and across dimensions of learning.	3.2.1. Educators design curricula in cognitive, affective, aesthetic, social, and leadership domains that are challenging and effective for students with gifts and talents. 3.2.2. Educators use metacognitive models to meet the needs of students with gifts and talents.
3.3. Talent Development. Students with gifts and talents develop their abilities in their domain of talent and/or area of interest.	3.3.1. Educators select, adapt, and use a repertoire of instructional strategies and materials that differentiate for students with gifts and talents and that respond to diversity. 3.3.2. Educators use school and community resources that support differentiation. 3.3.3. Educators provide opportunities for students with gifts and talents to explore, develop, or research their areas of interest and/or talent.
3.4. Instructional Strategies. Students with gifts and talents become independent investigators.	3.4.1. Educators use critical-thinking strategies to meet the needs of students with gifts and talents. 3.4.2. Educators use creative-thinking strategies to meet the needs of students with gifts and talents.

Student Outcomes	Evidence-Based Practices
	3.4.3. Educators use problem-solving model strategies to meet the needs of students with gifts and talents. 3.4.4. Educators use inquiry models to meet the needs of students with gifts and talents.
3.5. Culturally Relevant Curriculum. Students with gifts and talents develop knowledge and skills for living and being productive in a multicultural, diverse, and global society.	3.5.1. Educators develop and use challenging, culturally responsive curriculum to engage all students with gifts and talents. 3.5.2. Educators integrate career exploration experiences into learning opportunities for students with gifts and talents, e.g. biography study or speakers. 3.5.3. Educators use curriculum for deep explorations of cultures, languages, and social issues related to diversity.
3.6. Resources. Students with gifts and talents benefit from gifted education programming that provides a variety of high quality resources and materials.	3.6.1. Teachers and administrators demonstrate familiarity with sources for high quality resources and materials that are appropriate for learners with gifts and talents.

Gifted Education Programming Standard 4: Learning Environments

Introduction

Effective educators of students with gifts and talents create safe learning environments that foster emotional well-being, positive social interaction, leadership for social change, and cultural understanding for success in a diverse society. Knowledge of the impact of giftedness and diversity on social-emotional development enables educators of students with gifts and talents to design environments that encourage independence, motivation, and self-efficacy of individuals from all backgrounds. They understand the role of language and communication in talent development and the ways in which culture affects communication and behavior. They use relevant strategies and technologies to enhance oral, written, and artistic communication of learners whose needs vary based on exceptionality, language proficiency, and cultural and linguistic differences. They recognize the value of multilingualism in today's global community.

Standard 4: Learning Environments

Description: Learning environments foster personal and social responsibility, multicultural competence, and interpersonal and technical communication skills for leadership in the 21st century to ensure specific student outcomes.

Student Outcomes	Evidence-Based Practices
4.1. Personal Competence. Students with gifts and talents demonstrate growth in personal competence and dispositions for exceptional academic and creative productivity. These include self-awareness, self-advocacy, self-efficacy, confidence, motivation, resilience, independence, curiosity, and risk taking.	4.1.1. Educators maintain high expectations for all students with gifts and talents as evidenced in meaningful and challenging activities. 4.1.2. Educators provide opportunities for self-exploration, development and pursuit of interests, and development of identities supportive of achievement, e.g., through mentors and role models. 4.1.3. Educators create environments that support trust among diverse learners. 4.1.4. Educators provide feedback that focuses on effort, on evidence of potential to meet high standards, and on mistakes as learning opportunities. 4.1.5. Educators provide examples of positive coping skills and opportunities to apply them.
4.2. Social Competence. Students with gifts and talents develop social competence manifested in positive peer relationships and social interactions.	4.2.1. Educators understand the needs of students with gifts and talents for both solitude and social interaction. 4.2.2. Educators provide opportunities for interaction with intellectual and artistic/creative peers as well as with chronological-age peers. 4.2.3. Educators assess and provide instruction on social skills needed for school, community, and the world of work.
4.3. Leadership. Students with gifts and talents demonstrate personal and social responsibility and leadership skills.	4.3.1. Educators establish a safe and welcoming climate for addressing social issues and developing personal responsibility. 4.3.2. Educators provide environments for developing many forms of leadership and leadership skills. 4.3.3. Educators promote opportunities for leadership in community settings to effect positive change.
4.4. Cultural Competence. Students with gifts and talents value their own and others' language, heritage, and circumstance. They possess skills in communicating, teaming, and collaborating with diverse individuals and across diverse groups.[1] They use positive strategies to address social issues, including discrimination and stereotyping.	4.4.1. Educators model appreciation for and sensitivity to students' diverse backgrounds and languages. 4.4.2. Educators censure discriminatory language and behavior and model appropriate strategies. 4.4.3. Educators provide structured opportunities to collaborate with diverse peers on a common goal.
4.5. Communication Competence. Students with gifts and talents develop competence in interpersonal and technical communication skills. They demonstrate advanced oral and written skills, balanced biliteracy or multiliteracy, and creative expression. They display fluency with technologies that support effective communication	4.5.1. Educators provide opportunities for advanced development and maintenance of first and second language(s). 4.5.2. Educators provide resources to enhance oral, written, and artistic forms of communication, recognizing students' cultural context. 4.5.3. Educators ensure access to advanced communication tools, including assistive technologies, and use of these tools for expressing higher-level thinking and creative productivity.

1 Differences among groups of people and individuals based on ethnicity, race, socioeconomic status, gender, exceptionalities, language, religion, sexual orientation, and geographical area.

Gifted Education Programming Standard 5: Programming

Introduction

The term programming refers to a continuum of services that address students with gifts and talents' needs in all settings. Educators develop policies and procedures to guide and sustain all components of comprehensive and aligned programming and services for PreK-12 students with gifts and talents. Educators use a variety of programming options such as acceleration and enrichment in varied grouping arrangements (cluster grouping, resource rooms, special classes, special schools) and within individualized learning options (independent study, mentorships, online courses, internships) to enhance students' performance in cognitive and affective areas and to assist them in identifying future career goals. They augment and integrate current technologies within these learning opportunities to increase access to high level programming such as distance learning courses and to increase connections to resources outside of the school walls. In implementing services, educators in gifted, general, special education programs, and related professional services collaborate with one another and parents/guardians and community members to ensure that students' diverse learning needs are met. Administrators demonstrate their support of these programming options by allocating sufficient resources so that all students within gifts and talents receive appropriate educational services.

Standard 5: Programming

Description: Educators are aware of empirical evidence regarding (a) the cognitive, creative, and affective development of learners with gifts and talents, and (b) programming that meets their concomitant needs. Educators use this expertise systematically and collaboratively to develop, implement, and effectively manage comprehensive services for students with a variety of gifts and talents to ensure specific student outcomes.

Student Outcomes	Evidence-Based Practices
5.1. Variety of Programming. Students with gifts and talents participate in a variety of evidence-based programming options that enhance performance in cognitive and affective areas.	5.1.1. Educators regularly use multiple alternative approaches to accelerate learning. 5.1.2. Educators regularly use enrichment options to extend and deepen learning opportunities within and outside of the school setting. 5.1.3. Educators regularly use multiple forms of grouping, including clusters, resource rooms, special classes, or special schools. 5.1.4. Educators regularly use individualized learning options such as mentorships, internships, online courses, and independent study. 5.1.5. Educators regularly use current technologies, including online learning options and assistive technologies to enhance access to high-level programming.

Student Outcomes	Evidence-Based Practices
	5.1.6. Administrators demonstrate support for gifted programs through equitable allocation of resources and demonstrated willingness to ensure that learners with gifts and talents receive appropriate educational services.
5.2. Coordinated Services. Students with gifts and talents demonstrate progress as a result of the shared commitment and coordinated services of gifted education, general education, special education, and related professional services, such as school counselors, school psychologists, and social workers.	5.2.1. Educators in gifted, general, and special education programs, as well as those in specialized areas, collaboratively plan, develop, and implement services for learners with gifts and talents.
5.3. Collaboration. Students with gifts and talents' learning is enhanced by regular collaboration among families, community, and the school.	5.3.1. Educators regularly engage families and community members for planning, programming, evaluating, and advocating.
5.4. Resources. Students with gifts and talents participate in gifted education programming that is adequately funded to meet student needs and program goals.	5.4.1. Administrators track expenditures at the school level to verify appropriate and sufficient funding for gifted programming and services.
5.5. Comprehensiveness. Students with gifts and talents develop their potential through comprehensive, aligned programming and services.	5.5.1. Educators develop thoughtful, multi-year program plans in relevant student talent areas, PK–12.
5.6. Policies and Procedures. Students with gifts and talents participate in regular and gifted education programs that are guided by clear policies and procedures that provide for their advanced learning needs (e.g., early entrance, acceleration, credit in lieu of enrollment).	5.6.1. Educators create policies and procedures to guide and sustain all components of the program, including assessment, identification, acceleration practices, and grouping practices, that is built on an evidence-based foundation in gifted education.
5.7. Career Pathways. Students with gifts and talents identify future career goals and the talent development pathways to reach those goals.	5.7.1. Educators provide professional guidance and counseling for individual student strengths, interests, and values. 5.7.2. Educators facilitate mentorships, internships, and vocational programming experiences that match student interests and aptitudes.

Gifted Education Programming Standard 6: Professional Development

Introduction

Professional development is essential for all educators involved in the development and implementation of gifted programs and services. Professional development is the intentional development of professional expertise as outlined by the NAGC-CEC teacher preparation standards and is an ongoing part of gifted educators' professional and ethical practice. Professional development may take many forms ranging from district-sponsored workshops and courses, university courses, professional conferences, independent studies, and presentations by external consultants and should be based on systematic needs assessments and professional reflection. Students participating in gifted education programs and services are taught by teachers with developed expertise in gifted education. Gifted education program services are developed and supported by administrators, coordinators, curriculum specialists, general education, special education, and gifted education teachers who have developed expertise in gifted education. Since students with gifts and talents spend much of their time within general education classrooms, general education teachers need to receive professional development in gifted education that enables them to recognize the characteristics of giftedness in diverse populations, understand the school or district referral and identification process, and possess an array of high quality, research-based differentiation strategies that challenge students. Services for students with gifts and talents are enhanced by guidance and counseling professionals with expertise in gifted education.

Standard 6: Professional Development

Description: All educators (administrators, teachers, counselors, and other instructional support staff) build their knowledge and skills using the NAGC-CEC Teacher Standards for Gifted and Talented Education and the National Staff Development Standards. They formally assess professional development needs related to the standards, develop and monitor plans, systematically engage in training to meet the identified needs, and demonstrate mastery of standard. They access resources to provide for release time, funding for continuing education, and substitute support. These practices are judged through the assessment of relevant student outcomes.

Student Outcomes	Evidence-Based Practices
6.1. **Talent Development.** Students develop their talents and gifts as a result of interacting with educators who meet the national teacher preparation standards in gifted education.	6.1.1. Educators systematically participate in ongoing, research-supported professional development that addresses the foundations of gifted education, characteristics of students with gifts and talents, assessment, curriculum planning and instruction, learning environments, and programming. 6.1.2. The school district provides professional development for teachers that models how to develop environments and instructional activities that encourage students to express diverse characteristics and behaviors that are associated with giftedness. 6.1.3. Educators participate in ongoing professional development addressing key issues such as anti-intellectualism and trends in gifted education such as equity and access. 6.1.4. Administrators provide human and material resources needed for professional development in gifted education (e.g. release time, funding for continuing education, substitute support, webinars, or mentors). 6.1.5. Educators use their awareness of organizations and publications relevant to gifted education to promote learning for students with gifts and talents.

Student Outcomes	Evidence-Based Practices
6.2. Socio-emotional Development. Students with gifts and talents develop socially and emotionally as a result of educators who have participated in professional development aligned with national standards in gifted education and National Staff Development Standards.	6.2.1. Educators participate in ongoing professional development to support the social and emotional needs of students with gifts and talents.
6.3. Lifelong Learners. Students develop their gifts and talents as a result of educators who are life-long learners, participating in ongoing professional development and continuing education opportunities.	6.3.1. Educators assess their instructional practices and continue their education in school district staff development, professional organizations, and higher education settings based on these assessments. 6.3.2. Educators participate in professional development that is sustained over time, that includes regular follow-up, and that seeks evidence of impact on teacher practice and on student learning. 6.3.3. Educators use multiple modes of professional development delivery including online courses, online and electronic communities, face-to-face workshops, professional learning communities, and book talks. 6.3.4. Educators identify and address areas for personal growth for teaching students with gifts and talents in their professional development plans.
6.4. Ethics. Students develop their gifts and talents as a result of educators who are ethical in their practices.	6.4.1. Educators respond to cultural and personal frames of reference when teaching students with gifts and talents. 6.4.2. Educators comply with rules, policies, and standards of ethical practice.

Note. From *NAGC Pre-K–Grade 12 Gifted Programming Standards: A Blueprint for Quality Gifted Education Programs* (pp. 8–13), by National Association for Gifted Children, 2010, Washington, DC: Author. Copyright 2010 by National Association for Gifted Children. Reprinted with permission.

The Association for the Gifted (TAG), a Division of the Council for Exceptional Children, and its Board of Directors have reviewed these standards and express support of the NAGC Pre-K-Grade 12 Programming Standards. April 2010.

About TAG

The Association for the Gifted (TAG) was organized as a division of The Council for Exceptional Children in 1958. TAG plays a major part in helping both professionals and parents work more effectively with one of our most precious resources: the gifted child. Visit http://www.cectag.org for more information.

COMMON CORE STATE STANDARDS AND GIFTED EDUCATION

BY ELISSA F. BROWN

Overview

Academic content standards are an important part of our education system, serving as the foundation for what teachers should teach and students should learn in our public schools. Over the last several decades, educators and policymakers have turned to standards-based reform to solve some of the nation's perceived educational challenges. Proponents argue that students benefit when school systems articulate clear expectations of what students should know and are expected to do at each phase of their educational development (American Federation of Teachers, 2001, 2008). In 2010, the state of academic content standards across the nation took a huge step forward with the development and release of the Common Core State Standards (CCSS) in English-language arts (ELA) and mathematics. The CCSS are K–12 content standards, developed in mathematics and ELA to be a set of clear, consistent, and rigorous academic standards that are focused on what students should know and be able to do at each grade level to ensure that they graduate from high school prepared for college and the workforce (see http://www.core standards.org). Developed through a state-led process facilitated by the National Governors Association (NGA) Center for Best Practices and the Council of Chief State School Officers (CCSSO), the CCSS draw upon the strengths of the best state standards in the country, are internationally benchmarked against academic standards in some of the highest performing countries in the world, and are based on evidence and research about what students need to know to be college- and career-ready. The standards are benchmarked against the Advanced Placement program as well as national and international frameworks, including the Third International Mathematics and Science Study (TIMSS), Program for International Student Assessment (PISA), and other international comparisons as well as national measures such as the National Assessment of Educational Progress (NAEP; Wiley, Wyatt, & Camara, 2010). These standards were an important resource in the development of the CCSS because they were based and benchmarked on empirical evidence related to college success.

Academic experts from around the country wrote the standards with multiple rounds of feedback from state education leaders, teachers, and other education experts during the development process. At the time of this writing, nearly every state has adopted either or both the English language arts and mathematics standards. Science standards are nearing release as well. Additionally, 42 states report either having plans or building plans to revise their teacher-evaluation systems to comport with the expectations of Common Core. Thirty states claim to have fully developed plans to change their instructional materials to align with the new standards (Smarick, 2013).

The CCSS are different from many states' existing standards in several important ways. The ELA standards, for instance, include literacy standards for science, history, and social studies that are intended to supplement content standards in those areas, helping to ensure that there is a shared responsibility among all teachers for developing students' literacy skills. In addition, there is as much focus in the ELA standards on the complexity of texts that students should be able to read at each grade level as there is on how students learn to read. The standards also contain a greater balance between developing students' abilities to read literature and informational texts, focusing more heavily on reading informational texts in the upper grades, which is important for success in college-level coursework. In writing, the standards focus more on argumentative and explanatory writing in the later grades and less on narrative writing.

Similar to many high-performing countries around the world, the mathematics standards focus on building a strong understanding of whole numbers and number operations in the early grades so that students are able to learn and apply more advanced mathematical concepts as they progress through the grade levels. The mathematics standards also emphasize mathematical modeling in middle school and high school so that students are able to analyze empirical situations to help in decision making (Confrey & Kuzak, 2006). Furthermore, the mathematics standards call on students to apply their mathematical skills to real-world problems, as they will be expected to do in college courses or in the workforce. An example of the difference in mathematical standards from the historical way U.S. standards used to be arranged and the CCSS are arranged can be found in Figures 2.1 and 2.2. Figure 2.1 displays the historical way U.S. math standards used to be arranged, giving equal importance to all four areas—like "shopping aisles." Each grade goes up and down the aisles, tossing topics into the cart, losing focus. Figure 2.2 displays the trajectory of numbers and operations across the K–12 continuum showing foundational building blocks.

With all of that in place, are the CCSS appropriate for our most able learners, those who are gifted and talented? With the wide adoption of these content standards across much of the country, it affords those involved in gifted education to pause and determine the degree to which these standards respond to the varying needs of a population of students, the majority of which are already performing beyond proficiency.

The National Association for Gifted Children (NAGC) has produced a position statement on the CCSS and many resources to assist teachers and administrators (NAGC, 2014; see http://www.nagc.org/index2.aspx?id=11370 and Appendix A). Many states and local school districts have begun work on aligning current teaching practices, documents, and frameworks to the new CCSS with gifted learners and other populations of learners.

Why Should Gifted Education Care About the CCSS?

Gifted students are diverse. They vary from their age mates and even from other gifted students in both the rate at which they learn and the areas or domains in which they are gifted. They are served in a variety of educational models such as general education self-contained classrooms, pull-out resource models, cluster groups, specialized schools, and special classes. In every educational context, gifted learners are expected to learn the content standards and be assessed on them. Tomlinson (1999) recognized the importance of using standards as a springboard for differentiating instruction, stating that teachers must know where they are going and standards provide a roadmap. Gifted education can ill afford not to be vested in CCSS since these standards and subsequently new assessments are being used as the roadmap to demonstrate college and career readiness. Additional reasons are as follows:

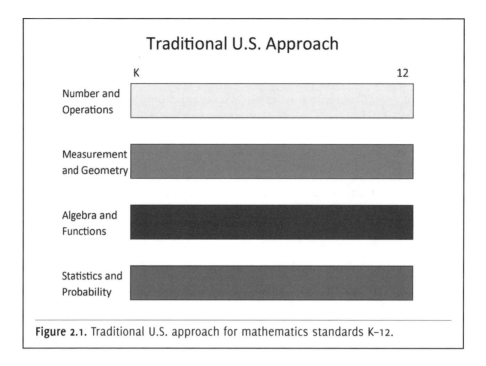

Figure 2.1. Traditional U.S. approach for mathematics standards K–12.

» International comparisons such as TIMSS, PISA, NAEP, as well as national measures, demonstrate that high-end learners in the U.S. are not making growth gains and are less competitive than their international peers.

» Most gifted students are "served" in general education classrooms and are required to adhere to state content standards and state assessments.

» Not all gifted students score proficient on summative, high-stakes assessments.

» In the current economic climate, gifted programs must integrate, collaborate, and be held accountable for student growth in order to demonstrate viability.

» CCSS provides an opportunity for growth and collaboration with regular education and within the field of gifted.

» The academic vocabulary, conceptual understandings, and content knowledge undergirding the CCSS are consonant with research-based best practices for meeting the needs of gifted learners (see Appendix A).

The ELA and mathematics standards each posit three fundamental shifts. The shifts in ELA are (a) building knowledge through content-rich nonfiction and informational text, (b) reading, writing, and speaking grounded in evidence from text, and (c) regular practice with complex texts and their shared vocabulary. The shifts in mathematics are (a) focus, (b) coherence, and (c) rigor. These shifts are

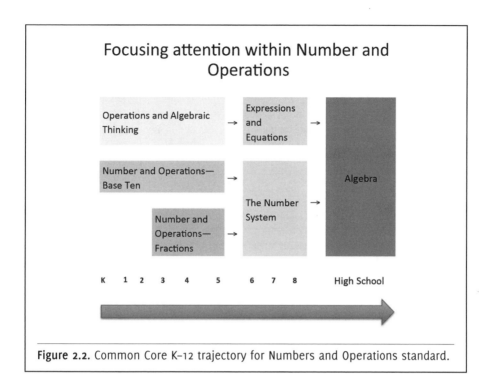

Figure 2.2. Common Core K–12 trajectory for Numbers and Operations standard.

implicit within the structure and intent of the CCSS. Tables 2.1 and 2.2 suggest some of the implications for teaching and assessing gifted learners relative to the ELA and mathematics shifts.

Employing Gifted Curricular Models to Differentiate the CCSS

There are many curricular and programmatic models supported by research that are appropriate for use with gifted students (VanTassel-Baska & Brown, 2009). Curriculum and instructional models provide a theoretical framework within which targeted learning activities and product and assessment demands can be planned and implemented (Davis, Rimm, & Siegle, 2011). The CCSS, in that way, become a launching pad for employing a variety of curricular and instructional strategies to provide rigor and relevance. The good news is that teachers have options. It is true that the CCSS are more explicit and descriptive than many of the previous state standard documents, but teachers still have tremendous flexibility with regard to implementation and approaches to learning. For gifted students, content standards play a significant role in the development of expertise and talent (Stambaugh, 2011) as long as they are implemented with the following best practices for differentiation (VanTassel-Baska, 2014):

TABLE 2.1

Shifts in Common Core ELA Standards and Their Implications
for Teaching and Assessing Gifted Students

CCSS ELA Shifts	Building knowledge through content-rich nonfiction and informational text
	Reading, writing, and speaking grounded in evidence from text
	Regular practice with complex texts and shared vocabulary
Implications for Teaching	► Employ above-level and professional levels of content ► Have a variety of informational and nonfiction texts, such as professional journals and manuals
	► Students engage in cross-disciplinary research projects ► Students take on a role of a key character in history and demonstrate through reading, writing, and speaking how the person influenced events in history and how history influenced changes in the individual's life over time ► Debate, persuasion, and speeches ► Employing strategies such as problem-based learning that allow students to ground their reasoning for problem resolution from several textual sources
	► Build text complexity to ensure students are on track each year for advanced coursework in college and career reading. For gifted students, text complexity could mean professional-level texts ► Systematically focus on the words that matter most—not obscure vocabulary, but the academic language that pervades complex texts and professional discourse
Implications for Assessment	► Simulate research on the assessment, including the comparison and synthesis of ideas across a range of informational sources linked to conceptual understandings

	► Focus on students rigorously citing evidence from texts throughout the assessment
	► Provide questions and assessments with more than one right answer to allow students to generate a range of rich insights that are substantiated by evidence from text(s)
	► Require writing to sources rather than writing to decontextualized expository prompts
	► Hold rigorous expectations for narrative writing, including accuracy and precision in writing in later grades
	► Provide students with author's claim in an assessment protocol and have students evaluate the argument, such as:
	  • Is the claim relevant? Why or why not?
	  • Is the claim valid? Why or why not?
	  • Is the evidence presented by the author sufficient? Why or why not?

	► Use complex, advanced-level content as assessment prompts; have students read and respond in authentic ways ► Have students, through assessments, demonstrate the vocabulary of the disciplines

TABLE 2.2
Shifts in Common Core Mathematics Standards and Their
Implications for Teaching and Assessing Gifted Students

CCSS Math Shifts	Focus: Strong
	Coherence: Think across grades and link to major topics
	Rigor: In the major work of the grade, require fluency, deep understanding, and application with equal intensity
Implications for Teaching	▸ Teachers spend more time on student understanding by going in depth rather than racing through to get to the next standard. Activities and assignments allow students to apply their understanding with less of a focus on computation ▸ Provide multiple opportunities for students to demonstrate their mathematical understanding, such as spatial visualization
	▸ Standards are designed around coherent progressions ▸ Each standard is not a new event, but an extension of previous learning ▸ There are key topics at each grade level ▸ Coherence is about making math sense and progressions of learning
	▸ Intensity calling for conceptual understanding of key elements so that math is not discrete procedures; the content standards require conceptual understanding and procedural fluency
Implications for Assessment	▸ Create performance-based assessments where students have to not only show the answer through pictures and/or words but articulate the reasoning behind it ▸ Incorporate the use of technology and mathematical demonstrations to provide rationale for problem solving and mathematical understanding
	▸ Instead of having students apply a rule, focus on important ideas and relationships involved. Skill acquisition can be achieved from the perspective of problem solving ▸ Students use heuristics to explain patterns
	▸ Regular use of complex application problems calling for students' ability to demonstrate reasoning and understanding ▸ Students demonstrate "mathematical habits of mind"

» experiences with challenging stimuli,

» understanding themes and concepts and higher order processes at a deeper level,

» emphasis on higher level thought processes that stress the simultaneity of elements of reasoning,

» instructional pacing matched to student abilities and competencies,

» making valid and important connections among disciplines,

» real-world applications that are problem- or issue-based,

» emphasis on open-ended yet guided questioning and project work,

» meaningful homework and project work grounded in advancing learning to deeper levels, and

» emphasis on metacognition and self-monitoring.

We cannot assume the wishful proposition that CCSS, coupled with differentiated instruction, would magically enable every teacher to succeed with every student in a mixed classroom, yet essential content understandings are core to understanding the discipline and critical to the learning needs of gifted students (VanTassel-Baska & Little, 2011).

Teachers can use a variety of differentiating approaches such as acceleration (e.g., preassessment, curriculum compacting, or providing advanced content at earlier grade levels, etc.), adding depth and complexity (e.g., studying issues, conducting research, engaging in real-world applications through the use of problem-solving models, etc.), building in enrichment activities (e.g., expand activities through student interests and creative options, etc.) or providing conceptual understandings (e.g., use of overarching concept, integrated learning across content domains, etc.), or a combination of these approaches. With any of these approaches, relevance to students is assumed. Rigor without relevance can result in students who do well academically but seem dysfunctional in the real world (Daggett, 2007). Although students must ultimately determine what is relevant to them, at times, teachers need to be explicit in making connections to specific content or skills relevant to students.

Figure 2.3 provides a framework for differentiating beginning with the content standard through process, product, concepts, and acceleration by implementation of differentiated task demands, product and assessment demands, conceptual understandings, and accelerating or compacting standards for gifted learners. This framework is driven by the relative content standard but implemented based on the readiness, skills, and interests of the learner (Tomlinson, 1999) as well as the capacity of the teacher and resources availability. Tables 2.3 and 2.4 provide examples in ELA and mathematics of a CCSS standard, a task demand for a typical learner, adaptations for a gifted learner, and which framework component is differentiated and in response to student readiness, skills, and interests. There are additional resources available with examples of task demands in using the CCSS in ELA and mathematics with gifted and advanced learners edited by VanTassel-Baska (2013) and Johnsen and Sheffield (2013), respectively (see https://www.nagc.org/nagc2/ngcShopper/).

This framework can be used as a tool for teachers and administrators in planning differentiated instruction. There are other resources and tools that have been developed. NAGC, many state education agencies, local school districts, content area specialists, and classroom teachers have all begun translating the CCSS to documents for classroom practice. Tools, resources, and guidelines are being cre-

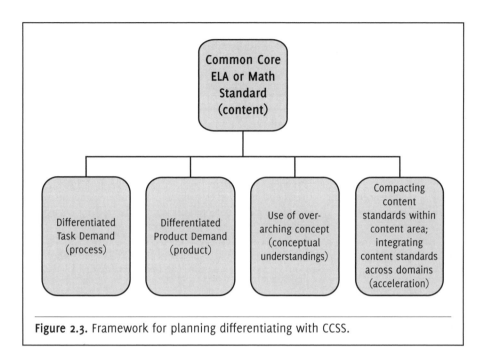

Figure 2.3. Framework for planning differentiating with CCSS.

ated and disseminated. Teachers and administrators should check with their state departments and central offices as well as national organizations for these tools.

Assessment Examples and Considerations

When considering the CCSS, teachers and schools need to take into account the assessments, under development, that will be implemented around the country in states that have adopted CCSS to assess students' level of proficiencies and growth. To date, there are two national assessment consortia engaged in developing assessments aligned to the CCSS in ELA/literacy and mathematics undergirded by the principle that these assessments will demonstrate college- and career-ready students. The states that have adopted CCSS are members of one or both consortia. Each assessment consortium professes that its assessment measure will be a comprehensive framework consisting of different question types, such as multiple choice, constructed response, computer adaptive, and performance-based. They have suggested that students would be better served by an integrated system where summative, interim, and formative components are built from common frameworks and cohere as a large information provision system. One consortium is called Smarter Balanced Assessment Consortium (SBAC). SBAC is a state-led consortium developing assessments aligned to the CCSS in ELA/literacy and mathematics that are designed to help prepare all students to graduate high school college- and career-ready. The other consortium is called

TABLE 2.3

Grade 5 ELA Differentiated Framework Component

English/Language Arts: Grade 5: Reading Standards for Literature Strand and Number: Key Ideas and Details #1	Common Core Standard	RL. 5.1 Quote accurately from a text when explaining what the text says explicitly and when drawing inferences from the text.
	Typical Learner	Students will *select a line* from Carl Sandburg's poem "Fog" and make an inference about what the author meant, drawing explicitly from the text.
	Advanced/Gifted Learner	Students will *define* personification, based on a line from Carl Sandburg's poem "Fog" and describe how Sandburg uses personification to enhance his meaning. Students will create their own personification poem using "Fog" as a model, or write how "Fog" supports the generalization that change occurs over time.
	Differentiation Framework Component	▸ Overarching concept ▸ Metacognition

Partnership for Assessment of Readiness for College and Careers (PARCC), a 22-state consortium to develop K–12 assessments in English and math.

For years, teachers have used a variety of assessments in implicit and explicit ways to drive curricular and instructional design and implementation. High-quality assessment can produce important and valid information about students' learning outcomes as well as provide some insight into the effectiveness of teachers' instruction. For gifted students, the use of performance-based measures that facilitate student learning provide useful data for instructional planning and systematically collecting data over time, and best demonstrates the effectiveness of any curricular model (VanTassel-Baska & Little, 2011). Consideration and employment of assessment protocols as assessment for learning (Stiggins, 2002) must be considered and used throughout the instructional process. This is especially important when working with diverse gifted learners who may not be able to demonstrate their abilities on more traditional standardized measures (VanTassel-Baska, 2008). Below are some examples from the two national assessment consortia. In reviewing the assessment examples in the sidebar, determine what knowledge and skills students are asked to demonstrate as well as considerations for classroom instruction and differentiating for gifted students.

TABLE 2.4
Grade 3 Mathematics Differentiated Framework Component

Math Grade 3: Domain: Number and Operations-Fractions		
	CC Standard	Standard 3.NF.2b Understand a fraction as a number on the number line; represent fractions on a number line diagram. Represent a fraction a/b on a number line diagram by marking off a lengths 1/b from 0. Recognize that the resulting interval has size a/b and that its endpoint locates the number a/b on the number line.
	Typical Learner	Give students the following fractions: 1/2, 1/3, 2/3, 1/4, 2/4, 3/4, 4/4, 2/6, 3/6, 5/6, 6/6 Have students locate each of the fractions on a number line.
		Have students put the fractions in order from least to the greatest.
	Advanced/Gifted Learner	Have students create a fraction by choosing a whole number between 1 and 50 for the numerator and a whole number between 2 and 98 for the denominator.
		Have students estimate where their fraction belongs on the number line and give a reason for their choice.
	Differentiating Framework Component	Product Demand (student choice)
		Task Demand Reasoning made explicit (Paul, 1992)

ELA and Mathematics Examples From PARCC and SBAC

Example 1: ELA
Grade 10 Prose Constructed-Response Item (PARCC, 2013, p. 2):

Use what you have learned from reading "Daedalus and Icarus" by Ovid and "To a Friend Whose Work Has Come to Triumph" by Anne Sexton to write an essay that provides an analysis of how Sexton transforms Daedalus and Icarus.

As a starting point, you may want to consider what is emphasized, absent, or different in the two texts, but feel free to develop your own focus for analysis.

Develop your essay by providing textual evidence from both texts. Be sure to follow the conventions of standard English.

Example 2: ELA
Final Grade 7 Prose Constructed-Response Item #2 (PARCC, 2012, p. 1):

You have read three texts describing Amelia Earhart. All three include the claim that Earhart was a brave, courageous person. The three texts are:
 + "Biography of Amelia Earhart"

- ◆   "Earhart's Final Resting Place Believed Found"
- ◆   "Amelia Earhart's Life and Disappearance"

Consider the argument each author uses to demonstrate Earhart's bravery.

Write an essay that analyzes the strength of the arguments about Earhart's bravery in at least two of the texts. Remember to use textual evidence to support your ideas.

Example 3: ELA
Grade 4 (SBAC, n.d.a., #43009)
The following is the beginning of a story that a student is writing for a class assignment. The story needs more details and an ending. Read the beginning of the story and then complete the task that follows.

Oliver's Big Splash
Oliver was a dog that lived in a small town near a lake. He loved to play outside. Oliver liked to play fetch, but his favorite thing to do was to chase leaves. He loved chasing leaves so much that his favorite time of year was fall when the leaves fell off the trees.

One beautiful fall day, Oliver and his owner, Jeff, went for a walk around the lake. They were enjoying the sunshine and the lake when suddenly a dragonfly flew past. For a moment, Oliver forgot where he and Jeff were and what they were doing. All of a sudden there was a big splash.

Write an ending for the story by adding details to tell what happens next.

Example 4: Mathematics
Grade 4: Problem Solving (SBAC, n.d.b., #43022)
A rectangle is 6 feet long and has a perimeter of 20 feet. What is the width of this rectangle? Explain how you solved this problem.

Example 5: Mathematics
Grade 6: Expressions and Equations 1 (SBAC, n.d.b., #43047)

Look at each expression. Is it equivalent to $36x + 24y$?
Select Yes or No for expressions A – C.
- A. $6(6x + 4y)$
- B. $30(6x - 6y)$
- C. $12(x + 2y + 2x)$

During much of the 20th century and the first decade of the 21st century, the main reason states administered standardized, large-scale measures was to permit comparative score interpretations among test-takers (Popham, 2008). Although much of that is still relevant to the upcoming CCSS assessments developed by the two national consortia, implicit within the assessment examples are higher order reasoning skills such as inferring and applying knowledge through constructed responses. Students throughout the year must have practice engaging in those types of assessment protocol as part of their instruction. The use of more authentic assessment item types suggests the integration of complex and in-depth understanding, creative production, and the use of alternative means of expression or performance that emulates professionals in a field of endeavor. Many of the curricular models employed in gifted education have a focus on product development (Renzulli & Callahan, 2008) and its appropriateness with gifted students. Conversations are occurring across the country and between teams of teachers with content-area experts in developing classroom assessments aligned to the CCSS to foster more in-depth analysis of student thinking.

Guiding Questions for Collaboration

Implementing the CCSS with fidelity for gifted learners allows an opportunity for gifted education professionals to collaborate with other educational and community partners. Although gifted education professionals would have a deep understanding of effective curriculum and instructional models, collaboration with others is paramount if optimal learning contexts are to be produced for talent development to emerge (Gubbins et al., 2002). Gifted education professionals play an important role in the implementation of the CCSS in the classroom by collaborating with other teachers, communicating with parents, and serving as a valuable resource for differentiated curriculum and assessment. The use of guiding questions may be helpful in shaping the conversation among professional learning communities, task forces, local gifted committees, and others engaged in implementing the CCSS across grade levels and content domains. Examples of guiding questions for intra- and interagency collaboration are as follows:

» What different resources are available in order to provide above-level content in general education classrooms for use with gifted students, as well as within other program models?

» How can fidelity of rigor, depth, complexity, and acceleration be ensured when employing the CCSS with gifted students across content domains and grade levels?

» If students can demonstrate an advanced mastery of the standards early in the year, what options are available for them?

» What types of training need to occur so that teachers are competent and comfortable with employing a variety of types of assessments (e.g., pre-, formative, performance, etc.) when working with gifted learners? What types of training need to occur for teachers to be able to make inferences from the assessments about student growth?

» What role do teachers of the gifted have within professional learning communities or other in-school and across-school models of teacher capacity building?

» If new policies and procedures are written about implementing CCSS, how do teachers ensure that gifted education is present?

» What supporting structures and impeding barriers are in place for implementing CCSS with gifted learners?

» In what ways can community and business partners foster meaningful extensions of the CCSS for gifted learners?

The adage of taking a village to raise a child has never been truer than in education today with the multitude of reform initiatives and demands placed upon administrators and teachers. In order to implement CCSS and ultimately sustain it, it is paramount that collaboration among and between many stakeholders occurs and that teachers of the gifted as advocates become real partners (Roberts & Siegle, 2012). Without this, only pockets of excellence will continue to occur idiosyncratically rather than coherence, alignment, comprehensiveness, and shared ownership.

Implications

The key to any set of content standards lies not only in the intent but in the implementation of teaching and learning practices. Many states are rolling out extensive professional development materials, toolkits, and videos, and facilitating conversations among instructional staff and administrators. It is too early to tell whether implementation of the CCSS will be reduced to a laundry list of checking off which standards have been taught but rather a rising tide of intellectual capital. Additionally, the assessment protocols developed by the two assessment consortia are intended to reflect the diversity among students, in terms of demonstrating content knowledge and varying degrees of ability through a variety of multiple-choice questions, computer-adapted testing, performance-based measures, and constructed response items. The following are implications for teachers and programs when implementing CCSS with gifted learners.

Teachers

- » Assist students in developing schema and well-organized structures based in the discipline.
- » Focus on issues and conceptual learning that characterize the discipline.
- » Develop pre- and formative assessment task demands that integrate learning objectives and use ongoing assessment practices to guide instruction.
- » Teach to the intent of the standard.
- » Employ advanced content aligned to the CCSS.
- » Consider ways to enrich, accelerate, and extend the CCSS.
- » Collaborate with others in the building and community to address the individual needs of gifted learners.

Programs

- » Shore up how your gifted program aligns, supports, and extends the CCSS.
- » Provide and collaborate on professional development opportunities.
- » Develop communication vehicles for parent understanding.
- » Determine how your enrichment and/or acceleration options are value-add and find ways to measure their impact.
- » Consider additional supports for diverse gifted learners.
- » Strengthen partnerships between regular education, special education, and gifted education.
- » Students may access more rigorous standards throughout the day, which would impact direct gifted education services and ensure access to advanced education throughout the day. Recognize that optimal learning experiences need to occur all day, every day.
- » Make sure the CCSS align with and validate gifted education best practices, such as concept-based learning, integration of disciplines, and inquiry-based options.
- » Some gifted education classrooms focus on less robust content than in the general education classroom, because they are engaged in process skills such as critical thinking or creative thinking void of content.

The interface between gifted education and CCSS affects all gifted education program components. For the most part, students identified as gifted continue to receive the bulk of their instruction in general education classrooms and are required to take any commensurate state assessments. Within the next few years, gifted students, and all students, will be required to take a Common Core assessment currently under development by one of two national assessment consortia. General education teachers are expected to differentiate in order to meet their academic and social/emotional needs. They are typically identified in domain-specific areas such as reading and mathematics. Any curricular and instructional modifications, as well as augmented services such as a resource pull-out room must be connected to state standards. Differentiation is frequently employed through modifications such as content differentiation, high-level processes and products, accelerating or enriching the standard curriculum, or other strategies such as problem-based learning. All of these strategies are utilized with the curriculum framework provided by the state content standards. In addition, gifted students typically are college-bound and therefore competing against national and international peers, so the notion of "college-ready" takes on another level of meaning. Gifted education can ill afford not to embrace the CCSS in traditional content dimensions as core areas of learning for the gifted in all grade levels rather than treating these core areas as peripheral. Gifted education must view the CCSS as an opportunity to upgrade what we do—we must go through the standards to do it, and not around them.

Conclusion

Due to the relative newness of CCSS, it is too early to tell the degree to which these content standards offer real systemic change, optimal learning, and a trajectory of academic growth for gifted and talented students. Standards by themselves cannot raise student achievement. Standards are the catalyst through which highly effective teachers engage students in the teaching and learning process to improve student outcomes for all students, even those at the top end.

Despite the fact that the vast majority of states have adopted the CCSS, gifted education remains a state and local control issue and optimal learning situations and documentation of program effectiveness will not occur for these students, even with strong content standards, unless systematic efforts in funding, and coherence of curricula, teacher preparation, program delivery, and accountability are achieved (Spielhagen, Brown, & Hughes, in press).

This chapter has provided an overview of the CCSS, a rationale for why gifted education should care, ways to consider implementing CCSS with gifted learners through differentiating given a framework, assessment considerations, implications, and guiding questions for collaborating with others. There are many areas that were not explicitly discussed such as the role of teacher preparation, ways to address diverse populations of gifted students, or the role of technology to facilitate the implementation of CCSS. Practices that inform the teacher preparation and programming standards in gifted education related to assessment, curriculum, instruction, and grouping considerations are all embedded within the CCSS. The CCSS hold promise for gifted students but can never replace the need for services based on the learning needs of gifted students, which differ from those of other students. The academic and social-emotional needs of gifted students should be addressed through differentiation, a modification of curriculum, instruction, and assessment based on the assessed achievement and interests of individual students.

Teacher Statement

The adoption of the CCSS has caused educators to think about how we are supporting our gifted learners. The question of how these standards affect gifted students and what the implications of these standards will be is at the forefront of educators' minds, especially those who teach gifted and talented classes in enrichment programs, specialized classes or schools, or other programs for the gifted. As a gifted and talented second-grade teacher in a large urban public school, the information in this chapter proved to be extremely beneficial from a curricular planning lens as it proves how important assessment, planning, and differentiation are to instruction, especially under this new set of standards.

The CCSS are rigorous for all students. This chapter makes it clear that these standards provide teachers with a "road map." This metaphor was enlightening as I plan around these standards for my gifted class. It is imperative to remember this comparison because I need to think about not just this year and my group of students but where they are going. As this chapter states, "gifted educators must use these standards as a method to get students to where they need to be." As a result of this chapter, I view these standards as the destination we are going toward, but educators still need to give students the directions on how to get there. Although teachers may go in different directions to get to the end destination and use various educational experiences in order to reach these challenging goals, *we* must create an educationally meaningful voyage. The voyage must be relevantly rigorous, challenging, and build knowledge through content-rich texts and experiences. This chapter stresses the importance that the voyage needs to be one where there is continual assessment and differentiation in order to find students' academic strengths and weaknesses in efforts to meet individual needs. There are examples of ways to organize the content for gifted learners, conceptually and operationally. This chapter proves that the CCSS still allow for, if not more so than the standards they replaced, teachers to have the flexibility and the responsibility to modify and create meaningful experiences for learning to occur with our gifted students.

I now realize this is a critical time for gifted educators to focus and reflect on how we can better our practice in efforts to lead to higher level thinking and authentic assessments, rather than preparation for lower level test-prep type answers. With the new CCSS, it becomes critical for us to show how we are differentiating and assessing for gifted learners within a set of rigorous standards in all subject areas. It is a time for gifted educators to collaborate, share best practices, and communicate as a large group to meet the needs of gifted students.

—Second-Grade Gifted Teacher

References

American Federation of Teachers. (2001). *Making standards matter: A fifty-state report on efforts to implement a standards-based system*. Washington, DC: Author.

American Federation of Teachers. (2008). *Sizing up state standards*. Washington, DC: Author.

Confrey, J., & Kuzak, S. (2006). A thirty-year reflection on constructivism in mathematics education in PME. In A. Guttiérrez and P. Boero (Eds.), *Handbook of research on the psychology of mathematics education: Past, present, and future* (pp. 305–345). Rotterdam, the Netherlands: Sense.

Daggett, W. (2007). *The education challenge: Preparing students for a changing world* (Position paper). Rexford, NY: International Center for Leadership in Education.

Davis, G. A., Rimm, S. B., & Siegel, D. (2011). *Education of the gifted and talented* (6th ed.) Boston, MA: Pearson.

Gubbins, E. J., Westberg, K. L., Reis, S., Dinnocenti, S. T., Tieso, C. L., & Muller, L. M. (2002). *Implementing a professional development model using gifted education strategies with all students* (RM02172). Storrs: University of Connecticut, National Research Center on the Gifted and Talented.

Johnsen, S. K., & Sheffield, L. J. (Eds.). (2013). *Using the Common Core State Standards for mathematics with gifted and advanced learners*. Waco, TX: Prufrock Press.

National Association for Gifted Children. (2014). *Common Core and Next Generation Science Standards for gifted and talented students* (Position paper). Retrieved from http://www.nagc.org/index2.aspx?id=11370

Partnership for Assessment of Readiness for College and Careers. (2012). *Sample items for grade 7*. Retrieved from https://www.parcconline.org/sites/parcc/files/Gr%207%20PARCC%20ELA%20Item%203_0.pdf

Partnership for Assessment of Readiness for College and Careers. (2013). *Grade 10 sample items*. Retrieved from https://www.parcconline.org/sites/parcc/files/Grade10SampleItemSet10.30.13.pdf

Paul, R. (1992). Critical thinking: What, why, and how. *New Directions for Community Colleges, 1992*, 3–24.

Popham, W. J. (2008). *Transformative assessment*. Alexandria, VA: Association for Supervision and Curriculum Development.

Renzulli, J. S., & Callahan, C. M (2008). Product assessment. In J. VanTassel-Baska (Ed.), *Alternative assessments with gifted and talented students* (pp. 259–284). Waco, TX: Prufrock Press.

Roberts, J. L., & Siegle, D. (2012). Teachers as advocates: If not you—who? *Gifted Child Today, 35*(1), 58–61.

Smarick, A. (2013). *The common core implementation gap*. Retrieved from http://www.edexcellence.net/commentary/education-gadfly-daily/common-core-watch/2013/the-common-core-implementation-gap.html

Smarter Balanced Assessment Consortium. (n.d.a). *English language arts/literacy sample items*. Retrieved from http://sampleitems.smarterbalanced.org/itempreview/sbac/ELA.htm

Smarter Balanced Assessment Consortium. (n.d.b). *Mathematics sample items*. Retrieved from http://sampleitems.smarterbalanced.org/itempreview/sbac/index.htm

Spielhagen, F. R., Brown, E. F., & Hughes, C. E. (in press). Outliers: Political forces in gifted and special education. In B. S. Cooper, J. G. Cibulka, & L. D. Fusarelli (Eds.), *Handbook of education politics and policy* (3rd ed.). Mahwah, NJ: Lawrence Erlbaum.

Stambaugh, T. (2011). Aligning curriculum for the gifted with content standards and state assessments. In J. VanTassel-Baska & C. A. Little (Eds.), *Content-based curriculum for high-ability learners* (2nd ed., pp. 397–412). Waco, TX: Prufrock Press.

Stiggins. R. J. (2002). Assessment crisis: The absence of assessement for learning. *Phi Delta Kappan, 83,* 758–764.

Tomlinson, C. A. (1999). *The differentiated classroom: Responding to the needs of all learners.* Alexandria, VA: Association for Supervision and Curriculum Development.

VanTassel-Baska, J. (2008). *Alternative assessments with gifted and talented students.* Waco, TX: Prufrock Press.

VanTassel-Baska, J. (Ed.). (2013). *Using the Common Core State Standards for English language arts with gifted and advanced learners.* Waco, TX: Prufrock Press.

VanTassel-Baska, J. (2014). In J. A. Plucker & C. M. Callahan (Eds.), *Critical issues and practices in gifted education: What the research says* (2nd ed., pp. 377–386). Waco, TX: Prufrock Press.

VanTassel-Baska, J., & Brown, E. (2009). An analysis of curriculum models in gifted education. In F. Karnes & S. Bean (Eds.), *Methods and materials for teaching the gifted* (3rd ed., pp. 75–106). Waco, TX: Prufock Press.

VanTassel-Baska, J., & Little, C. A. (2011). *Content-based curriculum for high ability learners* (2nd edition). Waco, TX: Prufrock Press.

Wiley, A., Wyatt, J., & Camara, W. J. (2010). *The development of a multidimensional college readiness index* (College Board Research Report 2010-3). New York, NY: The College Board. Retrieved from http://professionals.collegeboard.com/profdownload/pdf/10b_3110_CollegeReadiness_RR_WEB_110315.pdf

Appendix A
NAGC Position Paper: Common Core and Next Generation Science Standards for Gifted and Advanced Students

The adoption of Common Core State Standards (CCSS) in English language arts and mathematics and Next Generation Science Standards (NGSS) for K-12 students by a large majority of states is having a profound influence on curriculum, instruction, and assessment in classrooms across the country. The content standards initiatives are part of a national effort to define critical elements of college and career readiness and to raise expectations for all learners. The content standards are intended to promote higher levels of learning for all students and to promote the kinds of instructional strategies that have long been advocated in gifted education, including emphasis on analytical thinking, reasoning, and problem-solving skills. Such efforts to promote high-level learning for all students show promise for improving student achievement across the United States, but the message that high-level learning experiences are important for all must be coupled with a recognition that even with increased rigor and higher standards, some students will still require experiences beyond what the standards specify to show ongoing learning growth. Even rigorous standards for all learners may result in limits on learning for advanced students if schools tie the benchmarks for student achievement too closely to grade-level expectations. Thus, while supporting the effort to promote rigorous content standards for all learners, the National Association for Gifted Children also calls for attention to the specific needs of gifted learners in the implementation of the national content standards and their corresponding assessments.

Gifted and talented students typically grasp curriculum concepts more quickly and deeply than their age peers. They achieve grade-level expectations earlier than specified in the standards and generally need far fewer instructional and practice experiences to achieve mastery. To make continuous progress in their areas of talent, gifted students need learning experiences that extend and enrich the standards and require students to apply complex, creative, and innovative thinking to authentic problems. The developers of the CCSS and NGSS have acknowledged individual differences of gifted students noting that some students will master the standards before grade 12, and that it is up to educators to extend the learning goals and objectives beyond the standards to meet their needs.

This acknowledgement means that effective implementation of the standards requires specific instructional strategies and curricular materials, including modified formative and summative assessments, for advanced and gifted students whose levels of learning exceed grade-level expectations. Effective instruction using CCSS and NGSS for gifted students will require extensive professional development on the standards and the assessment systems, sufficient materials and personnel resources to support implementation, and reasonable expectations regarding the time required for learning new instructional practices. In addition, effective and comprehensive implementation of the content standards requires systematic attention to the growth of each learner. For gifted learners, such opportunities for growth will require concerted efforts from states, school districts, and building leaders to support the implementation of curricula that are sufficiently advanced.

These recommendations reflect a number of concerns in the translation and implementation of the standards into classroom practice. For example, providing differentiated methods and materials in the typical classroom for a heterogeneous group of learners, including those who are struggling or below grade level, may diminish attention to the needs of gifted and advanced learners. Moreover, the assessment process may further limit attention to the needs of advanced learners, especially if the assessments do not support demonstration of above-grade achievement due to low ceilings and instead are linked only to specific grade-level standards and related performance indicators. Assessment developers must consider how student performance above expected levels may be assessed in ways that will provide information useful for instructional planning.

To ensure that gifted children receive the advanced content and experiences they need to grow and learn, NAGC calls on states, school districts, and curriculum and assessment developers to implement the standards in ways that respond to gifted learners' pace and depth of learning. Doing this effectively will require substantial opportunities for professional development, resources that address instructional practices for exceptional learners, and assessments that reflect sufficient room for student growth. Only with such comprehensive support can the standards—and the learners—achieve their potential.

Resources

Achieve, Inc. (2013). *The Next Generation Science Standards.* Retrieved from http://www. nextgenscience.org/next-generation-science-standards

Adams, C. M., Cotabish, A., & Ricci, M. C. (2013). *Using the next generation science standards with gifted and advanced learners.* Waco, TX: Prufrock Press.

International Reading Association Common Core State Standards Committee. (2012). *Literacy implementation guidance for the ELA common core state standards* [White paper]. Retrieved from http://www.reading.org/Libraries/association-documents/ ira_ccss_guidelines.pdf

Hughes, C. E., Kettler, T., Shaunessy-Dedrick, E., & VanTassel-Baska, J. (2013). *A teacher's guide to using the common core state standards with gifted and advanced learners in English language arts.* Waco, TX: Prufrock Press.

Johnsen, S., K., Ryser, G. R., & Assouline, S. G. (2013). *A teacher's guide to using the common core state standards with mathematically gifted and advanced learners.* Waco, TX: Prufrock Press.

Johnsen, S. K., & Sheffield, L. J. (2012). *Using the common core state standards for mathematics with gifted and advanced learners.* Waco, TX: Prufrock Press.

National Governors Association Center for Best Practices & Council of Chief State School Offices. (2010a). *Common core state standards for English language arts.* Washington, DC: Authors.

National Governors Association Center for Best Practices & Council of Chief State School Offices. (2010b). *Common core state standards for mathematics.* Washington, DC: Authors.

VanTassel-Baska, J. (Ed.). (2012). *Using the common core state standards for English language arts with gifted and advanced learners.* Waco, TX: Prufrock Press.

Note

This appendix was reprinted from "Common Core and Next Generation Science Standards for Gifted and Advanced Students," created by the National Association for Gifted Children (2014) retrieved from http://www.nagc.org/ index2.aspx?id=11370. Copyright 2014 NAGC. Reprinted with permission.

OVERVIEW OF CHARACTERISTICS AND NEEDS OF GIFTED LEARNERS

CHARACTERISTICS OF GIFTED LEARNERS

Chapter **3**

Varied, Diverse, and Complex

BY SALLY M. REIS, ERIN E. SULLIVAN, AND SARA J. RENZULLI

In an ideal world, a definitive and research-based list of characteristics of gifted and talented learners would both exist and provide a foolproof way to absolutely identify gifted and talented students. This list, in this perfect world, could also be used to develop, identify, and teach the perfect curriculum for the academic and artistic growth of this population. Unfortunately, no such list exists, for one of the unifying themes in research on characteristics of gifted learners is, in fact, the absolute diversity of this heterogeneous, varied, and unique group. Despite this diversity, research suggests that there are some traits that occur with greater frequency in gifted and talented students than in the general population. In this chapter, these characteristics are discussed to provide educators with an overview of characteristics displayed by some gifted and high-ability students. Also discussed is how these characteristics vary according to gender, sociocultural characteristics, having a hidden or overt disability, age, and whether a student is achieving or underachieving. It is impossible to provide a checklist of characteristics of students so that their teachers can help them to be identified as either "gifted" or "not gifted." Rather, the intent of this chapter is to provide educators with the tools to understand the diverse characteristics in a broad spectrum of children and young adults. To begin, the following illustrative case study is presented as an example of a highly gifted individual and his childhood history. This case study was created through a review of multiple biographies online as well as several websites that provide childhood backgrounds of Terence Tao, who was also studied in research on prodigies by Gross (1986).

Terence Tao is a professor of mathematics at UCLA, where, his website explains, he "works in a number of mathematical areas, but primarily in harmonic analysis, PDE, geometric combinatorics, arithmetic combinatorics, analytic number theory, compressed sensing, and algebraic combinatorics" ("Terence Tao," n.d., para. 1).

Professor Tao's father was a Chinese-born pediatrician and his mother, who was born in Hong Kong, studied physics and mathematics. Terence's parents met while they were studying at the University of Hong Kong and moved to Australia in 1972, where his mother, Grace, taught high school. They had three children. Terence is their oldest child, followed by two younger brothers, Trevor and Nigel. According to biographies of Terence, he was extremely precocious, as he taught himself to read at age 2, and by his ninth birthday, he was enrolled in college math classes. He completed his doctorate in mathematics by the age of 20 and is now considered one of the most prominent mathematicians in the world, studying both prime numbers and the compression of images. He has won a Fields Medal, often considered the Nobel Prize of mathematics, and is the recipient of a MacArthur Fellowship "genius" award. He is described as down-to-Earth, and he often is found at work in a sweatshirt, blue jeans, and sneakers. He is married to an engineer at the NASA Jet Propulsion Laboratory. His current research is focused on compressed sensing, but his best known mathematical work involves prime numbers.

Tao's proficiency with numbers appeared at a very young age, and he is reported to have said that he always liked numbers. As a child, he used blocks to show older children how to count. Although his parents placed him in a private school when he was 3, they removed him soon after because they believed his teacher was not able to teach a student as advanced as Terence.

When he was 5, Terence was enrolled in a public school, and his parents, administrators, and teachers implemented an individualized program that enabled him to master subjects at his own pace, quickly accelerating through several grades in math and science while remaining closer to his age group in other subjects.

Terence began attending math classes at the local high school when he was 7, and two years later, he began taking university-level math and physics classes. He did extremely well in international math competitions and enrolled at Flinders University in Adelaide, Australia, when he was 14, where he earned his bachelor's degree in 2 years, his master's degree in a year, and then matriculated at Princeton for his doctoral work in mathematics, where he also found a peer group.

Giftedness as a Construct

Understanding characteristics of giftedness means that educators must recognize many overlapping definitions of giftedness. The field of gifted education, in an attempt to serve diverse groups of learners, has embraced diverse definitions of its central constructs. Thus, the terms *giftedness*, *talent*, *intellect*, and *intelligence* are not easily defined. For many years, researchers and psychologists, following in the footsteps of Lewis Terman, equated giftedness with high IQ. In practice, this legacy survives to the present day, with some researchers, educators, and parents continuing to assume that psychometric intelligence is equivalent to giftedness.

More recently, a new generation of researchers has argued that giftedness is a multidimensional construct incorporating a variety of traits, skills, and abilities, and manifesting in manifold ways. This view is particularly evident in the examination and subsequent reexamination of giftedness in Sternberg and Davidson's (1986, 2005) edited editions of *Conceptions of Giftedness*, in which most contributors propose conceptions of giftedness that go beyond or minimize the importance of IQ. Rapid learning as compared to others in the population (Cross & Coleman, 2005); attention control, memory efficiency, and characteristics of perception (Heller, Perleth, & Lim, 2005); desire to develop one's gifts (Reis, 2005); and task commitment (Renzulli, 2005) all are proposed as aspects of giftedness in the models in *Conceptions of Giftedness*.

One of the earliest researchers to propose a multifaceted conception of giftedness was Renzulli (1978), whose "three-ring" conception suggested that gifted behaviors result from a synergy among several distinct intrapersonal characteristics:

> Gifted behavior consists of behaviors that reflect an interaction among three basic clusters of human traits—above average ability, high levels of task commitment, and high levels of creativity. Individuals capable of developing gifted behavior are those possessing or capable of developing this composite set of traits and applying them to any potentially valuable area of human performance. Persons who manifest or are capable of developing an interaction among the three clusters require a wide variety of educational opportunities and services that are not ordinarily provided through regular instructional programs. (Renzulli & Reis, 1997, p. 8)

Characteristics that may be manifested in Renzulli's three clusters are presented in Table 3.1.

REIS, SULLIVAN, AND RENZULLI

TABLE 3.1

Taxonomy of Behavioral Manifestations of Giftedness According
to Renzulli's "Three-Ring" Definition of Gifted Behaviors

Above-Average Ability (General)	‣ high levels of abstract thought ‣ adaptation to novel situations ‣ rapid and accurate retrieval of information
Above-Average Ability (Specific)	‣ applications of general abilities to specific area of knowledge ‣ capacity to sort out relevant from irrelevant information ‣ capacity to acquire and use advanced knowledge and strategies while pursuing a problem
Task Commitment	‣ capacity for high levels of interest, enthusiasm ‣ hard work and determination in a particular area ‣ self-confidence and drive to achieve ‣ ability to identify significant problems within an area of study ‣ setting high standards for one's work ‣ open to new experiences and ideas ‣ curious ‣ willing to take risks ‣ sensitive to aesthetic characteristics

Note. Adapted from *The Schoolwide Enrichment Model: A How-to Guide for Educational Excellence* (2nd ed., p. 9), by J. S. Renzulli and S. M. Reis, 1997, Waco, TX: Prufrock Press. Copyright © 1997 by Prufrock Press. Adapted with permission.

The United States' current federal definition of giftedness likewise takes a multidimensional approach. It states, as follows:

> Children and youth with outstanding talent perform or show the potential for performing at remarkably high levels of accomplishment when compared with others of their age, experience, or environment. These children and youth exhibit high performance capability in intellectual, creative, and/or artistic areas, possess an unusual leadership capacity, or excel in specific academic fields. They require services or activities not ordinarily provided by the schools. Outstanding talents are present in children and youth from all cultural groups, across all economic strata, and in all areas of human endeavor. (U.S. Department of Education, 1993, p. 26)

One conception of giftedness varies the most from those presented earlier. The 1991 Columbus Group defined giftedness as being focused on developmental trajectory and affective qualities:

> Giftedness is "asynchronous development" in which advanced cognitive abilities and heightened intensity combine to create inner experiences and awareness that are qualitatively different from the norm. This asyn-

chrony increases with higher intellectual capacity. The uniqueness of the gifted renders them particularly vulnerable and requires modifications in parenting, teaching and counseling in order for them to develop optimally. (Columbus Group, 1991)

The diversity of multiple definitions of giftedness clearly suggests that no single conception of giftedness exists, nor does any definitive list of characteristics of gifted students. This chapter summarizes research about various subgroups of gifted learners, presenting varied conceptions of the construct and the characteristics that describe these varied definitions.

Characteristics of Academically Gifted Students

Giftedness is often associated with those who perform well in academic situations, a talent Renzulli (2005) referred to as "schoolhouse giftedness or high academic giftedness," and others have labeled "cognitive ability" or "intellectual ability." Schoolhouse giftedness is generally characterized by students who learn efficiently, take tests well, and excel in traditional intellectual assessments. This section of the chapter deals with characteristics that may be associated with students who are academically gifted.

General Characteristics

Over the years, many researchers and textbook writers have summarized broad characteristics of academically gifted students. This extensive list of characteristics presented by Clark (2002) is generally culled from anecdotal evidence and is divided into different categories as listed below.

  » *cognitive (thinking) characteristics*, such as retention of large quantities of information, advanced comprehension, varied interests and high curiosity, and a high level of language development and verbal ability;
  » *affective (feeling) characteristics*, such as unusual sensitivity to the feelings of others, keen sense of humor, heightened self-awareness, feelings of being different, and idealism and sense of justice;
  » *physical (sensation) characteristics*, such as heightened sensory awareness, unusual discrepancy between physical and intellectual development, and low tolerance for lag between their standards and their athletic skills;
  » *intuitive characteristics*, such as being open to intuitive experiences and creativity apparent in all areas of endeavor; and
  » *societal characteristics*, such as being strongly motivated by self-actualization needs, advanced capacity for conceptualizing and solving

societal problems, leadership, and involvement with the meta needs of society (i.e., justice, truth, beauty).

Comparing Clark's (2002) list with other characteristics of gifted students identifies broad consensus on traits commonly found in this group. Bailey (2011) studied gifted high school students and found low rates of internalizing and externalizing behaviors, strong social skills, high levels of competence, and slightly above average levels of ego development based on age. Research by Renzulli (2005) and Reis (1989) identified characteristics such as the ability to learn more rapidly than other students, understanding of complex or abstract topics, and advanced verbal ability and problem-solving skills. Steiner (2006) also suggested that gifted students more consistently use advanced problem-solving strategies than other learners. Frasier and Passow (1994) identified characteristics of giftedness that were found to be cross-cultural, including problem-solving ability, as well as traits found on Clark's (2002) list such as motivation, sense of humor, creativity, and well-developed memory.

The most comprehensive, well-researched characteristics of talented students across numerous content areas and areas of strength are the Scales for Rating the Behavioral Characteristics of Superior Students (SRBCSS) by Renzulli and his associates (2002, 2013). The SRBCSS were expanded in 2002 to include scales in reading, math, and technology in addition to the original scales in the areas of learning, motivation, creativity, leadership, artistic, musical, dramatic, communication, and planning abilities. In addition to the more generic lists and syntheses of traits and characteristics discussed, other research has focused on characteristics of distinct subgroups within the population of students identified as high potential or above average. These include groups such as talented readers.

Traits Associated With Talented Readers

Identifying the characteristics of talented readers was the focus of a study by researchers at The National Research Center on the Gifted and Talented (Reis et al., 2004). Research has indicated that not all gifted students are talented readers and not all talented readers are academically gifted, but more than half of those identified as gifted are talented readers who demonstrate some or most of the characteristics summarized in Table 3.2.

Social and Emotional Traits

The question of whether gifted and talented learners have unique affective, social, and emotional characteristics has been a topic of lively debate for decades. A comprehensive review of existing research was conducted by a team of researchers, psychologists, and educators from the National Association for Gifted

TABLE 3.2
Characteristics of Talented Readers

Enjoyment in the Reading Process	▸ Read avidly and with enjoyment ▸ Use reading differently for different reading purposes ▸ Demonstrate thirst for insight and knowledge satisfied through reading ▸ Pursue varied interests in and curiosity about texts ▸ View books and reading as a way to explore the richness of life ▸ Seek and enjoy depth and complexity in reading ▸ Develop a deeper understanding of particular topics through reading ▸ Demonstrate preferences for nonfiction ▸ Pursue interest-based reading opportunities
Read Early and Above Level	▸ Read at least two grade levels above chronological grade placement ▸ Begin reading early and may be self-taught
Advanced Processing	▸ Retain a large quantity of information for retrieval ▸ Automatically integrate prior knowledge and experience in reading ▸ Utilize higher order thinking skills such as analysis and synthesis ▸ Process information and thoughts at an accelerated pace ▸ Synthesize ideas in a comprehensive way ▸ Perceive unusual relationships and integrate ideas ▸ Grasp complex ideas and nuances
Advanced Language Skills	▸ Enjoy the subtleties and complexities of language ▸ Demonstrate advanced understanding of language ▸ Use expansive vocabulary ▸ Use reading to acquire a large repertoire of language skills ▸ Use language for humor ▸ Display verbal ability in self-expression ▸ Use colorful and descriptive phrasing ▸ Demonstrate ease in use of language

Children (Neihart, Reis, Robinson, & Moon, 2002). This task force found only a limited research base from which to draw conclusions about whether gifted and talented learners actually have unique social and emotional characteristics. No evidence was found that gifted children or youth—as a group—are inherently any more vulnerable to psychological problems than any other group of students. In general, they have no higher (or lower) rate of serious maladjustment, suicide, delinquency, or severe behavioral disorders than do students not identified as gifted. Rather, many gifted young people possess assets that, when supported, may enhance their own resilience to negative life events and enable them to use their talents to achieve productive and satisfying lives. When troubling social and emotional traits do occur in gifted students, they often are the result of a poor fit between the individual and his or her academic or social environment (Gross, 2002; Neihart, 2002).

In support of this idea, a notable exception to the findings on social-emotional adjustment of gifted children is the research that suggests that children with exceptionally high IQ scores, that is, IQs over 160, and students gifted in the visual arts and writing, do indeed have more problems than other students (Gross, 2002; Hollingworth, 1926, 1942). It is unclear why artists and writers have more social and emotional difficulties, suggesting the need for additional research into factors that contribute to and protect against isolation and mental health issues in this population. In regard to social and emotional difficulties in students with exceptionally high IQs, Gross (2002) suggested that these children may be so different from their age-mates that they cannot fit in socially even when consciously attempting to underachieve. The skills and abilities of this group may so far outstrip grade-level material that only radical acceleration of several grades will yield positive outcomes, similar to the case study of Terence Tao summarized above.

Although there is limited consensus in research regarding whether social-emotional characteristics of gifted students differ from the norm, one theory does seem to hold promise. Over the years, a body of literature (Ackerman, 1997; Bouchet & Falk, 2001; Piechowski & Colangelo, 1984; Piechowski & Cunningham, 1985) has developed suggesting that Dabrowski's (1964) Theory of Positive Disintegration can be usefully applied to gifted students. The theory, which centers on developmental potential, posits that five personal intensities can contribute to an individual's personal growth. To paraphrase Mendaglio and Tillier (2006) and other researchers, these five "overexcitabilities" (OEs) are as follows:

» *Psychomotor overexcitability*: Psychomotor OE is a surplus of energy or a translation of nervous energy into a variety of psychomotor behaviors, such as tics, nail biting, broad gestures, or impulsive behavior.

» *Sensual overexcitability*: Sensual OE is a sensitivity to sensory input and a tendency to use sensory outlets to release tension. Sensual OE can include an interest in the aesthetics of appearance and other sense-oriented stimuli.

» *Intellectual overexcitability*: Intellectual OE is an intense focus on understanding, pursuit of the truth, academic interests, and intellectual achievement.

» *Imaginational overexcitability*: Imaginational OE is an affinity and talent for imagery, fantasy, invention, and other facets of the imagination and can manifest as daydreaming or distractibility.

» *Emotional overexcitability*: Emotional OE is characterized by intense feeling and may include heightened sensitivity to others' emotions, inhibition, or shyness; heightened ability to recall emotional experiences; anxiety; and fear of the unknown.

Some preliminary research has linked each of the overexcitabilities to giftedness, but Emotional OE is by far most commonly associated with giftedness across studies (Ackerman, 1997; Bouchet & Falk, 2001; Miller, Silverman, & Falk, 1994; Piechowski & Colangelo, 1984; Piechowski, Silverman, & Falk, 1985). Although further research is needed on this topic, it appears that some gifted students demonstrate characteristics of emotional intensity far more often than other students.

Personality and Giftedness

Some research has identified patterns in the personality traits of gifted students (Cross, Cassady, & Miller, 2006; Cross, Speirs Neumeister, & Cassady, 2007; Delbridge-Parker & Robinson, 1989; Harris, 2004). Cross et al. (2007) administered the Myers-Briggs Type Indicator (MBTI; Myers, 1962) to 931 gifted adolescents attending a residential school and found that many gifted adolescents demonstrate personality traits that are less commonly found in other students. The MBTI was designed to measure personality preferences on four dichotomous traits: Extroversion/Introversion (E/I), Intuition/Sensing (N/S), Thinking/Feeling (T/F), and Judging/Perceiving (J/P). Introversion versus Extroversion refers to the degree to which one is oriented to the outside world versus the internal world. Extroverts are energized by interactions with others and seek out social situations, while Introverts are described as being energized by time alone and may require less social interaction than Extroverts. Intuition versus Sensing describes one's preference for either focusing on abstract ideas (Intuition) or attending to concrete information gathered through the senses (Sensing). Thinking versus Feeling refers to one's preferred style for making decisions. According to the theory behind the MBTI, Thinkers prefer to make logic-based decisions that exclude subjective factors, while Feelers prefer to take others' feelings and personal values into account when making decisions. Finally, Judging types are reported to prefer order, structure, and deadlines, while Perceiving types prefer to be spontaneous, open, and free to change course as they see fit (Cross et al., 2007).

Cross et al. (2007) found that the most common type preferences for gifted adolescents in this study were INTJ, INTP, INFP, ENFP, and ENTP—all of which are types that prefer abstract thinking (Intuition) to focusing on the concrete (Sensing). In fact, almost 70% of these adolescents preferred Intuition to Sensing. Likewise, Perceiving was preferred to Judging by about 57% of the participants. Approximately 40% of participants had a combined preference for Intuition and Perceiving. In contrast, the most common types in adolescents not identified as gifted are ESTP, ESFP, ESTJ, and ESFJ. All of these types are sensing types, preferring concrete reality to abstract thought. Judging (a preference for order and structure) was about as common as Perceiving (preference for flexibility and openness) in this population.

This data echoes previous research (Delbridge-Parker & Robinson, 1989; Gallagher, 1990; Hawkins, 1997; Sak, 2004) that has likewise found a disproportionate number of Intuitive and Perceiving types among gifted students. Sak (2004) analyzed 14 studies with a total of 5,723 gifted adolescents and found Intuitive and Perceiving types to be the most common across studies. Similar to the work completed in the Cross et al. (2007) study, about 70% of gifted adolescents in the studies analyzed by Sak preferred Intuition to Sensing. By comparison, only about 30% of adolescents in the general population prefer Intuition. Approximately 60% of the gifted adolescents in Sak's analysis preferred Perceiving, as compared to 45% in the normative population. These data may suggest that many gifted adolescents have personalities and traits that differ in some key ways from other students.

Characteristics Associated With Creative Giftedness

Renzulli (2005) has found that creative/productive giftedness is reflected in individuals who tend to be producers (rather than consumers) of original knowledge, materials, or products, and who employ thought processes that are inductive and problem oriented. Whereas Renzulli suggested that many gifted students possess attributes of both schoolhouse giftedness and creative productive giftedness, research suggests that having a high IQ by no means ensures high creativity (Davis & Rimm, 1998; Milgram & Hong, 2009; Renzulli & Reis, 2014). A 2005 meta-analysis of 21 studies and 45,880 participants, for example, found that the correlation between IQ and creativity was negligible. The researcher noted that this finding casts doubt on the idea that an individual must meet a certain "threshold" of intelligence in order for high levels of creativity to occur (Kim, 2005). It appears that creatively gifted people often possess qualitatively different characteristics than those possessed by academically talented people (Selby, Shaw, & Houtz, 2005). Research reviewed by Selby et al. (2005) produced a long, varied, and sometimes contradictory list of characteristics of creative individuals; however, within the complexity of their collection, patterns emerge. For example, a variety of traits was listed that might be labeled "courage" or "independence," such as the ability to make independent judgments, assertiveness/dominance, limited use of suppression as a defense mechanism, relatively high levels of impulsivity, openness, self-acceptance, and willingness to see oneself as unconventional. Traits having to do with motivation included an affinity for complexity, aesthetic appreciation, intrinsic motivation, appreciation of challenge, and curiosity. Other characteristics were affective, such as relatively low sense of well-being, a tendency toward self-criticism, a high degree of empathy, and emotional instability.

Highly creative individuals have been found to possess originality, curiosity, open mindedness, attraction to complexity and novelty, and a willingness to take risks (Renzulli, 2005). On the other hand, some research demonstrates that some traits, such as a tendency to be emotional, to question authority, and to take little interest in detail, may be seen in a negative light by parents, educators, and peers of creative children and may lead to behaviors considered inappropriate. Interestingly, although there is a great amount of research dealing with academically gifted students' perceptions of their own abilities and the impact of those abilities on their social and emotional lives, little research explains how creatively gifted students feel about their talents and characteristics. Future research might explore creative students' perceptions of their traits, both those that may be seen as positive and those that could be viewed by some as problematic.

In summary, although creative and academic ability may overlap in some students, other highly creative students may exhibit distinctly different characteristics than those commonly seen in academically gifted children. As such, programming for social and emotional needs may likewise be different for these students.

Developmental Aspects of Giftedness

Developmental issues are an important consideration in the recognition of the diverse characteristics of talented and gifted individuals. Traits and behaviors seen in gifted learners at one developmental level may not hold true for students at other ages.

The Young Gifted Child

As might be expected, there is research to support the idea that early signs of precocity exist in some children (Vaivre-Douret, 2011), such as early language precocity. Some parents are quite capable of describing their child's early behaviors, although they may not necessarily identify the behaviors as precocious, and so, parents should be viewed by educators as important sources of information about children's talents (Robinson, 1987). Early language development and early reading are precocious behaviors that are easily identified and assessed in young children, and young gifted children are described by their parents as having broader knowledge and better understanding of concepts when compared to their same-age peers (Sankar-DeLeeuw, 2004). They are also described as excelling in reading, math, or spelling skills, and having excellent memory skills (Harrison, 2004; Sankar-DeLeeuw, 2004). Some parents describe their young highly able children as preferring to work alone or enjoying the company of older children (Freeman, 1994; Sankar-DeLeeuw, 2004). They are also described as highly observant, curious, humorous, creative, and persistent (Harrison, 2004;

Sankar-DeLeeuw, 2004). Teachers of young gifted children have also reported observing traits such as asynchronous development and emotional immaturity (Sankar-DeLeeuw, 1999).

Gross motor competence and reaction time also may identify young gifted children. Hemmelgarn and Kehle (1984), for example, assessed reaction time in 59 gifted elementary school students and found a significant inverse relationship between IQ and reaction time. These findings suggest that both motor abilities and nervous system response may be more highly developed in young gifted students. In general, however, assessing advanced abilities and talents in young children proves difficult and unreliable, especially when using traditional intelligence tests. According to Robinson (1987), several researchers have found that strength in very early novelty preferences, visual attention, and visual recognition memory during infancy can be somewhat effective predictors of intelligence in childhood. Because little research exists in this area as compared to research on older gifted students, parents and teachers should keep their "views broad and flexible if we are to identify reliable and significant indices of precocious development" (Robinson, 1987, p. 162). Feldman's (1993) research on child prodigies, defined as children usually younger than 10 years old who are performing at the levels of highly skilled adults, suggested that prodigies have highly focused talent, extreme motivation to develop the talent, and unusual self-confidence in their ability to do so. Psychometric intelligence plays a role in the development of a prodigy, but is not central to his or her development (Feldman, 1993).

Gifted Adolescents

Along with other challenges faced by adolescents, particular personality, intellectual, and social characteristics may present unique challenges to gifted and talented teenagers. Csikszentmihalyi, Rathunde, and Whalen (1993) conducted an in-depth longitudinal study of 200 talented teenagers and identified a strong core of personal attributes that distinguished the talented teenagers in their study from their average-ability counterparts. These included intellectual curiosity, active reception of information from the world, strong desire to achieve, perseverance to attain their goals, preference for leading and controlling, desire to display accomplishments and gain others' attention, and little questioning of their own worth. It is important to note, however, that some of these personality attributes were displayed by only one gender. For example, talented male teens, in comparison to average male teens, valued stability and predictability more, preferred to avoid physical risks, enjoyed arguments more, and had an unusual need for social recognition. The talented female teens, when compared to their average counterparts, were less inclined to identify with values often seen as "feminine," such as orderliness, neatness, and predictability. Overall, researchers found that the cluster of attributes that described the talented teens suggested an "autotelic" (self-directed or self-rewarding) personality. The teens in this study "entered adolescence with personality attributes well suited to the difficult struggle of establishing their mastery over a domain: a desire to achieve, persistence, and a curiosity and openness to experience" (Csikszentmihalyi et al., 1993, p. 82).

Karnes and McGinnis (1996) also found support for differences between academically talented adolescents and average adolescents. Their study indicated that their sample of academically talented adolescents had a more internal locus of control than average students. Locus of control is the extent to which individuals believe that their behavior causes subsequent reinforcement; individuals who perceive reinforcement as contingent upon behavior or characteristics usually have an internal locus of control.

Assouline and Colangelo (2006) noted that although gifted adolescents have relatively healthy self-concepts, gifted teens may have less positive self-concepts than younger gifted students. Gifted high school girls, in particular, may demonstrate this trend. In general, gifted adolescents also are more likely to report feeling anxious and isolated than younger gifted students. Both male and female gifted adolescents may have low estimations of their social abilities and suffer from lowered self-satisfaction. On the positive side, they tend to report high opinions for their intellectual and academic status. In addition to the factors mentioned above, many gifted adolescents are abstract thinkers with a strong preference for flexibility and freedom, as previously noted. These personality characteristics contrast with the personality preferences of most adolescents. They also may put gifted adolescents in conflict with school environments in general, which tend to favor students who excel in lesson learning (Renzulli, 2005).

Special Populations of Gifted Learners

The last few decades have been marked by an increasing interest in diverse gifted students, including those from ethnic, racial, and linguistic minorities, as well as those from economically disadvantaged homes. Research on gifted girls; gifted underachievers; gifted gay, lesbian, or bisexual students; and gifted students with disabilities is likewise growing, consistently finding that underrepresentation of these groups in gifted programs is pervasive. With increased awareness of this issue, some policy makers and educators have been seeking ways to ensure that diverse gifted students receive the same opportunities that other gifted students enjoy. Complicating the process, however, is the reality that many current identification and selection procedures may be ineffective and inappropriate for the identification of these young people. Certainly, limited referrals and nominations of culturally, linguistically, and economically diverse (CLED) students, as well as other diverse populations of gifted students, affect their low placement in programs (Frasier & Passow, 1994).

Research has suggested that part of the problem may be that gifted students in these populations demonstrate characteristics that are different from those of "typical" gifted students. Recognizing the need to acknowledge characteristics of different cultures in the identification of talent among diverse groups, Ford (2007) urged educators to avoid assessments that are culture-blind when working with students of color in favor of identification procedures that may be more sensitive to cultural differences. Ford and Moore (2006) described many ways that students may differ in behavior and expression style based on ethnicity and culture. They noted, for example, that Asian and Native American students may be less animated and expressive, speak more quietly, and generally use less personal space than Hispanic or White students. African American students may be more animated and expressive, speak more loudly, and take up more space than other students. Native Americans, Asians, and Hispanics may be less direct in their communication style than African American and White students, who may be quite direct. Native Americans, Asians, and Hispanics also may use less physical contact in communicating than African American and White students. Finally, White students may place value on tasks over relationships, while other cultural groups value relationships over tasks. Although these characteristics do not refer specifically to gifted students, they may nonetheless raise awareness of what types of overt behaviors educators, counselors, and others may see in gifted students of various ethnic and cultural backgrounds.

A study by researchers at The National Research Center on the Gifted and Talented explored the characteristics of culturally, linguistically, and economically diverse gifted students. Following 35 economically disadvantaged, ethnically diverse, talented high school students in an urban high school for 3 years, Reis, Hébert, Díaz, Maxfield, and Ratley (1995) found a number of common personal characteristics in participants who achieved despite the challenges they faced. These characteristics included motivation and inner will, positive use of problem solving, independence, realistic aspirations, heightened sensitivity to each other and the world around them, and appreciation of cultural diversity. A determination to succeed was consistently echoed by most of the high-achieving participants in this study, despite what could be considered prejudice leveled against them. One of the study participants, for example, said that she had experienced various types of prejudice in her community and occasionally in academic experiences. This prejudice occurred in school, from teachers as well as students, and in the summer programs she participated in for high-achieving students, which often are held at some of the most prestigious private schools in the state. She explained, "I know that people will occasionally look at me and say, when they find out that I'm smart, 'How can that be? She's Puerto Rican.'"

Each of the high-achieving participants in this study referred to an internal motivation that kept them driven to succeed in their urban environment. One participant referred to this drive as an "inner will" that contributed to the strong belief in self. Resilience also was exhibited by many of the participants in this study, the majority of whom came from homes that had been affected by periodic or regular unemployment of one or more parents; poverty; family turmoil caused by issues such as alcohol, drugs, and mental illness; and other problems. All participants also lived in a city plagued by violence, drugs, poverty, and crime. Their school district often has been called one of the worst in the country and had the dubious distinction of having the state eliminate the local board of education and take over the schools. Despite these challenges, high-achieving participants in this study accepted their circumstances and made the most of the opportunities given to them.

Gifted Girls

What factors cause some smart young girls with hopes and dreams to become self-fulfilled talented women in their later lives? For the last three decades, educators have speculated on the answers to this question, and while some research has addressed the issue, much more is needed. In this section, characteristics of some gifted and talented girls are discussed (Ford, 1992; Foust, Rudasill, & Callahan, 2006; Mendez & Crawford, 2002; Reis, 1998).

Reis (1998) found that some gifted females begin to lose self-confidence in elementary school, and this continues through college and graduate school. They may increasingly doubt their intellectual competence, perceive themselves as less capable than they actually are, and/or believe that boys can rely on innate ability, while they themselves must work hard. Talented girls in school may choose more often to work in groups, appear more concerned about teacher reactions, and are more likely to adapt to adult expectations and less likely than boys to describe themselves or to be described as autonomous and independent. Some bright girls also use affiliations and their relationships to assess their level of ability, and to achieve at higher levels, and often believe that their grades will be higher if their teachers like them. Some bright young women deliberately understate their abilities, try to appear to be like everyone else, and work to get good, but not outstanding, grades. Displaying academic talents may be problematic for females because of adverse social consequences. Some adolescent females believe that it is a social disadvantage to be smart because of the potential negative reactions this may generate from others. Encouragingly, a recent study of more than 500 gifted students by Foust et al. (2006) reported that gifted females were no more likely to use social coping mechanisms, such as denial of giftedness, conforming, or hiding giftedness, than boys.

Reis (1998) concluded that girls achieve well in school but that self-confidence and self-perceived abilities decrease and that professional and work-related achievement in life is generally lower than males of comparable ability. This may start in adolescence, when gifted girls may aim lower in their career goals than gifted boys. Research (Mendez & Crawford, 2002) has found that gifted adolescent boys aspire to careers that require greater educational attainment and carry more prestige than do gifted adolescent girls. Reis also found that some gifted females value their own personal achievements even less as they get older, indicating that the aging process has a negative impact on both the achievement and the self-confidence of gifted females. She also found, however, that as gifted females approach middle to later age, many of the emotional conflicts they faced as young women decrease and they are able to excel.

Recent research indicates that in some situations high-ability females exhibit more positive characteristics regarding their achievement and talents. Talented African American males and females in an urban school district expressed great support for the achievement ideology, and gifted females believed they had the highest teacher feedback on their efforts in one study by Ford (1992). Similar findings emerged in research conducted by Reis, Hébert, et al. (1995) with talented female adolescents in an urban environment. Characteristics of gifted and talented girls vary by age, cultural group, and circumstance, and it is not possible to generalize from one population to another or to use one characteristic of one gifted girl to describe another. Too many intervening variables affect the complex reasons that one girl grows up to be self-confident and able to achieve while another of similar ability but different personality and environment does not.

Gifted Students Who Are Gay, Lesbian, or Bisexual

Students who may be both gifted and gay may feel marginalized, both externally and internally. Although little is known about this population, Cohn (2002) indicated that there may be only 1–3 such students in 1,000, increasing the likelihood of social isolation, alienation, and masking. Even in a large urban high school of 3,000 or so students, one might expect to find only 3–9 students who are both gifted and gay. Spread across four grade levels, the likelihood of such individuals finding one another or feeling safe enough to seek others like themselves is small. Additional research is needed to identify characteristics of these students, as well as necessary programming and supports.

Gifted Students With Disabilities

Gifted students with learning disabilities. Too few educators understand the needs and characteristics of gifted students with disabilities, as they are a very heterogeneous group whose characteristics vary widely depending upon the environment and situation. For instance, a student with high cognitive ability who also has difficulty concentrating during a lesson may blurt out answers and be unable to sit quietly. Might this suggest the presence of ADHD to teachers and even parents, or is this about the absence of challenging content (Assouline & Whiteman, 2011)?

Many teachers and parents of academically talented students have questioned whether these students are displaying characteristics of Asperger's syndrome, as some of these students have limited or no social skills at all. Many young, extremely bright students with poor social skills but with in-depth interests have been found to exhibit behaviors associated with Asperger's syndrome as well as those pertaining to asynchronous, highly gifted students with overexcitabilities (Budding & Chidekel, 2012; Neihart, 2008; Webb & Lattimer, 1993). A simple observation of behaviors associated with a definition can lead to misidentification or underidentification without examining the context in which these behaviors occur and the ability to view the behavior through multiple lenses and possibilities (Baum, Olenchak, & Owen, 1998). The potential frustrations experienced by students with both high potential and learning disabilities may place them at risk for social and emotional problems. Identifying traits and characteristics of gifted and talented students with disabilities is complicated by the fact that abilities of gifted students often mask their disabilities, and, in turn, their disabilities may disguise their giftedness. As a result, students who are gifted and also have disabilities are at risk of underidentification or exclusion from both programs for students with learning disabilities and programs for gifted and talented students (Baum, Owen, & Dixon, 1991; Nielsen, 2002; Olenchak, 1994; Reis, Neu, & McGuire, 1995). This also is true of gifted students with other exceptionalities such as ADHD (Moon, 2002) and Asperger's syndrome (Neihart, 2000).

Nielsen (2002) conducted a record review of 315 identified twice-exceptional children, reviewing records from parents, teachers, and diagnosticians who cited characteristics of both giftedness and learning disabilities (LD) in these children. Gifted characteristics demonstrated by twice-exceptional learners included interests or talents outside of school domains, strong vocabulary, big-picture thinking, superior problem-solving skills, insight and comfort with complexity, creativity, curiosity, imagination, sense of humor, and manipulation of the world around them to compensate for weaknesses. Characteristics associated with LD included frustration with school, inconsistency in academic performance, low self-esteem, slow pace of work, poor short-term memory, inflexibility, gross- and fine-motor problems (including poor handwriting), poor organizational skills, impulsivity, social skills deficits, distractibility, and limited tolerance for frustration. These findings are supported by those of past research (Baum & Owen, 1988; Baum et al., 1991; Reis, Neu et al., 1995).

In a study of 112 high-ability LD students in grades 4–6, Baum and Owen (1988) found that the major characteristic distinguishing high-ability/LD students from both LD/average and high-ability (non-LD) groups was a heightened sense of inefficacy in school. The high-ability/LD students in their study also displayed high levels of creative potential, along with a tendency to behave disruptively and to achieve low levels of academic success. In addition, 36% of the students in their study who had been identified as having a learning disability simultaneously demonstrated behaviors associated with giftedness.

After a thorough review of the literature on gifted/LD students, Reis, Neu et al. (1995) compiled a list of characteristics of gifted/LD students that may hamper their identification as gifted. These characteristics are the result of the interaction of their high abilities and their learning disabilities and include those listed in Table 3.3. Many students in this group display more negative than positive characteristics. In addition, Reis, Neu et al. (1995) found that almost half of the postsecondary gifted students with learning disabilities they studied had sought counseling for social and emotional problems, ranging from mild depression to contemplation of suicide.

Students who exhibit characteristics of both the gifted and learning disabled populations pose challenges for educators. The misconceptions, definitions, and expected outcomes for these types of students further complicate the issues of creating appropriate programming for this population (Baum et al., 1991). Nonetheless, gifted/LD students require unique educational programs and services for both their academic and affective development. Behaviors contributing to success can be taught, and strategies exhibited by successful adults with learning disabilities can be reasonably applied to the education of gifted/LD students. Baum (1990) made the following recommendations for working with gifted students with learning disabilities: encourage compensation strategies, cultivate awareness of strengths and weaknesses, focus on developing the child's gift, and provide an environment that values individual differences.

Gifted students with ADHD. Gifted students with Attention Deficit/ Hyperactivity Disorder (ADHD) present a number of challenges to parents, educators, and researchers. One of the issues most frequently discussed in the literature is accurate diagnosis of these students. The fifth edition of the Diagnostic and Statistical Manual of Mental Disorders (DSM-5; American Psychiatric Association, 2013) states that, in order to be diagnosed with ADHD, a child must demonstrate at least six signs of inattention and/or hyperactivity to a degree that is developmentally inappropriate. Qualifying symptoms of inattention include difficulty sustaining focus, not only during school, but also possibly during play and leisure activities, avoidance of tasks that involve sustained cognitive effort, forgetfulness, failure to pay attention when others speak, a tendency to misplace things, disorganization, and distractibility. Qualifying signs of hyperactivity include fid-

TABLE 3.3
Characteristics of Gifted Students With Learning Disabilities

Characteristics That Hamper Identification as Gifted	▸ frustration with inability to master certain academic skills ▸ learned helplessness ▸ general lack of motivation ▸ disruptive classroom behavior ▸ perfectionism ▸ supersensitivity ▸ failure to complete assignments ▸ lack of organizational skills ▸ demonstration of poor listening and concentration skills ▸ deficiency in tasks emphasizing memory and perceptual abilities ▸ low self-esteem ▸ unrealistic self-expectations ▸ absence of social skills with some peers
Characteristic Strengths	▸ advanced vocabulary use ▸ exceptional analytic abilities ▸ high levels of creativity ▸ advanced problem-solving skills ▸ ability to think of divergent ideas and solutions ▸ specific aptitude (artistic, musical, or mechanical) ▸ wide variety of interests ▸ good memory ▸ task commitment ▸ spatial abilities
Social and Emotional Characteristics of Gifted/LD Students	▸ exhibit feelings of inferiority ▸ show an inability to persevere in the accomplishment of goals ▸ demonstrate a general lack of self-confidence ▸ exhibit confusion as they struggle to understand why they can know an answer, but are not able to say it or write it correctly ▸ have their abilities mask their disabilities ▸ have their disabilities mask their giftedness ▸ demonstrate a strong, personal need for excellence in performance and in outcomes that nears and often embodies unhealthy perfectionism ▸ exhibit an intensity of emotions ▸ have unrealistic expectations of self ▸ have a tendency to experience intense frustration with difficult tasks that often produces a general lack of motivation ▸ experience feelings of learned helplessness ▸ exhibit low self-esteem

Note. From *Talent in Two Places: Case Studies of High Ability Students With Learning Disabilities Who Have Achieved* (pp. 16–17), by S. M. Reis, T. W. Neu, and J. M. McGuire, 1995, Storrs: The National Research Center on the Gifted and Talented, University of Connecticut. Copyright ©1995 by NRC/GT. Adapted with permission.

geting, frequently getting out of one's seat, blurting out answers, interrupting or intruding on others, running and climbing when it's inappropriate to do so, and an inability to play quietly. Some of the behaviors must be present before the age of 12, must occur in at least two or more settings (e.g., home and school), and must significantly interfere with academic, work, and/or social functioning. Behaviors must also be present for 6 months or more before a diagnosis can be considered.

Despite these seemingly stringent guidelines for diagnosis, questions of misdiagnosis of ADHD in gifted children have persisted (Amend & Beljan, 2009; Assouline & Whiteman, 2011; Baum et al., 1998; Edwards, 2009; Hartnett, Nelson, & Rinn, 2004; Rinn & Nelson, 2008). Some researchers (Amend & Beljan, 2009; Baum et al., 1998; Hartnett et al., 2004; Rinn & Nelson, 2008) have suggested that there may be an elevated risk of educators mistaking the high energy and eagerness that can be associated with giftedness for symptoms of ADHD. Others, such as Assouline and Whiteman (2011), however, have noted that current special education laws and practices may result in a lack of educational diagnoses for gifted students with ADHD. The Individuals with Disabilities Education Improvement Act (IDEA) of 2004 requires symptoms present an "adverse" impact on educational performance in order for a student to qualify for an educational classification of ADHD. Because many gifted students with ADHD and other learning difficulties may continue to perform within the average range when compared to national norms, these students may never qualify for testing or intervention under current special education laws—regardless of behavioral or cognitive deficits (e.g., executive functioning deficits) that may interfere with achievement of potential. Unfortunately, there is minimal data to indicate whether gifted students are being over- or underdiagnosed with ADHD. Martin, Burns, and Schonlau (2010), for example, found no quantitative studies between 1983 and 2008 that directly compared rates of ADHD in gifted and nongifted youth. Without studies demonstrating diagnosis rates, it is difficult to begin to ascertain whether proper diagnosis is occurring.

There have been, however, several studies that have indirectly suggested cause for concern. Hartnett, Nelson, and Rinn (2004) gave 44 counseling graduate students a description of a hypothetical 7-year-old student demonstrating restlessness, repeated interruption of the teacher, a tendency to hand in messy work, and questioning of authority. When participants were asked to supply their own hypothesis for the cause of the behaviors, none suggested giftedness as a possibility, while 77% suggested ADHD. When participants were given a prompt suggesting giftedness, ADHD, both, or neither as possible diagnoses, results were more promising, with 46% indicating that giftedness or giftedness plus ADHD could be the cause of the behaviors. Four years later, Rinn and Nelson (2008) conducted a similar study and found that preservice teachers, when provided with a description of a child who could be demonstrating symptoms of either ADHD or giftedness, strongly tended to diagnose the student as having ADHD. More recently, Rinn and Reynolds (2012) found that characteristics of psychomotor overexcitability, sensual overexcitability, and imaginational overexcitability correlated significantly and positively with inattentive and/or hyperactive symptoms related to ADHD as measured by teacher behavior rating scales, again prompting the question of whether giftedness could be misdiagnosed as ADHD.

Research by Katusic et al. (2011) may shed light on the question of accurate diagnosis, as well as other questions related to gifted students and ADHD. In perhaps the broadest quantitative study of this topic in recent years, Katusic and colleagues studied comprehensive medical and school records from the Rochester Epidemiology Project (REP), a cohort of more than 5,700 children followed from birth to late adolescence, to determine whether there were differences between students of various cognitive ability levels in regard to treatment and outcomes for ADHD. Student records were first retrospectively identified by researchers as meeting criteria for ADHD, based on the DSM-IV, rating scale data, and other information. Some, but not all of these students had received diagnoses of ADHD from medical or school professionals. The pool of research-identified students (*N* = 379) were then separated into groups based on low IQ (recorded IQ score below 80), average IQ (recorded IQ score between 80 and 120), and high IQ (at least one IQ score on record higher than 120), and their records analyzed for information about how they fared in school and life.

Their findings suggested that, at least in this cohort, gifted students were not over- or underidentified in comparison to peers. In particular, researchers found no significant difference between the groups with regard to whether they received some sort of educational intervention, whether they were treated with stimulant medications, or the age at which such treatment began. Moreover, outcomes for the three groups were highly similar, suggesting that researchers had not falsely identified gifted students as having ADHD. Specifically, those identified by researchers as having high IQ and ADHD showed the same rates of comorbid learning disorders, psychiatric diagnoses, and substance abuse as those in the medium and low IQ ADHD groups. The only statistical differences found between the groups were level of mother's education (found to be significantly higher in the high IQ group) and level of achievement in reading (also found to be significantly higher in the high IQ group).

Other researchers have also demonstrated findings suggesting that gifted students with ADHD are similar in many ways to other students with ADHD, including demonstrating greater executive functioning deficits, interpersonal issues, and comorbid difficulties than peers with similar ability without ADHD (Antshel et al., 2008; Brown, Reichel, & Quinlan, 2009; Foley-Nicpon, Rickels, Assouline, & Richards, 2012; Fugate, Zental, & Gentry, 2013; Leroux, 2000). Leroux (2000), for example, suggested that the following traits may be found in gifted students with ADHD: characteristic hyperactivity, tendency to challenge authority, disruptive behavior, social-emotional problems, and a sense of being different from others. Antshel et al. (2008) also found that symptoms of ADHD and associated social and behavioral issues persisted across time at similar rates for average-IQ and high-IQ students with ADHD. Fugate et al. (2013) found that gifted students with ADHD characteristics demonstrated working memory deficits typical of students with ADHD when compared to peers of similar cognitive ability without ADHD. Foley-Nicpon et al. (2012) found that gifted students with ADHD had lower self-concept and self-esteem than gifted peers without ADHD, as well as lower overall happiness levels. These findings are similar to those of ADHD students not identified as gifted (Demaray & Elliott, 2001; Edborn, Granlund, Lichtenstein, & Larson, 2008). On a more positive note, Fugate et al. (2013), like other researchers (Cramond, 1995; Leroux, 2000; Moon, 2002; Webb & Latimer, 1993) found that gifted students with ADHD characteristics demonstrated higher creativity levels than gifted peers without ADHD, echoing past findings associating ADHD and creativity in nongifted students (Cramond, 1994; Zentall, 1988; Zentall, Kuester, & Craig, 2011).

Although there is evidence suggesting that gifted students with ADHD have characteristics and challenges similar to others with ADHD, there is also some indication that giftedness may be a protective factor with regard to the severity of ADHD symptoms. Chae, Kim, and Noh (2003) found that gifted students with ADHD made fewer errors on a test of continuous performance than typical ADHD students. Grizenko, Zhang, Polotskaia, and Joober (2012) studied characteristics and treatment of more than 500 students with ADHD, who were classified into groups based on high IQ, average IQ, and low IQ. Researchers found that students with ADHD and high IQ had fewer behavioral problems than average-IQ or low-IQ students with ADHD. They also found lower delinquency rates, social problems, and attention problems in the high IQ group in comparison to low IQ groups.

In addition to examining characteristics of ADHD students with various levels of cognitive ability, Grizenko et al. (2012) explored the impact of treatment on these students, an important focus for future research. Grizenko and colleagues focused on medical intervention, implementing a trial of stimulant medication across the three groups. They found that high-IQ students with ADHD showed the same degree of symptom improvement with medication as did low-IQ and average-IQ students. Other studies have suggested that higher IQ is actually associated with a better response to stimulant treatment (Owens et al., 2003; Van der Oord, Prins, Oosterlan, & Emmelkamp, 2008). In regard to nonmedical intervention, Van der Oord et al. (2008) found no differences in responses to medication plus multimodal therapy when compared to medication alone for students with ADHD, including those with high IQ. When results were collapsed across the two treatment groups, high IQ predicted slightly better response to intervention. Beyond these quantitative studies, there is little empirical evidence regarding effective intervention for gifted students with ADHD (Foley-Nicpon et al.,

2012). It is likely that both the relatively small number of students who are both gifted and ADHD (e.g., in comparison to students who fall into either group alone), and the ways we currently diagnose disabilities and allocate interventions in schools have each contributed to the paucity of research. Past recommendations include taking a highly individualized approach to intervening with these students, focusing not only on interventions that remediate deficits, but also those that emphasize these students' gifts (Baum et al., 1998; Foley-Nicpon et al., 2012; Leroux & Levitt-Perlman, 2000). An example of a current practice that might lend itself to this type of individualized approach is functional behavioral analysis, which allows educators to explore in depth why various behaviors are occurring and what environmental factors and motivators may be manipulated to allow students to be more successful.

As noted by Baum et al. (1991), when schools implement comprehensive programs that identify and develop individual gifts and talents, twice-exceptional students begin to behave socially, emotionally, and academically more like gifted students without disabilities than like nongifted students with learning difficulties. These findings, later corroborated by Bender and Wall (1994) and Olenchak (1994), indicated that as educators diminish the attention to and importance of the disability and concentrate instead on the gifts, many twice-exceptional students can become creatively productive.

Gifted students with behavioral problems. Gifted students with emotional and behavioral problems are rarely referred for gifted programs or are terminated from programming once situated due to disruptive actions (Reid & McGuire, 1995). Although more research is needed on this population, it is known that these children often experience periods of underachievement (Reid & McGuire, 1995), are frequently underchallenged in school, and experience high frustration with "dead time," in which they are forced to wait for peers to finish their work (Neu, 1993). In a review of the sparse research on this population, Reid and McGuire (1995) found that as a result of their emotional and behavioral disorders, these students may "unpredictably engage and disengage in learning opportunities, resulting in inconsistencies in academic skills and knowledge foundations" (p. 16). They also found that many of these students drop out of school when they come of age. Well-designed and careful research is needed on the characteristics and needs of this population to allow educators to better serve and retain them going forward.

Underachieving Gifted Learners

As noted by Siegle (2013), the concept of the "gifted underachiever" is surrounded by controversy regarding how we define both giftedness and underachievement. Currently, there are no formally agreed upon definitions of either construct. Nonetheless, he suggested, student performance that falls noticeably short of potential, especially in young people with high ability, is both perplexing and frustrating for parents and educators. According to a 1990 national needs assessment survey conducted by The National Research Center on the Gifted and Talented, most educators of gifted students identified the problem of under-achievement as their number one concern (Renzulli, Reid, & Gubbins, 1991). Today, there is still a lack of broad understanding of why gifted students under-achieve and how best to intervene once underachievement has begun.

A likely factor contributing to confusion about how best to prevent and reverse gifted underachievement is the complexity of the phenomenon. Gifted students who underachieve have a wide variety of characteristics and fail to thrive for a broad array of reasons. Reis and McCoach (2000) identified several categories of characteristics demonstrated by gifted underachievers: *personality characteristics*, such as pessimism, distrust, anxiousness, inattentiveness, and social immaturity; *internal mediators*, such as fear of failure and rebellious perfectionism; *maladaptive strategies*, such as poor self-regulation and coping strategies; and *positive attributes*, such as creativity and intense interests.

Some students underachieve for reasons largely out of their control, such as family problems (Baker, Bridger, & Evans, 1998; Csikszentmihalyi et al., 1993) or poverty (Moore, Ford, & Millner, 2005; Renzulli & Park, 2002; Wyner, Bridgeland, & DiIulio, 2007). Some have poor self-regulation skills or lack moti-vation (Baslanti & McCoach, 2006; Matthews & McBee, 2007; McCoach & Siegle, 2003; Siegle & McCoach, 2005). Some simply may not find school mean-ingful or relevant (McCoach & Siegle, 2003; Rubenstein, Siegle, Reis, McCoach, & Burton, 2012). McCoach and Siegle (2003), for example, compared gifted achievers and gifted underachievers and found that underachievers showed lower value of academic goals and lower motivation to achieve. Low academic self-concept and self-efficacy are also characteristics that have been associated with gifted underachievement (Matthews & McBee, 2007; Siegle & McCoach, 2005), although at least one study (McCoach & Siegle, 2003) found that gifted underachievers did not suffer from low academic self-concept. As previously noted, some gifted underachievers may suffer from either obvious or hidden dis-abilities, including psychological and/or psychiatric disorders. Grobman (2006) reported that anxiety, depression, and self-destructive behavior plague some gifted underachievers.

Gender also appears to be a factor in underachievement. Currently, gifted boys are two to three times more likely to underachieve than gifted girls (Siegle, 2013), with environment potentially playing a role in this phenomenon. Hartley and Sutton (2013) found that both boys and girls believe that boys perform more poorly than girls in school, and that reinforcing or discounting this idea prior to assigning an academic task significantly impacted boys' performance.

Across genders, how students view teachers' behaviors and beliefs has been shown to impact achievement in gifted students, as has overall view of environment. Specifically, underachievers are more likely to hold negative attitudes about teachers, classes, and school and/or are more likely to blame the environment for failure (McCoach & Siegle, 2003; Rubenstein et al., 2012; Siegle & McCoach, 2005). In his 2013 book on underachievement, Siegle identified a variety of factors contributing to gifted underachievement that may also offer opportunities for intervention. These included:

- » teaching bright children about the role of hard work in achievement;
- » discouraging perfectionism by teaching gifted children that they are valued for who they are, not for what they produce;
- » finding ways to make school more meaningful to students;
- » coordinating interventions across home and school;
- » identifying and exploring faulty perceptions students may have about environmental factors impeding achievement;
- » helping students to increase their academic self-efficacy; and
- » teaching students strategies for self-regulation.

There is a tremendous need on the part of researchers and educators to continue to explore these and other strategies to intervene with gifted underachievers and to add to the body of knowledge on how to reverse underachievement in bright students. As with gifted students with disabilities, there is also a need for policies and/or clarifications of policies that would promote, rather than discourage, these types of interventions in schools.

Diversity in Talent Development and Emergence of Gifts

The way society approaches the study of people with gifts and talents in our culture could easily lead the casual reader to believe that giftedness is an absolute condition that is magically bestowed upon a person in much the same way that nature endows us with particular physical traits such as complexion and coloring (Renzulli, 1980). This position is not supported by the research cited in this chapter. Multiple lists of traits and characteristics exist with some for girls and some for boys; some for students from the majority culture, others for students from diverse cultural backgrounds; some for students with disabilities, others for students with no such problems. The misconception persists that somehow the right combination of traits can be found that prove the existence of giftedness and allow us to easily pick the lucky students from the crowds. The use of terms such as *truly gifted, highly gifted, moderately gifted,* and *borderline gifted* has only served to confound the issue.

Most of the confusion and controversy surrounding characteristics of giftedness can be placed into proper perspective if a few key questions are examined. How are specific characteristics of one group of people used to identify another group? Are the characteristics of giftedness reflected in high-ability Puerto Rican students in Hartford, CT, the same characteristics of giftedness as those demonstrated by above-average Mexican American students in Texas? Are there characteristics common to each group? If so, how are they exhibited? What happens to a child who consistently manifests these characteristics when he or she is in the primary grades but who learns to underachieve in school because of an unchallenging curriculum? What about a gifted child with a learning disability whose disability masks his or her talents? Are characteristics of giftedness static (i.e., you have or you don't have them) or are they dynamic (i.e., they vary within persons and among learning/performance situations)?

These questions have led educators to advocate for a fundamental change in the way characteristics and traits of giftedness are viewed. The characteristics of advanced learners should be identified in as many educational contexts and populations as possible to ensure a well-rounded and more accurate picture of how people with gifts and talents develop. This information then should be used to help identify students who need a level of service not currently provided, or even a continuum of services to develop to their fullest potential (Renzulli & Reis, 2014). Broadening ideas about the characteristics of gifted students in this way should, ideally, provide new flexibility in both identification and programming. This flexibility in turn may increase the inclusion of diverse students in gifted programs, which is a crucial issue in the field.

Once participation of diverse students in gifted programs is increased, challenges in equitable education will remain. Refining and understanding the types of characteristics that suggest talents and gifts in diverse populations may help us to identify services that are necessary to keeping these students in programs. Likewise, understanding the traits of a wide variety of gifted students may help to identify the types of programs that will best fit their needs. This, in turn, will help to develop programs that are internally consistent. At a very minimum, it must be understood that characteristics of giftedness are manifested differently across different populations, and it is critical that gifted and talented programs should be developed that both celebrate and develop the diversity of talents and gifts displayed by children and students of all backgrounds.

Teacher Statement

For the secondary school gifted course that I developed and teach, "Enrichment and Independent Study" (EIS), a single list of characteristics would not be adequate or appropriate to select students. Any identification practices should match the goals of a program. The goals of EIS are to provide multidisciplinary, stimulating, and challenging activities; build research and critical thinking skills; foster positive social and emotional development; and guide students through a long-term, in-depth study in their own interest area. The selection committee is composed of an administrator and the EIS teacher, as well as a content expert in the student's primary interest area. The committee considers multiple criteria, looking for an interaction among high ability, dedication to task/work ethic, and creative productivity or creative potential. It is easy for us to spot intellectual giftedness in the academic setting, but EIS is designed to serve all types of gifts and talents, so we look beyond subject grades (we do not use IQ or other standardized test scores) and pay equal attention to students' extracurricular and community involvement, portfolios, and teacher, parent, and self-nominations. The EIS curriculum is very student-centered, built around students' interests and talent areas, and it also offers many general enrichment and skill-building opportunities.

Because EIS is an elective class, it is important that students are internally motivated, can work independently, and are intellectually curious, but it is not necessary for them to be accomplished when they enter the class. EIS is meant to develop many kinds of gifts and talents, rather than just spotlighting existing talents. Furthermore, adolescents are in a constant state of developmental flux, and their interests and abilities change with age and experience. Cultural and gender differences, personality attributes, learning styles, ability, and aptitude—all of these factors and more have to be considered for the purpose of inclusion to EIS, rather than exclusion from it. I choose not to reduce the complexity of teaching and learning to a simplistic "one-list-fits-all" mentality so that there is diversity in the EIS class and, thus, different points of view. This chapter effectively conveys the diverse characteristics and traits that so many different gifted and talented students demonstrate.

—Meredith Greene

DISCUSSION QUESTIONS

1. Should there be a uniform definition of "giftedness" or list of characteristics to guide educators about the identification of gifted and high-potential students?

2. Given the variability demonstrated by gifted students, are book chapters, articles, and checklists providing information about gifted characteristics useful? Why or why not?

3. Is above-average performance in a domain or across domains a necessary characteristic of giftedness?

4. What can be done to help teachers more readily recognize potential in students who do not manifest some of the most common characteristics of giftedness?

References

Ackerman, C. M. (1997). Identifying gifted adolescents using personality characteristics: Dabrowski's overexcitabilities. *Roeper Review, 19,* 229–236.

Amend, E. R., & Beljan, P. (2009). The antecedents of misdiagnosis: When normal behaviors of gifted children are misinterpreted as pathological. *Gifted Education International, 25,* 131–143.

American Psychiatric Association. (2013). *Diagnostic and statistical manual of mental disorders* (5th ed.). Arlington, VA: Author.

Antshel, K. M., Faraone, S. V., Maglione, K., Doyle, A., Fried, R., Seidman, L., & Biederman, J. (2008). Temporal stability of ADHD in the high-IQ population: Results from the MGH Longitudinal Family Studies of ADHD. *Journal of the American Academy of Child & Adolescent Psychiatry, 47,* 817–825.

Assouline, S. G., & Colangelo, N. (2006). Social-emotional development of gifted adolescents. In F. A. Dixon & S. M. Moon (Eds.), *The handbook of secondary gifted education* (pp. 65–85). Waco, TX: Prufrock Press.

Assouline, S. G., & Whiteman, C. S. (2011). Twice-exceptionality: Implications for school psychologists in the post–IDEA 2004 era. *Journal of Applied School Psychology, 27,* 380–402. doi:10.1080/15377903.2011.616576

Baker, J. A., Bridger, R., & Evans, K. (1998). Models of underachievement among gifted preadolescents: The role of personal, family, and school factors. *Gifted Child Quarterly, 42,* 5–14.

Bailey, C. L. (2011). An examination of the relationships between ego development, Dabrowski's theory of positive disintegration, and the behavioral characteristics of gifted adolescents. *Gifted Child Quarterly, 55,* 208–222.

Baslanti, U., & McCoach, D. B. (2006). Factors related to the underachievement of university students in Turkey. *Roeper Review, 28,* 210–215.

Baum, S. (1990). *Gifted but learning disabled: A puzzling paradox* (ERIC Digest #E479). Reston, VA: Council for Exceptional Children.

Baum, S. M., Olenchak, F. R., & Owen, S. V. (1998). Gifted students with attention deficits: Fact and/or fiction? or, can we see the forest for the trees? *Gifted Child Quarterly, 42,* 96–104.

Baum, S., & Owen, S. V. (1988). High ability/learning disabled students: How are they different? *Gifted Child Quarterly, 32,* 321–325.

Baum, S., Owen, S. V., & Dixon, J. (1991). *To be gifted and learning disabled: From definitions to practical intervention strategies.* Mansfield Center, CT: Creative Learning Press.

Bender, W. N., & Wall, M. E. (1994). Social-emotional development of students with learning disabilities. *Learning Disabilities Quarterly, 17,* 323–341.

Bouchet, N., & Falk, R. F. (2001). Relationship among giftedness, gender and overexcitability. *Gifted Child Quarterly, 45,* 260–267.

Brown, T. E., Reichel, P. C., & Quinlan, D. M. (2009). Executive function impairments in high IQ adults with ADHD. *Journal of Attention Disorders, 13,* 161–167.

Budding, D., & Chidekel, D. (2012). ADHD and giftedness: A neurocognitive consideration of twice exceptionality. *Applied Neuropsychology: Child, 1,* 145–151.

Chae, P. K., Kim, J. H., & Noh, K. S. (2003). Diagnosis of ADHD among gifted children in relation to KEDI-WISC and TOVA performance. *Gifted Child Quarterly, 47,* 192–201.

Clark, B. (2002). *Growing up gifted* (6th ed.). Upper Saddle River, NJ: Merrill/Prentice Hall.

Cohn, S. J. (2002). Gifted students who are gay, lesbian, or bisexual. In M. Neihart, S. M. Reis, N. M. Robinson, & S. M. Moon (Eds.), *The social and emotional development of gifted children* (pp. 145–154). Waco, TX: Prufrock Press.

Columbus Group. (1991). Unpublished transcript. Columbus, OH.

Cramond, B. (1994). Attention-Deficit Hyperactivity Disorder and Creativity—What is the connection?. *The Journal of Creative Behavior, 28,* 193–210.

Cramond, B. (1995). *The coincidence of Attention Deficit Hyperactivity Disorder and creativity.* Storrs: University of Connecticut, The National Research Center on the Gifted and Talented.

Cross, T. L., Cassady, J. C., & Miller, K. A. (2006). Suicide ideation and personality characteristics among gifted adolescents. *Gifted Child Quarterly, 50,* 295–306.

Cross, T. L., & Coleman, L. J. (2005). School-based conception of giftedness. In R. Sternberg & J. E. Davidson (Eds.), *Conceptions of giftedness* (pp. 52–63). Cambridge, England: Cambridge University Press.

Cross, T. L., Speirs Neumeister, K. L., & Cassady, J. C. (2007). Psychological types of academically gifted adolescents. *Gifted Child Quarterly, 51,* 285–294.

Csikszentmihalyi, M., Rathunde, K., & Whalen, S. (1993). *Talented teenagers: The roots of success and failure.* Cambridge, England: Cambridge University Press.

Dabrowski, K. (1964). *Positive disintegration.* Boston, MA: Little, Brown.

Davis, G. A., & Rimm, S. B. (1998). *Education of the gifted and talented* (4th ed.). Boston, MA: Allyn & Bacon.

Delbridge-Parker, L., & Robinson, D. (1989). Type and academically gifted adolescents. *Journal of Psychological Type, 17,* 66–72.

Demaray, M. K., & Elliott, S. N. (2001). Perceived social support by children with characteristics of attention-deficit/ hyperactivity disorder. *School Psychology Quarterly, 16,* 68–90.

Edborn, T., Granlund, M., Lichtenstein, P., & Larson, J. (2008). ADHD symptoms related to profiles of self-esteem in a longitudinal study of twins: A person-oriented approach. *Journal of Child and Adolescent Psychiatric Nursing, 21,* 228–237.

Edwards, K. (2009). Misdiagnosis, the recent trend in thinking about gifted children with ADHD. *APEX: The New Zealand Journal of Gifted Education, 15*(1), 29–44.

Feldman, D. H. (1993). Child prodigies: A distinctive form of giftedness. *Gifted Child Quarterly, 37,* 188–193.

Foley-Nicpon, M., Rickels, H., Assouline, S. G., & Richards, A. (2012). Self-esteem and self-concept examination among gifted students with ADHD. *Journal for the Education of the Gifted, 35,* 220–240.

Ford, D. Y. (1992). Determinants of underachievement as perceived by gifted, above-average, and average Black students. *Roeper Review, 14,* 130–136.

Ford, D. Y. (2007). Teacher referral as gatekeeping: Cultural diversity training is one key to opening gifted education doors. *Gifted Education Press Quarterly, 21*(3), 2–5.

Ford, D. Y., & Moore, J. L. (2006). Being gifted and adolescent: Issues and needs of students of color. In F. A. Dixon & S. M. Moon (Eds.), *The handbook of secondary gifted education* (pp. 113–136). Waco, TX: Prufrock Press.

Foust, R., Rudasill, K. M., & Callahan, C. M. (2006). An investigation into the gender and age differences in the social coping of academically advanced students. *Journal of Advanced Academics, 18,* 60–80.

Frasier, M. M., & Passow, A. H. (1994). *Towards a new paradigm for identifying talent potential.* Storrs: University of Connecticut, The National Research Center on the Gifted and Talented.

Freeman, J. (1994). Some emotional aspects of being gifted. *Journal for the Education of the Gifted, 17,* 180–197.

Fugate, C. M., Zentall, S. S., & Gentry, M. (2013). Creativity and working memory in gifted students with and without characteristics of Attention Deficit Hyperactive Disorder: Lifting the mask. *Gifted Child Quarterly, 57,* 234–246.

Gallagher, S. A. (1990). Personality patterns of the gifted. *Understanding Our Gifted, 3,* 11–13.

Grizenko, N., Zhang, D. D. Q., Polotskaia, A., & Joober, R. (2012). Efficacy of methylphenidate in ADHD children across the normal and the gifted intellectual spectrum. *Journal of the Canadian Academy of Child and Adolescent Psychiatry, 21,* 282.

Grobman, J. (2006). Underachievement in exceptionally gifted adolescents and young adults: A psychiatrist's view. *Journal of Secondary Gifted Education, 17,* 199–210.

Gross, M. U. M. (1986). Radical acceleration in Australia: Terence Tao. *Gifted Child Today, 45,* 2–11.

Gross, M. U. M. (2002). Social and emotional issues for exceptionally intellectually gifted students. In M. Neihart, S. Reis, N. M. Robinson, & S. Moon (Eds.), *The social and emotional development of gifted children: What do we know?* (pp. 19–29). Waco, TX: Prufrock Press.

Harris, J. A. (2004). Measured intelligence, achievement, openness to experience, and creativity. *Personality and Individual Differences, 36,* 913–929.

Harrison, C. (2004). Giftedness in early childhood: The search for complexity and connection. *Roeper Review, 26,* 78–84.

Hartley, B. L., & Sutton, R. M. (2013). A stereotype threat account of boys' academic underachievement. *Child development, 84,* 1716–1733.

Hartnett, D. N., Nelson, J. M., & Rinn, A. N. (2004). Gifted or ADHD? The possibilities of misdiagnosis. *Roeper Review, 26,* 73–76.

Hawkins, J. (1997). Giftedness and psychological type. *Journal of Secondary Gifted Education, 9,* 57–67.

Heller, K. A., Perleth, C., & Lim, T. K. (2005). The Munich model of giftedness designed to identify and promote gifted students. In R. Sternberg & J. E. Davidson (Eds.), *Conceptions of giftedness* (pp. 147–170). Cambridge, England: Cambridge University Press.

Hemmelgarn, T. E., & Kehle, T. J. (1984). The relationship between reaction time and intelligence in children. *School Psychology International, 5,* 77–84.

Hollingworth, L. S. (1926). *Gifted children: Their nature and nurture.* New York, NY: Macmillan.

Hollingworth, L. S. (1942). *Children above 180 IQ (Stanford-Binet): Origin and development.* Yonkers-on-Hudson, NY: World Book.

Individuals with Disabilities Education Improvement Act, Pub. Law 108-446 (December 3, 2004).

Karnes, F. A., & McGinnis, J. C. (1996). Self-actualization and locus of control with academically talented adolescents. *Journal of Secondary Gifted Education, 7,* 369–372.

Katusic, M. Z., Voigt, R. G., Colligan, R. C., Weaver, A. L., Homan, K. J., & Barbaresi, W. J. (2011). Attention-Deficit/Hyperactivity Disorder in children with high IQ:

Results from a population-based study. *Journal of developmental and behavioral pediatrics: JDBP, 32,* 103.

Kim, K. H. (2005). Can only intelligent people be creative? A meta-analysis. *Journal of Secondary Gifted Education, 16,* 57–66.

Leroux, J. A. (2000). The gifted child with attention deficit disorder: An identification and intervention challenge. *Roeper Review, 22,* 171–176.

Leroux, J. A., & Levitt-Perlman, M. (2000). The gifted child with attention deficit disorder: An identification and intervention challenge. *Roeper Review, 22,* 171–176.

Martin, L. T., Burns, R. M., & Schonlau, M. (2010). Mental disorders among gifted and nongifted youth: A selected review of the epidemiologic literature. *Gifted Child Quarterly, 54,* 31–41.

Matthews, M. S., & McBee, M. T. (2007). School factors and the underachievement of gifted students in a talent search summer program. *Gifted Child Quarterly, 51,* 167–181.

McCoach, D. B., & Siegle, D. (2003). Factors that differentiate underachieving gifted students from high-achieving gifted students. *Gifted Child Quarterly, 47,* 144–154.

Mendaglio, S., & Tillier, W. (2006). Dabrowski's Theory of Positive Disintegration and giftedness: Overexcitability research findings. *Journal for the Education of the Gifted, 30,* 68–87.

Mendez, L. M., & Crawford, K. M. (2002). Gender role stereotyping and career aspirations: A comparison of gifted early adolescent boys and girls. *Journal of Secondary Gifted Education, 13,* 96–107.

Milgram, R., & Hong, E. (2009). Talent loss in mathematics: Causes and solutions. In R. Leikin, A. Berman, & B. Koichu (Eds.), *Creativity in mathematics and the education of gifted students* (pp. 149–163). Rotterdam: Sense Publishers.

Miller, N. B., Silverman, L. K., & Falk, R. F. (1994). Emotional development, intellectual ability, and gender. *Journal for the Education of the Gifted, 18,* 20–38.

Moon, S. M. (2002). Gifted children with attention-deficit/hyperactivity disorder. In M. Neihart, S. M. Reis, N. M. Robinson, & S. M. Moon (Eds.), *The social and emotional development of gifted children: What do we know?* (pp. 193–204). Waco, TX: Prufrock Press.

Moore, J. L., Ford, D. Y., & Milner, H. R. (2005). Recruitment is not enough: Retaining African American students in gifted education. *Gifted Child Quarterly, 49,* 51–67.

Myers, I. B. (1962). *The Myers-Briggs Type Indicator manual.* Princeton, NJ: Educational Testing Service.

Neihart, M. (2000). Gifted children with Asperger's syndrome. *Gifted Child Quarterly, 44,* 222–230.

Neihart, M. (2002). Gifted children and depression. In M. Neihart, S. M. Reis, N. M. Robinson, & S. M. Moon (Eds.), *The social and emotional development of gifted children: What do we know?* (pp. 93–102). Waco, TX: Prufrock Press.

Neihart, M. (2008). Identifying and providing services to twice exceptional children. In *Handbook of giftedness in children* (pp. 115–137). New York, NY: Springer.

Neihart, M., Reis, S. M., Robinson, N. M., & Moon, S. M. (Eds.). (2002). *The social and emotional development of gifted children. What do we know?* Waco, TX: Prufrock Press.

Nielsen, M. E. (2002). Gifted students with learning disabilities: Recommendations for identification and programming. *Exceptionality, 10,* 93–111.

Neu, T. W. (1993). *Case studies of gifted students with emotional or behavioral disorders.* Unpublished doctoral dissertation, University of Connecticut, Storrs.

Olenchak, F. R. (1994). Talent development: Accommodating the social and emotional needs for secondary gifted/learning disabled students. *Journal of Secondary Gifted Education, 5*(3), 40–52.

Owens, E. B., Hinshaw, S. P., Kraemer, H. C., Arnold, L. E., Abikoff, H. B., Cantwell, D. P., & Wigal, T. (2003). Which treatment for whom for ADHD? Moderators of treatment response in the MTA. *Journal of Consulting and Clinical Psychology, 71,* 540.

Piechowski, M. M., & Colangelo, N. (1984). Developmental potential of the gifted. *Gifted Child Quarterly, 28,* 80–88.

Piechowski, M. M., & Cunningham, K. (1985). Patterns of overexcitability in a group of artists. *Journal of Creative Behavior, 19,* 153–174.

Piechowski, M. M., Silverman, L. K., & Falk, R. F. (1985). Comparison of intellectually and artistically gifted on five dimensions of mental functioning. *Perceptual and Motor Skills, 60,* 539–545.

Reid, B. D., & McGuire, M. D. (1995). *Square pegs in round holes—these kids don't fit: High ability students with behavioral problems.* Storrs: University of Connecticut, The National Research Center on the Gifted and Talented.

Reis, S. M. (1989). Reflections on policy affecting the education of gifted and talented students: Past and future perspectives. *American Psychologist, 44,* 399–408.

Reis, S. M. (1998). *Work left undone: Choices and compromises of talented females.* Mansfield Center, CT: Creative Learning Press.

Reis, S. M. (2005). Feminist perspectives on talent development: A research-based conception of giftedness in women. In R. Sternberg & J. E. Davidson (Eds.), *Conceptions of giftedness* (pp. 217–245). Cambridge, England: Cambridge University Press.

Reis, S. M., Gubbins, E. J., Briggs, C., Schreiber, F., Richards, S., Jacobs, J. K., . . . Renzulli, J. S. (2004). Reading instruction for talented readers: Case studies documenting few opportunities for continuous progress. *Gifted Child Quarterly, 48,* 315–338.

Reis, S. M., Hébert, T. P., Díaz, E. I., Maxfield, L. R., & Ratley, M. E. (1995). *Case studies of talented students who achieve and underachieve in an urban high school.* Storrs: University of Connecticut, The National Research Center on the Gifted and Talented.

Reis, S. M., & McCoach, D. B. (2000). The underachievement of gifted students: What do we know and where do we go? *Gifted Child Quarterly, 44,* 152–170.

Reis, S. M., Neu, T. W., & McGuire, J. M. (1995). *Talent in two places: Case studies of high ability students with learning disabilities who have achieved.* Storrs: University of Connecticut, The National Research Center on the Gifted and Talented.

Renzulli, J. S. (1978). What makes giftedness?: Reexamining a definition. *Phi Delta Kappan, 60,* 180–184.

Renzulli, J. S. (1980). Will the gifted child movement be alive and well in 1990? *Gifted Child Quarterly, 24,* 3–9.

Renzulli, J. S. (2005). The three-ring conception of giftedness: A developmental model for creative productivity. In R. J. Sternberg & J. E. Davidson (Eds.), *Conceptions of giftedness* (pp. 53–92). Cambridge, England: Cambridge University Press.

Renzulli, J. S., & Park, S. (2002). *Giftedness and high school dropouts: Personal, family, and school-related factors* (RM02168). Storrs: University of Connecticut, The National Research Center on the Gifted and Talented.

Renzulli, J. S., Reid, B. D., & Gubbins, E. J. (1991). *Setting an agenda: Research priorities for the gifted and talented through the year 2000.* Storrs: University of Connecticut, The National Research Center on the Gifted and Talented.

OVERVIEW OF CHARACTERISTICS AND NEEDS OF GIFTED LEARNERS

Renzulli, J. S., & Reis, S. M. (1997). *The schoolwide enrichment model: A how-to guide for educational excellence* (2nd ed.). Waco, TX: Prufrock Press.

Renzulli, J. S., & Reis, S. M. (2014). *The schoolwide enrichment model: A how-to guide for talent development* (3rd ed.). Waco, TX: Prufrock Press.

Renzulli, J. S., Smith, L. H., White, A. J., Callahan, C. M., Hartman, R. K., & Westberg, K. L. (2002). *Scales for rating the behavioral characteristics of superior students* (Rev. ed.). Mansfield Center, CT: Creative Learning Press.

Renzulli, J. S., Smith, L. H., White, A. J., Callahan, C. M., Hartman, R. K., & Westberg, K. L. (2013). *Scales for rating the behavioral characteristics of superior students* (Rev. ed.). Waco, TX: Prufrock Press.

Rinn, A. N., & Nelson, J. M. (2008). Preservice teachers' perceptions of behaviors characteristic of ADHD and giftedness. *Roeper Review, 31*(1), 18–26.

Rinn, A. N., & Reynolds, M. J. (2012). Overexcitabilities and ADHD in the gifted: An examination. *Roeper Review, 34,* 38–45.

Robinson, N. M. (1987). The early development of precocity. *Gifted Child Quarterly, 31,* 161–164.

Rubenstein, L. D., Siegle, D., Reis, S. M., McCoach, D. B., & Burton, M. G. (2012). A complex quest: The development and research of underachievement interventions for gifted students. *Psychology in the Schools, 49,* 678–694.

Sak, U. (2004). A synthesis of research on psychological types of gifted adolescents. *Journal of Secondary Gifted Education, 15,* 70–79.

Sankar-DeLeeuw, N. (1999). Gifted preschoolers: Parent and teacher views on identification, early admission and programming. *Roeper Review, 21,* 174–179.

Sankar-DeLeeuw, N. (2004). Case studies of gifted kindergarten children: Profiles of promise. *Roeper Review, 26,* 192–207.

Selby, E. C., Shaw, E. J., & Houtz, J. C. (2005). The creative personality. *Gifted Child Quarterly, 49,* 300–315.

Siegle, D. (2013). *The underachieving gifted child: Recognizing, understanding, & reversing underachievement.* Waco, TX: Prufrock Press.

Siegle, D., & McCoach, D. B. (2005). Making a difference: Motivating gifted students who are not achieving. *Teaching Exceptional Children, 38*(1), 22–27.

Steiner, H. H. (2006). A microgenetic analysis of strategic variability in gifted and average ability children. *Gifted Child Quarterly, 50,* 62–74.

Sternberg, R. J., & Davidson, J. E. (1986). *Conceptions of giftedness.* Cambridge, England: Cambridge University Press.

Sternberg, R. J., & Davidson, J. E. (2005). *Conceptions of giftedness* (2nd ed.). Cambridge, England: Cambridge University Press.

Terence Tao. (n.d.). *UCLA bios.* Retrieved from http://www.math.ucla.edu/~tao/

United States Department of Education, Office of Educational Research and Improvement. (1993). *National excellence: A case for developing America's talent.* Washington, DC: U.S. Government Printing Office.

Vaivre-Douret, L. (2011). Developmental and cognitive characteristics of "high-level potentialities" (highly gifted) children. *International Journal of Pediatrics, 2011,* 1–14.

Webb, J. T., & Latimer, D. (1993). ADHD and children who are gifted. *Exceptional Children, 60,* 183–184.

Wyner, J. S., Bridgeland, J. M., & DiIulio, J. J. (2007). *The achievement trap.* Washington DC: The Jack Kent Cooke Foundation.

Zentall, S. S. (1988). Production deficiencies in elicited language but not in the sponta-neous verbalizations of hyperactive children. *Journal of Abnormal Child Psychology*, *16*(6), 657–673.

Zentall, S. S., Kuester, D. A., & Craig, B. A. (2011). Social behavior in cooperative groups: Students at risk for ADHD and their peers. *The Journal of Educational Research*, *104*(1), 28–41.

Author Note

Please visit the National Research Center on the Gifted and Talented's website (http://www.gifted.uconn.edu/nrcgt.html) for information about studies related to traits and characteristics of gifted and talented students.

SECTION

INSTRUCTIONAL PLANNING AND EVALUATION

AN ANALYSIS OF GIFTED EDUCATION CURRICULUM MODELS

BY JOYCE VANTASSEL-BASKA AND ELISSA F. BROWN

Much of gifted education as a field rests on the approaches that are used to serve gifted students in schools and other contexts. Consequently, the importance of programmatic and curriculum models cannot be overestimated. The purpose of this chapter is to systematically review existing program/curriculum models in the field and to determine the evidence for their use and their effectiveness with gifted populations. Although originally conceived as a study more than a decade ago, the models contained herein have been updated with more recent research support as it has become available and as related work on appropriate curriculum for the gifted has been conceptualized.

History of Curriculum Models

The history of curriculum development for the gifted has been fraught with problems, similar to the general history of curriculum development in this country. Some of the most successful curriculum models for gifted learners have been developed based on acceleration principles for advanced secondary students (VanTassel-Baska, 1998). Many educators worldwide perceive the International Baccalaureate (IB) program and the College Board's Advanced Placement (AP) program as representing the highest levels of academic attainment available. These programs are thought to provide important stepping stones to successful college work because they constitute the entry levels of such work. Thus, one approach to curriculum development for the gifted may be seen as a "design down" model, where all curricula at the K–12 level are organized to promote readiness for college and the process is both accelerated and shortened along the way for the most apt.

Alternatives to this viewpoint abound, however, and tend to focus on learning beyond, or in lieu of, traditional academics. Most of the curriculum models cited in this chapter ascribe to an enriched view of curriculum development for the gifted, a view that addresses a broader conception of giftedness, taking into account principles of creativity, motivation, and independence as crucial constructs to the development of high ability. These enrichment views also tend to see process skills, such as critical thinking and creative problem solving, as central to the learning enterprise, with content choices being more incidental. Evidence of student work through high-quality products and performances also is typically highly valued in these models.

Most of the enrichment-oriented approaches to curriculum development for the gifted emanated from the early work of Hollingworth (1926) and her curriculum template for New York City's self-contained classes. Strongly influenced by Deweyian progressivism, she organized curriculum units that allowed students to discover connections about how the world worked and what the role of creative people is in societal progress by having students study biographies, and to promote the role of group learning through discussion and conversation about ideas. In some respects, contemporary curricular development efforts fall short of Hollingworth's early work in scope, purpose, and delivery.

Accelerative approaches to learning owe much to the work of Terman and Oden (1947), Pressey (1949), and early developers of rapid learning classes that enabled bright students to progress at their own rates. Early educational examples of autodidacticism and tutorials also encouraged a view of learning that promoted independent interest and a self-modulated pace (VanTassel-Baska, 1995). Thus, current curriculum models are grounded in a history of research, development, and implementation of both accelerative and enrichment approaches, typically used in self-contained classes because the level of content instruction could be modified based on the group. Chief differentiation approaches, early in the history of this field, incorporated attention to differences between gifted and nongifted populations. One might argue that today's views of differentiation tend to center far more on individual differences among the gifted than on the group difference paradigm for curricula employed both in and out of school.

Definition of a Curricular Model: Subjects for Analysis

One of the issues in the field of gifted education rests with the differences between a program model and a curricular model. Several of the models that were researched in this study could be said to cut both ways: They met the criteria for a curricular model, but they also worked as a broad program framework. Others were clearly developed with curriculum as the organizing principle. The operational definition of a curricular model used for the study was one that had the following components:

» *A framework for curriculum design and development*: The model had to provide a system for developing and designing an appropriate curriculum for the target population. As such, it had to identify elements of such a design and show how these elements interacted in a curriculum product.

» *Transferable and usable in all content areas*: The model had to be utilitarian in that it was easily applied to all major areas of school-based learning.

» *K–12 applicability*: The model had to be flexible with respect to the age groups to which it would be applied. The central elements would have to work for kindergarten-age gifted children, as well as high school students.

» *Applicable across schools and grouping settings*: The model had to have relevance in multiple locations and learning settings. It would need to work in tutorials, as well as large classes.

» *Incorporates differentiated features for the gifted/talented learner*: The model had to spell out ways in which it responded to the particular needs of the gifted for curriculum and instruction.

If models met this definition, they were included in the study. Obviously, some well-known curricula such as *Man: A Course of Study* (Bruner, 1970) would be excluded because it was not developed with the target population in mind. Other curricular models would be excluded because they focused in one subject area only, such as *Philosophy in the Classroom* (Lipman, Sharp, & Oscanyan, 1980) or *Junior Great Books*. Still others might be excluded because they were limited to particular grade levels, such as AP or IB programs. Originally, 20 models were identified and then sifted according to the definitional structure, yielding 11 models for continued analysis.

Criteria Used to Assess Model Effectiveness

At a second stage of the process, the researchers were interested in comparing the selected curriculum models according to criteria found in the curriculum literature to be important indicators of effectiveness. These criteria, taken together, constituted the basis for yielding the overall effectiveness of the model. The criteria employed were:

» *Research evidence to support use (student learning impact)*: Studies have been conducted to document the effectiveness of the curriculum with target populations.

» *Application to actual curriculum (products in use)*: The model has been translated into teaching units.

» *Quality of curriculum products based on the model*: The curriculum products based on the model have been evaluated by appropriate audiences and show evidence of critical curriculum design features (goals, objectives, activities, assessment, and resources).

» *Teacher receptivity*: Teachers have commented positively on the curriculum in implementation.

» *Teacher training component for use of the model*: The model has a defined training package so that practitioners can learn how to implement it.

» *Ease of implementation*: The model shows evidence of feasible implementation.

» *Evidence of application of model in practice*: The model can be seen employed in various schools.

» *Sustainability*: The model has been in operation in schools for at least 3 years.

» *Systemic (operational in respect to elements, input, output, interactions, and boundaries)*: The model is definable as a system.

» *Alignment or relationship to national standards*: The model has a defined relationship to the national content standards, including the Common Core State Standards (CCSS) and Next Generation Science Standards (e.g., American Association for the Advancement of Science, 1989, 1993; International Reading Association & National Council of Teachers of English, 1996; National Research Council, 1996).

» *Relationship to school-based core curricula*: The model has a defined relationship to other curricular emphases in schools.

» *Comprehensiveness*: The model applies broadly to all areas and domains of curricula and to all types of gifted learners at all stages of development.

» *Evidence of scope and sequence considerations*: The model has been applied using a progressive development of skills and concept approach across grade levels and subject areas.

» *Longitudinal evidence of effectiveness with gifted students*: The model has evidence of effectiveness over at least 3 years with a given student cohort.

» *Evidence of use in teacher-developed curricula*: The model shows evidence of being used to organize new curriculum that is teacher-developed.

Methodology

The approach employed to carry out the study was organized around four phases. Phase I constituted the search for models that fit the definition described. Several comprehensive texts were reviewed for potential models. Moreover, additional searches were made in the broader literature. Once models were selected, Phase II constituted a review of both ERIC and Psychological Abstracts for research and program data about the models published from 1990 onward. The researchers determined that the models had to be contemporary and currently in use in order to be judged effective; therefore, models written about in roughly the last 20 years would be found in this limited year search. After such material was located for each model, it was decided to contact each model's developer to ensure that no available research or technical data had been overlooked. This phase of the study took 5 months, utilizing a written query followed up by a telephone call to nonrespondents. All developers were asked to corroborate the findings, using the same checklist of criteria described earlier. Three of the developers did not respond directly about their work. Several of the developers sent additional data and suggested changes in the rating of their work, based on this new information. The original developers' interpretations of the criteria for judgment of the work have been acknowledged in the text by the incorporation of key ideas and studies.

Limitations of the Study

Although the curriculum study used established research procedures for investigation, there are clear limitations to the findings generated. No attempt was made to judge the technical adequacy of the various studies reported except where sample size or lack of comparison group was a clear problem. Consequently, meta-analytic techniques to arrive at effect sizes were not used, rendering the findings cautionary. A follow-up study still remains to be conducted on the seven models that have yielded research evidence to ascertain the integrity of the research designs and the power of the findings.

Discussion

Each of the models is discussed in the following sections according to the criteria used to assess effectiveness. The two programmatic models are described first, those of Stanley and Renzulli, because both have defined the major program and curriculum efforts of the gifted education field since the mid-1970s, and both also represent the persistent programmatic division in the field between accelerative and enrichment approaches. Moreover, each of these models has more than a decade of research, development, and implementation behind it.

The Stanley Model of Talent Identification and Development

The overall purpose of the Stanley model is to educate for individual development over the lifespan. Major principles of the model include (a) the use of a secure and rigorous testing instrument that taps into high-level verbal and mathematical reasoning to identify students; (b) a diagnostic testing-prescriptive instructional approach (DT-PI) in teaching gifted students through special classes, allowing for an appropriate level of challenge in instruction; (c) the use of subject matter acceleration and fast-paced classes in core academic areas, as well as advocacy for various other forms of acceleration; and (d) curriculum flexibility in all schooling. The model has been developed at key university sites across the country with some adoptions by local school districts that have established fast-paced classes.

The Study of Mathematically Precocious Youth (SMPY) officially started in September of 1971 at Johns Hopkins University (JHU) and has been continued since 1986 at Iowa State University. From 1972 through 1979, SMPY pioneered the concept of searching for youth who reason exceptionally well mathematically (i.e., a talent search). In 1980, the talent search was extended to verbally gifted youth by others at JHU. Also in 1980 and 1982, respectively, two new national centers were developed based on the talent search model at Duke and Northwestern Universities. These centers replicated the talent search and programs and services to learners in respective geographic areas of the country. In 1984, the University of Denver added a talent search center to service the Rocky Mountain area.

For the students identified by the talent searchers, SMPY provided educational facilitation by utilizing acceleration or curricular flexibility and by developing fast-paced academic programs. Gifted students in seventh and eighth grade can participate in these talent searches by taking the SAT or the ACT. Almost 150,000 gifted students do so every year. These centers and other universities and organizations also offer residential and commuter academic programs in several disciplines to qualified students.

The research work on SMPY, the longitudinal study, continued; new studies based on other aspects of the talent search model were initiated and have also continued. The research work of SMPY has been strong during the past four decades, with more than 300 published articles, chapters, and books about the model. Recent studies based on the SMPY longitudinal data highlight the creative output of the top 1% of the sample in comparison to less able cohorts, and the tilt of their profiles at seventh grade predicting future career clusters. Findings of these studies consistently have focused on the benefits of acceleration for continued advanced work in an area by precocious students (Stanley, Keating, & Fox, 1974), a clear rationale for the use of acceleration in intellectual development (Keating, 1976), and the long-term positive repeated impacts of accelerative opportunities (Benbow & Arjmand, 1990; Park, Lubinski, & Benbow, 2007). Case study research also has been undertaken to demonstrate how these processes affect individual students (Brody & Stanley, 1991). Other studies have focused more specifically on student gains from fast-paced classes (Lynch, 1992). The use of the model has been extensive across all of the United States and in selected foreign countries. Curriculum materials have been developed by talent search staff at various sites and by individual teachers in the summer and academic year programs. Especially noteworthy are the curriculum guides for teaching Advanced Placement courses developed at the Talent Identification Program at Duke University. Strong use of articulated course materials are employed on the way to Advanced Placement coursework and testing in mathematics, science, and the verbal areas, including foreign language. These materials have been reviewed by practicing professionals and content specialists.

During the entirety of its years of operation, the model has been well received by parents and students who constitute the major client groups; schools have been less receptive based on their conservative attitudes toward accelerative practices and the emphasis on highly gifted students in subject areas.

The model does not have a formal training component, although selection of teachers is a rigorous process carried out carefully in each university and school setting. Content expertise and work with highly gifted secondary students are primary considerations for selection. The model is easy to understand but difficult to implement in schools based on prevailing philosophies. The application of the model that has been most successful is in afterschool and summer settings where students complete the equivalent of a high school honors class in 3 weeks (Olszewski-Kubilius & Clarenbach, 2012).

The SMPY model has proven to be highly sustainable, exhibiting strong replication capacity. Even in countries that do not conduct talent searches, students from those countries routinely attend summer programs at talent search universities in the United States.

Because the model is content-based, it aligns well with the new Common Core State Standards (CCSS) in mathematics and English/language arts. The model also aligns well to the Next Generation Science Standards (NGSS). SMPY represents core curricula on an accelerated and streamlined level. The model is not totally comprehensive in that it addresses students in grades 3–12 who reason exceptionally well mathematically and verbally. Some studies on spatially gifted students at those levels also have been conducted and have been recommended, based on contemporary research on the helpfulness of knowing a student's spatial ability (Wai, Lubinski, & Benbow, 2009). Curriculum areas are comprehensive, including all of the 26 Advanced Placement course strands. Scope and sequence work has been articulated for grades 7–12 in some areas of learning. Northwestern University has developed a guide for educational options for grades 5–12 while Duke University has designed curriculum modules for online use that focus on topics that relate to the underlying abilities assessed on the SAT and other instruments calibrated to provide off-level assessment. A recent review of the data from talent search university summer programs continues to mount an impressive argument for the benefits that accrue to students in academic, social, and emotional areas of learning (Olszewski-Kubilius, 2006). A review of longitudinal studies on acceleration continues to demonstrate the positive results of accelerative practices and the lack of negative consequences, such as knowledge gaps or loss of interest (Swiatek, 2000).

Longitudinal data, collected during the past 20 years on 300 highly gifted students, have demonstrated the viability of the Stanley model in respect to the benefits of accelerative study, early identification of a strong talent area, and the need for assistance in educational decision making (Lubinski & Benbow, 1994). A 50-year follow-up study (1972–2022) is in progress at Vanderbilt University with 6,000 students in the sample. This study already rivals Terman and Oden's (1947) longitudinal study with respect to its longevity and exceeds it with regard to understanding the talent development process at work.

In a recent 25-year follow-up study of these graduates, Park, Lubinski, & Benbow (2008) demonstrated that the talent search mechanism has been highly predictive of adult creative production at age 38. By analyzing the accomplishments of the top half of the top 1% in SAT scores and comparing them to those in the top 5%, they found significant differences in education levels, attendance at prestigious institutions, tenure levels at university, number of patents, number of books, and nature and extent of awards, favoring the most able students identified at age 13. Moreover, other analyses of this dataset have uncovered patterns of preferences for career fields that set the stage for outstanding accomplishment (Ferriman-Robertson, Smeets, Lubinski, & Benbow, 2013).

The Renzulli Schoolwide Enrichment Triad Model

The Schoolwide Enrichment Model (SEM) evolved after 15 years of research and field testing by both educators and researchers (Renzulli, 1988). It combined the previously developed Enrichment Triad Model (Renzulli, 1977) with a more flexible approach to identifying high-potential students, the Revolving Door Identification Model (Renzulli, Reis, & Smith, 1981). This combination of services was initially field-tested in 11 school districts of various types (rural, suburban, and urban) and sizes. The field-tests resulted in the development of the SEM (Renzulli & Reis, 1985, 1997, 2014), which has been widely adopted throughout the country.

In the SEM, a talent pool of 15%–20% of above-average ability/high-potential students is identified through a variety of measures, including achievement tests, teacher nominations, assessments of potential for creativity and task commitment, as well as alternative pathways of entrance (e.g., self-nomination and parent nomination). High achievement test scores and IQ scores automatically include a student in the talent pool, enabling those students who are underachieving in their academic schoolwork to be considered.

Once students are identified for the talent pool, they are eligible for several kinds of services. First, interest and learning style assessments are used with talent pool students. Second, curriculum compacting is provided to all eligible students; that is, the regular curriculum is modified by eliminating portions of previously mastered content, and alternative work is substituted. Third, the SEM offers three types of enrichment experiences: Types I, II, and III. Type III enrichment usually is more appropriate for students with higher levels of ability, interest, and task commitment.

Type I Enrichment consists of general exploratory experiences such as guest speakers, field trips, demonstrations, interest centers, and the use of audio-visual materials designed to expose students to new and exciting topics, ideas, and fields of knowledge not ordinarily covered in the regular curriculum. Type II Enrichment includes instructional methods and materials purposefully designed to promote the development of thinking, feeling, research, communication, and methodological processes. Type III Enrichment, the most advanced level of the model, is defined as investigative activities and artistic productions in which the learner assumes the role of a firsthand inquirer: thinking, feeling, and acting like a practicing professional, with involvement pursued at a level as advanced or professional as possible, given the student's level of development and age.

One comparative case study (Heal, 1989) examined the effects of SEM in relation to other enrichment models or strategies on students' perceptions of labeling. Other studies report results using within-model comparisons (Delisle, 1981; Reis, 1981) or the SEM program as compared to no intervention (Karafelis, 1986; Starko, 1986). Because control or comparison groups of students participating in alternate or comparison models were not used, it is difficult to attribute various results to participation in the SEM.

Evaluation studies have been conducted in 29 school districts on the perceptions of the model with parents, teachers, and administrators. Researchers documented positive change in teacher attitudes toward student work when the model is used.

Delcourt (1988) investigated characteristics related to creative/productive behavior in 18 high school students who consistently engaged in firsthand research on self-selected topics within or outside school. Starko (1986) also examined the effects of the SEM on student creative productivity. Results indicated that students who became involved in independent study projects in the SEM more often initiated their own creative products both in- and outside of school than did students in the comparison group. In addition, multiple creative products were linked to self-efficacy.

Several studies have examined the use of the model with underserved populations. Emerick (1988) investigated underachievement patterns of high-potential students. Baum (1985, 1988) examined highly able students with learning disabilities, identifying both characteristics and programmatic needs. Findings suggest positive effects of the model with these populations. Two authors (Ford, 1999; Johnson, 2000) have theorized about the use of the model with minority underachieving learners, suggesting its emphasis on creative thinking as an antidote to underachieving behavior.

Compacting studies have sought to document the fact that gifted students are capable of rapidly progressing through regular school curriculum in order to spend time on Type III project work. Results demonstrate knowledge scores that were as high or higher on in-grade standardized tests than noncompacted peers (Reis & Purcell, 1993). Another study demonstrated that students (N = 336) utilizing curriculum compacting strategies resulted in no decline in achievement test scores (Reis, Westberg, Kulikowich, & Purcell, 1998).

Two SEM longitudinal studies (Delcourt, 1988; Hébert, 1993) have been conducted with 18 and 9 students, respectively. These studies showed that students in the sample maintained similar or identical career goals from their plans in high school, remained in major fields of study in college, and were satisfied in current project work. Moreover, the Type III process appeared to serve as important training for later productivity.

The SEM model is widely used in some form in schools nationally and internationally. Annual summer training on the model is available at the University of Connecticut. Renzulli perceives that the model is closely linked to core curricula, offers a scope and sequence within Type II activities, and has the potential to be aligned with new national standards. Both teachers and selected students are especially enthusiastic about the model. A special volume of the *Journal for the Education of the Gifted* was devoted to Renzulli's work, including the model, in 1999. In 1994, *Gifted Child Quarterly* published an article reviewing research related to the SEM spanning a period of 15 years.

More recent work on the use of the SEM model has been in the area of reading and mathematics education in Title I schools. Research on effective math interventions (Gavin et al., 2007) has suggested that the use of math materials that emphasize real-world problem solving and use the strategies that support this approach enhance learning at the elementary levels in low-income settings. Research on reading achievement with low-income students (Reis, Eckert, McCoach, Jacobs, & Coyne, 2008) has suggested that differentiated tasks can enhance fluency. These curricular emphases, along with others, have been incorporated into the work of the Renzulli Academy in an elementary school in

Hartford, CT. In 2012, Renzulli received a grant award from the Jack Kent Cooke Foundation to replicate his Renzulli Academy program at other sites throughout the country.

The Betts Autonomous Learner Model

The Autonomous Learner Model for the Gifted and Talented was developed to meet the diverse cognitive, emotional, and social needs of gifted and talented students in grades K–12 (Betts & Knapp, 1980). As the needs of gifted and talented students are met, the students will develop into autonomous learners who are responsible for the development, implementation, and evaluation of their own learning. The model is divided into five major dimensions: (a) orientation, (b) individual development, (c) enrichment activities, (d) seminars, and (e) in-depth study.

One of the criteria used for assessing the appropriateness of a curriculum model is the evidence of research to support its use with gifted and talented learners. To date, no research evidence of effectiveness has been shown with regard to this model's student learning impact or longitudinal effectiveness with gifted learners; however, several curricular units and guides have been produced as a result of the dissemination of its ideas. One article reviewed and described the model by presenting guidelines for developing a process-based scope and sequence, as well as independent study programs for gifted learners (Betts & Neihart, 1986). The model also has been included in a volume on work with twice-exceptional gifted learners as a strong framework for programming for this population (Kiesa, 2000).

Regardless of the paucity of research on this model, it is one of the most widely recognized and used in the United States (Betts, 1986). Teachers have commented positively on its implementation. The model has been employed at selected sites in the United States and in other countries. Formal teacher training occurs in 3- and 5-day segments annually. Its design suggests a 3-year timeline for model implementation. It does contain a degree of comprehensiveness in that the model applies broadly to all curricular domains and ages of learners; however, it does not incorporate any features of accelerated learning, thereby limiting one aspect of its comprehensiveness.

Gardner's Multiple Intelligences

Multiple intelligences (MI) as a curricular approach was built on a multidimensional concept of intelligence (Gardner, 1983). Seven areas of intelligence were defined in the original published work, with an eighth intelligence added by Gardner in 1999. They are (a) verbal/linguistic, (b) logical/mathematical, (c) visual/spatial, (d) musical/rhythmic, (e) bodily/kinesthetic, (f) interpersonal, (g) intrapersonal, and (h) naturalistic.

Evidence of research based on multiple intelligences translated into practice has been documented (Brand, 2006; Latham, 1997; Smith, Odhiambo, & El Khateeb, 2000; Strahan, Summey, & Banks, 1996). Most of the research, however, lacks control groups; therefore, generalizations about the model are difficult to infer (Latham, 1997). Longitudinal evidence of effectiveness with gifted students over at least 3 years has not been documented, although some research has been conducted on incorporating multiple intelligences with other forms of curricular models (Maker, Nielson, & Rogers, 1994).

The multiple intelligences approach has been used in the formation of new schools, in identifying individual differences, for curriculum planning and development, and as a way to assess instructional strategies. A plethora of curricular materials has been produced and marketed based upon MI theory. This approach holds widespread appeal for many educators because it can be adapted for any learner, subject domain, or grade level. The model is not easy to implement and does require teacher training, financial resources, and time. Best-known project sites for the model are the Key School in Indianapolis, IN, and the Atlas Project in New York City. Although the model has been readily adapted to curricula, it remains primarily a conception of intelligence applied broadly to school settings as a way to promote talent development for all learners.

Developer concerns about application fidelity of the ideas and variability in implementation quality are strong, leading to a new project specifically designed to monitor implementation of MI in classrooms nationally where positive impacts have been reported (Gardner, 1999). Newer studies still lack quality control in data collection in order to make valid empirical inferences about the value of the model.

The Purdue Three-Stage Enrichment Model for Elementary Gifted Learners and The Purdue Secondary Model for Gifted and Talented Youth

The concept of a three-stage model, initiated by Feldhusen and his graduate students, was first introduced as a course design for university students in 1973. It evolved into the Three-Stage Model by 1979. It is primarily an ordered enrichment model that moves students from simple thinking experiences to complex independent activities (Feldhusen & Kolloff, 1986):

» Stage I focuses on the development of divergent and convergent thinking skills,

» Stage II provides development in creative problem solving, and

» Stage III allows students to apply research skills in the development of independent study skills.

The Purdue Secondary Model is a comprehensive structure for programming services at the secondary level. It has 11 components supporting enrichment and acceleration options, with each component designed to act as a guide for organizing opportunities for secondary gifted students. They are (Feldhusen & Robinson-Wyman, 1986):

» counseling services,
» seminars,
» Advanced Placement courses,
» honors classes,
» math/science acceleration,
» foreign languages,
» arts,
» cultural experiences,
» career education,
» vocational programs, and
» extraschool instruction.

Research has documented gains with regard to enhancement of creative thinking and self-concept using the Three-Stage Enrichment Model for Elementary Gifted Students (Kolloff & Feldhusen, 1984), and one study was conducted documenting limited long-term gains of the elementary program (Moon & Feldhusen, 1994; Moon, Feldhusen, & Dillon, 1994).

The application and implementation of either the elementary or secondary models are not conclusive, yet they appear to be sustainable (Moon & Feldhusen, 1994). Teacher training has accompanied the site implementation of both the elementary and secondary models; however, it is difficult to ascertain the degree of widespread application beyond Indiana. Neither model utilizes a scope and sequence, and neither may be viewed as a comprehensive model in terms of applying broadly to all areas of the curriculum, all types of gifted learners, or all stages of development.

The Kaplan Grid

The Kaplan Grid is a model designed to facilitate the curriculum developer's task of deciding what constitutes a differentiated curriculum and how one can construct such a curriculum. The model uses the components of process, content, and product organized around a theme. *Content* is perceived to be the relationship between various displays of power and the needs and interests of individuals and groups, including societies (Kaplan, 1986). The *process* component utilizes productive thinking, research skills, and basic skills. The *product* component culminates the learning into a mode of communication.

Research evidence could not be found to support the effectiveness of this model with a target population. The quality of the curricular products that have been produced based upon this model has not been reported in the literature; however, there has been extensive implementation of the approach at both state and local levels.

Teacher training has been conducted throughout the United States, initially through the National/State Leadership Training Institute and now independently by the developer so that practitioners can learn how to implement it. Thousands of teachers have developed their own curricula based upon the model. The grid is intended as a developmental framework for curriculum planning for gifted learners, but it does not contain a scope and sequence. Additionally, within the model itself, no provisions are explicitly made for accelerated learning.

The Maker Matrix

The Maker Matrix, developed to categorize content, process, environmental, and product dimensions of an appropriate curriculum for the gifted, represents a set of descriptive criteria that may be used to develop classroom-based curricula (Maker, 1982). Additional work on the model primarily represents an enhancement of its problem-solving component. The Discover project is a process for assessing problem solving in multiple intelligences. The problem-solving matrix incorporates a continuum of five problem types for use within each of the intelligences (Maker et al., 1994):

» Type I and II problems require convergent thinking;
» Type III problems are structured but allow for a range of methods to solve them and have a range of acceptable answers;
» Type IV problems are defined, but the learner selects a method for solving and establishing evaluation criteria for the solution; and
» Type V problems are ill-structured, and the learner must define the problem, discover the method for solving the problem, and establish criteria for creating a solution.

The project typically is used by teachers for curricular planning and assessing a learner's problem-solving abilities.

Research on problem types currently is underway involving 12 classrooms in a variety of settings; however, to date, the results have not been published. A pilot study has shown that use of the matrix enhances the process of problem solving

(Maker, Rogers, Nielson, & Bauerle, 1996). Studies to evaluate the long-term validity of the process are in progress.

School systems in several states have applied the matrix as a framework for organizing and developing classroom-level curricula. There is evidence of an individual teacher-developed curriculum, and teachers have been receptive to its use. Some training exists for its application. The sustainability of the matrix model for at least 3 years is not known. It is not comprehensive in nature, yet it does have a strong emphasis in its relationship to core subject domains.

The Meeker Structure of Intellect Model

The Structure of Intellect model (SOI) for gifted education was based upon a theory of human intelligence called the Structure of Intellect developed by Guilford (1967). SOI describes 90 kinds of cognitive functions organized into content, operation, and product abilities. SOI applies Guilford's theory into the areas of assessment and training. The model is definable as a system and applies broadly to all types of gifted learners at varying developmental stages, but due to its comprehensiveness and emphasis on cognition, only a few sites have actually implemented the model. Those sites have used it for identifying students or for training teachers to view intelligence as a nonfixed entity.

Studies of the model do not include effectiveness data (Meeker, 1976); rather, they primarily focus on findings for its use as identification criteria, as a means for organizing information about a gifted child, or as a means for overall program design. SOI has been used successfully in selected sites for identification with culturally diverse students (Hengen, 1983) and preschool screening for multiethnic disadvantaged gifted students (Bonne, 1985).

Although now dated, SOI offered a means of understanding students by delineating profiles of their intellectual abilities. It contained a teacher-training component that used teacher modules designed to train one SOI ability at a time. Training materials included mini-lesson plans for group teaching and self-help modules for individualized instruction with selected students (Meeker, 1969).

The Parallel Curriculum Model

The Parallel Curriculum Model (PCM) is a model for curricular planning based upon the composite work of Tomlinson and colleagues (2002). The heuristic model employs four dimensions, or parallels, that can be used singly or in combination: the core curriculum, the curriculum of connections, the curriculum of practice, and the curriculum of identity.

The PCM assumes that the *core curriculum* is the basis for all other curricula and it should be combined with any or all of the three other parallels. It is the foundational curriculum that is defined by a given discipline. National, state, and/or local school district standards should be reflected in this dimension. It establishes the basis of understanding within relevant subjects and grade levels. The second parallel, the *curriculum of connections*, supports students in discovering the interconnectedness among and between disciplines of knowledge. It builds from the core curriculum and has students exploring those connections for both intra- and interdisciplinary studies. The third parallel, the *curriculum of practice*, also derives from the core curriculum. Its purpose is to extend students' understandings and skills in a discipline through application. The curriculum of practice promotes student expertise as a practitioner of a given discipline. The last parallel, the *curriculum of identity*, serves to help students think about themselves within the context of a particular discipline—to see how it relates to their own lives. The curriculum of identity uses curriculum as a catalyst for self-definition and self-understanding. The authors suggest that the level of intellectual demand in employing all or elements of the PCM should be matched to student needs.

To date, no research-based evidence of effectiveness has been shown with regard to this model's use with gifted or nongifted learners; however, several curricular units and guides have been produced as a result of a wide dissemination effort by the National Association for Gifted Children (NAGC). Additionally, the creation of curricular units currently is being designed by practitioners at various levels and guided by authors of the model. The model holds appeal for many educators because it can be adapted for any learner, subject domain, or grade level. The model, although flexible, is not easy to implement and does require a degree of teacher training. Professional development on the implementation of the PCM typically requires 2 days and may be adjusted depending on the needs of the employing school district. Implementation sessions have been offered for both regular classroom use, as well as a series of "trainer of trainer" offerings, sponsored by NAGC.

The Schlichter Models for Talents Unlimited Inc. and Talents Unlimited to the Secondary Power

Talents Unlimited was based upon Guilford's (1967) research on the nature of intelligence. Taylor, Ghiselin, Wolfer, Loy, & Bourne (1964), also influenced by Guilford, authored the multiple talent theory, which precipitated the development of a model to be employed in helping teachers identify and nurture students' multiple talents. Talents Unlimited features four major components (Schlichter, 1986):

» a description of specific skill abilities, or talents, in addition to academic ability that include productive thinking, communication, forecasting, decision making, and planning;

» model instructional materials;

» an in-service training program for teachers; and

» an evaluation system for assessing students' thinking skills development.

Talents Unlimited Inc. is the K–6 model, and Talents Unlimited to the Secondary Power is a model for grades 7–12.

Research has documented gains using the model in developing students' creative and critical thinking (Schlichter & Palmer, 1993), and Rodd (1999) used action research to demonstrate the model's effectiveness in an English setting with young children. Additionally, there is evidence that the use of the model enhances academic skill development on standardized achievement tests (McLean & Chisson, 1980); however, no longitudinal studies have been conducted.

Staff development and teacher training constitute a strong component of the model. Teachers may become "certified" as Talents Unlimited trainers. Due to the strong emphasis on teacher training, Talents Unlimited has widespread applicable student use across the United States and worldwide. Part of its implementation success came as a result of funding and membership in the U.S. Department of Education's National Diffusion Network.

The model has been used most effectively as a classroom-based approach with all learners, thus rendering it less differentiated for the gifted in practice than some of the other models.

Sternberg's Triarchic Componential Model

Sternberg's Triarchic Componential Model is based upon an information processing theory of intelligence (Sternberg, 1981). In the model, three components represent the mental processes used in thinking. The executive process component is used in planning, decision making, and monitoring performance. The performance component processes are used in executing the executive problem-solving strategies within domains. The knowledge-acquisition component is used in acquiring, retaining, and transferring new information. The interaction and feedback between the individual and his or her environment within any given context allows cognitive development to occur.

An initial study has shown the effectiveness of the triarchic model with students learning psychology in a summer program (Sternberg & Clinkenbeard, 1995). More recent work has been conducted in studies using psychology as the curriculum base with larger samples of students. Students continue to show growth patterns when assessment protocols are linked to measuring ability profiles (Sternberg, Ferrari, Clinkenbeard, & Grigorenko, 1996). Primary to these studies is the validation of the Sternberg Triarchic Abilities Test (STAT) and its utility for finding students strong on specific triarchic components. Other studies (Grigorenko, Jarvin, & Sternberg, 2002; Sternberg, Torff, & Grigorenko,

1998a, 1998b) focus on the use of triarchic instructional processes in classrooms at the elementary and middle school levels. Results suggest slightly stronger effects for triarchic instruction over traditional and critical thinking approaches. Descriptions of teacher-created curricula and instructional instrumentation processes were limited but clearly are organized along discipline-specific lines of inquiry. Sustainability of the curriculum model beyond summer program implementation and pilot settings is not known.

There is not a packaged teacher training or staff development component, in part because the model is based upon a theory of intelligence rather than a deliberate curriculum framework. It is a systemic but not a comprehensive model with some applications in selected classrooms.

VanTassel-Baska's Integrated Curriculum Model

The VanTassel-Baska (1986) Integrated Curriculum Model (ICM) was specifically developed for high-ability learners. It has three dimensions: (a) advanced content, (b) high-level process and product work, and (c) intra- and interdisciplinary concept development and understanding. VanTassel-Baska, with funding from the Jacob K. Javits Program, used the ICM to develop specific curricular frameworks and underlying units in language arts, social studies, and science.

Research has been conducted to support the effectiveness of these curricular units with gifted populations within a variety of educational settings. Specifically, significant growth gains in literary analysis and interpretation, persuasive writing, and linguistic competency in language arts have been demonstrated for experimental gifted classes using the developed curricular units in comparison to gifted groups not using them (VanTassel-Baska, Johnson, Hughes, & Boyce, 1996; VanTassel-Baska, Zuo, Avery, & Little, 2002). Other studies have shown that using the problem-based science units embedded in an exemplary science curriculum significantly enhances the capacity for integrating higher order process skills in science (VanTassel-Baska, Bass, Ries, Poland, & Avery, 1998), regardless of the grouping approach employed.

Findings from a 6-year longitudinal study that examined the effects over time of using the William and Mary language arts units for gifted learners in a suburban school district suggest that gifted student learning in grades 3–5 was enhanced at significant and educationally important levels in critical reading and persuasive writing. Repeated exposure over a 2–3 year period demonstrated increasing achievement patterns, and the majority of stakeholders reported the curriculum to be beneficial and effective (Feng, VanTassel-Baska, Quek, Bai, & O'Neill, 2005). An earlier study had documented positive change in teacher attitude, student motivational response, and school and district change (VanTassel-

Baska, Avery, Little, & Hughes, 2000) as a result of using the ICM science and language arts curricula over 3 years.

A subanalysis of the language arts data across settings suggested that it is successful with low-income students, can be used in all grouping paradigms, and that learning increases with multiple units employed (VanTassel-Baska et al., 2002).

Research on the use of the social studies units suggested that unit use significantly impacts critical thinking and content mastery, using comparison groups (Little, Feng, VanTassel-Baska, Rogers, & Avery, 2007). Moreover, positive changes in teacher behaviors for using differentiated strategies were noted in this study as well.

Teacher training and development in the use of specific teaching models is an integral component of the ICM model. Training workshops have been conducted in 30 states, and The College of William and Mary Center for Gifted Education offers training annually. There is a strong relationship to core subject domains, as well as national standards alignment. The curricula based on the model was developed using the national standards work as a template. Alignment charts have been completed for national and state standards work in both language arts and science. Newer alignment to the CCSS have been effected by the curriculum developer (Hughes, Kettler, Shaunessy Dedrick, & VanTassel-Baska, 2014) and her colleagues (Johnsen, Ryser, & Assouline, 2014). Next Generation Science Standards also reflect alignment to the model in the elements of scientific inquiry and concept development (Adams, Cotabish, & Ricci, 2014).

The ICM units are moderately comprehensive in that they span grades K–10 in language arts and K–8 in science. Social studies units are now available for grades 2–10 as well. Selected units of study in math are now available in grades 3–8. The ICM model has been used for specific school and district curriculum development and planning in Australia, Canada, New Zealand, Japan, Korea, and Taiwan, as well as selected districts in the United States and international schools abroad.

There is evidence of broad-based application, but some questions remain regarding the ease of implementation of the teaching units, and the fidelity of implementation by teachers remains an area of concern in many settings. Some districts use the units as models for developing their own curricula. The developer reported that 100 school districts are part of a National Curriculum Network using multiple content area units. Data on student impact have been collected from more than 150 classrooms nationally.

More recent Javits grants assessed the effectiveness of the ICM units in language arts at the elementary level and science at the primary level with low-income learners in Title I schools using critical thinking as one outcome variable of interest. In Project Athena, the language arts program, findings on both student learning and teacher learning appeared promising. Experimental students did significantly better than control students in both critical thinking and comprehension with all groups registering significant growth gains from using the curriculum regardless of ability, gender, or ethnic background (VanTassel-Baska, Bracken, Feng, & Brown, 2009). Experimental teachers scored significantly higher on both the frequency of use and effective use of differentiated strategies across 2 years. Growth gains for teacher use of differentiation strategies remained stagnant in the third year. Also of note, experimental teachers who had used the curriculum for 2 years and received commensurate training demonstrated significantly enhanced use of differentiated strategies over first-year experimental teachers (VanTassel-Baska et al., 2008).

As an outgrowth of Project Athena, *Jacob's Ladder*, a reading comprehension program intended to move students from lower order to higher order thinking skills in the language arts (VanTassel-Baska, Stambaugh, & French, 2004), was designed and developed for use in Title I schools. Supporting the implementation of the program was a series of workshops to aid teachers in implementation. Two studies support the use of *Jacob's Ladder* with students from low-income backgrounds (French, 2006; Stambaugh, 2007), suggesting growth in critical thinking and reading comprehension as well as enhancing interest in the reading process.

In another Javits grant that used the William and Mary language arts units, results suggested that enhanced learning also accrued for both teachers and students (Swanson, 2006).

Project Clarion, the primary science program, has produced important findings that relate to several areas of interest. Student learning gains have been strong, with students demonstrating critical thinking increases, science achievement increases, and science concept learning gains. Using quasi-experimental designs, the project has demonstrated significant and important learning gains in these dimensions with effect sizes ranging from .3–.6 (Kim et al., 2012). Additionally, teachers have demonstrated learning gains in using differentiation strategies in key areas that include critical thinking, creative thinking, and accommodation to individual differences (Stambaugh, Bland, & VanTassel-Baska, 2010; VanTassel-Baska, 2013a). Two other Javits grants also used the science units from Project Clarion with strong results, especially for enhancing the teaching of science at the primary levels.

Studies of effectiveness are ongoing in classrooms nationally. The curricula are reported to be used in all 50 states. Internationally, the model is being used in multiple countries as a model for design and development of quality curriculum for the gifted.

Key Findings

An important part of the curricular model analysis also was to compare the models to one another, using the same criteria as the basis for comparison. Some models were more organizational than curricular in nature, which helps teachers get started on differentiation in their classroom; others were more programmatic in nature and were intended as a defining framework in schools. Examples of the former were the Kaplan Grid and the Maker Matrix, both heavily used by practitioners as designs for teacher-made materials. No studies of effectiveness have been conducted to date, however, to show the benefits of such models in practice with gifted learners. The Tannenbaum model, dropped at the second level of analysis, exemplified the programmatic framework model as a supraorganizer at the school level, but not at the level of curriculum units or courses of study. Regrettably, no studies or evidence of application were found for this model.

Only seven models showed evidence of having been the focus of research studies. Of those, six of the models employed comparison groups where treatment might be attributed to the curricular or instructional approach employed. The Stanley, SEM, Feldhusen, ICM, Sternberg, and Talents Unlimited models all have some evidence of effectiveness with gifted populations in comparison to other treatments or no treatments. Although the Talents Unlimited Model has some evidence of effectiveness, much of the research base is on nongifted populations. In recent years, there is also evidence that some of these models continue to be actively employed by schools, based on the work of the primary developer and his or her associates, with new curriculum being subjected to efficacy studies. The models that fit that description are the SEM and the ICM. The model for talent search and development originated by Stanley continues to provide important insights on the talent development process longitudinally, going well beyond the other models described in terms of greater utility to the field of gifted education beyond curriculum.

Evidence for the translation of these curricular models into effective practice varies considerably. Seven models have training packages that provide staff development for implementation, whereas only four models explicitly consider scope and sequence issues. Betts and Renzulli consider scope and sequence within their models. For Betts, it is in the movement from one stage to another; for Renzulli, it occurs within Type II activities. Stanley and ICM both have developed scope-and-sequence models linked to Advanced Placement work. More recent work has focused on the design of talent trajectories that suggest curricular interventions for gifted learners at different stages of development, cutting across the use of models (VanTassel-Baska, 2013b).

Data on curricular and instructional practices with the gifted clearly favor advanced work in the subject areas of language arts, science, and mathematics, although the approach to content acceleration may vary. Although both the Stanley and ICM models have elements of acceleration within them, only the Stanley model has empirically demonstrated the clear impact of accelerated study on learning over time.

Curricula organized around higher order processes and independent study have yielded few studies of student impacts, nor are the findings across studies consistent. Even longitudinal studies, such as those of Feldhusen and the SEM, have produced limited evidence of outcomes relevant to clear student gains. Limited sample size and other confounding variables, such as lack of comparison groups, also render these studies less credible.

Conclusions

A strong body of research evidence exists supporting the use of advanced curricula in core areas of learning at an accelerated rate for high-ability learners. Some evidence also exists that more enrichment-oriented models are effective. This conclusion has not changed much in the past 30 years (Colangelo, Assouline, & Gross, 2004; Daurio, 1979). Moreover, meta-analytic studies continue to confirm the superior learning effects of acceleration over enrichment in tandem with grouping the gifted (Kulik & Kulik, 1993; Rogers, 2002; Swiatek, 2000). In comparison to other strategies, such as independent study, various modes of grouping, and problem solving, acceleration not only shows performance gains but also has a powerful treatment effect, meaning that the gains are educationally, as well as statistically, significant (Walberg, 1991). Despite the lack of convincing research to support their use, several of the enrichment models enjoy widespread popularity and are used extensively in schools.

General Implications

Several implications might be drawn from these findings, related to both research and practice in gifted education. Too frequently, it is assumed that if a model is written about and used enthusiastically, such popularity is sufficient for proclaiming its effectiveness. Nothing could be further from the truth. Research-based practice is critical to defensible gifted programs; therefore, practitioners must proceed carefully in deciding on curricula for use in gifted programs. The evidence strongly suggests that content-based accelerative approaches should be employed in any curriculum used in school-based programs for the gifted and that schools need to apply curricular models faithfully and thoroughly in order to realize their potential impacts over time.

In the area of research, it is clear that there is a limited base of coherent studies that can make claims about the efficacy of enriched approaches to curriculum for the gifted. Thus, an important direction for future research would be to conduct curricular intervention studies testing these models, as well as to replicate existing studies, in order to build a base of deeper understanding about what works well with gifted students in school programs. More research on differential student learning outcomes in gifted programs using different curricular approaches clearly needs to be undertaken.

Implications for Schools

Decisions about curricular approaches and their implications for classrooms need to be made with a sense of what works for our best learners in schools. This chapter has delineated a set of criteria for considering the state of the art in curricular interventions for gifted learners. These criteria are important considerations for schools in making curricular decisions. The fundamental questions upon which schools need to focus are:

»   Do gifted students show evidence of learning as a result of the curricular approach? What is the nature and extent of the evidence and how credible is it?

»   Are differentiated classroom materials available to use in implementation?

»   Is training in the use of differentiated curricular materials available for school staff?

Teacher Statement

I first read this chapter during a time when I was both working with elementary gifted and talented students and pursuing a master's degree in education with a specialization in gifted and talented education. This chapter was one of many assigned from the previous edition of this text for a graduate course that covered various instructional strategies and models implemented in gifted education programs.

I found the chapter to be helpful because it provided a clear and concise overview of the most widely used program and curriculum models in the field of gifted education. Specifically, it emphasized the research evidence for each of the models discussed and their effectiveness with gifted students. The evidence presented in this chapter contributed positively to my instructional decision-making process by influencing me to incorporate more accelerative curriculum and instructional strategies related to student ability and interests.

This chapter also emphasized the caution with which educators should embrace new models and theories. After reading this chapter, I became more aware of and interested in the research behind instructional strategies and curriculum materials I incorporate into teaching. It encouraged me to ask for more evidence of effectiveness with gifted students or appropriateness for meeting the needs of gifted students.

I recommend this chapter to all educators in the field of gifted education, as well as parents and others interested in the program and curricular models used in a community's gifted education program. The authors provide useful information about prominent models used in the field of gifted education as well as guidelines and procedures for evaluating other programs and curricular models that might be implemented with gifted students.

—Bess B. Worley II

DISCUSSION QUESTIONS

1. Based on research evidence, what models appear to be most successful?

2. What models appear to work with special populations? Why?

3. What models lack research studies of effectiveness?

4. Why do you think the research base is so limited on curricular interventions with gifted students?

5. What features across models are critical to employ in a curriculum, according to your understanding of their characteristics and needs?

6. How can professional development in the field become more influential in helping curricular models become institutionalized?

INSTRUCTIONAL PLANNING AND EVALUATION

Teacher Resources

Websites

Schoolwide Enrichment Model—http://www.gifted.uconn.edu/sem

Integrated Curriculum Model (ICM), College of William and Mary, Center for Gifted Education—http://www.cfge.wm.edu

References

Adams, C. M., Cotabish, A., & Ricci, M. C. (2014). *Using the Next Generation Science Standards with gifted and advanced learners.* Waco, TX: Prufrock Press.

American Association for the Advancement of Science. (1989). *Science for all Americans.* New York, NY: Oxford University Press.

American Association for the Advancement of Science. (1993). *Benchmarks for science literacy.* New York, NY: Oxford University Press.

Baum, S. (1985). *Learning disabled students with superior cognitive abilities: A validation study of descriptive behaviors* (Unpublished doctoral dissertation). University of Connecticut, Storrs.

Baum, S. (1988). An enrichment program for gifted learning disabled students. *Gifted Child Quarterly, 32,* 226–230.

Benbow, C. P., & Arjmand, O. (1990). Predictors of high academic achievement in mathematics and science by mathematically talented students: A longitudinal study. *Journal of Educational Psychology, 82,* 430–431.

Betts, G. T. (1986). The autonomous learner model for the gifted and talented. In J. S. Renzulli (Ed.), *Systems and models for developing programs for the gifted and talented* (pp. 27–56). Mansfield Center, CT: Creative Learning Press.

Betts, G., & Knapp, J. (1980). Autonomous learning and the gifted: A secondary model. In A. Arnold (Ed.), *Secondary programs for the gifted* (pp. 29–36). Ventura, CA: Ventura Superintendent of Schools Office.

Betts, G. T., & Neihart, M. (1986). Implementing self-directed learning models for the gifted and talented. *Gifted Child Quarterly, 30,* 174–177.

Bonne, R. (1985). *Identifying multi-ethnic disadvantaged gifted.* Brooklyn, NY: Community School District #19.

Brand, S. T. (2006). Facilitating emergent literacy skills: A literature-based multiple intelligence approach. *Journal of Research in Childhood Education, 21,* 133–149.

Brody, L. E., & Stanley, J. C. (1991). Young college students: Assessing factors that contribute to success. In W. T. Southern & E. D. Jones (Eds.), *Academic acceleration of gifted children* (pp. 130–148). New York, NY: Teachers College Press.

Bruner, J. (Ed.). (1970). *Man: A course of study.* Newton, MA: Education Development Center.

Colangelo, N., Assouline, S. G., & Gross, M. (2004). *A nation deceived: How schools hold back America's brightest students* (Vol. 1). Iowa City: University of Iowa, The Connie Belin & Jacqueline N. Blank International Center for Gifted Education and Talent Development.

Daurio, S. P. (1979). Education enrichment versus acceleration: A review of the literature. In W. C. Gregory, S. J. Cohn, & J. C. Stanley (Eds.), *Educating the gifted: Acceleration and enrichment* (pp. 13–63). Baltimore, MD: Johns Hopkins University Press.

Delcourt, M. A. B. (1988). *Characteristics related to high levels of creative/productive behavior in secondary school students: A multi-case study* (Unpublished doctoral dissertation). University of Connecticut, Storrs.

Delisle, J. R. (1981). *The Revolving Door Identification Model: Correlates of creative production* (Unpublished doctoral dissertation). University of Connecticut, Storrs.

Emerick, L. (1988). *Academic underachievement among the gifted: Students' perceptions of factors relating to the reversal of the academic underachievement pattern* (Unpublished doctoral dissertation). University of Connecticut, Storrs.

Feldhusen, J. F., & Kolloff, M. B. (1986). The Purdue Three-Stage Model for Gifted Education. In J. S. Renzulli (Ed.), *Systems and models for developing programs for the gifted and talented* (pp. 126–152). Mansfield Center, CT: Creative Learning Press.

Feldhusen, J. F., & Robinson-Wyman, A. (1986). The Purdue Secondary Model for Gifted Education. In J. S. Renzulli (Ed.), *Systems and models for developing programs for the gifted and talented* (pp. 153–179). Mansfield Center, CT: Creative Learning Press.

Feng, A. X., VanTassel-Baska, J., Quek, C., Bai, W., & O'Neill, B. (2005). A longitudinal assessment of gifted students' learning using the Integrated Curriculum Model (ICM): Impacts and perceptions of the William and Mary language arts and science curriculum. *Roeper Review, 27,* 78–83.

Ferriman-Robertson, K. F., Smeets, S., Lubinski, D. & Benbow, C. P. (2013). Beyond the threshold hypothesis: Even among the gifted and top math/science graduate students, cognitive abilities, vocational interests, and lifestyle preferences matter for career choice, performance, and persistence. *Current Directions in Psychological Science, 19,* 346–351.

Ford, D. Y. (1999). Renzulli's philosophy and program: Opening doors and nurturing potential. *Journal for the Education of the Gifted, 23,* 117–124.

French, H. (2006). A pilot study of the Jacob's Ladder Reading Comprehension Program with gifted and potentially gifted learners in grades 3, 4, and 5. *Dissertation Abstracts International, 66,* 10.

Gardner, H. (1983). *Frames of mind: The theory of multiple intelligences.* New York, NY: Basic Books.

Gardner, H. (1999). *Intelligence reframed: Multiple intelligences for the 21st century.* New York, NY: Basic Books.

Gavin, M. K., Casa, T. M., Adelson, J. L., Carroll, S. L., Sheffield, L. J., & Spinelli, A. M. (2007). Project M3: Mentoring mathematical minds: A research-based curriculum for talented elementary students. *Journal for the Education of the Gifted, 18,* 566–585.

Grigorenko, E. L., Jarvin, L., & Sternberg, R. J. (2002). School-based tests of the triarchic theory of intelligence: Three settings, three samples, three syllabi. *Contemporary Educational Psychology, 27,* 167–208.

Guilford, J. P. (1967). *The nature of human intelligence.* New York, NY: McGraw-Hill.

Heal, M. M. (1989). *Student perceptions of labeling the gifted: A comparative case study analysis* (Unpublished doctoral dissertation). University of Connecticut, Storrs.

Hébert, T. P. (1993). Reflections at graduation: The long-term impact of elementary school experiences in creative productivity. *Roeper Review, 16,* 22–28.

Hengen, T. (1983, November). *Identification and enhancement of giftedness in Canadian Indians.* Paper presented at the annual meeting of the National Association for Gifted Children, New Orleans, LA.

Hollingworth, L. (1926). *Gifted children.* New York, NY: World Book.

Hughes, C. E., Kettler, T., Shaunessy Dedrick, E., & VanTassel-Baska, J. (2014). *A teacher's guide to using the Common Core State Standards with gifted and advanced learners in the English/language arts.* Waco, TX: Prufrock Press.

International Reading Association, & National Council of Teachers of English. (1996). *Standards for the English language arts.* Urbana, IL: National Council of Teachers of English.

Johnsen, S. K., Ryser, G. R., & Assouline, S. G. (2014). *A teacher's guide to using the Common Core State Standards with mathematically gifted and advanced learners.* Waco, TX: Prufrock Press.

Johnson, G. M. (2000). Schoolwide enrichment: Improving the education of students (at risk) at promise. *Teacher Education Quarterly, 27*(4), 45–61.

Kaplan, S. (1986). The Kaplan grid. In J. S. Renzulli (Ed.), *Systems and models for developing programs for the gifted and talented* (pp. 56–68). Mansfield Center, CT: Creative Learning Press.

Karafelis, P. (1986). *The effects of the tri-art drama curriculum on the reading comprehension of students with varying levels of cognitive ability* (Unpublished doctoral dissertation). University of Connecticut, Storrs.

Keating, D. P. (Ed.). (1976). *Intellectual talent: Research and development.* Baltimore, MD: Johns Hopkins University Press.

Kiesa, K. (2000). *Uniquely gifted: Identifying and meeting the needs of twice-exceptional students.* Gilsum, NH: Avocus.

Kim, K. H., VanTassel-Baska, J., Bracken, B. A., Feng, A., T., Stambaugh, T., & Bland, L. (2012). Project Clarion: Three years of science instruction in title I schools among K–third grade students. *Research in Science Education, 42,* 813–829. doi:10.1007/s11165-011-9218-5

Kolloff, M. B., & Feldhusen, J. F. (1984). The effects of enrichment on self-concept and creative thinking. *Gifted Child Quarterly, 28,* 53–57.

Kulik, J. A., & Kulik, C.-L. (1993). Meta analytic findings on grouping programs. *Gifted Child Quarterly, 36,* 73–77.

Latham, A. S. (1997). Quantifying MI's gains. *Educational Leadership, 55*(1), 84–85.

Lipman, M., Sharp, A. M., & Oscanyan, F. F. (1980). *Philosophy in the classroom.* Philadelphia, PA: Temple University Press.

Little, C. A., Feng, A. X., VanTassel-Baska, J., Rogers, K. B., & Avery, L. D. (2007). A study of curriculum effectiveness in social studies. *Gifted Child Quarterly, 51,* 272–284.

Lubinski, D., & Benbow, C. P. (1994). The study of mathematically precocious youth: The first three decades of a planned 50-year study of intellectual talent. In R. Subotnik & K. D. Arnold (Eds.), *Beyond Terman: Contemporary longitudinal studies of giftedness and talent* (pp. 375–400). Norwood, NJ: Ablex.

Lynch, S. J. (1992). Fast-paced high school science for the academically talented: A six-year perspective. *Gifted Child Quarterly, 36,* 147–154.

Maker, C. J. (1982). *Curriculum development for the gifted.* Rockville, MD: Aspen.

Maker, C. J., Nielson, A. B., & Rogers, J. A. (1994). Multiple intelligences: Giftedness, diversity, and problem solving. *Teaching Exceptional Children, 27*(1), 4–19.

Maker, C. J., Rogers, J. A., Nielson, A. B., & Bauerle, P. R. (1996). Multiple intelligences, problem solving, and diversity in the general classroom. *Journal for the Education of the Gifted, 19,* 437–460.

McLean, J. E., & Chisson, B. S. (1980). *Talented unlimited program: Summary of research findings for 1979–80.* Mobile, AL: Mobile County Public Schools.

Meeker, M. (1969). *The structure of intellect: Its interpretation and uses.* Columbus, OH: Merrill.

Meeker, M. (1976). *A paradigm for special education diagnostics: The cognitive area* (Report No. EC082519). Paper presented at the annual meeting of the American Educational Research Association, San Francisco, CA. Retrieved from ERIC database (ED121010)

Moon, S., & Feldhusen, J. F. (1994). The program for academic and creative enrichment (PACE): A follow-up study 10 years later. In R. Subotnik & K. D. Arnold (Eds.),

Beyond Terman: Contemporary longitudinal studies of giftedness and talent (pp. 375–400). Norwood, NJ: Ablex.

Moon, S. M., Feldhusen, J. F., & Dillon, D. R. (1994). Long-term effects of an enrichment program based on the Purdue Three-Stage Model. *Gifted Child Quarterly, 38,* 38–48.

National Research Council. (1996). *National science education standards.* Washington, DC: National Academies Press.

Olszewski-Kubilius, P. (2006). The role of summer programs in developing talent. In J. VanTassel-Baska (Ed.) *Serving gifted learners beyond the traditional classroom* (pp. 13–33). Waco, TX: Prufrock Press.

Olszewski-Kubilius, P., & Clarenbach, J. (2012). *Unlocking emergent talent: Supporting high achievement of low-income, high-ability students.* Washington, DC: National Association for Gifted Children. Retrieved from http://www.nagc.org/uploaded-Files/Conventions_and_Seminars/National_Research_Summit/Unlocking%20Emergent%20Talent%20FULL%20No-Tint.pdf

Park, G., Lubinski, D., & Benbow, C. P. (2007). Contrasting intellectual patterns for creativity in the arts and sciences: Tracking intellectually precocious youth over 25 years. *Psychological Science, 18,* 948–952.

Park, G., Lubinski, D., & Benbow, C. P. (2008). Ability differences among people who have commensurate degrees for scientific creativity. *Psychological Science, 19,* 957–961.

Pressey, S. L. (1949). *Educational acceleration: Appraisal and basic problems.* Columbus, OH: The Ohio State University Press.

Reis, S. M. (1981). *An analysis of the productivity of gifted students participating in programs using the revolving door identification model* (Unpublished doctoral dissertation). University of Connecticut, Storrs.

Reis, S. M., Eckert, R. D., McCoach, D. B., Jacobs, J. K., & Coyne, M. (2008). Using enrichment reading practices to increase reading fluency, comprehension, and attitudes. *Journal of Educational Research, 101,* 299–314.

Reis, S. M., & Purcell, J. H. (1993). An analysis of content elimination and strategies used by elementary classroom teachers in the curriculum compacting process. *Journal for the Education of the Gifted, 16,* 147–170.

Reis, S. M., Westberg, K. L, Kulikowich, J. M., & Purcell, J. H. (1998). Curriculum compacting and achievement test scores: What does the research say? *Gifted Child Quarterly, 42,* 123–129.

Renzulli, J. S. (1977). *The Enrichment Triad Model: A guide for developing defensible programs for the gifted and talented.* Mansfield Center, CT: Creative Learning Press.

Renzulli, J. S. (Ed.). (1988). *Technical report of research studies related to the Revolving Door Identification Model.* Storrs: Bureau of Educational Research, University of Connecticut.

Renzulli, J. S., Reis, S. M., & Smith, L. (1981). The Revolving-Door Model: A new way of identifying the gifted. *Phi Delta Kappan, 62,* 648–649.

Renzulli, J. S., & Reis, S. M. (1985). *The Schoolwide Enrichment Model: A comprehensive plan for educational excellence.* Mansfield Center, CT: Creative Learning Press.

Renzulli, J. S., & Reis, S. M. (1997). *The Schoolwide Enrichment Model: A comprehensive plan for educational excellence* (2nd ed.). Waco, TX: Prufrock Press.

Renzulli, J. S., & Reis, S. M. (2014). *The Schoolwide Enrichment Model: A comprehensive plan for educational excellence* (3rd ed.). Waco, TX: Prufrock Press.

Rodd, J. (1999). Encouraging young children's critical and creative thinking skills: An approach in one English elementary school. *Childhood Education, 75,* 350–354.

Rogers, K. (2002). *Re-forming gifted education: How parents and teachers can match the program to the child.* Scottsdale, AZ: Great Potential Press.

Schlichter, C. (1986). Talents unlimited: Applying the multiple talent approach in mainstream and gifted programs. In J. S. Renzulli (Ed.), *Systems and models for developing programs for the gifted and talented.* Mansfield Center, CT: Creative Learning Press.

Schlichter, C. L., & Palmer, W. R. (Eds.). (1993). *Thinking smart: A premiere of the talents unlimited model.* Mansfield Center, CT: Creative Learning Press.

Smith, W., Odhiambo, E., & El Khateeb, H. (2000, November). *The typologies of successful and unsuccessful students in the core subjects of language arts, mathematics, science, and social studies using the theory of multiple intelligences in a high school environment in Tennessee.* Paper presented at the annual meeting of the Mid-South Educational Research Association, Bowling Green, KY.

Stambaugh, T. (2007). Next steps: An impetus for future directions in research, policy, and practice for low-income promising learners. In J. VanTassel-Baska & T. Stambaugh (Eds.), *Overlooked gems: A national perspective on promising students of poverty.* Washington, DC: National Association of Gifted Children.

Stambaugh, T., Bland, L., & VanTassel-Baska, J. (2010). *Innovation in schools: The Project Clarion follow-up.* Paper presented at the annual University of Iowa Wallace Symposium, Iowa City.

Stanley, J. C., Keating, D., & Fox, L. (1974). *Mathematical talent: Discovery, description, and development.* Baltimore, MD: Johns Hopkins University Press.

Starko, A. J. (1986). *The effects of the Revolving Door Identification Model on creative productivity and self-efficacy* (Unpublished doctoral dissertation). University of Connecticut, Storrs.

Sternberg, R. (1981). A componential theory of intellectual giftedness. *Gifted Child Quarterly, 25,* 86–93.

Sternberg, R., & Clinkenbeard, P. R. (1995). The triadic model applied to identify, teach, and assess gifted children. *Roeper Review, 17,* 255–260.

Sternberg, R. J., Ferrari, M., Clinkenbeard, P., & Grigorenko, E. L. (1996). Identification, instruction, and assessment of gifted children: A construct validation of a triarchic model. *Gifted Child Quarterly, 40,* 129–137.

Sternberg, R. J., Torff, B., & Grigorenko, E. L. (1998a). Teaching for successful intelligence raises school achievement. *Phi Delta Kappan, 79,* 667–699.

Sternberg, R. J., Torff, B., & Grigorenko, E. L. (1998b). Teaching triarchically improves school achievement. *Journal of Educational Psychology, 90,* 374–384.

Strahan, D., Summey, H., & Banks, N. (1996). Teaching to diversity through multiple intelligences: Student and teacher responses to instructional improvement. *Research in Middle Level Education Quarterly, 19*(2), 43–65.

Swanson, J. (2006). Breaking through assumptions about low-income, minority gifted students. *Gifted Child Quarterly, 50,* 11–24.

Swiatek, M. A. (2000). A decade of longitudinal research on academic acceleration through the study of mathematically precocious youth. *Roeper Review, 24,* 141–144.

Taylor, C. W., Ghiselin, B., Wolfer, J., Loy, L., & Bourne, L. E., Jr. (1964). *Development of a theory of education from psychology and other basic research findings* (Final Report, USOE Cooperative Research Project, No. 621). Salt Lake City: University of Utah.

Terman, L. M., & Oden, M. H. (1947). *The gifted child grows up*. Stanford, CA: Stanford University Press.

Tomlinson, C. A., Kaplan, S. N., Renzulli, J. S., Purcell, J., Leppien, J., & Burn, D. (2002). *The parallel curriculum: A design to develop high potential and challenge high-ability learners*. Washington, DC: National Association for Gifted Children.

VanTassel-Baska, J. (1986). Effective curriculum and instruction models for talented students. *Gifted Child Quarterly, 30,* 164–169.

VanTassel-Baska, J. (1995). A study of life themes in Charlotte Brontë and Virginia Woolf. *Roeper Review, 18,* 14–19.

VanTassel-Baska, J. (1998). *Excellence in educating the gifted*. Denver, CO: Love.

VanTassel-Baska, J. (2013a). Project Clarion. In C. M. Adams & K. L. Chandler (Eds.), *Effective program models for gifted students from underserved populations* (pp. 103–116). Waco, TX: Prufrock Press.

VanTassel-Baska, J. (ed.). (2013b). *Using the Common Core State Standards for English language arts with gifted and advanced learners*. Waco, TX: Prufrock Press.

VanTassel-Baska, J., Avery, L. D., Little, C. A., & Hughes, C. E. (2000). An evaluation of the implementation: The impact of the William and Mary units on schools. *Journal for the Education of the Gifted, 23,* 244–272.

VanTassel-Baska, J., Bass, G. M., Ries, R. R., Poland, D. L., & Avery, L. D. (1998). A national study of science curriculum effectiveness with high ability students. *Gifted Child Quarterly, 42,* 200–211.

VanTassel-Baska, J., Bracken, B., Feng, A., & Brown, E. (2009). A longitudinal study of reading comprehension and reasoning ability of students in elementary Title I schools. *Journal for the Education of the Gifted, 33,* 7–37.

VanTassel-Baska, J., Johnson, D. T., Hughes, C. E., & Boyce, L. N. (1996). A study of the language arts curriculum effectiveness with gifted learners. *Journal for the Education of the Gifted, 19,* 461–480.

VanTassel-Baska, Stambaugh, T., & French, H. (2004). *Jacob's Ladder reading comprehension program*. Williamsburg, VA: College of William and Mary, Center for Gifted Education.

VanTassel-Baska, J., Zuo, L., Avery, L. D., & Little, C. A. (2002). A curriculum study of gifted student learning in the language arts. *Gifted Child Quarterly, 46,* 30–44.

Wai, J., Lubinski, D., & Benbow, C. P. (2009). Spatial ability for STEM domains: Aligning over fifty years of cumulative psychological knowledge solidifies its importance. *Journal of Educational Psychology, 101,* 817–835.

Walberg, H. (1991). Productive teaching and instruction: Assessing the knowledge base. In H. C. Waxman & H. J. Walberg (Eds.), *Effective teaching: Current research* (pp. 33–62). Berkeley, CA: McCutchan.

DIFFERENTIATION OF PROCESSES FOR THE GIFTED

5

Chapter

BY ROYAL TOY

The process of educating a gifted student is as involved and complex as the daily interaction of a bustling marketplace on a busy day. The classroom teacher is working with an ever increasingly diverse population. Each student comes with more variance in culture, learning style, social maturity, and academic readiness. Although a carefully crafted lesson may inspire one student to work diligently and one day become a professional botanist, the very same instruction may leave a different learner frustrated and bored. Teachers must work to monitor and adjust the learning environment as well as the strategies used to engage gifted learners to assist in talent development. Culturally responsive teaching is necessary in order to reach the diverse school population of today. Teaching methods that recognize and acknowledge students' differences will provide opportunities for classroom activities that help to foster student self-worth (Green, 2007).

Differentiation has become an educational buzzword that has pervaded the media and educational platforms of all teacher preparation programs. It is always on an agenda or mentioned in professional development and is advocated for by teachers, students, parents, and administrators alike. Educators and researchers of the gifted have reported this need based on many arguments such as the various abilities students possess or by their interests/passions (Gallagher, 2002; Johnsen, Haensly, Ryser, & Ford, 2002; Tomlinson, 2001). According to Winebrenner (2001), process is defined as the way that learners come to understand concepts, generalizations, and/or required standards. She explained that differentiation of the process for gifted students typically occurs through grouping, multiple intelligences or learning styles, or complexity of content or of research methodology. Gagné (2004) discussed "provisions" for educating the gifted that include a wide diversity of individual or group interventions that have traditionally been subdivided into three groups: enrichment, grouping, and acceleration. These groups are not mutually exclusive and are not at odds with each other but are rather a way that professionals have tried to segregate the varied processes involved in educating the gifted. Gagné noted that all experiences should be enriching and that by separating and delineating the processes into the three categories, the message of enrichment may become confused.

The Regular Classroom

Process intervention options may begin with early entrance to kindergarten or first grade. For students who are ready, this may be the very best option available, as it allows for students to begin their school careers with their academic peers and establish patterns of expectations for achievement early. The current process for entrance in to kindergarten or first grade seems based on an actuarial table relating to age by a specific date, which seems to be reinforced by other arbitrary measures, such as physical size.

Good communication must be in place in order to ensure that early entrance to school is successful. Parents and teachers need to objectively consider the social and emotional development of the child that is involved in the process. If the child is not ready for the placement, then parents must be willing to accept that it may not be the best placement for the child. On the other hand, teachers must be careful not to stigmatize the child based on preconceived expectations of other factors such as the child's size, gender, or physical development, as these may not be indicators that impact the child's readiness for school.

Another strategy that differentiates the process for the gifted learner relates to the structure of the peers in the environment. There are several types of grouping strategies that are common in the general classroom for the gifted.

Grouping

Flexible grouping is a strategy used to divide students into groups for an indeterminate period of time. This may be done as a result of an assessment or by choice to provide for review, remediation, enrichment, or reteaching. This grouping could be for a single lesson, objective, unit, or term. The groups may work together for a few minutes at a time or extended periods. The key is that the groups are not permanent, and it may be possible to have students move between groups even before the completion of the specified goal is met. One of the major benefits to this structure is that it allows for potential change of peers, and this variety can be welcome in the classroom. Flexible groups can be collaborative or independent, allowing the teacher to determine the amount of desired interaction between the students for a particular setting. As a temporary placement for students in the classroom, learners can move between groups and the teacher can be less concerned about the grouping and more focused on the development of the learning and outcomes of the particular unit or module. If a student is in a group that is found to have a poor fit, neither the teacher nor the student is forced to remain in the grouping situation.

Heterogeneous groups are beneficial when the students are diverse. Several types of activities can include opportunities that would allow for all students to participate and provide valuable information to the class. Examples may include critical thinking, brainstorming, thematic/multidisciplinary unit work, open-ended discussions, experiments, and problem-based learning. In each of these types of activities, students' various backgrounds, experiences, and other differences are valued and contribute to the outcome. In some situations, teachers want to consider grouping students so that there is less diversity. When students are randomly assigned to a group, these are typically heterogeneous. The benefit is that the groups will most closely mirror the general population of the classroom.

Homogeneous groups are most beneficial when working with students on advanced content, group practice in a single tier of instruction, or when working to achieve mastery of criterion-referenced expectations at the same time. Various ways are appropriate for selecting a homogeneous group such as ability grouping, where students are grouped as a result of performances based in a specific subject or domain. As a practice, this helps to eliminate some of the diversity in the skill or content to be taught, allowing the teacher to focus more on advancing the content as the students will remain together for the instruction or activity. Another closely aligned grouping is by readiness. When students are grouped by readiness, the content can be mastered in less time, as there are opportunities to adjust the curriculum for these learners. This opportunity speeds the process of instruction that could not be accomplished in the regular classroom with heterogeneous groups, as some tasks or performances that are required may need all students to have met certain developmental milestones or have mastered competencies to achieve them. Grouping by readiness provides the opportunity to avoid the time that would be required in waiting for some students to prepare for the prerequisite requirements. Typically, individuals do not begin their driving experience by being placed in a stock car to drive for the first time; rather, the individual would demonstrate readiness by achieving the appropriate competencies before sitting in the seat of the stock car to drive. Some groups are assigned by profile rather than academic readiness or ability. In these situations, students who are grouped by profile have other characteristics or commonalities that were of interest in the grouping process. It may be that the students were grouped by learning modality or preference. It is also possible that students could be grouped for multiple intelligences, as the activities they will be engaged in require certain entry points for access in the intelligence.

Cluster grouping is where students are grouped based on overall performance in all areas, or due to another factor. In some cases where other services for the gifted are not provided, schools will attempt to cluster gifted students in classrooms to allow teachers to differentiate for them based on this grouping strategy. Cooperative groups can be separated by ability as a homogenous group, or they can remain heterogeneous depending on the need of the project, task, or assignment. Grouping by choice can be of value to the learning environment, as typically the task commitment of the learner is high and will allow for completion of the objectives. This is also true of interest-based groups.

Although each type of grouping has strengths and weaknesses, it is important to select the grouping strategy that is appropriate for the gifted learners that are part of the overall class. Successful grouping practices will allow for variety and choice, and will keep the group members engaged in the learning that is occurring rather than becoming a distraction or burden to the students.

Components of differentiated process for gifted learners in the regular classroom also include enriching opportunities that help to keep the curriculum meaningful and relevant. Curriculum compacting is a process whereby material that is already known by the learner is removed from the curriculum, thus allowing the learner to move into deeper or more complex curricular options. In order for curriculum compacting to work, the facilitator must know the essential outcomes for the curriculum and develop a pretest of the material. The pretest is administered to the learner and the material that is already mastered is then removed from the curriculum for that learner. In some cases, the learner may be excused from instruction where material has been mastered and be provided opportunities for independent study or anchor activities. Tiered assignments are another process in differentiating the challenge to the learner by grouping the curriculum into multiple levels for adequate challenge.

Variety and Choice

One of the greatest strengths of the gifted classroom is the opportunity to add variety to the instructional strategies. Traditional lecture, reading the text, and writing papers may discourage highly able underachieving students (Neu, Baum, & Cooper, 2004; Nielson, 2002). It becomes important for the teacher of the gifted to incorporate varied instructional strategies into the design of the unit and the daily routine of the classroom. Some examples of instructional practices that can differentiate processes are:

» *Five plus one (5+1)*: This is a direct instruction technique with the facilitator typically instructing for 5 minutes. After the direct instruction, learners share experiences, interaction with the content, etc. and/or reflect for one minute, and then the process returns to the facilitator to repeat the direct instruction.

» *Active learning*: This process is generally attributed to techniques such as matching instruction to students' interests, understandings, and developmental levels. Active learning also focuses on hands-on activities where the environment and instruction are conducive to engagement from the learner rather than allowing passive "sit-and-get" interaction with the curriculum.

» *Advanced organizers*: These are designed to activate the prior knowledge of the learner and will allow the learner to become more receptive to the learning that is to follow.

» *Alphabet summary*: Each learner is given a different letter of the alphabet and asked to generate a word starting with the letter relating to the topic. These words are used in the summary.

» *Predictions*: Learners predict what may come next in a text or in classroom curriculum. This process is typically used as a reading strategy to assist emerging readers. Predictions are also used in the development of creativity and thinking skills.

» *Choice boards*: This practice allows learners to vary the process by selecting the curricular materials that they come into contact with as well as varying the products they produce. The exact choices available on the choice board are controlled by the teacher to ensure that all of the necessary outcomes or competencies are met.

» *Field trips*: Field trips are one way to vary the environment for the learner. The content can be taught in the classroom or on location. The learners are benefitted by experiencing additional locations that are beyond the typical classroom environment.

» *Learning contracts*: This process provides flexibility to the learner as well as the facilitator. The contracts provide the opportunity for the learner to become independent for part of his or her instructional time and to negotiate the learning outcome, process, and product with the facilitator as appropriate.

» *Service learning*: Developing civic engagement has been a part of many programs for the gifted. Lee, Olszewski-Kubilius, Donahue, and Weimholt (2008) claimed that service learning and active civic engagement are beneficial to the students. This instructional practice provides opportunities to apply curriculum to the community and encourages learners to apply the information they are engaged in to have an impact on others.

» *Learning centers*: These can be designed to be challenging and meaningful to the learner. They provide an opportunity for the facilitator to include tiered materials that are appropriate for multiple learners at once, and thus can provide room for additional flexibility within the classroom.

The Gifted Classroom

One provisional service to meet in differentiating the process for gifted learners is to change their environment and place them in a resource classroom or to serve them through pull-out classes. Typically these services are for a few hours out of a school day or week and the interventionist is tasked with providing a curriculum for the gifted learner. Often the resource classroom is the location for the services and the interventionist may provide options similar to Renzulli's Type II or Type III Enrichment (Renzulli & Reis, 2014). One of the most important conditions in educating the gifted is the opportunity to learn with similar peers (Bate, 2012; Rogers, 2002), thus the pull-out classroom has an intrinsic benefit that may be missing in the general education classroom.

In cases where a district has a systemwide program in place, pull-out classrooms may include a specific grade-level curriculum that scaffolds and builds from year to year, providing a continuum of services approach. Another approach that may be used would be for the general education teacher and the teacher of the gifted to coordinate their curriculum and provide extension of the core curriculum in the pull-out resource. This would provide for additional depth and enrichment for the students (Delisle & Lewis, 2003).

The full-day special class for the gifted may be another programming option. In cases where this is the process, instruction can typically focus on the advanced content, as students who will be identified for these services are typically grouped with intellectual peers. Whether learners are placed in a full-day special class or other placements, it is important that learners receive opportunities to collaborate with peers with similar ideals and provide solutions for realistic problems (Neu et al., 2004; Nielsen, 2002). The full-day grouping should be beneficial to the learner yet intellectually challenging as the learners work to meet their full-time educational goals.

Ericsson, Roring, and Nadagopal (2007) stated that specialized training in a specific area over a long time would be beneficial to students. The focus on the domain would allow for the ability within the learners to be uncovered and tapped to enable their potential. They found that specialized training in excess of 10 years has been demonstrated as typical before emerging eminence could be noted. Early intervention is typically beneficial, as foundational and critical skills can be taught correctly without barriers to interfere with rapid mastery. This then provides a foundation for further advanced development relying on cemented foundational skills.

Gagné (2011) described Academic Talent Development (ATD) as a content-based enriched course; however, this approach may be difficult for some students and parents to understand after implementation. The major hang-up is related to grading, as it is possible that grade inflation may have occurred in the regular classroom prior to ATD and students' grades may be more accurate using ATD. As the process proceeds and enriches the curriculum, the learners are faced with more appropriate academic challenges than a typical class. This is due to curriculum compacting (Reis, Bums, & Renzulli, 1992), which is at the heart of the process. By providing this framework for curriculum and instruction, there is more room in the curriculum for depth, complexity, and enrichment.

Newman (2008) claimed that society recognizes the need for students to learn to solve problems and become creative producers of knowledge. One model that leads to the development of these sets of skills for the gifted is the Talents Unlimited Model (Taylor, 1967). The model is important to address as it is used initially to teach thinking skills as part of everyday activities and is then an integrated part of the process for the gifted. The five talent areas are productive thinking, decision making, planning, forecasting, and communication. This model can provide not only an opportunity for students to master creative and critical thinking skills but to also provide a framework that can be used by the teacher of the gifted and the general education teacher to open a dialogue about student growth and the processes in both the gifted classroom and the regular education classroom.

Learner Profiles

During the process of educating the gifted, a great deal of time is spent in assisting the learner come to understand his or her self in order to come to understand the construct of gifted. Gregoric (2006) arranged a model of the mind into a set of four items. Two items relate to perception, concrete and abstract, while the other two relate to how information or ideas are ordered, random and sequential. This mental model then provides the teacher and learner with four very different combinations, allowing for differentiation based on preference.

Gardner (1999) provided a view that individuals have various intelligences rather than a general intelligence that pervades their being. The intelligences are verbal-linguistic, logical-mathematical, visual-spatial, interpersonal, intrapersonal, bodily-kinesthetic, musical-rhythmic, naturalist, and existential. Differentiating for gifted students requires coming to understand what the unique makeup of the individual is and how the intelligences within the individual interact. Each of these intelligences can be nurtured or strengthened through use and focused effort. The intelligences can also be weakened. It is important to note that each of Gardner's intelligences does not remain static, and that an inventory or assessment of preference does not necessarily mean that one would score the same way even a few hours later, as context can influence many of the inventories used to assess multiple intelligences. When working with a student who is struggling in a content area, it is beneficial to assist the student to access to the content using an entry point. Focusing on an intelligence that the student has a preference for, or that the student has strength in, as a way of accessing the curriculum can be used to improve task commitment for the activity. For students who are gifted with learning disabilities, it is important to ensure that focus is placed on a student's area of strength and that entry points are used more frequently (Reis & Ruban, 2005).

The Munich Model of Giftedness (Heller & Perleth, 2004; Heller, Perleth, & Lim, 2005; Zeigler & Heller, 2000) discusses the interaction of personality characteristics, environmental conditions, and individual ability. Examples of individual ability come from four domains—three of which are described as global: perception, cognition, and physical. The final ability factor is knowledge in a particular area of human expertise such as math, science, or art. Examples of personality characteristics that influence these innate abilities are motivation, coping mechanisms, learning strategies, or belief. The Munich Model of Giftedness (see Figure 5.1) provides a graphic representation of these connections as described. Most examples in the model of the environmental conditions relate to the interaction of a school or business, such as motivation for achievement and mentorships, but certainly would also include other factors, including socioeconomic status and opportunity. When learners are engaged through the active learning process, exceptional achievement in performance areas or disciplines may be achieved more readily. Examples of these achievements could include exceptional status in a profession, the creation of innovative technologies, or eminence in a particular field (Ziegler & Perleth, 1997).

When conditions are favorable and the personality of the learner is conducive to the interaction, growth and learning occur over time and exposure. When this

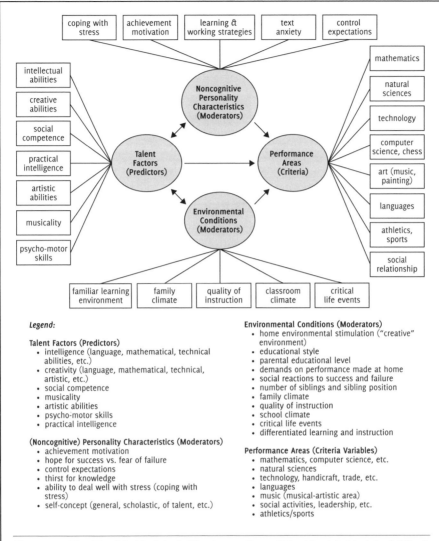

Figure 5.1. The Munich Model of Giftedness. From "The Munich Model of Gifted-ness Designed to Identify and Promote Gifted Students" (p. 149) by K. Heller, C. Perleth, & T. K. Lim, 2005, in R. J. Sternberg & J. E. Davidson (Eds.), *Conceptions of giftedness* (2nd ed.). New York, NY: Cambridge University Press. Copyright 2005 by Cambridge University Press. Reprinted with the permission of Cambridge University Press.

happens for a prolonged period of time and students are exposed to multiple domains, they will exhibit performances that are not limited to one particular context (Rostan, 2005). The model describes the interaction of the various contexts over educational periods to demonstrate the increasing complexity of the interactions and impact on a learner (Perleth, 2001). In essence, the innate abilities of an individual are impacted by moderators that may enhance an existing ability, allowing gifted performances or creative production to be evident. The Munich Process Model of Giftedness (see Figure 5.2) provides a graphic representation of the processes involved in process of developing talent and/or eminence.

Strategies

One of the ever expanding areas of interest in the U.S. when it comes to skills necessary for eminence and success outside of school is the combined areas of science, technology, engineering, and mathematics or STEM, and more recently the inclusion of arts (STEAM), as a vehicle for learning and engagement (Jones, 2011). The inclusion of the arts in STEM fields is a response for the need to develop individuals to be more creative and innovative in their respective fields (Eger, 2013). The integration of the arts provides an opportunity for learners to develop new types of thought through whole brain learning. This conceptualization that curriculum can and should be taught through an interdisciplinary approach rather than material that is taught independent of other subjects provides evidence that the traditional view of the classroom is changing. The arts allow learners to mimic the creativity of others while developing the skills necessary to contribute to the art form that is studied. At the highest level, the involvement in the arts, individuals are able to transform raw materials into expressions of creativity that can be appreciated by others. Often artists need to break away from traditional forms to create new art forms and to innovate when methods or materials have not been fully explored (Maeda, 2013). The inclusion of the arts into the STEM disciplines supports the idea that innovation is a product of creativity and that it is a necessary component for success today (McLaughlin, 2011). Unfortunately, current instruction in the critical areas of creative and spatial talent is rarely found at any level (Coxon, 2012) and is imperative in the STEAM fields. There is evidence to support the improvement of spatial ability (Coxon, 2012; Lim, 2005; Lohman, 1993; Onyancha, Derov, & Kinsey, 2009; Potter et al., 2009; Sorby, 2005; Urhahne, Nick, & Schanze, 2009; Verner, 2004), if students are provided challenging and meaningful educational experiences. Unfortunately, neither creativity nor spatial talents are included in the No Child Left Behind Act of 2001. It is important for us to move forward to develop creativity, as for the past 20 years creativity scores in the U.S. have declined (Bronson & Merryman, 2010).

Directly teaching tacit knowledge is important for a curriculum or a profession. This is true for all students but especially true for students with exceptionalities, who may view the world with a different perspective. Students should be taught effective note-taking strategies; test-taking preparation; library skills; written expression, reading, and mathematical processing; and how to organize their

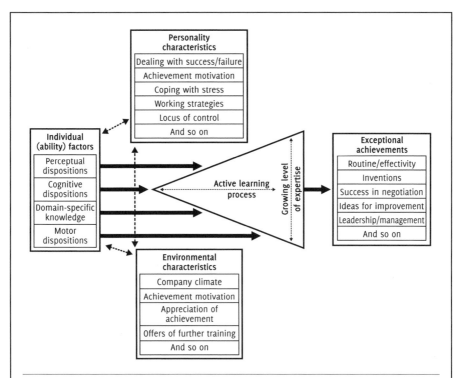

Figure 5.2. The Munich Process Model of Giftedness. From "The Munich Model of Giftedness Designed to Identify and Promote Gifted Students" (p. 150) by K. Heller, C. Perleth, & T. K. Lim, 2005, in R. J. Sternberg & J. E. Davidson (Eds.), *Conceptions of giftedness* (2nd ed.). New York, NY: Cambridge University Press. Copyright 2005 by Cambridge University Press. Reprinted with the permission of Cambridge University Press.

time (Reis & Ruban, 2005). Although in the past these "tricks of the trade" were often passed down as trade secrets, with the ever-increasing number of expectations placed on students, it is beneficial for the teacher of the gifted to directly instruct these items. Some may be complex, relating to shortcuts in curriculum, while others may be operational details or "passports" for success in various classrooms (Subotnik, Edmiston, Cook, & Ross, 2010). An example of one of these "tricks" could be the use of binder tabs to organize information by section. When a learner is taught to organize information and keep it accessible for future use, less time is spent in frustration for both the learner and the teacher. Another example could be instruction in the use of observation, attention to detail, and deduction to inform communication. If a student is taught how to use clues to engage in conversation with others, specifically instructors, it is possible to influence reactions and improve their perceptions of the student.

If teachers are not careful in the preparation of students, the learners may be stymied, as they should grow as thinkers and communicators because thinking and communication are limited by vocabulary (Nunan, 2005). Many educators assume that students who are gifted have a large vocabulary and that they know how to use the words in their lexicon appropriately. Many students have been left bereft of the direct instruction in vocabulary that could greatly benefit their academic success. In some cases, classrooms for the gifted are places where students are asked what they want to learn, how they want to learn, and what the product will be. They are then to go forth and learn. Unfortunately this process is not always used in conjunction with the opportunity to ensure that the students always have the necessary skills to conduct the learning they describe. This can lead to disengagement and frustration for the student, leaving him or her wondering what went wrong. Educators need to be watchful and to ensure that they are deliberate in the instruction used with students. They also need to be aware of the questioning strategies that they employ to help gifted learners come to understand what is required in their own study and what may be required as they further pursue independent and autonomous learning (VanTassel-Baska, 2012). Campbell and Walberg (2011) found that when students were involved in competitions to assist in the development of talent in gifted youth, it was possible to see a long-term impact. They reported that 52% of the 345 cases they studied had earned doctoral degrees. This demonstrates one additional way that skill instruction is necessary and an additional process by which skills can be taught. Typically, competitions provide a strong framework for the desired outcome with clearly defined rules and procedures. The procedures often prescribe some of the requisite skills needed to participate and allow the coach to further focus on the path to completion for the learners.

Metacognition

Efland (2002) stated that instruction should use metacognitive strategies, including similarities and differences between tasks and domains. Cukierkorn (2008) described developing a "habit of mind." This may be achieved through cooperative tasks that require transferrable skills and abilities in planning. It is important for the learner to move beyond the content of the material and make greater connections. By thinking about thinking, or how to use the appropriate strategy for problem solving or learning, students will better be able to master content and may also benefit by understanding who they are through necessary self-assessment (Reis & Ruban, 2005). Self-mastery and self-identity can be two great byproducts of teaching and developing metacognition. When connections between thoughts and actions related to various contents are employed, transfer to personal choices and actions should be developed in order to assist students in future development.

In order to develop metacognition within a content area, a change in teaching methodology may be necessary. In the domain of visual art, it may be necessary to move beyond the typical engagement with various media in isolated and superficial ways. If painting, drawing, and sculpture are all taught in isolation and only at the very basic level, then teaching metacognition is not possible. Teaching with an emphasis on finding and making connections across the various media through a directed process will help the learner develop advanced knowledge in the discipline as well as connectivity to other disciplines (Rostan, 2005).

Assessment

As a necessary component of differentiating processes, formative assessment must be ongoing. Without feedback on student progress and engagement in the curriculum, differentiating for learning cannot occur. Employing the various processes for learning at random may be no better than the typical sit-and-get lecture, as there is no way of knowing the effectiveness of the process employed. Value-added assessment is one way teachers can measure their effectiveness over time. This assessment process is typically conducted by comparing current student grades or performances to those of students in a prior year. Fulcher and Willse (2007) stated that there is benefit to a value-added assessment that can be administered to the students to examine the change score, which is used to determine the impact of the intervention. Change scores are simply the differences between the scores on the assessments. These can be used along with comparative gain scores to see what students knew before their instruction and what they knew after the intervention. Although it is impossible to rule out all outside factors that may influence these scores, the difference in the scores could provide baseline data to evaluate the effectiveness of the interaction between the student and the instruction, the curriculum, and the classroom/institution. Formative assessment is a necessary component that assists in curriculum planning, development of instructional strategies, and development of the various competencies in gifted students. Different types of formative assessment are necessary for process differentiation, but typically these can be delineated by the length of the time used for the formative assessment. Generally there are cycles or lengths of time that are used to determine the type and use of a formative assessment. Short-cycle assessments may be from a few seconds to a few hours. These assessments are what classroom teachers typically think of in relation to formative assessment. Data are used to impact the classroom practice and influence student engagement. Medium-cycle assessments may range from one week to a month. These data are also used to improve student performance; however, they may be more focused on helping the teacher measure student involvement and/or how the teacher is thinking about the learning that is taking place in the classroom. Finally, long-cycle formative assessments typically run from a month to a year and are typically used more for overall student monitoring or curriculum alignment (Black, Harrison, Lee, Marshall, & Wiliam, 2003).

Cassady et al. (2004) developed the Differentiated Classroom Observation Scale (Figure 5.3) to assist the classroom teacher. The instrument is designed to examine the various learning activities and classroom experiences that are differentiated for the learner. The development of this instrument is important for the classroom teacher in that it provides an overall classroom focus for the teacher rather than relying on individual assessments and allows for the investigation of the effects of specific instruction in the class in relation to other factors important to student growth and development.

Learning Environments

One of the greatest challenges that the classroom teacher has in developing the classroom environment is that in many cases the environment outside the classroom is not conducive to academic achievement (Ford, Harris, Tyson, & Trotman, 2002). This may be complicated further for some students, particularly those who are already at a disadvantage in school, as academic success is not socially valuable and may be viewed as a denial of one's culture or heritage (Rowley & Moore, 2002). This is particularly problematic when the current trend of raising achievement test scores also seems to be directly correlated to the amount of skill practice and "drill and kill" exercises in the general education classroom. This increase of skill practice makes it increasingly difficult for learners with advanced potential to succeed in the classroom (Stewart, 1981). It also works against the need for gifted students to demonstrate growth at the highest levels because they spend longer amounts of time in the regular classroom reviewing already mastered material, which decreases the academic rigor and the amount of time that could be dedicated to complex content (Southern, Jones, & Stanley, 1993).

Subotnik and colleagues (2010) found that students who are deeply interested in the sciences benefited from the opportunity to experience the intensity of full-time immersion in the catalyst program. The students benefited from the socialization of the scientists, as well as the opportunity to work with professionals with various career stages and other diversities. They also note that the focus on a singular domain should not exclude others, but rather should work to enhance the pursuit at hand.

Appendix A
Differentiated Classroom Observation Scale Protocol

Pre-Observation Phase

Before going to the teacher, the observer will contact the teacher to find a time that is convenient for the observation. The following will need to be arranged before the observation date:

- Permission to observe from teacher
- Copy of lesson plan
- Teacher will visually identify targeted group of students in classroom (with color-coded name tags or teacher's chosen strategy)

- Teacher is made aware that there is a brief (5 minutes or so) pre-observation interview, and a short post-observation debriefing.

Pre-Observation Interview

Before beginning the interview, please arrange to have the following questions answered. Some of this will be facilitated with prior contact with the teacher. In particular, having a copy of the lesson plan in advance would make the following questions less laborious for the teacher to answer prior to the observation period. This is an informal interview that is merely to gain essential descriptive information.

1. Is this lesson tiered?
   ___ Yes (based on identification status)
   ___ Yes (not based on identification status)
   ___ Not explicitly, but cluster grouping will be used
   ___ No, all students completing same activities

2. Who developed this lesson?
   ___ This teacher
   ___ Other: _____

3. How closely will you be following the pre-designed lesson plan?

4. Have you used this lesson before?
   What success have you noted with this lesson regarding this identified population?

5. Are learning contracts being used?
   ___ Yes (multiple identified students)
   ___ Yes (single identified student)
   ___ Yes (not related to identified status)
   ___ Yes (DEP-determined)
   ___ No

6. Has any of this lesson been compacted for any child?
   If so, please explain the alternate learning activities that are substituting for the lesson.

7. What are the goals/objectives of this lesson?

8. Anything else the teacher wants to add before the observation: _____

Classroom Observation Phase

School: _____   Teacher: _____   Time of observation: _____

Total number of students: ____   Number from identified group: ____

List additional adults in room, including time in room, role, and number of children served:

_____

Five-Minute Segment Scoring (use DCOS Scoring Sheet)
During the observation period, please indicate for each 5-minute segment which of the following instructional activities were in practice. There will be at least one per segment, and each segment will likely have more than one. The segment ratings should be marked separately for the two groups of students: "Identified" and "Not identified." In the event that there is no way to distinguish between the two groups, make whole-group ratings in the "Not Identified" group location only.

In addition to the instructional activities, please also rate student engagement, cognitive level, and "Learning Director" for each 5-minute segment.

Figure 5.3. Differentiated Classroom Observation Scale Protocol. From "The Differentiated Classroom Observation Scale" by J. C. Cassady, K. L. Speirs Neumeister, C. M. Adams, T. L. Cross, F. A. Dixon, & R. L. Pierce, 2004, *Roeper Review*, 26, pp. 144–145. Copyright 2004 *Roeper Review*. Reprinted with permission.

Instructional Activity Codes

Instructional Activity	Code	Description
Lecture	L	Teacher lecturing to group of students
Lecture with Discussion	LD	Teacher-led lecture, with periodic student discussion (recitation)
Class Discussion	CD	Discussion in class, students are primary discussants
Small Group Discussion	GD	Discussion in class, but in small groups, not whole group
Problem Modeling by Teacher	PM	Teacher demonstrating how to execute a task (e.g., working a math problem on board)
Student Presentation	SP	Student(s) presenting information to the class (either planned presentation or on-demand task)
Demonstration by Teacher	D	Teacher demonstrating a procedure to the class (e.g., how to safely use lab equipment)
Questioning by Teacher	Q	Teacher asking question of student(s) in group setting
Student Responding	SR	Student(s) answering questions posed by teacher (choral response included in this category)
Manipulates	M	Student(s) working with concrete materials to illustrate abstract concepts (e.g., math blocks)
Cubing	C	Student(s) working with cubing curriculum materials (differentiated, see Adams & Pierce [in press] for details)
Learning Center(s)	LC	Student(s) working at planned learning center(s) individually or in small groups (computer stations can be included if they are planned activities)
Anchoring activity before lesson	AB	Use of lesson-anchoring materials prior to teacher presentation of content, (see Adams & Pierce [in press] for details)
Anchoring activity during lesson	AD	Use of lesson-anchoring materials during teacher presentation of content
Anchoring activity after lesson	AA	Use of lesson-anchoring materials after teacher presentation of content
Seat work-Individual	SWI	Student(s) working at desk on academic materials (independently)
Seat work-Group based	SWG	Student(s) working at desk on academic materials (groups)
Cooperative learning	CL	Students working in a planned cooperative structure to complete a task
Role Playing	RP	Student(s) engaged in role play exercises (e.g., "playing store" to practice counting change)
Teacher interacting with individual student	TIS	Teacher working with/talking to/helping individual student
Teacher interacting with small group	TIG	Teacher working with/talking to/helping small group of students
Technology use-Students	TS	Technology being used by students for related learning activities
Technology use-Teacher	TT	Technology being used by the teacher for presenting instructional content
Assessment activity	A	Student(s) engaged in a formalized assessment activity (e.g., test; performance)
Pull-out activity, individual or group	PO	Student(s) removed from the room - no observation of these students possible
Other	O	List "other" activities

Student Engagement, Cognitive Activity, & "Learning Director"

Figure 5.3. Continued.

These are global ratings for each 5-minute segment. Thus, each segment will have only one rating for each of these two domains, the rating that is most representative of that time period for that group.

Student Engagement	Cognitive Activity	"Learning Director"
L Low engagement = 20% or fewer of students engaged in learning M Moderate engagement = 21–79% of students engaged in learning H High engagement = 80% or more of students engaged in learning	Remember Understand Apply Analyze Evaluate Create Ratings are made in each segment following the given scale: 1 Not evident 2 Evident 3 Well-represented	Who directs the learning, or makes the decisions about the learning activities? Use the following scale for making your segment ratings for the identified groups: 1 Teacher directs all learning. 2 Teacher directs most learning. 3 Teacher and student share learning decisions. 4 Student directs most learning. 5 Student directs all learning.

Figure 5.3. Continued.

Acceleration

Acceleration is perhaps one of the most underutilized resources in the current educational system. Although some forms of acceleration such as Advanced Placement courses have been readily accepted, there is still a resistance to the acceleration of a student through their formative years. When students require less practice or learn at a faster pace, they have a need for greater educational challenge (Coleman & Cross, 2001). Kulik (2004) found that accelerated students perform similar to their older classmates on achievement tests. In addition, they usually outperformed older classmates on the exams. This is further supported by a study conducted by Rogers (2004). Academic acceleration was found to be beneficial for students when either whole grade acceleration or subject-based acceleration were used for achievement purposes. Gross and van Vliet (2004) expressed the sensitive and careful planning necessary if a learner is radically accelerated. Several factors are necessary in order for the learner to be successful, such as persistence, advanced skills, and motivation. The school and teacher will also have to be aware that timing, flexibility, and accommodation of students' affective and intellectual needs are also necessary. The family will also need to be included so that all stakeholders are involved in ensuring that the options are tailored to the individual.

One of the major benefits of acceleration is the opportunity to place the student in a curricular experience that is already at the level of the learner and in place within a particular school system. Placing students in this system can allow for early development of skills and rapid expansion of preparation in a domain to facilitate the early development of expertise. Acceleration provides a need that was expressed by Walberg, Williams, and Zeiser (2003), in that it provides an efficient procedure for the development of learning that may open the door to extraordinary accomplishments. Weisberg (2006) also noted that there is compelling evidence that extensive practice has a positive relationship to eminent performance in a domain. Although most forms of acceleration in school are driven by careful academic testing and monitoring, there are times when educators may need to observe the intensities and passions of a particular student to allow what Cohen (2011) termed natural acceleration. In this way, the student becomes the driving force behind the opportunity rather than the school system. On another note, educators need to be aware that students who may be economically disadvantaged are at risk, as they may be overlooked for acceleration. It is important to provide opportunities for resilience and pride at overcoming the obstacles that may be in the way of success (Hrabowski, Maton, Green, & Greif, 2002).

Guidance and Counseling Needs

According to Elijah (2011), many experts in the field have expressed the need for counseling services for the gifted in order for students to reach their academic potential (Gentry, 2006; Moon, 2002, 2004; Reis & Renzulli, 2004). This is further complicated as the intellectual and academic needs of gifted and talented students are different than those of their classmates (Cottrell & Shaughnessy, 2005). Gifted students need to learn personal, social, and cultural competence. Their social and emotional needs needs are not static and fixed, but rather influenced greatly by their environment and culture (Cross, 2011). Without counseling supports and the best efforts of the teacher of the gifted, it may be difficult to mitigate some of the varied differences in the classroom of the gifted. Educators may provide foundational instruction in coping skills, stress management, or other mechanisms, but collaboration with the school counselor to inform opportunities for growth are warranted. There is often very little support for self-concept in general education programming (Gallagher, 2003), which is why it is imperative that educators of the gifted work diligently to support the change. The school counselor is also an excellent resource in helping the student develop an understanding of career choice, as many gifted students have difficulty narrowing the scope because they are capable in many areas (Greene, 2002). Career counseling is ever increasing in importance as part of the educational experience for gifted learners. It should be a lifelong process that is an extension of talent development. Involving collaboration with peers, mentors, coaches, and other interested stakeholders can help in the development of an accurate self-concept. This should lead to a realistic understanding of abilities, potential, and achievement (Greene, 2006).

Some academically talented students may have yet to face a setback from which recovery may be difficult. Many students may not be willing to risk taking challenges and persist through the difficulty. Subotnik and colleagues (2010) found that out-of-school programs may provide a safer environment to allow students to take risks, use unconventional problem solving, and recover self-concept.

Conclusion

The educator of today is expected to respond to the immediacy of the classroom, perform in a public environment, and prepare learners for lifelong pursuits of learning that will require proficiencies that are constantly changing. Educators need to be able to work flexibly with technology as it changes and continues to lead to new innovations in the future. Although it is important to set a broad foundation and have specific skills and facts that can be recalled, the major focus on skills for today's learners are on skills that can be used in multiple settings. Creativity, adaptability, collaboration, consultation, communication, and the ability to problem-solve provide us a springboard for success (Temmerman, 2008). For students to be successful, it is important to remember that practice and preparation are required for achievement in any field or discipline (Campbell & Feng, 2011).

Teacher Statement

When I entered the gifted classroom, I was shocked by the diversity among my students. From their academic ability levels to vocabulary to their learning styles and interests, I could not imagine any greater variance in such a small group of children. This chapter will be invaluable to regular classroom and gifted teachers alike, as it offers research-based approaches to differentiation.

In our district, regular classroom teachers are expected to document differentiation in each lesson plan, yet my coworkers expressed anxiety about how to do that for their intellectually advanced students. The objective seems much clearer when tailoring instruction to meet the needs of struggling students, but aside from simply assigning more work, there have not been clear options given to teachers regarding ways to promote the independent thinking and creativity that are crucial to the intellectual development of gifted learners. Some of the grouping options in this chapter, particularly "readiness" grouping and curriculum compacting, could be wonderful assets in the regular classroom, as so many of my students get frustrated at the length of time spent on instruction that they have already mastered. I utilize a number of grouping methods in my gifted pull-out program, and I have found that customizing my instruction to the interests and intelligences of my students yields more enthusiasm and active learning throughout instructional units.

I have taken away from this chapter a renewed desire to advocate for the academic rigor and the opportunities for intellectual growth that my students deserve. The children in my classes frequently voice concerns and frustrations because of the misconceptions so many of their educators and peers have about what it means to be gifted. I agree wholeheartedly that more counseling options need to be offered to prepare gifted learners for social, emotional, as well as academic success. Furthermore, meaningful professional development needs to take place in order for gifted learners to truly receive instruction differentiated for their needs.

—Sara Beth Honsinger

DISCUSSION QUESTIONS

1. Describe three different scenarios in which you would need to use grouping strategies for gifted learners, and provide appropriate grouping strategies for your learners in each scenario.

2. Describe how modifying one or more of your current instructional processes in the classroom may lend to more productive formative assessment of your learners.

3. Provided that metacognition has been described as part of the process of educating the gifted, discuss whether this process is really important, or if educators should focus strictly on singular domains, ignoring connections.

4. Thinking about your students, what specific information does your school counselor need from you to support the development of the gifted learner in developing personal, social, and cultural competence?

5. Consider the use of information from learning profiles in your classroom. What are four examples of meaningful data that are gathered from learning profiles that help you to provide individualized "process instruction" for your learners?

6. Describe the process you feel would be necessary to develop a pretest to compact the curriculum in your content, and if the time involved preparing the assessment would be worth the value of the impact on your instruction.

INSTRUCTIONAL PLANNING AND EVALUATION

TOY

References

Bate, J. (2012). Going beyond the school gates for our gifted. *New Zealand Principal, June,* 22–24.

Black, P., Harrison, C., Lee, C., Marshall, B., & Wiliam, D. (2003). *Assessment for learning: Putting it into practice.* Berkshire, England: McGraw-Hill Education.

Bronson, P., & Merryman, A. (2010, July 10). The creativity crisis. *Newsweek.* Retrieved from http://www.newsweek.com/2010/07/10/the-creativity-crisis.html

Campbell, J. R., & Feng, A. X. (2011). Comparing adult productivity of American mathematics, chemistry, and physics Olympians with Terman's longitudinal study. *Roeper Review, 33,* 18–25.

Campbell, J. R., & Walberg, H. J. (2011). Olympiad studies: Competitions provide alternatives to developing talents that serve national interests. *Roeper Review, 33,* 8–17.

Cassady, J. C., Speirs Neumeister, K. L., Adams, C. M., Cross, T. L., Dixon, F. A., & Pierce, R. L. (2004). The Differentiated Classroom Observation Scale. *Roeper Review, 26,* 139–146.

Cohen, L. M. (2011). Natural acceleration: Supporting creative trajectories. *Roeper Review, 33,* 218–227.

Coleman, L. J., & Cross, T. L. (2001). *Being gifted in school: An introduction to development, guidance, and teaching.* Waco, TX: Prufrock Press.

Cottrell, S., & Shaughnessy, M. F. (2005). *An interview with Dr. Edward R. Amend: About the emotional needs of gifted kids.* Retrieved from http://www.senggifted.org/articles_index.shtml

Coxon, S. V. (2012). Innovative allies: Spatial and creative abilities. *Gifted Child Today, 35,* 277–284.

Cross, T. L. (2011). *On the social and emotional lives of gifted children: Understanding and guiding their development* (4th ed.). Waco, TX: Prufrock Press.

Cukierkorn, J. R. (2008). Talented young artists. *Gifted Child Today, 31*(4), 24–33.

Delisle, J., & Lewis, B. A. (2003). *The survival guide for teachers of gifted kids: How to plan, manage, and evaluate programs for gifted youth K–12.* Minneapolis, MN: Free Spirit Press.

Eger, J. (2013). STEAM . . . now!. *The STEAM Journal, 1*(1), Article 8.

Efland, A. D. (2002). *Art and cognition: Integrating the visual arts in the curriculum.* New York, NY: Teachers College Press.

Elijah, K. (2011). Meeting the guidance and counseling needs of gifted students in school settings. *Journal of School Counseling, 9*(14), 1–19.

Ericsson, K. A., Roring, R. W., & Nadagopal, K. (2007). Giftedness and evidence for reproducibly superior performance: An account based on the expert performance framework. *High Ability Studies, 18*(1), 3–56.

Ford, D. Y., Harris, J. J., III, Tyson, C. A., & Trotman, M. F. (2002). Beyond deficit thinking: Providing access for gifted African American students. *Roeper Review, 24,* 52–58.

Fulcher, K. H., & Willse, J. T. (2007). Value added: Back to basics in measuring change. *Assessment Update, 19*(5), 10–12.

Gagné, F. (2004). Transforming gifted into talents: The DMGT as a developmental theory. *High Ability Studies, 15,* 119–147.

Gagné, F. (2011). Academic talent development and the equity issue in gifted education. *Talent Development & Excellence, 3*(1), 3–22.

Gallagher, J. (2002). Gifted education in the 21st century. *Gifted Education International, 16,* 100–110.

Gallagher, J. (2003). Issues and challenges in the education of gifted students. In N. Colangelo & G. A. Davis (Eds.), *Handbook of gifted education* (3rd ed., pp. 11–23). Boston, MA: Allyn & Bacon.

Gardner, H. (1999). *Intelligence reframed.* New York, NY: Basic Books.

Gentry, M. (2006). No child left behind: Gifted children and school counselors. *Gifted Child Quarterly, 10*(1), 73–81.

Green, S. L. (2007). Preparing special educators to work with diverse student populations: Culturally responsive teaching and its alignment with the teaching of social studies. *Black History Bulletin, 70*(1), 12–18.

Greene, M. J. (2002). Career counseling for gifted and talented students. In M. Neihart, S. M. Reis, N. M. Robinson, & S. M. Moon (Eds.), *The social and emotional development of gifted children: What do we know?* (pp. 223–235). Waco, TX: Prufrock Press.

Greene, M. J. (2006). Helping build lives: Career and life development of gifted and talented students. *Professional School Counseling, 10*(1), 34–42.

Gregoric, A. F. (2006). *The mind styles model: Theory, principles, and application.* Columbia, CT: Gregoric Associates.

Gross, M. U. M., & van Vliet, H. E. (2004). *Radical acceleration of highly gifted children: An annotated bibliography of international research on highly gifted young people who graduate from high school three or more years early.* Sydney, Australia: University of New South Wales, Gifted Education Research, Resource, and Information Centre.

Hrabowski, F. A., Maton, K. I., Green, M. L., & Greif, G. L. (2002). *Overcoming the odds: Raising academically successful African American young women.* London, England: Oxford University Press.

Heller, K., & Perleth, C. (2004). Adapting conceptual models for cross-cultural applications. In J. R. Campbell, K. Tirri, P. Ruohotie, & H. Walberg (Eds.), *Cross-cultural research: Basic issues, dilemmas, and strategies* (pp. 81–101). Hameenlinna, Finland: Hame Polytechnic.

Heller, K., Perleth, C., & Lim, T. K. (2005). The Munich model of giftedness designed to identify and promote gifted students. In R. J. Sternberg & J. E. Davidson (Eds.), *Conceptions of giftedness* (2nd ed., pp. 147–170). New York, NY: Cambridge University Press.

Johnsen, S., Haensly, P., Ryser, G., & Ford, R. (2002). Changing general education classroom practices to adapt for gifted students. *Gifted Child Quarterly, 46*(1), 45–63.

Jones, C. (2011). Children's engineering and the arts. *Children's Technology & Engineering, 16*(1), 3–17.

Kulik, J. A. (2004). Meta-analytic studies of acceleration. In N. Colangelo, S. G. Assouline, & M. U. M. Gross (Eds.), *A nation deceived: How schools hold back America's brightest students* (pp. 13–22). Iowa City: The University of Iowa, The Connie Belin & Jacqueline N. Blank International Center for Gifted Education and Talent Development.

Lee, S., Olszewski-Kubilius, P., Donahue, R., & Weimholt, K. (2008). The civic leadership institute: A service-learning program for academically gifted youth. *Journal of Advanced Academics, 19,* 272–308.

Lim, K. Y. T. (2005). Augmenting spatial intelligence in the geography classroom. *International Research in Geographical and Environmental Education, 14,* 187–199.

TOY

Lohman, D. (1993). *Spatial ability and g.* Paper presented at the Spearman Seminar, University of Plymouth. Retrieved from http://faculty.education.uiowa.edu/docs/dlohman/spatial_ability_and_g.pdf?sfvrsn=2

Maeda, J. (2013). STEM + art = STEAM. *The STEAM Journal, 1*(1). Article 34.

McLaughlin, C. (2011). Art and technology. *Children's Technology & Engineering, 16*(1), 2–15.

Moon, S. M. (2002). Counseling needs and strategies. In M. Neihart, S. M. Reis, N. M. Robinson, & S. M. Moon (Eds.), *The social and emotional development of gifted children: What do we know?* (pp. 213–222). Waco, TX: Prufrock Press.

Moon, S. M. (Ed.). (2004). *Social/emotional issues, underachievement, and counseling of gifted and talented students.* Thousand Oaks, CA: Corwin Press.

Neu, T. W, Baum, S. M., & Cooper, C. R. (2004). Talent development in science: A unique tale of one student's journey. *Journal of Secondary Gifted Education, 14*(1), 30–36.

Newman, J. L. (2008). Talents are unlimited: It's time to teach thinking skills again! *Gifted Child Today, 31*(3), 34–44.

Nielsen, E. M. (2002). Gifted students with learning disabilities: Recommendations for identification and programming. *Exceptionality, 10*(2), 93–112.

No Child Left Behind Act of 2001, 20 U.S.C.§6319 (2008).

Nunan, S. L. (2005). Forgiving ourselves and forging ahead: Teaching grammar in a new millennium. *English Journal, 94*(4), 70–75.

Onyancha, R. M., Derov, M., & Kinsey, B. L. (2009). Improvements in spatial ability as a result of targeted training and computer-aided design software use: Analyses of object geometries and rotation types. *Journal of Engineering Education, 98,* 157–167.

Perleth, C. (2001). Follow-up-Untersuchungen zur Münchner Hochbegabungsstudie [Follow-ups to the Munich Study of Giftedness]. In K. A. Heller (Ed.), *Hochbegabung im kindes- und jugendalter* [High ability in children and adolescents] (2nd ed., pp. 357–446). Göttingen, Germany: Hogrefe.

Potter, C., Van der Merwe, M., Fridjhon, P., Kaufman, W., Delacour, J., & Mokone, M. (2009). Three dimensional spatial perception and academic performance in engineering graphics: A longitudinal investigation. *South African Journal of Psychology, 39*(1), 109–121.

Reis, S. M., Bums, D. E., & Renzulli, J. S. (1992). *Curriculum compacting: The complete guide to modifying the regular curriculum for high-ability students.* Waco, TX: Prufrock Press.

Reis, S. M., & Renzulli, J. S. (2004). Current research on the social and emotional development of gifted and talented students: Good news and future possibilities. *Psychology in the Schools, 41*(1), 119–130.

Reis, S. M., & Ruban, L. (2005). Services and programs for academically talented students with learning disabilities. *Theory Into Practice, 44,* 148–159.

Renzulli, J. S., & Reis, S. M. (2014). *The Schoolwide Enrichment Model: A how-to guide for talent development* (3rd ed.). Waco, TX: Prufrock Press.

Rogers, K. (2002). *Re-forming gifted education.* Scottsdale, AZ: Great Potential Press.

Rogers, K. (2004). The academic effects of acceleration. In N. Colangelo, S. G. Assouline, & M. U. M. Gross (Eds.), *A nation deceived: How schools hold back America's brightest students* (pp. 47–57). Iowa City: University of Iowa, The Connie Belin & Jacqueline N. Blank International Center for Gifted Education and Talent Development.

Rostan, S. (2005). Educational intervention and the development of young art students' talent and creativity. *Journal of Creative Behavior, 39,* 237–261.

Rowley, S. J., & Moore, J. A. (2002). When who I am impacts how I am represented: Addressing minority student issues in different contexts. Racial identity in context for the gifted African American student. *Roeper Review, 24,* 63–67.

Sorby, S. (2005). Assessment of a "new and improved" course for the development of 3-D spatial skills. *Engineering Design Graphics Journal, 69*(3), 6–13.

Southern, W. T., Jones, E. D., & Stanley, J. (1993). Acceleration and enrichment: The context and development of program options. In K. A. Heller, F. J. Mönks, & A. H. Passow (Eds.), *International handbook of research and development of giftedness and talent* (pp. 387–410). Oxford, England: Pergamon Press.

Stewart, E. (1981). Learning styles among gifted/talented students: Instructional preferences. *Exceptional Children, 48,* 134–138.

Subotnik, R. F., Edmiston, A. M., Cook, L., & Ross, M. D. (2010). Mentoring for talent development, creativity, social skills, and insider knowledge: The APA catalyst program. *Journal of Advanced Academics, 21,* 714–739.

Taylor, C. W. (1967). Questioning and creating: A model for curriculum reform. *Journal of Creative Behavior, 1*(1), 22–33.

Temmerman, N. (2008). Arts/music learning and the development of learners' life-long creative capacity. *Australian Journal of Music Education, 1,* 38–43.

Tomlinson, C. (2001). Differentiated instruction in the regular classroom: What does it mean? How does it look? *Understanding Our Gifted, 14*(1), 3–6.

Urhahne, D., Nick, S., & Schanze, S. (2009). The effect of three-dimensional simulations on the understanding of chemical structures and their properties. *Research in Science Education, 39,* 495–513.

VanTassel-Baska, J. (2012). Curriculum issues using questions to elevate thinking. *Gifted Child Today, 35*(1), 68–69.

Verner, I. M. (2004). Robot manipulations: A synergy of visualization, computation and action for spatial instruction. *International Journal of Computers for Mathematical Learning, 9,* 213–234.

Walberg, H. J., Williams, D. B., & Zeiser, S. (2003). Talent, accomplishment, and eminence. In N. Colangelo & G. Davis (Eds.), *Handbook of gifted education* (3rd ed., pp. 350–357). Boston, MA: Allyn & Bacon.

Weisberg, R. W. (2006). *Creativity: Understanding innovation in problem solving, science, invention, and the arts.* Hoboken, NJ: John Wiley & Sons.

Winebrenner, S. (2001). *Teaching gifted kids in the regular classroom: Strategies and techniques every teacher can use to meet the academic needs of the gifted and talented.* Minneapolis, MN: Free Spirit Publishing.

Ziegler, A., & Heller, K. A. (2000). Conceptions of giftedness from a meta-theoretical perspective. In K. A. Heller, F. Mönks, R. Sternberg, & R. Subotnik (Eds.), *International handbook of giftedness and talent* (2nd ed., pp. 3–21). Oxford, England: Elsevier.

Ziegler, A., & Perleth, C. (1997). Schafft es Sisyphos, den stein den berg hinaufzurollen? Eine kritische bestandsaufnahme der diagnose- und fördermöglichkeiten von begabten in der beruflichen bildung vor dem hintergrund des Münchner Begabungs-Prozeß-Modells [Will Sisyphus be able to roll the stone up the mountain? A critical examination of the status of diagnosis and promotion of the gifted in occupational education set against the Munich Talent Model]. *Psychologie in Erziehung und Unterricht, 44,* 152–163.

PRODUCT DEVELOPMENT FOR GIFTED STUDENTS

BY KRISTEN R. STEPHENS AND FRANCES A. KARNES

Karen, a second-grade girl, proudly wears the T-shirt she designed to reflect what she learned across the various science units she explored during the school year. Jack, a seventh-grade boy, writes a script, designs a costume, and creates a set for a performance to depict the life, accomplishments, and impact of Abraham Lincoln on America. These are both examples of positive student products.

Meanwhile, David, an eighth-grade boy, writes his 10th book report this year. He has not been exposed to the variety of other products that would serve to demonstrate his learning.

Creative products are essential to curricula for the gifted. They allow students to express themselves and convey their ideas and knowledge in unique and complex ways. Product development also serves to motivate students, and it provides practical contexts in which they can develop knowledge, skills, and essential understandings within and across disciplines. This chapter provides teachers with the information necessary to assist students through the various stages of successful product development in the classroom.

What Is a Product?

Maker and Nielson (1996) defined a product as the "tangible evidence of student learning" (p. 186). The transformation of knowledge and new ideas into creative products is a critical goal for gifted students (Feldhusen & Kolloff, 1988; Renzulli, 1977). The types of products expected from such students should be highly creative and perhaps abstract. In other words, products created by gifted students should be comparable to those developed by professionals in the designated field. Product development is a vital phase in the learning process. Through the creation of products, students are able to move beyond mere acquisition of knowledge to application, analysis, and synthesis of content, concepts, and ideas, as products provide a means for students to transfer what they have learned into a new and meaningful format appropriate for sharing with others.

Ensuring Meaningful, Relevant Products

Products can be valuable tools for assessing student progress in that product development requires the application of new skills and concepts rather than mere retrieval and recall of knowledge and facts. Products also can assist teachers in determining the degree to which students are understanding and processing new information and content. Wiggins and McTighe (2005) indicated that products provide an "appropriate means of evoking and assessing *enduring* understandings" (p. 152).

Products developed in the classroom also should have very specific purposes that are closely aligned with curricular goals. In an age of increased accountability, teachers must ensure that the products students are creating are relevant and connected to curricular goals rather than just specific to an individual lesson. In other words, teachers must think as "assessors" rather than as "activity designers" when assigning products in the classroom. Emphasis should be placed on those performance tasks that will focus instructional work rather than on those projects students just might like to do on a particular topic (Wiggins & McTighe, 2005).

When assessing student understanding, it is critical that performance-based tasks are authentic. A project or task is authentic when it (Wiggins & McTighe, 2005):

» simulates the way in which an individual's knowledge is tested in the real world;
» requires students to develop a plan and procedure for solving a problem;
» asks students to simulate the kind of work done by professionals in the field;
» replicates real, complex challenges that adults may face in the workplace;

» requires students to use a repertoire of knowledge and skills to complete complex tasks; and

» allows students the opportunity to practice, obtain feedback, and refine their products and performances.

Student Attributes for Product Development

Before students can successfully engage in product development, they must have a disposition that encourages and allows for effective problem solving. If students do not enter the product development experience with the essential skills and mindset, the outcomes expected by teachers may not be achieved.

The fundamental goal of product development should be to help students *produce* new knowledge and ideas rather than *reproduce* or regurgitate existing knowledge. In order for students to successfully achieve this endeavor, they must possess the dispositions and attributes necessary to approach, think about, and resolve problems.

Costa and Kallick (2000) described 16 Habits of Mind that must be developed and employed by students for new knowledge and ideas to incubate and thrive. These 16 attributes follow with details regarding how each are specifically related to creative product development.

1. *Persisting*: Students must be able to stick to a task until it is completed. When developing products that require an extended focus and time commitment, some students may be too quick to abandon their efforts before completion. Other students may become frustrated when their product is not turning out how they initially envisioned and resort to haphazardly throwing something together so they can be done with it. Students must be encouraged to employ alternative strategies in problem solving when their initial methods fail. Knowing how to approach and sustain the problem-solving process over time is a fundamental skill in maintaining persistence.

2. *Managing Impulsivity*: Before students dive head first into developing their products, they must have a vision and a plan of action that details their goal. Teaching students how to slow down and effectively reflect on each alternative and consequence also will help eliminate the number of errors along the way.

3. *Listening to Others—With Understanding and Empathy*: Many products that students will create in the classroom are the result of group rather than individual work. Students need to develop skills in group dynamics and become astute in listening, understanding, and considering other people's perspectives relative to a specific problem. Such skills will allow

students to build upon others' ideas, resulting in a more sophisticated and complex product.

4. *Thinking Flexibly*: In order to produce creative products, students must be willing to explore various perspectives and approach problems from different angles. Flexible thinking also requires students to consider and ponder various points of a problem, avoid making a rush to judgment, and tolerate ambiguity.

5. *Thinking About Our Thinking (Metacognition)*: Perhaps one of the most beneficial aspects of creative product development is the mental processes that are developed while students are engaged in the activity of production. Through each stage of the process, students are planning, reflecting, and monitoring their progress toward established goals. Students need to be encouraged to think about the mental processes they are using as they work through the steps of a problem and how these steps and their sequence might be altered to improve performance.

6. *Striving for Accuracy and Precision*: Many times students strive for expedience rather than excellence. It is important for students to learn to value the craftsmanship of their work. The finished product should meet predetermined criteria and be of a quality similar to professionals.

7. *Questioning and Posing Problems*: In order to produce new knowledge, students must be able to ask effective and relevant questions. Teachers can help develop student questioning skills by modeling intriguing questioning in the classroom. Questions need to engage students so they want to put forth the effort in attempting to answer them. A good question is essential to the research and creative product development process.

8. *Applying Past Knowledge to New Situations*: Students should be encouraged to make connections between new and past knowledge. Teachers can aid this process by making both inter- and intradisciplinary connections with the content being taught. Helping students assimilate new ideas with old knowledge fosters greater retention and understanding. Connections within and across disciplines also help students consider content in creative and novel ways.

9. *Thinking and Communicating With Clarity and Precision*: When students develop products with an audience in mind, they must consider the best methods for explaining their knowledge and ideas to others. Presenting their products to authentic audiences also helps students build communication skills.

10. *Gathering Data Through All Senses*: The act of creating a product allows students to utilize a variety of senses, both within and outside of their preferred learning style. The opportunity to manipulate materials and actively engage with the content enhances understanding.

11. *Creating, Imagining, and Innovating*: Through creative product development, students are able to generate original ideas and strive for improvement by eliciting and welcoming constructive feedback of their work. Students also must have the flexibility to fine-tune and explore their ideas in greater depth.

12. *Responding With Wonderment and Awe*: When students engage in product development they are able to explore the problems they are most passionate about. Teachers can model lifelong learning for their students by encouraging curiosity, enthusiasm, and inquiry in the classroom.

13. *Taking Responsible Risks*: Some students may be reluctant to take risks in their product development. For example, they may stick with creating those products for which they have experienced the most success. Teachers should encourage students to take intellectual risks by delving into new, uncertain areas. Students are more likely to experience growth if they try out new ideas and products rather than just stick to what is safe. Students should welcome new challenges.

14. *Finding Humor:* Through product development, students must convey their information and ideas to others. Knowing when and if the incorporation of humor is appropriate to the topic and tone of a presentation is vital to the creative problem-solving process. In addition, teachers can help students learn to laugh at mistakes they make along the way and move on while learning to appreciate that human error is a fundamental part of the learning process. Humor also can help alleviate the stress that some students may feel as they engage in the product development process—particularly anxiety related to presenting in front of an audience.

15. *Thinking Interdependently*: Interaction with others can greatly enhance a learning experience. Whether a student is working independently or in a group, the activity of bouncing ideas off others can help refine and shape one's thoughts. Product development should be a social event in the classroom. Even if students are each working on their own projects, teachers still can encourage students to elicit suggested strategies and feedback from their peers along the way.

16. *Learning Continuously*: Even after a product has been created, a grade assigned, and a new topic introduced, students can continue to reflect and act on the ideas generated from the product development process. Teachers should encourage students to continue to explore alternatives and refine their solutions, as this is the essence of inquiry.

These Habits of Mind proposed by Costa and Kallick (2000) should be points of departure for any intellectual activity. Introducing and nurturing these attributes in the classroom will instill the characteristics of a lifelong learner in students and provide the foundation needed for successful product development in the classroom.

The Importance of Product Development in Gifted Education

Product modifications that can be made to better address the needs of gifted learners include allowing students to develop products that (a) result from real problems, (b) address and are evaluated by real audiences, (c) represent a transformation of content, and (d) are self-selected and allow for a variety of types of products to be considered (Maker & Nielson, 2005).

The act of product development is multifaceted in scope and sequence, and through the production process, gifted students can develop, enhance, and evaluate a wide spectrum of content and process skills, thus adding to the advancement of self-esteem, self-analysis, and self-actualization. Products can encompass all areas of human endeavor and provide a seamless way to integrate the arts, humanities, mathematics, science, literature, religion, and other subject matter.

Product development can help prepare students for future success in work and life. The Partnership for 21st Century Skills' (P21, 2011) vision for student success in a new global economy contains learning outcomes that can be realized through product development. For example, the P21 learning and innovation skills of critical thinking, communication, collaboration, and creativity can all be addressed through engagement in product development. The P21 life and career skills of flexibility and adaptability, initiative and self-direction, social and cross-cultural skills, productivity and accountability, and leadership and responsibility can also be honed through the creation of products. Additional process skills related to oral and written communication, scientific and library research, and social and personal development can be refined with each new product created, and the organizational skills of planning, time management, record keeping, and delegating also will be enhanced, as they play a crucial role in the process of achieving the intended goal.

Through product design, gifted youth become responsible for their own learning, thus fostering independence and accountability. Moreover, product development allows learners to explore, investigate, design, and formulate their own ideas, feelings, and thoughts, which encourages risk-taking and stimulates creativity. Students are allowed to proceed at their own established pace through selected activities that accommodate their individual learning styles. Finally, through research of a selected problem, presentation of solutions, and self-evaluation to assess demonstrated outcomes, students are exposed to authentic learning experiences.

Benefits for Twice-Exceptional Learners

Product development helps to individualize learning experiences so students can express themselves in ways that are most relevant to their own style of information processing. As such, the development of products can be an ideal way for twice-exceptional students to express what they have learned. Oftentimes, students with learning disabilities have difficulty adequately demonstrating their mastery of new material through traditional methods (e.g., essay, oral report, test). Product development provides such students the opportunity to capitalize on their strengths and reveal what they have learned through different media. Providing successful learning experiences to these students helps create an environment where stress and anxiety are reduced, thus allowing students to maintain their motivation to learn and participate. Product development also allows for mobility and fosters kinesthetic activities that may be of benefit to students with diagnosed Attention Deficit/Hyperactivity Disorder, as they are afforded the flexibility they need in order to be successful.

Creativity, Innovation, and the Common Core

In recent years, creativity and innovation have emerged as important elements for the future economy of the United States. Pink (2005) said we are entering an age where it is no longer sufficient to just create a product for function, but it is crucial to consider design and create something that is "beautiful, whimsical, and emotionally engaging" (p. 4). For this reason, creativity is an essential component in student product development. Students should be developing products that infuse their own thoughts and ideas, thus connecting the cognitive and affective domains rather than just replicating products that lack a personal connection to the creator.

In discussions pertaining to creativity and innovation, the development of talent in science, technology, engineering, and mathematics (STEM) has been emphasized by policy makers. U.S. competitiveness within a global economy will require schools to address and nurture those creative talents that are required to innovate. One means of cultivating such talent is through the development of spatial ability (Coxon, 2012a, 2012b). Lohman (1996) defined spatial ability as "the ability to generate, retain, retrieve, and transform well-structured visual images" (p. 98), and such "transformations" can be realized through creative product development. Hands-on engagement that also provides students the opportunity to grapple with real-world problems should be an essential component of a school's curriculum to ensure students are adequately prepared for careers in the future. Wai, Lubinski, and Benbow (2009) further acknowledged the importance of high spatial ability to success in fields such as engineering, computer science, and medicine. Nonetheless, such abilities are often overlooked in designing curriculum and instruction within schools (National Science Board, 2010).

The implementation of the Common Core State Standards across 44 states and the District of Columbia provides additional opportunities for the infusion of creative product development within English language arts and mathematics. The standards do not mandate a specific process by which curricular goals should be reached, thus teachers have considerable flexibility in determining how to help their students meet the standards. The Common Core State Standards for English Language Arts (National Governors Association (NGA) Center for Best Practices & Council of Chief State School Officers (CCSO), 2010a) offer the following portrait of students who meet the standards: independent; strong content knowledge; responsive to demands of audience, task, purpose, and discipline; discerning; constructively use evidence/reasoning; strategically use technology and digital media; and value others' perspectives. Many of these characteristics are also evident among successful product designers, and the creation of products is necessary to further develop these traits.

The Common Core State Standards for Mathematics (NGA & CCSSO, 2010b) emphasize an *understanding* of mathematics. What does such an understanding look like? Creative products can help make such understandings transparent to the teacher, as students have to transfer their knowledge in the content area into a new and meaningful context. Mathematical expertise that teachers should seek in students and that can be achieved through product development include: making sense of problems and persevering in solving them, reasoning abstractly and quantitatively, constructing viable arguments and critiquing the reasoning of others, modeling with mathematics, using appropriate tools strategically, attending to precision, and making use of structure, patterns, regularities, and repetitions (NGA & CCSSO, 2010b).

Types of Products

Products have long been used to assess student progress. Unfortunately, many classrooms are still limited to products such as written reports and posters. However, the variety of products that students can create is abundant. Figure 6.1 lists an assortment of products that students can produce to display knowledge from their research (Karnes & Stephens, 2009). The list of products in Figure 6.1 can be divided into several categories: written, visual, performance, oral, and multicategorical products. Several examples of each type of product are listed below.

» *Written*: letter of inquiry, persuasive essay, poem, research paper, friendly letter, newspaper story, report, business letter, description, explanation,

Abstract	Coat of arms	Essay	Internet search
Acronym	Collage	Etching	Interview
Activity sheet	Collection	Evaluation checklist	Invention
Advertisement	Coloring book	Event	Investigation
Alphabet book	Comedy skit	Exhibit	Itinerary
Altered book	Comic strip	Experiment	Jewelry
Animation	Commemorative	Fact file	Jigsaw puzzle
Annotated	stamp	Fairy tale	Jingle
bibliography	Commentary	Family tree	Joke
Aquarium	Commercial	Field experience	Journal
Archive	Competition	Field guide	Journal article
Art gallery	Computer	Film	Journal entry
Audiotape	document	Finger puppet	Kit
Autobiography	Computer program	Flag	Laser show
Ballad	Conference	Flannel board story	Law
Banner	presentation	Flier	Learning center
Bibliography	Construction	Flip book	Lecture
Big book	Cookbook	Flow chart	Lesson
Biography	Cooked concoction	Folder game	Letter
Blog	Costume	Fractal	Limerick
Blueprint	Crest	Game	List
Board game	Critique	Game show	Literary analysis
Book	Cross section	Geocache	Log
Book jacket	Crossword puzzle	Geodesics	Logic puzzle
Book report	Dance	Geometric model	Logo
Book review	Database	Glossary	Machine
Booklet	Debate	Graph	Magazine
Bookmark	Demonstration	Graphic	Magazine article
Broadcast	Design	Graphic organizer	Magic show
Brochure	Diagram	Greeting card	Manual
Budget	Dialogue	Guide	Manuscript
Bulletin board	Diary	Handbook	Map with key
Bumper sticker	Dictionary	Handout	Mask
Business plan	Digital story	Hidden picture	Matrix
Button	Diorama	Histogram	Menu
Calendar	Display	Hologram	Metaphor
Campaign	Document	How-to book	Mime
Cartoon	Documentary	Hypermedia	Mini-center
Carving	Doll	Hypothesis	Mobile
Catalog	Dramatization	Illuminated	Mock interview
Celebration	Drawing	manuscript	Mock trial
Characterization	Editorial	Illusion	Model
Charade	Electronic	Illustrated story	Monologue
Chart	scrapbook	Illustration	Montage
Checklist	ePortfolio	Index cards	Monument
Club	Equation	Instructions	Mosaic

Figure 6.1. List of possible products. From *The Ultimate Guide to Student Product Development* (2nd ed., pp. 4–5) by F. A. Karnes and K. R. Stephens, 2009, Waco, TX: Prufrock Press. Copyright 2009 by Prufrock Press. Reprinted with permission.

Motto	Photojournalism	Relief map	Storyboard
Multimedia presen-tation	Photograph	Report	Summary
	Pictograph	Resume	Survey
Mural	Pictorial essay	Riddle	Survival guide
Museum	Picture dictionary	Role-play	Table
Musical	Picture story	Routine	Tape recording
Musical composi-tion	Pie chart	Rubber stamp	Television show
	Plan	Rubbing	Terrarium
Musical instrument	Plaque	Rubric	Tessellation
Musical perfor-mance	Play	Samples	Test
	Podcast	Sand casting	Textbook
Mystery	Poem	Scavenger hunt	Theory
Myth	Pointillism	Scenario	Three-dimensional model
Narrative	Political cartoon	Science fiction story	
Needlecraft	Pop-up book	Scrapbook	Time capsule
Newsletter	Portfolio	Script	Timeline
Newspaper	Portrait	Sculpture	Toy
Newspaper article	Position paper	Self-portrait	Trademark
Novel	Poster	Seminar	Travelogue
Oral report	PowerPoint	Service project	Triptych
Organization	Prediction	Shadow box	Venn diagram
Origami	Presentation	Shadow play	Video
Ornament	Program	Short story	Video game
Outline	Project cube	Sign	Virtual field trip
Overhead transpar-ency	Prototype	Silk screening	Virtual museum
	Puppet	Simulation	Vocabulary list
Packet	Puppet show	Sketch	Wall hanging
Painting	Questionnaire	Skit	Watercolor
Pamphlet	Quilt	Slide show	Weaving
Panel discussion	Quotations	Sociogram	Web page
Pantomime	Radio show	Song	Webbing
Papier mâché	Rap	Speech	Webinar
Pattern	Rebus story	Spreadsheet	WebQuest
Performance	Recipe	Stage setting	Wiki
Personal experience	Recitation	Stained glass	Woodworking
Petition	Recording	Stencil	Word puzzle
Photo album	Reenactment	Stitchery	Written paper
Photo essay	Reflection	Story	

Figure 6.1. Continued.

story, advertisement, book report, classified advertisement, creative writing, critique, diary, dictionary, editorial, essay, checklist, script, glossary, journal, magazine article, musical composition, play, puppet show, questionnaire, test, worksheet, book, biography, song

» *Visual*: book jacket, drawing, poster, story map, bar graph, concept cube, timeline, pie chart, tree chart, web, collage, flow chart, Venn diagram, advertisement, blueprint, brochure, bulletin board, bullet chart, multimedia project, cross-section, film, graph, illustration, map, mobile, mural, cartoon, storyboard, carving, costume, diorama, photograph, quilt, sculpture

» *Performance*: dance, monologue, puppet show, demonstration, skit, dramatization, simulation, comedy sketch, experiment, musical performance, play

» *Oral*: debate, oral report, persuasive speech, roundtable discussion, class discussion, mock interview, newscast, oral book report, informative speech, panel discussion, description/show and tell, "how-to" talk, reading to the class, audiotape, conference presentation, documentary, group discussion, lecture, commentary, seminar, speech, trial

» *Multicategorical* (products that require the use of two or more of the above product types): exhibit, game, invention, multimedia slideshow, oral history, television show, video, website, broadcast, computer program, museum, time capsule, podcast

Students' learning styles may influence which types of products they prefer to create. For example, a student who excels in writing might select a product from the written category, whereas one who enjoys hands-on activities would probably favor those products in the performance or multicategorical areas.

The role technology plays in creating products has advanced in recent years. Housand and Housand (2012) stated that today's learners use technology as a fundamental tool in their lives, so it is only natural that this use is also incorporated in various aspects of the product development process. From computers to cell phones to Mp3 players, there are many different types of technology that can be incorporated within the development of creative products. Besnoy, Dantzler, and Siders (2012) discussed creating a "digital ecosystem" in the classroom that affords students the opportunity to "experience, create, and transform knowledge" (p. 306). Although Microsoft PowerPoint is frequently used by both students and teachers for presentations, there has been an emergence of other presentation options like LiveBinders™ (http://www.livebinders.com) and Voice Thread (http://www.voicethread.com). These new platforms help move students from static to more interactive presentations (Siegle, 2011).

Assessing Interests, Learning Style, and Product Preference

To determine the type of product a student prefers, Kettle, Renzulli, and Rizza (1998) devised My Way . . . An Expression Style Inventory, an instrument used to gather information on the types of products students are interested in creating. Students are asked to rate their interests in various activities on a Likert-type scale. The Expression Style Inventory divides products into 10 different categories: written, oral, artistic, computer, audio-visual, commercial, service, dramatization, manipulative, and musical. Students determine which type of product they would most likely be interested in developing by adding up the total of their responses to the 50 items on the inventory.

An online assessment of interests, learning style, and product preference is available through the Renzulli Learning System (http://www.renzullilearning.com). Schools can purchase site licenses to access the system. Students simply log in and complete a questionnaire to assess their interests, learning styles, and product preferences. Personalized enrichment experiences (e.g., virtual field trips, books, research opportunities) are then provided based on each student's profile. Teachers have access to student profiles and can use this information to easily group students by interest, learning style, and product preference. Parents also can access their child's profile and can be assured that the websites that their child is visiting are safe and recommended by educational experts.

Although information relating to the type of product a student would like to create is important, other circumstances also must be considered before selecting one. For example, with what audiences will this product be shared? What subject matter is the product attempting to display? Although a puppet show might be appropriate to teach young children about the importance of recycling, it might not be suitable to convince community leaders about the necessity of a detailed plan to improve inner-city environments.

It is important for teachers to encourage students to explore a variety of products. Even though a student who is an outstanding artist prefers to engage in products involving drawing and painting, it also is important that he or she be assisted in developing his or her skills in other areas through the creation of an assortment of products. For example, the student might include illustrations with a written story or design a set for a performance. Assisting gifted students in applying their strengths to a variety of areas encourages them to see connections and expand their developing concepts. Also, by encouraging students to develop a type of product that may be out of their comfort zone, they become engaged in healthy risk-taking. Neihart (1999) suggested that such intellectual risk-taking helps to "increase self-esteem, confidence, and courage in gifted youth" (p. 289). Challenging students' limitations is necessary to foster high levels of achievement and leadership (Neihart, 1999).

Design and Product Development

Burnette, Norman, and Browning (1997) described design as "a way of think-ing and doing that is both creative and practical . . . and [is] the key to innovative thinking and invention" (p. 11). Before students begin their product endeavors, it is necessary that they have a preliminary knowledge of the processes, principles, and elements of design. Oftentimes, it is assumed that students already possess most skills necessary for product design; however, they need prior instruction and guidance in such skills, from the basic uses of stencils, rulers, compasses, and pro-tractors, to the selection of appropriate colors, sizes, and shapes, to the recogni-tion of other aesthetic elements such as the more complex skills of superimposed imaging, voice synthesizing, and computer-generated graphics.

An introduction to the design process will assist students in planning for future product development. Davis, Hawley, McMullan, and Spilka (1997) described the following steps in the design process:

1. identifying and defining the problem,
2. gathering and analyzing information,
3. determining performance criteria for successful solutions,
4. generating alternative solutions and building prototypes,
5. evaluating and selecting appropriate solutions,
6. implementing choices, and
7. evaluating outcomes.

Another model depicting the design process is the I/DEPPE/I model (Burnette et al., 1997). This model is an acronym for the following dimensions:

» Intending—committing to a goal,
» Defining—identifying the problem,
» Exploring—generating possible solutions,
» Planning—making and communicating decisions,
» Producing—doing and making what is required,
» Evaluating—assessing the product and determining if you attained the goal, and
» Integrating—accommodating what was learned from the entire experi-ence with previous knowledge.

Both of the above models almost mirror the stages involved in product devel-opment and creative problem solving. Keep in mind that design is not restricted to any one discipline. It can be applied to anything where problems are solved. Designing is something that everyone does and can learn to do more effectively.

In addition to an introduction to the design process, students should become familiar with the elements and principles of design. Elements such as color, line, value, shape, form, balance, and texture must be explored, as well as the principles of repetition, unity, emphasis, economy, proportion, and variety.

Instructional materials and other resources that assist in teaching the process, principles, and elements of design are listed at the end of this chapter. Consult with the arts or technology instructor or department for additional resources and information at your school.

Stages of Product Development

There are several stages a student goes through when creating a product (Karnes & Stephens, 2009). Each step assists students in developing and practicing numerous skills. These stages are as follows:

1. formulation of a topic,
2. organization of production aspects,
3. transformation of content,
4. communication through products,
5. evaluation,
6. celebration, and
7. reflection.

Formulation of a Topic

The first stage in developing a product is selecting a topic to investigate. It may be selected through brainstorming or creating a web. It can be content-specific, such as pirates, Egypt, wolves, or architecture, or it may be concept-related, such as freedom, leadership, change, or cultures.

Narrow it down. It is important for students to narrow the topic from broad to specific. For example, the topic of astronomy might be focused to the Big Dipper or black holes. This will assist students in focusing research questions to the selected topic.

Build new knowledge. Students must be encouraged to select a topic from which they can learn new knowledge. One who has read every book about tornadoes and has already developed several products pertaining to tornadoes should select a different topic from which new knowledge can be gained.

Select an area of interest. Students should choose topics in which they have a genuine interest. This will serve as a motivator for the student to carry out product development to completion. Those who have been interested in tornadoes, for example, might find the topic of hurricanes fascinating as well.

Make sure resources are available and credible. A topic should be selected that requires utilizing more than a single source of information during the research process. In other words, students must select a topic using a variety of sources, including books, encyclopedias, the Internet, films, interviews, newspapers, primary source documents, atlases, experiments, and so forth. Students also should be able to determine which sources of information are credible. Although the Internet provides a wealth of resources, it also contains information that is inaccurate and biased. For example, the online encyclopedia, Wikipedia (http://www.wikipedia.com), has become quite popular with students; however, the site itself acknowledges that "significant misinformation, unencyclopedic content, or vandalism" (2007, para. 3) may exist in newer entries.

Organization of Production Aspects

The second phase, the organization stage, runs the length of the product-producing experience. Several organizational techniques can be utilized to help keep students focused and provide structure to daily activities relating to product development. For example, Figure 6.2 illustrates how students might document their production plan. Keep in mind that a well-developed organizational plan teaches students the necessity of setting and achieving both short- and long-term goals. Never assume that students have already acquired methods for organizing their work. Organizational skills need to be taught and can benefit students in a variety of academic endeavors. The following sections include examples of some organizational techniques that can be applied by students.

Timelines. Before getting too deep into a project, it is important to generate a timeline with a reasonable date for project completion. For example, daily activities may be placed on a calendar to build time-management skills. This will assist students in staying on task and will further allow them to visualize an end to their means. Furthermore, they should reflect on their accomplishments at the end of each day and evaluate their progress toward meeting their established goals. By staying organized and working toward a projected date, students demonstrate the ability to be responsible for their own learning.

Logs. Students can record daily progress toward completion of goals and plan activities for the next day in a project log. This will encourage them to think in advance about what materials they will need to bring to the subsequent class session in order to complete the next planned stage of product development. Logs can be kept in a spiral notebook or on a product log form, which can be designed by the teacher or student. Such forms may require students to answer questions pertaining to current progress and future agendas. Sample questions on a product log form might include the following: What did I accomplish today? What do I plan to do next class session? What materials will I need to bring? By answering these questions, students will further enhance their organizational and planning skills.

Let's Get Organized!		

Name: _____ Date: _____
Topic: _____ Product: _____

Description and components of proposed product		
Resources and contact people		
Criteria to meet: What are my goals?		
Materials I will need and where I might obtain them		
Possible audiences	Within school	Outside school

Figure 6.2. Product planner.

Research readiness. "Research readiness" refers to the organizational activities that precede the research process. Research readiness can include generating a list of questions pertaining to the topic, which will help guide research. The development of a KWL chart (What I **K**now? What I **W**ant to Know? What I **L**earned?) may be beneficial at this stage. Furthermore, students may want to produce a list of resources in which they might possibly locate the answers to formulated questions.

Students may be engaged in more than one research endeavor at a time. It is essential for them not only to conduct research about the topic they are investigating, but also to conduct research regarding the development of their product. For example, a student researching the roles of women in ancient Egypt will be reading books and surfing the Internet for information regarding Egyptian women during this period. If the student has selected to design a costume that is representative of what Egyptian women wore, then he or she also may be reading books and interviewing costume designers to gather information about fabrics, patterns, sewing techniques, and so forth. Essentially, two different types of research are going on simultaneously: research to gather content knowledge and research to gather product knowledge.

Determining audiences. Before students decide what type of product will best convey their new knowledge, it is essential that they create a list of possible audiences with whom to share their creations. Consider possible audiences both inside and outside of school. The characteristics of the audience, along with the information to be conveyed, will greatly influence the type and complexity of the product selected. Possible audiences might include peers, community leaders, younger students, retirement communities, the school board, clubs, and so forth.

Product selection. Once the audience and presentation content have been selected, students can determine which type of product will be most suitable. Media are the modes through which ideas are communicated. Selecting appropriate forms of media may be a complicated step for some students. They often tend to select media that reflect their particular learning style. As mentioned previously, authors will write and artists will illustrate.

Atwood (1974) described the three levels of media forms as demonstrative, representational, and symbolic. Demonstrative media, the most literal form of communication, might include displays, step-by-step procedures, and experiments. Representational media, which are used to represent reality when it is not easily displayed, might include sculptures, photographs, models, plays, and drawings. Symbolic media, which are considered translations of reality, might include speeches, advertisements, dances, graphs, maps, and computer programs.

Depending on the content of the project and the audience, gifted students must decide what form of media is most suited to communicating learned ideas accurately. Sometimes, the medium that will best demonstrate, represent, or symbolize an idea may not be the one the student would have normally selected. Keeping a list of possible products, as found in Figure 6.1, may help students choose varied media that will communicate their thoughts most effectively.

Material gathering. Once the product type has been selected, students should generate a list of materials needed to complete the proposed products. Students may need to make accommodations for certain materials due to expense and availability. These accommodations allow them to utilize their creative problem-solving abilities in authentic situations. Furthermore, materials that students first thought were appropriate may not work as planned. Through substitution and experimentation with alternate materials, they will enhance their problem-solving abilities.

Evaluation criteria. Before creating their product, students should develop criteria with which to evaluate the finished work. By establishing product criteria for evaluation early on, students are made aware of the standards set for them.

Because product types vary, different criteria will need to be established for each type.

Students may consult with an expert in the topic field in order to develop a list of components and exemplary characteristics for the proposed product. For example, a cartographer or geography professor may be an excellent resource for a student who desires to create a map; a genealogist would provide information relating to the components and characteristics of an ideal family tree; and a local reporter may offer advice on how to conduct a professional-quality interview. Baker and Schacter (1996) suggested using adult expert performance as a benchmark for assessment. The Center for Research on Evaluation, Standards, and Student Testing (CRESST) employed expert models to assess student performance in a variety of content areas. In addition, Wiggins (1996) suggested that teachers look for "exemplars" or "anchors," which are examples of a particular product that demonstrate an exceptional standard. These exemplars can serve as a basis for setting performance standards for students. The following is a suggested list of specific products with the experts that may be consulted when developing evaluation criteria:

»	blueprint	→	architect
»	brochure	→	marketing consultant
»	debate	→	speech-debate teacher
»	exhibit	→	museum curator
»	experiment	→	scientist
»	family tree	→	genealogist
»	magazine	→	editor
»	map	→	cartographer or geographer
»	musical composition	→	music professor
»	photograph	→	photographer
»	play	→	actor or professor of theater
»	sculpture	→	local artist
»	webpage	→	computer expert

Experts are everywhere. Many can be found in your local community through the following sources:

» colleges and universities,
» businesses,
» clubs and organizations,
» friends,
» craft guilds,
» local media,
» the Internet,
» the telephone directory, and
» the library.

The Internet is a valuable source of experts if they cannot be found within your community. For instance, students can send questions related to a specific discipline to experts in that field. Links to "Ask an Expert" sites across disciplines can be found at http://www.ciese.org/askanexpert2.html.

Transformation of Content

Because the attainment of higher level thinking skills is an essential focus in gifted programs, the type of products expected from students should be highly creative and perhaps abstract. Products should represent more than the mere acquisition of new knowledge. They should convey a genuine application of synthesis and analysis. This process of transformation allows the student to turn new knowledge into something more meaningful. Maker and Nielson (1996) outlined several elements of transformation: viewing from a different perspective, reinterpreting, elaborating, extending, and combining simultaneously. When evaluating a product, it is important to look for some of these elements in students' work. Students should turn learned content into their own creation instead of repeating or summarizing general information. Forster (1990) described the process of project development as "the act of surprising oneself with new ideas" (p. 40). The ultimate goal of product development is to transform student research into new thoughts, ideas, and perspectives.

Transformation involves many steps and processes. Students should be taught these steps and the types of activities in which they need to be engaged as they move through the process. The steps include:

1. *Research*: The student locates, comprehends, and classifies information in order to gain knowledge.
2. *Information filtration*: The student processes, interprets, refines, and extrapolates the knowledge and ideas gained from research.
3. *Idea generation*: From the selected information, the student emphasizes and analyzes various elements, concepts, and ideas of interest.
4. *Centralization*: The student selects, decides, and focuses on a specific element or idea.
5. *Reflection*: The student considers, ponders, and judges the selected idea.
6. *Manipulation*: The student tests and experiments with the idea and changes, improves, and adapts it as necessary.
7. *Execution*: The student decides, organizes, prepares, and produces a product to display the idea.
8. *Communication*: The student shares, performs, displays, or disseminates the product to an authentic audience.

A model of the above transformation process appears in Figure 6.3.

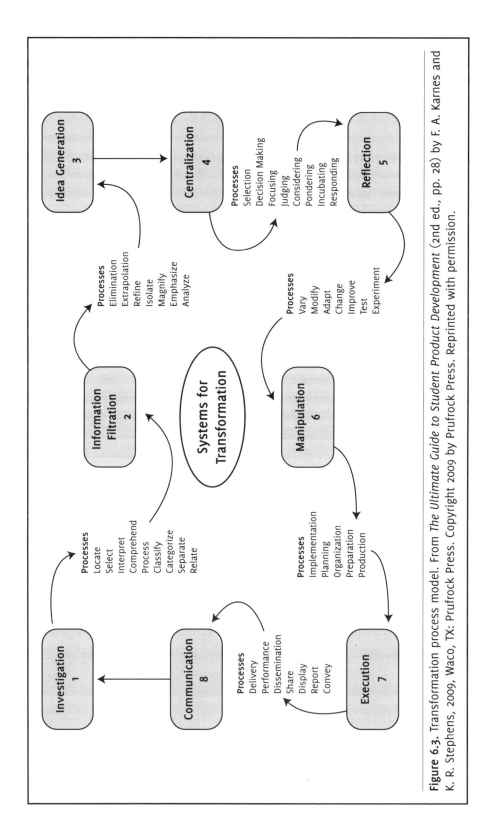

Figure 6.3. Transformation process model. From *The Ultimate Guide to Student Product Development* (2nd ed., pp. 28) by F. A. Karnes and K. R. Stephens, 2009, Waco, TX: Prufrock Press. Copyright 2009 by Prufrock Press. Reprinted with permission.

It is important to note the percentage of time students are spending in each phase of the transformation model. Typically, students spend little time planning and dive into the actual creation of their product. How often have students been observed with a fresh piece of poster board and a box of markers getting to work immediately without planning, sketching a draft, or constructing a prototype? How would the quality of what they are able to produce be impacted if more time and consideration were devoted to these initial steps? The steps in the transformation model should be taught to students, and each phase should receive ample time and consideration. Perhaps one of the first goals in fostering successful product development in students is teaching them how to slow down and think and plan prior to acting. When introducing the model, it is suggested that the teacher initially designate an amount of time to be spent by students at each step (e.g., three class periods for investigation, two class periods for information filtration); however, keep in mind that, depending on the complexity and depth of the topic being researched, time periods for each step may vary. Spending a thorough amount of time researching and reflecting on the topic will help students generate novel ideas. Otherwise, they will likely resort to a mere regurgitation of what they read from a book—which is not transformation.

The Transformation Model easily can be adapted for use with younger students. Teachers can rename each step and provide further elaboration so that younger students have a better understanding of the type of activities that need to be occurring along the way. For example:

- » explore the topic in depth (investigation),
- » determine what is important (information filtration),
- » record your thoughts and ideas (idea generation),
- » decide which idea you like best (centralization),
- » think about your idea overnight (reflection),
- » develop a draft or prototype (manipulation),
- » design your product (execution), and
- » share the results (communication).

Communication Through Products

During the communication stage, students share their ideas and products with a selected audience. Sharing the final product with an audience gives added purpose to the product. Instead of being stored in the back of a closet to collect dust, student products can provide valuable learning opportunities for many types of audiences.

Speaking skills. Speaking skills will be enhanced through the continued exposure to a wide variety of audiences. Eye contact, clear speech, and confidence are a few components of an effective presentation. Students should become more comfortable with practice and experience in presenting their products and ideas. Never assume that a student who is unable to give an effective presentation has not synthesized and analyzed information from his or her study. Presenting the product in class should be the first step, followed by audiences within the school and community. Younger students will need time to feel comfortable expressing themselves in front of others. It is advisable to keep audiences small and familiar for younger students until they build confidence presenting to larger, more unfamiliar groups.

Authentic audiences. It is important for students to share their products and ideas with authentic audiences. These may vary from product to product and student to student. Potential audiences may be peers, teachers, family members, topic experts, clubs, the school board, retirement community, or town council, to name a few. Students should be involved in selecting the audience.

Other sharing showcases. Products also can be attractively displayed in many areas throughout the community. This gives a sense of pride and importance to the student while serving as a great public relations tool by introducing to the rest of the world the excitement and learning that is being generated in the gifted classroom. Some places that student products may be displayed in your community include:

- » bank lobbies,
- » public and school libraries,
- » shopping malls,
- » airports,
- » restaurants,
- » stores,
- » newsletters,
- » real estate offices,
- » hospitals,
- » fairs or festivals,
- » PTA meetings,
- » post offices,
- » colleges and universities,
- » governmental offices,
- » clubs and organizations,
- » train and bus stations,
- » school administrative offices,
- » magazines,
- » newspapers,
- » retirement communities,
- » preschools,
- » town halls,

»   school board meetings, and

»   business offices.

Students also may choose to enter their products in various competitions. Information related to specific academic areas, as well as fine and performing arts, leadership, and service learning, can be found in the book *The Best Competitions for Talented Kids* (Karnes & Riley, 2013). The possibilities of potential audiences and display areas are abundant.

Evaluation

Evaluation of student products should be multidimensional so that students can receive helpful and extensive feedback from a wide array of sources. Assessment may be determined by the teacher using preselected criteria, self-evaluation by the students, and feedback from an audience. Forster (1990) suggested that projects should have self-regulatory and constant evaluation methods so that students can stay on course throughout the duration of the project. Students may wish to develop questionnaires to determine their audiences' perceptions of their products and presentations. Before beginning their projects, it also is advisable that students choose a support person with whom they can conference periodically to share progress and receive feedback. Gibbons (1991) suggested that this support person be an expert in the particular topic, if possible.

Establishing criteria. Students should be involved in establishing the criteria for product evaluation. If students are familiar with the criteria prior to beginning work on the projects, they will be more apt to produce successful products. Establishing criteria for evaluating products that are complex in nature can be difficult. Byrnes and Parke (1982) developed the Creative Products Scale, an easy-to-use scale for creative products such as drama, poetry, music, and dance. The scales contain glossaries of the important components of these unique products, making them easy for students and teachers to use effectively. Topic experts also can be asked to assist in developing criteria for certain products. Renzulli, Reis, and Smith (1981) developed the Student Product Assessment Form, which rates eight factors in product development: purpose; problem focusing; level of resources; diversity of resources; appropriateness of resources; logic, sequence, and transition; action orientation; and audience.

When each student in a class is engaged in developing a different product, the task of evaluating each one can overwhelm teachers. How does one evaluate a diorama, a skit, or an illustration objectively? Therefore, getting students involved in the process of developing an effective evaluation instrument is crucial. It not only assists them in developing goals and criteria for the anticipated outcome, but it also holds them accountable in working toward and meeting these goals. Rubrics can be designed for every type of product. You can practice creating rubrics as a class and then have students develop their own rubrics for their products.

Creating rubrics. A rubric is a framework for evaluating products on an established scale. The first step in constructing a rubric is to list all of the components of the proposed product. For example, if the product is a poster, the basic components might include title, labels, graphics, and layout.

Components will vary according to the expected complexity of the product and the abilities of the student. For example, older students may wish to add additional components beyond the basic ones. Students may need to conduct research related to their proposed product in order to determine the components. It is important that students learn and use the terminology associated with their product so they acquire the same vocabulary of a professional who might design this same type of product. For example, *legend, topography, scale, orientation, neatline,* and *cartographer* are terms that might be associated with a map.

After a list of components has been generated, exemplary characteristics of each component should be listed. For example:

Title
» legible, neat
» prominent, visible
» representative of topic, appropriate
» correct spelling/grammar

Labels
» legible, neat
» appropriate placement
» correct spelling/grammar

Graphics
» clear, visible
» appropriate to theme
» securely attached

Layout
» balanced
» noncluttered
» interesting
» appropriate emphasis

Students may want to examine good examples of a particular product to determine the exemplary characteristics of each component. It may be helpful for students to find out who is considered to be exemplary producers of this particular product. For example, students might investigate the work of Frank Lloyd Wright for an architectural product or the poetry of Phillis Wheatley if they choose to write a poem.

Once the exemplary characteristics of each component have been listed, a scale for each characteristic must be set. It is recommended that a 4- or 6-point scale be used, rather than one that is odd-numbered. With odd-numbered scales, there is a tendency for the rater to select the middle value. In addition, if using a numbered scale, each value should be clearly defined. For example, a "1" may be designated as "Poor" or "Incomplete," and a "4" may designate "Superior" production (Karnes & Stephens, 2009).

Figure 6.4 is an example of a rubric that was created using the above procedure. Many ready-made rubrics can be found in books and on the Internet. *The Ultimate Guide for Student Product Development and Evaluation* (Karnes & Stephens, 2009) contains ready-made rubrics for more than 40 unique products, each of which can be modified and enhanced as needed. A great website that can assist in rubric development is Rubistar (http://rubistar.4teachers.org), which is free to use and supported by the U.S. Department of Education. You can customize the rubrics generated by the site to meet your specific purposes. In addition, resource books related to specific products are helpful in determining the components of, and terminology associated with, particular products. Several product-related books are included at the end of this chapter.

Teachers can create separate rubrics to evaluate content knowledge and process skills demonstrated during the research and product development phase, or they can incorporate all items related to content, process, and product into one rubric.

Evaluators. As mentioned earlier, evaluation of student products should be multidimensional, which can be achieved by having a variety of evaluators. These might include peers, audience members, teachers, the student, topic experts, or school administrators.

Celebration

What better motivator to work diligently and produce a high-quality product than to have the chance to celebrate and reflect upon your accomplishments? Gibbons (1991) suggested that students have a party and share their products with one another informally, which allows them to see the wide variety of products they are capable of producing. Students can share the thought processes that went into designing their products and perhaps even have the opportunity to explore the topic further, as more questions are generated when minds meet.

Poster Product Guide								
Component	**Exemplary Characteristics**	**Ratings**						
Title	▸ Legible, neat	1	2	3	4	5	6	
	▸ Prominent, visible	1	2	3	4	5	6	
	▸ Representative of content, appropriate	1	2	3	4	5	6	
	▸ Correct spelling/grammar	1	2	3	4	5	6	
Labels	▸ Legible, neat	1	2	3	4	5	6	
	▸ Appropriate placement	1	2	3	4	5	6	
	▸ Correct spelling/grammar	1	2	3	4	5	6	
Graphics	▸ Clear, visible	1	2	3	4	5	6	
	▸ Appropriate to theme/content	1	2	3	4	5	6	
	▸ Add interest, enhance poster	1	2	3	4	5	6	
Layout	▸ Balanced	1	2	3	4	5	6	
	▸ Noncluttered	1	2	3	4	5	6	
	▸ Interesting	1	2	3	4	5	6	
	▸ Emphasis is appropriately placed	1	2	3	4	5	6	

1 = Incomplete   4 = Emerging
2 = Needs Improvement   5 = Good
3 = Fair   6 = Superior

Figure 6.4. Sample rubric for a product. From *The Ultimate Guide to Student Product Development* (2nd ed., pp. 37) by F. A. Karnes and K. R. Stephens, 2009, Waco, TX: Prufrock Press. Copyright 2009 by Prufrock Press. Reprinted with permission.

Product fair. Celebration is an important component of product development. It allows students to build confidence and feel good about their achievements. A product fair can provide students with the opportunity to share their products in a completely different type of stress-free setting. Renzulli and Reis (1991) suggested an end-of-year product fair, which includes coverage by local newspapers and television and radio stations. Such coverage would expand the students' audience and provide excellent public relations for the gifted program. Through such an event, students also can share the stages in the development, implementation, and evaluation of their products.

Reflection

As students pack up their products on the bus and depart for home, the time for reflection begins. They should be encouraged to reflect on the entire process of creating their product from beginning to end. Is there anything else about the topic that needs further research? What could have been done differently? What really worked? These reflections will be a valuable contribution toward improvement as students begin a new journey into another product frontier. They will learn from both their successes and failures. In a sense, they will learn a great deal about themselves and others. Often, people reflect on things without even realizing it, but, by purposely doing so, a great deal can be learned that will be of value in the future.

Reflection also is a skill that needs to be taught. Dewey (1933) recognized that it is not the experience but the reflection on the experience that leads to learning. Too often, this stage in product development is overlooked, but it is essential that adequate time be provided for students to reflect.

Product journals. One method students can use to reflect on their product-producing experience is keeping a detailed journal. This will help them keep track of the steps of product development and also will serve as a way for them to remember and reflect on the entire process. Students will have gained an abundance of new knowledge through their research, planning, and creative problem-solving experiences.

How to Foster Product Development in the Classroom

There are many ways teachers can encourage and promote creative product development within their classrooms. By providing the necessary resources, creative ideas are more likely to be generated.

Posting a Product List

A simple way to encourage product development is by merely posting a list of products as seen in Figure 6.1 on the wall in the classroom. When students need an idea for a product, they can go to this list and select something that is appropriate to their topic and audience. By displaying the list, students are motivated to try their hand at a variety of different products beyond the report and poster.

Product Portfolios and Inventories

Teachers can keep product portfolios and inventories on each student. This will allow teachers across grade levels to see what types of products a particular student has made during his or her school career. Visually, product portfolios provide an excellent way for students to see their growth and progress over the years. Figure 6.5 displays a technique that can be used to keep track of the various products a student develops.

Name:			
Date	Type of Product	Academic Subject	Grade Level/Teacher

Figure 6.5. Student product inventory.

Don't Throw It Away

Teachers throughout the school can send a notice home asking parents to donate a variety of items to the school or classroom that inspire creative product development. A designated corner in the classroom or closet within the school can house these materials. By having them available, students will be encouraged to use their creative abilities. Requested materials might include:

»   egg and milk cartons;
»   aluminum foil;
»   buttons;
»   boxes (shoe, jewelry);
»   yogurt cups;
»   ribbon;
»   toilet paper tubes;
»   wire coat hangers;
»   nuts, bolts, screws;
»   greeting cards;
»   newspapers;
»   clothespins;
»   broken costume jewelry;
»   cans (coffee, soup);
»   fabric scraps;
»   plastic berry baskets;
»   microwave meal trays;
»   butter tubs;
»   wrapping paper;
»   paper towel tubes;

»   packaging popcorn;

»   colored paper scraps;

»   old magazines;

»   old keys;

»   yarn/string; and

»   beads.

Product Resource Files

When students complete a product, they can take a photograph of it and write on a special form the directions and materials necessary for creating it (see Figure 6.6). This form and photograph can be stored in a product resource file to be used by other students to obtain ideas for new products. Students should be encouraged not merely to copy someone else's idea, but to expand on it. How might they make that particular product better? How might they display information related to the topic using a similar product?

Many of the products on the list may be unfamiliar to students, like a geodesic or triptych. Having a photograph and generic directions on how to create these unfamiliar products may assist students in better understanding what they are and how they are created.

"How-To" Library

Having a library of books that describe how to create various products may further inspire students. Books designed for both students and professionals can be used to provide an abundance of information. See the Student and Teacher Resources at the end of this chapter for book recommendations.

Summary

Product development is an excellent way to encourage both creative and independent learning. Students can create original products to extend an idea or thought pertaining to a particular topic of interest and, in the process, learn the value of flexibility when meeting time and material restraints during product construction. They engage in creative problem solving as they overcome obstacles during the process, and they learn that careful planning and organization can assist in making the product-producing experience a positive one. In addition, the dispositions essential for lifelong learning are fostered as students engage in product development. The development of products is an essential component in any gifted education program that meets the complex and advanced needs of gifted students as they become tomorrow's creative problem solvers and thinkers (Stephens, 1996).

STEPHENS AND KARNES

Name: _____ Subject: _____

Product: _____

Materials: What You Need, and Where to Get it!

	What	Where
1.		
2.		
3.		
4.		
5.		
6.		

The Process: Procedures for Production

	What	Where
1.		
2.		
3.		
4.		
5.		
6.		
7.		
8.		
9.		
10.		

Comments:

Pros:

Cons:

Advice:

* Attach a photo of product to this form *

Figure 6.6. Product description.

Teacher Statement

Products students have created in my class contain meaningful work in the subject areas. The rubrics for evaluation are in place and are solid ones. Many students have told me they enjoyed the assignments and learned lots from them. So, why am I not satisfied with the results? Why haven't I encouraged an even higher quality product from my students? Up until now, it was because I didn't know where to start, where to look for information, how to structure a more meaningful assignment, or how to get started on my own.

Information from this chapter has given me a solid framework and direction to make the changes that give my students opportunities for additional growth, creativity, and learning with ownership. I must understand that I do not have to start from scratch in revising what I do. There is no failure in using the good, well-researched information given within this chapter to help lighten my load and produce better outcomes. Change is difficult. I expect my students to push their comfort levels in order to grow. I plan to start with one product opportunity and build from there. I think the framework set forth in this chapter just might work for me as I set the stage for new learning opportunities for my students. Ready, set, I'll grow right along with my students—together we'll learn a lot!

—Eloise Williamson

DISCUSSION QUESTIONS

1. What strategies can be used to foster transformation of content into creative products and avoid mere repetition of what students have read pertaining to their topic?

2. Discuss the variety of process skills that are developed and enhanced through creative product development.

3. In what ways does the knowledge of design elements and principles enhance student products?

4. Think about your classroom and the units of study you currently teach. How can the incorporation of creative product development enhance your students' learning experiences?

5. How does creative product development help to differentiate learning experiences for gifted students?

6. What strategies can be implemented by teachers to assist them in evaluating the variety of products generated by students?

7. In what ways can technology support product development in the classroom?

Student and Teacher Resources

Amara, P. (2012). *So, you want to be a comic book artist?* Hillsboro, OR: Beyond Words.

Bentley, N., & Guthrie, D. (1996). *Putting on a play: The young playwright's guide to scripting, directing, and performing.* Brookfield, CT: Millbrook Press.

Bidner, J. (2011). *The kids' guide to digital photography: How to shoot, save, play with & print your digital photos.* New York, NY: Sterling.

Carreiro, C., & Jourdenais, N. J. (2005). *Make your own puppets & puppet theaters.* Nashville, TN: Williamson Books.

Court, R. (2005). *How to draw cartoons.* Chanhassen, MN: The Child's World.

Craig, D. (1997). *Making models.* Brookfield, CT: Millbrook Press.

Dearing, S. (1992). *Elegantly frugal costumes.* Colorado Springs, CO: Meriwether Pub.

Diehn, G. (2006). *Making books that fly, fold, wrap, hide, pop up, twist & turn.* New York, NY: Lark Books.

Draze, D., & Palouda, A. (1992). *Design studio.* Waco, TX: Prufrock Press.

Dunleavy, D., & Kurisu, J. (2004). *The jumbo book of drama.* Toronto, ON, Canada: Kids Can Press.

Fletcher, R. (2007). *How to write your life story.* New York, NY: Harper Collins.

Gallagher, M. (2010). *Speaking out: An introduction to public speaking.* Colorado Springs, CO: Meriwether Pub.

Harbour, J. S. (2012). *Video game programming for kids.* Boston, MA: Course Technology PTR.

Hambleton, V., Greenwood, C., & Hambleton, V. (2012). *So, you want to be a writer?: How to write, get published, and maybe even make it big!* New York, NY: Aladdin.

Hamby, V. (2012). *Seize the story: A handbook for teens who like to write.* Waco, TX: Prufrock Press.

Harrison, D. L. (2004). *Writing stories: Fantastic fiction from start to finish.* New York, NY: Scholastic.

Henry, S., & Cook, T. (2011). *Making masks.* New York, NY: PowerKids Press.

Horn, G. M. (2006). *Writing, producing, and directing movies.* Milwaukee, WI: Gareth Stevens.

Kasper, J. E., & Feller, S. A. (2001). *The complete book of holograms: How they work and how to make them.* Mineola, NY: Dover Publications.

Kronenwetter, M. (1995). *How to write a news article.* New York, NY: Franklin Watts.

Levine, G. C. (2006). *Writing magic: Creating stories that fly.* New York, NY: HarperCollins.

Robins, D. (2004). *Stencils and prints.* Laguna Hills, CA: QEB.

Selfridge, B., Selfridge, P., & Osburn, J. (2009). *A teen's guide to creating web pages and blogs.* Waco, TX: Prufrock Press.

Thomas, I. (2005). *Sculpting.* Chicago, IL: Heinemann Library.

References

Atwood, B. (1974). *Building independent learning skills.* Palo Alto, CA: Learning Handbooks.

Baker, E. L., & Schacter, J. (1996). Expert benchmarks for student academic performance: The case for gifted children. *Gifted Child Quarterly, 40,* 61–65.

Besnoy, K. D., Dantzler, J. A., & Siders, J. A. (2012). Creating a digital ecosystem for the gifted education classroom. *Journal of Advanced Academics, 23,* 305–325.

Burnette, C., Norman, J. T., & Browning, K. (1997). *D-K12 designs for thinking.* Philadelphia, PA: The University of the Arts.

Byrnes, P., & Parke, B. (1982, April). *Creative products scale: Detroit public schools.* Paper presented at the annual meeting of the Council for Exceptional Children, Houston, TX. Retrieved from ERIC database. (ED218903)

Costa, A. L., & Kallick, B. (2000). *Habits of mind: A developmental series.* Alexandria, VA: Association for Supervision and Curriculum Development.

Coxon, S. V. (2012a). Innovative allies: Spatial and creative abilities. *Gifted Child Today, 35,* 277–284.

Coxon, S. V. (2012b). The malleability of spatial ability under treatment of a FIRST LEGO league-based robotics simulation. *Journal for the Education of the Gifted, 35,* 291–316.

Davis, M., Hawley, P., McMullan, B., & Spilka, G. (1997). *Design as a catalyst for learning.* Alexandria, VA: Association for Supervision and Curriculum Development.

Dewey, J. (1933). *How we think: A restatement of the relation of reflective thinking to the educative process.* Boston: D. C. Heath.

Feldhusen, J., & Kolloff, M. (1988). A three-stage model for gifted education. *Gifted Child Today, 11*(1), 53–58.

Forster, B. R. (1990). Let's build a sailboat: A differentiated gifted education project. *Teaching Exceptional Children, 22*(4), 40–42.

Gibbons, M. (1991). *How to become an expert: Discover, research, and build a project in your chosen field.* Tucson, AZ: Zephyr Press.

Housand, B. C., & Housand, A. M. (2012). The role of technology in gifted students' motivation. *Psychology in the Schools, 49,* 706–715.

Karnes, F. A., & Riley, T. L. (2013). *The best competitions for talented kids: Win scholarships, big prize money, and recognition.* Waco, TX: Prufrock Press.

Karnes, F. A., & Stephens, K. R. (2009). *The ultimate guide to student product development and evaluation.* Waco, TX: Prufrock Press.

Kettle, K. E., Renzulli, J. S., & Rizza, M. G. (1998). Products of mind: Exploring student preferences for product development using My Way . . . An Expression Style Inventory. *Gifted Child Quarterly, 42,* 49–60.

Lohman, D. F. (1996). Spatial ability and g. In I. Dennis & P. Tapsfield (Eds.), *Human abilities: Their nature and assessment* (pp. 97–116). Hillsdale, NJ: Erlbaum.

Maker, J. C., & Nielson, A. B. (1996). *Curriculum development and teaching strategies for gifted learners* (2nd ed.). Austin, TX: PRO-ED.

Maker, J. C., & Nielson, A. B. (2005). *Teaching models in education of the gifted* (3rd ed.). Austin, TX: PRO-ED.

Neihart, M. (1999). Systematic risk-taking. *Roeper Review, 21,* 289–293.

National Governors Association Center for Best Practices, & Council of Chief State School Officers. (2010a). *Common Core State Standards for English language arts.* Retrieved from http://www.corestandards.org/ELA-Literacy

National Governors Association Center for Best Practices, & Council of Chief State School Officers. (2010b). *Common Core State Standards for mathematics.* Retrieved from http://www.corestandards.org/math

National Science Board. (2010). *Preparing the next generation of STEM innovators: Identifying and developing our nation's human capital.* Arlington, VA: National Science Foundation.

Partnership for 21st Century Skills. (2011). *Framework for 21st century learning.* Retrieved from http://www.p21.org/storage/documents/1.__p21_framework_2-pager.pdf

Pink, D. (2005). *A whole new mind.* New York, NY: Penguin.

Renzulli, J. S. (1977). *The Enrichment Triad Model: A guide for development defensible programs for the gifted and talented.* Mansfield Center, CT: Creative Learning Press.

Renzulli, J. S., & Reis, S. M. (1991). Building advocacy through program design, student productivity, and public relations. *Gifted Child Quarterly, 35,* 182–187.

Renzulli, J. S., Reis, S. M., & Smith, L. H. (1981). *The Revolving Door Identification Model.* Mansfield Center, CT: Creative Learning Press.

Siegle, D. (2011). Technology: Presentations in the cloud with a twist. *Gifted Child Today, 34,* 54–58.

Stephens, K. R. (1996). Product development for gifted students: Formulation to reflection. *Gifted Child Today, 19*(6), 18–21.

Wai, J., Lubinski, D., & Benbow, C. P. (2009). Spatial ability for STEM domains: Aligning over 50 years of cumulative psychological knowledge solidifies its importance. *Journal of Educational Psychology, 101,* 817–835.

Wiggins, G. (1996). Anchoring assessment with exemplars: Why students and teachers need models. *Gifted Child Quarterly, 40,* 66–69.

Wiggins, G., & McTighe, J. (2005). *Understanding by design.* Alexandria, VA: Association for Supervision and Curriculum Development.

Wikipedia. (2007). *Wikipedia: About.* Retrieved from http://en.wikipedia.org/wiki/Wikipedia:About

7

Chapter

DIFFERENTIATING THE LEARNING ENVIRONMENT

BY TRACY RILEY

The response to giftedness and talent is not simply differentiation, but qualitative differentiation: doing different kinds of things, not more of the same things. Modifications to learning experiences are made in both degree and kind, marked by dissimilarity, not similarity. In a practical sense, this means gifted and talented students may need adaptations that are of a different kind altogether than their peers. Tomlinson (2001) stated, "Differentiated instruction is not just 'tailoring the same suit of clothes'" (p. 3). Teachers may use the same patterns—content, process, and product differentiation—but as these patterns are applied to different fabrics, textures, and materials, and adjusted to suit different sizes, shapes, and styles, the tailoring becomes personalized.

In classrooms, teachers adjust content (what students are taught and learn), processes (how students are taught and learn), and products (the outcomes, or ways in which students demonstrate what they have learned). In other words, concepts, information, ideas, and facts are presented to students through different learning activities using a range of teaching methods with the expectation of tangible and intangible results. Qualitative changes should be matched to students' abilities and qualities, capitalizing upon their strengths and interests.

Qualitative differentiation implies choice, variety, flexibility, relevance, complexity, depth, breadth, and rigor through enrichment and acceleration. Inclusion of cultural, gender, moral, ethical, and personal dimensions of content are explored through inquiry developed with caring, critical and creative thinking, research, self-reflection, and metacognition. Gifted and talented learners are encouraged to challenge old ideas and create new ones, using authentic, real methods, materials, and practices as they develop self-selected products for appropriate audiences.

Picture this type of learning in action and one can only conclude that qualitatively differentiating the content, processes, and products in the development and delivery of a curriculum for gifted and talented learners requires dramatic changes in the learning environment. In many ways, the principles of differentiation, when applied in classrooms, necessitate changes that almost occur naturally. Teachers who provide differentiation, it would seem, would, without thinking, adjust the learning environment, too, but, as this chapter will show, it takes more than gut instinct or good teaching to create a learning environment suitable for gifted and talented students.

Teachers need to focus time and attention on the classroom environment and structure, in the same way as for assessment, curricular development, planning for differentiation, and instructional materials. Gifted and talented students move physically and psychologically through their education, so teachers need to step back and analyze the physical space and affective atmosphere in the classroom. From the moment a child enters a classroom, the teacher is communicating, sending overt and covert messages about the value placed on learning, the acceptance of diversity, and the chance to be an individual. The classroom environment should, therefore, be responsive to individuals and invitational to learning.

This chapter explores the theory and research related to practices suitable for gifted and talented learners in all classrooms, including special programs that may be school-based or out-of-school. The chapter is contextualized in general education by examining theories drawn from differentiated instruction and invitational education. These generic principles are then applied to practices drawn from the specific characteristics of gifted and talented learners and based on a limited body of research examining their preferences. The chapter concludes by sharing the key features of a learning environment that is qualitatively different and responsive to the needs of gifted and talented children and young people.

Invitational Learning Environments

The invitational education movement, begun by William Purkey more than 20 years ago, "provides an alternative lens to view educational practices and bring enthusiasm to teaching and learning" (Kane & Fiedler, 2010, p. 2). Imagine being invited to learn. How might that look and feel? Purkey and Novak (2013) explained that, "Invitational education is the process by which people are cordially, creatively, and consistently summoned to realize their potential" (p. 7). The writers explain that invitations are issued in the messages given by the five Ps: people, places, policies, programs, and processes. These five Ps are based on respect, trust, optimism, and intentionality. In other words, people can realize their potential when they are valued in places, processes, policies, and programs specifically designed to invite development.

Intentionality is central to this theory, for Purkey and Novak (2013) strongly believed that the messages teachers send can "invite people to meet their potential, or they can be used to hinder someone" (p. 20). Teachers can analyze their practices using a four-level classification system, as explained below, but it is important to remember that the complex nature of human behavior means that we cannot pinpoint an exact level of intentionality (Purkey & Novak, 2013). Every person will occasionally send messages at all levels.

» *Intentionally Disinviting*: This level of functioning is the antithesis to developing potential as it intentionally demeans, diminishes, and devalues others. Behaviors, policies, programs, places, and processes that outwardly discriminate against gifted and talented learners are often based on personal biases, prejudices, or misinformation. As Kane and Fiedler (2010) explained, "If a teacher is unable to overcome a particular preconceived notion regarding a gifted child or group of children then those individuals could be easily stigmatized" (p. 7).

» *Unintentionally Disinviting*: At this level, harm is not intended, but through lack of reflection, the messages sent to students may be misinterpreted and misunderstood because they are rooted in insensitivity, abruptness, and lack of forethought. "These classrooms often are characterized by boredom, busywork, and lack of orchestration" (Purkey & Novak, 2013, pp. 21–22). Gifted students in unintentionally disinviting classrooms are frequently provided with work that is irrelevant and inappropriate but keeps them busy. The sensitivities and intensities of gifted learners make them particularly vulnerable to unintentional messages (Kane & Fiedler, 2010). A common example of this is seen when teachers make comments like, "but you are gifted . . ." or "since you are gifted . . . ".

» *Unintentionally Inviting*: Teachers functioning at this level are described as being good-natured and gregarious, but by doing what comes naturally, without thoughtful commitment and reflection, they are prone to accidental successes. Unintentionally inviting actions reap positive results, but because these are almost flukes, the lack of consistency may prevent successful repetition.

» *Intentionally Inviting*: At this highest level, teachers are committed to caring and democracy, as they consistently examine and modify their practices, developing a broad knowledge base and constantly growing professionally. Teachers of gifted and talented students who are intentionally inviting have a sense of purpose that is persistent, an imaginative resourcefulness, and courage not to give in to naysayers and cynics. Policies, programs, processes, and places invite gifted learners, making them feel worthwhile and valued (Kane & Fielder, 2010).

In practice, this theory translates to the specific design of gifted and talented education, which in today's environment can sometimes be difficult. But using the Five P's, a starfish analogy was developed, which shows that with constant, steady pressure from a number of points, any challenge can be overcome (Purkey, 2013). Practical strategies for applying an invitational approach have been developed by Kane and Fiedler (2010), as summarized in Table 7.1 on the next page.

As the table shows, one way to extend an intentional invitation to learning to all of our students is through differentiation.

Differentiated Learning Environments

"Differentiation advises teachers to respond to student needs with invitation, investment, opportunity, persistence, and reflection" (Sousa & Tomlinson, 2011, p. 32). Tomlinson (2003) elaborated upon these teacher responses to students' needs for affirmation, contribution, power, purpose, and challenge in her book, *Fulfilling the Promise of the Differentiated Classroom*. As she explained, "Differentiated instruction is responsive instruction" (Tomlinson, 2003, p. 2), and it develops from students' readiness, interests, and learning profiles. Teachers working to create responsive learning environments begin where students are, and, according to Tomlinson (2003), "They look beyond those things they *cannot* change toward the young people, learning environments, curricula, and instruction they *can* change" (p. 26).

Being able to change the environment to respond to needs is part of the philosophy of inclusive education, and as Gartin, Murdick, Imbeau, and Perner (2002) explained, a learning environment that is inclusive emphasizes respect for

TABLE 7.1.

Practical Strategies for Creating Invitational Learning Environments

The Five P's	Practical Strategies
People: every person in the school, from administrators to volunteers	► Advocate for gifted and talented students. ► Develop self-understanding amongst gifted learners. ► Encourage self-advocacy in students. ► Connect gifted learners with mentors. ► Determine students' interests and match learning to those. ► Include, rather than isolate, students in the classroom. ► Foster relationships in the classroom.
Places: physical aspects of a school, from the playground to classrooms	► Develop quiet, chill spots for introverts. ► Create conversation spots, chat corners, and pair-share areas for extroverts. ► Allow students to choose work for wall displays. ► Post quotes and signs promoting self-reflection. ► Provide materials for self-exploration and creative expression.
Policies: procedures and rules that are mainly written, but can be unwritten	► Establish a growth model that allows learning at a pace commensurate to abilities. ► Develop policies that allow students of similar abilities and interests to learn together. ► Engage students in school governance. ► Encourage self-advocacy and responsibility for learning by the gifted.
Programs: formal or informal, curricular or extracurricular	► Encourage collaboration rather than competition. ► Allow for individual pursuit of passions through independent study. ► Create mentoring programs—by and for gifted students. ► Seek inclusivity in selection and engagement.
Processes: collaborative community	► Show empathy toward learners' concerns. ► Create an atmosphere of positive regard for all learners. ► Advocate on behalf of students.

Note. From Kane and Fiedler (2010).

all learners and highly values their work as students. These writers also emphasized the importance of change and the role of the teacher in changing the physical environment, instructional groupings, and classroom climate. Tomlinson (2003) placed emphasis on these areas but also highlighted the need to differentiate through communication, routines, support systems, and responsibility. Clark (2013) differentiated the physical, social-emotional, and instructional learning environment. Most writers on differentiation do not address the learning environment beyond acknowledging the need for physical changes and psychological safety. Whatever distinctions or definitions one prefers, it is clear from perusing the literature on differentiated classrooms that the learning environment is often overlooked (Sousa & Tomlinson, 2011; Tomlinson, 2003).

"Learning environments are largely invisible yet permeate everything that happens in a classroom" (Sousa & Tomlinson, 2011, p. 30). This is because of the profound impact the classroom has on affective and cognitive outcomes for the learners who reside there. They may be included or alienated, encouraged or discouraged, satisfied or left hungry for more. In other words, the classroom has to be conducive to learning (Gartin et al., 2002). Furthermore, as Figure 7.1 shows, researchers have demonstrated links between the learning environment and the development of one's abilities. Clark (2013) believed the learning environment plays a leading role in differences students exhibit in their learning styles, paces, and levels; the motivation they bring to learning; and challenge and stimulation.

In addition to these biological connections between learning environments and students, Sousa and Tomlinson (2011) argued that learning cannot take place if students' basic needs are not identified and met, basing their assertions on Maslow's theory. Students must have their basic physiological needs of food, shelter, and sleep met before those of safety and security, belonging, respect, and self-actualization. As they explained, ". . . if the learning environment confounds student needs at any level . . . that creates barriers to students' academic success" (p. 32).

Sousa and Tomlinson (2011) encouraged teachers and administrators to reflect upon their students' needs by determining if they are attuned to basics, like hunger and sleep deprivation, as well as behaviors that might indicate a lack of safety and security. Being alert to and aware of physiological and psychological needs is the first step toward a differentiated learning environment. The next step is to reflect upon teacher actions in response to these basic and safety needs, and then teachers can put in place practical differentiated strategies to ensure students feel belonging, respect, and affection as they achieve. Differentiated teacher actions seen in classrooms that are inclusive and responsive to all students include (Sousa & Tomlinson, 2011):

» *Modeling*: demonstrating respect for others, using positive humor (rather than sarcasm), showing a love of learning;
» *Sharing*: telling students about experiences, facilitating opportunities for them to share with one another;
» *Listening*: ensuring students listen to one another and the teacher and that they are heard when they speak;
» *Collaborating*: giving opportunities for working together, including with like minds, ensuring students have the how-to skills of collaboration;
» *Contributing*: allowing equal opportunities to contribute by calling on all students and supporting their participation in the classroom;
» *Seeking*: asking students for their input, valuing diverse perspectives; and
» *Acknowledging*: celebrating all legitimate student successes, promoting competition against one's own goals as opposed to against other learners.

All of these recommendations are derived from what we know about individual needs, but what do we know about learners? What are the implications of

---

Did you know . . .

- stimulating learning environments may be responsible for more rapid and robust neuron development?
- development is reliant upon the interaction between biological inheritance and environmental opportunities to use that inheritance?
- learning environments that are flexible maximize cognitive development?
- stress caused by fear, threat, anxiety, and tension produces a biochemical reaction that slows down brain function?
- the environment has an impact upon attention and concentration?

Figure 7.1. Brain facts in relation to learning environments (Clark, 2013; Sousa & Tomlinson, 2011).

---

some of the differences learners bring to classrooms? Sousa and Tomlinson (2011) have outlined some of these differences and what they mean for differentiated classrooms, suggesting teachers reflect upon and discuss these as a faculty. These can be adapted for gifted students, as shown in Table 7.2.

Further evidence of a differentiated classroom learning environment is outlined by Shalaway (2005), based on work produced by the Association of Supervision and Curriculum Development:

1. Teachers and students accept and respect one another's similarities and differences.
2. Assessment is an ongoing diagnostic activity, and learning tasks are planned and adjusted based on assessment data.
3. All students participate in work that is challenging, meaningful, interesting, and engaging.
4. The teacher is primarily a coordinator of time, space, and activities rather than a provider of information.
5. Students and teachers collaborate in setting class and individual goals.
6. Students work in a variety of flexible group configurations, as well as independently.
7. Students often have choices about topics, activities, and assessment.
8. Teachers use various instructional strategies to target instruction to student needs.
9. Students are assessed in multiple ways, and each student's progress is measured at least in part from where that student began. (p. 106)

Roberts and Inman (2009) summarized these principles much more succinctly: "A differentiated classroom respects diversity . . . maintains high expectations . . . and generates openness" (p. 20).

Gartin and colleagues (2002) explained some of the practicalities of differentiated classrooms in terms of physical spaces, classroom organization, and a posi-

TABLE 7.2
Cognitive Traits of Gifted Learners and the
Environments That Support Those Traits

Because we know that . . .	Learning environments should . . .
Gifted students are active learners	Support production of ideas rather than consumption
Gifted students construct their own meaning	Promote active engagement and metacognitive learning
Gifted students set goals, plan, and rethink	Develop goal-setting, planning, and reflective skills
Gifted students work within an advanced bandwidth of readiness and ability	Provide for variation in readiness, including advanced abilities
Gifted student grow when challenged by others with like minds	Provide supportive peer, teacher, and mentor partnerships
Gifted students have different ways of learning	Be flexible in response to strengths and needs
Gifted students learn at a faster rate	Be flexible enough to adjust pace
Gifted students develop multiple and different problem-solving strategies	Promote experimentation and accept different responses
Gifted students learn best in like-minded communities	Provide opportunities for working collaboratively and teach the skills to do so
Gifted students learn with many tools, artifacts, and materials to support them	Be rich in materials and resources at a range of levels and variety of types

Note. From Sousa and Tomlinson (2011).

tive classroom climate. Differentiated classrooms allow for seating that is flexible, including quiet spaces and multiple use areas (e.g., group work spaces). Desks are not owned and the classroom arrangement varies depending on activities and the level of independence expected. Well-established classroom routines, clear rules, signals and cues for changing activities or moving to new spaces, access to materials, and directions given orally and in writing are signs of classroom organization that takes into account different learner needs. Teaching appropriate behaviors and the skills of independence, alongside many of the already mentioned strategies, ensures a positive classroom climate. One-on-one teacher time with every student on a daily basis enables teachers to be involved with, not isolated from, individual students.

Other writers have outlined practical strategies for differentiated learning environments, elaborating upon the physical, organizational, and affective aspects. For example, Yatvin (2004) described the need for ". . . elbow room, boundaries, and neutral passing zones to minimize distractions" (p. 14). She also recommended the use of round tables, rather than desks, complemented by cubicles, shelves, or bags for personal belongings. Similarly, Yatvin advocated for the creation of differentiated teacher spaces by eliminating the power and isolation of a desk and replacing it with a functional table with shelves and filing cabinets, a rolling chair, and a smaller adjacent table for student meetings. Classrooms with storage lofts and those cleared of books, furniture, and equipment no longer in use allow for more flexible spaces for learning.

Tomlinson (2003) described scenarios of teachers' conscientious decision making regarding physical spaces and ways of communicating in classrooms. For example, one teacher has a "Kids' Corner" with high-interest books, posters, and artifacts for exploration. This teacher also uses a range of different shapes, sizes, and types of furniture, including rugs and pillows, for a variety of activities and groups. Other scenarios described a teacher who purposefully greets students by physically being at the classroom door as they enter each day, another who intentionally teaches respectful listening and constructive criticism, and a teacher who cultivates the habit of not giving up or asking a question until trying to solve a problem at least three different ways. Gregory and Chapman (2002) emphasized the importance of using laughter and humor in classrooms, encouraging students to cheer and applaud one another, and turning on music to add energy or exude calm. As Tomlinson (2003) explained, "Just as the teacher is the primary architect of the physical attributes of the classroom, so he or she initiates the affective climate" (p. 38). It is this combination of physical attributes of the classroom with a philosophy of invitational or responsive learning that enables differentiation to occur.

Although these basic strategies ensure *some* differentiation for *all* learners, they do not specifically address the needs of gifted and talented students. "At a general level, these practices appear appropriate for students identified as gifted; however, in practice, they need to be tuned to respond to the capacities that distinguish the learning of students with high ability from their age mates" (Kanevsky, 2011, p. 282). Kanevsky (2011) explained that the differences between differentiation for the gifted and differentiation for all learners might indicate that these practices are really just good teaching. It is the differences in the practices that reflect the differences in students. In other words, she defers to the students' preferences as drivers of differentiated teaching and learning, referring to deferential differentiation.

Deferential Differentiation of the Learning Environment

Kanevsky (2011) explained differential differentiation as "occurring when curriculum modifications defer to students' learning preferences by recognizing and including them in the design process" (p. 279). In other words, differentiation is reliant on students' preferences, which are sought by simply asking them, and then teachers work with students to enhance their preferences, what they want to know, and how they want to learn. This type of differentiation can be applied to the learning environment. For example, Kane and Fiedler (2010) devised a set of questions for teacher reflection. They explained, "These questions can serve as a guide in moving forward consistently and consciously to create invitational educational environments" (p. 13). The questions include (Kane & Fiedler, 2010):

» Think about a time when learning was joyful for you.
» Who were the people involved?
» Picture the place in your mind's eye. How did you feel being there?
» Were there any policies that allowed for the learning to occur?
» What type of program contributed to your sense of well-being?
» What processes enhanced the experience and made it joyful and filled you with enthusiasm? (p. 13)

Differential differentiation would shift these questions away from the teacher's experiences and directly to that of the students. Asking students to describe in words, draw on paper, or design in cyberspace moments of joyful learning and the places these occurred would give teachers a clear image of learners' preferences. As Prior (2011) reminded teachers, "One way to know what students who are gifted experience in their classroom is to ask them" (p. 125). It is from their insider perspectives that teachers gain insight into gifted students' preferences, and from those, rather than their own, they can differentiate the learning environment. Differential differentiation begins with the student's voice, a growing area of research in gifted education.

Kanevsky (2011) reported a study of more than 600 students in grades 3–8 (Canada and United States), of which approximately two thirds were in gifted pull-out programs. The students completed the *Possibilities for Learning Survey*, which queried their preferences for learning based on principles of curriculum differentiation. The findings from this study are almost overwhelming in detail and far too extensive to report in this chapter; however, there are important implications for developing a learning environment. Teachers might be surprised to discover that all students in this study, gifted or not, showed similar preferences for differentiated strategies.

As Kanevsky (2011) explained, "their preferences differed in degree rather than kind" (p. 295). The students in the study made it clear that the learning environment must be flexible enough for learners to spend the time they need, with peers of their choosing. The students "shared a desire to control the pace of their learning, the topics, methods and choice of workmates" (p. 295). There were differences, however, for gifted students: more wanted to work with others *some* of the time and fewer wanted to sit alone; they enjoyed complex, interconnected topics; they did not enjoy waiting for others to catch up or having to ask for help; and they liked having choice in a range of products. Importantly, Kanevsky has demonstrated the value in asking students for their preferences, for, as she explained, by asking students their preferences, they, too, become self-aware.

Other studies have focused more specifically on students' preferences in classroom learning environments. For example, Rayneri, Gerber, and Wiley (2006) conducted a study examining the relationship between classroom environment and learning style preferences amongst a sample of American gifted middle school students. These students leaned toward learning preferences that enabled mobility and flexibility, such as informal seating arrangements. Kinesthetic and tactile learning preferences were also reported, and the authors recommended field trips, hands-on activities, and time with mentors as ways to meet their need for mental and physical challenges. Other preferred classroom factors included having dim lights, eating and/or drinking while learning, and learning during the afternoon or evening. Interestingly, the study concluded that most typical classroom elements were not perceived by the gifted and talented students in this study as conducive to their learning.

In another study of secondary gifted students studying chemistry in Singapore, there is further support for open-endedness in teaching (Quek, Wong, & Fraser, 2005). These students also called for better-equipped labs and resources, suggesting a variety of materials that can be used to provide divergent learning in an intellectually stimulating classroom. The students in this study sought a learning environment for experimentation and creativity akin to a rich playground for learning. The gifted students in this study perceived their actual classrooms more favorably than their nongifted peers, a finding confirmed in a similar study undertaken by Rita and Martin-Dunlop (2011). This raises the question of attribution, suggesting that gifted learners who are successful achievers may be able to only partially blame external factors, like the learning environment, whereas their nongifted peers may externalize their failings more readily (Rita & Martin-Dunlop, 2011).

Nonetheless, the findings of the Rita and Martin-Dunlop (2011) study also presented some practical preferences of gifted students in science classrooms: a preference for more opportunities for investigations and more goal-oriented classrooms. Some of the secondary biology students in this study seemed to equate classroom goals as the knowledge and skills needed to pass assessments. They felt their teachers set these goals and determined who achieved them by "giving" grades. Other students seemed aware of the goals but questioned why they exist. This shows some possible differences in interpretations of classroom goals, but more importantly, highlights the need for differentiated learning goals that are personally meaningful and relevant. "As an intervention, a teacher could make a greater effort to clearly define objectives and goals for lessons and also allow students more opportunities to design experiments to test questions stemming from class discussions" (Rita & Martin-Dunlop, 2011, p. 35).

Although there have been numerous research studies on gifted and talented education, those investigating students' perspectives, by simply asking them, have been limited. When the question asks students about their preferences for a differentiated learning environment, the field of information narrows. What these limited studies show is that gifted and talented students' needs differ in degree from their peers (Kanevsky, 2011; Maker & Schiever, 2005), and this is why qualitatively differentiated learning environments should be considered.

Qualitatively Differentiated Learning Environments

For more than three decades, gifted and talented education specialists have advocated for qualitative differentiation. The modifications to content, processes, products, and learning environments have been argued based almost exclusively upon how gifted students differ from the norm as a group, rather than on a personal level (Olenchak, 2001). Research conducted by Olenchak (2001) at the turn of the century indicated that personalized differentiation was rare, and not surprisingly, he advocated for more opportunities based on individual needs. Although Olenchak's research looked more generally at differentiation, rather than only one aspect of it, his conclusions have implications for what is meant by qualitatively differentiated learning experiences: "the nature of differentiation, its interpretation, and its implementation are controversial" (2001, p. 195).

What this means in practice is that differentiation has often been based on a group's needs—in this case, the gifted group and their common characteristics—rather than on individual needs. And, as one of his research participants explained, "Differentiation has to mean something more than just changing the class around the group's needs" (Olenchak, 2001, p. 196). One way to tackle this problem is to talk with gifted and talented students, but another solution is to expand the criteria used for making decisions about differentiation. Maker and Schiever (2005) suggested three conditions be applied when deciding what modifications to make to the learning environment:

1. preference by most gifted students;
2. necessity for implementing content, process, and product differentiation; and
3. development built upon characteristics of gifted learners.

With these in mind, Maker and Schiever (2005) generated a set of eight modifications for qualitatively differentiating the physical and psychological learning environment for gifted students. As the list on the following page shows, these modifications have been presented as a dichotomy, but one could argue that a continuum might be the reality of how these are seen in practice. This is because not all gifted children are the same, which results in differences based on their characteristics, needs, and interests.

» *Learner-centered versus teacher-centered* classrooms focus on students' ideas generated in discussions and interactions led by them.

» *Independence versus dependence* in decision making and initiative is evidenced in an environment that is both tolerant and encouraging.

» *Open versus closed* physical and psychological environments allow for new materials, people, ideas, questions, and artifacts, as well as the freedom to take risks, speak freely, and even change directions.

» *Acceptance versus judgment* should be shown by accepting and understanding students' ideas, withholding and carefully timing value judgments, and evaluating both strengths and limitations.

» *Complex versus simple* materials and methods are part of the classroom climate and marked by their diversity, variety, complexity, and sophistication.

» *Varied versus similar groupings* allow for flexibility as students move in and out of groups based on abilities, interests, strengths, and needs, and based upon the purpose in the grouping and choices made by students and how groups are established, their relevant purposes, and who is engaged in them.

» *Flexibility versus rigidity* is evidenced in scheduling, requirements, criteria, and what is important in the classroom, and by allowing students extended periods of time for engagement, acknowledging the importance of working outside the classroom, and accepting the need for autonomy.

» *High mobility versus low mobility* is seen as students move in and out of the classroom, accessing the people, materials, equipment, and information needed to develop authentic products based on real processes.

Hunt and Seney (2001) reminded us that "by using these guidelines, environments are created which provide the comfort, autonomy, and opportunities gifted learners need for optimum growth and development" (p. 45).

Clark (2013) has developed an Integrative Education Model that incorporates a responsive learning environment as the first component of support for optimizing learning. Many of the elements she described have been previously discussed in the chapter, but some of her ideas are new. Describing the environment as a laboratory or workshop, she said it is ". . . rich in materials, with simultaneous access to many learning activities. The emphasis is on experimentation and involvement" (p. 327). Student involvement extends to being an active participant in all aspects of learning, with evidence of individualized activities and self-directed learning. Inquiry and invention are encouraged, and this requires physical spaces and patterns to support learning. As Clark (2013) explained, the environment is flexible, which is necessary for this sort of learning, but it is also complex in its organization so that each student's needs can be met.

Not surprisingly, whole-class lessons are minimized, with more opportunities for small groups of individuals. Learning is supported with materials geared at a range of levels, and enhanced with sensory stimuli, including color and sound. Importantly, the learning environment is a space open to teachers, students, and their families, all of whom work together to plan, implement, and evaluate differentiated learning. All of these elements are seen in the physical space, which features student work and evidence of their engagement in designing the room. In other words, the physical learning environment is designed with, by, and for the students. In a learning space occupied by gifted students, one would expect to see signs of complexity, depth, rigor, breadth, and sophistication on the walls, bulletin boards, notices, and student artwork, writing, inventions, and other products.

Importantly, for gifted students, Clark (2013) outlined an explicit set of "allowances" that result in optimal learning:

» Students assume some responsibility for their own learning.
» The skills for independent learning are taught and developed.
» Students learn at their own pace.
» Material is at each student's level.
» Teaching and learning strategies are offered in multiple modalities.
» Feedback is constructive, timely, and related to student's achievement goals.
» Students experience achievement and success, under their own control. (p. 331)

Teachers and administrators can reflect upon their classrooms in relation to Clark's (2013) Responsive Learning Environment Checklist in Figure 7.2. Does the physical, social-emotional, and instructional environment provide opportunities for differentiated learning for the gifted and talented students?

Conclusion

As this chapter has shown, the people, places, policies, programs, and processes of gifted and talented education have important roles in the creation of learning environments that are responsive to individual needs, strengths, and preferences. The principles and practices outlined in this chapter can be applied to all learning environments including the general classroom, special programs based in schools, and community-based, out-of-school programs. Teachers in general classrooms differentiate for all learners and need to develop a learning environ-

You will know that the physical environment is responsive when:

1. There is space for students to simultaneously participate in a variety of activities.
2. Students have access to materials with a range of levels and topics.
3. There is space for the students to engage in a variety of instructional groupings, and flexible grouping is used.
4. There are areas supportive of student self-management.
5. Desks are not individually owned.
6. The classroom has a comfortable, inviting ambience supportive of exploration, application, and personal construction of knowledge.

You will know that the social/emotional environment is responsive when:

1. The emotional climate is warm and accepting.
2. The class operates within clearly stated agreements decided upon cooperatively.
3. Instruction is based on each individual student's assessed needs and interests.
4. Student activities, products, and ideas are reflected around the classroom.
5. Student choice is evident in planning, instruction, and products of evaluation.
6. Building and practicing affective skills are a consistent and valued part of the curriculum and of each teaching day.
7. Students and teachers show evidence of shared responsibility for learning.
8. Empowering language is evident between teacher and student and among students.
9. Students show evidence of becoming independent learners with skills of inquiry and self-evaluation.

You will know that the instructional environment is responsive when:

1. The atmosphere is free of undue pressure and stress.
2. The lessons present novel challenges appropriate for the student's stage of development.
3. Stimulation to all of the senses is involved in the lessons.
4. Students have exposure to a broad range of skills and interests.
5. There is social interaction among intellectual peers.
6. Choices and the opportunity to choose are evident.
7. Exploration is an on going part of students' learning.

Figure 7.2. A responsive learning environment checklist. From *Growing up gifted* (8th ed.), by B. Clark, 2013, Boston, MA: Pearson. Copyright 2013 Pearson. Reprinted with permission.

ment that invites and includes gifted students. As Tomlinson (1999) reminded us, "principles of teaching guide us, but are not recipes" (p. 31). She suggested creating "healthy" classroom environments. As starting points, which she advocated can be revised, added to, or subtracted from, Tomlinson gave us these ingredients:

- » The teacher appreciates each child as an individual.
- » The teacher remembers to teach whole children.
- » The teacher continues to develop expertise.
- » The teacher links students to ideas.
- » The teacher strives for joyful learning.
- » The teacher helps students make their own sense of ideas.

» The teacher shares the teaching with students.
» The teacher clearly strives for student individuality.
» The teacher uses positive energy and humor.
» Discipline is more covert than overt. (p. 31–34)

These same principles of teaching can be applied by teachers in school-based programs for gifted students, including special classes and withdrawal programs, and in- and out-of-school opportunities, like university-based summer programs. Teachers in these specialized programs require professional development and support to ensure a qualitatively differentiated learning environment. This is because the principles and practices outlined in this chapter, although based upon the unique characteristics of gifted students, are not driven by a strong evidence base of research. The ideas in this chapter imply the need for careful planning of the learning environment, supported by policies and resources, and this planning should be driven by critical reflection and teacher inquiry. Asking gifted students about their preferences should be a central question in teacher inquiry and reflection.

When gifted students enter the learning environment, they bring their individual strengths, abilities, passions, and needs with them. Do teachers intentionally invite these differences? Do teachers actively seek gifted and talented learners' preferences for learning, creating people spaces and playgrounds for intellectual, creative, and social-emotional development? Do teachers step back, and using the mind's eye, assess the effectiveness of the learning environment in response to gifted and talented students?

DISCUSSION QUESTIONS AND ACTIVITIES

1. Reflect upon your teaching of gifted students. Do you intentionally invite learning? What enables those invitations and what are the barriers you sometimes face?

2. Conduct an assessment of the learning environment in which you teach by doing a SWOT analysis. What are the strengths, weaknesses, opportunities, and threats for differentiation?

3. Ask the students you teach about their classroom preferences using some of the questions outlined in this chapter or ask them to design the perfect learning space.

4. Based upon your assessment and the information from students, create an action plan for changing your learning environment to better meet their needs.

Teacher Resources

Books

Clark, B. (2013). *Growing up gifted* (8th ed.). Boston, MA: Pearson.

Gregory, G. H., & Chapman, C. (2002). *Differentiated instructional strategies. One size doesn't fit all*. Thousand Oaks, CA: Corwin Press.

Heacox, D. (2002). *Differentiating instruction in the regular classroom*. Minneapolis, MN: Free Spirit.

Maker, J., & Schiever, S. W. (2005). *Teaching models in the education of the gifted* (3rd ed.). Austin, TX: Pro-Ed.

Roberts, J., & Inman, T. F. (2015). *Strategies for differentiating instruction: Best practices for the classroom* (3rd ed.). Waco, TX: Prufrock Press.

Sousa, D. A., & Tomlinson, C. A. (2011). *Differentiation and the brain: How neuroscience supports the learner-friendly classroom*. Bloomington, IN: Solution-Tree Press.

Tomlinson, C. A. (1999). *The differentiated classroom: Responding to the needs of all learners*. Alexandria, VA: ASCD.

Tomlinson, C. A. (2001). *How to differentiate instruction in mixed-ability classrooms* (2nd ed.). Alexandria, VA: Association for Supervision and Curriculum Development.

Tomlinson, C. A. (2003). *Fulfilling the promise of the differentiated classroom: Strategies and tools for responsive teaching*. Alexandria, VA: Association for Supervision and Curriculum Development.

Yatvin, J. (2004). *A room with a differentiated view: How to serve all learners as individual learners*. Portsmouth, NH: Heineman.

References

Clark, B. (2013). *Growing up gifted* (8th ed.). Boston, MA: Pearson.

Gartin, B. C., Murdick, N. L., Imbeau, M., & Perner, D. E. (2002). *How to use differentiated instruction with students with developmental disabilities in the general education classroom*. Arlington, VA: Council for Exceptional Children.

Gregory, G. H., & Chapman, C. (2002). *Differentiated instructional strategies. One size doesn't fit all*. Thousand Oaks, CA: Corwin Press.

Hunt, B., & Seney, R. (2001). Planning the learning environment. In F. A. Karnes & S. M. Bean (Eds.), *Methods and materials for teaching the gifted* (pp. 43–92). Waco, TX: Prufrock Press.

Kane, M., & Fielder, E. D. (2010). *Invitational learning: Classrooms with enthusiasm*. Retrieved from http://www.seisummit.org/Data/Sites/1/PDF/invitationallearning. pdf

Kanevsky, L. (2011). Deferential differentiation: What types of differentiation do students want? *Gifted Child Quarterly, 55,* 279–299.

Maker, J., & Schiever, S. W. (2005). The role of teaching-learning models in curriculum development for the gifted. In J. Maker & S. W. Schiever (Eds.), *Teaching models in the education of the gifted* (3rd ed., pp. 1–26). Austin, TX: Pro-Ed.

Olenchak, F. (2001). Lessons learned from gifted children about differentiation. *Teacher Educator, 36,* 185–198.

Prior, S. (2011). Student voice: What do gifted students who are intellectually gifted say they experience and need in the inclusive classroom? *Gifted and Talented International, 26*(1–2), 121–129.

Purkey, W. (2013). *The starfish analogy*. Retrieved from http://www.invitationaleducation. net/ie/starfish.shtml

Purkey, W. W., & Novak, J. M. (2013). *Invitational education*. Retrieved from http://www. invitationaleducation.net/ie/PDFs/Fastback1[1]%20Invitational%20education.pdf

Quek, C. L., Wong, A., & Fraser, B. (2005). Student perceptions of chemistry laboratory learning environments, student-teacher interactions and attitudes in secondary school gifted education classes in Singapore. *Research in Science Education, 35,* 299–321.

Rayneri, L. J., Gerber, B. L., & Wiley, L. P. (2006). The relationship between classroom environment and the learning style preferences of gifted middle school students and the impact on levels of performance. *Gifted Child Quarterly, 50,* 104–118.

Rita, R. D., & Martin-Dunlop, C. S. (2011). Perceptions of the learning environment and associations with cognitive achievement among gifted biology students. *Learning Environments Research, 14*(1), 25–38.

Roberts, J., & Inman, T. F. (2009). *Strategies for differentiating instruction. Best practices for the classroom* (2nd ed.). Waco, TX: Prufrock Press.

Shalaway, L. (2005). *Learning to teach* (3rd ed.). New York, NY: Scholastic.

Sousa, D. A., & Tomlinson, C. A. (2011). *Differentiation and the brain: How neuroscience supports the learner-friendly classroom*. Bloomington, IN: Solution-Tree Press.

Tomlinson, C. A. (1999). *The differentiated classroom: Responding to the needs of all learners*. Alexandria, VA: ASCD.

Tomlinson, C.A. (2001). *How to differentiate instruction in mixed-ability classrooms* (2nd ed.) Alexandria, VA: Association for Supervision and Curriculum Development.

Tomlinson, C. A. (2003). *Fulfilling the promise of the differentiated classroom: Strategies and tools for responsive teaching.* Alexandria, VA: Association for Supervision and Curriculum Development.

Yatvin, J. (2004). *A room with a differentiated view: How to serve all learners as individual learners.* Portsmouth, NH: Heineman.

8
Chapter

WRITING UNITS THAT REMOVE THE LEARNING CEILING

BY JULIA LINK ROBERTS AND RICHARD A. ROBERTS

Many children who are gifted and talented spend most of their time learning in classrooms with children who have varying levels of ability, multiple interests, and a range of readiness. This chapter presents a model for writing units to differentiate learning experiences by providing a starting point for teachers who primarily have been using one set of learning experiences for the whole class. The model is a framework for teachers to embark on differentiation in their classrooms.

All children and youth benefit when the learning ceiling is removed, as they need opportunities to become the best learners they can be. All children and youth must master essential skills and core content; yet, as they reach mastery, they need and deserve opportunities to continue learning at challenging levels. It is important for educators to design learning experiences with accommodations to ensure continuous progress. After all, no one can learn what he or she already knows. Yes, a teacher can teach what the child already knows, but a child cannot learn it if he or she already knows it. For all children to make continuous progress, learning experiences must be differentiated to lift the learning ceiling. Differentiation allows students to continue learning each day, whether they are at a basic level or ready to learn at a more complex level and faster pace.

All K–12 teachers have the responsibility to write and implement units of study. Hopefully, all teachers are striving to promote lifelong learning for all students, including those who are gifted and talented. Educators who plan units to allow for continuous progress expect all students to perform academically at the highest level possible by providing opportunities for those who demonstrate readiness for advanced learning as well as grade-level learning. They recognize that fairness is matching learning experiences to student need, rather than providing the same instruction for all. The title of Stanley's (2000) article, "Helping Students Learn Only What They Don't Already Know," sums up the goal of education: continuous progress.

Support for instruction that is differentiated to allow students to reach their potential comes from many sources. The Chairman of the National Science Board (2010) gave two reasons for embarking on the report *Preparing the Next Generation of STEM Innovators: Identifying and Developing Our Nation's Human Capital.*

1. The long-term prosperity of our Nation will increasingly rely on talented and motivated individuals who will comprise the vanguard of scientific and technological innovation; and

2. Every student in America deserves the opportunity to achieve his or her full potential. (p. iv)

Another report that highlights the need to provide more advanced learning opportunities in order for students to reach advanced levels is *Mind the (Other) Gap! The Growing Excellence Gap in K–12 Education* (Plucker, Burroughs, & Song, 2010). This report focuses on the excellence gap, examining the demographic subgroups of K–12 students who achieve at advanced levels on the National Assessment of Educational Progress. The first recommendation is to "make closing the Excellence Gap a national and state priority" (p. 30).

Providing challenging subject matter requires differentiating so that the content and process match the varying levels of readiness among children who are in the same age bracket. All children are not ready to achieve at the same high level and on the same time schedule any more than they are ready to wear the same size shoes when they reach a certain age. Teachers must address the needs of all children, including those who are gifted and talented in a specific academic content area or in all content areas. Learning to use their minds well speaks to providing challenging levels of thinking and problem solving, as well as intellectually stimulating content.

The No Child Left Behind Act (2001) has led to heightened interest in reducing achievement gaps. Emphasis is being placed on teaching children to achieve at grade level. Of course, grade-level achievement is important for children who are not there yet; however, if children are to learn to their potential, any child who enters a grade already achieving above grade level needs to have more challenging learning experiences to make continuous progress. Tomlinson (2002) wrote an article entitled "Proficiency Is Not Enough." In fact, proficiency may be no stretch at all—possibly regression—for a child who is gifted and talented. A gap between achievement and potential is unacceptable, and this can be addressed by using units that remove the learning ceiling, requiring teachers to plan so each child can learn at the highest level possible.

Prisoners of Time, the report released by the National Education Commission on Time and Learning in 1994, stated: "The strongest message this commission can send to the American people is that education must become a new national obsession as powerful as sports and entertainment if we are to avoid a spiral of economic and social decline" (p. 10). This vivid and ominous statement is worthy of reflection in this time of educational reform. If the focus in schools and classrooms is on learning and student achievement, educators must build flexibility into planning and implementing instruction to accommodate children who require less time to learn and who need more challenging content if they are to reach their potential for high-level learning, as well as those children who need more time to learn. All children benefit when a teacher implements a differentiated unit of study.

National Excellence: A Case for Developing America's Talent (U.S. Department of Education, 1993), the second national report on gifted and talented children and youth, emphasized the need for a rigorous curriculum. Highlighting the importance of working hard on challenging tasks, Winebrenner (2001) stated:

> When gifted students discover during elementary school that they can get high praise for tasks or projects they complete with little or no effort, they may conclude that being smart means doing things easily. The longer they are allowed to believe this, the harder it is to rise to the challenge when they finally encounter one. (p. 1)

Winebrenner (1999) also emphasized the critical need to challenge advanced learners because "self-esteem actually is enhanced when success is attained at a task that has been perceived as difficult or challenging" (p. 13). Differentiating the curriculum for students who already have mastered much of the content of a unit prior to its implementation allows them to work hard at challenging academic tasks and to enhance their self-esteem as capable learners.

The National Academy of Sciences, National Academy of Engineering, and Institute of Medicine (2007) made a clarion call in *Rising Above the Gathering Storm* to recommend what the United States must do in order to remain globally competitive. In the 21st century, it will be imperative to raise the level of education if our young people are to remain competitive. More U.S. students must take the most challenging classes available and do well in them if they will be prepared to assume positions as innovators, entrepreneurs, researchers, and leaders in the global competition.

Planning the Unit

Planning offers the key to effective differentiation. A unit that is planned on a day-to-day basis will lack the necessary components to preassess the students' knowledge and skills in relation to the unit's goals and objectives. Just being different or offering choices to students does not make an intentionally differentiated unit. A differentiated curriculum is well planned; otherwise, it would be impossible to match learning experiences to the students' needs, interests, and readiness levels. Good planning is the prerequisite to preparing a unit that is differentiated to address the wide range of learner needs in a classroom.

If children and young people are to study rigorous curricula and reach high state and national standards, units of instruction must provide continuous progress for all students so that learning becomes a way of life, not an end product. The teacher's focus for each unit must be on what students should know and be able to do, taking into account what students already know and are able to do prior to implementing the unit. What individual students know and are able to do in relation to the topic and content selected for the unit will guide the teacher in determining challenging learning experiences for individuals, clusters of students, or both. Teachers must be knowledgeable of the content and be student-centered in order to plan and implement units that will challenge each student appropriately.

Before a school year begins, teachers need to have an overview of the curriculum for the year, even though they often will design specific learning opportunities unit by unit. Each unit must fit into the alignment of content for the academic year. A unit does not imply a specific amount of time that will be needed, as some units may be planned for 2 weeks and others will need more time to optimize learning. Within a unit, the time individual students need to master the objectives also will differ; therefore, in planning the unit, the teacher must include options that allow all students to be challenged to work at high levels.

Planning must precede differentiation. Good planning is essential for appropriate differentiation just as it is for effective teaching. In fact, differentiation is a necessary component of effective teaching. Unless planning is conducted well, there is no basis for differentiating learning experiences. Good planning makes it possible to preassess student learning, which provides the basis for differentiating learning experiences in such a way that it can be documented and explained to parents and students. Without such documentation, differentiating learning experiences may be perceived as whimsical, and, in fact, such decisions often are made in ways that cannot be supported.

Model of the Relationship of Unit Components

The Model of the Relationship of Unit Components provides the broad overview for planning (see Figure 8.1). The model highlights the importance of the universal theme and generalizations that form the outer ring of the model, the unbroken ring encircling all other components. The theme and related generalizations provide the framework needed to develop a variety of topics within or across content areas. A theme and related generalizations encompass the topic and related content, the preassessment and postassessment, as well as all of the learning experiences. All of the components must relate to each other if the learning experiences are to be meaningful and appropriately challenging to the learners. If learning is to be maximized, unit planning must be focused on the components, because a unit is much more than a loosely connected set of learning experiences.

Steps in Planning a Unit

Selecting the universal theme or identifying the topic provides the starting place to begin the planning process of a differentiated unit of study. Once the topic is chosen, it is important to identify the universal theme and develop related generalizations. Both steps must be planned early in the unit writing process to ensure that the unit maximizes opportunities for learning. The topic and the universal theme work together to add power to a unit and offer the potential to remove the learning ceiling. Together, the topic and the universal theme provide the focus for the teacher to use when selecting and designing learning experiences for the unit.

Steps in Unit Planning

1. Select a universal theme.
2. Develop generalizations related to the theme.
3. Identify the topic of study.
4. Identify core content and complex content related to the topic.
5. Design the postassessment or culminating activity.
6. Plan/identify preassessment strategies.
7. Design learning experiences incorporating content (core and complex content), process (basic and higher level processes), and product (a variety of products).

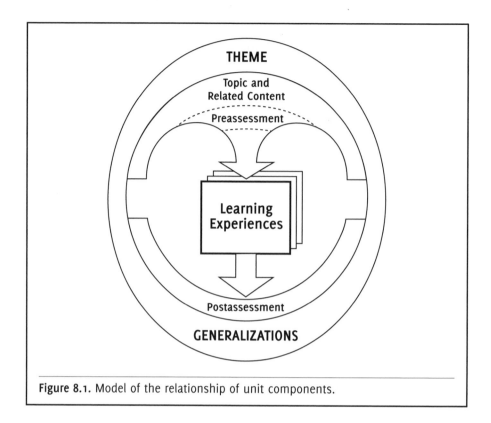

Figure 8.1. Model of the relationship of unit components.

The Universal Theme and Related Generalizations

A universal or broad-based theme maximizes learning potential because it can be used in various content areas to allow students to see how and where their learning in one content area applies to other content areas or situations. They can see how learning inside school connects to what they learn outside school and vice versa. Universal themes enhance the power of learning and help children and youth become lifelong learners. Kaplan (1993) provided the following criteria to assess a theme for its universal and broad-based nature:

1. Is the theme "universal" in its application?
2. Is the theme "timeless" in its application?
3. Is the theme equally usable across disciplines?
4. Is the theme appropriate for students across age groups?
5. Is the theme capable of "carrying" important information?
6. Is the theme useful in making connections between and among disciplines?
7. Are there generalizations (or big ideas) that can be used with the theme?

Universal themes add breadth and depth to learning. They are important in the Common Core State Standards, as they are big ideas that carry lots of important information and facilitate making interdisciplinary connections. Figure 8.2 illustrates the need for balance among the unit components and balance among content areas related to the universal theme.

Examining a few of the criteria for a universal or broad-based theme will demonstrate issues involved in its selection. First, the theme must be applicable for the past, present, and future, not being bound by time or space. For example, "The Roaring '20s" and "The Age of Dinosaurs" are topics, not universal themes, because they are limited by time and space. Second, the theme must be equally usable by teachers of all content areas, including mathematics, physical education, and the visual arts, without manufacturing content to "fit" into the theme. Requiring all teachers to base instruction on a topic (sometimes mistakenly called a theme) instead of a broad-based or universal theme often results in one or more teachers being forced to generate contrived learning experiences. For example, a physical education or mathematics teacher has a difficult time developing meaningful learning activities on "bears" or "holidays around the world." A universal theme promotes interdisciplinary learning, and it establishes an optimum situation for differentiating learning opportunities. Finally, the universal theme is capable of carrying important information; generalizations can be developed that link major concepts to important statements about the universal theme.

Examples of Universal Themes			
Change	Patterns	Structures	Adaptation
Systems	Exploration	Power	

Generalizations are statements related to the broad-based or universal themes that will hold true across time and space. Generalizations allow interdisciplinary connections to be discovered by students and modeled by teachers as they are applied to content across the disciplines. They can be amplified as the student matures in his or her thinking.

Themes and generalizations empower learners when teachers use them across content areas over time. A universal theme can be used by a single teacher; however, the impact of the theme is greater when employed by a team of teachers, at one grade level, or all of the teachers in the school using a theme that rotates by the year. For example, "change" may be the theme for the first school year, "patterns" for the next year, and "structures" for the third year. A schoolwide universal theme can be a powerful mechanism for enhancing interdisciplinary connection making. A theme and related generalizations can be used for an entire year, but they also may be planned for shorter periods of time.

Some themes, although not universal, allow for the use of generalizations that are appropriate for a limited number of content areas. "Revolutions," "expres-

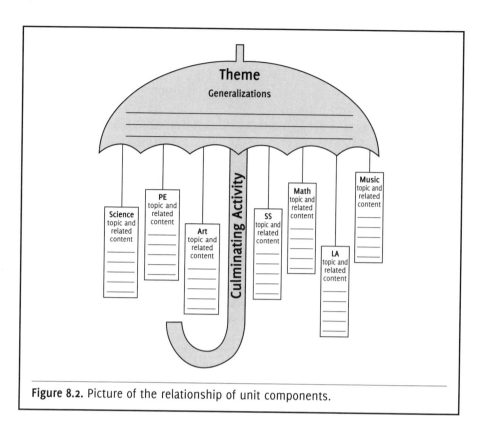

Figure 8.2. Picture of the relationship of unit components.

sion," and "culture" are examples of themes that apply to one or a few, rather than to all, content areas. These themes differ from universal themes in that they are not equally applicable in all content areas, yet they are capable of carrying important information through their generalizations. These content-specific themes can be useful in providing a focus in some content areas.

The Topic and Related Content

The topic describes the content of the unit in more specific terms. Examples of topics that are appropriate for various content areas at the elementary level include simple machines, folk tales and legends, rhythm and pitch, weather, and multiplication. Sample middle school topics include ecosystems, state government, perspective, and probability. Social issues, chemical reactions, medical technology, and mathematical notation are topics taught during high school. High school topics often are the same topics that were taught during earlier school years, but at a higher level that presupposes previous mastery. At all levels, topics are related to major concepts in specific disciplines. The power of topics to enhance student learning at all levels increases when they are linked to universal themes, thus facilitating the making of connections across disciplines.

Example of a Universal Theme and Related Generalizations

Change → 1. Change brings about change.
2. Change can have positive and negative results.
3. Change is universal.

There is no set number of generalizations, although three to five generalizations provide a reasonable number to pursue in one unit of study. Teachers should develop generalizations that provide a broad view of the content for their students.

Sources of Content

1. Local curriculum guidelines
2. State curriculum frameworks or guidelines
3. National curriculum standards

Selecting the basic and complex content follows the identification of the topic. Basic content is that which every student in the class is expected to master. Complex content relates to the core content, but goes beyond. It is more abstract and often relates to issues and problems tied to the core content. In a differentiated unit, all children are learning about the same topic, but some are learning core *content* whereas others, who have demonstrated that they already know the core content, are learning complex content. As all children share their learning experiences with the class, they are all tied to the same topic, concepts, and generalizations, and that sharing enhances learning for all.

The topic and the content of the unit come from three major sources: local curriculum guides, state curricular frameworks or guidelines, and the national curriculum standards. Local and state curricular documents are enhanced when used in conjunction with the national curriculum standards, including:

» Common Core State Standards in Mathematics and English Language Arts (National Governors Association Center for Best Practices & Council of Chief State School Officers, 2010a, 2010b),

» Curriculum Focal Points for Prekindergarten Through Grade 8 Mathematics: A Quest for Coherence (National Council of Teachers of Mathematics, 2006),

» National Geography Standards (Geography Education Standards Project, 1994),

» National Standards for American History (National Council for History Standards, 1994a, 1994b),

» National Standards for Arts Education (Consortium of National Arts Education Associations, 1994),

» National Standards for Civics and Government (Center for Civic Education, 1994),

» National Standards for World History (National Council for History Standards, 1994c),

» National Standards in Foreign Language Learning (National Standards in Foreign Language Education Project, 1996),

» Next Generation Science Standards (2013), and

» Standards for the English Language Arts (National Council of Teachers of English & International Reading Association, 1996).

Local, state, and national standards combine to provide the content to be considered when identifying topics and selecting the key content that will provide the focus of the unit.

Various content-based professional organizations have responded to the call for high standards by developing and issuing curriculum standards that spell out high-level content, including concepts and skills, to guide curriculum development. National standards establish the benchmarks for educators to use in their planning. For all children, they set high standards that will require quality teaching if they are to be met.

National standards provide the minimal standards for children who are gifted and talented. These standards should be in hand when planning curricula, as they provide the bottom line for the level of content and process that must be mastered by gifted and talented students who can learn at complex levels and at rapid paces. In line with the model presented in this chapter, preassessment for new units of instruction, related to the standards, will provide the important information needed to establish what students know and are able to do in order to match differentiated learning experiences to student needs. Only when preassessment results are analyzed can educators be certain that students are making continuous progress.

Postassessment

Also encompassed by the universal theme and generalizations in Figure 8.1 is the postassessment, which may be a culminating activity or an exit exhibition. The postassessment should be planned after the topic and related content have been specified, and it should provide the opportunity for students to demonstrate the breadth of their learning during the unit in a context typical of real-life situations. The postassessment should be planned before designing learning experiences because these experiences can be selected or developed to build skills and incorporate knowledge needed to complete the culminating or exit activity successfully. As a child learns to play a sport, he or she learns requisite skills one by one; however, the integration of knowledge and skills is necessary to play the sport well. The culminating activity requires a similar integration of what the student has learned and is able to do as a result of the learning experiences in the unit.

The postassessment or culminating activity is to the unit what a product is to the learning experience. In each case, the culminating activity and the product in the learning experience are the demonstration of what the student knows and is able to do; however, the postassessment encompasses what the student knows and is able to do at the conclusion of the unit, rather than being the result of a single learning experience. The postassessment may be designed by the teacher or by the student(s). The activity may be a problem-solving task that requires integrating knowledge (content) and skill (process) into a demonstration of what a student or students working together in a cluster know and are able to do to solve the problem. A well-constructed essay exam also can be an appropriate postassessment. A student or a cluster of students can design the culminating activity, a unique opportunity for students for whom the learning experiences have been differentiated in response to evidence that they already can meet the expectations of the core curriculum. Whether the teacher or the student(s) plans the postassessment, it is important to have a scoring guide or rubric that will set the standards for excellence.

Examples of Culminating Activities

A student or group of students writes a play/short story that ties together what they have learned about the culture, politics, and history of ancient Rome.

A student or group of students design and conduct an experiment to demonstrate that they understand the variables in the scientific process.

Preassessment

Once the goals and objectives for the unit have been established and the postassessment has been planned, the next step is to assess who already knows and can do what the unit is planned to teach. Assessment is the key to knowing for whom and when differentiated learning experiences are necessary. Prior to teaching a unit, teachers assess the students to find out who has already mastered the objectives or is close to doing so. Otherwise, teachers may not know how much their students already know about the topic and may assume that the assessment at the end of the unit revealed how much the students learned as the unit was taught. Preassessment provides key information for teachers to plan challenging learning opportunities for all children who demonstrate that they already know the basic or grade-level content and are ready to move on to more challenging learning experiences with more complex content. Of course, assessment at the conclusion of the unit provides additional information to inform planning for the next unit of instruction.

The Learning Experiences: Building Blocks of the Unit

Designing Learning Experiences

After the theme has been chosen, the generalizations have been identified, the topic and related content have been specified, the postassessment or culminating activity has been planned, and students have completed a preassessment, the next level of unit planning is the development of learning experiences. They are the building blocks of units, and they contain numerous learning opportunities designed to teach important content, processes, and products. The Elements of Learning Experiences, as shown in Figure 8.3, illustrate how a learning experience is built by combining content, process, and product.

The content is what the teacher wants the students to know at the end of the unit. Related content includes the concepts and knowledge to be learned to reach learning goals or outcomes for the unit. Content has been specified earlier in the unit planning process; each learning experience focuses on a concept or knowledge to be learned as the unit is implemented. If the concept to be taught is "the cell," then the cell becomes the content of the learning experience. If a new process skill is being introduced, that skill can become the content for that learning experience. In addition, teaching students how to produce a new or untried product can become the content for a learning experience. If the students have never produced a monologue, essay, or podcast, the new product would be the content of the learning experience. Likewise, process and skills may be built into or integrated into teaching the content.

The process is what the students are to be able to do cognitively with the content. The process includes thinking, problem solving, and research skills. The national curriculum standards include process, as well as content, within their standards. Bloom's (1956) Taxonomy of Educational Objectives in the cognitive

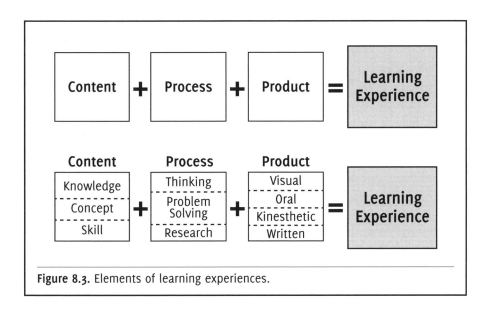

Figure 8.3. Elements of learning experiences.

domain represents a well-known way of developing process skills, and it provides a good starting point for teachers who are new to differentiation. The revision of Bloom's taxonomy (Anderson & Krathwohl, 2001) is used within the original model's framework, which makes it both useable and current: the nouns become verbs, which seems most appropriate for thinking or process skills. It involves two changes in the placement of the two highest levels: create (synthesis) and evaluate (evaluation). The revised Bloom's taxonomy provides a system for writing learning experiences at various levels of thinking. For example, on the level of remember/ understand (knowledge/comprehension), the desired outcome of a learning experience could be to explain the functions of the various parts of the cell. At the analyze (analysis) level, the student could compare and contrast the structure of plant and animal cells. At the evaluate (evaluation) level, the student could justify a position about continuing stem cell research. Another more comprehensive approach to process skills can be found in the Process Skills Rating Scales–Revised (Karnes & Bean, 2004).

Elements of a Learning Experience

Content: Plant and Animal Cells
Process: Analyze
Product: Venn Diagram (visual/written)

Objective of the learning experience: The student will compare and contrast the structure of plant and animal cells, producing a Venn diagram or an illustration.

The product is the means used to demonstrate what one has learned. In other words, the product is how the teacher wants students to show what they know and are able to do as the result of being involved in the learning experience. Karnes and Stephens (2009) described products as visual, oral, performance, written, or multicategorical. Roberts and Inman (2015) categorized products as visual, oral, kinesthetic, written, or technological. Providing a balance in the types of products allows students the opportunity to show what they have learned in a preferred way or with a learning style that reflects one of their strengths. Products that have been the traditional mainstays of the curriculum are papers (written), reports (oral or written), posters (visual), illustrations (visual), webpage (technological), and laboratory experiments (kinesthetic). However, the possibilities for products are much broader than those most frequently used. In fact, a wide array of products can motivate students by tapping into their learning interests and preferences. Today, products that incorporate technology are highly motivating to many students.

Using different combinations of content, processes, and products allows teachers to create learning experiences in which different student needs, abilities, and interests can be addressed. It is important to remember that many gifted students' needs are based on strengths, rather than weaknesses or deficiencies. A learning environment in which students have an element of choice and can engage in learning experiences that are matched to their needs and interests is a positive one for teachers and students.

Differentiating Learning Experiences

In order to differentiate the content of learning experiences, the following three curricular components must be in place:

1. The core content must be specified so that students know what they all should know and be able to do by the completion of the unit.
2. Strategies for ongoing assessment are planned in order to provide a solid rationale for compacting the curriculum and differentiating learning experiences.
3. Core and complex content, basic and higher order processes, and a variety of products must be identified/developed in order to plan differentiated learning experiences to match students' needs and prior knowledge/experiences.

Because of their importance, each of these components will be discussed in more detail.

Basic content. Identifying the basic content in the unit planning sequence is necessary before proceeding with planning to differentiate learning experiences. It is impossible to plan to differentiate appropriately without specifying what all children in a particular grade and content area are expected to know and be able to do with the topic and related content by the conclusion of the unit of study. The basic content must be specified so that both the teacher and students understand what all students should know and be able to do by the completion of the unit. Planning the topic and related content at the basic content level is a prerequisite for differentiation. Without this preplanning, there is no point of reference for compacting and differentiating the curriculum. Likewise, it is difficult to know if the teacher and students reach the unit goals if they are not stated in advance.

Topics usually are large enough that teachers could go in numerous directions, and it is not possible to teach all content that could be tied to the topic. For example, a unit on the Civil War could be taught chronologically or it could focus on battles, political events, or cultural history. Because it is possible to study the Civil War at the graduate level, it is impossible for students to master all of the content on a meaningful level during a 2- or 3-week unit. Narrowing the topic and focusing the related content will provide the rationale for selecting/developing some learning experiences over others. Likewise, the universal theme and generalizations will facilitate making interdisciplinary connections and provide criteria for designing learning experiences.

For example, if the universal theme of "change" is used and generalizations include "Change can be either good or bad" and "Change brings about change," a learning activity that examines the Civil War in light of the generalizations could ask students to compare and contrast life on a plantation in a Southern state before, during, and after the Civil War with a focus on evaluating whether these changes were good or bad and providing the rationale for the decisions. Product choices could include a written diary, a blog, a skit, or a series of illustrations. Thus, the learning experience is tied to the topic and basic content, yet it also relates to the universal theme and generalizations. Learning is more powerful and long-lasting if it is consciously tied to a universal theme and related generalizations.

Ongoing assessment. Strategies for ongoing assessment must be planned in order to provide a solid rationale for compacting the curriculum and differentiating learning experiences. Without evidence from assessment, differentiating learning experiences for students will appear capricious, and the teacher will be subject to criticism. The purpose of differentiation is to match a learning experience to the need(s) of a student or a cluster of students for whom the learning experiences are appropriately challenging. If everyone can complete the learning experiences planned for differentiation, then the learning experiences are not really appropriate for only some of the students, nor do they provide appropriately differentiated experiences. When assessment strategies demonstrate that the student already knows the content and is able to do what is expected at the conclusion of the unit, the rationale is provided for differentiation. Ongoing assessment can make it possible for all students to make continuous progress.

Examples of Preassessment Strategies

▸ Pretest
▸ Five Most Difficult Questions
▸ Mind Map
▸ Individual TWH Chart
▸ Open-Ended Question

Preassessment is a critical element in unit planning. Different strategies for preassessment can provide variety and bring in information on students' prior knowledge and interests relative to the content. Various assessment measures can be used to document what students know and what they might need for differentiation. Following are five examples:

» *Use a pretest, which may be the end-of-the-unit assessment given prior to teaching the unit.* The pretest will reveal what students already know about the topic and provide the documentation of the need for differentiated learning experiences. Because the postassessment is already planned, it is easy to use as a preassessment.

» *Ask the five most difficult questions to be learned before beginning the unit.* A student who can answer the five most difficult questions that the unit is planned to teach prior to the unit being taught deserves to have alternate learning experiences (Winebrenner, 1992, 2001).

» *Give students the opportunity to design a mind map.* A mind map (Buzan, 1983) provides the opportunity for students to map out visually what they know about the topic or focal subject matter of the unit, making connections between the major ideas or concepts. A mind map has some of the characteristics of webbing; however, the strategy depends upon using key words to detail what students already know about the topic. The mind map allows students who know a great deal about a topic to share the information, as well as experiences they have had that relate to the topic or concept that will be studied. A mind map also allows students to show the relationships among concepts that they understand about the topic.

» *Allow students to tell/write what they already know about a topic and what they would like to know through a "Think, Want, How" (TWH) assessment or chart.* Another assessment measure that will show the need for differentiation is an individual TWH chart on which the student details what he or she thinks about the topic (T), wants to find out or learn about the topic (W), and how he wants to learn (H) the concepts and skills in the unit (Roberts & Boggess, 2011). Having the student provide the T, W, and H provides direction for differentiated learning opportunities.

» *Ask open-ended questions about the topic for the unit.* This can reveal how much the student already knows or is able to do prior to beginning the study. Such a preassessment is easy to prepare and easy to assess.

With each of these five methods of preassessment, students bring what they have learned about a topic both in and outside of school to the forefront so the knowledge and skills can be taken into account when matching learning experiences to students. The value of the preassessment depends on how the teacher uses the information to allow individual students or clusters of students to learn more complex content and to have differentiated learning experiences based on what they already know and are able to do.

Planning for Differentiated Learning Experiences

- Identify/select the core content.
- Assess student knowledge of core content.
- Identify/plan core and complex content, basic and higher level processes, and a variety of products.

Content, process, and product. Learning experiences are designed by combining content, process, and product. During planning, basic and complex content, basic and higher order processes, and a variety of products must be identified and developed in order to provide differentiated learning experiences. Learning experiences can be differentiated on one, two, or all three dimensions—content, process, and product.

Complex content includes abstract concepts, issues and problems, and advanced knowledge related to the core content, universal themes, and related generalizations. Complex/abstract content related to the basic content allows students to continue learning about the same topic or universal theme with the rest of the class; however, it elevates the level of the content to match the students' advanced knowledge of the content and readiness to process the information at higher levels.

Differentiated learning experiences must be appropriately matched to the students' readiness to learn more complex content, use higher level processes to demonstrate what they have learned, and develop a wide range of products. The same students may not always need differentiation in all subjects or in all topics within a content area. If preassessment confirms that the basic content is known at the 80% level or above, the content needs to be compacted to include differentiated learning experiences with a focus on complex content.

Many states are specifying core content that requires thinking and problem solving for all children. All children need to use their minds well. National curriculum standards include content and process standards that all children and youth should reach before exiting specific grades. Because thinking and problem solving are expectations for all children, more complex and challenging experiences must be available for children who have mastered these process skills. The content for those gifted students who are ready for differentiated learning experiences must be complex, providing for continuous progress and the development of their academic capabilities. A variety of products can be used to demonstrate mastery of complex content.

To facilitate the planning process, the Planning Form for Learning Experiences was developed (see Figure 8.4). This form can be used to plan differentiated learning experiences with both basic and complex content. The planning form allows the planner to see the theme and related generalizations, as well as the topic and related content, as he or she designs learning activities. The layering of the learning experiences boxes suggests that numerous learning experiences can be developed in relationship to the content. A check in the content area box allows the teacher to use the same planning form for differentiated learning experiences with basic or complex content.

The revised cognitive taxonomy (Anderson & Krathwohl, 2001) is used for the process dimension of this model. Figure 8.5 highlights the revised taxonomy and the changes it makes to the original—nouns to verbs and switching the top two categories.

It should be noted that the process skills of remember, understand, apply, analyze, evaluate, and create are not arranged in the usual linear hierarchy. Instead, knowledge and comprehension form the foundation for all other process skills. A student cannot apply, analyze, evaluate, or create using criteria without knowledge of the topic. Starting with remember and understand, learning experiences can be developed that require students to utilize the full range of process skills while addressing core and complex content. Each time the student applies, analyzes, evaluates, or creates the content, he or she adds to the knowledge base.

Sample units provide examples of the finished product resulting from the steps described in this chapter. The completed planning forms for topical units on Patterns (primary) in Figure 8.6, the Rainforest (intermediate) in Figure 8.7, and Ancient Egypt (middle school) in Figure 8.8 illustrate how the basic learning experiences are planned in relationship to the universal themes and related generalizations. Examples of differentiated learning experiences with complex content show how the planning form can be used to remove the learning ceiling. The layered boxes on the form indicate that there can be several learning experiences at each level with the same content, but with a variety of products. The examples can be expanded to provide more student choice and to take the learning into greater depth.

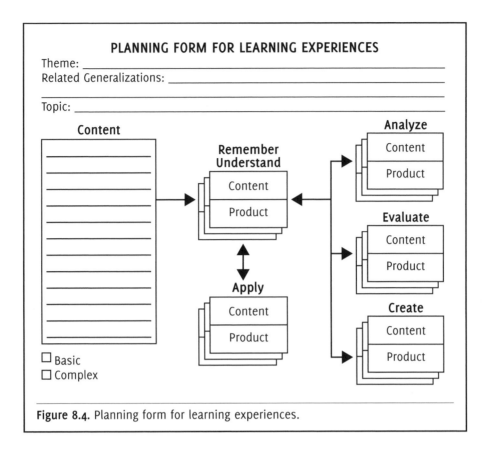

Figure 8.4. Planning form for learning experiences.

The Six Categories of the Cognitive Process Dimension

1. REMEMBER—Retrieve relevant knowledge from long-term memory
2. UNDERSTAND—Construct meaning from instructional messages, including oral, written, and graphic communication
3. APPLY—Carry out or use a procedure in a given situation
4. ANALYZE—Break material into constituent parts and determine how parts relate to one another and to an overall structure or purpose
5. EVALUATE—Make judgments based on criteria and standards
6. CREATE—Put elements together to form a coherent or functional whole, reorganize elements into a new pattern or structure

Figure 8.5. The six categories of the cognitive process dimension. *Note.* From *Strategies for Differentiating Instruction: Best Practices for the Classroom* (p. 53), by J. L. Roberts and T. F. Inman, 2007, Waco, TX: Prufrock Press. Copyright © 2007 by Prufrock Press. Reprinted with permission.

The sample units illustrate how differentiation can be planned for individual students or clusters of students based on information from the preassessment. They also show how learning experiences can be matched to needs, interests, and abilities. Not all children need to complete all learning experiences; rather, the match is the key to removing the learning ceiling. All children, including those who are gifted and talented, need challenging learning experiences in all content areas on an ongoing basis. They need to have the floor to learning raised and the ceiling removed.

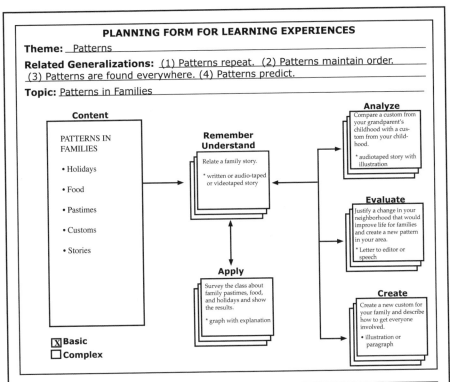

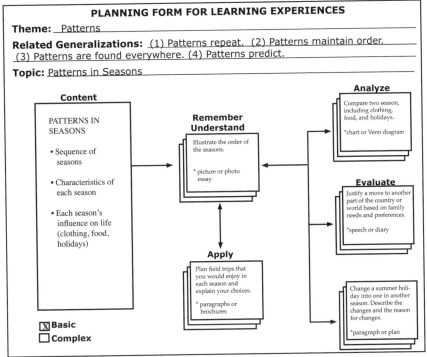

Figure 8.6. Example of completed planning form for learning experiences: Patterns.

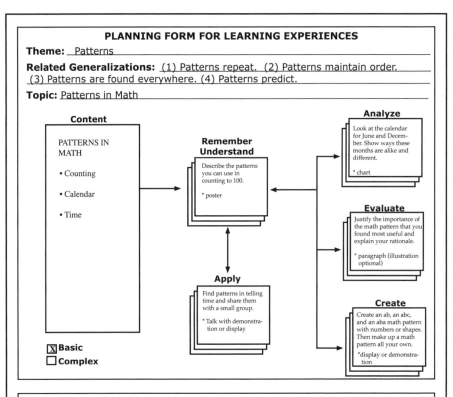

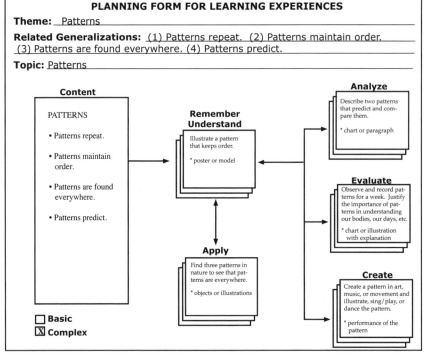

Figure 8.6. Continued.

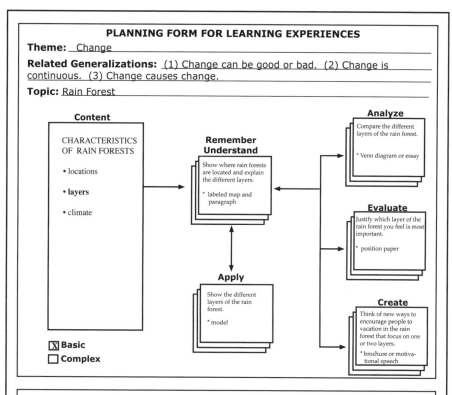

PLANNING FORM FOR LEARNING EXPERIENCES

Theme: Change

Related Generalizations: (1) Change can be good or bad. (2) Change is continuous. (3) Change causes change.

Topic: Rain Forest

Content

CHARACTERISTICS OF RAIN FORESTS

• locations

• **layers**

• climate

☒ Basic
☐ Complex

Remember Understand

Show where rain forests are located and explain the different layers.

* labeled map and paragraph

Apply

Show the different layers of the rain forest.

* model

Analyze

Compare the different layers of the rain forest.

* Venn diagram or essay

Evaluate

Justify which layer of the rain forest you feel is most important.

* position paper

Create

Think of new ways to encourage people to vacation in the rain forest that focus on one or two layers.

* brochure or motivational speech

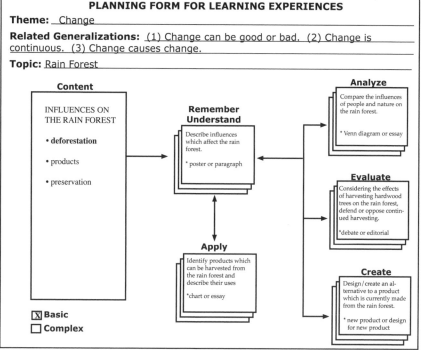

PLANNING FORM FOR LEARNING EXPERIENCES

Theme: Change

Related Generalizations: (1) Change can be good or bad. (2) Change is continuous. (3) Change causes change.

Topic: Rain Forest

Content

INFLUENCES ON THE RAIN FOREST

• **deforestation**

• products

• preservation

☒ Basic
☐ Complex

Remember Understand

Describe influences which affect the rain forest.

* poster or paragraph

Apply

Identify products which can be harvested from the rain forest and describe their uses

*chart or essay

Analyze

Compare the influences of people and nature on the rain forest.

* Venn diagram or essay

Evaluate

Considering the effects of harvesting hardwood trees on the rain forest, defend or oppose continued harvesting.

*debate or editorial

Create

Design/create an alternative to a product which is currently made from the rain forest.

* new product or design for new product

Figure 8.7. Example of completed planning form for learning experiences: Change.

LINK ROBERTS AND ROBERTS

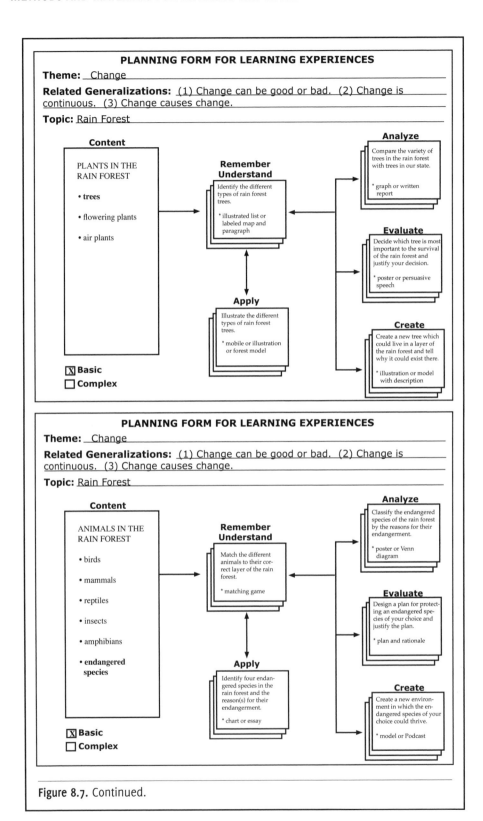

Figure 8.7. Continued.

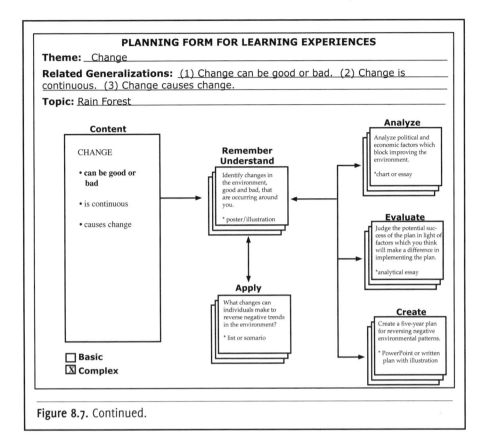

PLANNING FORM FOR LEARNING EXPERIENCES

Theme: Change

Related Generalizations: (1) Change can be good or bad. (2) Change is continuous. (3) Change causes change.

Topic: Rain Forest

Content

CHANGE

- **can be good or bad**
- is continuous
- causes change

☐ **Basic**
☒ **Complex**

Remember Understand

Identify changes in the environment, good and bad, that are occurring around you.

* poster/illustration

Apply

What changes can individuals make to reverse negative trends in the environment?

* list or scenario

Analyze

Analyze political and economic factors which block improving the environment.

*chart or essay

Evaluate

Judge the potential success of the plan in light of factors which you think will make a difference in implementing the plan.

*analytical essay

Create

Create a five-year plan for reversing negative environmental patterns.

* PowerPoint or written plan with illustration

Figure 8.7. Continued.

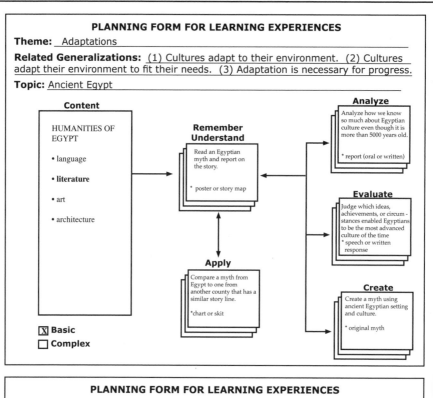

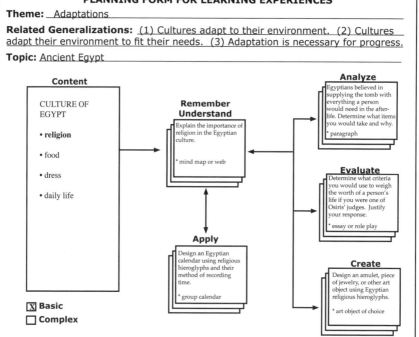

Figure 8.8. Example of completed planning form for learning experiences: Adaptations.

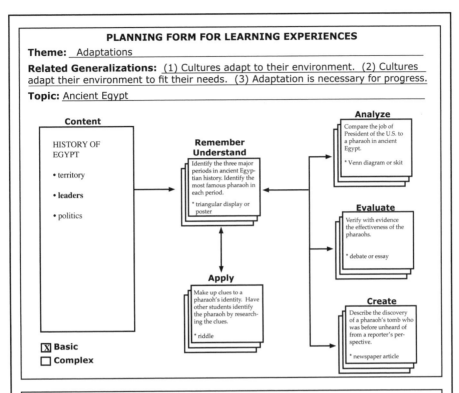

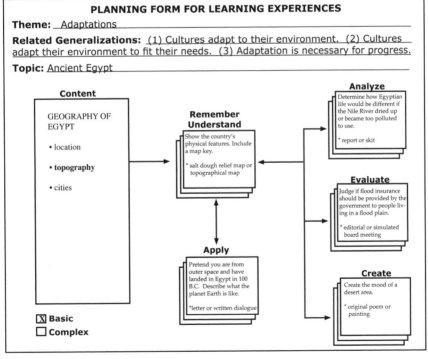

Figure 8.8. Continued.

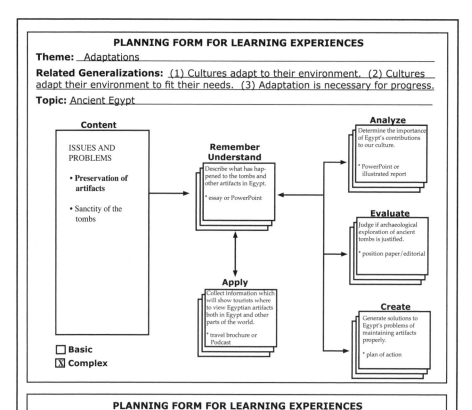

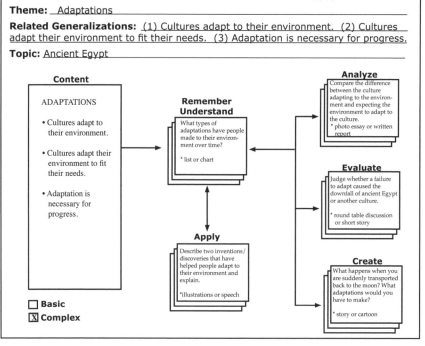

Figure 8.8. Continued.

Teacher Statement

Julia Roberts' and Dick Roberts' unit planning model provides teachers with a framework for planning differentiated lessons that allow all students the opportunity to work at an intellectually appropriate pace while providing students with learning experiences that match their needs, interests, and abilities. As a former teacher, current curriculum coordinator, and GT consultant, I have found this model consistently applicable for any teacher that removes the guesswork out of differentiation. Often times we, as teachers, are more reactive when planning for differentiation. We may give a preassessment we created after our lesson planning, copying of material, etc., only to realize that some students have already mastered or exceeded the state/national standard. As a result, we become reactive to their differentiated need. Sound familiar? We all have experienced situations such as this. How great is it that through the use of this model we become proactive and intentional when planning a unit providing intentional, complex material that is both rigorous and relevant? Moreover, one that also provides learning experiences that match students' needs, interests, and abilities, allowing us to know that we are truly meeting the educational essentials of our students. By following Roberts' and Roberts' step-by-step process, you will no longer feel inadequate or overwhelmed. You will be amazed by how engaged your students will become, resulting in a positive classroom environment that is conducive to student learning and active student engagement.

In order to achieve higher student achievement gains, it is imperative to follow all facets of the model. Through intentional use of this process, students will be provided with an overall understanding of a universal theme related to the topic, resulting in student recognition of details, trends, ethical considerations, different perspectives, points of view, and comparison of applicable events. Through collaboration with other teachers, I have also found that students gain a deeper understanding of a given topic when connected to a theme, especially when integrated across all disciplines. Further, the Planning Form for Learning Experiences template is very thorough and intentional, allowing teachers to focus on higher order thinking, utilizing Bloom's taxonomy. By providing a hierarchy of levels, this model can assist teachers in designing learning experiences, crafting questions, and providing feedback on student work. The examples provided in the chapter are an excellent resource that all educators can follow and may modify regarding student needs, keeping in mind, as noted in the chapter, that not all students need to complete all learning experiences.

In closing, if you have not already noticed, I am a huge advocate of Roberts' and Roberts' model, as it lends itself to intentional planning, which meets the needs of all students. I will reiterate, that when implementing this model, you will spend more time on planning for differentiated needs than you have ever before. However, keep in mind that the time you spend on planning will make up for itself when you begin implementation of the unit. No longer will you have to guess where the student need is; rather, you will have an intentional planning unit that appeals to all learner needs. You will become the facilitator and will be amazed at how the students guide you in their learning. I can only stress how intentional planning makes students feel that you took the time to take each of their individual needs into consideration. I know I was astounded when I first implemented the model.

—Natalia D. Estes

DISCUSSION QUESTIONS

1. What factors in a classroom or school create a learning ceiling?

2. What can teachers and school leaders do to remove the learning ceiling for a student or for a cluster of students?

3. What are the benefits of removing the learning ceiling? You may want to interview a couple of gifted students and their parents while considering the benefits.

4. Julian Stanley (2000) wrote an article entitled "Helping Students Learn Only What They Don't Already Know." Would teachers in your school agree or disagree with that idea? Why or why not?

5. What methods have you used to assess your students' knowledge and skills prior to teaching a unit, and how did you use that information to ensure continuous progress for each student in your class? How could you use that preassessment information to guide future instruction?

6. If you were observing in a classroom in which the teacher was differentiating the curriculum, what teacher behaviors could you observe?

7. If you were observing in a classroom in which the curriculum was being differentiated, what could you observe students doing?

8. Various professional organizations stress the importance of providing a rigorous curriculum to students. Think about the students you teach. What does providing a rigorous curriculum mean to each student in your class? Does the meaning of what a rigorous curriculum is differ from one student to another?

9. Rigor, relevance, and relationships—These terms have taken on great importance in schools. How do you increase rigor, relevance, and relationships as you differentiate learning experiences, matching learning experiences to learner readiness, interests, and learning preferences?

Teacher Resources

Publications

Center for Gifted Studies. (1996). *Incorporating broad-based thematic units into the curriculum* [Videotape]. Bowling Green, KY: Western Kentucky University.

Center for Gifted Studies. (1996). *Opening up the curriculum: Getting rid of the ceiling* [Videotape]. Bowling Green, KY: Western Kentucky University.

Clarke, C. L., & Agne, R. M. (1997). *Interdisciplinary high school teaching: Strategies for integrated learning.* Needham Heights, MA: Allyn & Bacon.

Kaplan, S. N. (1993). *Developing thematic interdisciplinary curriculum for middle schools.* Bowling Green, KY: Western Kentucky University.

Karnes, F. A., & Stephens, K. R. (2009). *The ultimate guide for student product development and evaluation* (2nd ed.). Waco, TX: Prufrock Press.

Roberts, J. L., & Boggess, J. R. (2012). *Differentiating instruction with centers in the gifted classroom.* Waco, TX: Prufrock Press.

Roberts, J. L., & Boggess, J. R. (2011). *Teacher's survival guide: Gifted education.* Waco, TX: Prufrock Press.

Roberts, J. L., & Inman, T. F. (2015). *Assessing differentiated student products: A protocol for development and evaluation* (2nd ed.). Waco, TX: Prufrock Press.

Roberts, J. L., & Inman, T. F. (2015). *Strategies for differentiating instruction: Best practices for the classroom* (3rd ed.). Waco, TX: Prufrock Press.

Roberts, J. L., & Inman, T. F. (2013). *Teacher's survival guide: Differentiating instruction in the elementary classroom.* Waco, TX: Prufrock Press.

Samara, J., & Curry, J. (1994). *Developing units for primary students.* Bowling Green, KY: Association for Gifted Education.

Samara, J., & Curry, J. (1995). *Product guides.* Austin, TX: The Curriculum Project.

Websites

American Association for the Advancement of Science: Benchmarks for Science Literacy—http://www.project2061.org/tools/benchol/bolframe.htm

American Council on the Teaching of Foreign Languages: National Standards for Foreign Language Education—http://www.actfl.org/i4a/pages/index.cfm?pageid=3392

Center for Civic Education: National Standards for Civics and Government— http://www.civiced.org/standards

Common Core State Standards for English Language Arts—http://www.corestandards.org/ELA-Literacy

Common Core State Standards for Mathematics—http://www.corestandards.org/Math/

Framework for Social Studies Standards—http://www.ccsso.org/Resources/Publications/Vision_for_the_College_Career_and_Civic_Life_Framework_for_Inquiry_in_Social_Studies_State_Standards.html

National Center for History in the Schools: National Standards for History Basic Edition, 1996—http://nchs.ucla.edu/standards

National Center for History in the Schools: National Standards for World History Grades 5–12—http://www.sscnet.ucla.edu/nchs/standards/worldera1.html

National Council for the Social Studies: Curriculum Standards for Social Studies—http://www.socialstudies.org/standards

National Council of Teachers of English: Standards for the English Language Arts—http://www.ncte.org/standards/ncte-ira

National Council of Teachers of Mathematics: Principles and Standards for School Mathematics—http://standards.nctm.org/document

National Council for Geographic Education: Geography for Life: National Geography Standards, Second Edition—http://www.ncge.org/geography-for-life

National Academies Press: National Science Education Standards—http://www.nap.edu/openbook.php?record_id=4962

The Kennedy Center: ARTSEDGE: National Standards for Arts Education—http://artsedge.kennedy-center.org/educators/standards/standards

References

Anderson, L. W., & Krathwohl, D. R. (Eds.). (2001). *A taxonomy for learning, teaching, and assessing: A revision of Bloom's taxonomy of educational objectives* (Abridged ed.). New York, NY: Longman.

Bloom, B. (Ed.). (1956). *Taxonomy of educational objectives: The classification of educational goals. Handbook I: Cognitive domain.* New York, NY: Longmans Green.

Buzan, T. (1983). *Use both sides of your brain.* New York, NY: Dutton.

Center for Civic Education. (1994). *National standards for civics and government.* Calabasas, CA: Author.

Consortium of National Arts Education Associations. (1994). *National standards for arts education: What every young American should know and be able to do in the arts.* Reston, VA: Music Educators National Conference.

Geography Education Standards Project. (1994). *National geography standards: Geography for life.* Washington, DC: National Geographic Society.

Kaplan, S. N. (1993). *Developing thematic interdisciplinary curriculum for middle schools.* Bowling Green: Western Kentucky University.

Karnes, F. A., & Bean, S. M. (2004). *Process skills rating scales–Revised.* Waco, TX: Prufrock Press.

Karnes, F. A., & Stephens, K. R. (2009). *The ultimate guide for student product development and evaluation* (2nd ed.). Waco, TX: Prufrock Press.

National Academy of Sciences, National Academy of Engineering, and Institute of Medicine. (2007). *Rising above the gathering storm: Energizing and employing America for a brighter economic future.* Washington, DC: The National Academies Press.

National Council for History Standards. (1994a). *National standards for United States history: Expanding children's world in time and space, grades K–4.* Los Angeles, CA: National Center for History in the Schools.

National Council for History Standards. (1994b). *National standards for United States history: Exploring the American experience, grades 5–12.* Los Angeles, CA: National Center for History in the Schools.

National Council for History Standards. (1994c). *National standards for world history: Exploring paths to the present, grades 5–12.* Los Angeles, CA: National Center for History in the Schools.

National Council of Teachers of English, & International Reading Association. (1996). *Standards for the English language arts.* Urbana, IL: NCTE.

National Council of Teachers of Mathematics. (2006). *Curriculum focal points for pre-kindergarten through grade 8 mathematics: A quest for coherence.* Reston, VA: Author.

National Education Commission on Time and Learning. (1994). *Prisoners of time.* Washington, DC: Author.

National Governors Association Center for Best Practices, & Council of Chief State School Officers. (2010a). *Common Core State Standards for English language arts.* Retrieved from http://www.corestandards.org/ELA-Literacy

National Governors Association Center for Best Practices, & Council of Chief State School Officers. (2010b). *Common Core State Standards for mathematics.* Retrieved from http://www.corestandards.org/math

National Science Board. (2010). *Preparing the next generation of STEM innovators: Identifying and developing our nation's human capital.* Arlington, VA: National Science Foundation.

National Standards in Foreign Language Education Project. (1996). *Standards for foreign language learning: Preparing for the 21st Century.* Yonkers, NY: Author.

Next Generation Science Standards. (2013). *Next generation science standards.* Washington, DC: Achieve Inc. Retrieved from http://www.nextgenscience.org/next-generation-science-standards

No Child Left Behind Act, 20 U.S.C. §6301 (2001).

Plucker, J. A., Burroughs, N., & Song, R. (2010). *Mind the (other) gap?: The growing excellence gap in K–12 education.* Bloomington, IN: Center for Evaluation and Education Policy.

Roberts, J. L., & Boggess, J. R. (2011). *Teacher's survival guide: Gifted education.* Waco, TX: Prufrock Press.

Roberts, J. L., & Inman, T. F. (2015). *Assessing differentiated student products: A protocol for development and evaluation* (2nd ed.). Waco, TX: Prufrock Press.

Stanley, J. C. (2000). Helping students learn only what they don't already know. *Psychology, Public Policy, and Law, 6,* 216–222.

Tomlinson, C. A. (2002, November 6). Proficiency is not enough. *Education Week, 22,* 36, 38.

U.S. Department of Education, Office of Educational Research and Improvement. (1993). *National excellence: A case for developing America's talent.* Washington, DC: U.S. Government Printing Office.

Winebrenner, S. (1992). *Teaching gifted kids in the regular classroom.* Minneapolis, MN: Free Spirit.

Winebrenner, S. (1999). Shortchanging the gifted. *The School Administrator, 56*(9), 12–16.

Winebrenner, S. (2001). *Teaching gifted kids in the regular classroom* (Rev. ed.). Minneapolis, MN: Free Spirit Press.

MAKING THE GRADE OR ACHIEVING THE GOAL?

9
Chapter

Evaluating Learner and Program Outcomes in Gifted Education

BY CAROLYN M. CALLAHAN

While planning and outlining instruction, administrators and teachers are apt to consider the general goals of the educational program and the day-to-day objectives of instructional activities. Exemplary teachers are also tuned in to the selection of activities that students will find engaging; however, in planning instruction for gifted students, educators should also consider other fundamentally important questions such as: "How will I assess what the students have learned?" and "How will I document the degree to which students are achieving the outcomes of instructional efforts?" Effective planning at the classroom and program level involves asking these questions:

» Are gifted students achieving goals and objectives they would not otherwise achieve if not for this instruction?
» Are student achievements new achievements?
» Is instruction leading to high-level student performance?
» Do the students know and understand the content of the curriculum?
» Can they effectively use the skills they are learning?

For educators to assess the degree to which they are making a difference with gifted students or judge whether the students are benefiting from the curriculum and instruction offered, they must collect reliable and valid data about the impact of curricular choices, instructional planning, and delivery of instruction. Measuring student achievement of objectives in the cognitive domain (knowledge and understanding of the disciplines and the development of skills in a variety of tasks) is one important aspect of this evaluation process, but educators should also assess the ways in which variables such as student attitudes, sense of self, and other affective domains are influenced by instruction. Classroom assessment of student achievement is important for feedback to students and communication with parents about student progress.

Student learning outcomes are also indicators of program success, and data collected on student growth are one source of information critical to various stakeholders in determining whether the investment of money, teacher time, and student time is warranted. Although student learning is a part of summative judgments of program success, full understanding of the factors contributing to overall student and program success, or lack of success, contributes to effective and efficient use of resources. Evaluating the ways in which the design and delivery of particular aspects of a gifted program and its related services contribute to the ultimate goal of gifted student growth and development will lead to greater likelihood of maximizing student academic success and to positive development in social and emotional realms as well. Hence, to ensure full and complete attention to quality educational services for gifted students, educators must assume responsibility for evaluating all components of the services offered to gifted students. To come full circle, effective evaluation in gifted programs requires the collection of valid data about both the immediate outcomes of ongoing day-to-day classroom instruction and student achievement relative to the long-term goals and objectives of the program. Teachers can make more effective decisions about student learning and lesson effectiveness when they plan for quality assessment of lesson objectives, and administrators can make good program decisions when they collect appropriate information and correctly interpret data about various components of service delivery modes, particularly those features of the program that positively influence the accomplishments of students and those that detract from maximum achievement.

Of course, determining whether or not a program is successful in achieving its targets relative to student outcomes rests on the willingness and skill of teachers and administrators to delineate clear long-term goals and intermediate benchmarks that indicate progress toward those goals. Only then can they assess the degree to which those benchmarks and goals are achieved and modify the program to enhance the probability for success.

The Importance of Careful Classroom Assessment in the Instructional Process

Assessment of students throughout the instructional process provides the greatest opportunity to assure that student learning is maximized. The collection of valid and reliable student data is critical: (a) prior to planning instruction (pre-assessment), (b) during the instructional process (formative assessment), and (c) at the conclusion of an instructional unit (summative or outcome assessment to determine the success of the teaching process and the extent of student learning).

Preassessment

Theorists and researchers have demonstrated that the greatest student learning will occur when learning activities are designed so that the tasks presented are not already within the repertoire of the learner. After all, students are not learning if they are just doing what they already know how to do, yet the learning activity must not be so far beyond the student's current knowledge or understanding that efforts to engage in the learning activity would prove futile. Learning is maximized when successful performance of a task is just within the students' reach, giving students an opportunity to develop new knowledge, skills, or understandings built on existing frameworks (content and skill knowledge already mastered). The "newness" in a learning task may include the attainment of new ideas, concepts, principles, or generalizations. Newness may also be derived from structuring a task based on the students' current levels of discipline mastery, but requiring them to use more advanced skills in applying that knowledge to a new, more advanced problem, consideration of an issue that requires transfer of knowledge, or production of a product that goes beyond replication. The task may also press students to probe for deeper and more complex understanding of familiar concepts, principles, or generalizations from the discipline.

The difference between what a given child can do on his or her own and what can be accomplished with a little assistance and processing is called "the zone of proximal development" (Vygotsky, 1986). Vygotsky believed instruction should be aimed just outside the limits of what a learner currently knows and can do, so in order to fashion appropriate curricula for any group of children, teachers must gather information about the current state of the learners' expertise by engaging in careful preassessment and ongoing formative assessment. For gifted students, this process is critical because their current levels of knowledge and skills are likely to be out of the normative range of their age or grade peers and the speed with which they attain new proficiencies more rapid than the average student. Teachers cannot rely on traditional assumptions about the developmental accomplishments or curricular achievements of the average fourth grader as a guide to the appropriate instructional level for a gifted fourth grader. Similarly, teachers cannot make the mistake of assuming that all gifted students of the same age level are alike or that a group of gifted students is equally advanced across all disciplines or potential talent domains. They cannot assume that a child identified as gifted has attained equal levels of achievement across all discipline areas. A child with very advanced skills in reading may not have achieved advanced levels of mastery of mathematics concepts and skills. He or she may be achieving on grade level in mathematics. Hence, success in preparing instructional activities for gifted students requires recognition of and planning for the great variability in achievement and aptitude across gifted students and within the individual gifted child.

Preassessment of the content domain should encompass both measures of knowledge and understanding as well as evaluations of process skills and those in product production. Preassessment may take place using informal activities or formal assessment tools. Accordingly, the sources of data a teacher can use for preassessment of levels of achievement range from test data, to self-reported data, to observation of student performance. In addition, results of summative assessments in prior units may provide valuable information about individual students for planning entry level instruction, needed scaffolding, and/or areas of mastery that need not be addressed by some students in a subsequent unit. Assessment data collected at the end of one unit of instruction about attained level of knowledge, skill, and understanding also can be critical to informing the next stage of instruction. To gather preassessment data using self-reports, students can be presented a simple checklist or rating scale on which they indicate their familiarity with the concepts within the unit to be taught or with the expected skills. For example, students can be asked to indicate if they have never heard of the topic (or know nothing about this topic), have learned some basic things about the topic ("I know a little about this"), or feel ready to teach others about it ("I am an expert in this topic"). An informal preassessment activity can include a concept map where the teacher gives each child the unifying concept of instruction (e.g., energy in science) and asks the students to create a diagram of all of the examples they can think of or all of the other concepts or ideas to which they think energy is related. Such a diagram will reveal the level of understanding and breadth of knowledge about the topic/construct. See Figures 9.1 and 9.2 for examples of preassessment tools.

Formative or In-Process Assessment

Gifted students are not a homogeneous group, and they learn at different rates and respond differently to the set of activities designed to lead to particular learning outcomes. For gifted students, the assumption that they all are learning at the same rate or are processing and producing products at the same rate may

We are going to be studying unique ways that poets use language to create images and feelings. I need to know what you already know so I can make the lessons most interesting for you. There may be some terms you have heard of and maybe some you have studied before, but I think many of these words will be new to you. This is not a test for a grade, but I do hope you will try your very best.

For each of the terms below (called poetic devices) circle the number in the Self-Evaluation column that shows me what you know about this term. You may choose 1, 2, 3, or 4 **OR** you may choose 3 and 4 if both describe you.

Poetic Device	Self-Evaluation
Tone	1-I never heard of this term. 2-I have heard of it, but I don't know very much at all. 3-I am very familiar with this term and can identify tone in poems. 4-I am very familiar with this term and can use it in writing my own poetry.
Stanza	1-I never heard of this. 2-I have heard of it, but I don't know very much at all. 3-I am very familiar with this term and can identify a stanza in poems. 4-I am very familiar with this term and can use it in writing my own poetry.
Simile	1-I never heard of this. 2-I have heard of it, but I don't know very much at all. 3-I am very familiar with this term and can identify similes in poems. 4-I am very familiar with this term and can use it in writing my own poetry.
Metaphor	1-I never heard of this. 2-I have heard of it, but I don't know very much at all. 3-I am very familiar with this term and can identify metaphors in poems. 4-I am very familiar with this term and can use it in writing my own poetry.
Personification	1-I never heard of this. 2-I have heard of it, but I don't know very much at all. 3-I am very familiar with this term and can identify personification in poems. 4-I am very familiar with this term and can use it in writing my own poetry.
Alliteration	1-I never heard of this. 2-I have heard of it, but I don't know very much at all. 3-I am very familiar with this term and can identify alliteration in poems. 4-I am very familiar with this term and can use it in writing my own poetry.
Hyperbole	1-I never heard of this. 2-I have heard of it, but I don't know very much at all. 3-I am very familiar with this term and can identify hyperbole in poems. 4-I am very familiar with this term and can use it in writing my own poetry.

Figure 9.1. A sample preassessment for a series of lessons on the use of poetic devices in a unit on poetry.

Poetic Device	Self-Evaluation
Symbol	1-I never heard of this. 2-I have heard of it, but I don't know very much at all. 3-I am very familiar with this term and can identify symbols in poems. 4-I am very familiar with this term and can use it in writing my own poetry.
Onomatopoeia	1-I never heard of this. 2-I have heard of it, but I don't know very much at all. 3-I am very familiar with this term and can identify onomatopoeia in poems. 4-I am very familiar with this term and can use it in writing my own poetry.
Imagery	1-I never heard of this. 2-I have heard of it, but I don't know very much at all. 3-I am very familiar with this term and can identify imagery in poems. 4-I am very familiar with this term and can use it in writing my own poetry.
Speaker/Voice	1-I never heard of this. 2-I have heard of it, but I don't know very much at all. 3-I am very familiar with this term and can identify voice in poems. 4-I am very familiar with this term and can use it in writing my own poetry.

Figure 9.1. Continued.

be an erroneous assumption that leads to some students not being challenged because they "get it" the first time a concept is presented and others needing more instruction or practice than has been offered to master the concept. Hence, "taking the temperature" of students frequently during a unit of instruction—even during or after a given day's activity—can help guide decision making. Teachers may have students fill out an exit card labeled "What I learned today (this week) in math" at the end of the day or week to gauge students' learning, or they might give students a checklist with important concepts and ask them to check all those for which they are ready to be "tested." Or, they may give students red, yellow, and green cards (with white backgrounds) that they can flash when a question is asked to indicate to the teacher whether they are following the discussion or are making progress comfortably toward the objective for the day. Although the white background makes the response anonymous if students are sitting in rows and only show the color forward to the teacher, alternative seating arrangements might make the use of such cards threatening to students. In those cases, teachers can give students colored sticky notes to stick to the desk or another unobtrusive place.

Many of the models of curriculum development in gifted education suggest product development as core to the model (e.g., Azano, 2013; Kaplan, 2013;

We are going to be studying unique ways that poets use language to create images and feelings. I need to know what you already know so I can make the lessons most interesting for you. There may be some terms you have heard of and maybe some you have studied before, but I think many of these words will be new to you. This is not a test for a grade, but I do hope you will try your very best.

In the left column, I have listed some of the words we use to describe terms called poetic devices. Some of these terms are also used to describe use of language in other writing so you may have heard of them before. In the right hand column are examples. Please write the letter of the example that best matches the term on the blank beside the term.

_____ Simile

_____ Metaphor

_____ Personification

_____ Alliteration

_____ Onomatopoeia

_____ Hyperbole

_____ Symbol

a. Peter Piper picked a peck of pickled peppers.

b. Mary had a little lamb its fleece was white as snow.

c. The only sounds are the snip, snip of scissors and the hum of sewing machines.

d. I have told you a thousand times not to do that.

e. All the world's a stage.

f. The leaves danced in the wind on the cold October afternoon.

g. Life is a roller coaster.

Figure 9.2. Alternative preassessment.

Renzulli, 2013; Tomlinson, 2013). Successful student planning and execution of a project also requires formative assessment; it is a fallacious assumption that students, even gifted students, have the prerequisite skills to complete a product that demonstrates advanced learning using sophisticated product production skills. A teacher may choose to distribute a brief survey to students as they engage in the preparation of a project or product. Or, a teacher may elect to have checkpoints at which students submit work completed up to the point of review. Formative assessment is not intended for grading or final evaluative purposes. It should be used to help teachers *and* students gauge progress toward attaining learning objectives. See Figure 9.3 for an example of a quick formative assessment of students' progress.

Outcome Assessment

Collecting evaluative information serves to provide students and their parents with feedback about student growth and achievements in response to the learning activities and in relation to expected outcomes and levels of performance. Carefully developed and clear procedures for evaluating students provide information about what students have achieved, their areas of strengths and weaknesses, and how their performance relates to standards of excellence. Informing

In today's class we looked at how poets use *metaphors* to create images in their poems. I am interested in finding out about how successful this lesson was. Please check all of the items below that describe how you feel after today's class.

____ I can define a metaphor.
____ I can find examples of metaphors in poems.
____ I understand how a metaphor is used to create an image by a poet.
____ I could write a metaphor that would enhance my poem's imagery.

Please write an example of a metaphor in the space below. Please create a metaphor that was not examined in class today.

_____

_____

_____

_____

Figure 9.3. Sample formative assessment.

students of standards of performance, rewarding efforts to achieve, and providing guidance in the next steps in further growth and development toward expertise are very important to ensuring that students get the most from their learning experiences.

Assessing student learning does not just provide information about the achievement of the students. Teachers may also learn a great deal about the quality of the curriculum or the instruction. A teacher should not assume that an instructional activity or a series of activities that make up an instructional unit all will be equally successful or equally successful with all gifted students. Making accurate judgments about what students have learned in response to any curricular segment provides essential information about the relative success of individual students *and also about the instruction.* Often, in focusing on the "holes" or gaps in student achievement, the only evaluation that is made reflects on students. The data also may be important in judging the success of lessons/activities, units of study, or overall curricular framework.

Assessment may yield data about unintended outcomes, as well. For example, a negative unintended consequence occurs when study of a unit results in increased scores in the achievement domain, but at the same time students lose interest in the study of a topic or even a domain of study because of the nature of the activities. As a case in point, some science units reflecting physics principles are taught using machines with which males tend to be familiar and or intrigued (e.g., automobile engines). Females in the class may learn the principles but decide that physics is not something they wish to pursue because of their stereotypic judgments about the discipline that are reinforced by the learning activities. Thus, evaluation information provides critical data about what to teach next to an individual gifted child and to groups of gifted children, as well as the cognitive and affective changes that occur as a result of the instruction.

Outcome, or summative evaluation, not only informs about individual students, it also provides valuable information about the effectiveness of curriculum development and instructional activities in contributing to the overall growth and development of gifted students. In particular, educators should use outcome assessment to judge whether the program and services being provided for gifted students result in achievements that would not otherwise be possible. The evaluation of learner outcomes serves many purposes. It provides students and their parents with information about the quantity and quality of student learning and performance. Evaluation of learner outcomes also serves as a basis for assessing the effectiveness of instruction, is one variable to consider in future instructional planning, and is a critical cornerstone of good program evaluation.

In order for the learner outcomes to be meaningfully assessed, whether at the program or classroom level, educators must carefully plan the evaluation process beginning with clearly articulated goals and objectives. Of course, there are often unintended outcomes, both positive and negative, that cannot be anticipated, but evaluation must begin with a clear sense of expectations for learning.

One of the most challenging tasks for educators in the field of gifted education is the specification of the expected outcomes of instruction. To assess the degree to which an instructional activity or a curricular unit has been successful, educators must be able to specify the ways in which they expect the learner to be different as a result of the teaching/learning process. The level of specificity of outcomes ranges from broad, general, and long-term statements of expectations as program goals, to specific activity-guiding objectives for teachers to use on a daily basis. Teachers must be able to specify what students will be expected to know, understand, and do as a result of the experiences provided by the instructional program.

Classroom assessment usually relates to specified learner outcomes relating to units of instruction; however, in a well-developed gifted program, those objectives should relate to the overarching goals of the program. Accordingly, in this chapter, the discussion of program and curricular model goal statements precedes discussion of specific classroom objectives and measurement.

Sources of Program Goal Statements Relating to Learner Outcomes: Program and Curricular Models

Many of the models proposed for developing programs or curricula for gifted students have explicitly stated goals, while many others imply goals. For example, a program basing its instruction on the Schoolwide Enrichment Model (Renzulli & Reis, 2013) would be expected to have learner outcomes specifying that students will be able to:

- » apply interests, knowledge, creative ideas, and task commitment to a self-selected problem or area of study;
- » acquire advanced level understanding of the knowledge (content) and methodology (process) used within specific disciplines, artistic areas of expression, and interdisciplinary studies;
- » develop authentic products that are primarily directed toward bringing about a desired impact on a specified audience;
- » develop self-directed learning skills in the areas of planning, organization, resource utilization, time management, decision making, and self-evaluation; and
- » develop task commitment, self-confidence, and feelings of creative accomplishment. (p. 202)

In programs based on the Autonomous Learner Model (Betts, 1986) students would be expected to:

- » comprehend the dynamics of the group process; and
- » apply the dynamics of group process to their environment. (p. 39)

Kaplan's (1986, 2005, 2013) Depth and Complexity curricular model, derived from the Principles of Differentiated Curriculum for the Gifted and Talented, implies that students will:

- » develop skills in conducting a project, action research and/or independent study reflecting in-depth learning within a self-selected study topic;
- » comprehend, investigate, and/or analyze new subject matter using critical, creative, logical, or problem-solving skills;
- » "think like a disciplinarian"—understand the language of the discipline, learn and organize the details of the discipline, recognize patterns and trends in the discipline, and bring about change using complex, abstract, and/or higher level thinking skills;
- » research skills and methods; and
- » create products that will challenge existing ideas and produce "new" ideas.

Further, students should attain goals such as:

» recognize classical ideas of a discipline;
» identify associations (connections, relationships, and links) that exist within, between, and among areas or disciplines of study;
» recognize key concepts that guide inquiry into content;
» define the point of initiation or beginning of a pattern; and
» establish the relationship between contributions in a discipline and rules of a discipline.

Specific curricular units to be used in a classroom based on models such as these should reflect the overall goals of the model or program, but more specific objectives are needed to guide year-to-year, month-to-month, and day-to-day instruction. Specificity may come from fitting the goal into more narrowly defined parameters, specifying a level of achievement, or defining the discipline within which a process will be applied. For example, a unit based on Kaplan's (1986, 2005, 2013) model includes the following specific objective:

> Students will define, explain, and exemplify the statement that "systems follow rules, procedures, and an order" by studying the communications system of writing, the ecological system of the rain forest, the governmental system of how a bill becomes a law, and the mathematical system of measurement. (California Department of Education, 1996, p. 1–2)

Another example from Kaplan (2013) would be:

> Students will define the trends leading to the Industrial Revolution and comparatively relate these trends to patterns of another revolution. They will read primary and secondary resources to determine the effects of the Industrial Revolution over time in order to support the big idea that "Revolutions can provide both a beginning and an ending." Students will be prepared to debate the big idea using the language of the discipline. (p. 282)

A program focusing on Renzulli's (2013) Schoolwide Enrichment Model might elect to specify certain Type II outcomes (process skill development) during a given time period in which students are exposed to the kinds of work that historians pursue. For example, the teachers might focus on objectives such as making sure that students are able to:

» generate clear, researchable, correctly worded hypotheses about the influences on historical events;
» discriminate between primary and secondary sources; and

» evaluate the relative reliability and validity of historical documents.

Programs not based on specific models must generate their own goals and objectives. Furthermore, model-independent programs still need to specify outcome expectations. Such a program might operate from a set of outcomes such as ensuring that students:

» exhibit improved critical thinking and problem-solving skills,
» demonstrate greater independent learning,
» produce creative products,
» demonstrate greater self-esteem,
» demonstrate positive attitudes toward school,
» value excellence in learning, and
» demonstrate in-depth understanding of the epistemology of at least one discipline (Callahan & Caldwell, 1993).

Even these goals need to be translated into specific objectives that are clearly delineated and evaluated in the classroom for each unit of instruction. For example, Burns (1993) broke critical thinking skills into specific objectives. Students will:

» recognize statements within an argument that reflect appraisals of worth that cannot be documented through objective means,
» recognize the various individuals or groups that may have differing sets of observations or priorities that influence their perspectives on a given argument,
» recognize information within an argument that is value laden or stereotypical, and
» distinguish between statements in an argument that can be proven and those statements that reflect personal beliefs or judgments. (p. 10)

Sources of Program Goal Statements Relating to Learner Outcomes: National and State Standards

Program and curriculum models provide one set of goals and objectives for gifted student learning. In addition, two current trends in education have implications for the instruction and assessment of gifted students. First, many schools are implementing service delivery models for gifted students based on differentiation within the regular classroom. Second, current emphasis on national and state standards, particularly the Common Core State Standards (CCSS) initiative and 21st-century skills has impacted instruction at all levels.

The challenge to the classroom teacher is to find ways (a) to differentiate the instruction that will challenge all learners while addressing these standards and (b) to create measures of achievement that reflect the students' level of learning. In these cases, teachers need to adapt their instruction to ensure student attainment of the basic content knowledge and rudimentary skills while modifying tasks and assessment to reflect mastery of multiple levels of sophistication of the increasingly more complex objectives. For example, because all students would be likely to master objectives such as "Fluently add and subtract multi-digit whole numbers using the standard algorithm" (National Governor's Association [NGA] Center for Best Practices & Council of Chief State School Officers [CCSSO], 2010d) or "Explain major differences between poems, drama, and prose, and refer to the structural elements of poems (e.g., verse, rhythm, meter) and drama (e.g., casts of characters, settings, descriptions, dialogue, stage directions) when writing or speaking about a text" (NGA & CCSSO, 2010b), the teacher likely would use common paper-and-pencil or simple performance assessments to measure outcomes, which would be the same for all students. On the other hand, if the objective is to "Compare and contrast the treatment of similar themes and topics (e.g., opposition of good and evil) and patterns of events (e.g., the quest) in stories, myths, and traditional literature from different cultures" (NGA & CCSSO, 2010b), assessments likely would be more complex and differentiated in order to assess different levels of expected sophistication in choice of texts, complexity and subtlety of themes and patterns, and depth of understanding of the meaning.

Whether the program is directed by goals specified by models in gifted education, by goals and objectives that emanate from the administrators or teachers, and/or by state and national standards, the outcomes specified for learners should come from both the cognitive and affective domains, and, sometimes, from the psychomotor domain.

The Cognitive Dimension: Content, Process, and Product Outcomes

Content Assessment

The content dimension is the first of the three dimensions that comes to mind when most classroom teachers consider the evaluation of cognitive outcomes for gifted students. Although the dimensions of process, product, and content should be integrated in the instructional plan and often can be most efficiently and effectively evaluated in a single product or performance task, they are presented separately here for ease of discussion. There also are occasions when it is appropriate to assess the dimensions separately. These occasions would include attempts to assess the ways in which particular aspects of the instructional process have been effective in achieving specific goals in one of the domains.

When measuring remembering, understanding, and simple application of facts, concepts/skills, procedures, and metacognitive skills (e.g., recounting stories, including fables, folktales, and myths from diverse cultures; NGA & CCSO, 2010a), then one dimension only is typically assessed; however, it is usually more efficient to measure content, process, and product outcomes in some combination using more sophisticated assessment tasks because high levels of cognition normally require an integration of these domains in the thinking and production process (Anderson & Krathwohl, 2001).

Outcome evaluation will be more valid if the teacher is able to specify the aspects of content, process, and product that will be evaluated. The examples that have been given thus far have suggested specific content. Within the example from the Kaplan model above, the content to be assessed would come from the areas of mathematics, ecology, government, and communication. The teacher would identify the specific concepts, principles, and generalizations to be taught and assessed.

Content objectives that can be used to form the basis of instruction and assessment from the specific disciplines are available from compendia developed as part of the CCSS (NGA & CCSSO, 2010c); the national standards projects in mathematics (National Council of Teachers of Mathematics, 1993), science (American Association for the Advancement of Science, 1993; National Research Council, 1995), social studies (National Council for History in the Schools, 1995), and the arts (Consortium of National Arts Education Associations, 1994); or state standards. The highest levels of learning described by these documents reflect the discipline outcomes appropriate for gifted learners. Gifted programs based on both enrichment and acceleration models easily can find specific outcome statements within these standards documents to guide teaching and assessment of learner performance. These references also indicate the ways in which content should be acted upon by learners to help them effectively incorporate the content into their cognitive structures, make meaning of the learning, apply the content to meaningful situations, and create new ideas and products. This leads to the second domain of cognitive assessment: process assessment.

Process Assessment

Within the process dimension, developers of curricula for gifted learners should consider the domains of accomplishment relating to the application of critical thinking, creative thinking, and problem-solving skills (or the analysis, evaluation, and creation levels of the new Bloom's taxonomy) and the outcomes identified in the Framework for 21st Century Learning (see http://p21.org). Educators need to determine the accomplishments of students in the realm of using, making sense of, and evaluating the new knowledge they encounter. They also need to evaluate the ways in which students use new and already mastered information to create new solutions, products, and ideas. Outcomes such as the ability to generate clearly stated and researchable hypotheses, to discriminate between primary and secondary sources, and to evaluate the relative reliability and validity of secondary sources, represent objectives in the process domain. Although the dimensions of process, product, and content are addressed independently in some assessments to be discussed in this chapter, it is nearly impossible to separate process from content. Students think about something, they create products in some domain, and they critically examine evidence and ideas about some content. The CCSS incorporate process skills with content skills; for example, "Apply the formulas $V = l \times w \times h$ and $V = b \times h$ for rectangular prisms to find volumes of right rectangular prisms with whole-number edge lengths in the context of solving real world and mathematical problems" (NGA & CCSSO, 2010e).

Therefore, in classrooms, process skills generally are measured within a content domain. For example, the item in Figure 9.4 illustrates how the process objectives mentioned above might be assessed within the social studies domain.

One excellent source of process skill objectives relating to the development of critical thinking skills is the work of Ennis (1985, 1993). Ennis and his colleagues created a comprehensive list of skills in the critical thinking domain and developed tests that measure critical thinking skills (Ennis, Millman, & Tomko, 1985). Ennis has also created a valuable website that contains information on critical thinking and an "Annotated List of Critical Thinking Tests" (http://faculty.education.illinois.edu/rhennis/TestListRevised11_27_09.htm). Faculty at Northeastern Illinois University (2005) developed a generic rating scale that can be used across disciplines (see Figure 9.5). Burns and Reis (1991) created a scope and sequence of process skills specific to instruction for gifted learners. Another useful assessment of process skills is the Process Skills Rating Scales–Revised (Karnes & Bean, 2004).

Performance/Product Assessment

Some designs for gifted programs explicitly call for performance or product outcomes. For example, the Enrichment Triad Model and the Schoolwide Enrichment Model (Renzulli & Reis, 2013) call for Type III activities as hallmarks of appropriate curricular activities for the gifted. These activities are characterized as individual or small-group "real-life" investigations on a real problem with a real audience in mind. The definition of the expected product in the

Criteria	Exemplary (8-10)	Proficient (5-7)	Needs Improvement (3-4)	Unacceptable (0-2)
Identification of Controversy Score _____: Comments:	Clearly and completely identifies and explains controversy	Identifies and explains controversy with minor lack of clarity or completeness (a maximum of one missing minor aspect of the controversy)	Does not clearly identify or explain the controversy, or identification and explanation are very unclear or incomplete	Lacks identification and explanation of the controversy or the controversy is misrepresented
Accuracy of Information Score _____: Comments:	Information is accurate throughout the paper	Information is generally accurate throughout the paper with minor errors that do not detract from overall effect	The inaccurate information detracts from overall effect	So much information is inaccurate that the rest of the paper cannot be defended
Perspective/Position Score _____: Comments:	Cleary and completely identifies and defends a policy position	Identifies and defends a policy position with minor inconsistencies	The policy position is either unclear or the defense is lacking in completion and/or clarity or the defense is illogical	A policy position is not stated or not defended
Incorporation of Jurisprudential Model Score _____: Comments:	Clearly and completely elaborates on all required elements of the jurisprudential model	Elaborates on all elements of jurisprudential model; lacks some clarity or completeness	Omits one or two elements of the jurisprudential model or fails to elaborate clearly and/or completely	Does not incorporate the jurisprudential model at all
Organization and Clarity of Writing Score _____: Comments:	Organization is logical and clear; writing is clear and easy to understand; both are easy to follow; would characterize the paper as articulate	Organization is generally logical and clear; writing is clear and easy to understand; minor difficulties in communicating ideas	Either organization is illogical and unclear or writing is unclear and difficult to follow	Organization is illogical and unclear; writing is unclear; both are difficult to follow
Grammar/Spelling Score _____: Comments:	Paper is free from any grammatical or spelling mistakes	Minimal grammar and spelling errors (less than 5)	Multiple grammar and spelling errors (more than 5; less than 10)	Many grammar and spelling errors

Figure 9.4. Rubric to score a public policy paper for implementing the jurisprudential model in a government class (developed by Mary Swanton).

Quality/Macro Criteria	No/Limited Proficiency (D&E)	Some Proficiency (C)	Proficiency (B)	High Proficiency (A)	Rating (A,B,C,D)
1. Identifies & Explains Issues	Fails to identify, summarize, or explain the main problem or question Represents the issues inaccurately or inappropriately	Identifies main issues but does not summarize or explain them clearly or sufficiently	Successfully identifies and summarizes the main issues, but does not explain why/how they are problems or create questions	Clearly identifies and summarizes main issues and successfully explains why/how they are problems or questions; and identifies embedded or implicit issues, addressing their relationships to each other	
2. Distinguishes Types of Claims	Fails to label correctly any of the factual, conceptual and value dimensions of the problems and proposed solutions	Successfully identifies some, but not all of the factual, conceptual, and value aspects of the questions and answers	Successfully separates and labels all the factual, conceptual, and value claims	Clearly and accurately labels not only all the factual, conceptual, and value, but also those implicit in the assumptions and the implications of positions and arguments	
3. Recognizes Stakeholders and Contexts	Fails accurately to identify and explain any empirical or theoretical contexts for the issues Presents problems as having no connections to other conditions or contexts	Shows some general understanding of the influences of empirical and theoretical contexts on stakeholders, but does not identify many specific ones relevant to situation at hand	Correctly identifies all the empirical and most of theoretical contexts relevant to all the main stakeholders in the situation	Not only correctly identifies all the empirical and theoretical contexts relevant to all the main stakeholders, but also finds minor stakeholders and contexts and shows the tension or conflicts of interests among them	
4. Considers Methodology	Fails to explain how/why/which specific methods of research are relevant to the kind of issue at hand	Identifies some but not all methods required for dealing with the issue; does not explain why they are relevant or effective	Successfully explains how/why/which methods are most relevant to the problem	In addition to explaining how/why/which methods are typically used, also describes embedded methods and possible alternative methods of working on the problem	

Figure 9.5. General Education Critical Thinking Rubric from Northeastern Illinois University. From "Critical thinking rubric" by Northeastern Illinois University General Education Committee, 2005, CTL Bulletin, 11, 1–2. Copyright 2005 by NEIU General Education Committee. Reprinted with permission.

Quality/Macro Criteria	No/Limited Proficiency (D&E)	Some Proficiency (C)	Proficiency (B)	High Proficiency (A)	Rating (A,B,C,D)
5. Frames Personal Responses and Acknowledges Other Perspectives	Fails to formulate and clearly express own point of view, (or) fails to anticipate objections to his/her point of view, (or) fails to consider other perspectives and position	Formulates a vague and indecisive point of view, or anticipates minor but not major objections to his/her point of view, or considers weak but not strong alternative positions	Formulates a clear and precise personal point of view concerning the issue, and seriously discusses its weaknesses as well as its strengths	Not only formulates a clear and precise personal point of view, but also acknowledges objections and rival positions and provides convincing replies to these	
6. Reconstructs Arguments	Fails to identify the major components of the main arguments at stake and to show their logical relations	Identifies a few of the premises but confuses the conclusion of the main argument in support of the position under consideration (his or her own, or that of others)	Correctly analyzes the arguments and theories; restates its component propositions and reconstructs their relationships correctly	Not only correctly reconstructs the main argument but does the same for subsidiary arguments and theories, and correctly identifies the kind or status of each of them	
7. Interprets Content	Fails to identify and choose between the possible meanings of the key terms and propositions included in the arguments and theories in use	Clarifies the meaning of a few but far from all of the key terms and propositions involved	Convincingly explains the meaning of all the key terms and main propositions involved in the arguments and theories involved	Offers fined-grained and original interpretations of a crucial term or proposition involved in the issue	
8. Evaluates Assumptions	Fails to identify and evaluate any of the important assumptions behind the claims and recommendations made	Identifies some of the most important assumptions, but does not evaluate them for plausibility or clarity	Identifies and evaluates all the important assumptions, but not the ones deeper in the background – the more abstract ones	Not only identifies and evaluates all the important assumptions, but also some of the more hidden, more abstract ones	
9. Evaluates Evidence	Fails to identify data and information that counts as evidence for truth-claims and fails to evaluate its credibility	Successfully identifies data and information that counts as evidence but fails to thoroughly evaluate its credibility	Identifies all important evidence and rigorously evaluates it	Not only identifies and rigorously evaluates all important evidence offered, but also provides new data or information for consideration	
10. Evaluates Inferences	Fails to identify and explain mistakes in the reasoning of others and fails to avoid them in his or her own reasoning	Successfully identifies and avoids some common mistakes of reasoning but misses less common ones, and does not explain why or how they are mistakes	Identifies and avoids all mistakes of reasoning and explains some of them	Not only identifies and avoids all mistakes of reasoning but gives clear explanations of why they are mistakes.	

Figure 9.5. Continued.

Schoolwide Enrichment Model provides an outline of the expectations for evaluation. Similarly, Kaplan's (2013) framework for curriculum development includes a component calling for products that serve as both tools of learning and verification of learning. The Parallel Curriculum Model includes specific directions in each parallel for the development of products (Tomlinson et al., 2009), and the CLEAR model for development of curriculum (Continuous formative assessment, clear Learning goals, data-driven learning Experiences, Authentic products, and Rich curriculum; Azano, 2013) similarly requires students to complete products that reflect high level analysis, application, and extension of content and skills acquired in a unit of study. Because the models of gifted education and the goals for their achievement are so often tied to sophisticated performance and products, educators have been urged to use authentic assessments to evaluate and provide feedback to gifted students (Reis, 1984; Renzulli & Callahan, 2008; VanTassel-Baska, 2008).

The keys to making the use of product assessments meaningful in gifted programs are twofold. First, creators of the assessment tools must find ways to set appropriate benchmarks for gifted learners. The benchmarks used in the assessment of gifted learners should be differentiated just as the curricular goals and objectives are differentiated. As Baker and Schacter (1996) suggested, the process of setting standards may require several stages, including:

»   finding ways to set the high standards to be attained by looking for good descriptions of expert performance,
»   describing that performance level in terms understood by both the teachers and their students, and
»   translating the performance standards into scoring rubrics that are valid reflections of the standards.

Standards of excellence for gifted students too often have been set as "better than others of the same age," rather than as the level of performance of those who are accomplished in the disciplines represented by the performance or the product. As Wiggins (1993) indicated, it is critical to set high standards representing professional levels of performance even though, at a given grade level, the teacher may not have expectations that all students, or even any students, at a given age level will attain the standard. He noted the important distinction between expectations and standards. Standards are set representing the highest level of performance, while expectations represent how far a teacher might presume a given student will move toward achieving the standard at a particular point in time. Interestingly, children with talent in athletics and the arts learn at a very young age to look to models of adult accomplishment as their standard. They watch and seek to emulate LeBron James or Wynton Marsalis. Similar models can be created in the sciences, social sciences, mathematics, and the humanities.

	Rework	Near Completion	Publishable	Classic
Sound: Music in the words (i.e., rhythm, speed of lines, alliteration, repetition, consonance, assonance)	Words and lines do not follow the principles of rhythm and rhyme. The sound of the poem does not enhance its meaning.	Most words and lines follow the principles of rhythm and rhyme. The sound of the poem supports its meaning.	Words and lines follow the principles of rhythm and rhyme. The sound of the poem supports its meaning.	*I never saw a moor, I never saw the sea; Yet I know how the heather looks And what a wave must be.* —Emily Dickinson
Imagery: Words that hint at the magic of the world (i.e., metaphor, simile, symbols, pictures for the senses)	The imagery is confused, clichéd, or ineffective.	The imagery is effective in places but ineffective in others.	The imagery is effective and successfully extends the meaning of the poem.	*My bull is like the silver fish in the river white like the simmering crane bird on the river bank White like fresh milk* —Dinka Tribe

Figure 9.6. Rubric exemplifying professional standards of performance. *Note.* From *Rubric for Scoring a Poetry Unit*, by M. Libernetz, unpublished manuscript, National Research Center on the Gifted and Talented, University of Virginia, Charlottesville.

Not only do students need to know the standard, but to make performance assessment meaningful, they must come to know and understand the steps necessary to achieve that standard. Looking at professional work without a sense of the progressive growth and development necessary to achieve the standard may frustrate both student and teacher. Well-developed rubrics will reflect stages of development toward the highest standards. An example of a rubric used to score poetry in Figure 9.6 exemplifies how a standard can be translated for students so they can see the progression toward professional excellence and the way it is manifested.

Affective Outcomes

Outcome goals for gifted students often include many objectives drawn from the affective domain, as well as the cognitive domain. They may include outcomes relating to students' social behaviors, emotional adjustments, habits of mind, or all three. Group process goals, such as those illustrated by the outcome expectations stated earlier from the Autonomous Learner Model, would fall in this

For each student, rate his or her group work according the following scale.

0   Behavior is never observed or contrary behavior is observed. For example, rather than attending to the comments and suggestion of others, the student ridicules or puts down the comments of others.

1   Behavior is only observed on rare occasions. You have hardly ever observed the behavior.

2   Behavior is observed less than half the time, but at least every now and then.

3   Behavior is exhibited about half the time.

4   Behavior is observed frequently. More than half the time.

5   Student nearly always exhibits this behavior.

	Javier	Corinne	Jacob	Annalissa
Listens to the comments and suggestions of other students respectfully and with indications of paying attention to the comments				
Offers constructive suggestions to help others solve problems				
Responds appropriately to the ideas of others				
Accepts help and suggestions from others graciously				
Willingly shares materials and resources				
Shares ideas respectfully and compromises as needed				
Offers encouragement to others				

Figure 9.7. Rating collaborative group behavior.

category. These goals also might reflect expectations that students will learn social skills, such as the ability to offer and accept constructive criticism, accept the role of leader and follower in a group as appropriate, and respect the ideas of others (see Figure 9.7). Also within the realm of affective goals are self-concept, self-esteem, and self-efficacy goals.

Educators also might wish to assess the degree to which students' attitudes toward school and learning, in general or specific academic areas, are influenced by the services offered, the curriculum that is taught, and the instructional experiences of the students. After all, of what value is helping students achieve high levels of performance in a given domain if the students simultaneously develop a dislike for and aversion to ever studying this content again?

Another group of outcomes that is not easily categorized as cognitive or affective is the set of behaviors that includes accepting responsibility for one's own

	Master	Apprentice	Novice	Dependent
Planning Skills	Student creates a reasonable timeline, can work backward from due date to create specific task deadlines and plan of action. All goals reflected.	Student creates timeline and sees sequence appropriately, but timeline does not reflect all important goals.	Student creates unreasonable timelines with few checkpoints; can see a progression of tasks is necessary, but misses critical steps; needs considerable help in creating plan.	Student doesn't know where to begin task plan; must have deadlines created by others to complete the task.
Meeting deadlines	Student meets all deadlines or can present "mitigating circumstances."	Student fails to meet 1–2 deadlines; progress is consistent.	Student fails to meet 1–2 deadlines; progress is inconsistent.	Student fails to meet 3 or more deadlines; fails to make progress toward the goal.
Uses class time wisely	Student consistently and independently uses class time toward completion of assignment; can adapt when obstacles occur.	Student consistently uses class time wisely; stymied when obstacles arise.	Student uses class time wisely only when directed to do so.	Student fails to use time wisely even when directed by teacher.

Figure 9.8. Student independence.

learning; becoming an independent learner, as in Treffinger's (1986) model for self-directed learning; or becoming autonomous learners (Betts, 1986). See Figure 9.8 for an illustration of several items on a rubric relating to this type of outcome.

Also within the scope of expected outcome behaviors for gifted students are those that are categorized as habits of mind, including openness to considering new evidence, willingness to consider varying viewpoints, looking for connections and relationships, disposition to consider or speculate on possibilities, and assessing the value both socially and personally.

Psychomotor Outcomes

Within the academic domain, students are often required to create products and perform tasks that require the use of psychomotor skills, but teachers neglect to evaluate achievement of those skills (e.g., use of laboratory equipment such as a microscope or using video equipment to produce products). In the arts areas, many skills are reflected in production or performance (e.g., dramatic perfor-

Demonstrates or Projects Sensory Awareness

0   The child does not use any indicators of sensory awareness.

1   The child uses his or her body and facial features in the most basic way to indicate the sense, but is somewhat exaggerated. For example, the child's eyes are squinted to show difficulty in seeing, moves head from side to side or up and down to show looking behavior, cocks head to show listening behavior, chewing behavior for eating.

2   The child uses slightly more sophisticated facial and bodily indicators—more in proportion to the dramatic event—and exhibits the secondary characteristics of the sense. For example, facial expressions indicate sweetness, sourness, goodness, or unpleasantness of taste; eyes move to follow an object or look intently at an object; or the child is very still with appropriate facial expression to show listening intentions.

3   The child exhibits sophisticated indicators of sensory awareness. For taste, the child can show stickiness or other texture of food; for sight, there is appropriate reaction to what is seen (laughter, fear, etc.); for sound, there is a reaction to what is being heard (e.g., rhythmic reaction to music).

Emotional Responsiveness

0   The child is wooden and deadpan or maintains an unchanging facial expression with no change in emotion throughout.

1   The child changes only facial expression using only the common and broad expression associated with simple emotions (e.g., smiling or frowning), with some exaggeration.

2   The child uses facial expression and some part of the body in expressing the emotion (e.g., shrugging shoulders for indifference), but still seems somewhat forced.

3   The emotion is expressed more subtly and appears to emanate naturally from within the child.

Figure 9.9. Sample item for scoring children's dramatic performance.

mance and musical performance). Sample items from a drama rating scale are presented in Figure 9.9.

Individual vs. Group Outcomes

In many curricular frameworks designed for gifted learners and in many instructional strategies used in gifted classrooms, there are specific opportunities for the students to work in groups either by direction of the teacher or by choice. Sharan and Sharan's (1992) Group Investigation Model and Cohen and colleagues' (1994) model for cooperative learning are specifically structured so that the students are required to do tasks that reflect individual strengths, and individual contributions are combined for the greatest success in completion of the task. One of the critical issues for assessment of cooperative learning is the clear specification of how the individual student will be evaluated in these settings. Slavin (1994) recommended that there be clear individual accountability and assessment, as well as group assessments. The students should be clearly informed regarding the ways in which they will be evaluated, both individually and collectively. Further, if the group process is to be evaluated along with the group product, the teacher needs to clearly communicate the criteria and expectations for good group work to students at the introduction of the task.

Creating or Selecting the Tools to Use in Classroom Assessment

One of the critical steps in the assessment process is ensuring that the level of specificity and definition of expected outcomes will lead to using a valid assessment tool. For example, to say that one wishes to measure creativity is too broad and nebulous. Does this mean that the intent is to measure the student's creative productivity/products? What will be the specific characteristics of that productivity? To what degree are novelty, appropriateness of solution to the problem, technical quality of the product, and so forth important in assessing the product? To what degree is it appropriate to include the process that the student uses in creating the product? What about attitudes and dispositions? Before selecting or constructing an instrument to assess student growth and achievement in any of the areas discussed thus far, we must specify exactly what will be assessed with clear meanings for the terms used.

The process of selecting or constructing the appropriate tools for assessing student progress toward achieving specified goals and objectives must be based on two critical judgments. First, the instrument or tool must be valid. That is, it is important to ensure that there is evidence that the selected instrument, procedures, or both truly measure the specified objectives (hence the need described above for careful and exact language in specifying goals and objectives). Second, it is important to pay close attention to ensuring that any tool selected or constructed is reliable. That is, the score or rating given on one day should not be overly affected by how the student felt on that day, the scorer's mood on that day, error from confusion regarding directions, and so forth. The measure should yield consistent scores regardless of who administers or scores the test, performance, or product.

Types of Instruments

In the assessment process, the teacher will have to choose between formal or informal instruments and procedures; a standardized or nonstandardized instrument; self-report, peer evaluation, or teacher report; and paper-and-pencil or performance or observational tools. These categories are not always mutually exclusive.

For example, a formal assessment is one that is planned with specific guidelines for gathering information, while informal assessments are conducted in the course of everyday classroom activities. An observation, therefore, may be formal or informal. Teachers always informally observe learners throughout the course of the day, but at times they may observe for specific behaviors and record their observations using a formal rating scale or checklist to document that particular behaviors are or are not exhibited and to provide systematically collected data for reporting or planning purposes. For example, a teacher might use the rating scale that was illustrated earlier in Figure 9.7 in observing students working in a group.

Standardized instruments are those that are developed to be administered and scored according to specific guidelines, including the manner in which directions are given and the timing of the test. Most published achievement, personality, and aptitude tests are considered formal and standardized. A teacher's classroom test is usually formal, but not standardized. The reliability and validity, as well as the advantages and disadvantages, of each approach depend to some degree on the outcomes to be measured, the purpose for which data are being collected, the audience for the evaluation information collected, and the time available to construct and use the instrument or procedures.

Use of Tests to Assess Learner Outcomes

Up until the last several years, paper-and-pencil tests dominated classroom assessment. These instruments included true/false, multiple choice, matching, fill-in-the blank, and short and extended essay questions. The advantage of using multiple choice, such as the social studies process items illustrated earlier, or other objective formats in assessment are threefold: (a) The range of topics or behaviors that can be assessed in a short period of time is very large, (b) the instruments can be administered to large groups and scored relatively quickly, and (c) they are very reliable. The disadvantages of such assessments, particularly in measuring many of the goals and objectives of gifted programs, are the limited range of outcomes measured and the mismatch between the goals of a gifted program and the types of outcomes that can be measured by such tests.

Performance and Product Assessments

Many of the goals and objectives characterizing gifted programs cannot be assessed by traditional paper-and-pencil tests. Any goals that suggest creative productivity, the investigation of authentic problems, the use of alternative means of expression, or performance that emulates or represents the performance of professionals must be assessed using performance and product assessments. These products or performances may be stimulated or elicited by specific task descriptions that reflect extensions (e.g., in-depth, complexity, abstractness) or enrichment of the traditional curriculum. They allow for all students to engage in the activity with clear standards representing appropriate expectations for gifted students and ways of dealing with advanced content, sophisticated process, and authentic products. As Wiggins (1993) noted, performance assessments for the gifted should reflect the work of the professional in the discipline. An example of a structured prompt for such an assessment is presented in Figure 9.10.

The content disciplines have provided guidelines for consideration in the construction of such tasks. For example, the National Council of Teachers of Mathematics (Schulman, 1996) suggested asking:

» Does this task address important mathematical ideas?
» How can responses to this task be used to inform instruction?
» In what ways does this task call for a variety of response options and modes of response?
» Do students have adequate guides for knowing what is expected of them in this task?
» Is the student required to provide evidence for inferences made?
» Does this task align with learning goals and instructional interventions provided?

Other products or performances to be evaluated may result from long-term assignments or projects such as those described earlier as part of the Schoolwide Enrichment Model or the CLEAR curriculum. An example of one item on a rating scale to evaluate products produced by students completing a Type III activity is provided in Figure 9.11.

It is not sufficient to create the task and leave the definition of expectations and standards to chance or to comparative evaluation (comparing students' performances to each other and giving the best products A's, the next best A minus, etc.). As noted earlier, it is critical in evaluating gifted students that teachers explore what is considered the highest level of performance in the domain. Once appropriate standards of excellence or expert performance have been identified, educators must ensure that the rubrics (scoring guidelines) used to evaluate the student clearly describe for the learner the progression of development from novice-level performance to expert performance. Schack (1994) effectively outlined such a rubric for adolescent research projects. The dimensions along which research projects should be evaluated include (a) formulating the research question, (b) generating hypotheses, (c) determining sample selections, (d) selecting and implementing data-gathering techniques, (e) representing and analyzing data, (f) drawing conclusions, and (g) reporting findings. Before students get to the level at which they would do original research, they must be able to gather information, evaluate

The Best of Times

Throughout history, progress (social, technological, artistic, etc.) has led people to believe that the time in which they are living is, in many ways, the "best of times."

Travel back in time to [the teacher would fill in the appropriate year here depending on the unit of study]. Develop a role for yourself. Are you male or female? How old are you? What race are you? What are your ethnic origins? Where do you live? How long has your family lived in this region? Are you employed? What is your occupation? If you are a kid, what are your aspirations? What do you want to do when you grow up?

Think about ways your life is better than it was for people in years past.

From the perspective of your role, write an essay or develop a monologue to be presented in class that will convince others that, for you, these are the best of times. In doing this, describe your life relative to *at least three* of the following areas:

- ► Art
- ► Civil Rights Movements/Social Movements
- ► Economic Circumstances
- ► Military Conflicts
- ► New Inventions/Technology
- ► Politics

In collecting information for this task, you may use any electronic or print material you like, but you are to go beyond the information provided in your textbook. Please prepare a written reference list detailing your sources of information and how you located them.

Evaluation Criteria

Your project will be evaluated using the following criteria:

- ► Historical accuracy (How accurate are your facts?)
- ► Perspective/Point of view (How true are you to your role? Do the opinions you present correspond to the life and circumstances of the individual you are portraying?)
- ► Persuasiveness (How convincing are you? Does the reader/listener believe you are from this time period?)
- ► Thoroughness (To what extent did you use a variety of information-gathering techniques? Do you rely primarily on primary resources?)
- ► Referencing skills (Do you report your references in a standardized format?)

Figure 9.10. A sample performance assessment task. *Note.* From *The Best of Times*, by E. Coyne, n.d., unpublished manuscript, The National Research Center on the Gifted and Talented, University of Virginia, Charlottesville. Reprinted with permission.

its importance, and organize the information collected. Figure 9.12 illustrates the levels of performance that can be used to evaluate the degree to which students are learning the skills of reporting in a secondary-level research project.

Wiggins (1996) provided generic, initial dimensions or criteria for scoring the products of gifted students. He suggested considering impact by evaluating the degree of effectiveness, the level of quality of the product, and the process of creating the product:

In this rating scale, an example of performance is given that would represent the highest level of expectation.

Level of Resources
Is there evidence that the student used resources, materials, or equipment that are more advanced, technical, or complex than materials ordinarily used by students at this age/grade level?

For example, a sixth-grade student utilizes a nearby university library to locate information about the history of clowns from the 12th through the 16th century in major European countries.

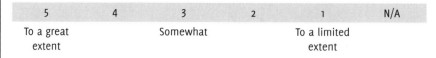

5	4	3	2	1	N/A
To a great extent		Somewhat		To a limited extent	

Figure 9.11. One dimension of a rating scale to evaluate Type III products. *Note.* From *The Schoolwide Enrichment Model: A Comprehensive Plan for Educational Excellence* (pp. 474–476), by J. S. Renzulli and S. M. Reis, 1985, Mansfield Center, CT: Creative Learning Press. Copyright © 1985 by Creative Learning Press. Adapted with permission.

» Does the product created solve the problem? Does it persuade an audience? (Degree of effectiveness)
» Is the product outstanding in its class? Is it novel? Is it ethical? (Level of quality)
» Is the process of creation purposeful? Was the process efficient? Was it adaptive? Was the creator self-critical? (Process)
» Is the process of creation thoughtful? Does it reflect consideration (considerate, responsive, inquisitive, etc.)?
» And, finally, does the student use the appropriate skills? These skills would be those linked to the task and product and would be situation-specific for each product.

Wiggins (1996) also suggested that the form of the product be rated. He recommended looking to see if the product is well-designed by asking questions such as:

» Does form follow function?
» Is the product authentic?
» Is it elegant?
» Is it clever?

To determine whether a product is well-crafted, he provided guidelines for considering organization, clarity, and mechanical soundness. Another dimension

Category	Exemplary	Proficient	Partially Proficient	Incomplete
Identification of Research Questions	• Identified clear, relevant, and innovative research question(s) that were easily understood, relevant to the topic, and "answerable"	• Research questions were clear and relevant, but were not new or novel. Questions were relevant to the topic	• Questions were somewhat vague, were poorly worded, and were only tangentially related to the topic	• Questions were not clear and focused, were poorly stated, and/or were not related to the topic
Identification and Selection of Sources	• Identified appropriate sources for the research questions posed and in sufficient numbers to allow for verification of information; used sources representing a variety of formats (books, journals, electronic sources) as appropriate to the research questions • Relied primarily on original sources	• Identified mostly appropriate sources with an attempt to verify most information using a variety of formats (books, journals, electronic sources) if appropriate • Used some original sources but too often relied on secondary sources	• Identified too few appropriate sources and made little attempt to balance format types • Used only secondary sources	• Identified no appropriate sources in any format • Used only secondary sources
	• Extracted relevant information	• Extracted mostly relevant information	• Extracted a lot of irrelevant information	• Extracted irrelevant information
Note-Taking and Keywords	• Notes were comprised of key facts, ideas, concepts, and hypotheses that directly addressed or answered all of the research questions. All notes were paraphrased or were clearly quoted • All notes were cited appropriately	• Notes included details that addressed or answered nearly all of the research questions • Most notes were paraphrased or clearly quoted • All notes were cited appropriately	• Notes included both relevant and irrelevant information • Some notes that were copied word for word directly from the original source were not cited as quotations • Notes did not include appropriate citations for paraphrased or quoted information	• Most notes were irrelevant and/or no citations for most sources
Organization and Presentation of Ideas	• Content was clearly organized with a concise and logical presentation of ideas and argument • All ideas accompanied by supporting evidence or represented a logical extension of information collected • Organized to allow for new ideas to emerge from a synthesis of findings • No redundancies	• Content was organized with just a few instances where logic was not clear. • Most ideas were accompanied by supporting evidence. • No new ideas • A few redundant ideas	• Lack of organization made the logic of the paper difficult to follow at many times	• The paper was very difficult to read and understand. The content was not focused in clearly developed paragraphs or with clear sequencing of ideas from paragraph to paragraph. Ideas not supported with evidence

Figure 9.12. A rubric for scoring research projects at the middle school level.

he listed as important is style. He recommended considering such aspects of voice as authenticity and grace. And, of course, Wiggins (1996) considered the content to be important. He included accuracy, sophistication, and focus in this category. To help in setting the highest level of performance that might be required for gifted students, Wiggins provided examples of ways in which exemplary models have been constructed and suggested looking at the products of older students to identify models for younger students and examining the models of experts for more advanced students. Others have suggested that students also identify accomplished works and derive the criteria from their own understanding of excellence.

Arter and McTighe (2001) have outlined other generic rubrics for performance-based assessment and the Internet has innumerable sources of guidelines for creating rubrics in general and websites that have screened some of those sources (e.g., http://freepdfdb.com/pdf/sources-of-performance-assessment-tasks-rubrics-and-samples-of-3342125.html). These rubrics are generated to evaluate the standard level of performance, and teachers should be prepared to modify those rubrics to encourage higher levels of performance in gifted students.

Specific learner outcomes should be reflected in the tasks and the rubrics used to assess them. A rubric designed to evaluate a task called "The Best of Times" and structured to address the range of performance possible in a heterogeneous classroom that includes highly able learners is presented in Figure 9.13.

Sometimes, teachers wish to use a common rubric across many products over the course of a year's instruction to be able to show student growth in particular areas. Several items from one teacher's rubric for scoring creative writing products illustrate this principle (see Figure 9.14). The scoring rubrics in these examples are particularly exemplary in that they describe the levels of expected performance at the top, middle, and bottom of the scale with very explicit language that can guide the learner in preparation of the product.

Although all of these scales were designed for teacher assessment of student progress, students should be encouraged to use them to evaluate their own work and that of their peers. These skills in self-evaluation provide a base for students to develop intrinsic/internalized standards of performance. Using the scales to evaluate others also can be valuable in helping students understand the standards by seeing models of each level and discussing the meaning of the levels of performance.

Observations

Certainly, the observation of musical, artistic, and other performances that may represent a student product will use carefully developed rubrics such as those described as performance assessment; however, as mentioned earlier, teachers may do more informal assessments of student behaviors relevant to the goals

	Exceeds Expectations	Meets Expectations	Below Expectations
Perspective/ Point of View	Views and opinions expressed consistently reflect both the time period and the character's circumstances.	Views and opinions are mostly appropriate to the time period and the character's circumstances. Minor inconsistencies do not detract from the overall effect.	There are many or major inconsistencies between the views expressed and the character's time period, circumstances, or both.
Persuasiveness	Multiple methods (vocabulary, tone, costume, etc.) are effectively used to convince the reader/ audience of the character's authenticity. You make us feel we know the person.	You use more than one method (vocabulary, tone, costume, etc.) to persuade the reader/listener that the individual is from the target period, but you have not completely gotten into character.	Little or no effort is made to convince the reader/audience that the character is from the time period portrayed.

Figure 9.13. Sample dimensions of the rubric for scoring the "The Best of Times" task. *Note.* From *The Best of Times*, by E. Coyne, n.d., unpublished manuscript, The National Research Center on the Gifted and Talented, University of Virginia, Charlottesville. Reprinted with permission.

of instruction. In particular, outcomes that are in the affective realm are often assessed using more informal observational strategies. Checklists or rating scales are often used to accomplish this assessment in a systematic fashion. An example of a teacher checklist used to evaluate social outcomes, particularly in group work, was provided in Figure 9.7. Figure 9.15 provides an example of a rating scale that might be used by students to evaluate themselves on their social behavior in class.

The Importance of Evaluating Programs for Gifted Students

The evaluation of learning outcomes is obviously also a critical component of program evaluation. The major stakeholders in education programs for gifted students (the identified gifted students, their parents, the funding agencies, and the teachers and administrators) are interested in the degree to which the expenditure of resources (including student time, teacher effort, and money) results in student learning and achievement that would not be possible without the program.

Standardized tests often are considered first in deciding how to measure the outcomes of gifted programming efforts. The major shortcomings of these tests are twofold. First, very few standardized tests measure the intended outcomes of gifted programs (a question of test validity). Second, ceiling effects may ham-

The full rating scale is divided into two sections. The first is substance and includes clarity of ideas, fluency, description, and overall effectiveness. The second section is grammar and includes sentence structure, spelling, and neatness. The first two items illustrated in this figure are from the substance section; the third is from the grammar section.

Fluency

4   The writing is very fluent and melodic. The writer uses language very effectively to create flow. Choice of words often is unusual and imaginative, but appropriate. The composition is not filled with clichés. The writer is not afraid to experiment with words or sentence structure and does so effectively.

3   For the most part, the choice of words and sentence structure is successful. A few mistakes do not distract from the overall beauty and flow of the language of the piece.

2   The writer uses clichés. The piece does not surprise the reader with its choice of words. The composition flows smoothly and is technically fluent, but it is not powerful because the language and wording is conventional. The writer uses no particularly descriptive or unusual words or seems to have used a thesaurus inappropriately.

1   The writer uses words very poorly. There is no regard at all for whether the choice of words is suitable. The writing is disjointed and inappropriately short. Words are inappropriately simple or common.

Description

4   The writer uses descriptive language well. Imagery is creative, imaginative, unusual, and clearly conveys a sense of that which is described. The reader can see or feel or taste that which is described. The setting for the theme is well developed. You are there. A clear mood is set. The characters and setting are vivid and three-dimensional.

3   The writer provides a setting, describes character, and uses imagery, but the descriptions are sometimes flat. The choice of descriptive words sometimes brings a vivid image to mind, but sometimes common image.

2   The writer provides a setting, describes character, and attempts imagery, but the descriptions are flat. The choice of words does not pull the reader into the setting or give the character life. The settings, characters, and scenes are not fully developed. You have an idea of where the writer wants you to be, but you are not there. The description lacks imagination.

1   There is neither setting nor imagery. Characters are identified in the most mechanical terms. The writer makes no effort to set a scene or provide descriptive language.

Sentence Structure

4   There are no major errors and only one or two minor errors in sentence structure (such as split infinitives). The sentence structure is correct regardless of the complexity of the sentence.

3   There are very few major or minor errors in sentence structure; they occur in very complex sentences.

2   There are a few serious errors in sentence structure and many minor errors, but the meaning remains clear. Errors occur in very complex and simpler sentences.

1   The sentence structure is so full of errors that the meaning of the text often is obscured.

Figure 9.14. Selected items from a rating scale to score creative writing compositions. *Note.* Adapted from *Creative Writing Compositions*, by A. Moss, 1977, unpublished manuscript.

Being a Good Classroom Citizen

Directions: Think carefully about the ways you participate in our classroom. Then check the box that best describes how you believe you interact with and respond to others.

	Always or nearly always	Usually (more than half the time)	Sometimes	Seldom or never
I participate in class activities without prodding.				
I listen carefully to what my classmates say.				
I let others finish before I begin speaking.				
I respect others' opinions.				
I try to be a cooperative group member.				
I finish tasks I am assigned when working in a group.				

Figure 9.15. Student assessment rating scale.

per assessment. A ceiling effect occurs when one cannot accurately assess the full extent of growth in gifted students because they answer all questions correctly on the pretest. Not only is there no room for growth, they may have more advanced knowledge, skill, and understanding than is even measured at that point. That is, when gifted students score at the very top of an instrument on the pretest, there is little room to show growth because very few additional items remain for them to answer correctly on the posttest (sometimes all items are answered correctly on the pretest). Ceiling effects also may occur because the instrument does not sufficiently measure a broad enough range of content or process or contain enough difficult items to tap the full extent of student growth on a posttest.

Validity is also an issue. In most cases, standardized achievement tests measure the traditional curriculum, with most items focusing on grade-level knowledge, often with an emphasis on low-level understandings and processes. Gifted students often demonstrate mastery of grade-level expectations before instruction; therefore, if instruction has been modified to go above grade level or to enrich outside the scope of grade-level content, an on-grade-level test will not measure the impact of instruction. In some cases where acceleration is the service offered to gifted students, out-of-level testing may be used to demonstrate mastery of more advanced levels of learning within the traditional curriculum.

There are a limited number of tests of process skills that claim to be discipline independent, and nearly all of those depend on reading and fluency with language. Further, most were developed and normed in the 1980s and 1990s, so the user must be cautious in the use of the instruments. Issues of cultural bias and inapplicability of the norms are obvious concerns. The most widely used are the Ross Test of Higher Cognitive Processes (Ross & Ross, 1976), the Torrance Tests of Creative Thinking (Torrance, 1998), the New Jersey Test of Reasoning Skills (Shipman, 1983), the Watson-Glaser Critical Thinking Appraisal (Watson & Glaser, 1980), the Cornell Critical Reasoning Test (Ennis et al., 1964), and the Cornell Critical Thinking Test (Ennis et al., 1985). Other sources of instruments that measure process skills used within specific disciplines are available through professional organizations such as the National Council for the Social Studies, which published *Selected Items for the Testing of Study Skills and Critical Thinking* (Morse, McCune, Brown, & Cook, 1971) or by searching journals in the teaching disciplines. The Process Skills Rating Scales–Revised (Karnes & Bean, 2004) can be used to assess process skills in a variety of areas. Teachers may, of course, construct their own classroom tests to assess the success of gifted children in achieving instructional goals and objectives. These are not considered standardized tests.

Some programs may choose to measure student outcomes by using data such as scores on Advanced Placement exams or tests and product ratings of the International Baccalaureate Program. Use of college admissions data, awards and competitions won, or other data related to program goals may supplement test data in assessing the degree of success of program offerings.

In the domain of affective outcomes, there are a variety of instruments that have been used to assess changes in students as part of program evaluation. Self-concept has been measured by such instruments as the Piers-Harris Children's Self-Concept Scale (2nd ed.; Piers Harris 2; Piers, Harris, & Hertzberg, 2002), the Tennessee Self-Concept Scale: Second Edition (TSCS2; Fitts & Warren, 1998), the Perceived Competence Scale for Children (Harter, 1982), and the Self-Description Questionnaire III (Marsh & O'Neil, 1984). One cautionary note in using these scales and expecting to document improved self-concept: Because gifted children generally exhibit relatively more positive self-concepts than average peers (Hoge & Renzulli, 1991; Robinson, 2002), expectations for growth may be unrealistic. Educators should monitor programming efforts to ensure that they do not have detrimental effects on students.

One affective area of concern that often is identified by parents, teachers, and counselors who work with gifted children is the stress and burnout a child might face in a gifted program. Instruments that have been used to monitor such effects are the Student Stress Inventory and the Maslach Burnout Inventory (Fimian, Fastenau, Tashner, & Cross, 1989). When concerns are raised about social adjustment of gifted students (ability to create and sustain friendships and good working relationships with age and intellectual peers), these outcomes can be assessed through the use of sociograms.

Just as the paper-and-pencil assessments are limited in measuring student outcomes for reporting individual student assessment, they are limited in program evaluation. If the goals of the program go beyond the types of outcomes measured by the instruments discussed above, then instruments must be designed that will more closely match the program's expected outcomes. Measures such as those described for classroom assessment can be developed with high reliability and validity for assessing program outcomes, but developers must take care to assure reliability and validity of measurement.

Learner outcomes are important, but they represent only one of the many critical dimensions that should be considered when evaluating programs or services for the gifted. Although program excellence only can be verified through the collection of data demonstrating the many goals and objectives of the program, including learner outcomes, one cannot expect to achieve high levels of student achievement if other components of the program do not work as expected. It is most disappointing to find students have not achieved at levels expected, but even more distressing when there are no means of identifying the underlying reasons why they were not successful. Therefore, questions that address the quality of related functions or the program operational dimensions must be asked. For example, have regular classroom teachers developed the skills that allow for development of curriculum and instructional practice that are likely to lead to development of students' full potential and demonstration of a wide range of talents? Are goals and objectives for gifted programs clearly specified at the district and classroom level? Achievement of unknown or vague goals is highly unlikely. Does the curriculum represent the most current theory and research about appropriate differentiation for the gifted? Have sufficient time and resources been dedicated to program implementation? Answers to these questions and others relating to the quality of all dimensions of gifted services are critical in ensuring that educators are making the best use of resources.

Program evaluation can be used to answer these questions accurately and makes it possible to validate those components of a program that are working and to modify those that are not. That is, a carefully planned program evaluation will help administrators and teachers plan and modify services that are most likely to lead to expected outcomes.

In the process of developing or modifying programs for gifted students and in the development of curricular frameworks and instructional practice, the process of planning for evaluation is a critical parallel function that should be given serious and concentrated attention. Doing program evaluation planning should not be an afterthought. In fact, good program evaluation planning can be a very helpful program planning aid. If administrators collect the kinds of evidence necessary to provide students with complete and accurate pictures of their accomplishments, if educators examine the degree to which their instructional efforts have been successful, and if they are aggressive in documenting the outcomes of programmatic efforts, then they will be more likely to provide the highest quality programs to gifted students. Neglecting to plan for accurate data gathering at the time program frameworks, curricula, and instructional strategies are developed may result in the failure to collect the most complete, necessary, significant, and meaningful information.

Assessment of Other Program Components

Whereas learner outcomes are one critical set of goals for gifted programs, there are many other important aspects of a gifted program that also must be evaluated. These commonly fall in the categories of identification and selection of students to be served, the adequacy of a definition of giftedness and philosophy of gifted education, teacher selection and training, curriculum development and implementation of instructional strategies, management of the program, and communication. Although each program will have different specific goals, examples of general evaluation concerns and questions that fall into each of these categories are given below.

» *Definition and philosophy*: Do the definitions of giftedness and the philosophy of gifted education reflect current theory, research, and practice in the field? Are they defensible? Are they well-articulated to administrators, teachers, parents, students, and the community?

» *Identification and placement of students*: Is the identification process effective and efficient in identifying students who reflect the stated definition of giftedness? Is the identification process equitable?

» *Teacher selection and training*: Does the staff development program provide teachers with the will and the skills to develop and implement an instructional program appropriate for gifted students?

» *Curriculum development and implementation*: Does the curriculum meet the "could, would, and should" test of Passow (1982)? Is this a curriculum in which only gifted students could, should, and would be successful? Does the curriculum and instructional practice reflect sound principles of differentiation? Is the curriculum implemented as developed? Are the components of a differentiated curriculum being implemented in the classroom?

» *Management*: Are there adequate resources and facilities to implement this program? Are program administrators well prepared in the area of gifted program management and the current state of the art in gifted education?

» *Communication*: Does the plan for communication provide parents with sufficient information about their children's experiences, expectations, and the evaluation of student achievements?

Determining Areas of Concern and Evaluation Questions

Although there are hundreds of evaluation questions that can be asked about a program, resources for doing an evaluation are limited, so focusing on critical areas that will provide the most useful decision-making data is important. The principle guides used in selecting priority areas for program evaluation are:

» Does this area of concern or question reflect an *important* outcome of the program?

» Will the information collected about this area of concern or question be of use to the key decision makers?

» Is this an area of concern or question of critical concern to the stakeholders in the program, those most affected by program decisions?

» Can studying this area of concern help improve services to the students?

To decide which questions fit these criteria, it is very useful to establish an advisory committee made up of representatives of key decision makers and stakeholder groups.

In formulating the key evaluation questions, it also is critical to consider formative or in-process questions such as, "Is the program being implemented as described and intended?" Outcome or summative questions are, of course, also important. An example of an outcome question asked about implementation of the Schoolwide Enrichment Model might be, "Did the students in this program use the tools of the discipline to produce creative, authentic products that addressed a real problem and were presented to a real audience?" For an in-depth discussion regarding the selection of evaluation concerns and questions, see Callahan and Caldwell (1993).

Sources of Information

The next stage in program evaluation is identifying sources that will provide valid and reliable information. Several sources of data regarding student outcomes have been discussed in detail in the earlier section of this chapter, including tests, performance and product rating scales, and observations. Student performance on both formal and informal assessments can become part of the program evaluation process. It also is possible to use other data such as the results of Advanced Placement (AP) or International Baccalaureate (IB) exams; performance in competitions; awards and special recognition; and surveys and interviews of students, parents, and teachers regarding student performance.

Parents are particularly good sources of information about the program's communication, the degree of challenge provided by the curriculum, and their children's reactions to program components. Teachers, both gifted specialists and those in the regular classroom, and school administrators also are good sources of information about areas of concern regarding communication, as well as program management and the identification process.

Program documents could be reviewed by experts to determine whether the definition, philosophy, identification process, and curriculum meet the standards reflecting best practices in the field. Of course, it also is critical to determine whether practice reflects program documents; therefore, in most cases, observation of classrooms will be necessary. An example of a document review form is found in Figure 9.16.

Data Collection

One of the primary issues in program evaluation is the question of who evaluates the program. Is it best to have an external evaluator (someone outside of the program or district)? Or, should school staff do the evaluation? The answer to this question depends on the purposes to be served, the demands of the audiences, and the expertise of staff.

In high-stakes situations or if the program staff is presumed to be biased, then it is wise to consider bringing in an outside evaluator to choose or create the outcome instruments, construct and administer surveys and interviews, observe classes, analyze data, and interpret findings. Similarly, if the staff does not have expertise in the fields of evaluation, survey construction, interviewing, and data analysis, then outside expertise should be sought. Teachers are in the best position to administer surveys to their students. They also are the most appropriate people to administer tests because students will be comfortable with this arrangement; however, it may be necessary to have scoring done by individuals considered less biased. One final consideration is staff time. If the evaluation will be done hurriedly with little attention to detail and accuracy, then the results will be useless at best and damaging if bad decisions are made based on unreliable or invalid assessments or interpretations.

Quantitative and qualitative data. Quantifiable data are the data derived from test scores, frequency counts of responses on surveys or questionnaires, scores on performance assessment scales, and responses on observational scales. Qualitative data are derived from interviews, observations, analyses of program documents, and open-ended questions on surveys. When analyzing qualitative data, evaluators are looking for common themes and deeper insights into the perceptions, understandings, and explanations surrounding the program.

	Novice	Apprentice Level I	Apprentice Level II	Master
Evidence of preassessment of student readiness	No evidence of preassessment.	Some non-systematic assessment.	Assessment data collected systematically, but not used to assign tasks.	Systematic data collection and clear match of readiness to task difficulty.
Uses a variety of materials other than standard text	No suggestion of alternative resources or materials.	One or two alternatives, but with no range of challenge or interest. All in same medium (e.g., all printed material).	Multiple alternatives, but with limited range of challenge, reflecting limited interests, or a limited range of media.	Many options with appropriate variability in challenge, types of resources, and match to interests.

Figure 9.16. Sample items from a document review form.

Surveys. Surveys are the most common source of quantitative data in gifted program evaluations. A survey to one sample of constituents may be used to address many evaluation questions, or it may focus on one topic.

Rating scales. Experts may use a rating scale to evaluate the quality of the curriculum that has been developed for use with a gifted population. Figure 9.17 is an example of an instrument designed for such use.

Other objective assessment strategies. A useful strategy for assessing social adjustment, an affective outcome, is the sociogram. If there is concern that the way in which services are provided to gifted students is creating problems of isolation, a simple technique is to administer three questions: Who would you most like to sit near? With whom would you most like to play? With whom would you most like to work? Ask the students to list their three top choices with all names written on the blackboard so fear of misspelling does not influence choice. Then, ask the same three questions in the negative form (e.g., Whom would you least like to sit near?). Strategies for constructing and analyzing sociograms can be found in most introductory assessment textbooks or at http://www.users.muohio. edu/shermalw/sociometryfiles/socio_are.htmlx#how.

Qualitative data collection. Interviews (individual and/or focus group) and observations form the basis for nearly all qualitative data collections. The process may be highly structured with specific interview questions or guides for observation, or they may be more open-ended, leaving the structure of the interview or observation open to the discretion of the person collecting the data. The choice of a structured interview and observation is most appropriate when there are specific

In evaluating this curriculum document, please indicate the degree to which the framework addresses each principle. 1 = no attention to this principle, 2 = minimal attention to this principle (surface features only), 3 = some attention to the principle with good likelihood of substantial effectiveness, 4 = substantial and effective attention to the principle, N/A = not applicable

1. The framework suggests an appropriate level of involvement of the gifted learner in decisions concerning choice of educational experience.   1   2   3   4   N/A

2. Individual responsibility for learning is promoted.   1   2   3   4   N/A

3. The teaching strategies selected and recommended replace the traditional superior/authority/dispenser of knowledge role of the teacher with the knowledgeable facilitator role.   1   2   3   4   N/A

4. There is appropriate integration of content, process, and product goals.   1   2   3   4   N/A

5. Included instructional strategies use hypothesizing, collecting and verifying data, predicting, and synthesizing at the level of sophistication appropriate for gifted children of this age.   1   2   3   4   N/A

6. The curriculum allows for differentiation for gifted learners who are at different levels of sophistication.   1   2   3   4   N/A

7. Problem solving using the methodologies of professionals in this discipline is included.   1   2   3   4   N/A

8. Recognition, analysis, and revisions of the process used to generate products receive as much focus as the evaluation of the product itself.   1   2   3   4   N/A

9. Authentic problems are included when appropriate.   1   2   3   4   N/A

10. Authentic or real products are encouraged as appropriate.   1   2   3   4   N/A

11. Opportunities are provided for gifted and talented students to pursue areas of their own selection—individually or collectively.   1   2   3   4   N/A

12. Content reflects a level of abstraction appropriate for gifted learners.   1   2   3   4   N/A

13. Content reflects a level of depth and complexity appropriate for gifted learners.   1   2   3   4   N/A

14. The process dimension of instruction reflects a level of depth and complexity appropriate for gifted learners.   1   2   3   4   N/A

15. Pacing of learning is appropriate for gifted learners.   1   2   3   4   N/A

16. The curriculum allows for students of different ethnic, socioeconomic, or racial backgrounds to become engaged in learning.   1   2   3   4   N/A

17. The content, process, and product dimensions of the curriculum reflect learning experiences that other students either could not, would not, or should not do.   1   2   3   4   N/A

18. Students will have a better understanding of the epistemology of the discipline.   1   2   3   4   N/A

19. Learning experiences require students to engage in the transformation of information, rather than mere memorization.   1   2   3   4   N/A

20. Creative productivity is encouraged.   1   2   3   4   N/A

Figure 9.17. A rating scale for use by experts in assessing curricular quality.

areas about which the evaluator is seeking data. When the purpose is to explore a more general sense of overall effectiveness and process, then a more open-ended approach should be used.

Data Analysis

The analysis of quantitative and qualitative data is the subject of whole courses in statistical and qualitative evaluation design courses. Questionnaire or survey data usually are analyzed by presenting descriptive statistics or frequency counts of responses. And on rating scales, means and standard deviations of responses are presented if there is a sufficiently large number (more than 25 respondents) to make interpretation meaningful. These same strategies are used to report on ratings of curricula and other elements of a gifted program.

For reporting student outcome data, inferential statistics comparing the learning of students receiving services with similar groups not receiving services may be used if there is a control or comparison group. However, most often, results are compared to a standard or norm established by the program.

The issues involved in using qualitative data has been the subject of many books, and those who are interested in pursuing this line of data collection and analysis should consult a source such as Savin-Baden and Major (2013) or Denzin and Lincoln (2005).

Decision Making

Whichever line of data collection and analysis is used for exploring program evaluation, the critical element is the use of the data. The evaluation data must reach appropriate decision makers for their use in evaluating the degree to which the program is functioning as intended. It must be presented in such a way that decision makers can assess the degree to which results achieved match the program's goals. It should be clear enough that they can use the information to direct the program toward improvement in delivering appropriate curricula and high-quality learning experiences to gifted students.

All of these evaluation efforts, either at the classroom or program level, are to no avail unless the data is fed back into the decision-making process to allow for the teacher or administrator to do the most effective instructional and program planning. Further, the most effective planning will occur when the evaluation processes in the classroom and across program components are carried out regularly and systematically. Hence, planning for instruction and for program modification must begin and end and begin again with effective evaluation.

The Instructional Circle

Too often, evaluation is viewed as the end process of instruction or the inevitable evil that accompanies schooling. Effective educators adopt a different framework and philosophy. The effectiveness of efforts to provide the highest quality services to gifted students will be greatest when:

» the assessment and evaluation process becomes part of a cycle where information is used to provide feedback to teachers on the effectiveness of instruction and for planning the next stage of instruction,

» the assessments provide students with useful information on how they are growing and changing,

» parents are given meaningful information on the accomplishments of their children, and

» decision-makers are able to use valid and reliable data to adjust program parameters to ensure the maximum effectiveness of services offered.

For these goals to be accomplished, each of the individuals responsible for the delivery of services must assume responsibility for specifying the expected outcomes of instruction, defining quality in programming, and selecting or designing and then using assessment tools that will reliably and validly assess the important learning outcomes and the effectiveness of related program components. To educate without systematically assessing students' readiness for instruction and to fail to evaluate the results of instructional efforts is an injustice to students and the community.

Teacher Statement

As Callahan points out, educators of the gifted, like others in the field of education, all too often view the evaluation process as a necessary evil, a course of action that must be carried out, but one that is not fully understood. When these educators become involved in an evaluation process that is properly utilized, however, they understand its impact upon the entire learning community.

When is an evaluation process properly utilized in gifted education? First of all, an effective evaluation process directly impacts the focus of gifted education: the gifted learner. An effective evaluation process enables teachers of the gifted to ensure that the learning of new material is taking place at the appropriate level. Whether the material is new in terms of depth, difficulty, or originality, the gifted learners are required to build upon prior knowledge to achieve. Effective evaluation also enables teachers of the gifted to recognize that gifted students perform at different levels and possess different interests, which, in turn, helps these teachers plan appropriate instruction. Additionally, a properly utilized evaluation process helps students, their parents, and their teachers monitor the students' progress.

How can a properly utilized evaluation process directly impact instruction? Teachers and administrators who use the evaluation process effectively choose curricular models that lend themselves to the evaluation of their effectiveness with individual learners and learner groups in the cognitive, affective, and psychomotor domains. Selected curricular models contain appropriate objectives that are measurable and utilize a wide array of assessments that are valid and reliable.

What other gains result from properly utilizing the evaluation process? An effective evaluation process goes beyond the achievement of the individual gifted learner and the effectiveness of classroom instruction to an evaluation of the gifted program as a whole. This evaluation examines the effectiveness of the identification process, the appropriateness of the curriculum, the skill of the teachers, the quality of the instructional delivery, and the effectiveness of communication with the entire learning community.

Educators and other stakeholders in gifted education wanting to develop and maintain strong and effective gifted programs monitor the learning outcomes of the students in their programs and make the necessary modifications to ensure the programs' continued success. Ultimately, effective educators of the gifted view the evaluation process as a way to make the most of their instructional efforts.

—Trudy P. Cook

DISCUSSION QUESTIONS

1. What do you consider as important cognitive learning outcomes for a gifted program? How could you measure those outcomes?

2. List at least four affective outcomes of instruction for gifted programs. How could you measure those outcomes reliably and validly?

3. What are some examples of performance assessment that you have experienced in your school career? What were the positive and negative aspects of your experience with performance assessments as compared to traditional testing? When could assessment data that are collected for student classroom performance evaluation also be used for program evaluation?

4. Consider a unit you might teach. What do professionals in that discipline do with the knowledge, skills, and understandings in that unit? How can you use that information in constructing a performance assessment?

5. Consider a product that you might ask students in your classroom to produce. What would be the most important dimensions of that product to assess? Describe at least three levels of performance on one of those dimensions.

6. How do you fairly grade gifted students in a heterogeneously grouped classroom? In a special pull-out program for gifted students?

References

American Association for the Advancement of Science. (1993). *Benchmarks for science thinking.* New York, NY: Author.

Anderson, L. W., & Krathwohl, D. R. (Eds.). (2001). *A taxonomy for learning, teaching and assessing: A revision of Bloom's taxonomy of educational objectives: Complete edition.* New York, NY: Longman.

Arter, J., & McTighe, J. (2001). *Scoring rubrics in the classroom: Using performance criteria for assessing and improving student performance.* Thousand Oaks, CA: Corwin Press.

Azano, A. (2013). The CLEAR curriculum. In C. M. Callahan & H. L. Hertberg-Davis (Eds.), *Fundamentals of gifted education: Considering multiple perspectives* (pp. 301–314). New York, NY: Routledge.

Baker, E. L., & Schacter, J. (1996). Expert benchmarks for student academic performance: The case for gifted children. *Gifted Child Quarterly, 40,* 61–65.

Betts, G. T. (1986). The autonomous learner model for the gifted and talented. In J. S. Renzulli (Ed.), *Systems and models for developing programs for the gifted and talented* (pp. 27–56). Mansfield Center, CT: Creative Learning Press.

Burns, D. E. (1993). *The teaching of thinking skills in the regular classroom: A six-phase model for the explicit teaching if thinking skills.* Storrs: University of Connecticut, The National Research Center on the Gifted and Talented.

Burns, D. E., & Reis, S. N. (1991). Developing a thinking skills component in the gifted education program. *Roeper Review, 14,* 72–79.

Callahan, C. M., & Caldwell, M. S. (1993). *A practitioner's guide to evaluating programs for the gifted.* Washington, DC: National Association for Gifted Children.

Cohen, E. G., Lotan, R. A., Whitcomb, J. A., Balderrama, M. V., Cossey, R., & Swanson, P. E. (1994). Complex instruction: Higher order thinking in heterogeneous classrooms. In S. Sharon (Ed.), *Handbook of cooperative learning methods* (pp. 82–96). Westport, CT: Greenwood.

Consortium of National Arts Education Associations. (1994). *National standards for art education: What every young American should know and be able to do in the arts.* Reston, VA: Music Educators National Conference.

Denzin, N. K., & Lincoln, Y. S. (Eds.). (2005). *The Sage handbook of qualitative research* (3rd ed.). Thousand Oaks, CA: Sage.

Ennis, R. H. (1985). A logical base for measuring critical thinking skills. *Educational Leadership, 43*(2), 44–48.

Ennis, R. H. (1993). Critical thinking assessment. *Theory Into Practice, 32*(1), 79–86.

Ennis, R. H., Gardiner, W. L., Guzzeta, J., Morrow, R., Paulus, D., & Ringel, L. (1964). *Cornell Conditional Reasoning Test.* Champaign, IL: Illinois Critical Thinking Project.

Ennis, R. H., Millman, J., & Tomko, T. (1985). *Cornell Critical Thinking Test.* Pacific Grove, CA: Midwest Publications.

Fimian, M. J., Fastenau, P. A., Tashner, J. H., & Cross, A. H. (1989). The measure of classroom stress and burnout among gifted and talented students. *Psychology in the Schools, 26,* 139–153.

Fitts, W. H., & Warren, W. L. (1998). *Tennessee Self-Concept Scale* (2nd ed.). Los Angeles, CA: Western Psychological Services.

Franker, K. (2011). *Research process—Middle school.* Retrieved from http://www2.uwstout. edu/content/profdev/rubrics/middlelschresearchrubric.html

Harter, S. (1982). The Perceived Competence Scale for Children. *Child Development, 53,* 87–97.

Hoge, R. D., & Renzulli, J. S. (1991). *Self-concept and the gifted child.* Storrs: University of Connecticut, The National Research Center on the Gifted and Talented.

Kaplan, S. N. (1986). The grid: A model to construct differentiated curriculum for the gifted. In J. S. Renzulli (Ed.), *Systems and models for developing programs for the gifted and talented* (pp. 180–193). Mansfield Center, CT: Creative Learning Press.

Kaplan, S. N. (2005). Layering differentiated curricula for the gifted and talented. In F. A. Karnes & S. M. Bean (Eds.), *Methods and materials for teaching the gifted* (2nd ed., pp. 107–132). Waco, TX: Prufrock Press.

Kaplan, S. N. (2013). Depth and complexity. In C. M. Callahan & H. L. Hertberg-Davis (Eds.), *Fundamentals of gifted education: Considering multiple perspectives* (pp. 277–286). New York, NY: Routledge.

Karnes, K. A., & Bean, S. M. (2004). *Process skills rating scales–Revised.* Waco, TX: Prufrock Press.

Marsh, H. W., & O'Neil, R. (1984). Self-Description Questionnaire III: The construct validity of multi-dimensional self-concept ratings by late adolescents. *Journal of Educational Measurement, 21,* 153–174.

Morse, H. T., McCune, G. H., Brown, L. P., & Cook, E. (1971). *Selected items for the testing of study skills and critical thinking.* Washington, DC: National Council for the Social Studies.

National Council for History in the Schools. (1995). *National standards for history.* Los Angeles, CA: Author.

National Council of Teachers of Mathematics. (1993). *Curriculum and education standards for mathematics.* Reston, VA: Author.

National Governors Association Center for Best Practices, & Council of Chief State School Officers. (2010a). *English language arts standards: Reading: Literature: Grade 3.* Retrieved from http://www.corestandards.org/ELA-Literacy/RL/3

National Governors Association Center for Best Practices, & Council of Chief State School Officers. (2010b). *English language arts standards: Reading: Literature: Grade 4.* Retrieved from http://www.corestandards.org/ELA-Literacy/RL/4

National Governors Association Center for Best Practices, & Council of Chief State School Officers. (2010c). *Implementing the Common Core State Standards.* Retrieved from http://www.corestandards.org/

National Governors Association Center for Best Practices, & Council of Chief State School Officers. (2010d). *Standards for mathematical practice: Grade 4: Numbers and operations in base 10.* Retrieved from http://www.corestandards.org/Math/Content/4/NBT

National Governors Association Center for Best Practices, & Council of Chief State School Officers. (2010e). *Standards for mathematical practice: Grade 5: Measurement and data.* Retrieved from http://www.corestandards.org/Math/Content/5/MD

National Research Council. (1995). *National science education standards.* Washington, DC: Author.

Northeastern Illinois University General Education Committee. (2005, April). Critical thinking rubric. *CTL Bulletin, 11,* 1–2. Retrieved from http://www.neiu.edu/~ctl/bulletins/Bulletin11.pdf

Passow, A. H. (1982). Differentiated curricula for the gifted/talented. In S. Kaplan & National/State Leadership Training Institute on the Gifted and Talented (Eds.),

Curriculum for the gifted/talented: Selected proceedings of the First National Conference on Curriculum for the Gifted and Talented (pp. 4–20). Ventura, CA: Ventura Superintendent of Schools.

Piers, E. V., Harris, D. B., & Herzberg, D. S. (2002). *Piers-Harris Children's Self-Concept Scale* (2nd ed.). Los Angeles, CA: Western Psychological Service.

Reis, S. M. (1984). Avoiding the testing trap: Using alternative assessment instruments to evaluate programs for the gifted. *Journal for the Education of the Gifted, 7,* 45–59.

Renzulli, J. S. (2013). The multiple menu model: A guide for developing differentiated curriculum. In C. M. Callahan & H. L. Hertberg-Davis (Eds.), *Fundamentals of gifted education: Considering multiple perspectives* (pp. 263–276). New York, NY: Routledge.

Renzulli, J. S., & Callahan, C. M. (2008). Product assessment. In J. VanTassel-Baska (Ed.), *Alternative assessment with gifted and talented learners* (pp. 259–284). Waco, TX: Prufrock Press.

Renzulli, J. S., & Reis, S. M. (2013). The Schoolwide Enrichment Model: A focus on student creativity, productivity, strengths and interests. In C. M. Callahan & H. L. Hertberg-Davis (Eds.), *Fundamentals of gifted education: Considering multiple perspectives* (pp. 199–211). New York, NY: Routledge.

Robinson, N. M. (2002). Individual differences in gifted students' attributions for academic performances. In M. Neihart, S. M. Reis, N. M. Robinson, & S. M. Moon (Eds.), *The social and emotional development of gifted children: What do we know?* (pp. 61–69). Waco, TX: Prufrock Press.

Ross, J. D., & Ross, C. M. (1976). *Ross Test of Higher Cognitive Processes.* Novato, CA: Academic Therapy.

Savin-Baden, M., & Major, C. (2013). *Qualitative research: The essential guide to theory and practice.* New York, NY: Routledge.

Schack, G. D. (1994). Authentic assessment procedures for secondary students' original research. *Journal of Secondary Gifted Education, 6,* 38–43.

Schulman, L. (1996). New assessment practices in mathematics. *Journal of Education, 178,* 61–71.

Sharan, Y., & Sharan, S. (1992). *Expanding cooperative learning through group investigation.* New York, NY: Teachers College.

Shipman, V. (1983). *New Jersey Test of Reasoning Skills.* Upper Montclair, NJ: Institute for the Advancement of Philosophy for Children.

Slavin, R. E. (1994). Student-teams-achievement divisions. In S. Sharon (Ed.), *Handbook of cooperative learning methods* (pp. 3–19). Westport, CT: Greenwood Press.

Texas Education Agency. (2010). Assessing process skills for science, social studies, and mathematics. Retrieved from http://www.tea.state.tx.us/student.assessment/staar/socstudies/

Tomlinson, C. A. (2013). Differentiated instruction. In C. M. Callahan & H. L. Hertberg-Davis (Eds.), *Fundamentals of gifted education: Considering multiple perspectives* (pp. 287–301). New York, NY: Routledge.

Tomlinson, C. A., Kaplan, S. N., Renzulli, J. S., Purcell, J. H., Leppien, J. H., Burns, D. E., & Imbeau, M. B. (2009). *The parallel curriculum: A design to develop learner potential and challenge advanced learners* (2nd ed.). Thousand Oaks, CA: Corwin Press.

Torrance, E. P. (1998). *Torrance Tests of Creative Thinking norms-technical figural (stream-lined) forms A & B.* Bensenville, IL: Scholastic Testing Service.

Treffinger, D. J. (1986). Fostering effective, independent learning thorough individual programming. In J. S. Renzulli (Ed.), *Systems and models for developing programs for the gifted and talented* (pp. 429–460). Mansfield Center, CT: Creative Learning Press.

VanTassel-Baska, J. (2008). Using performance assessment to document authentic learning. In J. VanTassel-Baska (Ed.), *Alternative assessment with gifted and talented learners* (pp. 285–308). Waco, TX: Prufrock Press.

Vygotsky, L. S. (1986). *Thought and language* (A. Kozuin, Trans.). Cambridge MA: MIT Press. (Original work published 1934)

Watson, G., & Glaser, E. M. (1980). *Watson-Glaser critical thinking appraisal.* San Antonio, TX: The Psychological Corporation.

Wiggins, G. P. (1993). *Assessing student performance: Exploring the purposes and limits of testing.* San Francisco, CA: Jossey-Bass.

Wiggins, G. P. (1996). Anchoring assessment with exemplars: Why students and teachers need models. *Gifted Child Quarterly, 40,* 66–69.

SECTION

STRATEGIES FOR
BEST PRACTICE

TEACHING ANALYTICAL AND CRITICAL THINKING SKILLS IN GIFTED EDUCATION

BY SANDRA PARKS

Analytical and Critical Thinking Instruction for Gifted Students

The significant trait that differentiates gifted students from their age peers is their exceptional capacity to process information and use it productively. Thinking process instruction extends the unusual cognitive abilities of gifted students in all talent areas and promotes types of thinking that talented young people may need for success and satisfaction in their fields.

For academically or intellectually gifted students, the advanced information processing skills that have warranted differentiated instruction are refined and used effectively in academic tasks. They practice creative and critical thinking skills that may not have been assessed or that may be underdeveloped. Students then apply all types of thinking processes in complex academic or practical problem-solving tasks.

Students with creative or artistic talent refine the perceptual and divergent-production skills that produce excellent work in their fields. They employ critical or analytical thinking in critique and explain their work effectively. Students with leadership talent learn to be more skillful in making judgments and become more creative as they learn to consider more innovative solutions.

Once students are placed in gifted programs, their teachers must organize and implement higher order thinking instruction. Critical thinking skills are seldom measured effectively in most identification procedures. Although students may be asked some "common sense" questions, placement tests do not commonly evaluate their ability to make well-founded judgments.

Although educators showed considerable interest in critical thinking during the 1980s and 1990s, processes and principles of sound reasoning are seldom addressed meaningfully in curriculum guides or textbooks. Because few teacher education programs offer courses on teaching critical thinking, teachers of the gifted are challenged to select or design instruction to teach abstract reasoning processes that sometimes require a technical understanding of logic.

The methods, materials, and programs described in this chapter promote analytical and critical thinking, decision making, and problem solving. Resources for creative thinking skills and processes are described in the chapter on creativity.

Use and Misuse of Bloom's Taxonomy

Teachers and curriculum developers have relied on versions of Bloom's taxonomy (Bloom, Englehart, Furst, Walker, & Krathwohl, 1977) to organize higher order thinking instruction. However, several practices involving the use of Bloom's taxonomy have resulted in designing curriculum that falls short of the intent and intellectual rigor of the model. During the 1980s, staff development and teacher education materials interpreted Bloom's taxonomy in oversimplified terms. Teachers of the gifted believed that they were implementing the Bloom model by asking questions or planning activities that used verbs correlated to analysis, synthesis, and evaluation. This practice resulted in lessons that were somewhat challenging and interesting, but the resulting instruction did not promote the depth of understanding or level of abstract reasoning that the Bloom model was designed to produce.

A second problem in implementing the Bloom model (Bloom et al., 1977) left students poorly prepared for meaningful higher order thinking. Teachers and curriculum developers commonly overlooked or poorly articulated the knowledge, comprehension, and application competencies in the Bloom model that underlie more abstract content objectives. According to Bloom's taxonomy, analysis and evaluation tasks involve many knowledge-level skills:

1.20 Knowledge of the ways of organizing, studying, judging and criticizing ideas and phenomena;

1.21 Knowledge of conventions, knowledge of characteristic ways of treating and presenting ideas and phenomena;

1.22 Knowledge of the processes, directions, and movements of phenomena with respect to time; and

1.23 Knowledge of the classes, sets, divisions, and arrangements which are regarded as fundamental or useful for a given subject field, purpose, argument, or problem. (Bloom et al., 1977, pp. 69–71)

Therefore, students often lacked the factual or procedural knowledge for meaningful analysis or evaluation.

A third misconception involved designating comprehension thinking processes as analysis skills, leading teachers to believe that such tasks were " higher order thinking." In the 1980s, many gifted education writers interpreted Bloom et al.'s (1977) analysis of elements or relationships to include definition, compare/contrast, sequencing, classification, part/whole analysis, and analogy. However, in Bloom's actual publication, the analysis of elements really involves much more reasoning. Processes such as recognizing unstated assumptions, distinguishing fact from hypothesis, and distinguishing a conclusion from supporting statements require more thought than distinguishing between two concepts.

Similarly, the analysis of relationships in the original Bloom model (Bloom et al., 1977) includes recognizing the factors that are relevant to the validation of a judgment, distinguishing cause-and-effect relationships from other sequential relationships, checking the consistency of hypotheses with given information and assumptions, and recognizing logical fallacies (Bloom et al., 1977). These inferences are much more abstract and time consuming than putting events in chronological order. Moreover, believing that they were complying with the model, teachers gave less attention to challenging processes that require more thoughtful consideration.

A fourth problem in using the Bloom model (Bloom et al., 1977) has been lack of clarity about critical thinking processes, lack of explicitness in teaching them, and underdeveloped standards for evaluating one's thinking about complex issues. Students were asked to analyze ideas in activities that applied higher order thinking, but they were not taught the processes or standards for skillful thinking. Evaluating a work, an idea, or a principle without knowledge of the criteria, procedures, and principles for making such determinations results in an unsubstantiated opinion or statement of preference, rather than an informed, well-founded judgment.

Critical thinking is commonly defined as evaluation tasks in the Bloom model (Bloom et al., 1977). According to Bloom et al., an evaluation task, the most complex form of higher order thinking, involves:

> . . . making judgments about the value, for some purpose, of ideas, works, solutions, methods, materials, etc. It involves the use of criteria, as well as standards for appraising the extent to which particulars are accurate, effective, economical, or satisfying . . . it is regarded as being a relatively late stage in a complex process which involves some combination of all the other behaviors of Knowledge, Comprehension, Application, Analysis, and Synthesis. (p. 185)

To make an informed evaluation, students should know some basic conventions for making judgments in various fields and must conduct certain types of analysis, all of which are generally regarded as critical thinking:

1.24　Knowledge of the criteria by which facts, principles, opinions, and conduct are tested and judged;

1.25　Knowledge of the methods of inquiry, techniques, and procedures employed in a particular subject field, as well as those employed in investigating particular problems and phenomena (Bloom et al., 1977, p. 71);

4.1　Analysis of elements: the ability to recognize unstated assumptions, to distinguish facts from hypotheses, and to distinguish a conclusion from the statements that support it; and

4.2　Analysis of organizational principles: the ability to infer an author's purpose, point of view, or traits of thought and feeling as exhibited in his work or to infer the author's concept of science as exemplified in his practice. (Bloom et al., 1977, p. 146)

According to the Bloom model (Bloom et al., 1977), evaluation behaviors include judgments based on internal and external criteria. Judgments in terms of internal standards include assessing accuracy in reporting facts based on the exactness of statement, documentation, and proof; applying given criteria to the judgment of the work; and indicating logical fallacies. Judgments based on external criteria include applying the techniques, rules, or standards by which such works are generally judged, as well as how effective the work is in terms of efficiency, economy, and utility (Bloom et al., 1977).

Clearly, the analysis and evaluation objectives in the Bloom model (Bloom et al., 1977) express critical thinking in action. Critical thinking, as defined by Paul and Scriven (Foundation for Critical Thinking, 2008), includes, but is broader than, Bloom's evaluation category:

> Critical thinking is the intellectually disciplined process of actively and skillfully conceptualizing, applying, analyzing, synthesizing, and/or evaluating information gathered from, or generated by, observation, experience, reflection, reasoning, or communication as a guide for belief and action. In its exemplary form it is based on universal intellectual values that transcend subject matter divisions: clarity, accuracy, precision, consistency, relevance, sound evidence, good reasons, depth, breadth, and fairness.
>
> It entails the examination of those structures or elements of thought implicit in all reasoning: purpose, problem, or question-at-issue; assumptions; concepts; empirical grounding; reasoning leading to conclusions; implications and consequences; objections from alternative viewpoints; and frame of reference. (para. 1–2)

In short, as curriculum development for the gifted has become more evolved, teachers and teacher educators have realized (a) that analytical and critical thinking is more complex and intellectually challenging than our curricula currently articulate; and (b) that Bloom's taxonomy (Bloom et al., 1977), as it was written, is much more abstract than our implementation of it presently demonstrates. If gifted programs continue to use this classic model, it should be expressed fully, requiring that curriculum developers, teachers, and students have clear understanding of the inferential thinking described in the model.

New Developments in Improving Students' Thinking

During the last decade, four significant curriculum innovations have informed instruction to improve students' thinking: revisions of Bloom's Taxonomy of Educational Objectives; recognition of the significance of metacognition in thought processes; incorporating effective thinking instruction in complex, meaningful contexts; and the emphasis on inferential reasoning in the Common Core State Standards (CCSS). These developments warrant review and reconsideration of gifted curricula in order to align instruction with best practices in teaching thinking processes.

Using the New Taxonomies

Anderson and Krathwohl's (2001) and Marzano and Kendall's (2007) revisions of Bloom et al.'s (1977) model redefine how thinking processes are organized in content instruction. In both taxonomies, some of the skills commonly called *analysis skills* (defining, sequencing, part/whole analysis, analogy) have been designated as skills of understanding or comprehension. Therefore, some of the most common thinking tasks that many teachers believed were higher order thinking are now more correctly described as basic skills of conceptualization.

In *A Taxonomy for Learning, Teaching, and Assessing*, Anderson and Krathwohl (2001) presented a two-dimensional model to describe the cognitive processes involved in learning various types of knowledge. Each of the six levels of Bloom's model (remember, understand, apply, analyze, evaluate, and create), slightly modified, is applied to different forms of knowledge: factual knowledge, conceptual knowledge, procedural knowledge, and metacognitive knowledge.

The Anderson and Krathwohl (2001) taxonomy recategorized analysis skills to create more abstract and challenging instruction. Whereas classification is described as understanding conceptual knowledge, other thinking processes, such as definition, compare/contrast, sequencing, part/whole analysis, and analogy, may be considered skills for understanding factual knowledge, leaving much more abstract reasoning in the analysis category (Anderson & Krathwohl, 2001).

The Marzano and Kendall (2007) revision, *The New Taxonomy of Educational Objectives*, also operates in two dimensions: levels of processing and domains of knowledge. The levels of processing include retrieval (recognizing, recalling, and executing); comprehension (integrating and symbolizing); analysis matching (classifying, analyzing errors, generalizing, and specifying); knowledge utilization (decision making, problem solving, experimenting, and investigating); metacognition (specifying goals, process monitoring, monitoring clarity, and monitoring accuracy); and self-system thinking (examining importance, efficacy, emotional response, and motivation). Each level is applied to three kinds of knowledge: information, mental procedures, and psychomotor procedures (Marzano & Kendall, 2007).

This model categorizes compare/contrast and classification as analysis skills, along with the more inferential tasks of analyzing errors, generalizing, and specifying. Other mental processes commonly referred to as analysis (definition, sequencing, part/whole analysis, and analogy) more closely fit the Level 1 retrieval skills. Depicting those relationships in a graphic organizer makes the process a "symbolizing" task in Level 2 comprehension skills (Marzano & Kendall, 2007).

Two new curriculum frameworks are used in general education and gifted curricula. *The Framework for 21st Century Learning* (Partnership for 21st Century Skills, 2011) was developed by technology companies to include the creative and critical-thinking and problem-solving skills required for business success and innovation. Embraced by several state departments of education and professional associations, including the Association for Supervision and Curriculum Development, this framework emphasizes information technology, provides critical thinking objectives, and encourages methods that promote critical thinking (see http://www.p21.org for more information).

The Rigor/Relevance Framework®, developed by the International Center for Leadership in Education (Dagett, 2014: see http://www.leadered.com/our-philosophy/rigor-relevance-framework.php), depicts instructional objectives in two dimensions: Knowledge and Application. The Knowledge Taxonomy is based on the Bloom model. The Application Model describes five levels of application: acquire knowledge in one discipline; apply knowledge in one discipline; apply knowledge across disciplines; apply knowledge to real-world predictable situations; and apply knowledge to real-world unpredictable situations.

The model organizes both dimensions into four quadrants:

A. Gather, store, remember, and understand information.
B. Solve problems, design solutions, and complete work.
C. Extend and assimilate knowledge and use it to analyze and solve problems.
D. Apply and adapt complex and extensive knowledge to create solutions and take action that further develops their skills and knowledge.

Critical and creative thinking instruction occurs in Quadrants C and D of the model and is applied to complex issues and real-life decisions. Because the model has just four quadrants, teachers can easily evaluate the level of rigor and relevance in specific lessons and determine that units meaningfully address higher order thinking. Like the Framework for 21st Century Learning, this model stresses action and problem solving, preparing students for present and future demands of businesses, organizations, and governments for innovation and equipping them to use increasing technological complexity.

All four of these new taxonomies reflect current understanding of thinking processes and organization of curriculum. Using any of these models, teachers should assure that their instructional units include explicit instruction in analysis and critical thinking, as well as adequate and meaningful metacognition about thinking processes and content. The decision to choose one of these models should depend on which model:

»   is used in the general education program in the district;
»   best reflects the goals of state and local gifted education curricula; and
»   leads to effective differentiation.

Metacognition

When the Bloom taxonomy (Bloom et al., 1977) was developed in the mid-20th century, little was written about the role of metacognition in thinking and learning. Informed by brain research and effective practice, one of the most significant developments of the thinking skills movement of the 1990s was the increased understanding of the importance of metacognition and the development of strategies to teach students to manage their own thinking and learning.

In current professional literature and text material, metacognition commonly is understood as "thinking about thinking," pausing in the thinking and learning process to consider how one is thinking through a process or principle, to evaluate how adequately one is reasoning or understanding the content, and to modify how one mentally processes the concept or issue. Research and reflective practice about teaching thinking has indicated that metacognition is essential for students to transfer a thinking process to another context. Unless students remind themselves of the thinking process that they have practiced, it may become so embedded in the content that students may not recall standards of clear thinking when called upon to carry out that kind of thinking in another context.

Both new revisions of Bloom et al.'s (1977) taxonomy emphasize metacognition. In the Anderson and Krathwohl (2001) taxonomy, metacognitive knowledge is expressed across all cognitive processes. The simplest form of metacognitive knowledge is *strategic knowledge*—knowing general strategies for thinking, learning, and problem solving. Teaching thinking processes explicitly, which includes most of the thinking programs and materials featured in this chapter, falls into this category.

Two other forms of metacognitive knowledge are featured prominently in the model. Knowledge about cognitive tasks refers to understanding the type of thinking process that various tasks require, such as knowing that recalling is more difficult than recognition. The third type of metacognitive knowledge is self-knowledge: understanding one's own cognitive strengths and weaknesses, the depth and breadth of one's understanding, and the effect of one's personal values on learning, such as motivation, interest, and utility.

In the Marzano and Kendall (2007) model, two of the five levels of mental operations include forms of thinking about one's thinking: metacognition about the accuracy, clarity, and purpose of the content; and self-system thinking about one's motivation, emotional response, efficacy, and the personal importance of what is learned. These two forms of metacognition are expressed in processing information, mental procedures, and psychomotor procedures.

In both taxonomies, metacognition about what one is learning, how well one is processing the content, and one's personal reaction to it, has become a significant factor in planning curriculum and conducting instruction. For most gifted programs, this emphasis on metacognition means that teachers and gifted program specialists should now review and revise their existing curricula to promote gifted students' management of their own thinking. Both taxonomies offer detailed guidance to incorporate metacognition into instructional units.

Although both new taxonomies feature metacognition, the Marzano and Kendall (2007) taxonomy gives more guidance and emphasis to self-reflection and self-monitoring. By applying metacognitive processes to all three domains—information, mental processing, and psychomotor—it integrates the three domains of the Bloom model (Bloom et al., 1977), two of which (affective and psychomotor) were seldom addressed.

Currently, teachers and curriculum developers have three choices to integrate metacognition into their instruction:

1. upgrade the use of the Bloom taxonomy, apply the model meaningfully, and add metacognition as described by the new taxonomies;

2. select one of the two new taxonomies, correlate it to the district's current gifted program curriculum, and add instruction needed to promote metacognition; and

3. add the explicit teaching of thinking and metacognition to the Framework for 21st Century Learning, the Rigor/Relevance model, or the Understanding by Design model (McTighe & Wiggins, 1998) described in the next section.

A New Model for Instruction to Improve Students' Thinking

The third factor in promoting students' thinking involves identifying rich contexts for embedding instruction in thinking skills and intelligent behaviors. In the 1970s, teachers commonly believed that challenging instruction taught students to think. However, such activities offered little guidance in teaching the thinking processes embedded in the content. In the 1980s, educators emphasized teaching thinking processes explicitly. Teachers of the gifted taught analytical and critical thinking explicitly as content-indifferent or interdisciplinary lessons. *Philosophy for Children* (Lipman, 1979) and *Critical Thinking* (Harnadek, 1976, 1980), both developed for general classroom use, were widely used in gifted programs.

As educators became experienced in teaching thinking processes, two new concerns emerged. Students often did not recognize when to use the thinking skills that they had been taught or were not disposed to do so when the occasion arose. Secondly, teachers and students did not transfer the thinking processes into content for which both teachers and students were accountable. Considering thinking instruction as an add-on, teachers were less willing to spend instructional time teaching thinking.

Over the last two decades, program directors and curriculum specialists have recognized the significance of improving thinking dispositions—the habits of mind or behaviors that thoughtful people engage in when making import- ant judgments. Implementation of such instruction has shown that intelligent behaviors can be taught or promoted. Students who are taught thinking strategies develop competence and confidence in their reasoning. However, knowing how to think skillfully is not sufficient for effective reasoning and decision making. Students must be willing to be reflective about their own mental processing and modify their conclusions and behavior accordingly. Similarly, teaching students effective habits of mind is not sufficient if their thinking processes are fuzzy, dis- organized, or incomplete.

Paul's taxonomy (Paul & Elder, 1999; Paul, Martin, & Adamson, 1989) described the essential intellectual traits involved in sound reasoning: intellec- tual humility, intellectual courage, intellectual empathy, intellectual auton- omy, intellectual integrity, intellectual perseverance, confidence in reason, and fair-mindedness.

Costa and Kallick (2000a, 2000b, 2000c, 2008, 2009) identified Habits of Mind that they termed "intelligent behaviors," and worked with teachers to develop multiple handbooks to understand these dispositions, to plan instruction to promote them, and to evaluate students' growth. The 16 Habits of Mind in the Costa and Kallick model include (a) persisting; (b) managing impulsivity; (c) listening to others with understanding and empathy; (d) thinking flexibly; (e) thinking about our thinking (metacognition); (f) striving for accuracy and preci- sion; (g) questioning and posing problems; (h) applying past knowledge to new situations; (i) thinking and communicating with clarity and precision; (j) gather- ing data through all senses; (k) creating, imagining, and innovating; (l) respond- ing with wonderment and awe; (m) taking responsible risks; (n) finding humor; (o) thinking interdependently; and (p) learning continuously (Costa, 2001).

Paul, Binker, Jensen, and Kreklau (1990) prepared handbooks for remodeling lessons that feature questioning strategies to prompt elements of thought, which include purpose, information, inferences, conclusions, concepts, assumptions, implications, consequences, points of view, and questions, as well as essential intellectual traits described earlier.

Paul's critical thinking program has been adapted as questions and graphics in the William and Mary model for designing curriculum. Based on the Integrated Curriculum Model (VanTassel-Baska, 1986), the program offers guidelines for advanced content units that feature interdisciplinary concepts, issues, and themes. Each unit includes questions that teachers should ask to address the elements of Paul's model in content-specific contexts. The curriculum units and the graphic organizers used to implement the lessons are available on the Center for Gifted Education website (http://cfge.wm.edu).

The Understanding by Design program developed by McTighe and Wiggins (1998) stressed identifying contexts in which students display their understanding of significant concepts, principles, or issues by a variety of performance assessments:

» *explanation*: thorough, elegant, and inventive account, fully supported, verified, and justified; deep and broad; goes well beyond the information given.

» *interpretation*: a powerful and illuminating interpretation and analysis of the importance/meaning/significance; tells a rich and insightful story; provides a rich history or context; sees deeply and incisively any ironies in the different interpretations.

» *application*: fluent, flexible, and efficient; able to use knowledge and skill and adjust understanding well in novel, diverse, and difficult contexts.

» *perspective*: a penetrating and novel viewpoint; effectively critiques and encompasses other plausible perspectives; takes a long and dispassionate, critical view of the issues involved.

» *empathy*: disposed and able to see and feel what others see and feel; unusually open to and willing to seek out the odd, alien, or different.

» *self-knowledge*: deeply aware of the boundaries of one's own and others' understanding; able to recognize one's prejudices and projections; has integrity, is able and willing to act on what one understands (McTighe & Wiggins, 2005, pp. 76–77).

Project Bright Idea, a Javits-funded program implemented by the North Carolina Department of Public Instruction and the American Association for Gifted Children at Duke University, employed all three elements for effective thinking instruction. It modified the Understanding by Design curriculum model and employed instruction in thinking skills and intelligent behaviors. This program for students in kindergarten through second grade was intended to close the achievement gap and to increase the number of underserved populations in gifted programs. Thinking instruction featured Beginning Building Thinking Skills (Parks & Black, 2008), a direct instruction program that infuses defining, comparing/contrasting, sequencing, classifying, and analogy into mathematics, science, and social studies content. The program also included instruction in Habits of Mind (Costa & Kallick, 2000a, 2000b, 2000c, 2008, 2009) and has developed a procedure for screening potentially gifted students based on intelligent behaviors.

Bright Idea teachers developed 125 interdisciplinary units to infuse thinking skills and intelligent behaviors into content instruction. Implemented with more than 4,000 students, the program demonstrated highly statistically significant gains in reading and mathematics and increased minority student participation in gifted programs.

Thinking Process Instruction and the CCSS in Gifted Education

The fourth development in improving students' thinking is the growing implementation of the CCSS, guidelines for curriculum development and assessment initiated by the National Governors Association Center for Best Practices (NGA) and the Council of Chief State School Officers (CCSSO). Designed to prepare students for college and work, the CCSS set forth common benchmarks for language arts and mathematics instruction, stress critical reading and mathematical reasoning, and require students to explain their conclusions and their thought processes in reaching those judgments (see http://corestandards.org; NGA & CCSSO, 2010a, 2010b).

The CCSS in English Language Arts require more inferential reasoning than current instruction and state assessment tests. Implementation of the CCSS in the United States impacts gifted education programs in three significant respects. Teachers in gifted programs must re-evaluate whether the critical thinking instruction in core curriculum courses is qualitatively differentiated. They may have to upgrade the level of abstract reasoning in enrichment courses. They may be expected to provide professional development in teaching critical thinking for their colleagues.

Critical thinking, as expressed in state and district gifted education curricula, will become implemented in language arts and English classes, making thinking instruction in gifted programs less "differentiated." Teachers of the gifted must increasingly monitor how critical thinking is addressed in local language arts/English classes in order to assure that critical thinking in gifted classes is more rigorous, more structured, and different in content and/or technique. Teachers of the gifted may employ one of the stand-alone critical thinking programs or use instructional methods to promote thinking, such as those techniques described in this chapter. However, they may be expected to assess critical and creative thinking skills and to articulate to colleagues and parents how critical thinking instruction in the gifted program is qualitatively different.

Reading and writing in enrichment courses should reflect the CCSS principles. Enrichment courses (such as global studies or accelerated science courses) and foreign language classes should follow the CCSS guidelines, employing nonfiction texts, using texts of increasing complexity, emphasizing critical reading and writing, and developing advanced academic vocabulary in those content disciplines.

As districts integrate thinking instruction into language arts instruction, teachers of the gifted may be called upon to help other teachers upgrade the inferential level of instruction that the CCSS require. Understanding the nature of these inferential shifts will be helpful in planning one's instruction in gifted classes, as well as assisting other teachers in complying with the CCSS.

What are the CCSS shifts in language arts and English? The CCSS promote increasing the proportion of nonfiction texts from 50% at grade 4 to 70% by grade 12 (NGA & CCSSO, 2010a). Nonfiction texts typically provide rich contexts for critical thinking, offering teachers ample opportunities to provide such instruction. Because enrichment courses usually feature nonfiction sources, such instruction can be easily modified to upgrade inferential reasoning.

The second shift involves content area literacy in science, history/social studies, and technology. Students must use primary sources, interpret statistical data, and understand the research processes of various disciplines. Because gifted curricula already feature these objectives, expanding them should be relatively straightforward.

The third shift requires using texts of increasing complexity and drawing inferences from what the text says and means. Because gifted students typically read more abstract material, this provision is already common in gifted instruction. Increasing the frequency and level of abstract reasoning, as well as the means of assessing critical thinking, should differentiate gifted program objectives from general education guidelines.

The fourth shift involves drawing evidence from the text to formulate interpretations or conclusions and to formulate students' questions about the material. This process is similar to the higher order questioning strategies of Junior Great Books, but applied to nonfiction. Informed assessment of the reliability of primary and secondary sources becomes a key factor in evaluating such evidence.

The fifth shift involves forming arguments or conclusions and supporting them with evidence, as compared to creative or personal narrative writing. Critical thinking processes, such as causal explanation, evaluating generalizations, evaluating strong and weak arguments, and deductive reasoning, are basic in making such judgments.

The sixth shift involves acquiring academic vocabulary within and across disciplines. For teachers of the gifted, this provision is more commonly addressed in science, technology, engineering, and math (STEM) and information literacy instruction. Now gifted students will become more knowledgeable of basic terminology to other fields, particularly in advanced and enrichment courses.

The lesson in Figure 10.1 to teach drawing inferences from comparing and contrasting to historical figures illustrates the shifts. In this lesson, students are asked to compare and contrast Abraham Lincoln and Frederick Douglass with regard to their leadership in ending slavery in America. Students begin by identifying the factors that one should take into account in evaluating leadership. Using a specialized graphic organizer for focused compare and contrast, they gather

Sample Student Responses • Lincoln and Douglass • Focused Compare and Contrast

FOCUSED COMPARE AND CONTRAST

LINCOLN	DOUGLASS

GOALS: To clarify how Lincoln and Douglass contributed to ending slavery in the United States

FACTORS TO CONSIDER: Goals, priorities, attitudes towards slavery, methods, accomplishments, effectiveness

FACTORS CONSIDERED IN THIS ACTIVITY:

HOW ALIKE?

Goals	They opposed slavery.
Methods	They both used language persuasively.
Effectiveness	Both influenced a great many people to oppose slavery.

HOW DIFFERENT?

Priorities	To save the Union and uphold the Constitution while opposing slavery	Abolition of slavery
Attitudes towards slavery	Belived slavery was unacceptable, (though it was legal)	Believed that no person could own another
Methods	Legal means; the power of the presidency	Oratory and writings; any means acceptable
Accomplishments	The Emancipation Proclamation	Newspaper and his own writings
Effectiveness	Legally freed slaves in southern states.	Increased public awareness of the plight of slaves

CONCLUSION OR INTERPRETATION:
While both Lincoln and Douglass worked towards the goal of ending slavery, Lincoln was constrained by legal considerations, regarding slaves as property, that Douglass did not accept, but ultimately Lincoln used the power of the presidency to work within the law to free slaves.

Figure 10.1. Focused compare and contrast task on Abraham Lincoln and Frederick Douglass. From *Infusing the Teaching of Critical and Creative Thinking Into Content Instruction: A Lesson Design Handbook for the Elementary Grades* (p. 128) by R. Swartz & S. Parks, 1994, Pacific Grove, CA: Critical Thinking Press and Software. Copyright 1994 by Critical Thinking Press and Software. Reprinted with permission.

information, individually and collectively, about the two leaders, asking how each similarity or difference is significant. Drawing on the research organized on their graphic notations, they then express their interpretations or conclusions about the two leaders and use the information summarized on the graphic to write an essay explaining their judgments.

Teaching Moral Reasoning

Promoting critical thinking ultimately involves teaching moral reasoning—principles of ethical reasoning and decision making. Similarly, character education programs explain good character traits, describe individuals that demonstrate those traits, and prompt students to demonstrate those qualities. Like critical thinking, moral reasoning and character education are not commonly taught in teacher education courses and may require the guidance of specialists in order to offer meaningful instruction.

Because gifted students often exhibit a heightened sense of fairness and concern for ethical outcomes, principles of moral reasoning should be included in the gifted program curriculum. Examples of moral reasoning and character education programs are included in the Teacher Resources section at the end of this chapter.

Approaches to Teaching Analytical and Critical Thinking

The three approaches in the teaching of critical thinking, summarized in Figure 10.2, include (Swartz & Parks, 1994):
- » teaching thinking processes directly in a structured course of study,
- » infusing analytical and critical thinking into content instruction, and
- » using methods that promote thinking about content learning.

These approaches also have proven effective in gifted education classes for different reasons, emphases, and results. Deciding which approach to use is determined primarily by the gifted and talented service model employed in a specific gifted program: homogeneous content-based classes, homogeneous resource programs focused on process instruction, cluster grouping, or mixed-ability classrooms.

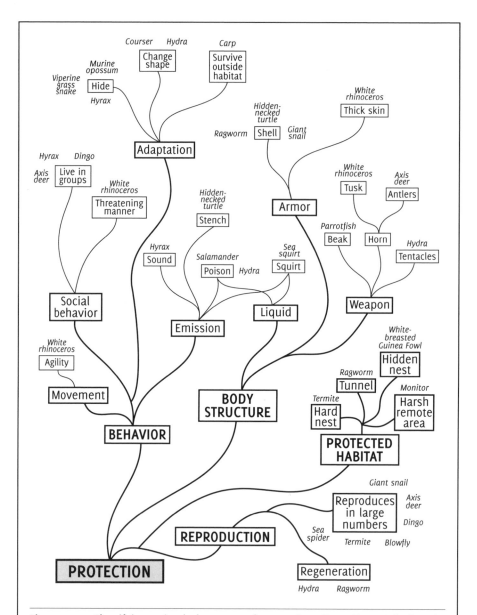

Figure 10.2. Classifying animals by types of protection. *Note.* From *Infusing the Teaching of Critical and Creative Thinking into Content Instruction: A Lesson Design Handbook for the Elementary Grades* (p. 162), by R. Swartz and S. Parks, 1994, Pacific Grove, CA: Critical Thinking Books and Software, (800) 458-4849. Copyright ©1994 by Critical Thinking Books and Software. Reprinted with permission.

Teaching Analytical and Critical Thinking Directly in a Structured Course of Study

Although current practice suggests that thinking processes should be taught in rich contexts, a thinking program with a clearly developed structure may be preferable in resource programs in which instructional time is limited and process, rather than content, objectives are more significant. The systematic teaching of thinking processes is particularly effective for special populations whose cognitive development or language acquisition warrant direct instruction. Gifted students who are bilingual, hearing impaired, and learning disabled benefit from sequentially developed cognitive instruction. Such programs offer practice in metacognition and teach students to express themselves in the language of thinking.

The pool of potentially gifted minority students can be enlarged by thinking skills instruction in elementary grades. For more than three decades, the Teaching Enrichment Activities to Minorities (TEAM) program in Dade County (Florida) Public Schools (Miami-Dade County Schools, 2012–2013; Rito & Moller, 1989) has demonstrated that direct instruction in thinking skills has increased the number of minority students placed in gifted programs.

In the TEAM program, teachers identify minority students who exhibit the behaviors of being gifted, but typically score only in the fifth and sixth stanines in achievement testing. These students were placed in classes where they received daily instruction in analysis skills. Approximately 25%–30% of these students scored the 130 IQ required for placement in Florida's gifted programs. Follow-up studies showed that these students perform as successfully in gifted and advanced academic classes as students identified by intelligence testing.

Like the North Carolina Bright Idea project, The TEAM program uses *Building Thinking Skills* (Black & Parks, 1985), a cognitive development curriculum of figural and verbal lessons that develop key skills to promote understanding (defining, compare and contrast, sequencing, classification, and analogy). Lessons are sequenced by increasing complexity and promote vocabulary acquisition for gifted students who have limited English proficiency or a learning disability. *Building Thinking Skills* provides cognitive objectives, practice exercises, content transfer, and suggestions for metacognition. It is evaluated using normed cognitive skills tests and the mathematics comprehension, mathematics problem solving, and reading comprehension subtests of the Stanford Achievement Test.

Critical thinking instruction as a separate course usually involves teaching logic, ethics, or aesthetics. *Critical Thinking I* (Harnadek, 1976) and *Critical Thinking II* (Harnadek, 1980) are two student books for specialized instruction in formal and informal logic. The symbolic logic lessons may be taught in mathematics classes and the informal logic taught in English instruction. The actual implementation of the complete course requires at least 60 hours of instructional time. *Critical Thinking I and II* have been widely used by gifted education classes (grades 5–9) for more than 30 years (see https://www.criticalthinking.com for these products).

Critical thinking courses have three common features:

» their objectives are cross-disciplinary or supplementary to language arts objectives;

» they involve a structured sequence of instruction to build competence in thinking skills; and

» they rely heavily on class discussion of specialized student materials.

Thinking objectives are clearly stated and measurable with cognitive abilities or critical thinking tests or performance assessments, such as debate or writing tasks.

Thinking courses are used primarily in resource rooms or enrichment classes because of their versatility across the curriculum and because a dedicated amount of time can be spent on them on a regular basis. A variety of direct instruction programs are listed in the summary of organizations and networks in the Teacher Resources section.

Infusing Teaching Analytical and Critical Thinking Into Content Instruction

The infusion approach involves teaching thinking processes explicitly within content lessons. It involves structured questions to reach sound judgments and graphic organizers to hold evidence and to guide students' thinking. Infusion instruction involves direct instruction of thinking processes and instructional methods that promote thinking in rich curriculum content.

Swartz and Parks (1994) developed thinking strategy maps and graphic organizers to infuse thinking instruction into content lessons. For example, students must use analysis principles from Bloom's taxonomy (Bloom et al., 1977) to evaluate whether or not an observation report is reliable. Figure 10.3 shows questions students generated about Percival Lowell's observations of Mars, in which the famous astronomer reported seeing lines that he described as canals. Students listed questions they wanted satisfied in order to decide whether the observation report was reliable. From their list of questions, they generated a critical thinking strategy of the factors that they would take into account whenever they evaluate the reliability of any observation report.

Using lines and color markers, students created a strategy map by aligning their questions with the types of questions represented on their list. Questions generally fell in four main categories: (a) questions about the observer, (b) the observation itself, (c) the nature of the report, and (d) evidence that other observers corroborate the findings.

Questions	Types of Questions			
	Observer	Observation	Corroboration	Report
What is his background?				
What is his scientific reputation?				
For whom was the report written?				
What kind of equipment did he use?				
Did he use the same equipment for all sightings?				
What was his state of mind? Was he clear-headed?				
Where was he when he made his observation?				
Did other accounts corroborate his report?				
In what form or publication did the report appear?				
Was the report a translation or his own words?				
What were the weather conditions?				
In what year did he make the observation?				
When did he write the report?				
Did he have normal sight?				
Was the equipment appropriately maintained?				
Was he typically trustworthy?				
What did he expect to see?				
Did he know how to use the equipment?				
How often did he observe it?				
Is the lens scratched?				
How long did he observe it?				
Did he believe in life on Mars prior to the observation?				
Did he make accurate observations of other planets?				
Was he drinking before he made the observations?				
Was a model made to verify how formations should look?				
Was he paid for this account? If so, by whom?				

Figure 10.3. Questions about reliability of source information. *Note.* From *Infusing the Teaching of Critical and Creative Thinking Into Content Instruction: A Lesson Design Handbook for the Elementary Grades* (p. 159), by R. Swartz and S. Parks, 1994, Pacific Grove, CA: Critical Thinking Books and Software, (800) 458-4849. Copyright ©1994 by Critical Thinking Books and Software. Reprinted with permission.

Once the types of questions were established and criteria for reliability were clarified, students then applied the strategy to evaluate the reliability of Lowell's account of his observations. The example in Figure 10.4 shows that students decided that the technology available to Lowell and his predisposition to believe that there were canals on Mars biased his observation and outweighed his credentials and other scientific achievements.

Teaching the analysis and evaluation processes shown in this example involves more than teacher-directed questions that the instructor asks and students may or may not remember. In this lesson, students derive and explicitly implement a strategy for evaluating an observation report: the questions that a thoughtful person must ask and answer with evidence before believing that an observation is reliable enough to trust. The thinking strategy and the graphic organizers that hold the details of the evidence can then be used in other contexts.

The infusion approach emphasizes systematic thinking and metacognition about the thinking strategies students have experienced. Clarity about the thinking processes allows for clear transfer, in contrast to the more situation-specific questioning that may be so embedded in the content that students may not recognize or remember the thinking involved.

Infusion lessons also employ the instructional methods described in the next section, including cooperative or problem-based learning, using graphic organizers, and asking higher order questions. Such techniques model reflective thinking and result in engaging instruction.

Unlike separate courses, the infusion approach involves redesigning content lessons to fully employ the thinking strategy. Teachers also plan sufficient transfer applications to assure that students understand the thinking process and can use it independently. This approach is more commonly used in homogeneous or cluster-grouped classes because of the depth of understanding, research, and discussion involved in infusion lessons and the planning time required to create and teach infusion lessons. Enrichment units, such as global studies, information technology, and anthropology, provide thought-provoking contexts that are easily modified for infusion lessons.

Using Methods That Promote Thinking About Content

Using instructional methods to stimulate students' thinking in content learning is commonly practiced in gifted education. Staff development for teachers of the gifted frequently includes teaching cooperative learning; using graphic organizers; asking higher order questions; employing Socratic dialogue or shared inquiry; using interactive computer software; designing instruction to honor multiple intelligences or various learning styles, hands-on mathematics and process

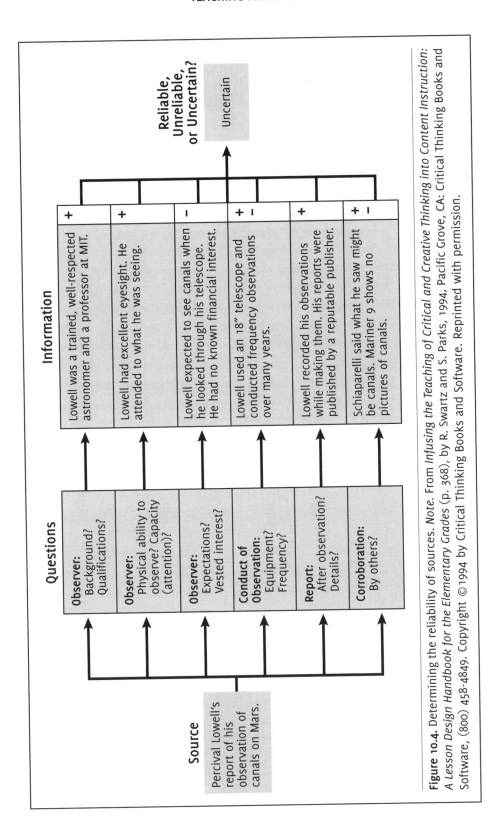

Figure 10.4. Determining the reliability of sources. *Note.* From *Infusing the Teaching of Critical and Creative Thinking into Content Instruction: A Lesson Design Handbook for the Elementary Grades* (p. 368), by R. Swartz and S. Parks, 1994, Pacific Grove, CA: Critical Thinking Books and Software, (800) 458-4849. Copyright ©1994 by Critical Thinking Books and Software. Reprinted with permission.

science, and inquiry or problem-based learning; and integrating art into other content areas.

Although these instructional methods may be used in any gifted education service model, they are especially useful in heterogeneous classes and cluster-grouped classes. Such methods promote deep understanding of content for all students, resulting in stimulating classroom activities. However, gifted students may utilize them at a more advanced level and with greater effectiveness. Gifted students demonstrate more complex applications of these techniques in classroom activities, discussions, and assessment tasks.

For more than four decades, teachers of the gifted learned to ask higher order questions and conduct meaningful dialogue through training in the Junior Great Books program. Teachers facilitate discussions in which students examine great works of children's literature, using techniques of shared inquiry about the novels. Although Junior Great Books is commonly employed in single-language, advanced academic programs, it also has been effective in gifted programs that include large numbers of second-language learners

Problem-based learning engages students in instruction that addresses real problems. As in the Renzulli (1977) Enrichment Triad Model, students exercise critical and creative thinking to develop solutions for real problems, producing real products for a real audience. Programs for problem-based and experiential learning are listed in the Teacher Resources section.

Using Graphic Organizers

In previous examples, the teaching of thinking processes has been supplemented by graphic organizers. Specialized diagrams depict how information is related, picturing issues to guide informed interpretations or judgments. By using graphic organizers, teachers and students can access, organize, and display complex information involved in evaluating issues, solving problems, or making decisions. Graphic organizers also may be used to guide or stimulate thinking, to plan projects, and to assess students' learning.

Specially designed graphic organizers depict questions that thoughtful people ask and answer when they think critically: assessing the reliability of sources of information, evaluating reasons for conclusions, reasoning by analogy, evaluating causal explanation, making informed predictions, evaluating or forming generalizations, and using conditional or categorical reasoning. Notations on the graphic organizer summarize the information or evidence required in making such judgments and depict the steps in the evaluation process by symbols and design elements such as arrows, circles, boxes, colors, and so forth.

Graphic organizers may be used for several purposes:

» to hold and organize information for research and evaluation,

» to show relationships, and

» to stimulate or guide thinking.

Graphics that hold and organize information. Matrices are commonly used in textbooks, newspapers, and periodicals to organize complex information. The matrix in Figure 10.5 contains information involved in considering what energy sources our nation should develop and use. This matrix on alternative energy sources serves as a data retrieval chart—a graphic organizer to guide students' research and observations for conducting inductive reasoning. Students are not given this data but instead use the matrix to organize their research. The empty cells of the diagram remind students of the kind of data needed in order to make an informed judgment and to provide a record of their research.

As shown in Figure 10.5, students listed options (types of energy sources) down the left side of the diagram. They labeled each column with a kind of consequence that should be considered in deciding energy use—availability, impact on the environment, cost to use and produce, etc. Each student group researched and reported its findings about an energy source on the matrix. A huge bulletin board can be used to organize and display the class's combined research on sources of energy.

As shown in Figure 10.6, having organized this mass of information, students must interpret its meaning. Individually, in small groups, or as a whole class, students summarized information in each row and created a summary statement about a particular form of energy. For example, the student group responsible for gathering the data on solar energy prepared its summary statement to synthesize the important information that its research uncovered about solar energy.

Then students summarized the information in each column to state a generalization that addresses the next important question: What kinds of consequences are more important than others? This summary statement addresses which factors in considering energy use warrant greater weight than others. By reflecting on the summary statements for the rows and the columns, students prepared a recommendation about which types of energy sources our nation should utilize.

Graphics that show relationships. Most of the graphic organizers featured in textbooks or magazines are designed to show how information is related. Commonly used graphics are those such as matrices, flowcharts, Venn diagrams, branching diagrams, and concept maps. These graphics depict these types of relationships:

» sequence,

» rank,

» classification,

» subdivision,

» analogy,

| Options | Relevant Consequences | | | |
	Ease of production	Environment	Cost	Availability

Solar
  Active
  Passive
  Photovoltaic				

Nuclear				
Petrochemical				
Coal				

Figure 10.5. Blank decision-making matrix. *Note.* From *Infusing the Teaching of Critical and Creative Thinking Into Content Instruction: A Lesson Design Handbook for the Elementary Grades* (p. 62), by R. Swartz and S. Parks, 1994, Pacific Grove, CA: Critical Thinking Books and Software, (800) 458-4849. Copyright ©1994 by Critical Thinking Books and Software. Reprinted with permission.

» part/whole relationships, or
» attribution.

Thinking Maps® (Innovative Sciences, Inc., 1995), based on Upton's (1940) book *Design for Thinking*, include eight diagrams that show classification, attributes, compare/contrast, sequencing, cause/effect, part/whole, and analogy relationships. Concept maps, also called *bubble maps* or *web diagrams*, can be used to show a variety of relationships, can stimulate creative thinking, and are versatile for numerous instructional or personal uses.

Graphics that stimulate or guide thinking. Graphic organizers can be used to analyze or create a metaphor. Class discussions recorded on graphic organizers show how metaphors serve as idea bridges to convey other characteristics or images with playfulness and richness. Consider the cat metaphor in Carl Sandburg's poem "Fog." Using the diagram shown in Figure 10.7, students named a characteristic of a cat that was also true of fog, such as "silence." Students brainstormed words for silence, associated with either a cat or fog, and wrote these details or descriptors in the boxes on each side of the diagram. They then used the

Options	Relevant Consequences			
	Ease of Production	Environment	Cost	Availability
Solar Active Passive Photovoltaic	‣ Easy, if location, latitude, and weather conditions are favorable. ‣ Little maintenance. ‣ Limited service for repairs. ‣ Photovoltaic not cost-effective until improved technology makes it more efficient.	‣ No undesirable air or water pollution. Unsightly equipment or circular fields of mirrors. ‣ Loss of trees. Environmental impact of manufacturing materials and equipment or disposing of batteries.	‣ Start up is costly (could be reduced by mass manufacture). ‣ Low maintenance and repair. ‣ Operation costs are minimal. ‣ Research and development costly.	‣ Limited by location, latitude, and weather. ‣ Seasonal in some areas. ‣ Distributing and storing resulting electricity is limited. ‣ Renewable.
Nuclear	‣ Complex, requiring sophisticated instruments, specialized technicians, and unusual safety measures. ‣ Waste disposal is risky and requires long-term safeguards.	‣ Radiation danger. ‣ Mining erosion and toxic tailings are produced to secure uranium. ‣ Storage of waste may result in radiation contamination. ‣ Production structures are huge.	‣ Protective measures in operation and start-up costs are high. ‣ Licensing, certifying, and inspecting plants are expensive. ‣ Maintenance costs.	‣ Uranium is scarce. ‣ Breeder reactors are controversial and limited.
Petrochemical	‣ Complex, but commonly practiced.	‣ Risk of oil spills. ‣ Depletion of the oil supply. ‣ Hydrocarbons pollute the air, damage the ozone layer, and create acid rain. ‣ Processing pollutes air.	‣ Exploration, research, distribution, and clean-up costs are high. ‣ Importing is costly; depends on international pricing. ‣ Valuable for uses other than energy.	‣ Limited regional supplies. ‣ Nonrenewable.
Coal	‣ Complex, but commonly practiced.	‣ Strip and shaft mining scars the land. ‣ Use creates a grey film in the surfaces. ‣ Particulate emissions pollute air. ‣ Acid rain pollutes air and water.	‣ Research and development of soft coal use is costly. ‣ Labor, transportation, and conservation are costly.	‣ Diminishing supply. ‣ Underutilize soft coal.

Figure 10.6. Completed decision-making matrix. *Note.* From *Infusing the Teaching of Critical and Creative Thinking into Content Instruction: A Lesson Design Handbook for the Elementary Grades* (p. 62), by R. Swartz and S. Parks, 1994, Pacific Grove, CA: Critical Thinking Books and Software (800) 458-4849. Copyright ©1994 by Critical Thinking Books and Software. Reprinted with permission.

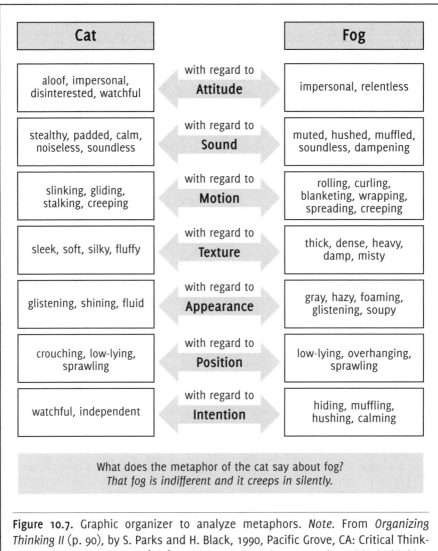

Figure 10.7. Graphic organizer to analyze metaphors. *Note.* From *Organizing Thinking II* (p. 90), by S. Parks and H. Black, 1990, Pacific Grove, CA: Critical Thinking Books and Software, (800) 458-4849. Copyright ©1990 by Critical Thinking Books and Software. Reprinted with permission.

information on the graphic to critique the effectiveness of the cat metaphor or to create a poem that used fog as a metaphor for a cat.

Computer Software and Technology Tools

Today's technology offers access to an array of information resources, promotes interactivity between people, and allows users to manipulate images and information on a scale unprecedented in human thought.

Interactive software allows the user to engage in inductive thinking. The Higher Order Thinking Skills (HOTS) program (initially developed by Pogrow in 1980) demonstrates the effectiveness of using computer software with higher order questioning to increase the basic skills development of low-performing students. Students interact with carefully selected interactive software and discuss the thinking process that they used, developing both thinking skills and metacognition. Commonly used with learning disabled or Title I students in grades 4–8, HOTS also has been effectively used with gifted students in the primary grades. The company still produces updates of its software; current HOTS software and research about the program can be found at http://www.hots.org.

Because using graphic organizers allows us to depict ideas quickly and easily, computer software helps us "download" ideas onto diagrams. Using graphics software stimulates creative thinking, decision making, and planning. Inspiration Software (2014) as shown in Figure 10.8, is programmed to reproduce standard design elements of graphic organizers—flowchart symbols, arrows, boxes, ovals, icons, and clip art—allowing students to doodle with a computer. The resulting visual display can be reproduced as a standard verbal outline with a keystroke. The software has been updated to include multiple new versions, including Kidspiration for grades K–5 and Inspiration Maps and Kidspiration Maps, the latter two of which are available as apps for the iPad at a lower cost.

Standardized spacing and size features in Inspiration allow the user to depict complex relationships almost as quickly as one could sketch them on paper, producing a first-draft diagram of surprisingly good craftsmanship. Another commonly used simple mind-mapping software free to educators is called bubbl.us (see http://bubbl.us). Helping students use drawing software like these to depict their thinking and learning improves their motivation to show what they know. It models the "thinking with a computer" skills that are increasingly common in the workplace.

Video technology can provide the context for students to develop problem-solving skills contextualized in real-world problems. The Vanderbilt Learning Technology Center developed a series of videos that presents complex, but authentic problems in which students must generate and solve many subproblems in order to resolve the larger issue. One video, *The Adventures of Jasper Woodbury: Episode One* (Learning Technology Center, 1996), presents a situation in which Jasper must decide what to do to get his boat home late in the afternoon, realizing that his boat has no lights. Based on a principle of embedded data design, the video provides relevant and irrelevant data such as time of sunset, a river map, weather conditions, etc. that middle school students use to define and solve Jasper's problem. The design features of this video are a CD-ROM format with random access capability, embedded data, and a context in which students must define problems, select mathematics operations, and exercise problem-solving

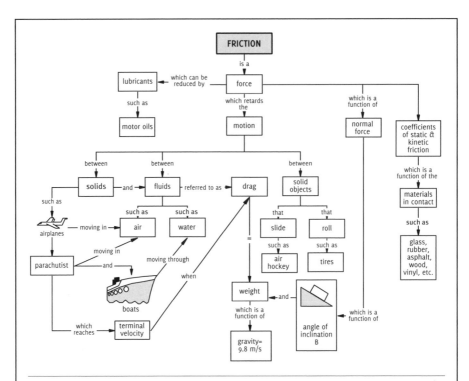

Figure 10.8. Organizer created with graphic software. *Note.* From *Inspiration* (p. 10), by Inspiration Software, graphic created by Paul Rutherford, Science Coordinator, Lee's Summit K–7 School District, Lee's Summit, MO, 1997, Portland, OR: Inspiration Software. Copyright ©1997 by Inspiration Software. Reprinted with permission.

skills. Such software provides a rich source of data not commonly available in middle school mathematics classes and offers an authentic, cooperative problem-solving experience for students.

Using computer software meaningfully offers enrichment opportunities that most teachers of the gifted, particularly those in rural areas, cannot otherwise access. Computer software that poses problems that require critical thinking, practical problem solving, and decision making can be used in all types of gifted program services. Selection should be based on both the content and process objectives of the program, whether software is used independently or in class discussion, the time available for student access to computers, and the individual interest and abilities of gifted students.

Assessing Analytical and Critical Thinking

Assessing Students' Thinking in Writing

The effectiveness of analytical and critical thinking instruction is demonstrated dramatically in the quality of students' writing. One's writing is the hard copy of one's thinking. If a student's thinking is fuzzy, disorganized, and incomplete, his or her writing will be similarly flawed. Improvement in the quality of students' writing is the most dramatic and direct assessment of the effectiveness of analytical and critical thinking instruction. Figure 10.9 shows the correlation of thinking processes to various kinds of writing prompts. Although the questions in the thinking strategy may serve as standards for creating rubrics, students' thinking often is implicit, rather than explicit. Unless teachers review students' prewriting notes, one may not know whether or not students have employed thinking strategies when preparing their papers.

Writing assessment increasingly involves using graphic organizers. Students frequently submit prewriting material so that the teacher can understand the process, as well as the product, of students' composition. Evaluating students' writing can be made more flexible by incorporating these tools into portfolio and performance assessment.

Assessing Thinking and Learning

Performance assessment offers the most meaningful evaluation of higher order thinking. *Understanding by Design* (McTighe & Wiggins, 2005) explained how to design assessments at the outset of unit design. It provides suggestions, procedures, and rubrics for performances of understanding. *The Understanding by Design Guide to Creating High-Quality Units* (Wiggins & McTighe, 2011) takes the Understanding by Design process further to help teachers create units independently and includes fillable PDF worksheets for the process.

One of the most complex issues in evaluating students' critical thinking and understanding involves planning appropriate assessment tasks and weighing students' work to assign a grade. For teachers in gifted classes in core subjects, grading is always difficult, especially when class time and students' assignments have emphasized critical thinking. Higher order thinking is often demonstrated in performance assessments that requires considerable time and preparation for the students.

The diagram in Figure 10.10 shows how evaluation procedures can be weighted accordingly:

Types of Writing	Thinking Strategy
Narrative Create a story about this situation: _____.	Decision Making
Expository Compare and contrast _____ and _____. Describe the events that lead to _____. What caused _____. What would happen if _____.	Compare and Contrast Sequencing Causal Explanation Prediction
Persuasive Why should _____ do _____? Why did _____ do _____? Develop an argument for _____. What should be done to _____?	Reasons/Conclusions Causal Explanation Reasons/Conclusions and Uncovering Assumptions Decision Making
Creative Create a poem or story about _____.	Create a Metaphor Generating Possibilities
Descriptive Describe a _____. Describe how to _____.	Parts of a Whole or Classification Sequencing

Figure 10.9. Correlated thinking strategies to types of writing. *Note.* From *Design for Understanding*, by S. Parks, 1999, unpublished manuscript.

> » evaluation tasks that involve critical or creative thinking require products that take considerable time and preparation and therefore receive the most credit;
> » analysis tasks can be evaluated in forms that require less preparation and thought; and
> » knowledge, comprehension, and application tasks can be evaluated in test form, taking less time, requiring less thought, and receiving the least credit.

Staff Development on Improving Critical Thinking Skills

Although staff development for teachers of the gifted commonly features analytical and critical thinking strategies, meaningful implementation of higher order thinking instruction requires a long-term personal and professional development process. Teaching critical thinking requires that teachers themselves are clear about the criteria, terminology, and procedures of sound reasoning. Because teacher education rarely offers sufficient background in critical thinking instruction, professional development requires considerable in-service instruction.

Critical thinking by its nature requires evaluating one's own strengths and weaknesses in higher order thinking, as well as reflective practice regarding the quality of the critical thinking instruction that one offers students. Individual

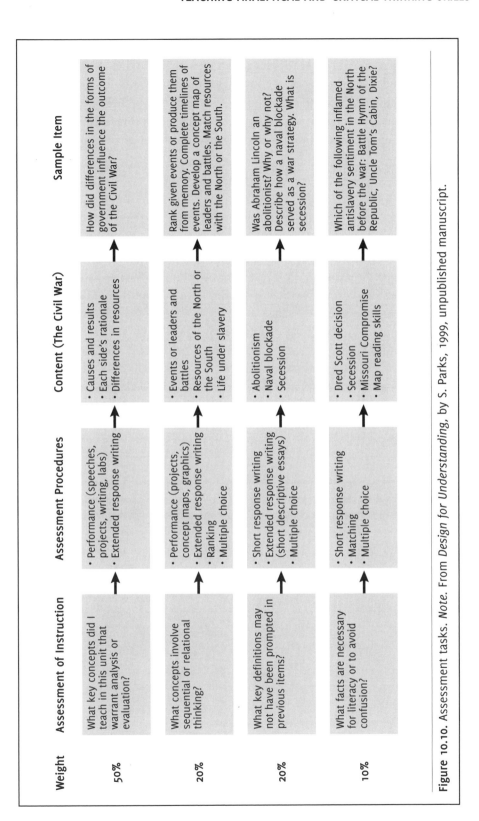

Figure 10.10. Assessment tasks. *Note.* From *Design for Understanding*, by S. Parks, 1999, unpublished manuscript.

Weight	Assessment of Instruction	Assessment Procedures	Content (The Civil War)	Sample Item
50%	What key concepts did I teach in this unit that warrant analysis or evaluation?	• Performance (speeches, projects, writing, labs) • Extended response writing	• Causes and results • Each side's rationale • Differences in resources	How did differences in the forms of government influence the outcome of the Civil War?
20%	What concepts involve sequential or relational thinking?	• Performance (projects, concept maps, graphics) • Extended response writing • Ranking • Multiple choice	• Events or leaders and battles • Resources of the North or the South • Life under slavery	Rank given events or produce them from memory. Complete timelines of events. Develop a concept map of leaders and battles. Match resources with the North or the South.
20%	What key definitions may not have been prompted in previous items?	• Short response writing • Extended response writing (short descriptive essays) • Multiple choice	• Abolitionism • Naval blockade • Secession	Was Abraham Lincoln an abolitionist? Why or why not? Describe how a naval blockade served as a war strategy. What is secession?
10%	What facts are necessary for literacy or to avoid confusion?	• Short response writing • Matching • Multiple choice	• Dred Scott decision • Secession • Missouri Compromise • Map reading skills	Which of the following inflamed antislavery sentiment in the North before the war: Battle Hymn of the Republic, Uncle Tom's Cabin, Dixie?

teachers must self-assess and self-select the thinking processes that fit their disciplines and own teaching styles. Then teachers must invest in their own intellectual growth, as well as expanding their knowledge of teaching techniques.

The summaries of programs and centers in the Teacher Resources section of this chapter indicate sources of training and research to improve the quality of students' thinking and to enhance teachers' own personal and professional growth.

Teacher Statement

In our all-day pull-out gifted program, my fifth graders participate in shared inquiry discussions using Junior Great Books. After reading a piece of literature from Junior Great Books, the students basically lead their own thorough discussion of the piece and write an essay requiring critical thinking, creative thinking, or a combination of the two. Their favorite part? The discussions—and they would continue for much longer if our class met daily.

We also study an interdisciplinary thematic unit called "Our Germanic Roots." In it, the students are introduced to many aspects of the country: its history, geography, language, people, animal life, plant life, natural resources, education systems, economy, politics, arts, music, sports, foods, and even its hopes for the future. They investigate these topics through intensive research using many resources in our school's media center. The students work in small groups creating projects to present their research findings. If two or more students find opposing facts about a topic, they must consider the reliability and biases of the sources and reach a consensus as to which side to rely upon for their information. Students critically evaluate their projects and presentations using rubrics they create in class. They score their peers, themselves, and the class as a whole. They also make suggestions about how to improve both the projects and the presentations for future reference.

In another learning unit, the children study economy, business, and advertising techniques. They create their own imaginary business within budgetary guidelines I provide, and then they make a website to advertise it. The websites must meet guidelines the students select prior to beginning their technological projects. The culminating activities include class presentations of the websites followed by peer- and self-evaluations of the sites according to the criteria and guidelines the students chose as their standards for acceptable projects.

My students also enjoy matrix logic puzzles. Whenever they enter our gifted program (even in early primary grades), they are taught to solve these types of puzzles. By the fifth grade, the children are very comfortable solving relatively complex ones. To stretch their critical thinking skills, I also ask the students to create original matrix logic puzzles of their own. Each must make the matrix, a suitable introduction, a set of clues, and an answer sheet, and then they test each other's puzzles for solvability and logic.

—Tina Goggans Gay

DISCUSSION QUESTIONS

1. Why is it important for teachers to incorporate analytical and critical thinking skills into gifted curriculum?

2. Why do you think analytical and critical thinking skills have been neglected in the gifted curriculum? What is your strategy for changing this?

3. Compare and contrast various strategies for incorporating analytical and critical thinking skills into the curriculum for gifted students. Which strategies would work best for your program and population of gifted learners?

4. How may your students clarify and demonstrate intelligent habits of mind in classroom activities?

5. Examine the screening and identification instruments that are used for identifying critical and analytical thinking skills in gifted students. How can that information be used in planning instruction?

6. What professional development and planning workshops do you need to provide meaningful instruction in thinking skills, habits of mind, and rich, complex content?

Teacher Resources

Assessments

CTB-McGraw Hill. (1993). *Test of cognitive skills* (2nd ed.). Monterey, CA: Author.

Bennett, G. K., Seashore, H. G., & Wesman, A. G. (1990). *Differential aptitude tests* (5th ed.). San Antonio, TX: The Psychological Corporation.

Lohman, D. F., & Hagen, E. P. (2001). *Cognitive abilities test (Form 6)*. Itasca, IL: Riverside.

Web Addresses—Assessment of Thinking

Pearson Assessment Training Institute—http://ati.pearson.com
Foundation for Critical Thinking—http://www.criticalthinking.org

Web Addresses—Cooperative Learning

Center for the Social Organization of Schools—http://www.csos.jhu.edu
Cooperative Learning Institute—http://www.co-operation.org
Intercultural Development Research Association—http://www.idra.org
Kagan Professional Development—http://www.kaganonline.com
Shared Learning Inc.—http://sharedlearninginc.com

Web Addresses—Critical Thinking

Australian Thinking Skills Institute—http://www.austhink.com
Great Books Foundation—http://www.greatbooks.org
Institute for the Advancement of Philosophy for Children—http://www.montclair.edu/pages/iapc/home.html
Teaching SMART—http://www.teachingsmart.com
TregoED—http://www.tregoed.org

Web Addresses—Experiential or Problem-Based Learning

BIE—http://www.bie.org
Outward Bound—http://outwardbound.org

Web Addresses—Improving Thinking Through Science and Technology

Coalition for Science Literacy—http://www.csl.usf.edu
The Council of Scientific Society Presidents—http://www.cssp.us
Higher Order Thinking Skills (HOTS)—http://www.hots.org

Web Addresses—Improving a Variety of Thinking Processes

The Choices Program—http://www.choices.edu
Future Problem Solving Program International—http://www.fpsp.org
The Institute of General Semantics—http://www.generalsemantics.org
The National Center for Teaching Thinking—http://www.nctt.net
The National Research Center on the Gifted and Talented—http://www.gifted.uconn.edu/
   nrcgt/
Project Zero—http://pzweb.harvard.edu

Web Addresses—Moral/Character Education

Character Development Group—http://www.charactereducation.com
The Character Education Partnership—http://www.character.org
Characterplus—http://www.characterplus.org
The Council for Spiritual and Ethical Education—http://www.csee.org
Educators for Social Responsibility—http://www.esrnational.org
Facing History and Ourselves—http://www.facing.org
The Kenan Institute for Ethics—http://www.kenan.ethics.duke.edu

References

Anderson, L., & Krathwohl, D. (Eds.). (2001). *A taxonomy of learning, teaching, and assessing.* New York, NY: Longman.

Black, H., & Parks, S. (1985). *Building thinking skills.* Pacific Grove, CA: Critical Thinking Books and Software.

Bloom, B., Englehart, M., Furst, E., Walker, H., & Krathwohl, D. (Eds.). (1977). *Taxonomy of educational objectives: The classification of educational goals. Handbook 1: Cognitive domain* (2nd ed.). New York, NY: Longman.

Costa, A. L. (Ed.). (2001). *Developing minds.* Alexandria, VA: Association for Supervision and Curriculum Development.

Costa, A. L., & Kallick B. (2000a). *Assessing and exploring habits of mind.* Alexandria, VA: Association for Supervision and Curriculum Development.

Costa, A. L., & Kallick B. (2000b). *Discovering and exploring habits of mind.* Alexandria, VA: Association for Supervision and Curriculum Development.

Costa, A. L., & Kallick B. (2000c). *Integrating and sustaining habits of mind.* Alexandria, VA: Association for Supervision and Curriculum Development.

Costa, A. L., & Kallick B. (2008). *Learning and leading with habits of mind: 16 essential characteristics for success.* Alexandria, VA: Association for Supervision and Curriculum Development.

Costa, A. L., & Kallick B. (2009). *Habits of mind across the curriculum: Practical and creative strategies for teachers.* Alexandria, VA: Association for Supervision and Curriculum Development.

Daggett, W. R. (2014). *Rigor/relevance framework: A guide to focusing resources to increase student performance.* Rexford, NY: International Center for Leadership in Education.

Foundation for Critical Thinking. (2008). *Defining critical thinking.* Retrieved from http://www.criticalthinking.org/aboutCT/definingCT.cfm

Harnadek, A. (1976). *Critical thinking I.* Pacific Grove, CA: Critical Thinking Books and Software.

Harnadek, A. (1980). *Critical thinking II.* Pacific Grove, CA: Critical Thinking Books and Software.

Innovative Sciences, Inc. (1995). *Thinking maps.* Cary, NC: Author.

Inspiration Software. (1997). *Inspiration.* Portland, OR: Author.

Inspiration Software. (2014). *Inspiration 9.* Portland, OR: Author. Retrieved from http://www.inspiration.com/inspiration

Learning Technology Center. (1996). *The adventures of Jasper Woodbury: Episode one.* Nashville, TN: Vanderbilt University.

Lipman, M. (1979). *Philosophy for children.* Montclair, NJ: Institute for the Advancement of Philosophy for Children.

Marzano, R., & Kendall, J. (2007). *The new taxonomy of educational objectives* (2nd ed.). Thousand Oaks, CA: Corwin Press.

McTighe, J., & Wiggins, G. P. (1998). *Understanding by design.* Alexandria, VA: Association for Supervision and Curriculum Development.

McTighe, J., & Wiggins, G. P. (2005). *Understanding by design* (2nd ed.). Alexandria, VA: Association for Supervision and Curriculum Development.

Miami-Dade County Public Schools. (2012–2013). *Guidelines for implementing the Teaching Enrichment Activities to Minorities (TEAM) program.* Retrieved from http://

briefings.dadeschools.net/files/73021_2012-2013_Guidelines_for_Implementing_TEAM.pdf

National Governors Association Center for Best Practices, & Council of Chief State School Officers. (2010a). *Common Core State Standards for English language arts.* Washington, DC: Author.

National Governors Association Center for Best Practices, & Council of Chief State School Officers. (2010b). *Common Core State Standards for mathematics.* Washington, DC: Author.

Parks, S. (1999). *Design for understanding.* Unpublished manuscript.

Parks, S., & Black, H. (1990). *Organizing thinking II.* Pacific Grove, CA: Critical Thinking Books and Software.

Parks, S., & Black, H. (2008). *Building thinking skills: Primary.* Pacific Grove, CA: Critical Thinking Books and Software.

Partnership for 21st Century Skills. (2011). *Framework for 21st century learning.* Retrieved from http://www.p21.org/storage/documents/1.__p21_framework_2-pager.pdf

Paul, R., Binker, A. J. A., Jensen, K., & Kreklau, H. (1990). *Critical thinking handbook: 4th–6th grades.* Dillon Beach, CA: The Foundation for Critical Thinking.

Paul, R., & Elder L. (1999). *The miniature guide to critical thinking concepts and tools.* Dillon Beach, CA: The Foundation for Critical Thinking.

Paul, R., Martin, D., & Adamson, K. (1989). *Critical thinking handbook: High school.* Dillon, CA: The Foundation for Critical Thinking.

Pogrow, S. (1980). *Higher order thinking skills.* Tucson, AZ: Thinking With Computers.

Renzulli, J. (1977). *Enrichment triad model: A guide for developing defensible programs for the gifted.* Mansfield Center, CT: Creative Learning Press.

Rito, G. R., & Moller, B. W. (1989). Teaching enrichment activities to minorities: TEAM for success. *Journal of Negro Education, 58,* 212–219.

Swartz, R., & Parks, S. (1994). *Infusing the teaching of critical and creative thinking into content instruction: A lesson design handbook for the elementary grades.* Pacific Grove, CA: Critical Thinking Press and Software.

Upton, A. (1940). *Design for thinking: A first book in semantics.* Stanford, CA: Stanford University Press.

VanTassel-Baska, J. (1986). Effective curriculum and instruction models for talented students. *Gifted Child Quarterly, 30,* 164–169.

Wiggins, G., & McTighe, J. (2011). *The understanding by design guide to creating high-quality units.* Alexandria, VA: Association for Supervision and Curriculum Development.

CULTIVATING CREATIVE THINKING

11
Chapter

BY BONNIE CRAMOND, SARAH SUMNERS, DONG GUN AN,
SARAH MARIE CATALANA, LAURA ECKE, NOPARAT SRICHAROEN,
SUEHYEON PAEK, HYERI PARK, BURAK TÜRKMAN,
AND SONYA TÜRKMAN

Why Should Educators Cultivate Creative Thinking?

In the summer of 2010, *Newsweek* magazine dropped a bomb on the U.S. by reporting in a cover story that creativity in our country is declining (Bronson & Merryman, 2010). Based in large part on a recent study by Kim (2012), the story concluded that creative thinking had been steadily declining from 1990 to 2010 in Americans of all ages, especially in primary school children. Although it did not have quite the same impact on American education as the Sputnik scare of 1957, it did wake up many educators to a possible problem with our schools. Accordingly, Massachusetts, Oklahoma, and California have begun to develop measures of schools' opportunities for creativity development (Robelen, 2012).

Without further research, it is impossible to determine whether this crisis is real and what the cause may be. However, it seems logical that the recent emphasis on testing under the No

Child Left Behind Act (2001) and the Race to the Top Grant Program, part of the American Recovery and Reinvestment Act (2009), would have a negative impact on creativity. Renzulli (2005) warned that such highlighting of tests and basic skills neglect the needs of America's most gifted, creative, and innovative young people. Such neglect could threaten our nation's preeminence, and leave us with a "dearth of scientists, engineers, inventors, entrepreneurs and creative contributors to all areas of the arts and sciences" (Renzulli, 2005, p. 40).

While the U.S. has been moving toward more testing and an emphasis on basic skills, other countries have been putting more emphasis on the development of creativity. For example, a former South Korean minister of education, Byong-man Ahn (2012), marveled recently in *Education Week* that while others see South Korean education as enviable, South Koreans see it as the nation's biggest problem because of its emphasis on memorization. He went on to explain that educational reform in that country revolves around "creating the type of education in which creativity is emphasized over rote learning, diversity over uniformity, and self-determined education over other-determined education" (p. 39). Similarly, Hua Zhang, one of the leaders of the Chinese school reform movement, has indicated that the Chinese culture of testing has harmed its students both physically, evidenced by lack of sleep and the number of student suicides, and intellectually, evidenced by the degree of passive learning occurring in the schools (Pierik, 2013). Likewise, an online survey of teachers in the 27 states of the European Union (Cachia et al., 2009) resulted in 10,000 responses that overwhelmingly indicated that teachers valued creativity as an important and transversal skill.

Even the recent emphasis on science, technology, engineering, and mathematics (STEM) subjects in school is being transformed into STEAM by adding art to the formula to emphasize the complementary importance of creativity in different domains (cf. http://stemtosteam.org; http://steam-notstem.com). This emphasis shows that creativity is not exclusive to the arts, but is enriched in all subjects through inclusion of the arts.

In addition, many schools are emphasizing creativity in response to the increased pressures of the global economy. In 2007, the National Center on Education and the Economy released a report calling for the first redesign in a century of the American education system in order to maintain our standard of living. The report emphasized that the U.S. must educate students as the future workforce for creative work because routine work will be done by machines or outsourced to people in less developed countries.

More recently, IBM's (2010) Institute for Business Value conducted a survey of 1,500 chief executive officers from 60 countries and 33 industries and found that they identified an increasingly complex world as the biggest challenge and creativity as the most important leadership competency for business success.

Scientific progress and economic pressures are not the only reasons for cultivating creative thinking in schools. Society depends on creative ideas to solve increasingly complex social problems, improve lifestyles, and make the world a more beautiful, enjoyable, and harmonious place to live. If it is possible to develop this kind of thinking in students, don't educators have a responsibility to do so? Schools must also consider the costs of neglecting the needs of the highly creative. Creative thinking fosters self-actualization and mental health, and blocking the drive to create fosters the opposite (Runco & Richards, 1997).

What Is Creativity?

An excellent collection of original writings on various views of creativity (Rothenberg & Hausman, 1976) illustrated the diversity of conceptions of the nature of creativity. In this compilation of original writings, they show how the psychoanalytic view of creativity as described by Freud and others explains creative expression as a regression to a childlike way of thinking or as a way to express aggressive or sexual thoughts safely. Conversely, humanists such as Rogers (1954) or Maslow (1968) differentiated self-actualizing creativity as part of optimal mental health from special talent creativity that may accompany mental problems. Behaviorists, led by Skinner (1972), have argued that creativity is simply a learned response to stimuli, and many cognitive psychologists, such as Guilford (1967), explained that creativity is a way of thinking that can be taught.

Some scholars think of creativity as a system that incorporates the person, process, product, and the environment (e.g., Feldman, Csikszentmihalyi, & Gardner, 1994; Sternberg, 1988). These system views grant that, within each of the four dimensions listed above, there are many variables that determine the if, when, how, who, what, where, and why of creativity. For example, a person may be born with perfect pitch, a good auditory memory, and the creative capacity to write new music, but not have the opportunity for music lessons, the manual dexterity to play an instrument, or the time, money, and encouragement to pursue a musical interest. Such a person would have some of the components necessary for the expression of musical creativity, but not others. So many variables must coincide at the same time for creativity to be expressed: inborn talent, creative motivation, opportunity, environmental supports, persistence, creativity, and so forth.

Others believe that creativity can be viewed hierarchically (Taylor, 1959). In Taylor's model, outlined in Figure 11.1, the expressive artwork of a child can be considered creative; however, it is not as high on the scale as a creative invention. The highest level, emergenative creativity, involves changing the structure of the field or starting a new field or movement. The hierarchical model of creativity is similar to the ideas of little "c" and Big "C" creativity. Everyday creativity, or

CRAMOND, SUMNERS, AN, CATALANA, ECKE, SRICHAROEN, PAEK, PARK, TÜRKMAN, AND TÜRKMAN

Emergenative Creativity—entirely new principles or assumptions around which new schools, movements, and the like can flourish.

Innovative Creativity—improvement through modification involving conceptualizing skills.

Inventive Creativity—ingenuity is displayed with materials, methods, and techniques.

Productive Creativity—artistic and scientific products within restrictions.

Expressive Creativity—spontaneous drawings of children.

Figure 11.1. Taylor's levels of creativity.

---

little "c," can be accessed by most everyone (Runco & Richards, 1997), such as a dancer with a new style of dancing, a teacher with a new intervention in solving students' learning problems, or a medical technologist with a fast and easy way to diagnose a disease. On the other hand, big "C" creativity is descriptive of eminent forms of creative achievement (Beghetto & Kaufman, 2007) such as Mozart's musical compositions, Einstein's theories of physics, Shakespeare's writings, and Freud's psychoanalysis.

With different interpretations of creativity abounding, it is not surprising that there is some confusion in schools about the concept. The assumption that creativity is limited to artistic expression and doesn't include problem solving is a large contributor to this confusion. In recognition of this bifurcated conceptualization, creativity may be divided into two types for definition purposes: expressive and adaptive (Cramond, 2002). Expressive creativity is the type that is used to communicate the creator's emotional and aesthetic senses. It is creative if it is judged to be original and valuable. Nonetheless, adaptive creativity is the type that addresses a worthwhile problem and results in a novel and appropriate solution. Torrance (1988) said, "When a person has no learned or practiced solution to a problem, some degree of creativity is required" (p. 57). This is the type that is used to make scientific discoveries, solve social problems, and keep restless children entertained on a rainy day.

The debates over domain-specific versus domain-general theories of creativity are another source of confusion. Several researchers advocate that creativity is a generalized ability that is not tied to subject domains (Guilford, 1959; Hocevar, 1976; Milgram, 1990; Plucker, 1998; Torrance, 1966). Put simply, some people are just more creative than others regardless of the subject, medium, or domain. To foster general creativity, teachers could use a picture book to enhance students' creativity and to develop students' divergent thinking. On the other hand, if one regards creativity as domain-specific, it should be fostered within a particular context of talent areas (Plucker, 1998). To illustrate, teachers have to explicitly teach or guide students about how creative strategies or thinking can be applied to solve problems or create original products in a particular lesson; however, the consideration of using both definitions in nurturing ones' creativity is also promising (Kaufman & Baer, 2005; Simonton, 2007).

Further confusion surrounds the operational definition of creativity. Originality and effectiveness are the main criteria to determine whether ideas or products are creative according to the standard definition of creativity (Runco & Jaeger, 2012). Originality of ideas or products is considered as a result of creativity when they also contain good reasons, values, or appropriateness. For example, an impromptu performance of a jazz musician at a party demonstrates a level of creativity because the originality and the effectiveness of the performance are demonstrated by the audience's appreciation. In everyday life, individuals generate many original ideas, but not all of the ideas turn out to be good. That's why effectiveness of ideas is also important.

Who Is Creative?

When people talk about creative individuals, they are talking about people who express a high level of creative ability, just as when they talk about intelligent individuals. So, in thinking of the creative person, it is important to consider whether there are common characteristics of creative individuals (e.g., risk-taking, preference for complexity, persistence, openness to experience, etc.), or if the characteristics are particular to the domain. One might argue that both are true.

Consequently, educators need to provide students with a variety of opportunities to explore their aptitudes and to develop diverse capacities and dispositions. In fact, extremely creative persons often seek convergence among different domain-specific traits and experiences. Highly eminent scientists usually engage in artistic hobbies such as painting, photography, sculpting, poetry, and singing (Root-Bernstein, Bernstein, & Garnier, 1995). Planck (1949) observed, that in order to be creative in the sciences, one "must have a vivid intuitive imagination, for new ideas are not generated by deduction, but by an artistically creative imagination" (p. 109).

Persistence, motivation, and determination—the common affective factors of eminent creators—would be enhanced by focusing on what each individual enjoys. Educators need to observe and analyze students' preferred inquiry methods, information representation types, and motivations in order to discover their creative interests. This will enable students to discover and develop their individual aptitudes by considering the different characteristics of subdomains.

Finally, because many of the characteristics indicative of creative individuals may also be used in identifying learning and behavioral problems, teachers should be wary of attributing a negative cause to a child's "differentness." For example, an examination of the similarity in the behaviors attributed to both highly creative individuals and those diagnosed with Attention Deficit/Hyperactivity Disorder (ADHD) indicates the possibility of an overlap in the conditions (Cramond, 1994, 1995). Both individuals who are creative and those who have been diagnosed with ADHD may manifest similar characteristics such as daydreaming, high energy, risk-taking, preoccupation, difficult temperament, and poor social skills.

To foster creativity and enhance creative abilities in students, the role of creative environments is crucial.

Enhancing Creativity Through the Environment

Most of the research on environments that foster creativity and innovation come from the business world; however, the same supportive principles may apply to educational environments. For example, one well-known instrument was developed by Ekvall (1999) in Sweden, then refined and validated with others in the U.S. Ekvall's environmental assessment is composed of nine factors that can be grouped into three categories: personal motivation, resources, and exploration.

Personal Motivation

Intrinsic motivation refers to motivation that comes from within, not from an external source or as a result of others' expectations. Amabile (1996) pointed out that intrinsic motivation has the power to support people to reach difficult or previously unattained goals. Like Amabile, many other researchers recognize the central relationship between creativity and intrinsic motivation (Sternberg & Lubart, 1991; Woodman & Schoenfeldt, 1990). In a 22-year longitudinal study, Torrance (1987) empirically supported this relationship.

The big question for educators then becomes how to motivate students in the classroom. According to social learning theory, individual expectancies shape our creative behavior (Joy, 2004). Rotter (1975) pointed out that reinforcement from the environment influences an individual's motivation to seek alternative ways to overcome problems. Given this theoretical basis, educators should pay attention to the individual and create environments that reinforce creative behavior.

Another important component of motivation is students' perception of their ability and their power to change it. According to Dweck (2007), students who have a concept of their intellectual ability as fixed will not be as motivated as students who perceive that their effort can affect their achievement. It seems reasonable to assume that students who believe that everyone has creative ability, and that it can be increased through their efforts, are more likely to try to think creatively than those who believe that creativity is an inborn and stable ability that some have and some do not. Thus, a classroom that encourages the creativity of all students and helps students learn strategies to enable their creative thinking is more likely to motivate students to think creatively.

Amabile (1983) concluded that evaluation of performance is critical to creativity but must be carefully constructed. Even positive evaluation has the potential to diminish creativity because the expectation of a possible positive evaluation also carries with it the possibility of a negative one next time (Amabile, 1983). In some cases, the more positive the first evaluation, the harder it is to live up to it on subsequent tries. Thus, there is the writer who's blocked after one bestseller, or the artist who releases a one-hit recording and is never heard from again. Specific task related feedback is best, such as "You effectively isolated the critical variable" or "You have really expanded your range of color." Most importantly, the student should be encouraged to develop effective self-evaluation: "Did this story express what you were trying to say more effectively than the last one?"

Resources

Most teachers would probably agree that creativity is enhanced when students have time to think of ideas, receive support for their ideas, and are given challenges suitable to their abilities. In such an environment, the students are likely to be involved with the curriculum and learning.

Csikszentmihalyi (1990), a leading creativity theorist, found that creative ideas are found in the environments that enable flow. After interviewing more than 300 people involved in creative activities, he concluded that they described their experiences during the creative process with the same phenomenological characteristics. As several of them referred to being swept along or other such terms, he called the experience *flow*.

Flow experiences can be created where children work on independent projects, have some choices about what activities they do, or continue to work outside of school. This would include activities that come from the students' interests, have some degree of self-selection, and are extended over time with feedback.

Exploration

Part of developing an original idea requires taking a risk that you'll be wrong. The less severe the consequences, the more likely the risk will be assumed; therefore, there is some debate about the role of rewards in the fostering of creativity.

Rogers (1954) contended that individuals must feel psychologically safe in order to take the risks necessary to develop creative ideas, and such safety is developed through reinforcement and support as well as an absence of judgment. Accordingly, Cameron and Pierce (1994) found through meta-analysis that the environment has a direct psychological effect on students' motivation and creative thinking. If students find an environment where their teachers love and encourage them, they show better creative performance. This means that reinforcement and acceptance of the students' perspective help them to value themselves and produce their own original ideas.

An environment that encourages students to challenge ideas, debate issues, and have some freedom to develop and defend their own viewpoints encourages students to see that knowledge is transitory. Much of what was known has been proven false or has changed. Much of what is currently known to be true may be found lacking, too. If a student is to grow into an adult who challenges conventional wisdom to find new truths, that student should learn to do so in school.

One way to promote a positive school environment and encourage exploration is to develop empathy and self-understanding. A large part of this goes back to tolerance in recognizing and accepting people's similarities and differences. Creative children are especially prone to feeling like they don't fit in with their peers. In spite of their talents, they often suffer from low self-esteem. Discussion centered around good books can be very effective in guiding the emotional development of children because stories touch the emotions (Halsted, 2009). The key is to find personal factors that can be a part of the creative process and draw upon them with the environment.

Summary

An environment that is conducive to creativity is one that is attentive to personal motivation, provides open resources, and is sensitive to personal factors that build students' self-esteem. The relaxed atmosphere in these environments encourage students to engage in ideation, motivates them to play with ideas, and gives them the freedom and support to experiment with their thoughts. Thus, it is a psychologically safe place where the intrinsic rewards of accomplishment are emphasized over extrinsic rewards and controls, where students have opportunities to learn about their interests and pursue them with some autonomy, where there is a balance of stimulation and quiet time, and where challenges are matched to the abilities of the learners. Such an environment can be created for students at least some of the time, and they can learn to create such environments for themselves.

Strategies for Promoting Creativity in the Classroom

Although providing the proper environment is crucial for nurturing creativity, there are more active ways to promote creativity in the classroom. Through the use of specific creativity strategies, teachers can help students develop thinking skills and attitudes that are conducive to the creative process. Just as with critical thinking activities, creative thinking activities should be ingrained in all subjects if students are to see their worth and apply them when suitable.

Warm-Up

Just as it is important to warm up muscles before any vigorous exercise, so too is it important to warm up brains, especially for creative thinking. Ideas for warm-ups are almost limitless; teachers may use just about any simple activity that meets the primary principles of a warm-up—psychological safety, enjoyability, student engagement, creative possibilities, and easy accessibility.

A good, active, kinesthetic movement warm-up that encompasses these main criteria is one based upon complex machines. The teacher can explain that such a machine is like the one in the popular game Mousetrap, or show pictures of Rube Goldberg's (1968) inventions. Students are asked to volunteer to get in front of the group and make a repeated machine-like movement. Then, other students can come up one by one and add a motion to the machine. When all volunteers are up and moving, remaining students are asked to brainstorm what the machine is and how the various movements work together.

Creative learning should be meaningful for students and also easily accessible for teachers. If creative teaching is cumbersome for teachers, it will be hard for them and their students to blossom in the classroom. Thus, for the last principle, warm-ups should be simple and easily accessible. Humor is a simple and easy way to warm-up students for the creative process. A simple use of humor is to share appropriate jokes or cartoons with the class. Another idea is to have students propose captions for cartoons chosen from children's magazines (Ziv, 1983).

Ideation

Ideation is one of the most popular areas in creativity research (Runco, 2010), because it can be the basis of creativity in terms of generating creative ideas. Several ideation strategies can be used to rev up or restart creative thinking when things get bogged down. Brainstorming and SCAMPER are perhaps the best-known strategies for ideation.

The principles of brainstorming are simple: (a) there must be deferred judgment, and (b) quantity breeds quality. That is, while producing ideas, people must resist the urge to criticize their own ideas, as well as those of others. The goal is to produce as many ideas as possible so that at least one good creative idea will be generated. Sometimes, even one person's silly idea will spark a creative idea in another.

Brainstorming can be used for any class and can be adapted depending upon the purpose. Starters for brainstorming can be as simple as "Name all of the things that you can think of that are square." Although easy, the fun begins when one student realizes that the things need not be physically square. Boundary breaking ideas might include a square meal, a squared-off haircut, or even trying to fit a square peg into a round hole, suggesting a challenge. Brainstorming also can be as thought provoking as, "Just suppose there was no gravity on Earth." There are many ways to start this process that are appropriate for the age and sophistication of the group.

Another simple technique for encouraging ideation is called SCAMPER (Eberle, 1996). The letters of the acronym stand for different methods for considering things in order to think of new ideas. Stiff views restrain ideas, thereby limiting ideation. SCAMPER offers seven different angles that help bring about novelty. For example, take the question, "How can I invent a new type of backpack for my students?" The SCAMPER method might be used to brainstorm:

» Substitute (use Velcro to attach a pencil case and other stuff onto the backpack);
» Combine (attach a backpack to the underside of a skateboard);
» Adapt (add a GPS locator to track it easily);
» Magnify or minify (make a backpack that folds down to fit in your pocket);
» Put to other uses (transform used tarps and old seatbelts into a new backpack);
» Eliminate (eliminate the shoulder straps to reduce shoulder pain); and
» Reverse or rearrange (make it reversible with two different colors and materials).

Students could generate more original ideas. Some of them might work very well, while others may be unfeasible. Although this strategy does not guarantee original ideas, it could boost students to generate not only many ideas, but also a variety of ideas. Teachers should be careful, however, not to restrict students in only these seven angles. Sometimes the frame could inhibit creative thinking. Strategies are just tools to encourage ideation, but are not an aim per se.

Metaphorical or Analogical Thinking

Other creative strategies use metaphorical or analogical thinking. One technique is to begin with an incomplete statement: (Something) is like _____ because _____. Participants then complete the phrase with an unlikely object and tell how they are alike. Here is a stem and some sample responses from *A Whack on the Side of the Head* (von Oech, 1983):

Life is like . . .

. . . riding an elevator. It has a lot of ups and downs and someone is always pushing your buttons. Sometimes you get the shaft, but what really bothers you are the jerks (pp. 40–41).

A variation would be to have participants choose nouns at random by drawing word cards from a hat, picking words from a dictionary, or asking a classmate. They would then have to find ways to force-fit the two nouns to answer the question of how they are alike. For example, a student who chose a crayon and a brain might say, "A crayon is like a brain because they both can be sharpened." This would be a good way to involve students in using the vocabulary for a new unit of study. Teachers could intentionally design the choices to reach the specific educational goal.

Synectics

Gordon (1961) developed a method of systematically applying analogies in problem solving that he called *synectics*. Such thinking has been used in business for creating new products or improving existing products and has been a powerful tool to think and generate ideas.

According to Gordon (1961), four mechanisms are used to make the familiar strange in stating problems and then to force-fit generated responses into a realistic solution for the problem. The four types of analogies used are: (a) *direct* analogy, with the goal of making actual comparisons with similar situations in nature or elsewhere; (b) *personal* analogy, with the goal of having the problem solver identify with some aspect of the problem in order to look at it in an unfamiliar way; (c) *symbolic* analogy, with the goal of using an objective and impersonal image to represent some component of the problem, perhaps through putting two conflicting aspects of the problem together; and (d) *fantasy* analogy, which uses imaginary ideas to find ideal solutions (Gordon, 1961).

Visualization

Visualization is a type of exercise that can range from simple to complex. One way to promote visualization skills is through guided imagery. With this technique, students relax and close their eyes while the teacher verbally leads them through a succession of images. One language arts teacher in the urban Northeast took a group of middle school students on an imaginary trip to California's redwood forests. These students, who had never been in a dense forest, were led to imagine what the trees looked and smelled like, the crispness of the fresh air, the soft pillowy wet snow, and the soft hoot of an owl in the distance. The teacher used vivid sensory images to describe the scene. Then, she had the students write a story about a trip to the forest and was amazed at the length of the stories and the students' use of descriptive words and phrases.

Another activity that uses visualization is the encounter lesson. Encounter lessons are activities to stimulate creativity and positive feelings of worth. They are active lessons lasting from 15 to 20 minutes that involve sensory imagination. The structure of the lesson consists of five questions with lengthy pauses for the students to imagine their answers. Soft music can be played in the background. The type and order of the questions are: (a) question of identity; (b) question of awareness; (c) question of isolation; (d) question of risk or danger; and (e) question of wisdom.

Focusing on Attributes

Attributes are categories of characteristics. Attributes can include the physical, psychological, and social as well as other categories. For example, attributes of people include hair color, eye color, height, weight, temperament, ethnicity, talents, and so forth. According to Koberg and Bagnall (1991), "Attribute listing is easiest when you begin with general categories and work your way down to specifics" (p. 59). By focusing on attributes, problems can be solved in several ways. Four techniques that use attributes are attribute listing, attribute analogy chains, morphological analysis, and morphological synthesis.

To use attribute listing, list all of the components or elements of the given problem in one column. List all of the attributes or characteristics of each component in a second column. Generate ideas for improvement in a third column and positive and negative features in a fourth column. The problem should be stated in "how-to" fashion, for example, "How to improve the playground" (see Table 11.1). Using this model, each positive and negative feature then can be translated into a new element of the problem to be run through the entire process again, making the creative activity self-perpetuating (see Table 11.2).

Morphological analysis is another technique that uses attributes to develop new ideas. With this checkerboard technique, attributes from one dimension of the object are listed along the top and attributes of another dimension along the side. The new ideas are created when combinations are forced to fill in the squares of the grid (see Figure 11.2).

Morphological synthesis is a similar technique that requires the attributes of the situation to be listed. Below each attribute, participants then brainstorm as many alternatives as possible. When completed, they make many random runs across the lists of alternates, picking up a different one from each column and combining them into original forms. Here is one way to do this to get an idea for writing a story:

TABLE 11.1

Attribute Listing Chart—How to Improve the Playground

Element	Attribute	Ideas for Improvement	Positive/Negative
1. Swings	Too high	Lower them	Small kids can swing; if too low, little kids can get hurt easier
2. Ground	Blacktop	Soften with mats, artificial turf	Safety; increases number of games playable and cost; effects of weather on mats

TABLE 11.2

Second Attribute Listing Chart—How to Improve the Playground

Element	Attribute	Ideas for Improvement	Positive/Negative
1. Children	Different ages	Separate in areas	Safer for small ones; less interaction
2. Cost	High	Fundraiser	Effective; work

		Grain		
		Corn	Barley	Kasha
Fruit	Kiwi	Kiwi corn	Kiwi barley	Kiwi kasha
	Mango	Mango corn	Mango barley	Mango kasha

Figure 11.2. Morphological analysis grid.

Main Character	Supporting Characters	Conflict	Setting
dog	farm hands	property	mountain town
detective	circus acts	jealousy	Old West
murderer	talking animals	theft	New York
beauty queen	school children	international plot	Ancient Egypt
superhero	a family	war	farm
rock star	bikers	personal	TV station

Figure 11.3. Morphological synthesis grid.

» List the main attributes to be used for the story starter: main character, supporting characters, conflict, setting.

» Brainstorm as many ideas as possible under each attribute. In this case, there are six listed under each, but there are many more possibilities (see Figure 11.3).

» Randomly pick one option from each of the columns. One way to do this is to roll four dice. For example, if the dice turned up a 2, 6, 5, 1, choose the second option in column 1, the sixth in column 2, and so on. Because you may want to generate more options per column with older students, you might use a game spinner or a die with more than six sides (which can be purchased at hobby shops or online).

» Put the combination together. In this case, a detective would be involved in a war with a group of bikers in a mountain town. Some television plots have been written this way.

Lateral Thinking

Certainly, one of the most prolific authors in the area of creativity strategies has been de Bono, who coined the term *lateral thinking* and defined it as pattern switching, a new way of looking at the world (de Bono, 1985a). He explained that lateral thinking is not the same as creativity; rather, it is valueless, but it comprises both an attitude and a number of defined methods (de Bono, 1970).

Lateral thinking methods can be applied in social studies or science classes to strengthen students' creative thinking through a deliberate thinking process. Each of these methods is named with key letters that stand for the first letters in the words of the method. For example, EBS is a method that has participants *examine both sides* of an argument. A follow-up method called ADI has participants list the issues of the argument under the columns *agreement, disagreement,* and *irrelevance*. By practicing these methods, students' lateral thinking process can be fostered as they consider each other's different perspectives on an issue in an argumentative situation.

In *Six Thinking Hats* (1985b) and *Six Action Shoes* (1991), de Bono introduced practical techniques that help students explore different decision-making processes through deliberate thinking process. The six hats represent six different ways of thinking. White is worn by the neutral and objective thinker who is concerned with facts and figures. Red represents the emotional, intuitive view that acts on hunches and impressions rather than on logical reasons. Black points out the negative aspects of a situation, the errors in logic, and possible consequences of a course of action. Yellow maintains optimistic, positive thinking and focuses on benefits and constructive ideas. Green represents creativity, deliberate innovation, and new approaches to problems. Blue stands for control and organization of the thinking and of the other thinkers.

Students can be divided into groups, and each can be given a hat made from construction paper in one of the six colors. When presented with a problem to solve or an issue to discuss, the students must stay in the role according to the hat they are wearing. This method helps them to be aware of some of the ways in which people think about issues and to focus on deliberate thinking. One variation on this is to pair the students—white and red, black and yellow, green and blue—to discuss the issue. Another is to have them discuss for a certain amount of time, then switch hats.

Furthermore, the important point of the Six Thinking Hats Method is that students explore different points of view and develop thinking skills by switching the thinking hats. By "trying on" methods of thinking that may not be natural to them, students can learn how other people think about an issue and focus on deliberate thinking in problem solving.

Creative Problem Solving

The Osborn/Parnes Creative Problem Solving process is composed of five steps: fact finding, problem finding, idea finding, solution finding, and acceptance finding (Parnes, 1981). This process incorporates both *divergent thinking*, thinking of many possibilities, and *convergent thinking*, thinking of the one right or best solution. During *fact finding*, information is gathered about the situation. *Problem finding* means identifying the central or most salient problem and any underlying subproblems. *Idea finding* refers to the process of generating many possible solutions, usually by brainstorming. The *solution finding* step involves applying criteria to choose the best solution, and *acceptance finding* involves "selling" the solution to the key individuals involved in decision making.

For example, a teacher gives students a problem situation: A school gets its transportation budget curtailed so the administration needs to reduce the number of school buses; however, most students use school buses as the school is in a very rural area. "In what ways might we transport all of the children to and from school with our current budget?" One simple example is shown in Table 11.4.

As mentioned above, students should switch flexibly between divergent thinking and convergent thinking. Although these steps are presented in a logical order, in real problem solving, they do not always occur in this order. Sometimes, people are presented with a problem and have to go back and research the facts. Other times, people may be in a position to sell an idea to a constituency and find that the correct problem was not identified, so they have to go back to the problem-finding step. Teachers should not rush students to adhere to the linear order of the process.

TABLE 11.4
The Process of Creative Problem Solving

Phase	Step	Sample Activity
Explore the challenge	Objective finding	T: What is the goal? ▸ Every student should use transportation conveniently. ▸ Transportation should be financially independent from school budgets.
	Fact finding	T: What is the current situation? ▸ School will reduce the number of school buses. ▸ Students live far from the school.
	Problem finding	T: What is the key problem that we have? ▸ Students need transportation to and from school. ▸ Students should find alternative means of transportation. ▸ Students should find financial support to keep the current transportation service.
Generate ideas	Idea finding	T: What might we do to solve this problem? ▸ All students could move near to the school. ▸ Students can have a fundraising party. ▸ Parents can periodically offer transportation for the neighborhood students.
Prepare for action	Solution finding	T: What are good candidate ideas among your brainstormed ideas? Choose some of them and evaluate them with the criteria that you developed. ▸ Students develop an evaluation grid with critical criteria: acceptable, feasible, affordable, and so forth. ▸ Students evaluate each candidate's solutions and choose the best one.
	Acceptance finding	T: You can make the action plan for the implication. You should elaborate the when, who, what for implementing it. ▸ Students develop a full-fledged action solution.

Note. "T" indicates what teachers should say to lead students' activity.

Problem Finding

In creative problem solving, problem finding has been regarded as one of the critical components (Csikszentmihalyi & Getzels, 1971), since the quality of any creative solution is determined by the creative problem (Okuda, Runco, & Berger, 1991). Many creativity processes involve problem finding, giving the tactic diverse names, including being aware of problems, encounter, problem discovery, sensing gap, hypothesis formulation, and problem identifying (Hoover & Feldhusen, 1990; Runco & Okuda, 1988; Torrance, 1976; Wallas, 1926).

First of all, problem finding requires a prepared mind. Although problem finding sounds serendipitous (Runco, 1994), students cannot perceive problems even accidently without a prepared mind (Chumaceiro, 1997). The prepared mind needs more than skills; training should comprehensively cover cognitive skills, metacognition, and relevant knowledge. Therefore, comprehensive priming for problem finding must equip students with prepared minds through miscellaneous media of knowledge, such as books, mass media, and the Internet. This way is not simple and quick, yet it should be the fundamental approach.

A sense of discrepancy is also a very fundamentally valuable attitude for problem finding. Problem finding begins with sensing gaps between a current situation and an ideal situation (Torrance, 1962). A chart, a Venn diagram, or a table can be used to help students compare a current condition and a pursued state as visualized medium. For lower grades and warm-ups, teachers can provide fun games, such as finding the difference between two similar pictures.

In classes, teachers also can employ a simple problem-finding strategy. Problem finding is usually initiated from idea generation out of a vacuum. Although the Divergent Thinking tests were initially developed for research (Wakefield, 1985), they also have many implications in classes. As a warm-up activity, teachers can ask students to list uses or instances of a simple item, both as many as possible and as original as possible. Then, students are asked to list problems in a given situation in the same manner. This puzzle can serve both as problem generating practice and an activity prior to selecting a novel problem among a problem pool.

Even though problem finding might look incidental, it should be elaborately prepared. For better preparation, sufficient domain knowledge should be part of the process. It could also be necessary to imagine an original closing state and find a discrepancy. In classes, teachers should allow more flexible time for students to play with ideas in ill-structured tasks.

Role-Playing

Role-playing can be a wonderful outlet for creative expression, as well as an effective creative problem-solving technique. Role-playing and creative dramatics have been recommended as part of the curriculum for gifted children, especially in the language arts (Cramond, 1993; VanTassel-Baska, 1998). A survey of a group of gifted middle school students indicated that role-playing and creative dramatics were among their favorite activities in school (Martin & Cramond, 1983).

Even teachers who *do* recognize the value of engaging students in role-play may be reluctant to use it with students because they do not feel they have time. Although creative students enjoy acting out different parts and scenarios, role-play activities often are reserved for brief periods of time when all "important" work has been completed. Teachers feel that they cannot justify taking time out of their busy schedules for role-play with students when so much academic content is expected to be covered and documented during the year. Creative teachers know that they can use role-play, however, as a means of motivating students to learn new material and to reinforce material that already has been learned.

One example of an effective use of role-play is the following: Fifth-grade students who were beginning a unit of study on Innovative Inventors were informed that the culminating activity for the unit would be a "living wax museum." Each student could choose an inventor and could dress and act the part of that person in the class wax museum. Visitors to the museum could press a pretend button at the base of the living wax figure to hear memorized facts about the figure's life, but additionally, each student would thoroughly research the historical figure for more interesting and lesser known information. Students were encouraged to learn as much as possible about the historical figure when he or she was about 11 years of age. What would that person have been like in a fifth-grade classroom? What would he or she have known about various subjects at that age during that time period? What type of classroom management style would that 11-year-old have expected from his or her teacher? What would his or her fears have been at that age? What about games and hobbies and chores at home? What was that person hoping to become as an adult?

Fewer teachers seem to be aware of the need and methods for teaching problem solving through role-playing (Torrance, Murdock, & Fletcher, 1997). Based upon the techniques of sociodrama or psychodrama, role-playing in creative problem solving differs in the type of problem that is addressed and the depth of emotional involvement and disclosure of the participants. Although psychodrama can be a powerful tool for individuals to address serious psychological problems, sociodrama can be the same for groups. Problem solving through role-playing can use many of the same techniques with less personal problems. For example, students could role-play to convince the principal to consider their proposal to bring back the art class.

There are many more techniques and variations on this basic creative problem-solving method through role-playing (Torrance et al., 1997). Teachers are cautioned to be alert during the action for any sensitive matters or strong emotional reactions from students that may warrant professional counseling. If these arise, the action should be stopped until the matter is addressed. The key to this method is having students act out and be emotionally involved in the problem at hand, not to cause stress.

Removing Blocks

Another effective way to encourage creativity is to remove blocks to individuals' creativity. These blocks are described, with exercises designed to help remove them, in Adams' (1986) book, *Conceptual Blockbusting: A Guide to Better Ideas.*

Perceptual blocks include:

» seeing what you expect to see—stereotyping;
» difficulty in isolating the problem;

»   tendency to delimit the problem area too closely;

»   inability to see the problem from various viewpoints;

»   saturation; and

»   failure to utilize all sensory inputs.

One familiar example, the Nine Dot problem ("Draw four lines to connect all of the dots without lifting your hand.") shows how perceptual blocks can limit our thinking.

Emotional blocks include:

»   fear of making a mistake, failing, or taking risks;

»   inability to tolerate ambiguity—overriding desires for security, order, with "no appetite for chaos";

»   preference for judging ideas, rather than generating them;

»   inability to relax, incubate, and "sleep on it";

»   lack of challenge—problem fails to engage interest;

»   excessive zeal, overmotivation to succeed quickly;

»   lack of access to areas of imagination;

»   lack of imaginative control; and

»   inability to distinguish reality from fantasy.

How many students, especially bright ones, have difficulty suspending disbelief long enough to consider that the improbable may be possible? Torrance (1974) reported that the psychologist Thorndike presented prospective graduate students with an unlikely hypothetical situation and asked them to "just suppose" the outcome. Those who were unable to conjecture were considered too incurious for graduate study. For a class exercise, students can try a "just suppose" activity and the teacher can discuss how often each of the students has missed an opportunity because of a fear of failure. By sharing each other's experiences, students can learn how these blocks prevent them from exercising their creativity.

Cultural blocks include:

»   fantasy and reflection are a waste of time, lazy, even crazy;

»   playfulness is for children only;

»   problem solving is serious business, and humor is out of place;

»   reason, logic, utility, and practicality are good, while feelings, intuition, qualitative judgments, and pleasure are bad;

»   tradition is preferable to change;

»   any problem can be solved by scientific thinking and lots of money; and

»   taboos.

Adams (1986) gave an example of an activity that illustrates the power of taboos in thwarting problem solving.

Imagine that you are one of a group of six people in a bare room along with the following objects: 100 feet of clothesline, a carpenter's hammer, a chisel, a box of Wheaties, a file, a wire coat hanger, a monkey wrench, and a light bulb. A steel pipe is stuck vertically in the concrete floor with a ping-pong ball lying at the bottom of the pipe. The inside diameter of the pipe is just slightly larger than the diameter of the ping-pong ball. Your task is to get the ball out of the pipe without damaging the ball, tube, or floor. How many ways can you think of to do this? (p. 54)

The solution of urinating in the pipe to float the ball out is rarely suggested. When it is suggested, it is typically by a male, and it is often after there has been some whispering among the participants and laughing. Once that boundary has been breached, many other ideas come forth. This is not to say that these are the best ideas, but rather that taboos can keep us from even considering some ideas and can limit our creativity.

Environmental blocks include:

» lack of cooperation and trust among colleagues;
» autocratic boss who values only his or her own ideas and does not reward others;
» distractions (phone, easy intrusions, etc.); and
» lack of support to bring ideas into action.

It is easy to demonstrate environmental blocks if you work in a school setting. Have students discuss the things they find most distracting when they are trying to concentrate at home and at school. Then, have them sit silently for a prescribed amount of time in each location and record the number and types of distractions they observe. Finally, address how they may eliminate or mitigate against most distractions.

Intellectual and expressive blocks include:

» solutions formed by solving the problem using an incorrect language;
» inflexible or inadequate use of intellectual problem-solving strategies; and
» lack of, or incorrect, information and inadequate language skill to express and record ideas (verbally, musically, visually, etc.).

Most people have favorite languages (verbal, mathematical, visual, psycho-motor) with which they attempt to solve most problems. For most, verbal or mathematical skills are used most often to solve problems, probably because these are the kinds of problems usually solved in school. Few are equally adept in all areas or are even capable of identifying problems that require a different language to solve.

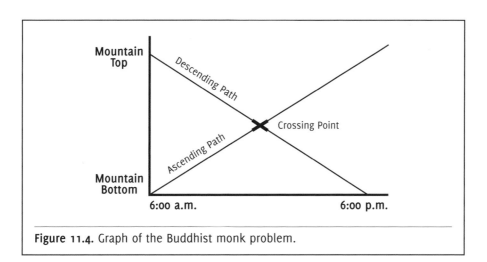

Figure 11.4. Graph of the Buddhist monk problem.

A favorite example is the Buddhist monk problem (Sternberg, 1986). A Buddhist monk walks up a mountain path to a temple at the top to pray. He leaves the bottom at 6 a.m., stops to eat lunch along the way, then continues until he reaches the top by 6 p.m. He prays and meditates through the night, then leaves at 6 a.m. the next morning to return to the bottom along the same path. Once again, he stops to rest and eat before arriving at the bottom near 6 p.m. The question: Is there a point along the path that the monk passes at the same time of day on both of the days of his trip?

Extremely bright adults struggle with the semantics or the numbers in trying to answer the question. The answer is "yes," and the proof is visual. Instead of 2 days, imagine that there are two monks on 1 day. Of course they would meet somewhere along the narrow path as one ascended and the other descended. Another way to visualize this is to draw a graph (see Figure 11.4).

The key is not whether that graph exactly represents the path that the monk took, but whether it is possible to draw any representative graph of his trip in which the lines do not intersect. The point of this exercise is to get people to realize that expert problem solvers spend time assessing the problem and devising a suitable strategy, rather than attacking every problem in the same way. Such flexibility in problem solving is an asset to creativity.

Competitive Creative Problem-Solving Programs

There are a myriad of competitive creative problem-solving programs that exist to foster critical and creative thinking skills in children. This section elaborates on three main creative problem-solving programs—Future Problem Solving Program International, Destination Imagination, and Odyssey of the Mind—

while also pointing the reader to several additional programs that exist to harness and develop creativity in children.

Future Problem Solving Program International

Perhaps the best-known creative problem-solving competition is the Future Problem Solving Program International (FPSPI), founded in 1974 by Torrance with the mission to "develop the ability of young people globally to design and promote positive futures using critical, creative thinking" (FPSPI, 2013, para. 1). Students compete at the local, state, and international levels in teams of four or as individuals at one of three age levels: Junior (grades 4–6), Intermediate (grades 7–9), or Senior (grades 10–12). The program contains three competitive components: Global Issues Problem Solving, Community Problem Solving, and Scenario Writing, which are all designed to appeal to students with various personalities and learning styles.

The diverse components of the program are meant to teach students *how* to think, rather than *what* to think (FPSPI, 2013). FPSPI helps raise students' awareness about global community issues by giving them a chance to develop their critical thinking as they scrutinize, evaluate, and propose the best solution for a particular issue. Such a process will also develop students' emotional needs, such as sensitivity, empathy, self-actualization, and resilience through the students' expressiveness about the issue.

Global issues problem solving. This component requires teams of four (students also have the option to work independently) to propose solutions to complex societal problems such as endangered species and water pollution. These problems, referred to as future scenes or "fuzzies," require students to project themselves into the future to propose solutions. Students work carefully through the Future Problem Solving Six Step Model, based on the Osborn/Parnes Creative Problem Solving process (CPS), to analyze future scenes in detail and present potential solutions.

Community problem solving component (CmPS). CmPS challenges students to identify a real need in their own community and solve it through the application of FPSPI skills. This component encourages problem-finding skills, because students must explore their environment and identify problems before progressing to problem solving (Runco, 1994).

Scenario writing. Here, students compose original futuristic stories related to their choice of the current year's future scenes. This component typically appeals to students who enjoy working independently and expressing their creative ideas verbally.

FPSPI also has a noncompetitive component, Action-based Problem Solving, which is designed to be implemented in regular classroom environments. This component encourages the application of creative problem-solving skills in more academic environments and can be effective in scaffolding the appropriate transfer of creative problem-solving skills from extracurricular to traditional academic environments.

Destination Imagination

Destination Imagination was formed in 1999, when it split from Odyssey of the Mind to continue as a nonprofit organization. Students work in teams of up to seven members in various age categories to solve one of six challenges in the following categories: technical, scientific, fine arts, improvisational, structural, and service learning. These challenges require students to conduct research and create solutions in skit form to be presented at competition. Challenges have several intricate requirements that students must incorporate in their performance, ranging from moving vehicles, structures that hold large amounts of weight, and intricate props and costumes.

The competition is based on two components: the Challenge Solution that the students work to solve all year, as well as an Instant Challenge, which is a short-term improvisational challenge solved the day of the tournament. Students are judged not only on their final product, but also on their teamwork and the technique they use to solve the problem.

Odyssey of the Mind

Odyssey of the Mind is an international creative problem-solving program quite similar to Destination Imagination. Teams of up to seven children in various age groups work yearlong to solve problems in one of the following categories: mechanical, classics, performance, structure, and technical performance. All problem solutions require some sort of presentation, which is presented at competition. Teams also compete in Spontaneous Problems, in which they must use their creative thinking and teamwork skills to solve problems in less than 10 minutes. Similar to the Instant Challenge portion of Destination Imagination, teams are judged by how well they work together to solve the problem, as well as the final product.

This review includes the most popular competitive creative problem-solving programs, but a multitude of other programs exist. Several programs are invention-based and require students to develop a new invention to improve everyday life.

In light of creativity research, competitive creative problem-solving programs can be highly effective in promoting creative thinking skills. The programs discussed address the four P's of creativity (process, product, person, and place) in various capacities (Rhodes, 1961). Each program suggests a unique problem-solving process, each of which coincide with Wallas's creative problem-solving stages: preparation, incubation, illumination, and verification (Wallas, 1926). Perhaps the most effective facet of competitive creative problem-solving programs is the focus on creating safe environments that meet individual student needs and encourage creative thinking.

The Incubation Model

The Incubation Model is, as the name says, a model, rather than a strategy for teaching creative thinking (Torrance & Safter, 1990). It was conceived as a way of addressing the whole of creativity, both rational and suprarational where the "individual consciousness transcends the boundaries of the deliberately rational creative process and experiences an altered state of consciousness, a holistic state of awareness, a state of instant communication among all the parts" (Torrance & Safter, 1990, p. vii). This suprarational creative process differs from the more linear stages of rational creativity and includes moments of "insight, intuition, and revelation" (Torrance & Safter, 1990, p. vii).

A great teacher goes beyond teaching students the rational creative thinking techniques and engages their curiosity, intuition, and emotions. Torrance considered incubation to be a vital part of the creative process. When solving problems creatively, the mind needs time to let the issue rest, to incubate, in the same way that mulling over a problem might allow one to see a clear solution over time. This model has the goal of fostering incubation in students by encouraging them to continue thinking about the lessons beyond the classroom. Many lesson plan formats have an initial activity, some developmental activities, and a culminating activity that often is some type of evaluation. With this type of lesson, the students' minds are opened up with the initial activity, then closed with the final, closing, or evaluation activity. The point of the Incubation Model is to open the students' minds and keep them open to learning about the topic after the formal lesson has ended. The three stages of "Heightening Anticipation," "Deepening Expectations," and "Keeping it Going" provide a framework for teachers to foster deep curiosity in students.

Stage 1: Heightening Anticipation

The purpose of Stage 1 is to warm-up students in a more profound way than the usual introductory activity of a lesson. Below is a list of learning activities that illustrate how teachers can intentionally design any content area start-up to create in students a desire to know more. In essence, the purpose of the Stage 1 activities is to: create the desire to know; heighten anticipation and expectation; get attention; arouse curiosity; tickle the imagination; and give purpose and motivation.

1. Confront ambiguities and uncertainties.

2. Heighten concern about a problem or future need.
3. Make the strange familiar or the familiar strange.
4. Look at the same information from different viewpoints.
5. Provide only enough structure to give clues and direction.
6. Warm up physically or bodily to the information to be presented.

Stage 2: Encountering the Expected and Unexpected and Deepening Expectations

Once a student's interest is awakened, the teacher must find a way for this curiosity to find fulfillment. The following activities encourage students to delve more deeply into the content.

1. Heighten awareness of problems and difficulties.
2. Present information as incomplete and have learners ask questions to fill gaps.
3. Juxtapose apparently irrelevant elements.
4. Preserve open-endedness.
5. Make outcomes not completely predictable.
6. Encourage visualization.

Stage 3: Going Beyond and "Keeping It Going"

Eventually, students need the opportunity to do something with the knowledge they have acquired, in order to continue the creative process. It is time for the student to venture beyond the classroom. Students engage in information processing strategies such as humor or fantasy, finding personal meaning, imagining ideal solutions, finding inspiration, and relating the ideas to the future. The learning activities below can facilitate these goals.

1. Play with ambiguities.
2. Encourage elegant solutions, the solution of collision conflicts, unsolved mysteries.
3. Examine fantasies to find solutions to real problems.
4. Encourage future projections.
5. Entertain improbabilities.
6. Create humor and see the humorous in the information presented.
7. Encourage deferred judgment and the use of some disciplined procedures of problem solving.
8. Encourage the manipulation of ideas, objects, or both.
9. Confront and examine paradoxes.

The Incubation Model was presented last under techniques for creative thinking because it provides an organizing framework for the creative activities described in this chapter. For example, in teaching a lesson on density in a science class, the teacher heightens anticipation by showing the students a tub of water and two cans of soda of the same brand—one regular and one diet. She asks the students to speculate about whether the cans will float or sink, questioning them about some of the principles they've learned about density. After the students have discussed their predictions and reasons, the teacher drops the regular can of soda in the water and it sinks. By doing this, the teacher guides the students to encounter the expected, for those who guessed correctly, and unexpected, for those who did not, and deepen their expectations by predicting whether the can of diet soda will sink or float. When the students have made their predictions, the teacher drops the diet soda into the tub and it floats.

Most lessons would conclude at this point with a wrap-up and summary of why the two cans reacted differently; however, the idea of the Incubation Model is to keep it going, rather than wrap it up. Before class ends, the students may be asked to think about another test they could do to discover the principle behind the density difference. If students are intrigued enough, they will continue to think about the problem outside of class. Some may try to discover at home why some sodas sink and others float. Other students may propose another test to be conducted in class. With guidance, and a touch of drama, the teacher should be able to lead the students to discover that the sugar in the regular soda is what makes it denser than the diet soda. The students have learned about density, but they also have learned about problem solving, hypothesizing, testing ideas, and persisting with an idea beyond the boundaries of the classroom. The Incubation Model provides a way for creativity to flourish beyond the classroom experience.

Summary

Although this chapter has described and illustrated a number of strategies and activities to enhance creativity in the classroom, it is in no way exhaustive. A plethora of other sources of strategies and activities are available both commercially and on the Internet. A small sample of these are located in the Teacher Resources section at the end of this chapter. Be aware that in the digital age these resources are fluid and change rapidly. Such is the nature of creativity in the classroom, an ever (ex)changing landscape of thoughts, ideas, products, processes, strategies, and activities.

Conclusion

Before educators can begin to nurture creativity in students, they must first be able to recognize and value the role it plays in their own lives. It is only then that teachers can begin to create a classroom climate that is psychologically safe for creative exploration. Within this learning environment, there are several techniques to be used, first as warm-ups, but also exercises to promote ideation, visualization, analogical thinking, lateral thinking, group and individual problem solving, and going beyond the rational for incubation. These techniques and strategies can assist in removing blocks to creativity, exploring competitions and other outlets for children's creativity, while providing opportunities and encouragement for expressive and problem-solving creativity. It is at this intersection where teachers are truly able to foster creativity in students and become those teachers who "made a difference" (Torrance, 1981, p. 55).

Teacher Statement

As a student, I can remember that most classes had desks in rows, teachers in the front of the room, and an unspoken understanding that there should be silence when the bell rang. What inevitably followed in those rooms was the monotony and repetition that we students loathed, accompanying the idea that there should be very little input from those being taught. There was never any need, the teacher was the purveyor of information. The truth of the matter is that these were the classes I dreaded making my way to each day. Of course, I learned—but I know I could have done so much more.

In contrast, the classes that I remember as being the most engaging and interesting—the ones I remember fondly—were the few where we students were treated as an important piece of the learning. We were allowed to step outside the bounds of what was "normal" in the classroom. We were allowed to be creative and encouraged to use our own ideas—because after all, it was our learning. The teachers in those classrooms took risks and allowed us to take part in the day-to-day.

When I became a high school teacher, I promised myself that I would never allow my classroom to be one that students feared or dreaded coming to each day. I wanted to be counted among those that the students found interesting and engaging . . . I wanted them to learn, but equally as important I wanted them to enjoy their time in my room and take ownership in what they were doing.

Now, more than ever, it is vital for our students to be in an environment that doesn't stifle their chances for interaction, teamwork, and creativity. The world we are preparing our students to enter is one that is ever changing. Giving our students the tools to be successful when faced with new technology, new jobs, and new ideas in this ever-shrinking global society should be our top priority. This cannot be done by keeping creativity and innovation out of the building blocks of our classrooms. If we can't teach our students to take risks and use their own ideas, we're doing them a grave disservice.

Some would describe my classroom as disorganized. Some would describe my classroom as unruly. Some would describe my classroom as being too loud. I would describe my classroom to be one that welcomes the new idea, where there's not just one "correct" way of doing whatever "it" is. I would describe my classroom as a place where students can take risks and test their limits, a system of organized chaos. My goal each day is to encourage students never to shy away from sharing an opinion or trying something new. Because I've come to the conclusion that it's in these types of environments where students are allowed to spread their wings—using their own thoughts and creative ideas—that success is the result.

—Chris Turpin, High School Teacher

DISCUSSION QUESTIONS

1. What is your own definition of creativity? How does that definition influence your teaching?

2. Is creativity something that can and should be taught? Where does it fit into the curriculum?

3. How do you see the role of competition in education? Is it motivating or intimidating? Does it stifle creativity?

4. Design a warm-up activity for creative thinking. Why would it be a good warm-up?

5. How can you modify the environment in your classroom to encourage creative thinking?

6. What discussion topics can you think of for the six thinking hats method to facilitate students' creative problem solving?

7. What are the positive effects of role-playing on students' learning?

8. Have you ever experienced blocks to your creativity? What kind of blocks did you remove and how did it help you generate ideas or solve problems creatively?

9. In what ways can parents and teachers show they value the development of creativity?

Teacher Resources

Publishers

Creative Education Foundation—http://www.creativeeducationfoundation.org
Free Spirit Publishing—http://www.freespirit.com
Prufrock Press—http://www.prufrock.com

Competitions

Destination Imagination, Inc.—http://www.destinationimagination.org
Future Problem Solving Program International—http://www.fpspi.org
Odyssey of the Mind—http://www.odysseyofthemind.com

Websites

The American Creativity Association—http://www.aca.cloverpad.org
Cyberkids—http://www.cyberkids.com
Cyberteens—http://www.cyberteens.com
Creativity Based Information Resources (CBIR)—http://www.buffalostate.edu/orgs/cbir
Creativity Café—http://creativity.net
Creative Parents.com—http://www.creativeparents.com/librarynotes.html
Creativity Games.net—http://creativitygames.net/
Enchanted Mind—http://www.enchantedmind.com
Mycoted: Creativity and Innovation Techniques—http://www.mycoted.com/Category: Creativity_Techniques
The Torrance Center for Creativity and Talent Development—http://www.coe.uga.edu/torrance/

References

Adams, J. L. (1986). *Conceptual blockbusting: A guide to better ideas.* Reading, MA: Addison-Wesley.

Ahn, B. (2012, January). Education in the Republic of Korea: National treasure or national headache? *Education Week, 31,* 39.

Amabile, T. M. (1983). *The social psychology of creativity.* New York, NY: Springer-Verlag.

Amabile, T. M. (1996). *Creativity in context.* New York, NY: Springer-Verlag.

American Recovery and Reinvestment Act of 2009, Pub. Law 111-5. (2009).

Beghetto, R. A., & Kaufman, J. C. (2007). The genesis of creative greatness: Mini c and the expert performance approach. *High Ability Studies, 18*(1), 59–61.

Bronson, P., & Merryman, A. (2010, July 19). The creativity crisis. *Newsweek, 156*(3), 44–50.

Cachia, R., Ferrari, A., Kearney, C., Punie, Y., Van Den Berghe, W., & Wastaiu, P. (2009). *Creativity in schools in Europe: A survey of teachers.* Retrieved from http://ftp.jrc.es/EURdoc/JRC55645_Creativity%20Survey%20Brochure.pdf

Cameron, J., & Pierce, W. D. (1994). Reinforcement, reward, and intrinsic motivation: A meta-analysis. *Review of Educational Research, 64,* 363–423.

Chumaceiro, C. L. (1997). Serendipity and its analogues in Runco's problem finding, problem solving, and creativity. *Creative Research Journal, 10*(1), 87–89.

Cramond, B. (1993). Speaking and listening: Key components of a language arts program for the gifted. *Roeper Review, 16,* 44–48.

Cramond, B. (1994). Attention-Deficit Hyperactivity Disorder and creativity: What is the connection? *The Journal of Creative Behavior, 28,* 193–210.

Cramond, B. (1995). *The coincidence of ADHD and creativity* (Research-Based Decision-Making Series No. 9508). Storrs: University of Connecticut, The National Research Center for the Gifted and Talented.

Cramond, B. (2002). The study of creativity in the future. In A. G. Alienikov (Ed.), *The future of creativity* (pp. 83–86). Bensenville, IL: Scholastic Testing Service.

Csikszentmihalyi, M. (1990). *Flow: The psychology of optimal experience.* New York, NY: Harper Perennial.

Csikszentmihalyi, M., & Getzels, J. W. (1971). Discovery-oriented behavior and the originality of creative products: A study with artists. *Journal of Personality and Social Psychology, 19,* 47–52.

de Bono, E. (1970). *Lateral thinking.* New York, NY: Harper & Row.

de Bono, E. (1985a). *de Bono's thinking course.* New York, NY: Facts on File Publications.

de Bono, E. (1985b). *Six thinking hats.* Boston, MA: Little, Brown.

de Bono, E. (1991). *Six action shoes.* New York, NY: HarperCollins.

Dweck, C. (2007). *Mindset: The new psychology of success.* New York, NY: Ballantine.

Eberle, B. (1996). *Scamper: Creative games and activities for imagination and development.* Buffalo, NY: D.O.K.

Ekvall, G. (1999). Organizational climate for creativity and innovation. In G. J. Puccio & M. C. Murdock (Eds.), *Creativity assessment: Reading and resources* (pp. 147–164). Buffalo, NY: Creative Education Foundation.

Feldman, D. H., Csikszentmihalyi, M., & Gardner, H. (1994). *Changing the world: A framework for the study of creativity.* Westport, CT: Praeger.

Future Problem Solving Program International, Inc. (2013). *Welcome.* Retrieved from http://www.fpspi.org/index.html

Goldberg, R. (1968). *Rube Goldberg vs. the machine age: A retrospective exhibition of his work with memoirs and annotations.* New York, NY: Hastings House.

Gordon, W. J. (1961). *Synectics.* New York, NY: Harper & Row.

Guilford, J. P. (1959). Three faces of intellect. *American Psychologist, 14,* 469–479.

Guilford, J. P. (1967). *The nature of human intelligence.* New York, NY: McGraw-Hill.

Halsted, J. W. (2009). *Some of my best friends are books* (3rd ed.). Tucson, AZ: Great Potential Press.

Hocevar, D. (1976). Dimensionality of creativity. *Psychological Reports, 39,* 869–870.

Hoover, S. M., & Feldhusen, J. F. (1990). The scientific hypothesis formulation ability of gifted ninth-grade students. *Journal of Educational Psychology, 82,* 838–848.

IBM. (2010, May 18). *IBM 2010 Global CEO study: Creativity selected as most crucial factor for future success* [Press release]. Retrieved from http://www03.ibm.com/press/us/en/pressrelease/31670.wss#release

Joy, S. (2004). Innovation motivation: The need to be different. *Creative Research Journal, 16,* 313–330.

Kaufman, J. C., & Baer, J. (2005). *Creativity across domain: Faces of the muse.* Hillsdale, NJ: Lawrence Erlbaum.

Kim, K. H. (2012). The creativity crisis: The decrease in creative thinking scores on the Torrance Tests of Creative Thinking. *Creativity Research Journal, 22,* 285–295.

Koberg, D., & Bagnall, J. (1991). *The universal traveler: A soft-systems guide to creativity, problem solving, & the process of reaching goals.* Menlo Park, CA: Crisp.

Martin, C. E., & Cramond, B. (1983). Creative reading: Is it being taught to the gifted in elementary schools? *Journal for the Education of the Gifted, 6,* 70–79.

Maslow, A. H. (1968). *Toward a psychology of being.* New York, NY: Van Nostrand Reinhold Co.

Milgram, R. M. (1990). Creativity: An idea whose time has come and gone? In M. A. Runco & R. S. Albert (Eds.), *The theories of creativity* (pp. 215–233). Newbury Park, CA: Sage.

National Center on Education and the Economy. (2007). *Tough choices or tough times: The report of the New Commission on the Skills of the American Workforce.* Washington, DC: Jossey-Bass.

No Child Left Behind Act, 20 U.S.C. §6301 (2001).

Okuda, S. M., Runco, M. A., & Berger, D. E. (1991). Creativity and the finding and solving of real world problems. *Journal of Psychoeducational Assessment, 9,* 45–43.

Parnes, S. J. (1981). *The magic of your mind.* Buffalo, NY: Creative Education Foundation.

Pierik, R. P. (2013, Winter). Learning in China. *The magazine of the Harvard Graduate School of Education.* Retrieved from http://www.gse.harvard.edu/news-impact/2003/10/learning-in-chinafree-market-style/

Planck, M. (1949). *Scientific autobiography and other papers* (F. Gaynor, Trans.). New York, NY: Philosophical Library.

Plucker, J. (1998). Beware of simple conclusions: The case for content generality of creativity. *Creativity Research Journal, 11,* 179–182.

Renzulli, J. S. (2005, May 25). A quiet crisis is clouding the future of research and development. *Education Week, 24,* 32–33, 40.

Rhodes, M. (1961). An analysis of creativity. *The Phi Delta Kappan, 42,* 305–310.

Robelen, E. W. (2012, February 2). States mulling creativity indexes for schools. *Education Week, 31*(19). Retrieved from http://www.edweek.org/ew/articles/2012/02/02/19creativity_ep.h31.html

Rogers, C. R. (1954). Toward a theory of creativity. *ETC: A Review of General Semantics, 11,* 250–258.

Root-Bernstein, R. S., Bernstein, M., & Garnier, H. (1995). Correlations between avocations, scientific style, work habits, and professional impact of scientists. *Creativity Research Journal, 8,* 115–137.

Rothenberg, A., & Hausman, C. R. (Eds.). (1976). *The creativity question.* Durham, NC: Duke University.

Rotter, J. B. (1975). Some problems and misconceptions related to the construct of internal vs. external control of reinforcement. *Journal of Consulting and Clinical Psychology, 43,* 56–67.

Runco, M. A. (1994). *Problem finding, problem solving, and creativity.* Norwood, NJ: Ablex Pub.

Runco, M. (2010). Divergent thinking, creativity, and ideation. In J. Kaufman & R. J. Sternberg (Eds.), *The Cambridge handbook of creativity* (pp. 413–446). New York, NY: Cambridge University Press.

Runco, M. A., & Jaeger, G. J. (2012). The standard definition of creativity. *Creativity Research Journal, 24*(1), 92–96.

Runco, M. A., & Okuda, S. M. (1988). Problem discovery, divergent thinking, and the creative process. *Journal of Youth and Adolescence, 17,* 211–220.

Runco, M. A., & Richards, R. (Eds.). (1997). *Eminent creativity, everyday creativity, and health: Publications in creativity research.* Greenwich, CT: Ablex.

Simonton, D. K. (2007). Specialized expertise or general cognitive processes. In M. J. Roberts (Ed.), *Integrating the mind* (pp. 351–367). New York, NY: Psychology Press.

Skinner, B. F. (1972). From "A lecture on 'having' a poem." In B. F. Skinner, *Cumulative record: A selection of papers* (3rd ed., pp. 345, 350–355). Englewood Cliffs, NJ: Prentice-Hall.

Sternberg, R. J. (1986). *Intelligence applied: Understanding and increasing your intellectual skills.* New York, NY: Harcourt, Brace, Jovanovich.

Sternberg, R. J. (Ed.). (1988). *The nature of creativity: Contemporary psychological perspectives.* New York, NY: Cambridge University Press.

Sternberg, R. J., & Lubart, T. I. (1991). An investment of creativity and its development. *Human Development, 34,* 1–31.

Taylor, I. A. (1959). The nature of the creative process. In P. Smith (Ed.), *Creativity* (pp. 521–582). New York, NY: Hastings House.

Torrance, E. P. (1962). *Guiding creative talent.* Englewood Cliffs, NJ: Prentice-Hall.

Torrance, E. P. (1966). Nurture of creative talents. *Theory Into Practice, 5,* 168–202.

Torrance, E. P. (1974). *Norms-technical manual: Torrance Tests of Creative Thinking.* Lexington, MA: Ginn.

Torrance, E. P. (1976). *Future problem solving and career education.* Athens, GA: University of Georgia, Pre-Service Training in Career Education Project, College of Education.

Torrance, E. P. (1981). Predicting the creativity of elementary school children (1958–80) and the teacher who "made a difference." *Gifted Child Quarterly, 25,* 55–62.

Torrance, E. P. (1987). Future career image as a predictor of creative achievement in the 22-year longitudinal study. *Psychological Reports, 60,* 574.

Torrance, E. P. (1988). Creativity as manifest in testing. In R. J. Sternberg (Ed.), *The nature of creativity* (pp. 43–75). New York, NY: Cambridge University Press.

Torrance, E. P., Murdock, M., & Fletcher, D. (1997). *Creative problem solving through role-playing.* Pretoria, South Africa: Benedic Books.

Torrance, E. P., & Safter, H. T. (1990). *The incubation model of teaching: Getting beyond the aha!* Buffalo, NY: Creative Education Foundation Press.

VanTassel-Baska, J. (1998). *Excellence in educating gifted and talented learners* (3rd ed.). Denver, CO: Love.

von Oech, R. (1983). *A whack on the side of the head: How to unlock your mind for innovation.* New York, NY: Warner Books.

Wakefield, J. F. (1985). Towards creativity: Problem finding in a divergent-thinking exercise. *Child Study Journal, 15,* 265–270.

Wallas, G. (1926). *The art of thought.* New York, NY: Harcourt Brace and World.

Woodman, R. W., & Schoenfeldt, L. F. (1990). An interactionist model of creative behavior. *Journal of Creative Behavior, 24,* 279–290.

Ziv, A. (1983). The influence of humorous atmosphere on divergent thinking. *Contemporary Educational Psychology, 8,* 68–75.

DEVELOPING RESEARCH SKILLS IN GIFTED LEARNERS

BY KATE BROWN AND DANA SEYMOUR

Emily spends 6 hours each week in a university research laboratory alongside leading scientists in the field of breast cancer research. Working to identify an antibody that would assist in the body's defense against breast cancer, this team of researchers represents some of the top scientific minds in the country. Their study, funded by the National Science Foundation, holds real promise for minimizing the deadly effects of one particularly aggressive form of breast cancer. Analyzing biopsy slides and recording data, Emily confidently exchanges ideas and suggestions with the other scientists in the room. Although her advanced cell biology and human anatomy and physiology courses provided Emily with a strong foundational knowledge in the subject matter, the opportunity to conduct potentially life-saving studies crystallized her plans to select medical research as her field of study.

Thirty miles away, Marcus deposes a witness for an upcoming civil trial. He will transcribe the deposition from an audiotape and prepare a word-for-word written account of the testimony. Analyzing this deposition against those of six other major witnesses, Marcus will look for patterns, trends, and significant events that will help build a case for his client, a major manufacturing facility in the community. Assisting Marcus is both a senior and junior partner in a prestigious law firm. They exchange smiles as Marcus poses a pivotal question and the witness struggles to maintain composure. The partners are impressed with the calm yet probing manner in which Marcus questions the witness, and they continue to make notes as the deposition continues.

Hunched over a stack of photographs in the library's historical archive room, Thomas examines the fuzzy image in an old black and white photograph with a magnifying glass, carefully matching the features of one man in the photo to those of his research subject, Ira Bergman, hoping for a positive identification. Bergman, a Jewish businessman, played a key role in the reconstruction of this small southern town following the Civil War. His grave, marked by a small cross and engraved foot marker, sits in Friendship Cemetery, the reputed site where Memorial Day began. Thomas could recite from memory the story of confederate women placing wreaths of flowers on the graves of Yankee soldiers buried in Friendship Cemetery. He'd grown up with the stories, after all, and had always had a passion for history and tales of all kinds. One by one, Thomas and his colleagues were bringing to life the stories of those buried in Friendship Cemetery, buried and forgotten—their stories left untold. The goal of this original research project was to uncover and tell the stories of individuals who had lived and died in this community, giving these "tales from the crypt" as a gift to local residents and visitors from across the region, bringing history to life through authentic reenactment.

What is unusual about the stories of Emily, Marcus, and Thomas? They are not practicing professionals and they are not graduate students or doctoral candidates. Instead, they are high school juniors and seniors, students at the Mississippi School for Mathematics and Science (MSMS), a public, residential high school for gifted and talented students. Rarely would top students have the opportunity to assist with cutting-edge research; engage in rich, authentic mentoring experiences; or conduct original research projects, but at MSMS and other special schools for gifted learners across the country, these kinds of engaging learning experiences are more the rule than the exception. Leadership teams in these schools recognize the value of authentic research experiences: increased critical and creative thinking skills, motivation based on personal interest and drive, connections between schoolwork to real-world applications, and self-directed independent learning. Their experience with information gathering, source analysis and verification, synthesis of data and knowledge, drawing conclusions, and presenting findings enables these students to become producers of knowledge and positions them to lead in their fields of study, even at a relatively young age. This is true talent development, authentic recognition of potential, and clear best practice for nurturing gifted learners.

Gifted learners need opportunities for authentic learning experiences, including mentorships, research internships, and in-depth studies in areas of intense personal interest (Betts, 1985; Betts & Kercher, 1999; Maker & Nielson, 1996; Piirto, 2007; Renzulli, 1977; Renzulli & Reis, 2014; Robinson, Shore, & Enersen, 2007; Treffinger, 1975). Differentiation of content, process, and product can be facilitated through scaffolded learning experiences that develop research skills in gifted learners, experiences tailored to the unique characteristics and learning needs of the gifted. According to Renzulli (2013),

> The goal is to place students in situations in which they acquire, manage, and produce information in an organized and systematic fashion by applying the thinking and research process used to create this knowledge in the first place. When students have acquired a mature understanding of the methodology of the field, they are no longer passive recipients of information; they are able to begin the process of gaining and then generating knowledge within the field. (p. 271)

Feldhusen (1994a) also emphasized the important role of research in gifted education classrooms of all ages.

> The general rationale is that gifted learners have very high potential for creative activity and production in adulthood, and they should begin developing that potential as early as possible. A closely related goal is for gifted learners to become effective as high-level researchers and creators. To develop skills in research, these students need underlying competencies in creative thinking and problem solving, a knowledge base in the area or discipline in which they may conduct research, and some specific research skills (p. 313).

The Case for Developing Research Skills

The research process presents an open-ended, inquiry-based approach to learning that, if facilitated well, can lead to numerous positive student learning outcomes. Piirto (2007) defined inquiry as "a process of investigating phenomena, devising and working through a plan, and proposing a solution to the problem" (p. 502). In defining appropriate curriculum for the gifted, VanTassel-Baska (1989) outlined "essential curriculum components" including research as a process skill, and advocated introducing increasingly challenging and complex research skills beginning in kindergarten and progressing through high school. Incorporating research skills into the gifted curriculum increases rigor of learning, enhances critical and creative thinking skills, develops skills associated with autonomy and independent learning, and prepares gifted students to contribute in valuable ways to existing bodies of knowledge.

Increasing Motivation

Research projects on topics selected by students engage their interests and increase motivation to learn (Betts, 1985; Betts & Kercher, 1999; Piirto, 2007; Renzulli, 1977; Renzulli & Reis, 2014; Robinson et al., 2007; Schack & Starko, 1998; Treffinger, 1975). Schack and Starko, the authors of *Research Comes Alive* (1998), linked student research to motivation:

> We also believe involving students in original research contributes to increased motivation. This motivation comes when students are encouraged to investigate questions of genuine interest to them. Students also see the value of what they are learning in school when they recognize that it helps them answer questions they find relevant and compelling. Structuring learning so that students are actively involved in designing and carrying out research also gives them a more active role as learners (p. 2).

Students engaged in authentic, interest-based, relevant projects are more eager to learn and are more capable of directing their own learning. Increasing student motivation raises the ceiling for what gifted learners can accomplish. In allowing choice when facilitating the development of research skills, teachers of the gifted simultaneously amplify both the level of interest and the level of motivation.

Developing Skills of Autonomy

Skills of autonomous learning include independence, responsibility, goal setting, self-regulation, planning, time management, understanding of self and personal interests, intrinsic motivation, and understanding how knowledge is constructed (Betts, 1985; Betts & Kercher, 1999; Renzulli, 1977; Renzulli & Reis, 2014; Treffinger, 1975). The student-centered approach to research provides learners with the opportunity to pursue topics of interest, to self-manage with varying levels of scaffolding and support from the teacher-facilitator, to think independently, and to evaluate their own work. According to Maker and Nielson (1996),

Developing independence is an essential factor in the education of gifted students. Among the process modifications, we stress the importance of freedom of choice and open-endedness. These changes, along with establishment of a learner-centered environment, encourage students to be more independent . . . Tolerance and encouragement are reflected in many ways in the classroom, including academic factors such as student choice of what to learn, how to learn, and how to evaluate that learning. (p. 39)

Developing Critical and Creative Thinking Skills

The research process with its many levels of complexity can be used to address the scope and sequence of learning represented in the Common Core State Standards (CCSS; National Governors Association Center for Best Practices [NGA] & Council of Chief State School Officers [CCSSO], 2010a, 2010b) including content knowledge acquisition, synthesis of knowledge, and higher-order critical thinking. According to a leading pioneer in the field, critical thinking can be defined as "reasonable reflective thinking focused on deciding what to believe or do" (Ennis, 2000, p. 1). Ennis related critical thinking to steps commonly associated with the research process:

Under this interpretation, critical thinking is relevant not only to the formation and checking of beliefs, but also to deciding upon and evaluating actions. It involves creative activities such as formulating hypotheses, plans, and counterexamples; planning experiments; and seeing alternatives. (p. 1)

Over decades of work in the field of critical thinking, Ennis (2000) has isolated specific dispositions and abilities of ideal critical thinkers; the 12 key abilities of successful critical thinkers include being able to:
1. Focus on a question.
2. Analyze arguments.
3. Ask and answer questions of clarification and/or challenge.
4. Judge the credibility of a source.
5. Observe and judge observation reports.
6. Deduce and judge deduction.
7. Induce and judge deduction.
8. Make and judge value judgments.
9. Define terms and judge definitions.
10. Attribute unstated assumptions.

11. Consider and reason from premises, reasons, assumptions, positions, and other propositions with which they disagree or about which they are in doubt.

12. Integrate the other abilities and dispositions in making and defending a decision. (p. 2–8)

Ennis' list of abilities found in critical thinkers aligns closely with the skills utilized and developed through the research process. Student researchers integrate inductive and deductive thinking with skills of evaluation and judgment to gather accurate and reliable information, create research hypotheses and questions, analyze data, and draw conclusions. Schack and Starko (1998) asserted that the research process develops skills for critical thinking in students that otherwise may not be addressed in the standard school curriculum.

> . . . it is important to help students understand not just the content of the school curriculum (knowledge about), but also how professionals expand what is known and contribute new knowledge to the world (knowledge how). Content has traditionally been presented as a set body of knowledge to be learned. If, instead, it is approached as the end result of someone's research and creative productivity, students can gain a whole new perspective on both content and their own potential as knowledge producers. They also can gain tools for critical understanding. If they know what constitutes acceptable research, they can better judge information they encounter in the media, school, and among peers, etc. (p. 2)

Developing Expertise

Sternberg, Grigorenko, and Ferrari (2004) argued that intelligence may be described as developing expertise, which the researchers defined as "the ongoing process of the acquisition and consolidation of a set of skills needed for a high level of mastery in one or more domains of life performance" (p. 1).

Others in the field of gifted education recognize the importance of developing expertise in a particular area of interest or in a discipline (Betts, 1985; Betts & Kercher, 1999; Renzulli, 1977; Renzulli & Reis, 2014; Tomlinson et al., 2008). Developing domain expertise enables students to move beyond the role of learner and into the role of research, facilitator, teacher, and leader. Without a broad knowledge base of the subject, students cannot think critically about the ideas they encounter during research, nor can they pose high-quality research questions (Willingham, 2009).

Producing New Knowledge

Research encompasses more than the collection and perusal of information; it should move students from consumption of knowledge to its production. Research is a systematic process of inquiry and discovery, and as such, should ultimately direct students to hold sufficient expertise in a particular interest that they are able to develop new products, theories, ideas, practices, models, and techniques relevant to their field of study. According to Schack and Starko (1998),

> The focus of research is the discovery or production of new knowledge or understanding. This role is somewhat different for students who have traditionally been expected to consume information, not produce it. Researchers deal with questions without known answers, problems without effective solutions. Rather than re-examine what others have done, cutting-edge researchers add to the body of knowledge by producing new information. (p. 1)

Gifted Education Models Emphasizing Student Research

Several models frequently used in the field of gifted education incorporate student research as a key element. Often, this is in the form of independent studies, problem-based learning, or creative problem solving—all processes that require students to engage in research. As a group, these models treat the development of research skills as a process that students perfect over time and one that becomes increasingly rigorous and independent as expertise develops. Projects generally progress from the exploration of topics and ideas for possible study, to learning basic research skills, to conducting original research and generating new knowledge.

Autonomous Learner Model

The Autonomous Learner Model (Betts, 1985; Betts & Kercher, 1999) firmly establishes the important role of research in creating lifelong learners. Different levels of research skill development are incorporated in each of the five dimensions of the model, culminating in student-directed in-depth studies in the fifth and highest dimension. In the first dimension, the Orientation dimension, learners focus on deepening their understanding of giftedness, discovering self, exploring opportunities, developing potential, and building group interaction skills. The second dimension, Individual Development, provides for the development of the cognitive skills and attitudes necessary for lifelong learning and autonomy of learning. The role of technology in the research and learning processes is also covered. During Enrichment, the third dimension of the model, learners research and learn about topics of interest to them through *explorations*—broadening knowledge of many topics through exposure to new ideas, opportunities, or pursuits—and *investigations*—deepening understanding and knowledge of a few topics through targeted research. The fourth dimension, Seminars, requires further development of research skills as learners work in small groups to develop expertise in an area and to apply that expertise to create new ideas, products, or theories. Seminars are presented to real audiences comprised of peers, community members, practicing professionals, and other interested parties. Whereas seminars take place over a relatively short period of time and are undertaken by groups of learners, the fifth and highest dimension of the model, In-Depth Study, is distinguished by its depth of content and level of complexity as well as its individualization. In this dimension, learners are encouraged to conduct rigorous study and research in an area of great interest to them. Betts calls this "passion learning" and views it as the highest level of learning, a cornerstone to becoming an autonomous, lifelong learner. In-Depth Study requires learners to select an area of study, use research skills to develop a strong knowledge base, follow the example of professionals in the field to determine appropriate methodology, produce new knowledge through original work, and to self-assess their progress through the entire experience.

Enrichment Triad and Schoolwide Enrichment Models

The Enrichment Triad and Schoolwide Enrichment Models (Renzulli, 1977; Renzulli & Reis, 2014) delineate three separate types of learning for the gifted. Type I activities include general enrichment and exploratory activities designed to spark students' interest in further research or study. Examples of Type I activities include guest speakers, films/videos, representatives from community agencies, and field trips. Type II activities focus on the development of research skills and problem-solving strategies. Brainstorming, creative problem solving, problem-based learning, and experiments following the scientific method are all Type II activities. Type III activities consist of independent studies targeted at solving real-world problems and engaging in the behaviors of a practicing professional in the field. Usually conducted by individuals or in small groups, Type III activities should generate new ideas, skills, or products and involve gifted learners in the processes of developing, solving, and creating.

Parallel Curriculum Model

The Parallel Curriculum Model (PCM; Tomlinson et al., 2008) proposes four curriculum parallels designed to be used in tandem to develop potential and to effectively challenge gifted learners. Research skills are emphasized in all of the parallels of the PCM. In the Curriculum of Practice, students are asked to develop an understanding of the construct of the discipline, to analyze and emulate the behaviors and practices of professionals in the discipline, and to add new knowledge to the field through personal production and practice. The Curriculum of Identity encourages students to explore their possible roles in contributing to the discipline, to understand the ways in which their own interests and talents connect to the field, and to actively pursue engagement in learning and experiencing the discipline. To effectively challenge and engage gifted learners, the PCM suggests incorporating levels of "ascending intellectual demand," essentially a system of scaffolding tasks and content to increasingly higher levels of difficulty. Burns' (1993) Six-Phase Model for the Explicit Teaching of Thinking Skills is recommended as a catalyst for developing intellectually demanding learning activities because of its focus on the systematic development of analytical, critical, and creative thinking processes. Several steps in the typical research process connect directly to Burns' thinking skills model and naturally align with the development of higher order thinking skills as well as higher levels of rigor and intellectual demand: judging the accuracy of information, judging the credibility of a source, developing hypotheses, generalizing, decision making, planning, predicting, determining cause and effect, brainstorming, and creative problem solving.

Self-Directed Learning Model

The Self-Directed Learning Model (Treffinger, 1975) provides a scaffolded approach to increasing the autonomy and independent learning skills of students. Treffinger describes a systematic method for moving learners from a teacher-directed curriculum to a student-directed program of study. Level One of this model has students selecting research topics from a list prepared by the teacher. At this level, the teacher provides the structure, guidance, and evaluation for the project, while the student conducts the research project within those stipulated boundaries. When they reach Level Two, the teacher and student brainstorm together and select research topics, project requirements, and evaluation methods, essentially coplanning the learning. As students transition from one level to the next, they demonstrate mastery of basic skills related to self-directed learning: organizational skills, self-management, independence, judgment, motivation, and research skills. At Level Three, students have the freedom of choice and have exhibited the requisite skills to effectively plan, manage, and conduct self-directed learning projects. Although the teacher must approve the student's selections and decisions, the primary burden of organizing the learning experience resides with the student. At this level, students are actively engaged in choosing their research topic, developing a timeline, organizing their research, and creating their own system of evaluation.

Research Skills and the Common Core State Standards

The authors of the CCSS (NGA & CCSSO, 2010a, 2010b) pointed out that the standards do not explicitly address high-ability students and those who perform above grade level; these omissions are "intentional design limitations" that allow teachers to provide appropriate interventions for their gifted students (p. 6). Consequently, CCSS should not be considered a sufficient substitute for appropriate gifted education.

Although the standards do not specifically address the needs of gifted students, the strong research focus of the CCSS is well-tailored to best practices differentiation for gifted education. High-ability students may be afforded more autonomy and time to develop and produce research at appropriately advanced levels of complexity. Especially in schools without a dedicated gifted program, regular classroom teachers should capitalize on the research foci of the CCSS in English/language arts, science, mathematics, and social studies coursework; engaging gifted students in self-directed, supported research fits perfectly with the goal of CCSS, which is to produce sophisticated consumers and producers of knowledge for 21st-century success.

Constructing a Knowledge Base

Researchers require deep content knowledge to effectively plan and conduct well-designed studies and experiments and to make sense of the results (Willingham, 2009). Constructing a knowledge base is a foundational research skill. According to Feldhusen (1994b), a "knowledge base is essential before one can organize schemata and develop deep understanding. This means that gifted and talented youth must learn to be independent seekers of knowledge through reading and study" (p. 369). Student researchers develop a knowledge base through gathering information from a diverse range of sources, evaluating and verifying the reliability of sources and information, analyzing and synthesizing the information gathered, and aligning new information with existing understanding.

Accessing Information

Students today have many resources from which to draw when researching a particular topic. Only a few decades ago, finding enough information could be a challenge for researchers; today, the Internet contains immense amounts of information on nearly any topic. Those who grew up with Internet search engines may automatically rely on this singular method of information gathering, but significant challenges can arise if students have not learned to navigate the vastness of resources. Unfortunately, students often assume that information on websites is accurate; they need guidance, experience, and training in judging and evaluating sources and information of all kinds. Encouraging the use of multiple source types increases opportunities for student researchers to explore various information sources, examine differing viewpoints, and substantiate key information.

Types of Information Resources

Developing a strong knowledge base in a particular subject or field requires extensive reading and research and should reflect the use of many different sources of information. Drawing on a variety of rich resources that have been verified for authenticity and veracity provides a strong foundation from which student researchers are poised to develop more accurate theories and ideas, design more meaningful experiments, and conduct research projects of value and significance. According to Piirto (2007),

> Academically talented students should be challenged to organize the material for themselves, using general reference books, encyclopedias, and bibliographies, and several texts rather than just one. This training in research techniques will teach the academically talented child to distinguish between theoretical viewpoints and experiments, between surveys, anthologies, and original reports of data gathering. The academically talented child should learn by browsing, and by rapid surveying of material. (p. 455–456)

Generally, reference sources can be divided into four primary categories: (a) *documents*—which may be handwritten or typed, published or unpublished—represent written or printed texts; (b) *numerical records* include survey data, financial statements, test scores, and other quantifiable records; (c) *audio/visual records* consist of events experienced and/or observations conducted firsthand or video or audio recorded or photographed; and (d) *artifacts* represent physical objects that allow researchers to gain insight into their topics of study. Sample resources in each of these four areas are listed in Figure 12.1.

Artifacts	Audio/Visual Records	Documents	Numerical Records
▸ Artwork	▸ Films	▸ Magazines	▸ Census records
▸ Objects	▸ Photographs	▸ Encyclopedias	▸ Finance records
▸ Clothing	▸ Audio	▸ Books	▸ Scores
▸ Buildings	recordings	▸ Diaries	▸ Survey results
▸ Journals	▸ Observations	▸ Legal records	▸ Budgets
▸ Work samples	▸ Video	▸ Journals	▸ Databases
▸ Equipment	recordings	▸ Monographs	▸ Statistics
▸ Monuments	▸ Interviews	▸ Newspapers	▸ Charts/Tables
▸ Furniture	▸ News footage	▸ Research	▸ Graphs
▸ Models	▸ Oral histories	reports	▸ Calculations
▸ Structures	▸ Statements	▸ Research	▸ Algorithms
▸ Examples	▸ Stories	studies	▸ Codes
▸ Experiments	▸ Legends/Tales	▸ Public records	
▸ Websites	▸ Songs	▸ Databases	
	▸ Websites	▸ Government	
	▸ Maps	publications	
		▸ Websites	

Figure 12.1. Possible reference sources.

Evaluating Information Resources

Students must be taught to question the reliability of their sources. This process includes examining potential biases or conflicts of interest such as a website supporting a particular idea, cause, policy, or practice that is financially supported by a special interest group. This may also include publications, videos, and websites from various national organizations with specific agendas such as political parties, activist groups, or corporations. Students should ask several questions about the resource:

» Who sponsors, promotes, publishes, or provides this information?
» Does this organization have any motive to present one-sided or inaccurate information?
» What evidence do I have that this is a reputable source?
» What is the professional affiliation or reputation of this source?
» What qualifications and requirements had to be met for this resource to provide this information?

Evaluating Information Accuracy

Once the source has been evaluated and verified as acceptable, students should question the reliability of the material. Although the Internet and many print media offer ready access to information, not everything online or in print is true or accurate. Students can verify correctness by carefully examining the information, comparing it to evidence gathered from other sources, and triangulating key facts and ideas by locating the same claims in multiple sources. Key questions for evaluating the accuracy of information gathered include:

» Is there a conflict of interest or a potential for bias?
» How current is the material?
» Does the information align with what I already know to be true about this topic?
» Does the information contain any obvious errors?
» Can I find the same information in at least three places?

A sample student form for evaluating sources and verifying the accuracy of information is presented in Figure 12.2.

As students gather information from multiple sources, verify both the legitimacy of the source and the accuracy of the information, analyze and process key ideas about their topic, and synthesize the information, they develop a strong foundation of knowledge in their research topic. This development of a knowledge base is essential to planning and executing effective and thorough research projects. Students cannot clearly define a problem, generate rich research questions, or appropriately plan a study if they do not possess deep knowledge of the topic under study. For this reason, teacher-facilitators should allow ample time for this part of the process; the eventual quality of the research project is dependent on the breadth and depth of knowledge students possess about the domain in question.

Types of Research

Typically, teachers ask students to "research" a topic and prepare a report; often, this is a knowledge or comprehension level task where students paraphrase information gathered from an online search or gleaned from an encyclopedia. True research begins with the development of a deep and substantial knowledge base on a topic of intense interest and includes information gleaned from numerous sources that has been analyzed, evaluated, and synthesized to reflect a clear and complete picture of the problem or topic under study. This process of identifying and defining a problem, gathering information, verifying sources, developing a knowledge base, and synthesizing the information into a well-structured, useful format reflects foundational skills necessary for any researcher and should not be discounted. The development of research skills is an incremental process that students improve through experience and maturity (Betts, 1985; Betts & Kercher, 1999; Treffinger, 1975; VanTassel-Baska, 1989). Once students exhibit skills in

BROWN AND SEYMOUR

Verifying the Accuracy of Information

Name: _____ Date: _____

Research Topic: _____ Source: _____

Key Information: _____

Evaluating the Source:

1. Who sponsors, promotes, publishes, or provides this information?

   _____

2. What indications are there that this is a reputable source?

   _____

3. What is the professional affiliation or reputation of this source?

   _____

4. What qualifications and requirements had to be met for this resource to provide this information?

   _____

Evaluating Information Accuracy:

1. What possible conflicts of interest or a potential for bias exist?

   _____

2. Is the information current?   ____ Yes ____ No

3. Does the information align with what I
   already know to be true about this topic?   ____ Yes ____ Somewhat ___ No

4. Is this a reputable source?   ____ Yes ____ No

5. Does the information contain errors?   ____ Yes ____ No

6. Can I find the same information in at least three places?
   Verification 1: _____

   Verification 2: _____

   Verification 3: _____

Figure 12.2. Sample student form for evaluating information.

---

identifying appropriate research topics and developing a rich knowledge base, they are able to move into original research, generally grouped into three broad categories: historical research, descriptive research, and experimental research.

Historical Research

Historical research applies to any field and simply means to examine a problem, issue, idea, or event that occurred in the past. Often used in the social sciences, historical research helps better understand origins, growth, patterns, change, theories, sequences of events, and other phenomena that may be of interest or significance. Elementary students may practice historical research by interviewing grandparents to answer questions like "What was it like for African Americans before integration?" or "How did families spend their free time before televisions and the Internet?" A middle school student passionately interested in space exploration may conduct historical research to trace the major events influencing the national space program or the progression of technology in space exploration. Whatever the age or area of interest of the students, the important concept behind historical research is that they investigate something that has already occurred, something that is in the past. Methods of historical research include interviews, oral histories, and examination of audio/video recordings, documents, records, photographs, and other artifacts. In historical research, students examine all relevant and reliable sources of information to piece together answers to questions or solutions to problems. According to Fraenkel, Wallen, and Hyun (2011), historical research consists of four clearly defined steps: problem finding, information gathering, synthesis of information, and interpretation and presentation of findings.

Step 1: Problem finding. In this preliminary step, researchers recognize a particular historical problem or issue, often the lack of organized information or understanding of a culture or event that raises questions or creates ambiguity. The topic of investigation should be clearly defined and recognized as worthy of study and contributing to historical knowledge. Hypotheses, if appropriate, should be generated once the problem is clearly defined.

Step 2: Information gathering. Historical researchers gather as much relevant information about their topic of study as possible, examining primary documents whenever they can. Primary documents provide firsthand accounts by actual participants or witnesses whereas secondary documents recount the events secondhand and therefore are considered less reliable, but usually more readily available, sources of information. In this phase, researchers also verify the authenticity and reliability of their sources.

Step 3: Synthesis of information. Once sources are identified, verified, and combed for information, researchers organize information in order to identify major ideas, patterns, trends, and theories. Often, this is through the process of triangulation, a method of drawing conclusions based on a preponderance of evidence or information drawn from careful and thorough evaluation of all available historical data.

Step 4: Interpretation and presentation of findings. Historical researchers draw inferences about the past by interpreting patterns and themes identified in records. Evidence gathered in Step 2 and triangulated in Step 3 guides researchers to conclusions that are firmly rooted in historical fact, that are well-supported by documented sources, and that offer reasonable explanations or solutions. Historical researchers should next determine an appropriate audience and presentation method to share the findings of their research. This may be through formal or informal presentation or publication but should include the careful recording of the research process and the conclusions drawn from the project.

Students interested in events of historical significance, historical figures, elements of culture, social issues, or other topics suitable for historical research will find this is a rich and challenging research method, well suited to a questioning, analytical mind. Historical researchers dig and sift through documents and records to piece together a clear and accurate picture and often find the process of solving the mystery as rewarding as the end result. Student historical researchers need to be comfortable with a level of mystery and "fuzziness" as they explore because historical questions often cannot be answered in full and instead require careful and sustained examination of all available resources and some amount of logical conjecture. Depending on the resources available in the local community, students are often able to examine primary documents through historical societies, local archives, public libraries, amateur and professional historians, colleges and universities, and museums. They may also be able to conduct interviews or record oral histories with individuals directly related to their topics of study. Teacher-facilitators of this type of research can assist with identifying possible community resources and assisting student researchers in connecting with these sources of information. In the example at the beginning of the chapter, Thomas was acting as a historical researcher, piecing together the life story and significance of a man who lived and died in another century but who contributed in meaningful ways to the community in which Thomas lives.

Descriptive Research

Descriptive research aims to develop a better understanding of a topic, subject, or problem through careful gathering and analysis of data. As opposed to historical research, which is grounded in the past, descriptive research focuses on investigating the current or present status of a problem or phenomenon. A third-grade student may study and describe the feeding habits of hummingbirds congregating in the backyard while a middle school student may develop and conduct a survey to determine the shopping habits of teenagers. As with any form of research, descriptive studies focus on problems or issues specific to a discipline. In the field of marketing, this might include studies of name brand recognition, perceptions of consumers, or opinion polls. Psychology studies may focus on self-esteem, perceptions of self-efficacy, or risky behaviors of teens, and medical scientists may examine behaviors contributing to disease, attitudes toward exercise and wellness, or preferences toward homeopathic remedies versus traditional medicine. Drawing from varied sources and data gathering methods, descriptive researchers accumulate a wealth of understandings and explanations from which they are able to generalize about the population and/or develop theories to explain or predict. Researchers may use surveys and questionnaires to study the attitudes, preferences, behaviors, practices, or interests of individuals or groups. To more thoroughly understand the sample under study, researchers may also implement qualitative research methods including interviews, observations, and artifact analysis. Descriptive research is a logically structured process following a set of ordered steps similar to both historical and experimental research.

Step 1: Identify a problem or phenomenon worthy of study. Descriptive researchers begin by identifying problems or various phenomena of interest to them and deemed worthy of study in that discipline. The problem should be clearly defined, relevant, and appropriate for study using descriptive methods.

Step 2: Select an appropriate sample of participants to represent the population. Researchers use sampling to study a relatively small number of cases intended to represent an entire population. For this reason, sampling methods should be carefully considered to ensure an accurate representation of the population. Random selection may provide a stronger basis for generalizing results from the sample to the population, but often convenience sampling is more manageable. Researchers examine the pros and cons of various sampling methods before selecting the most appropriate method for each study, recognizing the limitations that exist within each method.

Step 3: Select or develop instruments to gather information. Descriptive researchers apply a variety of data-gathering methods to study a particular problem and sometimes find the need to create their own instruments to best fit the research question. Numerous surveys, questionnaires, interview protocols, and observation checklists are readily available to be used in descriptive research or to be modified to better match specific topics of study. To maximize the value of the study, methods of gathering data should be carefully aligned with the purpose of the research and the problem or phenomenon under study.

Step 4: Analyze the data and report the findings. Once information has been gathered through surveys, questionnaires, interviews, observations, and other methods, researchers analyze the data, attempting to paint as clear and accurate a picture as possible. Numerical data may be compiled using charts, tables, and graphs to better recognize trends and patterns. Basic computer programs like Excel allow researchers to manipulate data easily and view results in different ways to simplify the analysis and reporting step, but hand calculations are also an option. Major findings emerging from the analysis of data should be reported in ways consistent with those typically used by the discipline.

Step 5: Draw conclusions based on the findings of the study. Descriptive researchers use major findings to draw conclusions about the problem or phenomenon studied. Conclusions must be grounded in the research findings and should be supported with specific quantitative or qualitative examples. Theories, predictions, claims, and suggestions for further research generated by the researcher add to the body of existing knowledge in the field and validate the importance of the study.

Descriptive research is a logical choice for students who wish to measure or evaluate behaviors, perceptions, attitudes, and other patterns. With this form of research, students take the lead in determining their focus of study, identifying or developing measures to gather the necessary information, and using those data to generate conclusions, theories, or predictions. Students who appreciate clear and structured processes are able to see the "big picture" behind a trend or pattern, are detail-oriented, and want to understand a problem or phenomenon in a deeper way and will enjoy the descriptive method. Descriptive research allows students to identify and interpret trends and patterns and to draw meaningful conclusions. Teacher-facilitators of students who choose descriptive research can assist with finding, evaluating, or creating instruments for data gathering; identifying experts in the discipline to serve as mentors to guide the research process; and providing resources for the analysis of data to ensure accuracy. One element of descriptive research may be a mentorship experience during which a student develops a deeper understanding of his or her area of interest. Marcus, whose story unfolded at the beginning of the chapter, engaged in a mentorship in a local law firm to research and better understand the profession. This experience allowed him to interview, ask questions, and participate in professional activities that contributed to his understanding of civil law and led to knowledge he could use to describe characteristics of civil attorneys, civil cases, and other elements of civil law.

Experimental Research

Most often associated with the discipline of science, experimental research projects revolve around an experiment and focus on conducting studies and careful documentation to ensure that the experiment can be replicated by anyone interested in verifying the results or investigating similar questions using a different population or condition. The typical science fair project falls under the category of experimental research, requiring students to formulate a hypothesis, design an experiment, conduct the experiment several times, measure and analyze results, and draw conclusions. Rather than looking to the past or examining the present, experimental research allows students to demonstrate future thinking, asking "How?" and "What if?" Central to the practice of experimental research is the understanding that the best way to answer questions or solve problems regarding a particular topic may be to conduct an experiment or to test a theory. This is true for medical trials for new prescription drugs, educational interventions such as afterschool programs, and toxicity tests for pesticides. Although understanding the perceptions, attitudes, and behaviors of people or entities that these issues affect may also be important, ultimately, testing or experimentation is required in each of these areas. Students may be interested in studying a topic that has the potential to directly affect them, for instance, the value of ACT or SAT prep materials. To study the effects of a prep program on test scores, researchers would design an experiment to compare the scores of students who had used a prep program to students who had not or compare students who used one program to students who used a different program. Regardless of the approach, researchers use control groups (groups that receive no treatment whatsoever) to provide baseline data and to ensure that results can be directly attributed to the intervention and not some other variable. Experimental research involves the testing or manipulation of independent variables, for example the ACT prep program, while simultaneously measuring the effects of the independent variable on dependent variables, such as ACT scores. The scientific method is the most widely used and accepted approach to experimental research. Many variations of the scientific method exist in experimental research, but most methods include the following six steps: (a) select a problem or question to be studied; (b) generate hypothesis(es) or research question(s); (c) design the experiment; (d) conduct the experiment and gather data; (e) analyze the data and compile the findings; and (f) draw conclusions based on the findings.

Step 1: Select problem or question. Student researchers will likely generate multiple questions that they would like to answer about their topic and may identify several problems that exist. Beginning by brainstorming a list of research problems and/or questions, students examine the topic in different lights before deciding upon the problem or question to be addressed in their study. This process ensures that the underlying problem being studied is both clear and compelling.

Step 2: Generate hypothesis(es) or research questions. Hypotheses are statements of what the researcher expects to happen as a result of the experiment, and the testing process is designed to either prove or disprove the hypotheses. Research questions represent a different approach to experimental design; rather than proving or disproving a statement, the researcher attempts to answer a question or questions through experimentation. Using the ACT/SAT prep program example, a possible research hypothesis might be "The use of an ACT prep book will increase ACT scores." The experiment would be designed to measure whether or not students who used an ACT prep book demonstrated an increase in their ACT scores compared to those who did not. A possible research question might be "What are the effects of an ACT prep program on ACT scores?" and the study would be deliberately planned to answer this question. The two approaches are quite similar, and the process selected is determined by personal preference.

Step 3: Design the experiment. As discussed in Step 2, the experiment should be carefully and deliberately designed to either prove or disprove hypotheses or to fully answer research questions. The strongest experimental research designs make use of control groups and randomization—either random selection of test subjects or random assignment of subjects to the experimental or control groups. A written research plan helps ensure clear, thorough steps that will garner the desired results and be able to be replicated.

Step 4: Conduct the experiment and gather data. The experiment should be conducted and documented with precise and careful steps. The accuracy of the test depends on the exact progression from step to step and precision of measurement, implementation, and recording. Data are to be collected at logical points in the experiment and recorded in a clear and organized manner. Often, researchers gather more data than they anticipate needing to be able to answer additional questions as they arise during or following the study. Data may be collected in the form of journals, charts, notes, photographs, video and audio recordings, and other appropriate fashions.

Step 5: Analyze data and compile the findings. Data analysis often presents students with questions, and they may need to be connected with a mathematician or statistician to assist with the process. Data may be analyzed through relatively simple means like tallies and counts or can be more complexly manipulated through statistical tests, calculation of percents and ratios, or the application of logarithms or formulas. Once data are analyzed, experimental researchers organize the data into useful charts, tables, and graphs to facilitate easier interpretation of findings. Researchers look for patterns, trends, effects, and changes and examine the strength or significance of those findings.

Step 6: Draw conclusions based on the findings. Key results and findings from the study lead student researchers to draw logical and appropriate conclusions about the research topic. In this step, hypotheses (whether proven or disproven) are discussed or research questions answered to the fullest extent possible. If the experiment was carefully designed, included control groups, and used randomization, students may be able to offer generalizations about the topic based on the results of their analysis. For example, if a student conducted the ACT study discussed earlier and found mixed results, he may be able to conclude that although ACT prep programs did not increase scores for all students, there were significant score increases for weak readers. Even though the study did not accomplish what the student anticipated—higher test scores for all students using an ACT prep program—it did contribute important information about the topic and added new knowledge to the field.

Students who choose to conduct experimental research should follow steps that can be replicated and should describe all aspects of the study in sufficient detail so that the study can be accurately repeated. Experimental researchers test the effectiveness of an intervention or compare one or more interventions based on a set of established criteria, and often these studies are replicated multiple times to ensure accuracy of results. Gifted students who enjoy scientific, ordered processes are well-suited for experimental research. Often experimental research studies lead to additional studies in the same area, and are a good match for the student consumed with a problem, question, or issue and who is committed to solving it. Teacher-facilitators of student research can assist experimental researchers by helping them understand independent and dependent variables, experiment design, data collection, and data analysis as well as connecting them with practicing professionals in the field such as university researchers and scientists. The student researcher example of Emily at the beginning of this chapter demonstrates one option for experimental research: research internships. Through authentic internship programs, gifted middle and high school students engage in real-world research, partnering with experts in their field of interest, and contributing in meaningful ways to the body of knowledge in a particular area.

The Research Process

Whichever method a student chooses to conduct research, the basic process of developing research skills encompasses both skill and knowledge development as well as critical and productive thinking. To facilitate the development of research skills, teachers of the gifted should provide structured experiences beginning with explorations and investigations as advocated by Betts (1985) and Renzulli (1977). Figure 12.3 outlines the major steps in conducting research, depicted as a continuous cycle, an ongoing process that teachers should use with gifted students.

Discover, Explore, and Identify Topics of Interest

Exposing students to a multitude of topics and issues sparks student interest and engages learners in asking questions and attempting to solve problems. Teachers of the gifted should structure opportunities to further explore topics of interest and identify areas of passion or intense interest. Students may explore several topics of interest and may shift from one topic to another with little warning. This is a natural part of the process; student researchers need to find a topic they feel strongly about and in which they are highly interested, increasing motivation and engagement in the research process.

Build Knowledge Base

Once students have determined their area of interest, the next step is to develop a strong knowledge base—to become an expert in their area. Reading and learning about the subject prepares learners to identify gaps in what is known about their topics, formulate relevant research hypotheses and questions, and design effective studies. Verifying the reliability of sources and the veracity of information is a key skill associated with the building of a knowledge base. Evidence of knowledge

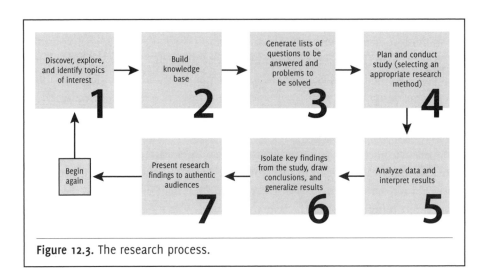

Figure 12.3. The research process.

and understanding does not have to be reflected solely in research papers; instead, it can be compiled into many different formats—electronic portfolios, displays, videos/films, models, websites, presentations, resource files, and more. Because this part of the research process is so critical, teacher-facilitators should allow for plenty of time, while verifying that the student is still focused on the topic. At this stage, sudden shifts of direction may occur as the student is introduced to new facets of the subject area; this is a normal part of the process, but one that the teacher should monitor.

Generate Lists of Potential Problems and Research Questions

Students who possess deep knowledge of a particular area are well-prepared to begin generating lists of possible problems to study and research questions to pose in future studies. Brainstorming numerous options allows students to analyze and judge the validity and relevance of their potential areas of study and to select and clearly define research topics that lead to rich and meaningful investigations and the increased likelihood of creating new knowledge. Figure 12.4 shows a method of generating problems to study by webbing key questions surrounding the topic.

Plan and Conduct the Study

The first step in planning any study is to select the most appropriate research method. Most problems and phenomena can be better understood using any of the three major models: historical research, descriptive research, or experimental research. Often, however, specific problems or research questions can be best addressed through one method over the others. A written research plan provides greater structure for student researchers as well as a format to follow for consis-

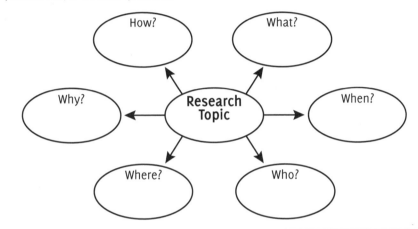

Problem Generator Web

Use the problem generator to web possible questions about your research topic. Consider how questions that examine ways to improve the topic and cause/effect relationships; what questions that help us understand more about the topic; why questions that seek to explain origins, reasons, and theories; when questions that attempt to chronologically order key events to better understand a topic; where questions that identify locations, origins, and sources and can help you identify possible resources for your project; and who questions that identify key figures in your area of study and may guide you to people in your community who can assist you.

Once you have questions in each area, you're ready to begin defining your research problem and/or research questions.

Figure 12.4. Problem/research question generator.

tent replications or authentications of the study. As students conduct their studies, documentation of steps taken and data gathered is essential. Students should maintain accurate reference lists of all sources utilized in their study as well as research records or journals.

Analyze Data and Interpret Results

All research studies produce data in varying amounts and types. Historical research reflects themes, patterns, and stories while descriptive research results in detailed assessments and reports of the subject of study, and experimental research generates data showing effectiveness or the nature of the relationship between variables. Analyzing data using methods appropriate to the methodology and the field of study leads to increased effectiveness in accurately interpreting results. Organizing data into charts, tables, and graphs may help students recognize patterns, trends, effects, and so forth. Drawing on the evidence grounded in the data they have gathered, student researchers clearly delineate and interpret the study results.

Isolate Key Findings, Draw Conclusions, and Generalize Results

Within the study results, students isolate key findings—evidence in support of or against their research hypotheses or answers to their research questions—and draw conclusions based on the results of the study. These conclusions may include modifying the existing theories or developing new ones, creating models for prediction or clarification, or making recommendations for further study. Students may also be able to generalize the results of their study to the population and substantiate the generalizations with evidence from the study.

Present Research Findings to Authentic Audiences

Providing opportunities for student researchers to share their findings with authentic audiences validates the importance of their work, allows them to find meaning in contributing to the field, and provides a venue for feedback. Prior to presenting their results, students should evaluate their work, reflect on its value, and note specific strengths and limitations of the study. Presentations should target audiences who recognize the significance of the research and who can offer constructive feedback. Other student researchers should also be included. Figure 12.5 provides suggestions for showcasing student research projects.

Planning documents provide a model and structure for students to plan independent research projects. Depending on the level of independence and readiness of the student, teacher-facilitators can require varying levels of detail in the planning document. Independent learning contracts may also be useful in facilitating student research projects. A sample student research planning document is provided in Figure 12.6.

Facilitating Student Research

Torrance and Safter (1990) described three primary results of incorporating the first step of research, problem finding, into the curriculum: (a) maintain a student-centered focus by drawing on student interest and generating enthusiasm and motivation for learning; (b) diminish teacher boredom by creating new topics of study each year due to the changing nature of problems and varying interests and pursuits of students; and (c) encourage facilitative behaviors among teachers as students gradually become more autonomous in their learning and require less direction and guidance. Torrance and Safter also identified specific teacher behav-

Showcasing Student Research Projects

- Science fair
- Social science fair
- Science carnival
- Ask the student expert
- Historical reenactment
- Documentary
- Website
- Electronic research portfolio
- Brochure

- Data fair
- Living history museum
- Student research forum
- Panel discussion
- Display
- Bound publication
- Professional presentation
- Performance
- Model/theory fair

Figure 12.5. Suggested presentation formats.

Research Project Planning Document

Name: _____ Date: _____

Research Topic: _____

Possible Research Questions/Hypotheses:

1. _____

2. _____

3. _____

Research Method Options:

Historical: _____

_____

Descriptive: _____

_____

Experimental: _____

_____

Possible Community Resources:

1. _____

2. _____

3. _____

Information Resources:

1. _____

2. _____

3. _____

4. _____

5. _____

Figure 12.6. Sample student research project planning document.

iors that lead to enhanced creative teaching methodologies and greater student success:

» Recognizing previously overlooked or misunderstood potential
» Facilitating opportunities for independent work
» Encouraging students to pursue areas of interest and to accomplish significant goals within those areas of interest
» Stifling criticism or judgment until students work through a problem and have the opportunity to generate solutions/ideas on their own
» Permitting students to work ahead of the group and/or pursue specific topics of interest more in-depth
» Engaging directly with students in planning and achieving individual learning and growth
» Accepting and promoting the need for student-directed learning experiences and deep interest in specific areas
» Facilitating the development of responsibility and constructive contribution
» Generating rich questions that require students to think in different ways

Teachers should determine their own readiness and skill for facilitating student research projects in the classroom. This reflective process provides opportunities to recognize areas of weakness and target improvement. Just as the development of research skills and autonomy are processes that mature with time and practice, so are the skills required for effective facilitation of student research projects. Expert facilitators develop these skills through a research process of their own: building a knowledge base through learning about best practices in student research; experimenting with practices, attitudes, support materials, and expectations for student-directed projects; and analyzing results to draw meaningful conclusions and inform practice. Use the self-assessment presented in Figure 12.7 to assess the current climate for student research in your classroom, reflect on current practice, and target areas for growth.

Conclusion

Teaching research skills to gifted learners represents a prime strategy for differentiating content, process, and product to meet the unique characteristics and learning needs of the gifted. Understanding the research process and developing skills as a facilitator of student research enables teachers to develop these important skills in their students. Few other processes require such high levels of critical and creative thinking and offer the benefits of motivating students, developing higher order thinking skills, fostering student autonomy, and preparing students to become producers of knowledge. The research process aligns with Sternberg's (1997) Triarchy of Thinking Abilities in that it encourages the development of creative, analytical, and practical intelligence skills. Gifted learners of all ages

How Research-Friendly Is Your Classroom?

Read each of the following statements and consider how often it is true in your classroom (*usually*—5, *sometimes*—3, or *rarely*—1). Circle the appropriate number for each question.

I recognize emerging potential in my students.	5	3	1
I facilitate opportunities for independent work.	5	3	1
I encourage students to pursue areas of interest.	5	3	1
I encourage students to achieve significant goals.	5	3	1
I withhold judgment, allowing students to solve problems.	5	3	1
I permit students to work ahead of the group.	5	3	1
Within a unit, my students pursue topics of interest in depth.	5	3	1
I work directly with students planning independent learning.	5	3	1
I accept and promote the need for self-directed learning.	5	3	1
I facilitate the development of responsibility and autonomy.	5	3	1
I expect my students to contribute new knowledge.	5	3	1
I generate rich questions that encourage critical thinking.	5	3	1

Total Score: _____

46–60: Highly Research-Friendly
You're already encouraging students to undertake independent learning projects and have the skills to facilitate such projects. Keep challenging students to pursue research projects.

27–45: Somewhat Research-Friendly
You may recognize the importance of student research but lack some of the knowledge and skills for facilitating the process. Intentionally incorporate independent learning projects for your students—with practice comes expertise.

12–26: Not Consistently Research-Friendly
You are not comfortable facilitating individual research projects. Undertake a research project of your own to learn more about the process and begin to implement research skill development activities. As you deepen your understanding of the process, you'll develop the skills necessary to effectively facilitate independent learning in your classroom.

Figure 12.7. Teacher self-assessment of research-friendly classroom climate. *Note.* Based on the work of Torrance and Safter (1990).

should be actively engaged in developing research skills in preparation for careers as productive mathematicians, scientists, physicians, artists, musicians, educators, lawmakers, and other roles as contributing citizens and members of a larger community.

Teacher Statement

As a teacher of gifted students, I find that research is a key teaching method to fight boredom, allow students to explore topics of interest, and provide the basis for development of writing and communication skills. My students enjoy doing research. Research projects often give them a feeling of accomplishment, while also encouraging further inquiry as one answered question leads to new questions.

The tools and methods offered by this chapter provide an important structure to the student research projects and direct the students toward deeper analysis and interpretation. Like past generations of students who thought that research consisted of summarizing encyclopedia articles, this generation is tempted to accept and report the findings of Internet searches without any critical analysis. Following the methods presented here will help the students learn to evaluate information sources, verify the accuracy of information, critically compare sources that present differing information and opinions, and create an analysis of the findings.

The Internet information explosion has allowed students access to the data that can form the basis of original research; however, they can be overwhelmed by information. I appreciate the manner in which the models offered in this chapter can help both the student and teacher in turning ordinary questions into research questions, finding the research methods to answer the questions, and then analyzing and communicating the findings. Research allows students to augment core-curriculum competencies with the critical analysis and problem-solving skills that they will need in their further educational experiences.

—Lisa Lindley

DISCUSSION QUESTIONS

1. How do research projects align with the CCSS or the curriculum and frameworks used in your district?

2. Develop and discuss tools for managing student research projects. How would you use these tools to provide support and structure for students engaged in independent research?

3. Develop a rubric for evaluating student research and discuss the appropriate use of assessment and evaluation of independent learning projects.

4. Describe the basic research process and discuss how it integrates critical and creative thinking skills.

5. Discuss why developing domain or background knowledge is so critical in the research process.

6. Select one research topic and provide examples of a study that might be conducted in each of three primary research methodologies. Briefly outline the steps that would be taken to carry out each study.

Teacher Resources

Publications

Benjamin, A. (2003). *Differentiated instruction: A guide for elementary school teachers.* Larchmont, NY: Eye on Education.

Betts, G. T., & Kercher, J. K. (1999). *Autonomous learner model: Optimizing ability.* Greeley, CO: ALPS.

Betts, G. T., Toy, R. E., & Vasquez, K. A. (2006). *The young gifted child and the autonomous learner model, Grades K–3.* Greeley, CO: ALPS.

Bransford, J. D., Brown, A. L., & Cocking, R. R. (1999). *How people learn: Brain, mind, experience and school.* Washington, DC: National Academy Press.

Heacox, D. (2002). *Differentiated instruction in the regular classroom: How to reach and teach all learners, Grades 3–12.* Minneapolis, MN: Free Spirit.

Northey, S. S. (2005). *Handbook on differentiated instruction for middle and high schools.* Larchmont, NY: Eye on Education.

Purcell, J. H., & Renzulli, J. S. (1998). *Total talent portfolio: A systematic plan to identify and nurture gifts and talents.* Mansfield Center, CT: Creative Learning Press.

Renzulli, J. S. (1977). *The enrichment triad model: A guide for developing defensible programs for the gifted and talented.* Mansfield Center, CT: Creative Learning Press.

Renzulli, J. S., Leppien, J. H., & Hays, T. S. (2000). *The multiple menu model: A practical guide for developing differentiated curriculum.* Waco, TX: Prufrock Press.

Renzulli, J. S., & Reis, S. M. (2014). *The schoolwide enrichment model: A how-to guide for talent development* (3rd ed.). Waco, TX: Prufrock Press.

Schack, G. D., & Starko, A. J. (1998). *Research comes alive: Guidebook for conducting original research with middle and high school students.* Mansfield Center, CT: Creative Learning Press.

Sternberg, R. J., & Grigorenko, E. L. (2000). *Teaching for successful intelligence: To increase student learning and achievement.* Arlington Heights, IL: Sky Light Professional Development.

Winebrenner, S. (2012). *Teaching gifted kids in today's classroom: Strategies and techniques every teacher can use* (3rd ed.). Minneapolis, MN: Free Spirit.

Willingham, D. T. (2009). *Why don't students like school? A cognitive scientist answers questions about how the mind works and what it means for the classroom.* San Francisco, CA: Jossey-Bass.

Zemelman, S., Daniels, H., & Hyde, A. (2005). *Best practices: Today's standards for teaching & learning in America's schools.* Portsmouth, NH: Heinemann.

Websites

Cultures/World Links—http://www.cultures.com
Google Earth—http://www.google.com/earth/index.html
Google Scholar—http://www.googlescholar.com
NASA—http://www.nasa.gov
National Academy of Sciences—http://www.nas.edu
National Endowment for the Humanities—http://www.neh.gov
National Gallery of Art—http://www.nga.gov

National Geographic Society—http://www.nationalgeographic.com
National Humanities Institute—http://www.nhumanities.org
National Register of Historic Places—http://www.nps.gov/history/nr/
National Science Digital Library—http://www.nsdl.org
National Science Foundation—http://www.nsf.gov
National Wildlife Federation—http://www.nwf.org
Neuroscience for Kids—http://faculty.washington.edu/chudler/neurok.html
Science Fair Project Resource Guide—http://www.ipl.org/div/projectguide/
Smithsonian Institution—http://www.si.edu
Social Science Research Network—http://www.ssrn.com/
United States Census Bureau Homepage—http://www.census.gov/#

References

Betts, G. (1985). *Autonomous learner model for the gifted and talented learner.* Greeley, CO: ALPS.

Betts, G. T., & Kercher, J. K. (1999). *Autonomous learner model: Optimizing ability.* Greeley, CO: ALPS.

Burns, D. E. (1993). *A six-phase model for the explicit teaching of thinking skills.* Storrs: University of Connecticut, The National Research Center on the Gifted and Talented.

Ennis, R. H. (2000, October 18). *An outline of goals for a critical thinking curriculum and its assessment.* Retrieved from http://www.criticalthinking.net/goals.html

Feldhusen, J. F. (1994a). Strategies for teaching the gifted. In J. VanTassel-Baska (Ed.), *Comprehensive curriculum for gifted learners* (2nd ed., pp. 366–378). Needham Heights, MA: Allyn and Bacon.

Feldhusen, J. F. (1994b). Thinking skills and curriculum development. In J. VanTassel-Baska (Ed.), *Comprehensive curriculum for gifted learners* (2nd ed., pp. 301–324). Needham Heights, MA: Allyn and Bacon.

Fraenkel, J. R., Wallen, N. E., & Hyun, H. (2011). *How to design and evaluate research in education* (8th ed.). New York: McGraw Hill.

Maker, C. J., & Nielson, A. B. (1996). *Curriculum development and teaching strategies for gifted learners* (2nd ed.). Austin, TX: Pro-Ed, Inc.

National Governors Association Center for Best Practices, & Council of Chief State School Officers. (2010a). *Common Core State Standards for English language arts.* Washington, DC: Author.

National Governors Association Center for Best Practices, & Council of Chief State School Officers. (2010b). *Common Core State Standards for Mathematics.* Washington, DC: Author.

Piirto, J. (2007). *Talented children and adults: Their development and education* (3rd ed.). Waco, TX: Prufrock Press.

Renzulli, J. S. (1977). *The enrichment triad model: A guide for developing defensible programs for the gifted and talented.* Mansfield Center, CT: Creative Learning Press.

Renzulli, J. S. (2013). The Multiple Menu Model: A guide for developing differentiated curriculum. In C. M. Callahan & H. L. Hertberg-Davis (Eds.), *Fundamentals of gifted education: Considering multiple perspectives* (pp. 263–276). New York, NY: Routledge.

Renzulli, J. S., & Reis, S. M. (2014). *The schoolwide enrichment model: A how-to guide for talent development* (3rd ed.). Waco, TX: Prufrock Press.

Robinson, A., Shore, B. M., & Enersen, D. L. (2007). *Best practices in gifted education: An evidence-based guide.* Waco, TX: Prufrock Press.

Schack, G. D., & Starko, A. J. (1998). *Research comes alive: Guidebook for conducting original research with middle and high school students.* Mansfield Center, CT: Creative Learning Press.

Sternberg, R. J. (1997). *Successful intelligence.* New York, NY: Plume.

Sternberg, R. J., Grigorenko, E. L., & Ferrari, M. (2004). *Giftedness and expertise: Intervention study I—Intelligence as developing expertise* (RM04198). Storrs: University of Connecticut, The National Research Center on the Gifted and Talented.

Tomlinson, C. A., Kaplan, S. N., Renzulli, J. S., Purcell, J., Leppien, J., Burns, D., Strickland, C., & Imbeau, M. (2008). *The parallel curriculum: A design to develop learner potential and challenge advanced learners* (2nd ed.). Thousand Oaks, CA: Corwin Press.

Torrance, E. P., & Safter, H. T. (1990). *The incubation model of teaching: Getting beyond the aha!* Buffalo, NY: Bearly Limited.

Treffinger, D. F. (1975). Teaching for self-directed learning: A priority for the gifted and talented. *Gifted Child Quarterly, 19,* 46–59.

VanTassel-Baska, J. (1989). Appropriate curriculum for the gifted. In J. Feldhusen, J. VanTassel-Baska, & K. Seeley (Eds.), *Excellence in educating the gifted* (pp. 175–192). Denver, CO: Love.

Willingham, D. T. (2009). *Why don't students like school? A cognitive scientist answers questions about how the mind works and what it means for the classroom.* San Francisco, CA: Jossey-Bass.

13
Chapter

ADAPTING PROBLEM-BASED LEARNING FOR GIFTED STUDENTS

BY SHELAGH A. GALLAGHER

Educational reform has spawned much experimentation in both curricula and instruction. One approach that has gained popularity over the past few decades is problem-based learning (PBL; Barrows, 1985; Gallagher, 2013; Stepien & Gallagher, 1993). With explicit attention to authentic problem solving, hands-on learning, and self-directed learning, many teachers have embraced PBL as a way to improve curricula and instruction for all of their students. Others have claimed that PBL is actually a "best fit" for gifted students. Can both of these viewpoints be true? If PBL is appropriate for all students, then it must be appropriate for gifted students as well; however, it does not necessarily follow that PBL is exactly the same for all students. Certainly, a fundamental similarity always will be present because the structural elements of PBL are the same in any setting. The substance inside a PBL unit, however, can and should be adapted to meet the individual needs of the students who will be working with the problem.

The purpose of this chapter is to present unique characteristics of gifted students as problem solvers and to show how PBL units can be adapted to extend their potential.

Matching Curriculum and Characteristics: Gifted Students and Expert Problem Solving

Gifted students have cognitive and affective characteristics that distinguish them from the regular population of students. Interestingly, many of these traits are similar to those that distinguish experts from novice problem solvers. The characteristics shared by gifted students and expert problem solvers provide a set of guidelines to use when thinking about adapting PBL for gifted students. Essentially, the goal of modifying PBL for the gifted is to narrow the gap between the potential possessed by the gifted child and the practice of expert adults. The similarities between expert problem solvers and gifted students are observed in four broad areas: knowledge base, conceptual reasoning, problem-solving strategies, and dispositions.

Gifted Students Have the Capacity to Build an Expert's Knowledge Base

The cornerstone of a problem solver's expertise is a large knowledge base. Experts acquire and retain large bodies of information by making connections among different facts (Hambrick & Engle, 2002; Steiner & Carr, 2003). The large knowledge base serves to make experts both better informed and more creative: Experts process knowledge in an efficient working memory (Hambrick & Meinz, 2011), finding unusual associations as they combine seemingly dissimilar facts and events. For example, an expert biologist (or to be specific, an ichthyologist) has a lot to remember in her study of fish. In order to ensure that she remembers all of the information associated with a given aquarium, such as the kinds of fish, temperature of the water, and compatible varieties of aquatic plants, she uses a unified point of reference like the fishbowl. When she remembers the shape of the fishbowl, she also remembers all of its elements. Using a fishbowl as a central point of reference, experts also can make associations with new information like gravel or fish food. In the future, when the expert needs this information, she need only recall the fishbowl, and all of the associated information will be retrieved as well.

Gifted children are uniquely suited to developing a large knowledge base, one of the bridges to expertise. The ability to absorb facts is one of the most frequently cited characteristics of gifted children (Clark, 2006; Gallagher, 2009;

VanTassel-Baska & Stambaugh, 2005). Longitudinal studies of learning suggest that, even as infants, gifted children are more likely to look for something new in their environment, make it familiar or "habituate" to it quickly, and then start seeking again (Carr, Alexander, & Schwanenflugel, 1996). In order to make their expert-like knowledge accessible, gifted students also would need the expert-like ability to organize and store this knowledge.

Gifted Students Practice Conceptual Reasoning

When searching for a helpful way to represent a problem, experts tend to look for its deep structure, using abstract concepts or principles to describe the heart of the dilemma. By contrast, novices tend to work with surface characteristics that may be more obvious but are less essential to developing an understanding of the heart of the problem. Returning to the previous example, differences between novice and expert scientists would emerge if there was a problem in the fishbowl; if, for example, the fish were dying. The novice would try to solve a problem of dying fish in a fishbowl by looking at the fish food and the water in the tank, obvious targets, but perhaps not the right ones. The expert, on the other hand, would look at the fishbowl as a water ecosystem. Recognizing that the elements in systems interact, the expert might look for interactions in and around the fishbowl and find that the gravel reflects sunlight, raising the water to a dangerously high temperature for the fish (Ericsson, Charness, Feltovich, & Hoffman, 2006).

Expert problem solvers and gifted students are similar in their tendency to look beyond the surface of the problem to find an underlying structure. Gifted students give evidence of conceptual and abstract reasoning at an earlier age than their age-mates (Berninger & Yates, 1993; Planche & Gicquel, 2000; Sriraman, 2003). After summarizing the research on how children acquire conceptual thinking, Berninger and Yates (1993) suggested that gifted students think conceptually as much as 3 years earlier than their age-mates.

Gifted Students Have Early Capacity for Problem Solving

While solving the problem of the fishbowl, the expert can switch easily from a content analysis of the water, to a dissection of a dead fish, to consultation with resources to bridge gaps in understanding. In other words, experts tend to have more problem-solving tools at their disposal than novices, and they know how to select among those skills according to their needs (Ericsson et al., 2006). Faced with a similar situation, the novice simply may conduct different variations of a single kind of water analysis. The novice's problem solving is limited because he or she doesn't have as many ways to delve into the problem. Having looked at the data from many perspectives, the expert also is more likely to come up with a more creative or sophisticated problem definition. The expert's capacity for creative problem definition, or problem finding, provides the foundation for unique solutions (Cherney, Winter, & Cherney, 2005; Getzels, 1979). Throughout the problem-solving process, experts make greater use of metacognitive reflection by monitoring and controlling their thinking (Ericsson et al., 2006) by reflecting on questions such as, "Have I considered all the possibilities?" "What assumptions am I making about the effect of lamp light on the fishbowl water?" and "Is this strategy working?" By contrast, novices might doggedly pursue the same unsuccessful strategy, unable to find their way out of a dead end.

Gifted students are more adept at problem finding than average-ability students (Heinze, 2005). Rogers (2004) found other similarities between the problem-solving behaviors of experts and gifted students, including careful selection of strategies. Gifted students also have an earlier grasp of problem-solving stages, know more problem-solving strategies, and select strategies more effectively. Gifted students are more inclined than regular students to select strategies associated with deep—rather than surface—level learning (Holschuh, 2000). When they can't think of what to do, gifted students are more likely to invent a strategy (Montague, 1991).

Although it is clear that metacognition is a component of expert thinking, gifted students do not show a clear-cut performance advantage. In fact, there are only a few areas where gifted students consistently show superior performance: (a) gifted students' awareness of their own strengths and weaknesses, (b) gifted students' knowledge about specific learning strategies, and (c) their inclination to use a skill in a new, unusual setting, also known as *far transfer* (Carr et al., 1996; Housand & Reis, 2008; Snyder, Nietfeld, & Linnenbrink-Garcia, 2011). Other studies of metacognition show inferior performance among the gifted, especially in the absence of challenging content (Dresel & Haugwitz, 2005).

Gifted Students Have Expert-Like Dispositions

Eminent authors, scientists, and historians all emphasize the importance of exploration and the disposition to seek the unknown to their success (Judson, 1980; O'Connor, 1962; Tuchman, 1966). With the inclination to search for the unknown, experts are more likely to use forward problem solving, because they assume that the answer to their problem does not exist. Novices, on the other hand, would be more likely to pursue more predictable questions with verifiable solutions.

Taking an open-ended approach to problem solving requires believing that some problems have no predetermined "right" answer. Students who believe that all problems have a single, absolute right answer are not likely to look for many alternative answers in an ill-structured problem. The belief that some questions have no single right answer is one factor that might determine a student's success in open-ended assignments. Studies of gifted children consistently report their inclination to be open to experience, a precursor to viewing a problem from multiple perspectives (Gallagher, 2013). A few studies directly investigating student dispositions have shown that gifted students are more likely to believe that some questions have no predetermined answers (Hofer & Pintrich, 2002; Thomas, 2008). In this attribute, gifted students are similar to adult experts.

Taken together, these research data give evidence that gifted students have a head start on their peers in developing expert problem-solving capabilities, as demonstrated in Table 13.1. At the same time, there is no doubt that gifted students have a long way to go in refining their raw potential into sophisticated skill. Having a head start is no guarantee of achieving the level of problem solving that a gifted student could well acquire. What must intervene is an education that moves gifted students from potential to skill and, hopefully, expertise along these dimensions.

It is clear that expertise involves much more than just a high IQ: "Although experts need sufficient general ability (IQ) to perform at a high level, other factors such as task commitment, a strong knowledge base and social support are more important for developing expertise and promoting achievement through expertise . . ." (Carr et al., 1996, p. 214). The list of requirements for expertise also includes perspective, forward problem solving, persistence, risk-taking, and tacit knowledge such as professional language and behaviors (Ericsson et al., 2006; Jarvin & Subotnik, 2006; Shore, 2000; Sternberg, 2003). There is evidence that information is retained more effectively when it is presented in a context that is meaningful to students (Driscoll, 2005). Conceptual reasoning is enhanced when a teacher models the kind of thinking that reveals the conceptual level of activities (Bransford, Brown, & Cocking, 2000). Conversely, we know that expert-like understanding will not develop in environments where instruction is oversimplified, presented from a single perspective, context-independent, rigidly compartmentalized into structures, and passively transmitted (Gamoran, 2000; King & Kitchener, 2002). In other words, success in complex thinking happens only with repeated practice in complex learning environments.

Problem-Based Learning: A Promising Road to Expertise

Problem-based learning provides the kind of complex learning environment that is well suited to developing expertise. The complex learning environment is created through the combined impact of the structural components of PBL: the ill-structured problem, the student as stakeholder, the self-directed learner, and the teacher as coach.

TABLE 13.1

Shared Qualities of Expert Problem Solvers and Gifted Students

Expert Problem Solver Qualities	Gifted Student Qualities
‣ Has broad knowledge base	‣ Acquires information quickly
‣ Looks for "deep structure" of problems	‣ Gives early evidence of conceptual thinking
‣ Has a large toolkit of skills; uses skills flexibly	‣ Carefully selects problem-solving strategies
‣ Monitors the problem-solving process	‣ Spontaneously uses metacognitive skills
‣ Uses dispositions supporting open-ended problem solving; uses forward-thinking problem solving	‣ Recognizes that many questions have no single, absolute right answer

The Ill-Structured Problem

Perhaps the most noticeable difference between traditional instruction and PBL is that a PBL unit begins with the presentation of an ill-structured problem. The differences between traditional well-structured problems and ill-structured problems are embodied in the following two examples:

> **Problem A:** You have two dozen oranges in your store. Mary comes in and buys six. Charles thinks about buying three but then changes his mind and gets six. If Teresa buys four oranges and Ryan buys eight, is Brenda justified when she complains to you about not being able to find any oranges in the produce department?
>
> **Problem B:** You are the owner of the local food co-op. Your favorite customers have all come in complaining about the insufficient supply of oranges. What should you do?

These two problems have some surface similarities: They both deal with oranges, shortages, and customer dissatisfaction. Their differences are far more important than their similarities, for they are the characteristics that distinguish a well-structured problem from an ill-structured one. Characteristics of the ill-structured problems include the following:

>   » *More information than is initially available is needed to understand the problem.* In the example, Problem A can be solved quite easily once the appropriate formula is in place. In Problem B, much more is needed to understand the problem. Why is there an insufficient supply of oranges? What do the clients mean by insufficient? Did we run out? What are some ways of keeping oranges (and other fruit) in stock? The quality of the ill-structured problem is frequently referred to as a *generative problem.* That is, the ill-structured problem actually generates questions.

» *No single formula exists for conducting an investigation to resolve the problem.* In Problem A, there is a specific set of operations to conduct in order to solve the problem; and, while some of the operations are reciprocal, there isn't much room for creative structure. In Problem B, however, there may be any number of different ways to deal with the clients' complaints, depending, in part, on the exact nature of the problem.

» *As new information is obtained, the problem changes.* In this case, Problem A has all of the information needed to solve the problem supplied in the brief paragraph. In Problem B, the problem could shift considerably if students were to find either that there were restrictions on the import of citrus fruit or, on the other hand, that a new "orange diet" had caused a run on the fruit.

» *Students can never be 100% sure they have made the "right" decision.* Problem A has a single, correct answer. In Problem B, the many possible options would have to be weighed to select the most reasonable one; and, even then, there would likely be negative, as well as positive, consequences to the solution. Only rarely would an answer be absolutely right.

An important point to be made about PBL is that students are solving problems that are central to a field of study and designed around specific educational goals. Indeed, research in medical PBL suggests that learning gains are highest when PBL problems are carefully designed with specific learning objectives in mind (Goodnough & Cashion, 2003; Sockalingam, Rotgans, & Schmidt, 2012). Because an important goal of PBL is to integrate core content with authentic problem solving, the problems used in the PBL classroom must meet additional criteria. To be considered educationally sound, PBL problems must:

» be designed to ensure that students cover a predefined area of knowledge, preferably integrated from many disciplines;

» help students learn a set of important concepts, ideas, and techniques;

» successfully lead students to (parts of) a field of study; and

» hold intrinsic interest or importance or represent a typical problem faced by the profession (Ross, 1991; Schmidt, Rotgans, & Yew, 2011).

Thus, PBL is considered to be a more effective way to teach the core curriculum. In Problem B, students would run into much more substantial content while trying to figure out why there are no oranges, including the growing cycle and different varieties of oranges, import-export laws, or diseases that might infest oranges. All of these are associated with basic learning objectives at different grade levels. Taken together, the qualities of the ill-structured problem lead students to pursue questions and, in the process, extend their knowledge base in a meaningful context. Much of the curriculum can be converted into problems if the task is approached with care (Stepien & Pyke, 1997).

Teachers who are accustomed to traditional, lecture-based instruction some-times balk at the thought of stepping away from delivering classroom content. The truth of the matter is that teachers don't step away from content, they just deliver it differently. Ill-structured problems developed for the classroom are ill-structured to students, but not necessarily to the teacher/developer. Instructors who have thought through how they want to present their problem to students will be able to predict most of the questions students will ask. Teachers deliver the content by carefully structuring the problem to elicit questions related to desired subject areas. Moreover, successful PBL teachers scaffold the learning environment, embedding supports and learning experiences that build their stu-dents' skills sets as they move through the problem. These supports can focus either on process skills, such as communication or self-directed learning, or on cognitive skills, such as critical thinking, conceptual reasoning, or understanding discipline-specific methods (i.e., experimental method; Gallagher, 2009; Hmelo-Silver, Duncan, & Chinn, 2007; Vardi & Ciccarelli, 2008). To demonstrate, let's go back to the example:

> **Problem B:** You are the owner of the local food co-op. Your favorite customers have all come in complaining about the insufficient supply of oranges. What should you do?

If the content focus was really supposed to be biology instead of economics, the problem might look like this instead:

> **Problem C:** You are the owner of the local orange grove. The weather report suggests that there will be bad weather tonight, creating a real problem for your crop. What should you do?

Problems B and C both focus on an orange shortage; both are ill-structured. When presented with Problem C, however, students are likely to ask questions including: What kind of bad weather could affect an orange crop? What is the point of no return when an orange crop is damaged? How bad does an orange have to be before it's ruined? Will oranges ripen if they are picked early? What has to be done to stimulate ripening? Problem B leads the students to mathematics, economics, and social studies, but Problem C leads to climatology, botany, and economics.

With a carefully constructed problem in hand, teachers are liberated from delivery and can work on developing reasoning skills, research techniques, and self-directed learning. Research in PBL suggests that taking on the tutor role is important; students learn more in PBL as tutors acquire more skill at facilitating self-directed learning, constructivist learning, and collaborative learning (van Berkel & Dolmans, 2006).

Student as Stakeholder

A second feature of PBL is the practice of placing students in a carefully selected stakeholder position. The stakeholder in a PBL unit is a person who has some level of authority, accountability, and responsibility for resolving some aspect of the problem. Students are assigned a specific role in each problem they encounter: a political advisor in a problem about district gerrymandering; a journalist in a problem about media in the courtroom; or a golf course groundskeeper in a problem about improving golf through grass selection. The goal of placing students in the shoes of a person actually involved in the problem is to make them an "apprentice" in that area. Like an artist's apprentice, students in a PBL problem experience the entire world of the problem solver and learn to adopt the appropriate dispositions, as well as content and skills. While in their apprenticeship, students learn many valuable lessons about problem solving from inside a discipline, including:

» the way problem solving is approached in different disciplines;
» the role of bias and perspective in the problem-solving process;
» the subjective nature of all real-world problem solving;
» the need to understand many different ways to solve a problem (economic, scientific, political, ethical); and
» the intricate process of weighing the priorities of different points of view in a complex problem.

Self-Directed Learner

The third change incorporated into the PBL classroom is that students are encouraged to take control of the learning process, thus becoming increasingly capable, self-reliant, and responsible learners. Teachers assist in this process by becoming a "tutor" who focuses on helping students develop a good toolkit of problem-solving skills, assisting students as they learn to use them, and engaging students in a process of reflection about their performance and the nature of problem solving.

The tutor also allows students to take on an increasing set of responsibilities, including setting the learning agenda, facilitating the group process, and setting timelines or deadlines. Using metacognitive questioning and modeling good inquiry, the tutor reveals to students how professionals approach similar problems, helps students focus on a problem's central concepts, and probes to ensure that all of the data gathered are understood. By reflecting on and evaluating their own thinking, students acquire better control over their thinking and feeling processes, ultimately resulting in better reasoning.

Problem-Based Learning and Student Achievement

Given the emphasis on accountability and meeting the requirements of the Common Core State Standards (CCSS; National Governors Association [NGA] Center for Best Practices & Council of Chief State School Officers [CCSSO], 2010a, 2010b), it is natural to want to know the effect of PBL on student achievement. A majority of studies both from medical schools and K–12 education show that PBL students can learn at least as much as traditionally instructed students (Gallagher, 2001; Hmelo-Silver, 2004; Sungur, Tekkaya, & Geban, 2006; Verhoeven et al., 1998; Wirkala & Kuhn, 2011), especially when the problem is carefully designed. Studies also show that PBL students retain what they learn over time (Strobel & van Barneveld, 2009). Because research and collaboration are integral to PBL, it is easy to meet skills-based CCSS requirements for nonfiction reading, research skills, MLA citation, writing, collaboration, and communication (see the English language arts standards; NGA & CCSSO, 2010a). Learning outcomes for PBL improve when (a) the problem is carefully designed around specific learning outcomes (Goodnough & Cashion, 2003; van Berkel & Dolmans, 2006), and (b) the tutor has either deep content knowledge or developed skill in cultivating students' self-directed learning. Adding lectures to PBL, however, does not seem to add to student achievement (van Berkel & Schmidt, 2005). Evidence also suggests that student achievement increases as students become more independently self-directed (van de Hurk, 2006). At the same time, PBL students learn more higher order thinking skills (Cruickshank & Olander, 2002) suggesting that PBL has learning value above and beyond content knowledge.

Adapting PBL for Gifted Students: New Applications of Familiar Recommendations

PBL is not inherently appropriate for gifted students; rather, it must be adapted and designed to match their unique needs. The appropriateness of PBL for gifted students depends on the kinds of adaptations that are built into the problem design and instruction. For average-ability students, the first order of business in PBL might be to acquire the basics of metacognition and self-direction, the nature of concepts, and the skills of problem solving. Gifted students, on the other hand, need a different level of challenge in PBL, one that refines and extends existing skills that are already in place. The five adaptations recommended here may sound quite familiar, because the same recommendations are made for all sorts of curricula for gifted students (Davis, Rimm, & Siegle, 2010; Gallagher, 2009; Maker & Schiever, 2005; VanTassel-Baska & Stambaugh, 2005). Recommended modifications of PBL for gifted students include:

» ensuring advanced content;
» working with complex concepts;
» demonstrating interdisciplinary connections;
» practicing good reasoning, habits of mind, and self-directed action; and
» discussing conflicting ethical appeals.

Changes in any one of these five dimensions make PBL problems more appropriate for gifted students; the benefits in learning accumulate as the number of adaptations increases. Perhaps the best way to demonstrate how a problem can be modified for instruction with gifted students is to work with a concrete example. For the purpose of discussion, consider the introduction to a problem involving an old oil platform, presented in Figure 13.1.

In this problem, students become stakeholders as the panel of scientists facing the problem of finding something to do with the defunct oil platform. After thinking about the problem, a group of gifted middle school students might use a Learning Issues Board to help sort their thinking into categories: What they Know, What they Need to Know, and an Action Plan, including steps they will take to answer their questions. An example of a Learning Issues Board is presented in Figure 13.2. Notice that the Learning Issues Board already suggests that students will have to conduct research, synthesize diverse information, and discuss the implications of their findings. This is baseline learning for all students, consistent with the mandates of the CCSS. Also notice that the list of questions go in different directions, allowing for differentiation by interest or learning style, consistent with best practice in the regular classroom (Tomlinson & Imbeau, 2010).

Modification 1: Ensuring Advanced Content

One essential component of any PBL curriculum is a problem designed around an important and worthy body of knowledge. More specifically, the problems designed for gifted students should lead to advanced investigations that broaden and deepen their knowledge base. Teachers can ensure the presence of complex information by choosing problems that require the study of advanced information. For example, middle school students will be more challenged by the Brent Spar problem in Figure 13.1 than by a problem about building a playground. Teachers also can arrange for students to "discover" resources with appropriately challenging information. In the case of the Brent Spar problem, this

The 40-story oil storage tank, named Brent Spar by its owner, the Shell Oil Company, is easy to spot, even in the cold choppy water of the North Sea. Its giant carcass, towering more than 90 feet above the surface and extending 370 feet below it, is temporarily anchored at 600 degrees north latitude, 50 kilometers west of the Shetland Islands. It has been there since June 1995. According to plans by Shell Oil, the storage tank should have been disposed of by now. But, Greenpeace became involved, and now the obsolete tank is riding the waves off Scotland.

The Brent Spar is now your problem! Shell Oil and Greenpeace have agreed to allow an impartial team of scientists to decide what to do with the platform. This is where you and your team come in.

Shell Oil no longer wants to use the old storage tank, or any of the more than 100 of the old platforms, built in the 1970s. Last June, Shell Oil and the British government agreed to allow the oil company to scuttle the platform and let it settle to the bottom of the ocean. When Greenpeace heard of the plan, it organized a boycott against Shell Oil gasoline in Europe and landed protesters on the platform itself. A small group of protesters are still on the tank.

You and your team must decide what to do with the Brent Spar. As the boat approaches the platform, your team assembles to begin discussing the situation. What are your first thoughts about the situation? What do you think the group should know more about to solve the problem of the Brent Spar?

Figure 13.1. Brent Spar problem. *Note.* From *Problem-Based Learning Across the Curriculum: An ASCD Professional Inquiry Kit* (Folder 4, Activity 1, p. 2), by W. J. Stepien and S. A. Gallagher, 1997, Alexandria, VA: Association for Supervision and Curriculum Development. Copyright © 1997 by ASCD.

might take the form of prompting a guest speaker to raise issues about regulating ocean waters that might not otherwise emerge.

The content in a PBL problem can be differentiated in a heterogeneous classroom. For example, in the Brent Spar problem, all students will encounter a foundation of understanding about the effects of oil on the ocean. During the course of small-group research, the teacher/coach could help a small group of gifted students understand more challenging information about the physics involved in different approaches to sinking the platform.

Modification 2: Complexity of the Concept

Problem-based learning and a concept-centered curriculum go hand in hand. In the Brent Spar problem, the concept of change is used to help students organize and think about the different components of the problem (Gallagher & Stepien, 1996). Discussion of the concept should not be reserved just for gifted students, because all students need to learn the fundamental nature of change. Gifted students, however, will be ready to appreciate the power of the concept at a more advanced level. Where regular students might benefit from a discussion centering around the fact that "Change causes change," gifted students are ready for a more

Hunches: What seems to be going on here?
           Shell Oil is trying to get out of a bind.
           The oil barge will pollute the water if it stays where it is.
           The barge should be towed ashore.

What We Know	What We Need to Know (Our Learning Issues)	Plan of Action
▸ Shell Oil owns the platform. ▸ It is not in use anymore. ▸ Greenpeace has protested on the barge. ▸ The barge is off the shore of Scotland. ▸ We are scientists. ▸ We are supposed to come up with a plan to get rid of the barge.	▸ Why is Greenpeace so upset? ▸ Who is going to pay for all this? ▸ What are the effects of sinking the barge? ▸ Why can't we just leave it out there? ▸ Could the barge be converted to another use? ▸ What are other ways of disposing of the barge? ▸ What kind of animal life is in the water?	▸ Build models of barges to sink. ▸ Look up information about the barge on the Internet. ▸ Interview a physicist about sinking things. ▸ Look up Greenpeace in magazine articles.

Figure 13.2. Sample learning issues board for Brent Spar.

sophisticated application of the problem, such as "Change is irreversible because it interacts with time." Concepts can be drawn into the problem as a part of coaching, in Problem Log assessments, or during problem debriefing. At a more advanced level, teachers can use a concept to tie several problems together and let the concept develop as students transfer it from one problem to the next. Seeing the same concept in action in several problems also should help students develop the habit of looking for a conceptual structure to the problem (Gallagher, Sher, Stepien, & Workman, 1995; Gallagher, Stepien, & Workman, 1996).

PBL in Action: Planet X

When pilot testing the PBL science units, commonly referred to as "the William and Mary units," "Planet X"* was of special interest to us. Students were placed in the role of "mission specialists," charged with the job of creating a plant ecosystem that would help save the dying planet. It was the first time PBL had been tested with very young children, so we were eager to document as much as possible. A graduate assistant was in the classroom nearly every day to videotape the problem at work. Initially, we would have been satisfied with a very modest success; but, before long, we realized that we were onto something very, very special. The teachers working with the second graders were natural PBL coaches, and soon they were all on an adventure in plant ecosystems.

One day, the students were discussing how they might communicate with personnel on Planet X. The planet was just opposite the Earth on the other side of the sun, and it had exactly the same tilt and rotation. Being on the other side of the sun, the children were faced with the dilemma of how to send messages to their colleagues on the planet. They knew that sound travels in a straight line, which means that messages "beamed" to the planet would always bump into the sun. Their coach gently encouraged students to consider alternatives—drawing the Earth on a chalkboard and marking the path of a sound wave; and in a corner of the room, barely audible, you could hear someone murmur, ". . . mirror . . ."

"What?" exclaimed the coach, seizing on the teachable moment. "What do you mean? Here, come up to the board and show us."

He handed the chalk to the second grader and stood back. The boy shuffled up to the chalkboard and drew a line above the picture of the Earth.

He said, "If we put a mirror up here . . ."

"Yes! Yes!" the nearest girl shouted. "This will work because when we experimented with light, we bounced light!"

"Ah," the coach stepped in. "You mean that sound might reflect like light reflects? Could we use something like a satellite to get sound by the sun to Planet X? Would that work?"

"Yes!" shouted the class, overjoyed with their own cleverness.

That was just one moment in an amazing 4 months of PBL. That's right: 4 months. The unit lasted that long; not because the problem got out of control but because the teachers and students were both enjoying it and learning so much, they decided to keep it going for as long as they could. Even after 4 months, the students were disappointed when the adventure ended.

Note. "Planet X" has since been revised into the problem "Dust Bowl."

Modification 3: Interdisciplinary Connections and Interactions

Most real-world problems are interdisciplinary, which makes the goal of revealing connections and interactions among disciplines quite natural; however, the degree to which a problem is interdisciplinary can vary as a function of problem design and tutor guiding. A likely goal for teachers of the gifted would be to help gifted students explore intricate interconnections. As with the development of the concept, several layers of interdisciplinary interactions could be explored in the Brent Spar problem. For example, while other students think about the interactions of the energy use on the environment, gifted students might investigate additional kinds of interactions, including the multifaceted interactions of energy dependence, global governmental regulation, and territoriality.

Modification 4: Higher Order Thinking Skills

A well-designed problem provides an environment where tutors can help students acquire sound inquiry skills (Hmelo-Silver, 2013). PBL provides an environment where students can be coached to improve their skills along many dimensions of good reasoning.

Critical thinking skills. Just as the problem can be designed to rely on more or less complex applications of a concept, so can students be encouraged to use more complex kinds of reasoning. Different phases of the problem draw on various kinds of reasoning skills. The first lesson of a problem, filling in the Learning Issues Board, requires analytical reasoning, discriminating between fact and inference, recognizing gaps in understanding, and prioritizing. Problem definition, on the other hand, requires skills that include analysis and synthesis of information, determining bias, and summarizing understanding.

Beyond the basic problem-solving and critical-thinking skills, students will have an opportunity to learn discipline-specific skills related to the content matter of the problem. In the Brent Spar problem, students have a natural opportunity to learn about posing scientific hypotheses, experimentation, and reporting. Students also will learn firsthand why it is important for scientists to be able to communicate with a variety of audiences, from other people in the science community, to the lay public, as they try to explain to the press the rationale behind their decision.

Habits of mind. Independent, self-directed, learning requires skills that go beyond critical thinking. Students also need effective habits of mind such as persistence, tolerance of ambiguity, thinking and communicating with clarity and precision, approaching information with a desire to question, and self-regulation (Costa & Kallick, 2008). PBL teachers have an opportunity to select specific habits of mind to work on in each PBL unit. For example, teachers could raise the issue of precision and accuracy with their students as they begin their experiments in the Brent Spar problem. Assessments of the experiment could be designed to make the standards of clarity and precision a priority. As students become increasingly self-directed, they should be expected to adopt not only skills, but also habits of mind, once again enhancing the complexity of the experience for gifted students.

PBL in Action: Student Perspectives

One of the questions that perpetually pesters teachers is whether or not students "get it." In the case of PBL, we might ask whether or not students "get" the idea of complex problem solving. Recently, in Project P-BLISS (Problem-Based Learning in the Social Sciences), we became very interested in this question. We were working with disadvantaged gifted high school students, looking for curricula that would excite them and motivate them to engage in complex thought. To see if the students "got" the idea of complex problem solving, we used this question in their Problem Log: "What do you know about problem solving that you didn't know before?" Here are some representative responses:

- This unit taught me that if you want to be a good problem solver, you must be totally unbiased and look at both sides of the problem. I also learned that everything in a problem is not always as it seems, and many times you have to look into the facts deeper before you can come to a conclusion.
- This unit taught me that the solving process takes a while and is also a lot of work; but, once you get into the flow, it's fun. This process taught me how to compare and contrast and how to choose the right one. It also taught me how not to take sides in the matter because before you can understand what's going on, you have to get both sides of the story.
- I learned that, to solve a problem, it helps to break it down into a bunch of smaller problems that can be solved one at a time. And, doing this, you make it so you don't miss any parts of the problem that could play a good part in making it right. I also learned that, if you try to solve a problem without breaking it down, you can end up with a huge mess.
- You have to have lots of patience. Because everyone might not agree, everyone is not going to agree, and you have to stop and see it in two ways. Sometimes, when you think you've got somewhere, you have to go back 'cause you might have overlooked something.
- I did not realize the extent of how hard it is to make everyone agree on one topic, even though we all wanted essentially the same outcome.

Disciplinary thinking. Stakeholder positions, or the roles students take during the problem, can provide more than career exposure. Immersion in the stakeholder point of view can be used to full benefit by requiring some reflection specifically about his or her role, introducing students to the kind of thinking and questioning that is representative of different fields. As scientists sent to investigate the Brent Spar problem, students should be encouraged to think like scientists and have firsthand experience with the difficulties of conducting science in a politically heated arena. Tutors maximize the apprenticeship by asking students to reflect about the scientist's dispositions: "As a member of the science team investigating the Brent Spar problem, what are your priorities?" "Why is careful data recording so important?" "What are you learning about the way scientists work?" Other questions could engage students in dialogue about the role of people who are involved in both science and community life: "What happens when business or government interferes in the course of science?" "If you are a scientist who works for the government or business, where is your first obligation: to the company or to the data?" Questions like these maximize the nature of the mini-apprenticeship created in the PBL classroom.

Metacognition. From the very beginning, students should be encouraged to reflect on their own problem-solving practices. Metacognition is important for all students. That is, all students need to learn how to self-assess their success in selecting priorities, implementing good problem-solving strategies, and using positive individual and cooperative work habits. As a part of the goal to promote self-directed learning, gifted students could be asked, either during discussion or in Problem Log activities, to reflect on their own attitudes toward problem solving and on key dispositions by asking them questions such as, "How do your own personal biases affect your problem solving?" "Is it ever possible that the least supported idea is the right idea?" "What happens when we close off our options too early or too late?" "What does it mean to have intellectual courage?" and "Why would that be important while solving a problem?"

Modification 5: Discussing Ethical Appeals

Complex, real-world problems often involve ethical dilemmas, and all students need to explore some dimensions of this side of any problem. Gifted students are unusually attuned to ethical issues and can benefit from discussions involving right, wrong, and best options. Gifted students also appreciate complexity and realize that ethical discussions presenting one perspective as right are often too simplistic. Rather than point to one preferable perspective, an effective way to discuss ethics with gifted students is to look at the different ethical appeals evoked in the problem. Brody (1988) defined six ethical appeals: to rights, to consequences, to justice, to virtues, to benefit/cost, and to personhood. Each presents a different paradigm from which to view the problem. By looking at the problem through these different vantage points, students learn how problems become more complicated when different parties are using a different basis for their actions. In the Brent Spar problem, students/scientists would first see that the ethical appeal of their own perspective is an appeal to consequences: "What will happen if the oil platform isn't removed?" In order to develop a reasonable solution, they also might have to see that others involved with the problem use different ethical appeals. Environmentalists might be more interested in personhood—in this case, the right of the individual to live in a clean, safe environment—and the owner of Shell Oil might be concerned about the benefit/cost of the spill.

Putting the Pieces Together

As mentioned above, changes in any one of the five recommended areas make the PBL environment more appropriate for gifted students. The degree of adaptation depends on the usual variables: teacher comfort and skill, student age and ability level, type of classroom adaptation, and everyone's familiarity with the PBL environment. Some teachers, working in heterogeneous groups, may only be able to adapt Problem Log activities for their gifted students, focusing on different kinds of self-reflection for different ability groups. Teachers in resource or self-contained settings may want to try more ambitious adaptations. A summary of all of the adaptations described above is presented in Table 13.2.

Where and When to Use PBL

Complexity, especially the kind found in PBL curricula, can be fun, but it's not always easy. Because it is built to be multifaceted and complex, PBL requires a certain amount of time and story continuity. This can be a challenge to teachers of gifted students, who often work in a number of different program configurations. Resource teachers can use PBL effectively, but it takes a little more organization and effort. The following section provides a brief set of guidelines to use when considering PBL for your classroom.

Continuous Instruction Classroom (Regular Classroom, Self-Contained Gifted Classroom, Daily Resource Program)

PBL is effective in any setting when students and teachers are together daily. Although using PBL in the regular or self-contained classroom offers different challenges to teachers, they are no different from the challenges presented by any curriculum. In the regular classroom, all students of varying abilities need to be stimulated; teachers can make judicious use of the Learning Issues Board to help differentiate assignments. Teachers may be surprised to see who rises to the challenge of an ill-structured problem. A study of PBL in the regular classroom demonstrated that the curriculum model was effective in helping teachers recognize students with advanced academic potential (Gallagher & Gallagher, 2013).

TABLE 13.2

Summary of Adaptations of PBL Problems for Gifted Students

Area of Adaptation	Baseline Goals for Regular-Ability Students	Additional Goals for Gifted Students
Content	‣ Roles governing ocean territories ‣ Monetary conversions (pound to dollar) ‣ Three alternative strategies to discard the Brent Spar ‣ The impact of pipeline technologies ‣ The impact of oil on the surrounding ocean ecosystem ‣ Water flow rates	‣ Chemical composition of metals and oils ‣ Radio nuclides ‣ Differences between intensity and duration effects ‣ Physics of fast and slow release options
Concept	‣ Most things change ‣ Change causes change	‣ Adaptation and transformation are two different kinds of change and have different effects ‣ Change is irreversible because of its interaction with time
Interdisci-plinary	‣ Interaction of science (methods of sinking the barge; environmental impact) and social science (economics of each disposal option; business interest in benefit/cost)	‣ More complex interactions of social science (global regulation versus local regulation of water/local decision making impacts global arena) and economics (monetary versus human and/or animal costs) ‣ Long-term effect of dependence on oil
Critical Thinking and Habits of Mind	‣ Experimentation, selection of problem-solving strategies, and progress through the problem, including collaborative group work	‣ Additional reflection about the nature of problem solving, about the biases and assumptions of people with different points of view

In the self-contained classroom or daily resource program, the whole problem should be adjusted to enhance the complexity of the content, thinking processes, and reflection built into the unit. At this level, the challenge in curriculum design is to avoid overloading the unit with an abundance of activity. Being intentional and selective in curriculum design is crucial to balancing the level of support and challenge in a PBL unit.

Resource Consultation

Another ideal configuration for PBL is resource consultation. Building on the collaborative relationship between the regular classroom teacher and the resource teacher (Landrum, 2001), the two adults can build the program together and then share responsibility for differentiating instruction. While in the classroom, the resource teacher could either work with the gifted students on a specific aspect of the problem or assist the regular classroom teacher with coaching strategies. The resource teacher also could help the regular classroom teacher develop assignments and activities to keep the high-ability students engaged with the problem between visits.

Resource Program, Occasional

The PBL model has been adapted successfully for resource programs where students meet less frequently, but modifications must be made. The nature of the problem must be adapted along at least two dimensions. First, the story must be a little more episodic. Especially important is the use of "kickers" or "twists" to keep the story alive for students from week to week. Research tasks assigned for the periods between meetings can help provide a link from one session to the next. Second, the problem must be somewhat less complex, because a huge, multifaceted problem would take the majority of the school year when students only meet once a week. Teachers who only see their students for an hour once a week may not be able to use PBL, but those with half-day blocks once a week will probably be successful if they think ahead about keeping the problem lively.

These guidelines are not meant to seem prescriptive, restrictive, exclusive, or exhaustive, but rather to serve as a helpful blueprint as teachers experiment with PBL. Most of all, they are designed to answer the question, "Isn't this for all kids?" Yes, PBL is for all students, but adaptations help maximize its usefulness for different groups of students. It is true that all students should learn important concepts, but they differ in levels of abstraction and complexity. Gifted students are likely to need more complex applications of concepts to be appropriately challenged. All students need to understand relationships among disciplines, but to different degrees of sophistication. All students should be taught to self-assess their ability to analyze information, but gifted students will be ready earlier to think about their capacity to show intellectual honesty or integrity in their reasoning. Gifted students, naturally oriented toward open-ended learning, complexity, and independent thought, appreciate the difference in their learning, as evidenced by the comments of some middle school gifted students following their first PBL experience (Horak & Haskins, 2012):

» It was fun to be able to have control of a situation and think for myself. Learning about the human side of [the black-footed ferret problem] helped me think deeply.

» You don't feel like you are learning but you are, you also remember the important parts better than by just studying. We didn't have to purposefully memorize everything we learned but soaked up the information so we could solve the problem.

» It was deeper than just learning from the textbook. It helped me understand interactions in ecosystems better. I also liked how the problem led to learning about other things, like niches.

With careful adaptation, teachers of the gifted can successfully use PBL to open the doorway to rich, challenging, and exciting learning experiences for gifted children.

Teacher Statement

Although I've had many experiences using problem-based learning, my first one is special to me. At the time I learned about PBL, I was teaching in a multiage (grades 4–6) Montessori classroom. As one of two teachers in the room, I had the opportunity to take a small group of gifted students to try out a PBL unit. The group, all girls, had a strong interest in environmental issues and science, a perfect combination for the ill-structured problem I had designed around their science curriculum. PBL can be either real or simulated; this problem was real and centered on a nonprofit botanical forest overpopulated with deer. The deer were enjoying all of the vegetation they could get, so the board decided to put up a fence to keep the hungry animals out. Of course, the girls knew nothing of this when one day they received a "fax" informing them that, as members of the board's Subcommittee on Fencing Recommendations (their stakeholder role), they had to present their fence design to the board in 2 weeks.

The girls wasted no time. With fax in hand, they immediately began to reread the details, take notes, and talk about the assignment. A key element of an ill-structured problem is that information presented is just vague enough to encourage students to ask natural questions: "What kind of fence?" "How high will it need to be?" "Will it keep other wildlife out, too?"

As the students contacted deer experts at zoos, salesmen at fence companies, and relearned (this time with a purpose) mathematical concepts like perimeter and costs per foot, they received a rather heated fax from the "Deer Lovers of America" insisting the fence would prevent these beloved creatures from enjoying their own natural habitat. The reaction to this PBL "kicker" was not at all expected. Despite their love of animals, the students had been assigned an important job: to design a fence that would protect the plants and trees of this forest. They had no intention of hurting any of the wildlife, nor were they going to cave into the pressures of an animal-lovers group. As one of the girls said, "There's plenty for them to eat outside the fence." Indeed, a trip to the forest (a true field trip) proved just that. The area owned by the nonprofit contained 200-year-old beech trees and other fragile vegetation that needed protection to survive. Plenty of forest remained for the deer to inhabit outside the property lines.

The kicker helped the girls recognize one new concern: the risk of injury to the deer should they try to jump the fence. Through careful research, the students became real experts in the abilities and tendencies of these animals. They also learned that no fence company had the perfect fence, so they designed their own. More importantly, they learned to be problem solvers in a world where sometimes problems have no predetermined right answer.

We all learned a lot with this unit. The girls learned content and worked with meaningful thinking skills. They learned how to act professionally outside of the classroom. They even learned how to present at a conference; their enthusiasm was so infectious I took them to the state gifted education conference to share their excitement about their PBL experience. For my part, I learned that even a novice PBL teacher can have a huge success. Every extra minute I spent in preparation was returned in extra enthusiasm and investment by my students.

—Christine H. Weiss

DISCUSSION QUESTIONS

1. Inquiry-based approaches such as problem-based learning have consistently demonstrated that students learn the same amount of content, if not more, than when they are taught through more traditional approaches. Even so, many teachers balk at the idea of using these highly effective strategies for fear that students will not perform as well on standardized tests. What do you think it would take to convince teachers that the data regarding inquiry and content acquisition are true and reliable?

2. Why is it important to think of problem-based learning as a curriculum and instruction model, rather than simply a new way to write curricula?

3. Teachers who are most successful trying PBL for the first time have generally put some effort into planning and support. What kind of advanced planning do you think you would need to do to before teaching a PBL unit? What kind(s) of support would you need and from whom?

4. Which of the following words do you think best describes problem-based learning: model, framework, or strategy? Why?

5. The chapter presents five ways of adapting PBL to make it more appropriate for gifted students: ensuring advanced content, complexity of the concept, interdisciplinary connections and interactions, higher order thinking skills, and discussing ethical appeals. Which of these do you think would be the best place to start making modifications?

6. Problem-based learning is an important part of any teacher's repertoire; however, debate continues over how frequently PBL should be used. Some medical school programs use PBL exclusively. Most K–12 teachers find this comprehensive approach extreme and unfeasible. Ideally, how many times a year do you think a teacher should use PBL?

7. What are the similarities and differences between problem-based learning and other approaches to problem solving (i.e., Parnes' creative problem solving)?

8. Given that PBL is only one of a number of ways to differentiate curricula and instruction for gifted students, think about which strategies would complement PBL in a well-rounded program for gifted students. How are the models you choose to go alongside PBL in your hypothetical program model complementary to PBL?

Teacher Resources

Publications: Model Curriculum Units and Guides

College of William and Mary Center for Gifted Education. (1997a). *Acid, acid everywhere*. Dubuque, IA: Kendall/Hunt.

College of William and Mary Center for Gifted Education. (1997b). *Dust bowl*. Dubuque, IA: Kendall/Hunt.

College of William and Mary Center for Gifted Education. (1997c). *What a find*. Dubuque, IA: Kendall/Hunt.

College of William and Mary Center for Gifted Education. (1997d). *Electricity city*. Dubuque, IA: Kendall/Hunt.

College of William and Mary Center for Gifted Education. (1997e). *Something fishy*. Dubuque, IA: Kendall/Hunt.

College of William and Mary Center for Gifted Education. (1997f). *No quick fix*. Dubuque, IA: Kendall/Hunt.

College of William and Mary Center for Gifted Education. (1997g). *Hot rods*. Dubuque, IA: Kendall/Hunt.

Gallagher, S. A. (2011). *Problem-based learning for classroom teachers*. Unionville, NY: Royal Fireworks Press.

Gallagher, S. A. (2011). *Black death*. Unionville, NY: Royal Fireworks Press.

Gallagher, S. A. (2009). *Excluded!: The Chinese exclusion laws*. Unionville, NY: Royal Fireworks Press.

Gallagher, S. A. (2008). *All work and no play: Child labor during the Progressive Era*. Unionville, NY: Royal Fireworks Press.

Gallagher, S. A., & Plowden, D. (2012). *A final appeal: The First Amendment and* To Kill A Mockingbird. Unionville, NY: Royal Fireworks Press.

Gallagher, S. A., & Plowden, D. (2012). *Ferret it out: A problem about endangered species and animal ecosystems*. Unionville, NY: Royal Fireworks Press.

Gallagher, S. A., & Plowden, D. (2012). *Hull House: Living democracy in the Progressive Era*. Unionville, NY: Royal Fireworks Press.

Kain, D. (2003a). *Problem-based learning for teachers, grades K–8*. Boston, MA: Allyn & Bacon.

Kain, D. (2003b). *Problem-based learning for teachers, grades 6–12*. Boston, MA: Allyn & Bacon.

Ronis, D. L. (2000). *Problem-based learning for math and science*. Arlington Heights, IL: Skylight.

Stepien, W. J., Senn, P., & Stepien, W. C. (2001). *The Internet and problem-based learning: Developing solutions through the Web*. Waco, TX: Prufrock Press.

Stepien, W. (2002). *Problem-based learning with the Internet: Grades 3–6*. Waco, TX: Prufrock Press.

Publications: Selected Readings

Barrows, H. (1985). *How to design a problem-based curriculum for preclinical years*. New York, NY: Springer.

Barrows, H. (1988). *The tutorial process.* Springfield: Southern Illinois University School of Medicine.

Barrows, H. (1994). *Practice-based learning.* Springfield: Southern Illinois University School of Medicine.

Benoit, B., McClure, T., & Kuinzle, R. (1997). Problem-based learning: Meeting real-world challenges. In J. H. Clarke & R. M. Agne (Eds.), *Interdisciplinary high school teaching: Strategies for integrated learning* (pp. 208–235). Boston, MA: Allyn & Bacon.

Boyce, L. N., VanTassel-Baska, J., Burruss, J. E., Sher, B. T., & Johnson, D. T. (1997). A problem-based curriculum: Parallel learning opportunities for students and teachers. *Journal for the Education of the Gifted, 20,* 363–379.

Cuozzo, C. C. (1996/1997). What do lepidopterists do? *Educational Leadership, 53,* 34–37.

Delisle, R. (1997). *How to use problem-based learning in the classroom.* Reston, VA: Association for Supervision and Curriculum Development.

Feng, A. X., VanTassel-Baska, J., Quek, C., Bai, W., & O'Neill, B. (2005). A longitudinal assessment of gifted students' learning using the Integrated Curriculum Model (ICM): Impacts and perceptions of the William and Mary language arts and science curriculum. *Roeper Review, 27,* 78–83.

Gallagher, S. A. (2000). Project P-BLISS: An experiment in curriculum for gifted disadvantaged high school students. *NAASP Bulletin, 84*(615), 47–57.

Gallagher, S. A. (2009). What do you need to know? Becoming an effective PBL teacher. In B. MacFarlane & T. Stambaugh (Eds.), *Leading change in gifted education: The festschrift of Dr. Joyce VanTassel-Baska* (pp. 337–350). Waco, TX: Prufrock Press.

Gallagher, S. A., & Gallagher, J. J. (2013). Using problem-based learning to explore unseen academic potential. *Interdisciplinary Journal of Problem-based Learning, 7*(1). Retrieved from http://dx.doi.org/10.7771/1541-5015.1322

Gallagher, S. A., & Horak, A. (2011). Somewhat like Sisyphus: Systematic implementation of PBL. *Gifted Education International, 27,* 247–262.

Gallagher, S. A., Sher, B. T., Stepien, W. J., & Workman, D. (1995). Implementing problem-based learning in the science classroom. *School Science and Mathematics, 95,* 136–146.

Gallagher, S. A., Stepien, W. J., & Rosenthal, H. (1994). The effects of problem-based learning on problem solving. *Gifted Child Quarterly, 36,* 195–200.

Stepien, W. J., & Gallagher, S. A. (1993). Problem-based learning: As authentic as it gets. *Educational Leadership, 50*(7), 25–29.

Stepien, W. J., Gallagher, S. A., & Workman, D. (1993). Problem-based learning for traditional and interdisciplinary classrooms. *Journal for the Education of the Gifted, 16,* 338–357.

Stepien, W. J., & Pyke, S. L. (1997). Designing problem-based learning units. *Journal for the Education of the Gifted, 20,* 380–400.

Torp, L., & Sage, S. (2002). *Problems as possibilities: Problem-based learning in K–12 classrooms* (2nd ed.). Reston, VA: Association for Supervision and Curriculum Development.

Films

Johnson, T. (Producer), & Murphy, M. (Regional Director). (1998a). *Problem-based learning: Using problems to learn* [Film]. (Available from Association for Supervision and Curriculum Development, 1703 N. Beauregard St., Alexandria, VA 22311–1714)

Johnson, T. (Producer), & Murphy, M. (Regional Director). (1998b). *Problem-based learning: Designing problems for learning* [Film]. (Available from Association for Supervision and Curriculum Development, 1703 N. Beauregard St., Alexandria, VA 22311–1714)

Websites

Exploring the Environment: Problem-Based Learning—http://www.cotf.edu/ete
> Part of NASA's Classroom of the Future initiative, this site gives a nice overview of the theory and structure of PBL along with several model science units.

The Illinois Mathematics and Science Academy (IMSA) PBL Network—http://pbln.imsa.edu/
> The IMSA hosts a number of resources for teachers through the IMSA Center for Problem-Based Learning. Included on their website are descriptions of the PBL process, sample problems, and, perhaps most importantly, access to ASCD's PBL Network, a network, newsletter, and listserv for teachers and other professionals involved with PBL.

Problem-Based Learning Initiative—http://www.pbli.org/shopping/book_ppapbl.htm
> Generally recognized as the modern father of PBL, Howard Barrows worked at the Medical School at Southern Illinois University until 2011. Anyone who is interested in PBL should be familiar with Dr. Barrows' work and philosophy of PBL. This site is the source of many seminal works by Dr. Barrows, including *The Tutorial Process*.

University of Delaware Problem-Based Learning—http://www.udel.edu/pbl
> This website is for people interested in the application of PBL in higher education (or for people looking for problems to use with advanced high school students). The University of Delaware is an example of an undergraduate institution that is proactive in its support of the transformation from traditional to PBL-structured classrooms. The website offers an impressive list of classes offered using the PBL model.

Interdisciplinary Journal of Problem-Based Learning—http://docs.lib.purdue.edu/ijpbl/
> An open-access online journal dedicated to scholarship in PBL at all levels of education. This is an excellent resource for anyone interested in current research and theory in PBL; it is edited by leaders in the field.

Royal Fireworks Press—http://www.rfwp.com/pages/shelagh-gallagher/videos/
> This website has links to several brief YouTube videos that walk viewers through the details of an actual PBL unit.

References

Barrows, H. (1985). *How to design a problem-based curriculum for preclinical years*. New York, NY: Springer.

Berninger, V., & Yates, C. (1993). Formal operational thought in the gifted: A post-Piagetian perspective. *Roeper Review, 15,* 220–224.

Bransford, J. D., Brown, A. L., & Cocking, R. R. (2000). *How people learn: Brain, mind, experience, and school.* Washington DC: National Academy Press.

Brody, B. A. (1988). *Life and death decision making.* New York, NY: Oxford University Press.

Carr, M., Alexander, J. M., & Schwanenflugel, P. J. (1996). Where gifted children do and do not excel on metacognitive tasks. *Roeper Review, 18,* 212–217.

Cherney, I. D., Winter, J., & Cherney, M. G. (2005). Nuclear physics problem solving: A case study of expert-novice differences. *Transactions of the Nebraska Academy of Sciences, 30*(1), 1–7.

Clark, B. (2006). *Growing up gifted: Developing the potential of children at home and at school* (7th ed.). Columbus, OH: Merrill/Prentice Hall.

Costa, A., & Kallick, B. (2008). *Learning and leading with habits of mind: 16 essential characteristics for success.* Alexandria, VA: Association for Supervision and Curriculum Development.

Cruickshank, B. J., & Olander, J. (2002). Can problem-based instruction stimulate higher order thinking? *Journal of College Science Teaching, 31,* 374–378.

Davis, G, A., Rimm, S. B., & Siegle, D. (2010). *Education of the gifted and talented* (6th ed.) Upper Saddle River, NJ: Pearson.

Dresel, M., & Haugwitz, M. (2005). The relationship between cognitive abilities and self-regulated learning: Evidence for interactions with academic self-concept and gender. *High Ability Studies, 16,* 201–218.

Driscoll, M. P. (2005). *Psychology of learning for instruction.* Upper Saddle River, NJ: Pearson.

Ericsson, K. A., Charness, N., Feltovich, P. J., & Hoffman, R. R. (2006). *The Cambridge handbook of expertise and expert performance.* New York, NY: Cambridge University Press

Gallagher, S. A. (2001). But does it work? Testing the efficacy of problem-based learning: A review of the literature and research agenda for educators of the gifted. In S. G. Assouline & N. Colangelo (Eds.), *Talent development IV: Proceedings from the 1998 Henry B. and Jocelyn Wallace National Research Symposium on Talent Development* (pp. 179–204). Scottsdale, AZ: Great Potential Press.

Gallagher, S. A. (2009). Designed to fit: Educational implications of gifted adolescents' cognitive development. In F. Dixon (Ed.), *Programs and services for gifted secondary students* (p. 3–20). Waco, TX: Prufrock Press.

Gallagher, S. A. (2013). Building bridges: Research on gifted students' personalities from three perspectives. In C. Neville, M. Piechowski, & S. Tolan (Eds.), *Off the charts: Asynchrony and the gifted child* (pp. 48–100). Unionville, NY: Royal Fireworks Press.

Gallagher, S. A., & Gallagher, J. J. (2013). Using problem-based learning to explore unseen academic potential. *Interdisciplinary Journal of Problem-based Learning, 7*(1), 111–131. Retrieved from http://dx.doi.org/10.7771/1541-5015.1322

Gallagher, S. A., Sher, B. T., Stepien, W. J., & Workman, D. (1995). Implementing problem-based learning in the science classroom. *School Science and Mathematics, 95,* 126–146.

Gallagher, S. A., & Stepien, W. J. (1996). Depth versus breadth in problem-based learning: Content acquisition in American studies. *Journal for the Education of the Gifted, 19,* 257–275.

Gallagher, S. A., Stepien, W. J., & Workman, D. (1996). Problem-based learning in traditional and interdisciplinary classrooms. *Journal for the Education of the Gifted, 16,* 338–357.

Gamoran, A. (2000). High standards: A strategy for equalizing opportunities to learn? In R. D. Kahlenberg (Ed.), *A notion at risk: Preserving public education as an engine for social mobility* (pp. 93–126). New York, NY: Century Foundation.

Getzels, J. W. (1979). Problem-finding: A theoretical note. *Cognitive Science, 3,* 167–171.

Goodnough, K., & Cashion, M. (2003). Fostering inquiry through problem-based learning. *The Science Teacher, 70*(9), 21–25.

Hambrick, D. Z., & Engle, R. W. (2002). Effects of domain knowledge, working memory capacity, and age on cognitive performance: An investigation of the knowledge-is-power hypothesis. *Cognitive Psychology, 44,* 339–387.

Hambrick, D. Z., & Meinz, E. J. (2011). Limits on the predictive power of domain-specific experience and knowledge in skilled performance. *Current Directions in Psychological Science, 20,* 275–279.

Heinze, A. (2005). Differences in problem solving strategies of mathematically gifted and non-gifted elementary students. *International Education Journal, 6,* 175–183.

Hmelo-Silver, C. (2004). Problem-based learning: What and how do students learn? *Educational Psychology Review, 16,* 235–266.

Hmelo-Silver, C. E. (2013). Creating a learning space in problem-based learning. *Interdisciplinary Journal of Problem-Based Learning, 7*(1), 24–39. Retrieved from http://dx.doi.org/10.7771/1541-5015.1334

Hmelo-Silver, C. E., Duncan, R. G., & Chinn, C. A. (2007). Scaffolding and achievement in problem-based and inquiry learning: A response to Kirschner, Sweller, and Clark (2006). *Educational Psychologist, 42,* 99–107.

Hofer, B. K., & Pintrich, P. R. (Eds.). (2002). *Personal epistemology: The psychology of beliefs about knowledge and knowing.* Mahwah, NJ: Lawrence Erlbaum.

Holschuh, J. P. (2000). Do as I say, not as I do: High, average, and low-performing students' strategy use in biology. *Journal of College Reading and Learning, 31*(1), 94–108.

Horak, A., & Haskins, J. (2012, November). *Evaluation of a problem-based learning unit for middle school students.* Presentation made at the annual meeting of the National Association for Gifted Children, Denver, CO.

Housand, A. M., & Reis, S. M. (2008). Self-regulated learning in reading: Gifted pedagogy and instructional settings. *Journal for Advanced Academics, 20*(1), 108–136.

Jarvin, L., & Subotnik, R. (2006). Understanding elite talent in academic domains: A developmental trajectory from basic abilities to scholarly productivity/artistry. In F. A. Dixon & S. M. Moon (Eds.), *The handbook of secondary gifted education* (pp. 203–220). Waco, TX: Prufrock Press.

Judson, H. F. (1980). *The search for solutions.* New York, NY: Holt, Rinehart and Winston.

King, P. M., & Kitchener, K. S. (2002). The Reflective Judgment Model: Twenty years of research on epistemic cognition. In B. K. Hofer & P. R. Pintrich (Eds.). *Personal epis-*

temology: The psychology of beliefs about knowledge and knowing (pp. 37–62). Mahwah, NJ: Lawrence Erlbaum.

Landrum, M. S. (2001). An evaluation of the catalyst program: Consultation and collaboration in gifted education. *Gifted Child Quarterly, 45,* 139–151.

Maker, C. J., & Schiever, S. (2005). *Teaching models in education of the gifted* (3rd ed.). Austin, TX: Pro-Ed.

Montague, M. (1991). Gifted and learning disabled gifted students' knowledge and use of mathematical problem solving strategies. *Journal for the Education of the Gifted, 14,* 393–411.

National Governors Association Center for Best Practices, & Council of Chief State School Officers. (2010a). *Common Core State Standards for English language arts.* Washington, DC: Author.

National Governors Association Center for Best Practices, & Council of Chief State School Officers. (2010b). *Common Core State Standards for Mathematics.* Washington, DC: Author.

O'Connor, F. (1962). *Mystery and manners.* New York, NY: Farrar, Straus & Giroux.

Planche, P., & Gicquel, M. (2000). L'accession à l'opérativité formelle chez les enfants intellectuellement précoces. *International Journal of Psychology, 35,* 219–227.

Rogers, K. B. (2004). The academic effects of acceleration. In N. Colangelo, S. Assouline, & M. U. M. Gross (Eds.), *A nation deceived: How schools hold back America's brightest students* (Vol. 2, pp. 47–57). Iowa City: The University of Iowa, The Connie Belin & Jacqueline N. Blank International Center for Gifted Education and Talent Development.

Ross, B. (1991). Towards a framework for problem-based curricula. In D. Boud & G. Feletti (Eds.), *The challenge of problem-based learning* (pp. 34–41). New York, NY: St. Martin's Press.

Schmidt, H. G., Rotgans, J. I., & Yew, E. H. J. (2011). The process of problem-based learning: What works? And why? *Medical Education, 45,* 792–806.

Shore, B. M. (2000). Metacognition and flexibility: Qualitative differences in how gifted children think. In R. C. Friedman & B. M. Shore (Eds.), *Talents unfolding: Cognition and development* (pp. 167–187). Washington, DC: American Psychological Association.

Snyder, K. E., Nietfeld, J. L., & Linnenbrink-Garcia, L. (2011). Giftedness and metacognition: A short-term longitudinal investigation of metacognitive monitoring in the classroom. *Gifted Child Quarterly, 58,* 181–193.

Sockalingam, N., Rotgans, J. I., & Schmidt, H. G. (2012). Assessing the quality of problems in problem-based learning. *International Journal of Teaching and Learning in Higher Education, 4*(1), 1–12.

Sriraman, B. (2003). Mathematical giftedness, problem solving, and the ability to formulate generalizations. *Journal of Secondary Gifted Education, 14,* 151–165.

Steiner, H. H., & Carr, M. (2003). Cognitive development in gifted children: Toward a more precise understanding of emerging differences in intelligence. *Educational Psychology Review, 15,* 215–243.

Stepien, W., & Gallagher, S. A. (1993). Problem-based learning: As authentic as it gets! *Educational Leadership, 50*(7), 25–28.

Stepien, W. J., & Gallagher, S. A. (1997). *Problem-based learning across the curriculum: An ASCD professional inquiry kit.* Alexandria, VA: Association for Supervision and Curriculum Development.

Stepien, W. J., & Pyke, S. (1997). Designing problem-based learning units. *Journal for the Education of the Gifted, 20,* 380–400.

Sternberg, R. J. (2003). A broad view of intelligence: The theory of successful intelligence. *Consulting Psychology Journal: Practice and Research, 55*(1), 139–154.

Strobel, J., & van Barneveld, A. (2009). When is PBL more effective? A meta-synthesis of meta-analyses comparing PBL to conventional classrooms. *Interdisciplinary Journal of Problem-Based Learning, 3*(1), 44–58. Retrieved from http://dx.doi.org/10.7771/1541-5015.1046

Sungur, S., Tekkaya, C., & Geban, Ö. (2006). Improving achievement through problem-based learning. *Journal of Biological Education, 40,* 155–160.

Thomas, J. A. (2008). Reviving Perry: An analysis of epistemological change by gender and ethnicity among gifted high school students. *Gifted Child Quarterly, 52,* 87–98.

Tomlinson, C. A., & Imbeau, M. (2010). *Leading and managing in a differentiated classroom.* Arlington, VA: Association for Supervision and Curriculum Development.

Tuchman, B. (1966). *The proud tower.* New York, NY: Macmillan.

van Berkel, H., & Dolmans, D. (2006). The influence of tutoring competencies on problems, group functioning and student achievement in problem-based learning. *Medical Education, 40,* 730–736.

van Berkel, H., & Schmidt, H. (2005). On the additional value of lectures in a problem-based curriculum. *Education for Health: Change in Learning & Practice, 18*(1), 45–61.

van de Hurk, M. (2006). The relation between self-regulated strategies and individual study time, prepared participation and achievement in a problem-based curriculum. *Active Learning in Higher Education, 7,* 155–169.

VanTassel-Baska, J., & Stambaugh, T. (2005). *Comprehensive curriculum for gifted learners.* Boston, MA: Allyn & Bacon.

Vardi, I., & Ciccarelli, M. (2008). Overcoming problems in problem based learning: A trial of strategies in an undergraduate unit. *Innovations in Education and Teaching International, 45,* 345–354.

Verhoeven, B. H., Verwijnen, G. M., Scherpbier, A. J., Holdrinet, R. S., Oeseburg, B., Bulte, J. A., & van der Vleuten, C. P. (1998). An analysis of progress test results of PBL and non-PBL students. *Medical Teacher, 20,* 310–317.

Wirkala, C., & Kuhn, D. (2011). Problem-based learning in K–12 education: Is it effective and how does it achieve its effects? *American Educational Research Journal, 48,* 1157–1186.

STRATEGIES FOR BEST PRACTICE

TEACHING GIFTED STUDENTS THROUGH INDEPENDENT STUDY

14
Chapter

BY SUSAN K. JOHNSEN AND KRYSTAL K. GOREE

A third-grade teacher announced to a small group of gifted students that they were going to begin their first independent study. She asked, "Does anyone know about independent study?"

A proud little girl immediately raised her hand and blurted, "It's when you write a research report!"

Most students might define an independent study in the same way as this third grader, but it is much more than reading books and writing papers. Independent studies may be used for solving community problems, uncovering new questions, creating a previously unknown history of a small neighborhood, and, most importantly, helping a student create a lifelong love affair with learning.

Independent study is the most frequently recommended instructional strategy in programs for gifted students and is included in the majority of introductory texts as a means for differentiating and individualizing instruction (Clark, 2012; Colangelo & Davis, 2002; Coleman & Cross, 2005; Davis, Rimm, & Siegle, 2010; Piirto, 2007). Independent study also is preferred by gifted students (Caraisco, 2007; Chan, 2001; Dunn

& Griggs, 1985; French, Walker, & Shore, 2011; Kanevsky, 2011; Renzulli, 1977a; Rogers, 2007; Stewart, 1981; Thomson, 2010).

When compared to learning preferences of more average students, gifted students like instructional strategies that emphasize independence such as independent study and discussion. Although gifted students like these methods, they do not always have the necessary skills that are essential to self-directed learning; consequently, they need to learn them. Once they have acquired critical independent strategies, gifted students are able to become lifelong learners, capable of responsible involvement and leadership in a changing world (Betts, 1985).

Johnsen and Johnson (2007a) defined independent study as:

> a *process* students use when they research a new topic by themselves or with others. This process is cyclical and includes a variety of steps that engage the student in acting like professionals, such as posing questions, gathering information related to the questions, organizing the information, and presenting the information to an audience. (p. 1)

Kitano and Kirby (1986) added the important elements of planning and teacher involvement: "Students conduct self-directed research projects that are carefully planned with the teacher and are monitored frequently" (p. 114). Both Betts (1985) and Renzulli and Reis (1991) emphasized the importance of "real-world investigations" in their definitions. "In-depth studies are life-like for they provide an opportunity to go beyond the usual time and space restrictions of most school activities" (Betts, 1985, p. 55). Type III research projects are " . . . investigative activities and artistic productions in which the learner assumes the role of a first-hand inquirer—thinking, feeling, and acting like a practicing professional" (Renzulli & Reis, 1991, p. 131).

In summary, independent study is a planned research process that (a) is similar to one used by a practicing professional or authentic to the discipline; (b) is facilitated by the teacher; and (c) focuses on lifelike problems that go beyond the general education class setting.

Independent Study Models

Models such as Renzulli's (1977a; Renzulli & Reis, 2014; Renzulli & Renzulli, 2010) Enrichment Triad Model, Feldhusen and Kolloff's (1986) Three-Stage Model, Treffinger's (1975, 1978, 1986) Self-Initiated Learning Model, and Betts and Kercher's (1999) Autonomous Learner Model have inspired teachers to include independent study as an important component of their gifted programming.

Renzulli's model (1977a) contains three qualitatively different phases: Type I enrichment or general exploratory activities introduce the student to a variety of topics and interest areas, Type II group training activities develop creativity and research skills, and Type III investigations encourage students to pursue real problems of personal interest to them (see Figure 14.1). Students move among and between the three types of activities based upon their interest in a particular question, topic, or problem. When students arrive at Type III activities, the teacher helps them identify specific questions and methods to use in pursuing their independent studies. The teacher also provides feedback and helps students find resources and audiences who might be interested in their products (Renzulli, 1979). Renzulli (1979) emphasized the importance of finding "real" problems and using "authentic" methods during the Type III activities.

Feldhusen and Kolloff's (1986) three-stage inquiry model focuses on the development of basic divergent and convergent thinking abilities at Stage 1, more complex creative and problem-solving activities at Stage 2, and independent learning abilities at Stage 3 (see Figure 14.2). In the independent learning stage, gifted students are involved in research projects that focus on defining problems, gathering data, interpreting findings, and communicating results. At this stage, the students' own interests and knowledge base serve "to stimulate a deep intrinsic interest in an area of investigation" (Feldhusen & Kolloff, 1986, p. 131). More recently, Feldhusen (1995) proposed The Purdue Pyramid (see Figure 14.3). Included in the wide array of learning experiences needed to develop talent and still occupying a prominent position is "independent study and original investigations" (Feldhusen, 1995, p. 92).

Treffinger (1975) developed a four-step plan for teaching increasing degrees of independent, self-initiated learning (see Figure 14.4). At the Teacher-Directed Level, the teacher prescribes all of the activities for individual students; at Level 1, the teacher creates the learning activities and the student chooses the ones he or she wants to do; at Level 2, the student participates in decisions about the learning activities, goals, and evaluation; and at Level 3, the student creates the choices, makes the selection, and carries out the activity. The student also evaluates his or her own progress.

More recently, Treffinger (2003) identified self-directed learning as one "style" that might be observed in a classroom (p. 14); see (Figure 14.5). The emphasis in the student-teacher contract style (i.e., contracting) and self-directed learning style (i.e., exploring) is on student-led or student-managed activities where the teacher acts as a facilitator of independent and group efforts. The other styles are controlled either by the teacher (i.e., command and task styles) or by the group (i.e., peer partner styles).

Betts and Kercher (1999) divided their Autonomous Learner Model into five major dimensions: orientation, individual development, enrichment activities,

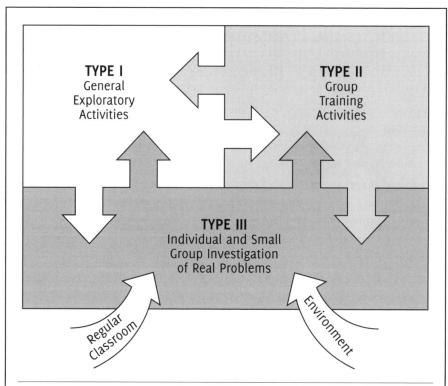

Figure 14.1. The Enrichment Triad Model. *Note.* From *The Enrichment Triad Model: A Guide for Developing Defensible Programs for the Gifted and Talented* (p. 14), by J. S. Renzulli, 1977a, Mansfield Center, CT: Creative Learning Press. Copyright ©1977 by Creative Learning Press. Reprinted with permission.

seminars, and in-depth study (see Figure 14.6). During orientation, the students learn about themselves and what the program has to offer. In individual development, the student focuses on developing skills, concepts, and attitudes that promote lifelong independent, autonomous learning. Enrichment activities assist students in deciding what they want to study independently. Seminars provide a forum for students in small groups to present their research to the rest of the group. Students learn how to promote understanding of their topics and facilitate the discussions. During the final in-depth study, students pursue areas of interest in long-term individual or small-group studies similar to Renzulli's Type III projects.

Although these and other models of independent study exist, empirical research is limited, with most of the studies focusing on Renzulli's model. For example, students who completed Type III investigations reported that they were better prepared for research assignments, "were able to manage their time efficiently, and plan their work to meet their desired goal" (Hébert, 1993, p. 27). They have higher self-efficacy with regard to creative productivity and are more

Stage I	
Divergent and Convergent Thinking Abilities	**Examples of Resources**
▸ Teacher-led short span activities ▸ Emphasis on fluency, flexibility, originality, elaboration ▸ Application of skills in various content areas ▸ Balance between verbal and nonverbal activities	▸ *Basic Thinking Skills* (Harnadek, 1976) ▸ *New Directions in Creativity* (Renzulli & Callahan, 1973; Renzulli et al., 2000) ▸ Purdue Creative Thinking Program (Feldhusen, 1983) ▸ *Sunflowering* (Stanish, 1977)
Stage II	
Development of Creative Problem-Solving Abilities	**Examples of Resources**
▸ Teacher-led and student-initiated ▸ Techniques of inquiry, SCAMPER ▸ Morphological analysis, attribute listing, synectics ▸ Application of a creative problem-solving model	▸ *CPS For Kids* (Stanish & Eberle, 1996) ▸ *Problems! Problems! Problems!* (Gourley & Micklus, 1982) ▸ *Design Yourself!* (Hanks, Belliston, & Edwards, 1977) ▸ *Hippogriff Feathers* (Stanish, 1981)
Stage III	
Development of Independent Learning Abilities	**Example of Resources**
▸ Student-led, teacher-guided individual or small group work on selected topics ▸ Application of research methods ▸ Preparation of culminating product for an audience	▸ *Big Book of Independent Study* (Kaplan, Madsen, & Gould, 1976) ▸ *Self-Starter Kit for Independent Study* (Doherty & Evans, 1980) ▸ *Up Periscope!* (Dallas Independent Schools, 1977) ▸ *Interest-A-Lyzer* (Renzulli, 1977b, 1997)

Figure 14.2. Purdue Three-Stage Model. *Note.* From "The Purdue Three-Stage Enrichment Model for Gifted Education at the Elementary Level," by J. F. Feldhusen and P. B. Kolloff, 1986, in J. S. Renzulli (Ed.), *Systems and Models for Developing Programs for the Gifted and Talented* (p. 131), Mansfield Center, CT: Creative Learning Press. Copyright © 1986 by Creative Learning Press. Reprinted with permission.

likely to pursue creative productivity outside of school (Garcia-Cepero, 2008; Starko, 1988; Troxclair, 2000). Delcourt (1993) and Mathisen and Bronnick (2009) reported that students were more internally motivated toward projects they wanted to do and viewed other types of projects such as regular and gifted class assignments as "routine" or "regular" and not a part of creative activities. Olenchak and Renzulli (1989) found that students enrolled in Schoolwide Enrichment Model (SEM) schools had numerous creative products that exceeded

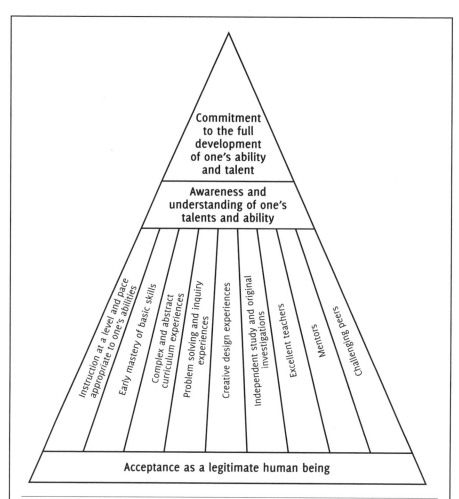

Figure 14.3. The Purdue Pyramid. *Note.* From "Talent Development: The New Direction in Gifted Education" by J. F. Feldhusen, 1995, *Roeper Review*, 18, p. 92. Copyright © 1995 by Roeper Review, P.O. Box 329, Bloomfield Hills, MI 48303. Reprinted with permission of Taylor & Frances, LTD., http://www.informaworld.com.

the norm of typical student creative production. Gifted students who have participated in these programs felt that independent study had a positive influence on their motivation and career, their study habits and thinking processes, the degree of challenge, and the opportunity for self-expression in school (Hertzog, 2003; Jin & Moon, 2006; Renzulli & Gable, 1976; Zimmerman & Martinez-Pons, 1990). In general, pursuing personal interests appears to contribute to positive attitudes, creative potential, and a sense of competence and self-determination or persistence (Caraisco, 2007; Chan, 2001; Fulk & Montgomery-Grymes, 1994; Runco & Chand, 1995; Ryan & Deci, 2000; Sayler, 2009; Selby, Shaw, & Houtz, 2005; Torrance, 1995; Vallerand, Gagné, Senecal, & Pelletier, 1994; Zimmerman

	Levels of Self-Direction			
Decisions to Be Made	Teacher-Directed	Self-Directed— Level 1	Self-Directed— Level 2	Self-Directed— Level 3
Goals and objectives	Teacher prescribes for total class or individuals.	Teacher provides choices or options for students.	Teacher involves learner in creating options.	Learner controls choices; teacher provides resources and materials.
Assessments of entry behaviors	Teacher tests, then makes specific prescription.	Teacher diagnoses, then provides several options.	Teacher and learner hold diagnostic conference; tests employed individually if needed.	Learner controls diagnosis; consults teacher for assistance when unclear about some need.
Instructional procedures	Teacher presents content, provides exercises and activities, arranges and supervises practice.	Teacher provides options for student to employ independently at his or her own pace.	Teacher provides resources and options, uses contracts that involve learner in scope, sequence, and pace decisions.	Learner defines project and activities, identifies resources needed, makes scope, sequence, and pace decisions.
Assessment of performance	Teacher implements evaluation procedures, chooses instruments, and gives grades.	Teacher relates evaluation to objectives and gives student opportunity to react or respond.	Peer partners used to provide feedback; teacher and learner conferences used for evaluation.	Learner does self-evaluation.

Figure 14.4. Model for self-directed learning. *Note.* From "Teaching for Self-Directed Learning: A Priority for the Gifted and Talented," by D. J. Treffinger, 1975, *Gifted Child Quarterly*, 19, p. 47. Copyright ©1975 by the National Association for Gifted Children. Reprinted by permission SAGE Publications.

& Martinez-Pons, 1990). Researchers suggest that students should be encouraged to select their own topics for projects that they enjoy (Collins & Amabile, 1999; Collins, Joseph, & Bielaczyc, 2004; Csikszentmihalyi, Rathunde, & Whalen, 1993; Douglas, 2004).

Using Kuhlthau's Information Search Process Model, Bishop (2000) reported that the most difficult stage in independent study is exploring and forming a focus for the project. This stage appears critical to the success of the process and shows the importance of the teacher's guidance in framing the problem and organizing information. Moreover, without direct teacher support and specific lessons, stu-

Teacher-Directed Styles	**Command Style** *Emphasis: Directing* The teacher controls decisions about goals and objectives, diagnostics, learning activities, and evaluation. This style is beneficial when the goals emphasize conveying information, teaching specific skills, or communicating basic declarative knowledge and concepts within a prescribed curriculum area. It may be appropriate for "enthusiastic beginners" who need considerable task direction.
	Task Style *Emphasis: Enabling* The teacher controls decisions about goals, objectives, diagnostics, and evaluation. The students have some choices regarding learning activities. This style is beneficial when the goals include content at varying levels of difficulty, or varying themes within a broad topic area. It still provides considerable task direction while offering some support for student choices. It is appropriate when the teacher begins teaching the students how to make choices and deal with mobility and freedom of movement.
Group-Directed Styles	**Peer Partner Styles With Two Substyles (Peer Teaching and Cooperative)** *Emphasis: Collaborating* These styles are highly interactive, as the teacher begins to involve the students in shared decisions about goals and objectives, diagnostics, learning activities, and evaluation. *Peer Teaching or Tutoring.* Members of the groups are dissimilar in relation to the task on which they are working. One (who is proficient in relation to the task) serves as the "teacher partner" or tutor, and the other is the "learner partner," for whom the task represents a new and important goal. The students begin to define and carry out the "teacher" role with a peer, before undertaking it for themselves. *Cooperative Groups.* The group members are relatively similar in relation to the task at hand. The group members work together in planning, carrying out, and evaluating learning activities, after conferencing with the teacher. The major purpose is to serve as a "prelude" for self-direction.
Self-Directed Styles	**Student-Teacher Contract Style** *Emphasis: Contracting* The student takes increasing control and responsibility for decisions about goals and objectives, diagnostics, and evaluation. Students negotiate specific contracts or learning agreements with the teacher, including all four areas of instructional decisions. There will be specific curriculum relevance or "pay-off" in the contracts; the teacher will involve students in individual and group evaluation, but retains final "approval" and evaluation authority.
	Self-Directed Learning Style *Emphasis: Exploring* Individuals or student-initiated teams pursue projects they have designed. They assume leadership for goals and objectives, diagnosis, activities, and evaluation. They are responsible for demonstrating the appropriateness and relevance of their plans in relation to acceptable educational goals or requirements and for documenting the quality and quantity of their work and results. They may involve outside resources or mentors.

Figure 14.5. Classroom teaching styles. *Note.* From *Independent, Self-Directed Learning: 2003 Update* (p. 14), by D. J. Treffinger, 2003, Sarasota, FL: Center for Creative Learning. Copyright ©2003 by Center for Creative Learning. Reprinted with permission.

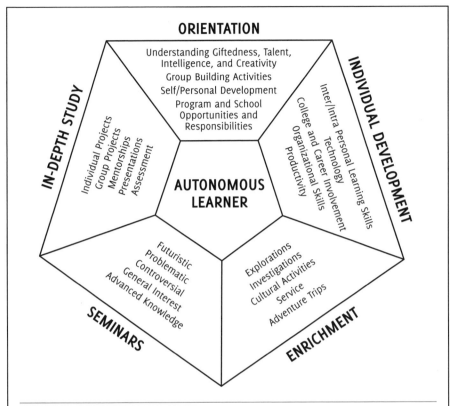

Figure 14.6. The Autonomous Learner Model. *Note.* From The Autonomous Learner Model: Optimizing Ability (p. 2), by G. T. Betts and J. J. Kercher, 1999, Greeley, CO: ALPS Publications. Copyright © 1996, ALPS Publications. Reprinted with permission.

dents are less likely to be successful in completing creative products (Newman, 2005; Trumbull, Scarano, & Bonney, 2006).

Guidelines for Independent Study

Although independent study is frequently used by teachers of gifted students, it also is one of the most abused strategies. Parents often find themselves struggling with their children's September-assigned research projects that are due in the spring. In these cases, teachers provide only grades with limited instruction and support. With effective independent studies, teachers are actively involved, facilitating each phase of the study as a student's interest emerges and develops. Teachers, therefore, need to remember the following guidelines when initiating independent studies with their students.

1. *Don't confuse aptitude with skill.* Although gifted students have a great aptitude for performing at high levels and producing complex products,

they may not have the necessary skills for completing independent study projects. For example, they may not know how to identify good study questions or select a sample or use a systematic study method or gather information from a variety of sources. The teacher will need to teach many of these skills, particularly during the first independent study.

2. *Identify independent study skills.* To facilitate the independent study, the teacher must be aware of the skills that are involved in every step of the process. For example, if the student is going to be conducting historical research, the teacher needs to know the specific steps in this method or be able to identify a historian.

3. *Adapt as the student changes.* Although the teacher needs to have a thorough understanding of the steps in the process, the student's interest *must* guide the study. An interest cannot always be "turned on" according to schedule. Some flexibility must be built into the process so that students have choices of what, when, how, and how much they want to explore a topic.

4. *Use different types of research.* When conducting research, most students go to the Internet first before other sources of information. Although the Internet is a great resource to students, they also need to learn about first-hand or primary learning sources such as interviewing, experimenting, field studies, observing, surveying, discussing, and brainstorming with others. The type of research should match the question and method of study and be authentic to the discipline. For example, if the student is interested in roller coasters, then he might study them using the tools of a physicist.

5. *Make it a part of a regular program, not an addition.* Sometimes independent study is something that students do when they finish the rest of their regular work. When this occurs, the student may never have enough time to pursue something of interest, may lose continuity, or worse yet, may view research as extra work. The teacher may wish to use acceleration or curriculum compacting to buy class time for independent study (Renzulli & Reis, 2014).

6. *Monitor progress and products.* Establish a regular time to meet with students to facilitate various phases and stages as they become more involved with their areas of study. This one-on-one time is important to identify needed research skills and to maintain each student's interest.

7. *Develop an appropriate assessment.* The assessment should match the characteristics of each step in the process and the student's experience with independent study. If the student is pursuing a topic independently for the first time, the teacher should consider this novice-level and use formative and summative assessments accordingly. Assessments should improve

a student's study skills, encourage his or her interests, and increase a love for learning. If assessments, particularly evaluations, are too harsh initially, students will quickly lose motivation and follow teacher rules rigidly to receive the desired grade. A better way to encourage the student is to develop an assessment together at the beginning of the study; this will help not only with accountability but also with the quality of the process and the final product or performance.

8. *Believe in the student's ability and be a model.* Nothing is more stimulating to students than others' interest in their independent studies. Teachers should make a point of noticing improvements and new ideas. Teachers who are engaged in their own research provide a model and can discuss their challenges in a collegial fashion with their students.

9. *Remember that independent study is only one way of meeting the needs of gifted students.* Programs for gifted students often are synonymous with independent studies because it is the only strategy that is used; however, students quickly become bored with a repetition of projects leading to more and more products. Teachers will want to include many different instructional strategies in their programs and limit independent studies to student-driven interests.

Steps in Independent Study

This section will describe nine steps that might be used in independent study (Johnsen & Johnson, 2007a). All of the steps may or may not be used in every independent study because the teacher and the student may already have defined some steps. For example, the teacher may present the problem and the students are primarily responsible for gathering information and sharing their results. In addition, the steps are not necessarily sequential, but are more cyclical and based on the student's progress (Johnsen & Johnson, 2007a). For example, in the seventh step, students are supposed to develop a product, but if they haven't gathered enough information to address their questions thoroughly, they may need to return to Step 6, gathering information. Similarly, students may begin to gather information about their questions and decide that they want to change or add another question to their study. Based on the student's performance, the teacher may decide to skip steps, guide the student through some of the steps, and/or allow the students to do some of the steps independently. The teacher will, therefore, want to use the independent study process as a framework based on the students' background and experiences.

Step 1: Introducing the Independent Study

In introducing the independent study, the teacher defines the process and gives each student a plan to manage his or her work. At this stage, the teacher describes (a) various steps that will be used during the study; (b) the dates when different stages of the study are due; (c) the criteria that will be used in assessing the study; and, if known, (d) the audience who will be interested in the results of their study. As mentioned earlier, the steps may vary depending upon the nature of the study. If the teacher has already identified the questions, the students may be focusing primarily on collecting information, developing and sharing a product, and assessing the process.

At this initial step, the teacher will want to identify, with the student, the criteria for assessing each of the steps and the final product or performance. These criteria can be used to guide the process, helping the teacher know when to intervene and offer direct instruction. In addition, the teacher will help the student understand expectations and when to seek assistance.

The teacher will want to help students learn how to manage their time in meeting deadlines by establishing due dates for each step in the process and the final due date. Depending upon the student, these due dates can be organized by week or even by the day. Students need to understand that although researchers often dream of unlimited time to pursue topics of interest, reality generally dictates a timeline for completion.

Students will be more involved in the independent study if the topic is of genuine interest to them and if they know it will be used or heard by an authentic audience. For example, when a second-grade gifted class was introduced to the problem of limited recycling in their community, they immediately pinpointed the lack of curbside services as a contributing factor. With the help of their teacher, they identified the city council as an important audience because the members held the budgetary power to make changes in the current recycling program. Their entire study then focused not only on researching various aspects of recycling but also on how to sell their ideas to the council. Their enthusiasm and their professional DVD were rewarded with the desired change. Curbside recycling indeed improved the recycling program within their community.

Step 2: Selecting a Topic

At this step, the students select something to study. It may be a problem they want to solve, an issue they want to debate, an opinion they want to prove, something they want to learn how to do, or simply something they want to know more about. Interesting ideas may be pursued immediately or collected over a period of time. For example, a bulletin board of expressed classroom opinions might be developed with the purpose of proving or disproving them later. Newspaper headlines can become issues or problems for community action studies. Ideas and new questions that grow from classroom units can be researched immediately or stockpiled for future investigations.

When students have difficulty selecting a single area for study, they may want to consider some of these questions: Which topic is most interesting to me? Which topic do I know the least about? Which topic do I know the most about? Which topic will be easy to find information? Which topic is the most unusual? Which topic will be the most useful to me? Which topic will be the most interesting to the audience?

This step frequently involves gathering more information about the topic. Students may investigate by contacting museums, agencies, universities, and state or national departments. They may send letters home to parents, distribute bulletins that request topic information, interview experts in the field, call public radio and television stations, or, of course, browse the Internet or school library. The teacher may also help by inviting experts to discuss their fields of study with the class, taking the class on field trips, or setting up learning centers that provide an overview of a specific topic. During this process, students may discover that they can't locate information about their topic, that the information is too technical or too difficult to understand, that the information is really not very interesting to them after all, or that another topic is more interesting. Throughout, the teacher lets the students know that seemingly good ideas don't work and that new ideas may appear accidentally or in unusual places. This step is important. If students are energized by their topics, the teacher may assume the role of facilitator rather than dictator.

For example, Alice happened to be in a fourth-grade resource room with five other gifted children—all of who were boys. The boys were very interested in discovering methods for designing new video games. Alice could not care less about games; instead, she was really interested in penguins. Although her choice created some difficulty for the teacher, who had wanted a group-designed project, she eventually acquiesced to Alice's interest. The result was a beautifully designed zoo for Emperor Penguins.

Step 3: Organizing the Study

Sometimes the teacher assists students in organizing or "mapping" their topics to help them find specific questions or problems. For example, if the teacher asks the students to brainstorm problems related to space explorations and the result includes only questions about UFOs and aliens, then this step is needed.

Organizational structures may include (a) descriptions, (b) comparisons, (c) causes and effects, or (d) problems and solutions. In describing space exploration, for example, the teacher might want to begin by creating categories for brainstorming. These categories may include space exploration's contributions, its future, its features, its history, its changes, its stages, or people's beliefs, feelings, or criticisms about it. Each of these broader categories form the hub of a wheel of student ideas and, eventually, questions.

Any of the descriptors generated about space exploration can be compared to other topics, models, theories, or rules. For example, the teacher might encourage the students to compare technological and human space exploration; historical and current beliefs about space exploration's contributions to science; or the features of early spacecraft with current or future ones. Again, questions begin to emerge from these comparisons or may lead to other organizational structures such as causes and effects or problems and solutions.

For example, if people have changed their feelings about space exploration, the student may want to consider the causes and effects of such a shift in attitudes. What might happen to space exploration's financial support? To scientific advances? To educational benefits? To scientists involved in cosmology? These effects may generate future problems. If financial support is withdrawn from space exploration, then the understanding of our solar system and the creation of a broader knowledge base may be limited.

All of these ways of examining a topic should lead to the most important step in the process: asking questions.

Step 4: Asking Questions

After doing some preliminary research and organizing their topics, the students are ready to ask questions. Good questions lead to quality independent studies. Teachers need to teach students the criteria for selecting good questions.

One criterion relates to its complexity. Can it be answered by a simple "yes" or "no" or by facts from a reference book? If so, the question may not be one that requires much research. Good study questions often produce several possible answers and may be pursued differently by various researchers. Two other criteria relate to practicality. Does the student have the time or resources to study the question? Finally, is the question useful or beneficial to the student or others? These criteria should help the student evaluate his or her questions.

Students may use their organizational categories to generate questions related to these stems: who, what, when, where, why, how, how much, how many, how long, how far, and what might happen if? For example, if a student were studying seals, he or she might ask descriptive questions such as, "What does a seal look like?" "Where does a seal live?" "When do seals breed?", comparison questions such as, "How are seals and penguins alike or different?", cause and effect questions such as "How do treaties protect seals?", or problem questions such as, "Why is there a disagreement among countries over the hunting of seals?" The process of including categories with "W + H" stems should produce a great many questions. The teacher might wish to have the student select several questions for study or have the student examine the level of thinking required by each question.

In the latter case, some teachers choose to teach their students a framework for asking questions such as Bloom's taxonomy (Anderson et al., 2001; Bloom, 1956). In this way, the student can determine the complexity of the question. One approach is to teach them the differences among "little thinking," "more thinking," and "most thinking" questions (Johnsen & Johnson, 2007a, 2007b). "Little thinking" (i.e., knowledge and comprehension; remember and understand) questions are those that the student can answer by simply copying or redoing something that someone else has done. "More thinking" (i.e., application and analysis; apply and analyze) questions are those that can be answered if the student uses the information in new situations. "Most thinking" questions are those that can only be answered if the student evaluates and creates new information. Giving students these evaluation tools helps them create more complex questions that, in turn, influence the overall quality of the independent study.

For example, in Alice's study of Emperor Penguins, she asked several "little thinking" questions such as, "What are the characteristics of Emperor Penguins?" "Where do they live?" "How do they breed?" and "What do they eat?" One "more thinking" question was, "How does the zoo in our city provide a habitat similar to the natural habitat of Emperor Penguins?" and one "most thinking" question was, "What might be an ideal zoo for an Emperor Penguin?"

Step 5: Choosing a Study Method

Most of the time, students are aware of only a limited number of methods for gathering information to study a question in an area of interest: the library and, more recently, the Internet. In both cases, students often feel that their research is not quite complete without referring to the venerable encyclopedia—whether online or in the library. This one-type-of-method approach may not even address their study questions. How might Alice answer the question, "How does the zoo in our city provide a habitat similar to the natural habitat of Emperor Penguins?" by gathering information in the library or even on the Internet? Alice is going to need to visit the city zoo, talk to the zookeepers, and interview experts who know about Emperor Penguins. In Alice's and other students' studies, the questions should determine the study method.

There are many different kinds of study methods. Some of these methods include descriptive, historical, correlational, developmental, ethnographic, action, experimental, and quasi-experimental research (Isaac & Michael, 1997). For example, if students want to know how different schools in their town were named, they would be interested in an historical study method. First, they might contact primary sources such as principals of different schools and people who were either at the school building when it was dedicated or know the person or place for whom/which the school was named. Second, they might locate secondary sources, such as newspaper stories that were written about the persons or places for which the schools were named. Third, they would interview their primary sources and take notes from their secondary sources. Fourth, they would review their interviews and notes, focus on facts, and delete biased or exaggerated information. Finally, they would verify information with their primary sources before sharing it with others.

Teachers will want to become acquainted with the research methods that address different kinds of questions so that their students will use authentic approaches that are practiced frequently by experts in each field. In addition, teachers will want to engage experts as mentors when students pursue topics in greater depth. What better way to study paleontology than to visit a "dig" with a practicing archaeologist? Or to learn about theater with a director of drama? Or to visit a courtroom with a practicing attorney? Authenticity is supported through the use of scientific methods, experts in various disciplines, a genuine student interest, and multiple approaches to gathering information, which is addressed in the next section.

Step 6: Gathering Information

Both the study method and the information are related to the questions. If a student is interested in the relationship between the number of study hours at home and grades in school, then he or she will use a correlational method of research and gather information from students related to study hours and grades. If students are interested in how an engineer spends his or her time during a workday, they will use a more ethnographic method of research to observe engineers during their workdays.

There are many ways of gathering information. Some of these include note taking, writing letters, surveying, interviewing, observing, reading, listening to focus groups, brainstorming with others, locating information on the Internet, going on field trips, and conducting controlled experiments in a laboratory. In each case, the teacher needs to clearly specify and teach the steps involved with the approach. For example, when interviewing, the student needs to know how to (a) select a person to interview; (b) make the initial contact and set up an appointment; (c) locate background information and prepare questions for the interview; (d) make a good impression during the interview; (e) ask questions and record information; (f) summarize interview notes; and (g) provide information to the interviewed person. With the advent of e-mail, interviews with experts are much more accessible for students. With the Internet, the interested researcher may even take virtual tours of museums all over the world. Again, the teacher plays a valuable role by assisting the student in using search engines, locating reliable sources of information and/or experts, and critically evaluating the information.

Younger gifted children often gather information through hands-on activities, oral interviews, or surveys. For example, in learning about structures, children might build bridges with various materials, testing the strength of each design by placing toy cars or other objects on top. In deciding what businesses are needed in a classroom "city," they might conduct a "market analysis" through a survey of their classmates.

Remember that gathering information or paraphrasing written materials is a difficult task and should be taught to older students before they begin the process of independent study. In this way, interest in the topic and pacing of the project are not delayed by the frequently perceived "drudgery" of writing notes and outlining information. They also need to learn about plagiarism and how to insert quotes in their work or cite references. If students are already proficient with these tasks, then their studies can flow at a rate that maintains their enthusiasm.

In summary, information that is gathered should relate to the question, be authentic within the field of study, be clearly defined and taught to the students, and be appropriate for the age of the researcher.

Step 7: Developing a Product

Whereas most students believe that "independent study" is synonymous with "written report," information may be organized in a variety of ways. Products include books, diagrams, dioramas, videos, computer programs, games, graphs, posters, puppet shows, reports, tape recordings, timelines, debates, dramatizations, models, newspapers, poems, speeches, and many others.

If the product is an option, then students may select one or more that match their original questions. For example, Albert had several questions that related to his topic of interest, bees. They included "What are the parts of a bee?", "What are the different kinds of bees?", and "Which wildflowers in my neighborhood do bees prefer?" Albert might have answered all of these questions with a written report or a PowerPoint presentation, but he wanted to organize a display for the parent open house. To answer the questions related to parts and kinds of bees, he drew a diagram of each one—comparing and contrasting coloration, size, and shape. He mounted these on a poster along with some photos in their natural habitats and labeled each part. For his study question that examined wildflower preferences among bees, he displayed his field notes, presenting the results in a series of graphs. He then prepared a PowerPoint in which he orally described the entire process of his independent study.

Similar to the step of gathering information, the product should be authentic within the field of study. For example, what product(s) might a naturalist develop to share his or her work? Did Albert share his bee study in a similar way? Indeed, a naturalist would keep a scientific journal, attach pictures or photos as examples, summarize results in a graph, and present information orally or in written form.

The teacher will want to teach each step of product development. For example, in designing a timeline, the student might (a) determine which years will be included; (b) decide whether the timeline will be horizontal or vertical; (c) decide whether to use pictures, drawings, special lettering, or other graphic designs; (d) decide the length of the line and each time period; (e) draw the line manually or use the computer; (f) divide the line into specific time periods; (g) write the dates and information beside the timeline and attach any pictures or drawings; and (h) write a title.

Finally, the way that the information is organized should again match the age of the youngster. Hands-on, visual, and oral products are easier for younger children than written ones. For example, in presenting information gathered about an ancient culture, a class of young gifted students created a museum of artifacts with videos of "experts" describing each display. The teacher will find many resources to help in organizing information into products (see Teacher Resources at the end of this chapter).

Step 8: Sharing Information

Although information may be shared informally, students need to learn that there is life beyond the product. The teacher might discuss with the students some of these reasons for sharing information: students can learn from one another; students can improve their products; others can help evaluate the product; and students can gather support for the product.

There are a variety of ways of sharing information with an audience: oral reports, demonstrations, performances, displays, or a combination of these. The best approach should be determined by the audience. Each step needs to be outlined and taught. For example, in designing an oral report, the student will need to (a) plan the report; (b) practice the report; (c) arrange materials in order; (d) stand in a visible spot; (e) introduce him or herself; (f) look at the audience; (g) speak loudly enough to be heard; (h) hold the product or visuals where they can be seen; (i) state major points; (j) keep the talk short; (k) ask for questions; (l) have the audience complete the evaluation; and (m) thank the audience.

For an oral report, students should practice before their peers. During these practice sessions, each student should provide at least two positive comments to every negative comment that relate to specific criteria. In this way, students' self-esteem and performance will improve.

Sometimes the process of independent study stops with the completion of a product. Products are graded, taken home, and eventually discarded. For products to live, students need to share their ideas, garner support, and develop new ideas that might intensify or create fresh interests in their topics. For example, Albert, who studied bees, might contact entomologists via e-mail or at a local university to discuss the results of his field study. He might improve his techniques through these communications or by actually working with an expert in planning his next study.

Step 9: Assessing the Study

The assessments of independent studies are both formative and summative. With formative assessment, students examine their performance as the study proceeds. Criteria might include the following statements:

- » I wrote a probing study question.
- » I developed a product that related to my questions.
- » I used a study method that related to my questions.
- » I collected information from more than one source.
- » The product I developed related to my research.
- » My product showed that I understood important concepts.
- » I considered the audience when I made my presentation.
- » The product was attractive, professional, and interesting to the audience.
- » The product was original—something I had never done before.
- » The product was advanced beyond my grade level.
- » Throughout the study, I used my time efficiently and followed my plan. (Johnsen & Johnson, 2007b, p. 44)

Similar criteria may be developed for other assessors, such as the teacher, peers, or both. The audience members may also contribute their assessment comments. All of the assessments can be collected and reviewed at a final teacher-student conference.

In addition to these types of formative assessments, the student and teacher will want to use summative evaluation in judging the independent study products. Checklists or rubrics can be designed with specific criteria listed for each type of product. For example, evaluation characteristics for a pictograph might include the following questions:

- » Did the pictures relate to the collected data?
- » Did the picture reflect the kind of information being expressed? (For example, if the graph is about money, money signs ($) or pictures of coins might be used.)
- » Did each symbol represent the same amount?

» Did partial symbols represent fractions of the amount?
» Were the symbols the same size?
» Were the symbols aligned next to the labels?
» Did the graph have a title that represented the question?
» Was each line of pictographs labeled?
» Was there a key that indicated the amount that each pictograph represented?
» Was the overall graph neat and attractive?

There are many assessment tools that may be accessed in the literature. One example is the Student Product Assessment Form (Renzulli & Reis, 2014), which examines the statement of the purpose; problem focus; level, diversity, and appropriateness of resources; logic, sequence, and transition; action orientation; and audience. Another is the Texas Performance Standards Project (Texas Education Agency, n.d.), which includes six components for grades K–8: (a) content, knowledge, and skills, (b) analysis and synthesis, (c) multiple perspectives, (d) research, (e) communication, and (f) presentation of learning; and nine components of assessment for grades 9–12: (a) content, knowledge, and skills, (b) analysis and synthesis, (c) multiple perspectives, (d) communication, (e) innovation and application, (f) ethics/unanswered questions, (g) methodology and use of resources, (h) relevance and significance, and (i) professional quality.

Assessments in independent studies should focus on what the student has learned and what he or she might do to improve the next research project. If assessments are positive, the student will be encouraged to continue his or her study, looking for new questions or new areas.

Conclusion

This chapter has provided a very brief overview of the critical steps involved in independent study and research. The reader is encouraged to use the resources at the end of the chapter to learn more about this important instructional strategy with gifted students.

Teacher Statement

As a teacher in a heterogeneously grouped classroom of second graders, differentiating the curriculum to meet the needs of individual learners was one of my greatest challenges. For me, independent study was the most effective strategy to use in addressing the needs of gifted learners in the group. It provided an opportunity for students to study topics of interest in-depth while learning and practicing a variety of skills. It also set the stage for lifelong learning, confidence, and success.

I quickly discovered that the most efficient way to introduce the independent study process was to take the entire classroom through the process as a group. As we worked together through the process, all children in the classroom became excited about the contributions they would make to the project.

After navigating the project together, children were prepared to delve into independent research on their own. I often involved mentors from the community to meet with students and provide expertise in the area chosen for study, making the experience more meaningful for the young researcher and validating his or her area of interest.

After completion of the study and sharing the products with selected audiences, children were listed in the campus library resource guide as experts on the topics they had studied. Teachers would then invite them into classrooms to share their knowledge when the class was studying the topic on which they had become an expert.

One student, Todd, was particularly excited about engaging in an independent study. He was a second grader who was immensely talented in the area of art and immediately decided that he wanted to study a topic that would enhance his understanding of art in society. As he began to gather information on the wide array of topics that could be considered, he became interested in studying the art of origami. Due to the fact that I was no expert in the field of art, I immediately began looking for someone who could be a valuable resource for Todd. I called the art center associated with a community college in the area and found that the director of the center was interested in origami and had studied it extensively. He was thrilled to have the opportunity to share his passion with a young person and agreed to meet with Todd two times, once to introduce Todd to the topic and once during the study to answer any questions that had come up since the initial meeting.

Having gone through the entire independent study process with his class as a group, Todd was familiar with the process and could work on the study independently during the school day. He learned a great deal as he conducted his study and chose his class as the audience for his product presentation when the study was complete. The art center director was in attendance for the presentation, and Todd proudly presented his findings related to the art of origami.

Following the presentation, the mentor talked to Todd's mother and me about him sharing his expertise with other children. Several months later, Todd appeared on the local PBS station, presenting short segments about origami between "Sesame Street" and "Mr. Roger's Neighborhood."

Several years later, I walked into the high school Todd attended. It was close to the holidays, and as I entered the building, I immediately noticed a beautiful tree decorated from top to bottom with intricately crafted origami ornaments. At the bottom of the tree was a small sign that said, "The ornaments on this tree were made by Todd Smith." Todd is now studying architectural design.

—Krys Goree

DISCUSSION QUESTIONS

1. In comparing each of the models, how might the implementation of independent study be similar and different?

2. From the perspective of the classroom teacher, what are the positive and negative aspects of implementing independent study as an instructional strategy for gifted learners? How might the negative aspects you listed be addressed?

3. There are nine steps of the independent study process described in the chapter. Which step do you think would be most difficult to facilitate as a teacher? Why?

4. Given a typical classroom with gifted and general education students, how might the teacher include independent study in the curriculum?

5. How might you design a community project that would include independent study?

6. What teacher characteristics are important in facilitating independent studies?

7. How might involving mentors who are experts in the fields enhance the independent study experiences of the students? How might a teacher find mentors to work with students on independent study projects?

8. What might be your philosophy and rationale for including independent study in a comprehensive curriculum?

9. Interview several gifted high school students. How do they describe their independent study experiences from elementary through high school? How are their experiences the same or different?

Teacher Resources

Publications

Betts, G. T., & Kercher, J. K. (1999). *The autonomous learner model: Optimizing ability.* Greeley, CO: ALPS.

>This 336-page book is a guide to the Autonomous Learner Model. It describes each of the five dimensions of the model and includes essential activities.

Blair, C. (2003). *Let your fingers do the searching.* Dayton, OH: Pieces of Learning.

>This book for grades 7–12 guides students in using 40 reference sources to conduct research. Grading tally sheets and record-keeping assignments are included.

Blachowicz, C. L., & Ogle, D. (2008). *Reading comprehension: Strategies for independent learners.* New York, NY: Guilford Press.

>This practical resource and widely used text presents a wealth of research-based approaches to comprehension instruction. The authors offer specific classroom practices that help K–9 students compare and evaluate print and online sources, develop vocabulary, build study and test-taking skills, and become motivated readers.

Blandford, E. (2009). *How to write the best research paper ever.* Dayton, OH: Pieces of Learning.

>This student workbook for grades 6–12 provides a framework for organizing a well-written research paper. Topics include choosing a subject, works cited, locating and using resources, developing a thesis sentence, outlining, evaluating opposing evidence, and constructing effective conclusions.

Conklin, W. (2012). *Strategies for developing higher-order thinking skills.* Huntington Beach, CA: Shell Education.

>Developed for grades 3–5, this resource provides teachers with strategies to build student mastery of high-level thinking skills, promote active learning, and encourage students to analyze, evaluate, and create. Model lessons are provided to provide guidance for teachers in how to integrate strategies including questioning, decision making, creative thinking, problem solving, and idea generating.

Doherty, E. J. S., & Evans, L. C. (2003). *Primary independent study.* Tucson, AZ: Zephyr Press.

>This resource guides educators and parents in providing the mature beginning reader and emergent reader an opportunity for independent study or instructing any student beginning his or her first independent study. Teaching strategies that supplement the self-starter kit and lesson plans for note taking, idea production, and location of library resources are included.

Draze, D. (2005). *Blueprints: A guide for 16 independent study projects.* Waco, TX: Prufrock Press.

>This book for students in grades 4–8 provides directions for a written report, speech, model, debate, experiment, poster, book, survey, demonstration, learning

center, multimedia project, problem solution, game, special event, display, and science project.

Draze, D. (2005). *Project planner: A guide for creating curriculum and independent study projects.* Waco, TX: Prufrock Press.

This 48-page book includes suggestions for high-interest topics, hands-on methods of investigation, techniques for processing information, and product ideas that guide teachers and students through project design and independent study.

Heacox, D. (2014). *Differentiation for gifted learners: Going beyond the basics.* Minneapolis, MN: Free Spirit Publishing.

Topics discussed in this resource include real-world problem solving, abstract thinking, interdisciplinary concepts, authentic products, learning autonomy, accountability, grouping practices, affective curriculum, 21st-century skills, Advanced Placement and Honors classes, IB programs, underserved populations, and twice-exceptional learners.

Johnsen, S. K., & Johnson, K. (2007). *Independent study program* (2nd ed.). Waco, TX: Prufrock Press.

This program for students in grades K–12 includes a teacher's guide with lesson plans for teaching research skills, student workbooks that correlate to the guide and are used for organizing the student's study, and reusable resource cards that cover all of the steps of basic research.

Kaplan, S., & Cannon, M. (2001). *Curriculum starter cards: Developing differentiated lessons for gifted students.* Waco, TX: Prufrock Press.

This book includes guidelines for independent study, creative student products, and higher level thinking skills as tools for building units of instruction that emphasize depth and complexity of curricula for gifted students in grades K–12.

Kent, R. (2000). *Beyond Room 109: Developing independent study projects.* Portsmouth, NH: Heinemann.

This book, placing student choice at the center of the classroom, extends learning outside of the classroom. The author shares models and work samples allowing readers to discover ways to implement a yearlong program that culminates in an independent study as high school students explore their areas of interest.

Kramer, S. (1987). *How to think like a scientist.* New York, NY: HarperCollins.

This book teaches students in grades 2–5 the steps in the scientific method: asking a question, collecting data/information, forming a hypothesis, testing the hypothesis, and reporting the results.

Laase, L., & Clemmons, J. (1998). *Helping students write the best research reports ever.* New York, NY: Scholastic.

This book contains mini-lessons that help students select meaningful topics, navigate references, take effective notes, paraphrase, organize materials, and write research reports that verify learning. Creative product ideas are included.

Leimbach, J. (2005). *Primarily research*. Waco, TX: Prufrock Press.

This 64-page book includes eight units for primary-age children. Each unit presents a different animal or pair of animals and includes interesting facts and activities for structuring research.

Leimbach, J., & Riggs, P. (1992). *Primarily reference skills*. Waco, TX: Prufrock Press.

This 65-page book helps students in grades 2–4 learn how to use the library. Reproducible worksheets teach the parts of a book, alphabetical order, dictionaries, encyclopedias, and how to find books.

Lester, J. D., Sr., & Lester, J. D., Jr. (2005). *The research paper handbook* (3rd ed.). Tucson, AZ: Good Year Books.

This book for students in grades 7–12 targets the writing process, from selecting a topic, to writing a polished paper. Examples and models that illustrate how to examine various subjects and sources, as well as tips on using computer searches and databases, are included.

Long, L. (2004). *Great graphs and sensational statistics*. Hoboken, NJ: John Wiley & Sons.

This book assists readers in learning about pictographs, bar graphs, pie charts, line graphs, map charts, and basic statistics in order to communicate information efficiently and effectively.

McGee, B. H., & Keiser, D. T. (2013). *Differentiated projects for gifted students: 150 ready-to-use independent studies*. Waco, TX: Prufrock Press.

This resource offers research-oriented activities for children in grades 3–5. The projects are fully integrated and allow students to use 21st-century skills to explore content more deeply through specific, intensive online research.

Merritt, D. (2007). *Independent study. Expanded edition with CD*. Dayton, OH: Pieces of Learning.

This book for grades 4–12 provides students with tools for planning studies, researching topics, presenting information, and assessing learning experiences. An overview to guide teachers in using the tools to design independent study experiences for students is included.

Mueller, M. (2000). *Great research projects step by step*. Portland, ME: Walch.

This book, which is recommended for grades 7–12, presents research as a thorough process that involves steps including topic selection, finding what students need to know, navigating systems that will help provide needed information, and conducting meaningful research.

Nottage, C., & Morse, V. (2000). *Independent investigation method: Teacher manual*. Grand Haven, MI: Active Learning Systems.

This manual for teachers working with children in grades K–8 provides instructions for two skill levels, reproducible work pages and assessment tools, sample research studies, and teacher resource pages. A poster set (sold separately) reinforces the vocabulary and flow of the process.

Patterson, K. (2009). *Text me a strategy: How to encourage students to develop skills they need to become independent learners.* Portland, ME: Pembroke.

Building on student interest in text messaging, this book offers practical tools that promote student learning and personal growth in the fast-paced information age. Included in the text are 100 strategies that are easily taught, reviewed, and reinforced by the teacher. The name of each strategy reflects its function, which makes the strategy easy to recall and easy to apply.

Polette, N. (2001). *The research book for gifted programs, K–8.* Dayton, OH: Pieces of Learning.

This 176-page book provides more than 150 projects for primary, middle, and upper grades. Critical thinking skills are stressed.

Polette, N. (2009). *Research without copying.* Dayton, OH: Pieces of Learning.

This book describes practical approaches for reporting on topics in diverse ways. Different types of research are illustrated along with models.

Polette, N. (1998). *Research reports to knock your teacher's socks off!* Dayton, OH: Pieces of Learning.

This book for grades 3–8 gives specific models and examples to show students different ways to organize information about animals, people, places, and events.

Renzulli, J. S., & Reis, S. M. (2014). *The schoolwide enrichment model: A how- to guide for educational excellence* (3rd ed.). Waco, TX: Prufrock Press.

This resource book includes a collection of useful instruments, checklists, charts, taxonomies, assessment tools, forms, and planning guides to organize, implement, maintain, and evaluate different aspects of the Schoolwide Enrichment Model in grades K–12.

Starko, A. J., & Schack, G. D. (1992). *Looking for data in all the right places.* Waco, TX: Prufrock Press.

This guidebook introduces different types of research and guides students in developing their own research questions, gathering and analyzing data, and presenting their results. Each chapter includes explanations, examples, and practice activities for various steps in the research process.

Wee, P. H. (2000). *Independent projects: Step by step.* Lanham, MD: Scarecrow Press.

This resource guides high school educators and their students in independent project development. It presents step-by-step methods for planning, development, and presentation of research.

Winebrenner, S., Brulles, D., & Winebrenner, S. (2012). *Teaching gifted kids in today's classroom: Strategies and techniques every teacher can use.* Minneapolis, MN: Free Spirit Publishing.

This book provides information on using technology for accelerated learning, managing cluster grouping, increasing curriculum rigor, improving assessments, boosting critical and creative thinking skills, and addressing gifted kids with special needs.

Websites

These websites will provide teachers and students with information about independent study topics.

Annenberg Learner—http://www.learner.org
> Sponsored by the Annenberg Foundation, this website offers numerous resources to support both educators and students in independent study in a variety of content areas including the arts, foreign language, literature and language arts, mathematics, science, and social studies.

Best Environmental Directories—http://www.ulb.ac.be/ceese/meta/cds.html
> This site highlights 650 topics and publications that focus on environmental and energy issues in society.

Curriki—http://www.curriki.org/
> Membership to this website is free and full of resources to assist in independent study. Members are granted access to numerous information sources and have the ability to add, create, and organize resources and store them for future use. In addition, members can share ideas and collaborate with one another.

iLoveLanguages: Your Guide to Languages on the Web—http://www.ilovelanguages.com
> This page is a catalog of language-related Internet resources. You may find online language lessons, translating dictionaries, native literature, translation services, software, language schools, or language information.

Independent Study—http://www.cde.ca.gov/sp/eo/is/
> This site, provided by the California Department of Education, provides information and multiple references concerning independent study in the classroom. It offers a quick guide to independent study, frequently asked questions, an operations manual, legal forms, an evaluation guide, and examples.

International Council of Museums—http://www.icom.museum/
> This site provides a comprehensive directory of online museums and museum-related resources. Museums are organized by country.

Ivy's Search Engine Resources for Kids—http://www.ivyjoy.com/rayne/kidssearch.html
> This page offers links to more than 10 search engines and more than 80 websites that are appropriate for children and young adults. Research sources are presented according to search engines, Web guides, and specialized searches for kids.

KidsOLR: Kids' Online Resources—http://www.kidsolr.com
> Numerous resources are provided on this page, including links to information sources that focus on discipline areas such as art, music, geography, history, language arts, math, science, and health and topics such as games/toys, kids of the world, and zoos/animals.

The Math Forum @ Drexel—http://mathforum.org/library

This forum contains math resources organized by topics, resource types, mathematics education topics, and education level. For example, when you select history and biography under math topics, you will find more than 600 items including the biographies of women mathematicians, Euclid's elements, famous problems in the history of mathematics, the Galileo project, and Mayan math.

Martindale's The Reference Desk—http://www.martindalecenter.com

Martindale has a variety of guides including astronomy, cars, chemistry, construction, engineering, fashion, food, health, international travel, language, music, and photography. For example, when selecting the photography center, you will find photography tools, photography courses, and teaching modules on topics such as depth of field, film development, broadcast cameras, microscopy cameras, photomicrography, and sunrise/sunset.

NASA—http://www.nasa.gov/audience/foreducators/index.html

NASA has provided an in depth resource for both students and teachers. This website, sponsored by NASA, provides an in-depth resource for both students and teachers that includes current news, missions, and connections to multiple resources. Content is arranged by grade level spans and includes videos, interactive programs, archived news clips, and much more.

National Geographic Kids—http://kids.nationalgeographic.com/kids/

This website, created by National Geographic, offers resources for children that provide access to information on numerous topics including animals, plant life, and countries around the world. Video clips, a photograph gallery, and current event summaries are just a few of the features presented.

PBS Teachers—http://www.pbs.org/teachers

The PBS Teachers website offers a variety of valuable resources and links to support educators in guiding students at every grade level in independent study and research.

Smithsonian Museums—http://www.si.edu/museums

The Smithsonian provides a link to all of its museums on this page. Some of the museums offer opportunities for exploring topics and specific exhibitions. For example, the National Museum of Natural History allows users to explore human origins, development of world cultures, ancient and modern mammals, birds, amphibians, reptiles, insects, and sea creatures.

Teacher Tap Internet Resources for Health, Fitness, and Physical Education—http://eduscapes.com/tap/taphealth.html

This site provides resources to help adults and children learn more about health and fitness. Specific links are provided for teachers, young adults, and children.

Teachnology History Sites to Use With Students—http://www.teach-nology.com/teachers/educational_technology/internet_in_class/students/history/

The major purpose of this site is to encourage the use of the Internet as a tool for learning and teaching and to help teachers locate and use resources. A wide selection of topics is included under the general headings such as archaeology, explorers, historic battles/wars, and lesson plans.

Thinkfinity—http://www.thinkfinity.org

The Verizon Foundation partners with various educational organizations to provide teachers with the latest tools in education on this website. A variety of resources and links to support independent study and research in numerous content areas are offered.

Yahoo!—http://www.yahoo.com

You may search for specific topics using this page or use the listed resources to help you find information. Listed resources relate to arts and humanities, business and economy, computers and Internet, education, entertainment, government, health, news and media, recreation and sports, reference, science, social science, and culture.

References

Anderson, L. W. (Ed.), Krathwohl, D. R. (Ed.), Airasian, P. W., Cruickshank, K. A., Mayer, R. E., Pintrich, P. R., et al. (2001). *A taxonomy for learning, teaching, and assessing: A revision of Bloom's taxonomy of educational objectives.* New York, NY: Longman.

Betts, G. T. (1985). *The autonomous learner model for gifted and talented.* Greeley, CO: ALPS Publications.

Betts, G. T., & Kercher, J. K. (1999). *The autonomous learner model: Optimizing ability.* Greeley, CO: ALPS Publications.

Bishop, K. (2000). The research processes of gifted students: A case study. *Gifted Child Quarterly, 44,* 54–64.

Bloom, B. S. (Ed.). (1956). *Taxonomy of educational objectives: The classification of educational goals. Handbook I: Cognitive domain.* New York, NY: Longmans Green.

Caraisco, J. (2007). Overcoming lethargy in gifted and talented education with contract activity packages "I'm choosing to learn!" *The Clearing House, 80,* 255–260.

Chan, D. W. (2001). Learning styles of gifted and nongifted secondary students in Hong Kong. *Gifted Child Quarterly, 45*(1), 35–44.

Clark, B. (2012). *Growing up gifted: Developing the potential of children at home and at school* (8th ed.). Upper Saddle River, NJ: Prentice Hall.

Colangelo, N., & Davis, G. A. (Eds.). (2002). *Handbook of gifted education* (3rd ed.). Upper Saddle River, NJ: Pearson.

Coleman, L. J., & Cross, T. L. (2005). *Being gifted in school: An introduction to development, guidance, and teaching* (2nd ed.). Waco, TX: Prufrock Press.

Collins, M., & Amabile, T. (1999). Motivation and creativity. In R. J. Sternberg (Ed.), *Handbook of creativity* (pp. 297–312). New York, NY: Cambridge University Press.

Collins, A., Joseph, D., & Bielaczyc, K. (2004). Design research: Theoretical and methodological issues. *Journal of the Learning Sciences, 13*(1), 15–42.

Csikszentmihalyi, M., Rathunde, K., & Whalen, S. (1993). *Talented teenagers: The roots of success and failure.* New York, NY: Cambridge University Press.

Dallas Independent School District. (1977). *Up periscope! Research activities for the academically talented student.* Dallas, TX: Author.

Davis, G. A., Rimm, S. B., & Siegle, D. (2010). *Education of the gifted and talented* (6th ed.). Upper Saddle River, NJ: Pearson.

Delcourt, M. A. B. (1993). Creative productivity among secondary school students: Combining energy, interest, and imagination. *Gifted Child Quarterly, 37,* 23–31.

Doherty, E. J., & Evans, L. C. (1980). *Self-starter kit for independent study.* Austin, TX: Special Education Associates.

Douglas, D. (2004). Self-advocacy: Encouraging students to become partners in differentiation. *Roeper Review, 26,* 223–228.

Dunn, R., & Griggs, S. (1985). Teaching and counseling gifted students with their learning style preferences: Two case studies. *G/C/T, 14,* 40–43.

Feldhusen, J. F. (1983). The Purdue creative thinking program. In I. S. Sato (Ed.), *Creativity research and educational planning* (pp. 41–46). Los Angeles, CA: Leadership Training Institute for the Gifted and Talented.

Feldhusen, J. F. (1995). Talent development: The new direction in gifted education. *Roeper Review, 18,* 92.

Feldhusen, J. F., & Kolloff, P. B. (1986). The Purdue three-stage enrichment model for gifted education at the elementary level. In J. S. Renzulli (Ed.), *Systems and models for developing programs for the gifted and talented* (pp. 126–152). Mansfield Center, CT: Creative Learning Press.

French, L. R., Walker, C. L., & Shore, B. M. (2011). Do gifted students really prefer to work alone? *Roeper Review, 33,* 145–159. doi: 10.1080/02783193.2011.580497

Fulk, B., & Montgomery-Grymes, D. (1994). Strategies to improve student motivation. *Intervention in School and Clinic, 30,* 28–33.

Garcia-Cepero, M. (2008). The enrichment triad model: Nurturing creative-productivity among college students. *Innovations in Education and Teaching International, 45,* 295–302.

Gourley, T. J., & Micklus, C. S. (1982). *Problems! Problems! Problems!* Glassboro, NJ: Creative Competitions.

Hanks, K., Belliston, L., & Edwards, D. (1977). *Design yourself.* Los Altos, CA: Kaufmann.

Harnadek, A. (1976). *Basic thinking skills: Critical thinking.* Pacific Grove, CA: Midwest.

Hébert, T. P. (1993). Reflections at graduation: The long-term impact of elementary school experiences in creative productivity. *Roeper Review, 16,* 22–28.

Hertzog, N. B. (2003). Impact of gifted programs from the students' perspective. *Gifted Child Quarterly, 47,* 131–143.

Isaac, S., & Michael, W. (1997). *Handbook in research and evaluation: A collection of principles, methods, and strategies useful in the planning, design, and evaluation of studies in education and the behavioral sciences* (3rd ed.). San Diego, CA: Edits.

Jin, S., & Moon, S. M. (2006). A study of well-being and school satisfaction among academically talented students attending a science high school in Korea. *Gifted Child Quarterly, 50,* 169–184.

Johnsen, S. K., & Johnson, K. (2007a). *Independent study program.* Waco, TX: Prufrock Press.

Johnsen, S. K., & Johnson, K. (2007b). *Independent study program student booklet.* Waco, TX: Prufrock Press.

Kanevsky, L. (2011). Differential differentiation: What types of differentiation do students want? *Gifted Child Quarterly, 55,* 279–299.

Kaplan, S., Madsen, S., & Gould, B. (1976). *The big book of independent study.* Santa Monica, CA: Goodyear.

Kitano, M., & Kirby, D. F. (1986). *Gifted education: A comprehensive view.* Boston, MA: Little Brown.

Mathisen, G. E., & Bronnick, K. S. (2009). Creative self-efficacy: An intervention study. *International Journal of Educational Research, 48*(1), 21–29.

Newman, J. L. (2005). Talents and type IIIs: The effects of the talents unlimited model on creative productivity in gifted youngsters. *Roeper Review, 27,* 84–90.

Olenchak, F. R., & Renzulli, J. S. (1989). The effectiveness of the schoolwide enrichment model on selected aspects of elementary school change. *Gifted Child Quarterly, 33,* 36–46.

Piirto, J. (2007). *Talented children and adults: Their development and education* (3rd ed.). Waco, TX: Prufrock Press.

Renzulli, J. S. (1977a). *The enrichment triad model: A guide for developing defensible programs for the gifted and talented.* Mansfield Center, CT: Creative Learning Press.

Renzulli, J. S. (1977b). *The Interest-a-Lyzer.* Mansfield Center, CT: Creative Learning Press.

Renzulli, J. S. (1979). The enrichment triad model: A guide for developing defensible programs for the gifted and talented. In J. C. Gowan, J. Khatena, & E. P. Torrance (Eds.), *Educating the ablest: A book of readings on the education of gifted children* (2nd ed., pp. 111–127). Itasca, IL: Peacock.

Renzulli, J. S. (1997). *The Interest-A-Lyzer family of instruments.* Waco, TX: Prufrock Press.

Renzulli, J. S., & Callahan, C. (1973). *New directions in creativity: Mark 3.* Mansfield Center, CT: Creative Learning Press.

Renzulli, J. S., Callahan, C., Smith, L. H., Renzulli, M. J., & Ford, B. G. (2000). *New directions in creativity package.* Mansfield Center, CT: Creative Learning Press.

Renzulli, J. S., & Gable, R. K. (1976). A factorial study of the attitudes of gifted students toward independent study. *The Gifted Child Quarterly, 20,* 91–99.

Renzulli, J. S., & Reis, S. M. (1991). The schoolwide enrichment model: A comprehensive plan for the development of creative productivity. In N. Colangelo & G. A. Davis (Eds.), *Handbook of gifted education* (pp. 111–141). Needham Heights, MA: Allyn & Bacon.

Renzulli, J. S., & Reis, S. M. (2014). *The schoolwide enrichment model: A how-to guide for talent development* (3rd ed.). Waco, TX: Prufrock Press.

Renzulli, J. S., & Renzulli, S. R. (2010). The schoolwide enrichment model: A focus on student strengths & interests. *Gifted Education International, 26,* 140–156. doi:10.1177/026142941002600303

Rogers, K. B. (2007). Lessons learned about educating the gifted and talented: A synthesis of the research of educational practice. *Gifted Child Quarterly, 51,* 382–396.

Runco, M., & Chand, I. (1995). Cognition and creativity. *Educational Psychology Review, 7,* 243–267.

Ryan, R. M., & Deci, E. L. (2000). Self-determination theory and the facilitation of intrinsic motivation, social development, and well-being. *American Psychologist, 55*(1), 68–78.

Sayler, M. F. (2009). Gifted and thriving: A deeper understanding of the meaning of GT. In L. Shavinina (Ed.), *International handbook on giftedness* (pp. 215–230). Amsterdam, The Netherlands: Springer.

Selby, E. C., Shaw, E. J., & Houtz, J. C. (2005). The creative personality. *Gifted Child Quarterly, 49,* 300–314.

Stanish, B. (1977). *Sunflowering.* Carthage, IL: Good Apple.

Stanish, B. (1981). *Hippogriff feathers.* Carthage, IL: Good Apple.

Stanish, B., & Eberle, B. (1996). *CPS for kids.* Waco, TX: Prufrock Press.

Starko, A. J. (1988). Effects of the revolving door identification model on creative productivity and self-efficacy. *Gifted Child Quarterly, 32,* 291–297.

Stewart, E. D. (1981). Learning styles among gifted/talented students: Instructional techniques preferences. *Exceptional Children, 48,* 134–138.

Texas Education Agency. (n.d.). *Texas Performance Standards Project.* Retrieved from http://www.texaspsp.org

Thomson, D. L. (2010). Beyond the classroom walls: Teachers' and students' perspectives on how online learning can meet the needs of gifted students. *Journal of Advanced Academics, 21,* 662–712. doi: 10.1177/1932202X1002100405

Torrance, E. P. (1995). Insights about creativity: Questioned, rejected, ridiculed, ignored. *Educational Psychology Review, 7,* 313–322.

Treffinger, D. (1975). Teaching for self-directed learning: A priority for the gifted and talented, *Gifted Child Quarterly, 19,* 46–49.

Treffinger, D. (1978). Guidelines for encouraging independence and self-direction among gifted students. *Journal of Creative Behavior, 12*(1), 14–20.

Treffinger, D. (1986). Fostering effective, independent learning through individualized programming. In J. S. Renzulli (Ed.), *Systems and models for developing programs for the gifted and talented* (pp. 429–460). Mansfield Center, CT: Creative Learning Press.

Treffinger, D. (2003). *Independent, self-directed learning: 2003 update.* Sarasota, FL: Center for Creative Learning.

Troxclair, D. A. (2000). Differentiating instruction for gifted students in regular education social studies classes. *Roeper Review, 22,* 195–198.

Trumbull, D., Scarano, G., & Bonney, R. (2006). Relations among two teachers' practices and beliefs, conceptualizations of the nature of science, and their implementation of student independent inquiry projects. *International Journal of Science Education, 28,* 1717–1750.

Vallerand, R., Gagné, F., Senecal, G., & Pelletier, L. (1994). A comparison of the school intrinsic motivation and perceived competence of gifted and regular students. *Gifted Child Quarterly, 36,* 68–72.

Zimmerman, B. J., & Martinez-Pons, M. (1990). Student differences in self-regulated learning: Relating grade, sex, and giftedness to self-efficacy and strategy use. *Journal of Educational Psychology, 82*(1), 51–59.

AFFECTIVE EDUCATION

Addressing the Social and Emotional Needs of Gifted Students in the Classroom

BY STEPHANIE K. FERGUSON

The affective characteristics of gifted individuals as well as the social-emotional needs related to those characteristics have been well documented by researchers in the field of gifted education (Clark, 2012; Cohen & Frydenberg, 2006; Cross, 2010; Roeper, 1995; Schultz & Delisle, 2013; Silverman, 1993). However, despite the evidence and support provided by the literature, proactive attention to the affective domain is still overlooked in many schools unless that attention is in reaction to some overt problem identified by teachers or the administration (Peterson, 2003).

What Is Affective Education?

"To be nobody-but-myself—in a world that is doing its best, night and day, to make you everybody else—means to fight the hardest battle which any human being can fight, and never stop fighting."—e. e. cummings

Affective education is the domain of the educational process that encompasses the attitudes, beliefs, feelings, and emotions of students as well as the effectiveness of their interpersonal relationships (Katz et al., 2002).

Theories Supporting the Affective Domain and Its Development

Theories advancing the social and emotional aspects of human development and their connection to cognitive processing are numerous. The idea of the affective domain as an important aspect of education originated in the humanistic-oriented psychology and psychotherapy of the 1950s (Katz et al., 2002). Many of these have direct influence on educational practices even though they may or may not have been developed with gifted individuals in mind.

Not all students arrive at the school's door ready to focus on the day's tasks. Maslow (1971) developed a hierarchy of human needs that maintains that in order for emotional development to be facilitated, the primary needs of food, shelter, safety, and sense of love and/or belonging must be met in order for the more complex needs of self-concept, self-actualization, and transcendence to be addressed. If a need at any level goes unmet, then all energies that would have been spent moving up in the hierarchy are refocused to fill the void. Thus, students who come to school hungry or homeless as well as those who are experiencing familial discord or dysfunction will have difficultly self-actualizing, let alone developing a positive self-concept. Gifted students who wonder where they fit in to the schema of school and the social cliques and hierarchies may have trouble forming a positive self-concept and reaching self-actualization.

Dabrowski's (1964) theory of positive disintegration and his theory of overexcitabilities (Dabrowski & Piechowski, 1977) both address affective development. Dabrowski's theory of positive disintegration (TPD) highlights the role emotions and struggles play in human development (Silverman, 1993). The theory suggests that tension created by inner conflict moves an individual toward higher levels of emotional development (see Figure 15.1). The levels of development progress from rigid, stereotypical structures and actions at the lowest level, through the emergence of an understanding of the difference between "what is" and "what ought to be," to the highest level manifested in altruism, compassion, and integrity (Mika, 2009). TPD is a comprehensive theory of personality development that has implications for the education of gifted students; however, Dabrowski did not suggest any strategies applicable for the classroom (Mendaglio, 2002).

The relationship between emotion and cognition are emphasized in Dabrowski's explanation of overexcitabilities (OEs; Silverman, 1993). An OE is a higher than average capacity [sensitivity] for experiencing stimuli, both internal and external, involving both psychological factors and nervous system sensitivity (Mika, 2009; Webb, 2013). Table 15.1 provides descriptions, possible manifestations, and suggested strategies for each OE.

Level V: Secondary Integration
organization, harmonization, and actualization of the personality and the personality ideal; the integration of personal values and ideals into one's everyday life; characterized by personal responsibility, compassion, authenticity, autonomy, and empathy

Self-aware

Altruistic

Level IV: Organized Multilevel Disintegration
conscious shaping and categorization of personal behavior; deliberate self-transformation and movement toward self-actualization; clarity of values and goals

Metacognitive Transformation

Level III: Spontaneous Multilevel Disintegration
emerging hierarchy of values and goals; awareness of inner conflict between "what is" and "what ought to be"; aspirations to grow toward the ideal

Positive Maladjustment

Level II: Unilevel Disintegration
influence stems from external societal mainstream values and peer group; ambivalence due to ambiguous internal values

Moral Relativity

Level I: Primary Integration
no inner conflicts; lack of empathy or self-reflection; impulsive actions characterized by lack of responsibility for one's actions

Egocentric

Nonreflective

Figure 15.1. Dabrowski's theory of positive disintegration.

Dabrowski identified five OEs (Mika, 2009; Silverman, 1993; Tolan, 1999):

» *psychomotor*: characterized by needing movement and/or having difficulty quieting one's mind in order to rest, may manifest in fast talking, gesturing, or nervous tics;

» *sensual*: characterized by powerful reactions to sensory stimuli (e.g., tastes, smells, sights, sounds, textures), may manifest in profound aesthetic awareness (e.g., crying in reaction to a television commercial);

» *imaginational*: characterized by visual and/or metaphorical thinking, may manifest through daydreaming or vivid memories of nightly dreams;

» *intellectual*: most identified with classic definitions of giftedness, characterized by logical prowess and reasoning skills, may manifest in aptitude for puzzles and logic games; and

» *emotional*: characterized by an intensity of emotion, a wider range of emotions, empathy, compassion, and a need for deep connections with others, may manifest in the creation and prolonged maintenance of imaginary friends.

The number and levels of OEs a person exhibits affects how he or she experiences the world around him or her (Mendaglio, 2002; Webb, 2013). Both TPD

TABLE 15.1
Dabrowski's Overexcitabilities, Manifestations, and Strategies

OE	Description	Possible Manifestations	Suggested Strategies
Psychomotor	A heightened tendency toward being active and energetic, either mentally, physically, or both	Less need for sleep Action oriented; restless Gesturing Rapid talk Preference for violent or fast games and/or sports Delinquent behavior Nervous tics Self-injurious behavior	Promote constructive release of excess energy (e.g., organized sports, trips, community activity) Employ relaxation and sensory integration techniques
Sensual	An increased capacity to experience sensory (i.e., sight, sound, taste, smell, touch) pleasure or displeasure	Strong aesthetic interests Need for physical contact; attention; companionship Dislike of loneliness Keen interest and curiosity in food Early signs of sexual interest and development	Promote empathy Teach techniques for desensitization to overwhelming stimuli Encourage self-control and reflection
Imaginational	A strong ability to produce creative thought and visualization	Associations of images and impressions Visual thinking Adept use of imagery and metaphor in expression Visualization skills Vivid daydreams, dreams, and nightmares Developed sense of humor Mixing of truth and fiction Highly developed internal fantasy world (e.g., imaginary friends) Maladjustment to external reality	Encourage adaptive creativity strategies rather than maladaptive isolation Teach the difference between reality and fantasy Provide time for creative production and relaxation
Intellectual	A capacity for sustained intellectual effort	Inquiry skills Theoretical thinking Search for truth; moral concern Extensive reading	Balance by encouraging the development of emotional and physical domains
Emotional	A heightened capacity for emotional depth and sensitivity	Need for connections with people, places, or things Empathy; compassion Heightened sense of responsibility Self-examination Need for security Exclusive relationships	Develop talents and encourage creativity Encourage healthy friendships Provide contact with nature Employ bibliotherapy Teach relaxation techniques

Note. Adapted from *Theory of Positive Disintegration*, by E. Mika, (2009), retrieved March 31, 2003, from http://www.nswagtc.org.au/ozgifted/conferences/TPD.html and *Dabrowski's Over-Excitabilities: A Layman's Explanation*, by S. Tolan (1999), retrieved October 22, 2003, from http://www.stephanietolan.com/dabrowskis.htm

and OEs provide a context with which to interpret common characteristics associated with giftedness such as asynchronous development, intensities of interest, emotion, creativity, movement, perfectionism, interpersonal dynamics, and some maladaptive behaviors.

Krathwohl, Bloom, and Masia (1964) developed the Affective Taxonomy to provide criteria with which to classify educational objectives according to the depth, complexity, and thinking skills required. As addressed in the taxonomy, the affective domain involves the manner in which individuals deal with emotions, demonstrating feelings, personal values, appreciation, enthusiasm, motivations, attitudes, and sensitivities to other people, things, or ideas (See Figure 15.2). The Affective Taxonomy is comprised of five categories (Maker & Schiever, 2005):

- » *receiving*: awareness and passive or selective attention;
- » *responding*: complying with given expectations, willingness to respond, and satisfaction in responding;
- » *valuing*: assessing worth of a person, thing, situation, or idea, ranging from acceptance to preference and, finally, commitment to a value or belief system;
- » *organizing*: categorizing and prioritizing values and resolving conflicts among competing values by comparing, relating, and synthesizing them; and
- » *characterizing*: internalizing the established value system and behaving in a manner that is consistent with that system.

Because emotions are not directly measurable, the criteria related to each category focus upon the demonstrated presence or absence of an emotion or attitude as it guides or controls one's behavior.

The aforementioned theories provide a foundation upon which definitions of affective education have been built; however, just as there is no standard definition of giftedness upon which all interested parties can agree, there are multiple facets associated with affective education, but no single definition.

Operationalizing the Definition of Affective Education

Although the cognitive domain encompasses the intellectual processes, the affective domain addresses emotional aspects. Researchers interpret the components of the affective domain differently. Some elements associated with affective education include:

- » individualized value systems (Krathwohl, Bloom, & Masia, 1964);
- » attitudes, beliefs, and values (Sellin & Birch, 1981);
- » interests and appreciations (Carin & Sund, 1978);
- » persistence, independence, and self-concept (Levey & Dolan, 1988);

FERGUSON

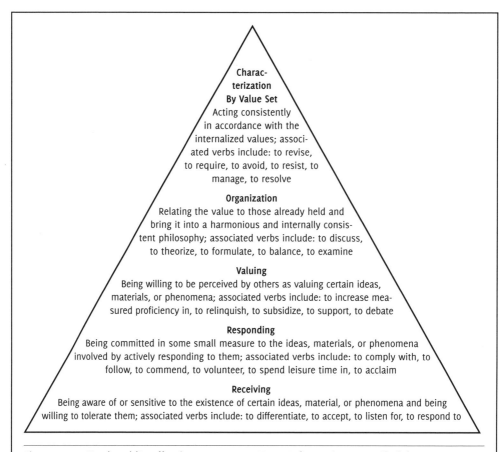

Figure 15.2. Krathwohl's affective taxonomy. *Note.* Information compiled from *Taxonomy of Educational Objectives: The Classification of Educational Goals. Handbook II: Affective Domain* (pp. 176–185), by D. Krathwohl, B. Bloom, and B. Masia, 1964, New York, NY: David McKay. Copyright © 1964 by David McKay.

- » feelings, emotions, and awareness of self and others (Treffinger, Borgers, Render, & Hoffman, 1976);
- » interpersonal relations (Treffinger et al., 1976);
- » humanitarianism (Weinstein & Fantini, 1970);
- » curiosity, risk-taking, complexity, and imagination (Williams, 1970); and
- » character and leadership (Delisle, 2002).

With so many factors linked to affective education, it is a wonder that schools continue to neglect the affective domain. Prior to crises or overt threats, schools have traditionally paid little attention to the social and emotional needs of the student body in general and gifted students in particular (Peterson, 2003).

Reasons Schools Neglect the Affective Domain

Researchers cite numerous causes behind schools choosing not to include the affective domain within their gifted curricula:

- » the lack of acknowledgement that the gifted have specific affective needs (Cross, 2010; Delisle, 1992; VanTassel-Baska, 1989a);
- » the traditional lack of concern in education for the affective domain (Tannenbaum, 1983; VanTassel-Baska, Cross, & Olenchak, 2009);
- » attitudes on the part of adults that emotions are to be dealt with at home rather than in the school (Elgersma, 1981);
- » fear of indoctrination (Bloom, Hastings, & Madaus, 1971);
- » the position that if the school meets the child's cognitive needs, affective development will automatically follow (Cross, 2010; Elksnin & Elksnin, 2006; Mehrens & Lehman, 1987);
- » lack of reliable and valid tools for assessing affective functioning (Elksnin & Elksnin, 2006; Levey & Dolan, 1988);
- » lack of clarity as to the optimal level of affective functioning to be attained (Elksnin & Elksnin, 2006; Levey & Dolan, 1988); and
- » the belief that healthy emotional development among the gifted is automatic (Blackburn & Erikson, 1986; Cross, 2010).

Teachers are continually challenged by other issues that impact teaching and learning beyond the cognitive: motivation and emotion, values and norms, physical and social. In addition, social and societal problems such as bullying, dropping out, at-risk behavior, racism, and prejudice require a more elaborated definition of education (Katz et al., 2002). Whatever reasons schools may give for not addressing the affective needs of gifted students within the curriculum, ultimately the effects of such shortsightedness may be evident in gifted students who do not reach their full potential (Galbraith, 1985; Lovecky, 1997; Roeper, 1988; Silverman, 1993; Sisk, 1982).

Why Include Affective Education in the Curriculum?

"I really must learn to read, except I'm afraid it will make it awfully hard for me in school next year if I know things. I think it will be better if people just go on thinking I'm not very bright. They won't hate me quite so much."—Charles Wallace from *A Wrinkle in Time* by Madeline L'Engle

Morelock (1992) defined asynchronous development in gifted individuals as an uneven rate of development in the cognitive, affective, and physical domains. When school curriculum focuses solely upon the cognitive realm, the uneven development of the other domains may be enhanced, thus emphasizing the gifted child's feeling of being "out of sync" with his or her peers (Silverman, 1993). Roeper (1995) contended that if asynchronous development is left unchecked, the adoption of unhealthy lifestyles (e.g., perfectionism, self-criticism, poor self-concept) or maladjustment (e.g., depression, eating disorders, antisocial behavior) may ensue. Beane (1993) pointed to the importance of integrating the affective domain in the total curricula. The integration of the affective domain with almost every other aspect of learning and schooling is essential for the positive development of the whole student. When affective issues are addressed and social-emotional needs met, gifted students face their challenges with emotional balance and appropriate coping mechanisms that promote success in reaching personal potential rather than failure to do so (Roeper, 1995).

Issues in the Affective Domain Facing Gifted Students

Gifted children have the same basic needs as any child—food, shelter, security, and a need for belonging (Maslow, 1943); however, gifted children often progress through developmental stages at a younger age and at a faster rate (Webb, 1994). Although all children face affective and developmental challenges, gifted children, due to their differentiating characteristics in the affective domain, may also face issues that their age-mates may not. Research suggests that the well-being of the gifted child is influenced by (a) his or her type and degree of giftedness, (b) educational fit or lack thereof, and (c) personal characteristics (Neihart, 1999).

Table 15.2 provides affective characteristics as articulated by Clark (2012), Webb (1994), Seagoe (1974), and VanTassel-Baska (1989b), social-emotional needs associated with specific characteristics, and possible negative behaviors that may appear if the social-emotional needs are not addressed.

All too often in school, gifted students are asked to put their emotions aside and focus on the cognitive task at hand. In the current atmosphere of accountability in education, many administrators and educators feel as though there aren't enough hours in the school day to address the academic standards set forth by local, state, and federal authorities. However, research suggests that there is a connection between cognitive and affective functioning (Goleman, 2006). Imagine the student who was ostracized during a game of kickball at recess. Is it any wonder that he or she brings a less than positive attitude into the classroom after recess? Everyone carries what amounts to their personal baggage with them, even in primarily cognitive arenas. This relationship has the potential to impact school performance on a variety of levels. Katz (1994) purported perceived social status,

TABLE 15.2

Affective Characteristics, Needs, and Manifestations of the Gifted

Affective Characteristic	Social-Emotional Needs	Negative Manifestations
Keen interest in understanding one's self and feelings of being "different"	To understand differences and similarities between themselves and others; To assert personal needs; To share with self and others as a means of self-clarification and validation	Tendency toward introversion, isolation; May result in peer rejection
High expectations of self and others	To learn to clarify one's own feelings as well as the expectations of others; To set reasonable goals and communicate feelings	Tendency toward intolerance, perfectionism, criticism, depression, distorted self-concept; Being overwhelmed by competing expectations
Highly developed sense of humor	To learn how one's own behavior may affect the feelings or behavior of others	May be misunderstood or misinterpreted by peers; Tendency toward verbal attacks on others
Early sense of idealism, emphasizing truth, justice, equity	To reconcile "what should be" with "what is"; To find causes to which one can commit and promote; To develop a personal value system	Tendency toward altruistic worrying or humanitarian concerns resulting in undue stress; Attempts toward unrealistic endeavors resulting in frustration
Development of inner locus of control; internal motivation and satisfaction	To self-monitor motivational issues; To prioritize personal value system in order to address potential conflicts	Tendency toward nonconformity, which may be perceived as a challenge to authority; Rejects external motivators
Heightened emotional intensity and depth; sensitivity; empathy	To process cognitively the emotional meaning of experience; To learn healthy ways of expressing emotions	Sensitivity to criticism and rejection; Vulnerable to giving too much to others without ensuring that one's own needs are met
Strong need for self-actualization	To pursue interests and seemingly divergent directions; To understand the process and demands of self-actualization	Lack of challenge, frustration, loss of undeveloped or underutilized talents
Ability to address and conceptualize societal, social, and environmental problems	To learn various problem solving frameworks; To experience meaningful involvement in real-world societal, social, and environmental problems	Tendency toward developing quick solutions without addressing the depth and complexity of the problem at hand; Those in authority may not value the contributions of children
Attraction to the aesthetic facets of society at large (e.g., truth, beauty, justice)	To explore and experience the highest levels of human thought, potential, and production	Tendency to be drawn to obscure organizations with questionable, narrow, or perfectionistic value systems

Note. Compiled from Clark (2012), Seagoe (1974), VanTassel-Baska (1989b), and Webb (1994)

perception of teachers, perception of peers, participation in class discussions, and self-direction in learning can be linked to either a positive or negative self-concept depending upon how those impressions are internalized and processed. Frey and Sylvester (1997) contended that successful exposure to affective education strategies can aid in the development of a positive self-concept.

Bullying. According to Peterson and Ray (2006), more than two-thirds of academically talented students claim to have experienced bullying and almost one-third of those had violent thoughts resulting from the bullying behavior they experienced. Bullying can take many forms—some direct, like name-calling, teasing, and pushing, and some indirect, like rumor-spreading and graffiti-writing. Students interviewed in the study identified depression, unexpressed rage, and school absenteeism as responses to the bullying they experienced (Peterson & Ray, 2006). Although students across all academic performance levels may experience bullying, gifted students often are singled out because of their academic performance—making their strength into a perceived weakness.

Cyberbullying. Move bullying behavior to the virtual world and cyberbullying is the result. Cyberbullying includes using computers, cell phones, or other electronic devices to inflict willful and repeated harm in the form of text messages, degrading postings on social networking sites, threatening e-mails, or websites specially created to target an individual (Hinduja & Patchin, 2010; Patchin & Hinduja, 2006; Smith, Dempsey, Jackson, Olenchak, & Gaa, 2012). According to Dempsey, Haden, Goldman, Strivinski, and Wiens (2011), it is possible that those who are aggressors in cyberbullying may also be engaged in traditional forms of bullying behavior because highly aggressive adolescents tend to seek multiple outlets for their aggression.

How Can the Affective Domain Be Addressed in the Classroom?

"You have brains in your head. You have feet in your shoes. You can steer yourself in any direction you choose."—Theodore Seuss Geisel (Dr. Seuss)

Teachers of the gifted have a unique opportunity to help their students address their own affective needs through classroom activities (Nugent, 2000). Lovecky (1992) delineated five social-emotional traits that are exhibited frequently by gifted students: divergent thinking ability, excitability, sensitivity, perceptiveness, and entelechy. These traits, when exhibited, may leave gifted students vulnerable in the social-emotional arena. Table 15.3 presents these traits, their possible manifestations, suggestions to help the student acclimate to the trait, and strategies to aid in that acclimation.

TABLE 15.3
Affective Traits and Acclimation Strategies

Affective Trait	Behavioral Manifestations	Affective Acclimation	Suggested Strategies
Divergent thinking—prefer the unusual, unique, and/or creative aspects of topics; pose curious questions and respond with unusual answers; exhibit fluency and/or flexibility of thought processes	Dislike of working in groups; appear to be disorganized and/or absent-minded; difficulty with goal setting and/or decision making; enjoy novelty; may be prone to fantasy; nonconformity	Adopting an atmosphere that welcomes play related to creativity	Develop activities that focus on the creative process rather than final product while also ensuring sufficient time for the activity
		Developing appropriate risk-taking behavior by promoting intrinsic satisfaction rather than extrinsic praise	Aid in constructing rubrics and evaluative criteria for work focusing on strengths and weaknesses rather than "good" and "bad"
		Promoting the idea there is something to be learned from any endeavor whether the result was expected or not	Incorporate biographies and other source material that illustrate how initial "failures" led to advancements in various fields
		Learning about social conventions	Create a safe environment where awareness of the requirements of social conformity can be discovered without fear of retribution
		Finding support of those who share similar dreams and aspects	Establish a mentor relationship with someone who possesses similar interests
Excitability—high levels of energy, emotional reactivity, and central nervous system arousal	High need to explore the environment; crave new experiences or novelty; may have difficulty completing projects; thrive on competition; may be either stimulus-seekers or stimulus-withdrawers	Maintaining comfortable levels of arousal with self-regulation	Develop healthy coping mechanisms like relaxation exercises, physically withdrawing from an interaction, and metacognitive strategies to reduce anxiety
		Completing projects within a timeline	Organize activities into structured "chunks" of time and promote intrinsic satisfaction from task completion
		Encouraging healthy aspects of competition	Develop activities where the focus is on doing one's best or personal performance (either individually or collectively) improvement rather than on winning
		Coping with overstimulation in advance of the situation as well as in the midst of it	Encourage strategies such as journal writing and creative visualization techniques in order to deal with extreme feelings
Sensitivity—depth of feeling that results in a sense of identification with others	Passion as evidenced by intense commitment to particular people and/or ideas; compassion related to a sense of caring for others; a focus on potential rather than faults; empathy	Learning to keep appropriate interpersonal distance	Facilitate the separation of their feelings from the feelings of other people by using mental imagery techniques (e.g., building a transparent wall)
		Giving altruistically without any thought of remuneration	Examine the basis for giving in each instance; aid in assessing when to give and when not to; encouraging an understanding of the obligatory response recipients of the gift may experience

Table 15.3 *Continued*

Affective Trait	Behavioral Manifestations	Affective Acclimation	Suggested Strategies
Perceptiveness—an ability to see multiple sides of a situation at once, assessing concomitant layers to see through to the core of an issue, intuition, insight	A need for truth; clear sense of honesty/dishonesty, right/wrong; low tolerance for perceived hypocritical behavior; low tolerance for the ordinary	Learning to be trusting (without being naïve) in an imperfect world	Engender trusting relationships based upon mutual respect incorporating strategies to help to examine what people really mean in given situations (e.g., studying body language, metaphor, etc.)
		Assessing the balance between truth and the importance of personal feelings	Engage in role-playing and/or thinking aloud about the feelings some words connote
		Realizing that immediate action to address an issue or right a wrong is not always possible	Study the techniques used by organizations like Amnesty International (e.g., witnessing from a distance and reporting observations; letter writing, etc.)
		Understanding the behavior of age-peers	Adopt the perspective of an anthropologist studying a culture or tribe
Entelechy—a particular type of motivation, need for self-determination and/or inner-strength to accomplish things even during difficult circumstances; striving to reach one's fullest potential	Highly motivated and often single-minded while in pursuit of personal goals; strong-willed; independent; inner spirit; willing to be responsible; can be lonely; at times taken for granted by peers and others	Recognize both the positive and negative aspects of being strong-willed	Create a pros and cons chart that delineates possible consequences of both positive and negative aspects
		Choosing which "battles" to fight with strength of will	Use hypothetical situations to underscore how to use negotiation, problem solving, and empathy
		Helping to find true friends	List qualities and characteristics desired in a friend as well as what the student is willing to give in return to the relationship

Note. Adapted from "Exploring Social and Emotional Aspects of Giftedness in Children," by D. Lovecky, 1992, *Roeper Review, 15*, 18–25.

It is essential for teachers to not only recognize, but also aid in developing appropriate acclimation of gifted students' affective traits in order for them to achieve their fullest potential.

Affective Instructional Strategies

Classroom climate. Once a comfortable classroom climate has been established, students are much more willing to share their own insights. An atmosphere of acceptance and personal responsibility rather than fear of retribution or negativity provides students with a safe haven where risk-taking and personal reflection can occur. One method for creating such an atmosphere within the classroom is the exploration and development of class parameters. Instead of dictating a set of rules and consequences to be used within the classroom, engage students in an open forum discussion of what kinds of behaviors promote their individual learning success and what types of behaviors undermine their learning. Have students brainstorm a list of acceptable and unacceptable behaviors. Combine and restructure the brainstormed items into a positively stated set of classroom parameters (See Table 15.4).

TABLE 15.4
Transforming Negative Statements Into Positive Parameters

Negative Statements	Positive Parameters
Do not criticize. Do not speak out of turn. Do not cheat. Lateness is not acceptable.	Provide positive, constructive feedback. Use respect and exercise good judgment. Adhere to the school's academic honesty policy. Show responsibility for your own learning by being prompt.

Then, follow the same process in order to develop the consequences for not adhering to the established parameters. In so doing, students become stakeholders in the classroom community. If parameters are exceeded, the students themselves have taken part in the development of the guidelines or rules as well as the consequences.

Another strategy to aid in the establishment of an affective classroom community is the identification of banished or dead words, those that are not acceptable to use in the classroom. Often, gifted students are inundated with a barrage of terms that their peers use as synonyms for "gifted" such as *nerd, brainiac, bookworm,* etc. These and other "offensive" words (e.g., *stupid, dumb, idiot*) are written on slips of paper and placed on a bulletin board or wall display. For a banished words theme, a jail cell motif could be used to imply that these words have been "put away." For a dead words topic, a headstone with "rest in peace" or a cemetery effect may be used.

Arts incorporation. Sometimes, no matter how inviting and nonthreatening a classroom environment is, some gifted students may not be comfortable with verbalizing their affective needs. Others may not even be cognitively aware that they have affective issues to address, and thus, they are at a loss when activities that require affective verbal disclosure arise. Incorporating art into a content area activity is one method that can be used to access the affective domain of gifted students when verbal strategies are ineffective or as a companion to verbal activities. The use of collage is one strategy that allows students of all artistic skill levels to participate in a creative activity that may be used as an affective outlet. For example, a discussion on the real versus the ideal has developed during a unit on justice. Using discarded magazines, ask students to create individual collages that depict what ought to be on one side and what is on the other. The pictures students choose to incorporate into their collages may reveal more about their perception of the real and the ideal than their discussion. Upon completion of the collages, allow students the opportunity to share their observations about their own work and the work of other students in the class. Debrief students on the applicable affective aspects of reconciling the real and the ideal such as perfectionism, body image, and multipotentiality.

Bibliotherapy. Bibliotherapy is the use of literature to help students understand and resolve personal issues (Halsted, 2009; Frazier & McCannon, 1981). Teachers can also use guided reading of literature to help gifted students develop coping skills and more realistic self-expectations (Hébert, 2011). The interaction between the reader and the story through identification or universal experience, catharsis, and insight appeals to many gifted students (Nugent, 2000). Gifted students whose strengths lie in their ability to conceptualize and generalize often find success through bibliotherapeutic reading (Adderholt-Elliot & Eller, 1989). It is one of the most effective affective strategies available to teachers, parents, counselors, and gifted students (Silverman, 1993). After careful selection of a book or short story, teachers should develop activities and guided inquiry questions to aid students in the understanding and internalization of the book and the bibliotherapeutic process.

Planning activities prior to the bibliotherapy session, like the sample provided in Figure 15.3, helps to ensure that guided discussion and/or structured activities take place. Short stories or novels used within the curriculum may also be used with bibliotherapeutic goals in mind depending upon the themes or issues presented within the context of the plot. Hébert (2011) included a list of literature to guide gifted students, with extensive lists of biographies for this purpose, in his text.

Cinematherapy. Like bibliotherapy, cinematherapy engages viewers in an interaction with the medium to examine specific issues. Using film portraying the gifted as characters, either major or minor, to address the affective needs of gifted students has been the focus of several articles within the field of gifted education (Nugent & Shaunessy, 2003). Milne and Reis (2000), Hébert and Neumeister (2001), and Newton (1995) concurred that teachers can effectively use film to help students understand themselves and cope with being gifted. Figure 15.4 provides a sample plan for using film clips in the classroom as a way to address specific affective issues.

When selecting film clips, teachers should identify which affective characteristics are to be targeted during instruction. As with bibliotherapy, film clips from cinematic versions of short stories or novels used in the curriculum may be applicable to cinematherapeutic strategies. Hébert (2011) provided a list of appropriate films to use for guided viewing with gifted students.

Character education. Anne Frank wrote in her diary, "The final forming of a person's character lies in their own hands" (as cited in Lewis, 1998, p. 2). Teachers of the gifted can help their students develop character not only through modeling positive character traits, but also through the integration of those traits in the content of daily curricula. For example, try regrouping the selections presented in the

Book: L'Engle, M. (1962). *A wrinkle in time*. New York, NY: Dell.
Grade Level: upper elementary, junior high

Major Characters:
- *Meg Murray:* An awkward, highly intelligent, but underachieving high school student who is insecure about her physical appearance and abilities and displays social immaturity, particularly not taking responsibility for her own actions.
- *Charles Wallace Murray:* The extraordinarily intelligent 5-year-old brother of Meg who has a strong interpersonal connection with Meg and his mother. He exhibits uncanny empathy and entelechy. He hides his brilliance from most of society.
- *Calvin O'Keefe:* A popular and athletic boy in Meg's high school. He also is very intelligent, but has never felt truly accepted for who he really is.
- *Mr. and Mrs. Murray:* Both brilliant scientists (a physicist and an experimental biologist, respectively) who instill a thirst for learning and independence in their children.
- *Sandy and Dennys Murray:* Meg and Charles Wallace's twin brothers, who are very athletic and popular in school.

Themes:
A Wrinkle in Time is a classic retelling of the battle between good and evil and the ultimate triumph of love. Additional motifs are encountered through the life lessons Meg learns as she completes her quest to find her father. They include overcoming her desire for conformity and appreciating her own uniqueness; realizing and accepting that one person cannot know everything; and understanding the importance of communication even when words are inadequate.

Suggestions for Use in Bibliotherapy:
Understanding Giftedness: Charles Wallace realizes he is different. Although he is intellectually gifted, he lacks the physical ability to do things like other boys in his class.
1. Have students define asynchronous development and give examples from their own life experiences when they have been touched by it.
2. Have students brainstorm the characteristics of an intellectually gifted child. Then, make a chart for each of the Murray children and Calvin O'Keefe and cite evidence from the book that indicates his or her giftedness.
3. Have students comment on the following quote from Charles Wallace: "I really must learn to read, except I am afraid it will make it awfully hard for me in school next year if I know things. I think it will be much better if people go on thinking I'm not very bright. They won't hate me quite so much." Have they ever felt the way Charles Wallace does as evidenced by this quote? What coping skills do they use to combat it?

Ownership of the Gift: Meg, Charles Wallace, and Calvin all have issues dealing with conformity and others' expectations of themselves.
1. Have students discuss or journal about the pressures they face to be like everyone else. Then, discuss, brainstorm, or present coping skills that can be employed to combat such pressures.
2. Using collages, poetry, or some other form of personal expression, have students illustrate their unique abilities, and the things that make them special.

Figure 15.3. Sample bibliotherapy guide.

Sample Film Clip Usage Guide

Film: *Billy Elliot* (2000, directed by Stephen Daldry)
MPAA: R (original rating of theatrical release); PG-13 (cut video version)—some mature material and language. Select scenes with content in mind.
Grade level: 5–9
Major characters:

- *Billy Elliot* (Jamie Bell): an 11-year-old boy who discovers a hidden talent for ballet during boxing practice and struggles to overcome obstacles to pursue his passion.
- *Mrs. Wilkinson* (Julie Walters): Billy's dance teacher, who senses his spark, raw talent, and passion. She teaches Billy and has faith in his potential.
- *Jackie Elliot* (Gary Lewis): Billy's dad is a conventional miner and initially does not approve of Billy's desire to dance rather than choosing another more typical athletic pursuit.
- *Tony Elliot* (Jamie Draven): Billy's older brother shares a room with him and is on strike from the mine along with his father.

Synopsis: In 1984, in the midst of a mining strike in his town, 11-year-old Billy Elliot tries to hide his dancing talent from his classmates in his working-class British town. Billy is artistic and he especially likes music. He tries to play piano like his mother, who is dead, once did. Billy is also rather mature and responsible; he takes care of his grandmother, who has memory problems and often wanders off. In Billy's family, boxing is the sport of tradition, but Billy becomes enamored with ballet. Billy becomes a rebel by secretly joining a ballet class without his family's knowledge. When his father finds out about his ballet class, it is up to Billy to show the world what he really cares about.

Pertinent scenes and suggested uses:
Conformity and Risk-taking: Billy's first encounter with ballet class. He is drawn to music and dance, but still shows reticence. This is a turning point. Will Billy take a chance to reach his potential or conform?

1. Share through discussion or journaling instances when each student has hidden his or her gift in order to conform. Discuss the context of the conformity and alternate coping mechanisms that could be used in the future.
2. Operationally define the term *potential*. Have students share through discussion, writing, or artistic creation what they feel their potential contribution to society is. Discuss goal-setting strategies to help students reach their potential.
3. Taking risks can be intimidating because there is a chance of not succeeding. Present instances of inventors who went through multiple iterations before landing on a successful invention or writers who experienced several rejection letters before having a manuscript accepted. Discuss ways that an unsuccessful attempt at something can lead to new knowledge, greater insight, and growth.

Overcoming challenges and resilience: Billy finally shows his dad what he is made of. Although he doesn't show it at first, Billy's dad is amazed by his talent and becomes committed to Billy's dream of attending ballet school and becomes inspired by it.

1. Discuss with students what it feels like when their interests are not supported by friends or family members. Use journaling or some other method to allow students to express their emotions regarding the issue. Brainstorm coping mechanisms to help them build their resiliency and action plans to overcome the next challenge they face by providing a hypothetical scenario for the class to work through as a group or in small groups to report back to the class.

Figure 15.4. Sample film clip usage guide for cinematherapy.

Gender roles and stereotyping: When Billy first broaches the topic of his ballet participation with his family, traditional gender roles and stereotypical prejudices regarding sports are revealed.

1. Gifted and creatively talented students often have traits that are out-of-sync with their peers. Similarly, they may have androgynous traits—traits that are associated with both genders, such as confident or aggressive personalities in girls or sensitivity in boys. They might be interested in areas typically "reserved" for the opposite gender. Billy Elliot shows all of these traits. He rebels against the conventional ideas for what boys should do and what his family expects of him, skipping boxing practice in order to take ballet instead. Depending upon the needs of your students, you can discuss these issues or choose what is most relevant to them. Students can write a journal entry to organize their thoughts and get out all of their personal ideas. They can relate Billy's quest to their own personal situation. After writing, they will be better prepared to participate in a class discussion.

Figure 15.4. Continued.

literature text by character themes like tolerance, justice, equality, and honesty. Use each theme as a prereading activity by defining it, having students describe what such behavior looks like and give examples of that character trait in action through current events or daily activities. If the content area's scope and sequence is not flexible enough to allow the reordering of selections, then be sure that a positive character theme is unveiled in the discussion of each selection. Other than language arts, character themes can be identified in units being covered in social studies (e.g., justice, loyalty), in science (e.g., ethics, integrity), and in physical education (e.g., cooperation, fairness).

Service learning. One affective characteristic that many gifted students share is a heightened emotional intensity and sensitivity toward societal and social problems (Clark, 2012). One way for students to address those feelings is to become proactive and "do something" about their chosen cause (e.g., homelessness, elder care, pollution). Service learning is a way to incorporate such proactive measures into the curricula. Service learning is a method whereby students learn and develop through active participation in thoughtfully organized service experiences that meet community needs while being integrated into the students' academic curriculum. It provides structured time for students to think, talk, or write about what they did and saw during the service activity and to use newly acquired skills and knowledge in authentic situations, thereby enhancing what they have learned in school through extending it beyond the classroom (Belbas, Gorak, & Shumer, 1993). The benefits of service learning extend well beyond the classroom as well to include the students, the school, and the community (see Table 15.5).

Making a difference is a need for many gifted students. Many times they bear the weight of the world on their shoulders as they empathize with the woes of our society and our environment. Through service learning, they have the opportunity to help. Because service-learning activities are open-ended, gifted students are often excited by the possibilities and experience the full effect of their cre-

TABLE 15.5

The Benefits of Service Learning

Benefits to Students	Benefits to the School	Benefits to the Community
‣ Improve self-esteem ‣ Become active citizens ‣ Exercise leadership ‣ Promote positive relationships between peers and adults ‣ Apply academic and social skills in a real-world setting ‣ Gain relevant skills and experience ‣ Explore careers	‣ Engender positive relationships with community ‣ Create positive images of students within the community ‣ Provide a vehicle for positive public relations ‣ Produce positive, active learners ‣ Develop partnerships within the community	‣ Provide a needed service ‣ Become a resource to the community ‣ Become stakeholders in the community

Note. Adapted from *Service Learning and Technology,* by S. Nugent, June 1998. Paper presented at the annual meeting of High Schools That Work, Tulsa, OK.

activity. In Massachusetts, a group of middle school students solved a community conundrum of stockpiling sludge from liquid wastes and, in the process, saved the community about $120,000 (Nugent, 1998).

Self-understanding. In order to reach their potential and move toward self-actualization, gifted students need to understand themselves and their abilities, both relative strengths and relative weaknesses. One way to begin the self-discovery process is to use a student questionnaire. Although many teachers use such questionnaires or inventories at the beginning of the school year to learn about their students and their interests, by using those instruments as a springboard for discussion, teachers can promote reflective and metacognitive behaviors as well as identify coping strategies in use or in need of instruction. Have students complete several open-ended statements (see Figure 15.5). Then, use their responses as a means to open sharing and group discussion (see Figure 15.6).

Upon completing the questionnaire, a discussion on reasons behind the responses and possible coping strategies would be appropriate. Lind (2003) suggested developing a feeling vocabulary by selecting a feeling and listing all of its synonyms. Then, have each student order them by intensity, mild to intense. Students could then volunteer to compare their word orders to promote discussion about specific word connotations and denotations. Coupling self-exploration activities with appropriate bibliotherapy, cinematherapy, character education, and/or service learning activities, teachers could develop an entire unit on the discovery of the gifted self.

Complete the following phrases to make true statements. Write your first instinctual response after reading the phrase.

I don't know why _____

If no one helps me _____

Some teachers _____

I hope I'll never _____

It makes me angry when _____

I'm happy when _____

Most people don't know _____

I'm tired of _____

I'm good at _____

I believe that _____

Figure 15.5. Open-ended response form.

Closing Thoughts

Addressing the affective domain within the curricula is appropriate for all students, but it is essential for gifted students whose affective traits may include divergent thinking, overexcitabilities, sensitivities, perceptiveness, and entelechy (Lovecky, 1992). In order to meet the program standards set forth by NAGC, gifted programs must incorporate the affective domain. Specific strategies to meet students' affective needs can be integrated into any subject area through individual activities, lessons, curricular units, or separate units. It is essential, however, that teachers who endeavor to address the affective aspects of giftedness be willing to follow up on issues that are inadvertently revealed. Whenever classroom activities touch upon the affective realm, it is important to remember that most teachers are not trained counselors. Teachers may not be prepared for all that is disclosed. A support system must be in place in the form of school counselors, school psychologists, and/or therapists.

I don't know why . . .
People make things harder than they are.
I can't sit still.
Nobody understands me.
Life's not fair.

If no one helps me . . .
I do it myself.
I do a whole lot better.
I'll be smarter.

Some teachers . . .
Don't teach to your level.

I hope I'll never . . .
Lose hope.
Become like my mom.
Get brain damage.

It makes me angry when . . .
People cheat off other people who do the work.
I get picked on.

I'm happy when . . .
It's complicated.

Most people don't know . . .
How smart I am.
How to reason.
The real me.
How to feel.

I'm tired of . . .
People asking stupid questions.

I'm good at . . .
Whatever I put my mind to.

I believe that . . .
People can do a lot if they are determined.
People can make the world better.

Figure 15.6. Sample responses of junior high school gifted students.

Teacher Statement

Affective education is a critical addition to teachers of gifted students. The author provides a thorough summary of the theoretical background supporting attention to affective aspects of children's personal development. Major theorists' writings are synthesized to succinct and manageable segments that enable educators to efficiently acquire a basic understanding of some of the significant themes in the field in a short time. Affective development manifests itself differently in gifted children. For example, the author maintains, gifted students are likely to show acute moral sensitivity ahead of their peers (e.g., before teachers might expect it). This chapter provides a detailed discussion of the importance of recognizing these variations in affective development and the necessity of incorporating opportunities in instructions for their exploration. Finally, and significantly, the author offers many pragmatic suggestions on integrating affective education into standard curricula including practical ideas for classroom activities that are easy for teachers to adopt.

—Robin Kyburg Dickson, Ph.D.

Dr. Ferguson states, "Making a difference is a need for many gifted students." Making a difference is also a need for teachers of the gifted. This chapter on affective education by Dr. Stephanie Ferguson will be a great asset in assisting educators to do just that. Apart from a broad ranging, clearly written overview and background on affective education, characteristics, social-emotional needs and manifestations in students, the instructional strategies provided will be of particular use to the practitioner. Bibliotherapy and cinematherapy are two perhaps lesser used but effective tools teachers could add to their classroom toolkits. A thorough and useful resource list of books, websites, and templates for curricular planning provide further support to teachers interested in strengthening the connection between cognition and affect with their gifted students. It is a delight to find such beneficial work collected in one chapter.

—Jane Englund, Ph.D.

DISCUSSION QUESTIONS

1. With respect to Maslow's Hierarchy of Needs, what programs are currently in place to help meet student's primary needs so that learning can take place? How could you help students move from primary need concerns to more complex needs within the context of your classroom?

2. By applying your knowledge of general characteristics of the gifted, which of Dabrowski's overexcitabilities seems to be the most common? Justify your response.

3. Develop your own comprehensive definition of affective education describing what it is and how it can be incorporated into the curriculum. Which theories, methods, and/or strategies did you include? Why?

4. Why are bullying and cyberbullying such difficult issues to address in schools?

5. Examine your own school setting (either the school you attended, your work setting, or your postsecondary school experience). How are/were students' affective needs met within the curriculum? Provide an example that illustrates the integration of the affective domain. If the affective domain is/was not addressed, suggest a way that it might be integrated.

6. Select one of the strategies provided within the chapter and develop an activity that addresses at least one of the affective characteristics listed in Table 15.2. How would you integrate this strategy into a specific content area? What are the goals and objectives? How would you assess the activity?

7. Which of the affective traits shown in Table 15.3 seem most prevalent in your experience with gifted individuals? Provide an example that supports your choice.

8. Select one of the quotes presented in the chapter. Explain how the selected quote applies to educational issues within the affective domain.

Teacher Resources

Affective Education Books

Cross, T. (2010). *On the social and emotional lives of gifted children* (4th ed.). Waco, TX: Prufrock Press.

> Dr. Cross addresses pertinent issues for today's gifted youth including social media and terrorism as well as how parents, teachers, and counselors can help guide these students through difficult times.

Elksnin, L.K., & Elksnin, N. (2006). *Teaching social-emotional skills at school and at home.* Denver, CO: Love.

> This book provides strategies for both teachers and parents to help children and youth become socially and emotionally competent. The research-based strategies are practical and easy to understand.

Hébert, T. P. (2011). *Understanding the social and emotional lives of gifted students.* Waco, TX: Prufrock Press.

> This text guides the reader through the theoretical underpinnings of affective development as well as supporting specialized populations of gifted learners and creating classroom environments that engender social and emotional development.

VanTassel-Baska, J. L., Cross, T. L., & Olenchak, F. R. (Eds.). (2009). *Social-emotional curriculum with gifted and talented students.* Waco, TX: Prufrock Press.

> This text contains chapters written by some of the leading scholars in the field of gifted education and contains theories, models, counseling tips, and strategies for supporting gifted learners.

Affective Education Websites

Ethics Resource Center—http://www.ethics.org

> The Ethics Resource Center is a nonprofit, nonpartisan educational organization whose vision is a world where individuals and organizations act with integrity. This site provides information that can be used in classrooms to prompt ethical dilemma discussions.

Kieve-Wavus Education—http://www.kieve.org

> Started in 1926, as a summer camp in Maine, the Kieve-Wavus Education has grown to include summer camps for both boys and girls, an ocean discovery program, science and wilderness programs, and a leadership program. They offer a free e-mail newsletter that is packed with informative strategies and suggestions.

The Society for Safe and Caring Schools and Communities—http://safeandcaring.ca/tools-resources-page/children-youth/

This site provides lesson plans and strategies to incorporate empathy and the affective domain into the curriculum and resources for teacher and students as well as workshops and research.

Classroom Climate Books

Canfield, J., & Wells, H. (1994). *One hundred ways to enhance self-concept in the classroom.* Needham Heights, MA: Allyn & Bacon.

This book offers more than 100 practical, class-tested exercises that can be integrated into the school day or used in specific self-esteem programs. The authors provide suggestions for organizing and sequencing the activities, which are based upon solid learning and psychological research.

Shoop, L., & Wright, D. (1999). *Classroom warm-ups: Activities that improve the climate for learning and discussion.* San Jose, CA: Resource Publications.

The easy-to-use activities in this book are quickly adaptable and easy to incorporate into a classroom, and most of all enjoyable to the students.

Freiberg, H. (1999). *School climate: Measuring, improving, and sustaining healthy learning environments.* New York, NY: Routledge Falmer.

This book provides a framework for educators to look at school and classroom climates using both informal and formal measures. Each chapter focuses on a different aspect of climate and details techniques, which may be used by heads or classroom teachers to judge the health of their learning environment.

Classroom Climate Website

Tribes Learning Community—http://www.tribes.com

Tribes is an organization and a program dedicated to promoting caring, safe, and comfortable learning environments. This site provides information and suggested bibliographies as well as staff development opportunities regarding the Tribes program.

Arts Incorporation Books

Gelb, M. (1998). *How to think like Leonardo daVinci.* New York, NY: Delacorte Press.

The author presents strategies for approaching challenges through problem solving, creative thinking, self-expression, aesthetic recognition, and goal setting.

McAuliffe, J., & Stoskin, L. (1993). *What color is Saturday?* Tucson, AZ: Zephyr Press.

Using analogies, this book encourages both cognitive and affective aspects of creativity. The strategies used in the book lend themselves well to arts incorporation in the curriculum.

Arts Incorporation Websites

Americans for the Arts—http://www.artsusa.org

This advocacy organization provides information on how to increase the coverage of arts in education. The site provides a wealth of information to help justify arts incorporation as well as links to local arts associations and agencies.

Arts Education Partnership—http://www.aep-arts.org

The Arts Education Partnership (AEP) is a national coalition of arts, education, business, philanthropic, and government organizations that demonstrate and promote the essential role of the arts in the learning and development of every child and in the improvement of America's schools. AEP was founded and is supported by the National Endowment for the Arts and the U. S. Department of Education. Partnership organizations affirm the central role of imagination, creativity and the arts in culture and society; the power of the arts to enliven and transform education and schools; and collective action through partnerships as the means to place the arts at the center of learning.

National Endowment for the Arts—http://www.nea.gov

This site provides links and information on grants and innovative funding ideas for arts education.

The Wallace Foundation—http://www.WallaceFoundation.org

The Wallace Foundation, nationally recognized today for its involvement in educational and cultural programs, traces its origins back a half-century to the philanthropic impulses of DeWitt and Lila Acheson Wallace, founders of The Reader's Digest Association. The Wallace Foundation seeks to support and share effective ideas and practices that will strengthen education leadership, arts participation, and out-of-school learning.

Bibliotherapy Books

Ayers, R., & Crawford, R. (Eds.). (2004). *Great books for high school kids: A teachers' guide to books that can changes teens' lives.* Boston, MA: Beacon Press.

This book includes an annotated list of nearly 400 titles, arranged by author with informative and entertaining descriptions as well as more than 70 subject, title, and author indexes.

Berthoud, E., & Elderkin, S. (2013). *The novel cure: From abandonment to zestlessness: 751 books to cure what ails you.* New York, NY: Penguin.

Categorized by "ailment," this book is a list of books to "cure" readers. Wonderful for those looking for thematic connections among titles or for just a little humor.

Hahn, D., Flynn, L., & Reuben, S. (Eds.). (2008). *The ultimate teen book guide: More than 700 great books.* New York, NY: Walker & Co.

Written from the teenager's perspective, this book contains recommendations from teen reviewers from classics to cult fiction.

Halsted, J. (2009). *Some of my best friends are books: Guiding gifted readers* (3rd ed.). Tucson, AZ: Gifted Psychology Press.

> Halsted provides background and research on the affective and cognitive needs of gifted students along with typical reading patterns of the gifted. Also included is an annotated bibliography of more than 300 books appropriate for gifted readers, indexed by topic.

Odean, K. (2002). *Great books for girls* (Rev. ed.). New York, NY: Ballantine.

> This resource provides more than 600 titles selected to encourage, challenge, and nurture girls. Each book is annotated and provided with a reading level range by grade. The selected books are indexed by author, title, and category.

Odean, K. (1998). *Great books for boys.* New York, NY: Ballantine.

> More than 600 titles have been carefully selected and annotated. Organized by reader age and genre, this is an excellent resource for parents, teachers, and librarians.

Stanley, J. (1999). *Reading to heal: How to use bibliotherapy to improve your life.* Boston, MA: Element.

> The first nonacademic book about bibliotherapy, it is an accessible, useful, and engaging tool that informs readers how to choose and use books for bibliotherapeutic processes.

Bibliotherapy Websites

Best Children's Books—http://www.best-childrens-books.com

> Provides a compendium of children's titles and summaries along with suggestions for use. Site can be navigated by category along with by recognized lists like Newbery Award winners.

Bibliotherapy Bookshelf—http://www.carnegielibrary.org/kids/booknook/bibliotherapy

> A service of the Carnegie Library of Pittsburgh, this site provides an extensive list of books categorized by issue. The site is updated frequently.

Bibliotherapy Education Project—http://bibliotherapy.ehs.cmich.edu/

> This site has resources and links to assist with evaluating materials for bibliotherapy work with children and adolescents, finding evaluated books for certain age groups and issues, and learning more about the use of books in therapy.

Cinematherapy Books

Hesley, J., & Hesley, J. (2001). *Rent two films and let's talk in the morning: Using popular movies in psychotherapy* (2nd ed.). New York, NY: Wiley and Sons.

> This book provides concise descriptions of dozens of popular films and shows how they can be used for address specific issues (e.g., divorce, substance abuse, personal responsibility). The volume also offers suggestions for selecting films and creating assignments.

Solomon, G. (2001). *Reel therapy: How movies inspire you to overcome life's problems.* New York, NY: Lebhar-Friedman Books.

This author suggests film titles to address life's emotional problems. This book provides analyses of films to aid viewers in comprehending the film on deeper, more emotional levels.

Cinematherapy Website

Cinematherapy.com—http://www.cinematherapy.com

This site is authored and hosted by Dr. Birgit Woltz. The site provides an index of films with suggestions for use as cinematherapy.

Character Education Books

DeRoche, E., & Williams, M. (1998). *Educating hearts and minds: A comprehensive character education framework.* Thousand Oaks, CA: Corwin Press.

This guide provides a framework to help design, organize, implement, and maintain a character education program that is successful for students, staff, and the community. The suggestions provided are easily adaptable and implemented including standards to aid in assessment of the program.

Lewis, B. (2005). *What do you stand for?: A kid's guide to building character.* Minneapolis, MN: Free Spirit.

This user-friendly book guides the reader through units grouped by character traits such as courage, honesty, sincerity, honor, and cooperation. Each chapter includes character dilemmas and activities promoting problem solving and values clarification.

Ryan, K., & Bohlin, K. (1999). *Building character in schools: Practical ways to bring moral instruction to life.* San Francisco: Jossey-Bass.

This book outlines the principles and strategies of effective character education and explains what schools and teachers must do to teach students the habits and attitudes that combine to define a person of character.

Character Education Websites

Character Counts/Josephson Institute for Ethics—http://www.charactercounts.org

This organization promotes the six pillars of character: trustworthiness, responsibility, respect, fairness, caring, and citizenship. The website offers free teaching materials and suggestions.

Character Education Partnership—http://www.character.org

The Character Education Partnership (CEP) is a nonpartisan coalition of organizations dedicated to developing moral character and civic responsibility. The site contains resource lists, virtual bulletin boards, and current news events related to character education.

Center for the 4th and 5th Rs—http://www2.cortland.edu/centers/character/
> This center, directed by Dr. Thomas Lickona, is based at the State University of New York at Cortland and promotes the 4th and 5th R's: respect and responsibility. The site contains valuable links to information and best practices for character education.

Good Character.com—http://www.goodcharacter.com
> This website offers free teaching guides specifically designed for high school, middle school, and elementary school students. In addition, the site provides specific information on character in sports, opportunities for action, school-to-work ethics, and links to other character education organizations.

The School for Ethical Education—http://www.ethicsed.org
> This site gives teachers strategies to put ethics into action and offers assistance and staff development for educators interested in character education.

Service Learning Books

Lewis, B. (1998). *The kid's guide to social action* (Rev. ed.). Minneapolis, MN: Free Spirit.
> Beyond providing real-life vignettes of students who have made a difference, the author outlines the skills and steps needed in developing, enacting, monitoring, and evaluating social action projects.

Eyler, J., & Giles, D. (1999). *Where's the learning in service-learning?* San Francisco, CA: Jossey-Bass.
> This book explores service-learning as a valid learning activity. The authors present data from two national research projects. Their studies include a large national survey focused on attitudes and perceptions of learning, intensive student interviews before and after the service semester, and additional comprehensive interviews to explore student views of the service-learning process. The book provides ideas for those interested in promoting service-learning projects in their own settings.

Lewis, B. (2007). *The teen guide to global action: How to connect with others (near & far) to create social change.* Minneapolis, MN: Free Spirit.
> This is a guide for kids who want to change the world now! It is filled with real-life vignettes as well as hand-on activities, tools, and resources to put their altruistic spirit into action.

Lewis, B., & Espeland, P. (1995). *The kid's guide to service projects: Over 500 service ideas for young people who want to make a difference.* Minneapolis, MN: Free Spirit.
> This book contains self-starter ideas for service projects for kids, from simple, small-scale projects to multiple-person, large-scale commitments.

Service Learning Websites

The GoodCharacter Service Learning Primer—http://www.goodcharacter.com/SERVICE/primer-1.html
>   This guide offers step-by-step instructions on how to create, implement, and assess service-learning projects.

The National Service-Learning Clearinghouse—http://gsn.nylc.org/clearinghouse
>   A searchable database of service learning opportunities for students.

Self-Understanding Books

Galbraith, J. (2013). *The survival guide for gifted kids: For ages 10 and under* (Rev. ed.). Minneapolis, MN: Free Spirit.
>   This book helps young gifted children construct their own understanding of what it means to be gifted. The book is filled with contributions from gifted kids written to gifted kids providing insight and advice.

Galbraith, J., & Delisle, J. (2011). *The gifted teen survival guide: Smart, sharp, and ready for (almost) anything* (4th ed.). Minneapolis, MN: Free Spirit.
>   This book is filled with strategies, advice, and insights from gifted adolescents from all over the country. Arranged by issues, the book can help students understand themselves and their giftedness.

Kincher, J. (1995). *Psychology for kids*. Minneapolis, MN: Free Spirit.
>   This book provides 40 Personality Style Inventories to help students learn about their own attitudes, opinions, beliefs, habits, choices, memories, ideas, feelings, and abilities. The PSIs are designed to help students understand themselves.

Kincher, J. (1995). *Psychology for kids II*. Minneapolis, MN: Free Spirit.
>   Volume II presents 40 experiments to help students learn about the beliefs, attitudes, perceptions, differences, and styles of learning of others. The tests are presented in a student friendly format and provide debriefing information as well as resources for further information if students' interest is sparked.

Schultz, R. A., & Delisle, J. R. (2013). *If I'm so smart, why aren't the answers easy?* Waco, TX: Prufrock Press.
>   This book includes surveys with more than 5,000 gifted young adults to share the experiences of those growing up gifted. Some of the topics covered include friendships and fitting in with peers, school struggles and successes, and worries about the future. The book also has journal prompts for students to use.

Webb, J. (2013). *Searching for meaning: Idealism, bright minds, disillusionment, and hope*. Tucson, AZ: Great Potential Press.
>   This easy-to-understand book helps gifted students and those who care about them understand their struggles.

Coping Strategies Books

Cohen, L., & Frydenberg, E. (2006). *Coping for capable kids: Strategies for parents, teachers, and students.* Waco, TX: Prufrock Press.

> This book provides practical strategies for those who need to find positive ways to cope with the social and emotional issues that confront gifted kids.

Forman, S. (1993). *Coping skills interventions for children and adolescents.* San Francisco: Jossey-Bass.

> The author details specific techniques for educators and/or parents to use and/or share with students.

Webb, J. (2013). *Searching for meaning: Idealism, bright minds, disillusionment, and hope.* Tucson, AZ: Great Potential Press.

> This book provides suggested coping strategies to help gifted students address their disillusionment and nurture hope, happiness, and contentment.

Coping Strategies Website

Coping Skills for Kids—http://www.copingskills4kids.net/

> This site provides online manuals for coping strategies in a number of areas including loss, betrayal, rejection, and humiliation.

Bullying Books

Beane, A. L. (2011). *The new bully free classroom: Proven prevention and intervention strategies for teachers K–8.* Minneapolis, MN: Free Spirit.

> Through examples and the use of scenarios, the book promotes the power of bystanders to stop bullies in their tracks. Digital content is included—handouts, PowerPoint presentation, and reproducible forms.

Coloroso, B. (2010). *The bully, the bullied, and the bystander: From preschool to high school—How parents and teachers can help break the cycle of violence.* New York, NY: Harper Collins.

> This book helps readers recognize the triad of bullying: the perpetrator, the target (who may become a bully), and the bystander. The author describes what bullying is and isn't, the differences between male and female bullies, how to tell if a child is being bullied, and four abilities that may help keep a child from succumbing to bullying.

Jacobs, T. A. (2010). *Teen cyberbullying investigated: Where do your rights end and consequences begin?* Minneapolis, MN: Free Spirit.

> Using a collection of current court cases, readers are asked whether they agree with the outcome and how the decision makes an impact upon their lives.

Romain, T. (1997). *Bullies are a pain in the brain.* Minneapolis, MN: Free Spirit Publishing.

> This book blends humor with the very serious subject of how to handle bullying behavior if it is directed at you.

Bullying Website

Stopbullying.gov—http://www.stopbullying.gov

This government-sponsored website provides current information about both bullying and cyberbullying, techniques for identification and prevention, and information about how to get help. The site also provides links to videos, free resources, policies and laws, and current news articles related to bullying and cyberbullying.

References

Adderholt-Elliot, M., & Eller, S. (1989). Counseling students who are gifted through bibliotherapy. *Teaching Exceptional Children, 22*(1), 26–31.

Beane, J. A. (1993). *A middle school curriculum: From rhetoric to reality* (2nd ed.). Columbus, OH: National Middle School Association.

Belbas, B., Gorak, K., & Shumer, R. (1993). *Commonly used definitions of service-learning: A discussion piece.* Retrieved from http://www.nicsl.coled.umn.edu/res/mono/def.htm

Blackburn, C., & Erikson, D. (1986). Predictable crises of the gifted student. *Journal of Counseling and Development, 64,* 552–554.

Bloom, B., Hastings, J., & Madaus, G. (1971). *Handbook of formative and summative evaluation.* New York, NY: McGraw-Hill.

Carin, A., & Sund, L. (1978). *Creative questioning: Sensitive listening techniques: A self-concept approach.* Columbus, OH: Merrill.

Clark, B. (2012). *Growing up gifted* (8th ed.). Upper Saddle River, NJ: Merrill Prentice Hall.

Cohen, L., & Frydenberg, E. (2006). *Coping for capable kids: Strategies for teachers, parents, and students* (2nd ed.). Waco, TX: Prufrock Press.

Cross, T. (2010). *On the social and emotional lives of gifted children* (4th ed.). Waco, TX: Prufrock Press.

Dabrowski, K. (1964). *Positive disintegration.* Boston, MA: Little, Brown.

Dabrowski, K., & Piechowski, M. (1977). *Theory of levels of emotional development* (Vols. 1 & 2). Oceanside, NY: Dabor Science.

Daldry, S. (Director). (2000). *Billy Elliot.* [Motion picture]. London, England: Working Title Pictures and Universal Studios.

Delisle, J. (1992). *Guiding the social and emotional development of gifted youth: A practical guide for educators and counselors.* New York, NY: Longman.

Delisle, J. (2002). Affective education and character development: Understanding self and serving others through instructional adaptations. In F. Karnes & S. Bean (Eds.), *Methods and materials for teaching the gifted* (pp. 471–494). Waco, TX: Prufrock Press.

Dempsey, A. G., Haden, S. C., Goldman, J., Strivinski, J., & Wiens, B. A. (2011). Relational overt victimization in schools: Associations with suicidality and violence. *Journal of School Violence, 10,* 374–392.

Elgersma, R. (1981). Providing for affective growth in gifted education. *Roeper Review, 3*(4), 6–8.

Elksnin, L.K., & Elksnin, N. (2006). *Teaching social-emotional skills at school and home.* Denver, CO: Love.

Frazier, M., & McCannon, C. (1981). Using bibliotherapy with gifted children. *Gifted Child Quarterly, 25,* 81–85.

Frey, K., & Sylvester, L. (1997). *Research on the second step program: Do student behaviors and attitudes improve?* Seattle, WA: Committee for Children.

Galbraith, J. (1985). The eight great gripes of gifted kids: Responding to special needs. *Roeper Review, 8*(1), 15–18.

Goleman, D. (2006). *Emotional intelligence: Why it can matter more than IQ* (10th ed.). New York, NY: Bantam Books.

Halsted, J. (2009). *Some of my best friends are books: Guiding gifted readers* (3rd ed.). Tucson, AZ: Gifted Psychology Press.

Hébert, T. (2011). *Understanding the social and emotional lives of gifted students.* Waco, TX: Prufrock Press.

Hébert, T., & Neumeister, K. (2001). Guided viewing of film: A strategy for counseling gifted teenagers. *Journal of Secondary Gifted Education, 12,* 224–227.

Hinduja, S., & Patchin, J. W. (2010). Bullying, cyberbullying, and suicide. *Archives of Suicide Research, 14,* 206–221.

Katz, E. (1994). *Self-concept and the gifted student.* Boulder, CO: Open Space Communications.

Katz, Y., Kontoyianni, A., Lang, P., Menezes, I., St. J. Neill, S., Puierula, A., . . . Vriens, L. (2002). North and south contrasted: Cultural similarities and differences in affective education. In C. A. Torres & A. Antikainen (Eds.), *The international handbook on the sociology of education: An international assessment of new research and theory* (pp. 362–380). Lanham, MD: Rowman and Littlefield.

Krathwohl, D., Bloom, B., & Masia, B. (1964). *Taxonomy of educational objectives: The classification of educational goals. Handbook II: Affective domain.* New York, NY: David McKay.

L'Engle, M. (1962). *A wrinkle in time.* New York, NY: Dell.

Levey, S., & Dolan, J. (1988). Addressing specific learning abilities in gifted students. *Gifted Child Today, 11*(3), 10–11.

Lewis, B. (1998). *What do you stand for?: A kid's guide to building character.* Minneapolis, MN: Free Spirit.

Lind, S. (2003). *Tips for parents: Developing a feeling vocabulary.* Retrieved from http://www.gt-cybersource.org/Record.aspx?NavID=2_2&rid=12298

Lovecky, D. (1992). Exploring social and emotional aspects of giftedness in children. *Roeper Review, 15,* 18–25.

Lovecky, D. (1997). Identity development in gifted children: Moral sensitivity. *Roeper Review, 20,* 90–94.

Maker, C. J., & Schiever, S.W. (2005). *Teaching models in education of the gifted* (3rd ed.). Austin, TX: Pro-Ed.

Maslow, A. H. (1943). A theory of human nature. *Psychological Review, 50,* 370–396.

Maslow, A. H. (1971). *The farther reaches of human nature.* New York, NY: Viking.

Mehrens, W., & Lehman, I. (1987). *Using standardized tests in education.* New York, NY: Longman.

Mendaglio, S. (2002). Dabrowski's Theory of Positive Disintegration: Some implications for teachers of the gifted. *AGATE, 15*(2), 14–22.

Mika, E. (2009). *Theory of Positive Disintegration as a model of personality development for exceptional individuals.* Retrieved from http://www.positivedisintegration.com/mika2.pdf

Milne, H., & Reis, S. (2000). Using videotherapy to address the social and emotional needs of gifted students. *Gifted Child Today, 23*(1), 24–29.

Morelock, M. (1992). Giftedness: The view from within. *Understanding Our Gifted, 4*(3), 1, 11–15.

Neihart, M. (1999). The impact of giftedness on psychological well-being. *Roeper Review, 22*(1), 10–17.

Newton, A. (1995). Silver screens and silver linings: Using theater to explore feelings and issues. *Gifted Child Today, 18*(2), 14–19, 43.

Nugent, S. (1998, June). *Service learning and technology.* Paper presented at the annual meeting of High Schools That Work, Tulsa, OK.

Nugent, S. (2000). Perfectionism: Its manifestations and classroom-based interventions. *Journal of Secondary Gifted Education, 11,* 215–221.

Nugent, S., & Shaunessy, E. (2003). Using film in teacher training: Viewing the gifted through different lenses. *Roeper Review, 25,* 128–134.

Patchin, J. W., & Hinduja, S. (2006). Bullies move beyond the schoolyard: A preliminary look at cyberbullying. *Youth Violence and Juvenile Justice, 4,* 148–169.

Peterson, J. S. (2003). An argument for proactive attention to affective concerns of gifted adolescents. *Journal for Secondary Gifted Education, 14,* 62–70.

Peterson, J. S., & Ray, K. E. (2006). Bullying among the gifted: The subjective experience. *Gifted Child Quarterly, 50,* 252–269. doi: 10.1177/001698620605000305

Roeper, A. (1988). Should educators of the gifted and talented be more concerned with world issues? *Roeper Review, 11*(1), 12–13.

Roeper, A. (1995). How the gifted cope with their emotions. In *Annemarie Roeper: Selected writings and speeches* (pp. 74–84). Minneapolis, MN: Free Spirit.

Schultz, R. A., & Delisle, J. R. (2013). *If I'm so smart, why aren't the answers easy?* Waco, TX: Prufrock Press.

Seagoe, M. (1974). Some learning characteristics of gifted children. In R. Martinson, *The identification of the gifted and talented.* Ventura, CA: Office of the Ventura County Superintendent of Schools.

Sellin, D., & Birch, J. (1981). *Psychoeducational development of gifted and talented learners.* Rockwell, MD: Aspen.

Silverman, L. (Ed.). (1993). *Counseling the gifted.* Denver, CO: Love.

Sisk, D. (1982). Caring and sharing: Moral development of gifted students. *Elementary School Journal, 82,* 221–229.

Smith, B. W., Dempsey, A. G., Jackson, S. E., Olenchak, F. R., & Gaa, J. (2012). Cyberbullying among gifted children. *Gifted Education International, 28*(1), 112–126. doi: 10.1177/0261429411427652

Tannenbaum, A. (1983). *Gifted children: Psychological and educational perspectives.* New York, NY: Macmillan.

Tolan, S. (1999). *Dabrowski's overexcitabilities: A layman's explanation.* Retrieved from http://www.stephanietolan.com/dabrowskis.htm

Treffinger, D., Borgers, S., Render, G., & Hoffman, R. (1976). Encouraging affective development: A compendium of techniques. *Gifted Child Quarterly, 20*(1), 47–65.

VanTassel-Baska, J. (Ed.). (1989a). *A practical guide to counseling the gifted in a school setting* (2nd ed.). Reston, VA: The Council for Exceptional Children.

VanTassel-Baska, J. (1989b). Counseling the gifted. In J. Feldhusen, J. VanTassel-Baska, & K. Seeley (Eds.), *Excellence in educating the gifted* (pp. 299–314). Denver, CO: Love Publishing.

VanTassel-Baska, J., Cross, T., Olenchak, F.R. (Eds.). (2009). *Social-emotional curriculum with gifted and talented students.* Waco, TX: Prufrock Press.

Webb, J. (1994). *Nurturing the social-emotional development of gifted children.* Arlington, VA: ERIC Clearinghouse on Disabilities and Gifted Education. (ERIC Digest No. E527)

Webb, J. (2013). *Searching for meaning: Idealism, bright minds, disillusionment, and hope.* Tucson, AZ: Great Potential Press.

Weinstein, G., & Fantini, M. (1970). *Toward humanistic education: A curriculum of affect.* New York, NY: Praeger.

Williams, F. (1970). *Classroom ideas for encouraging thinking and feeling* (2nd ed.). Buffalo, NY: D.O.K.

DEVELOPING THE LEADERSHIP POTENTIAL OF GIFTED STUDENTS

16
Chapter

BY SUZANNE M. BEAN AND FRANCES A. KARNES

A group of preschoolers negotiating the use of playground equipment . . . elementary-age students working on group projects . . . teenagers planning special events for the school . . . young people using social media to develop their own nonprofit movement to help those less fortunate . . .

These are examples of the experiences through which leadership potential is developed. Although the concept of leadership often is misunderstood and the type of leader needed in the next generation is changing, it is resolved that leadership skills can be developed and more intentional endeavors must be made to cultivate bright, young leaders for today's world.

The process of becoming a leader holds many valuable lessons in life. Interpersonal skills are necessary in every aspect of human endeavor—at home, school, work, and in the social arena. As one's leadership potential is nurtured, the ability to relate to others improves and skills in communication, conflict resolution, decision making, and goal achievement are refined.

Initiative and responsibility increase, and self-concept and personal fulfillment flourish. Basic human needs of belonging, accomplishment, and reaching one's potential can be realized through the development of leadership. Leadership skills can make the difference between talents being fully utilized or unfulfilled.

The personal rewards for developing one's leadership potential are many, but the societal benefits of effective leaders may be even more significant. The call for more effective leaders must not be ignored. Perhaps at no other time in history has there been a greater challenge for positive human interaction and ethical leadership. These goals are critical to the progress of humankind.

Definitions of Leadership

The word *leadership* means different things to many people. Most of the disagreement stems from the fact that leadership is a complex phenomenon involving the leader, the followers, and the situation. Some researchers have focused on the personality, physical traits, or behaviors of the leader; others have addressed the relationships between leaders and followers; still others have studied how aspects of the situation affect leaders' actions. Leadership is one of the most observed and least understood phenomena on Earth. It involves a range of experiences in the life of a person, which suggests the changing nature of this elusive concept.

Leadership has been defined in the following ways:

1. the process of persuasion or example by which an individual (or leadership team) includes a group to pursue objectives held by the leader or shared by the leader and his or her followers (Gardner, 1990);
2. an activity or set of activities, observable to others, that occurs in a group, organization, or institution involving a leader and followers who willingly subscribe to common purposes and work together to achieve them (Clark & Clark, 1994);
3. those who stimulate and inspire followers to both achieve extraordinary outcomes and, in the process, develop their own leadership capacity (Bass & Riggio, 2006);
4. the ability to create a vision for positive change, help focus resources on right solutions, inspire and motivate others, and provide opportunities for growth and learning (Martin, 2007);
5. the process of multiplying the intelligence and capability of people, which increases the brainpower of the organization to meet growth demands (Wiseman & McKeown, 2010); and
6. a process of social influence, which maximizes the efforts of others, toward the achievement of a goal (Kruse, 2013).

Although the definitions differ in many ways, it is important to remember that there is no single, correct definition. This variety points to the multitude of factors that affect leadership and the different perspectives from which to view it. There is some agreement, however, that changes in leadership definitions are focusing much more on today's need for collective, shared leadership.

Theories of Leadership

One of the earliest leadership theories was the Great Man theory, which maintained that leaders were distinguishable from followers by fixed, inborn traits that were applicable across all situations (Galton, 1869). Research focused on identifying these abilities and traits believed to separate leaders from followers, but, for the most part, these efforts failed to find conclusive evidence that leaders and followers were truly different (Stogdill, 1974).

Since the Great Man theory, research efforts have fluctuated with respect to issues like the behavior of leaders, the modifications they make based on the followers and the situation, and the characteristics and effects of transactional and transformational leaders. Situational Leadership theory inspired further analysis of the relationship among leader behaviors, followers' satisfaction and performance, and the situation of the leadership experiences (Blake & Mouton, 1985; Hersey & Blanchard, 1982). Stogdill (1974), Bass (1981), Avolio, Bass, and Jung (1999), Aarons (2006), and Northouse (2014) supported the notion that leadership effectiveness is highly dependent on the relationship between leader characteristics and the demands of specific situations. The past few decades have seen an interest in Transactional and Transformational Leadership theories (Bennis & Nanus, 1985; Hollander & Offerman, 1990; Yammarino & Bass, 1990). The basic difference in these two models is in the process by which the leader is thought to motivate followers. Transactional leaders motivate through contingency rewards and negative feedback, while transformational leaders inspire performance beyond ordinary expectations as they create a sense of mission and encourage new ways of thinking.

The Center for Creative Leadership offers an emerging theory of leadership that moves beyond a mainstream view of leadership toward a more connected or distributed view of leadership focusing on systems and processes that involve multiple people working together. This concept of leadership involves leaders leading laterally, across boundaries, or in nonauthority contexts. As opposed to traditional theories, which focus on the characteristics and abilities of individuals, the emerging view of leadership is one that requires relationship and community building as key aspects of producing leadership (Martin, 2007).

21st-Century Leadership

In the past two decades, the world has changed exponentially. Through various forms of technology and social networks, students have instant and constant access to each other and the world. According to the Kaiser Family Foundation at the Pew Research Center, children ages 8–18 spend 7 hours per day with media, and the typical teen sends 3,000 text messages per month (Media Literacy Clearinghouse, n.d.). There are 50 million tweets sent daily and 31 billion Google searches per month (Media Literacy Clearinghouse, n.d.). This digital interconnectedness offers invaluable opportunities to learn in multiple and creative settings, understand worldwide complexities, and ultimately, work as a global society.

Additionally, the increase in use of technology among today's youth might change the types of behaviors that build leadership potential. Although participation in athletics and clubs have been important in developing leadership skills of current leaders, the reliance of today's youth on social networking and online gaming may diminish the value of such activities for leadership development in the future. Reeves, Malone, and O'Driscoll (2008) discussed the importance of multiplayer online gaming in developing young people's sense of teamwork, mission accomplishment, and goal setting. The way in which children and adolescents learn how to interact with one another is also affected by computer and mobile technology. Social networking, blogs, e-mail, and instant messaging communication occurs at younger and younger ages, affecting communication preferences that will, in turn, affect communication preferences later in life (Murphy & Johnson, 2011).

Educator Karl Fisch (2012) stated that we are currently preparing students for jobs that don't exist, using technologies that haven't been invented, in order to solve problems we don't even know are problems yet. Gordon (2013) estimated that today's learner will have 10–14 jobs by the age of 38 and that many jobs that will be in demand in years to come may not exist today.

The Partnership for 21st Century Skills (P21) is a national organization that combines the efforts of education, business, and government to work toward a common vision of 21st-century learning for all students. The organization was formed in 2002 through the joint efforts of the United States Department of Education and many corporations, such as the AOL Time Warner Foundation, Apple, Microsoft, Cisco, Blackboard, the KnowledgeWorks Foundation, Dell, Junior Achievement, the Corporation for Public Broadcasting, and the National Education Association. The work of this movement indicates that the fundamental changes in the economy, jobs, and businesses are driving new, different skill demands and that today, more than ever, individuals must be able to perform nonroutine, creative tasks if they are to succeed. In 2010, P21, in conjunction with the American Management Association, surveyed more than 2,000 executives about the needs of the 21st-century workforce, and results showed that, overwhelmingly, the four skills seen as priorities for employee development and talent management are *critical thinking, communication skills, collaboration/team-building*, and *creativity/innovation*. These are today's survival skills, not only for career success, but for personal and civic quality of life as well. These are also the skills most needed for leaders in the 21st century.

P21 recognizes leadership as a part of the Life and Career Skills in its Framework for 21st Century Learning. The organization defines 21st-century skills of leadership as the ability to:

» Use interpersonal and problem-solving skills to influence and guide others toward a goal;

» Leverage strengths of others to accomplish a common goal;

» Inspire others to reach their very best via example and selflessness;

» Demonstrate integrity and ethical behavior in using influence and power; and

» Act responsibly with the interests of the larger community in mind. (P21, 2009, p. 7)

George (2010) reported that the hierarchical model of leadership is not as effective in today's world. The craftsman-apprentice model has been replaced by learning organizations, filled with knowledge workers who do not respond to "top down" leadership. Young people, seeking opportunities to lead, are not willing to spend 10 years waiting in line to lead. A new generation of leaders is reshaping the best-led global companies. Leadership for today is more holistic, centered in groups and organizations, rather than individuals. Next generation leaders engage the entire group or organization in heart, mind, spirit, and energy by aligning, empowering, serving, and collaborating toward common goals and sustained, long-term performance. With this people-centered paradigm, leadership development shifts from individual-centered to collective-centered; from a packaged curriculum to an evolving educational process focused on building relationships, embedded in concrete issues identified by participants in the process (Sandmann & Vandenberg, 1995).

Generational Differences and Leadership

In addition to the changing theories of leadership, it is important to consider generational differences and how they may affect students' perspective on leadership. For example, Bennis and Thomas (2002) investigated how one's formative era shapes the character of the leaders. Lee and King (2001) indicated that attitudinal changes between generations show differences in people's willingness to respect formal authority, indicating that today, more than ever, leadership is more about influence than authority. This generational change means that leaders of today will need to find new ways to motivate and meet the needs of this generation and those to follow. Leaders often are harder to recognize by their titles, and job descriptions of leaders may indicate a wide range of expectations for what the person in that job will actually do or the style he or she will use to lead.

Although commonalities across generations of leaders do exist, from Baby Boomers to Generation X, to the Millennials/Generation Y, each generation has developed its own paradigm of life and distinctive voice (Elmore, 2001; Howe & Strauss, 2000). While the leadership style of the Senior Generation was more directive and "command-and-control," Generations X and Y view leadership as less hierarchical and more participative. Figure 16.1, inspired by George Barna of the Barna Research Group and modified by Elmore (2001), depicts changing generations of thought since 1900. According to Elmore, the youth of today have always lived with fast-paced change. They can process visuals much faster than adults, are accustomed to multitasking, and get bored quickly. To Millennials, life is like a smorgasbord from which they may pick and choose as well as mix and match everything from music, to courses, to religion. With so many options available, the youth of today may need more guidance in critical thinking and decision making as they develop themselves as leaders. This generation is already engaged in community problem solving, and they want to fix the world. This view may cause them to seek out experiences that transform them as they take their place as leaders.

Trends in Leadership

In 2007, researchers at the Center for Creative Leadership asked 247 senior executives around the globe about 10 leadership trends (Criswell & Martin, 2007). From this study, important patterns emerged focusing on talent, innovation, collaboration, and globalization (see Table 16.1).

Given these emerging trends in leadership, educators must recognize the link between leadership and emotional intelligence. Key leadership skills and perspectives are related to one's intrapersonal skills, self-knowledge and understanding, and one's interpersonal skills (skills in building and maintaining relationships with others).

Emotional Intelligence and Leadership

In 2003, the Center for Creative Leadership published a report (Leslie, 2003) on the relationship between leadership skills and emotional intelligence. The sam-

		Seniors	Builders	Boomers	Generation X	Millennials
1.	Era They Were Born	1900–1928	1929–1945	1946–1964	1965–1983	1984–2001
2.	Worldview	Manifest destiny	Be grateful you have a job	You owe me	Relate to me	Life is a cafeteria
3.	Attitude to Authority	Respect them	Endure them	Replace them	Ignore them	Choose them
4.	Role of Relationships	Long-term	Significant	Limited; useful	Central; caring	Global
5.	Value Systems	Traditional	Conserva-tive	Self-based	Media	Shop around
6.	Role of Career	Loyalty	Means for living	Central focus	Irritant	A place to serve
7.	Schedules	Responsible	Mellow	Frantic	Aimless	Volatile
8.	Technology	What's that?	Hope to outlive it	Master it	Enjoy it	Employ it
9.	Market They Introduce	Commod-ities	Goods	Services	Experiences	Transforma-tions
10.	View of Future	Uncertain	Seek to stabilize	Create it	Hopeless	Optimistic

Figure 16.1. Generational changes.

ple for this study included 302 managers attending a leadership development program at the center in 2000. Each participant completed the Benchmarks® assessment, a 360-degree, multirater feedback tool and the BarOn EQ-i, a self-report measurement of emotional intelligence for adults. Benchmarks® is based on 15 years of work and research conducted by the center in the area of leadership and focuses on 16 key leadership skills and perspectives. The BarOn EQ-i (Bar-On, 1997) is the most widely used assessment of emotional intelligence and has a large body of scientific data showing its reliability and accuracy. The study found that higher levels of emotional intelligence are positively correlated with leadership performance in 10 of the 16 areas measured by Benchmarks®: (a) participative management, (b) putting people at ease, (c) self-awareness, (d) balance between personal life and work, (e) straightforwardness and composure, (f) building and mending relationships, (g) doing whatever it takes, (h) decisiveness, (i) confronting problem employees, and (j) change management.

Bradberry and Su (2006) examined the effect of emotional intelligence on the job performance of leaders, and they reported that emotional intelligence provides a good framework for people to understand and manage emotions. Bradberry and

TABLE 16.1
Trends in Leadership

Trend	Explanation	Educational Needs
The Rise of Complex Challenges	The breadth and intensity of change will continue to rise due to factors such as market dynamics, a shortage of talent, and globalization.	The need to develop new leadership skills such as co-inquiry, paying attention, risk-taking, adaptability, and navigating challenges.
The Innovation Revolution	Organizations are looking for the next big thing and people who have unique ideas to find that next big thing.	The need to develop more creative thinkers and people willing to take risks.
The Art of Virtual Leadership	Organizations are continually asked to bridge cultural, geographical, and functional boundaries, which require skills different from face-to-face leadership.	The need to develop people who have excellent written and oral communication skills.
Collaboration Nation	In a complex, global environment with new technology, collaboration is essential to the work of leaders.	The need to develop skills of relationship-building, collaboration, and innovation.
The World of Interruption	Leaders often exist in work environments in which they are frequently interrupted, thus decreasing productivity and increasing frustration.	The need to develop strategies for managing lives through maintaining focus and overcoming distractions.
Authentic Leadership	Authentic leaders are able to conduct their jobs without compromising their values, beliefs, or personality.	The need to develop intrapersonal skills, self-understanding, clarity of beliefs, and purpose.
Fallout From the Baby Boom and Filling the Leadership Void	With the approximate 83 million individuals who will start leaving the workforce in 4 years, organizations are likely to experience a loss of institutional vision, knowledge, networks, and historical context.	The need for organizations to find ways to attract and retain older workers and younger workers.
Leadership for Longevity	As leaders attempt to lead and live in an increasingly complex world, improved levels of stress, health, diet, and fitness will be necessary to ensure a productive and sustainable career.	The need to help young leaders understand the need for exercise, proper diet, sleep, and stress management.
The Shift From Autocratic to Participative Leadership	Leaders predict that future success of leaders will be the ability to collaborate and focus on the team rather than the individual.	The need to develop interpersonal skills and emotional intelligence.

Note. From *10 Trends: A Study of Senior Executives' Views on the Future*, by C. Criswell and A. Martin, 2007, Greensboro, NC: Center for Creative Leadership. Copyright ©2007 by Center for Creative Leadership.

Su (2006) also concluded that "leaders who use emotional intelligence to build solid relationships are likely to perform well in their jobs" (p. 65).

Research on Youth Leadership Development

Although the majority of research in the area of leadership addresses adults, studies focusing on leadership and youth are increasing. Newer studies have gained insight into factors that contribute to leadership development from ages 2–29.

In a recent study of early childhood and leadership, Popper and Mayseless (2007) identified developmental antecedents of leadership such as self-confidence, a prosocial and caring orientation, optimism, and openness/curiosity/flexibility. Murphy and Johnson (2011) posited that leadership behaviors can be observed in early childhood. Included in their model are precursors for individual variables, such as communication, personality, social-emotional intelligence; developmental factors, such as parenting styles and learning experiences; and self-management, such as self-efficacy, coping styles, and motivation. According to Murphy and Johnson (2011), these building blocks, in concert with the child's context of development, are related to leader behaviors, which, in turn, predict leader outcomes.

Another early temperament trait associated with leadership behavior is the approach/withdrawal dimension, which reflects the quality of the child's reaction to the new and unfamiliar, to novel stimuli such as people, places, food, toys, etc. Caspi and Silva (1995) found that children who were inhibited at age 3 also exhibited a restrained behavioral style and nonassertive interpersonal attitude at age 18. They preferred safe activities, were cautious, were submissive, and were not fond of leadership roles. When assessed again at age 26, Caspi et al. (2003) found those children who were inhibited at age 3 continued to prefer that others take charge and did not enjoy being the center of attention. Children who had demonstrated less inhibition at age 3, were found to score higher in extraversion and social skills at age 17 and again at 29, and these skills related to higher leadership potential, both in terms of leader work duties and transformational leadership (Guerin et al., 2011).

From a developmental psychology perspective, family structure and parenting can have a powerful influence on leadership in later life. According to Murphy and Johnson (2011) and Popper and Mayseless (2007), parents who are authoritarian, with firm rules and control, often have teenagers who are less likely to be leaders, with poor communication and decision-making skills. Neglectful, uninvolved parents tend to have teenagers with low social competence and weak self-control. Indulgent parents who provide warmth and few rules often produce teenagers with little self-control and low social competence. On the other hand, authoritative parents encourage independence with limits. They are assertive, but not intrusive and restrictive. Teens with authoritative parents tend to be more socially competent and self-reliant than teens raised under different parenting styles (Murphy and Johnson, 2011; Popper and Mayseless, 2007). Additionally, in the study of family environment's effects on leadership, Avolio, Rotundo, & Walumbwa (2009) found that exposing children and adolescents to experiences that promote self-management and emotional control, social skill development, team skills, and early leadership experiences may foster later leader development.

Factors related to children's birth order, family size, and parental attention can affect the type of leader one becomes (Murphy & Johnson, 2011). The child's age relative to peers might also influence leader development. In Gladwell's (2008) book, *Outliers*, he summarized research about the success that soccer and hockey players enjoy just by being older than others on their teams. Dhuey and Lipscomb (2008) found that high school students who are relatively old for their grades were more likely to emerge as leaders.

Murphy and Johnson (2011) have developed a lifespan approach to leader development, which includes developmental stages, societal expectations, and time in history. They conclude that leadership development occurs more readily in childhood and adolescence than in adulthood because one's behavior, personality, and skills are more malleable at a young age than they are in adulthood. They also state that one's development to become a leader is a self-reinforcing process, so as one gains greater leadership efficacy, or confidence in one's ability to lead a group, that individual is more likely to engage in leadership experiences, which will help increase leader effectiveness.

Intelligence is generally positively related to leadership, as those with stronger verbal skills, reasoning, and problem-solving abilities may contribute to leader capacity (Bass & Bass, 2008). The Fullerton Longitudinal Study (FLS) is an ongoing, long-term, and longitudinal research project designed to study participants from ages 2–29. According to Day (2011), the study traces, among other things, the developmental pathways from individual differences in early childhood to self-rated adult leadership potential, as well as leader emergence. FLS researchers Judge, Colbert, and Ilies (2004) argued that intelligence is important for leadership development due to the following: (a) the complexity of the leadership position requires higher levels of intelligence, (b) intelligent leaders are better problem solvers, and (c) intelligent leaders are more creative and motivate their followers to be more creative. Additionally, Guerin et al. (2011) concluded that, over time, adolescents with greater intellectual resources may pursue experiences that build their capacity to lead, qualify them to assume positions of leadership, or influence others' perceptions of them as leaders.

To determine aspects of personality that are building blocks of leadership, FLS researchers Judge, Bono, Ilies, and Gerhardt (2002) used the Five Factor Model (FFM), a taxonomy for classifying the following personality traits:

» openness to experience;
» conscientiousness;
» extraversion;
» agreeableness; and
» neuroticism.

Among the five dimensions of the FFM, Judge et al. (2002) determined that the dimension of extraversion "is the most important trait of leaders and effective leadership" (p. 773). Extraversion refers to the amount and quality of interpersonal interaction characteristic of an individual. Extraverts usually are warm, assertive, active, and talkative, and they like being around people, like excitement, and tend to be cheerful and energetic. Bono and Judge (2004) found that extraversion was the strongest correlate of ratings of transformational leadership and extraverted adolescents more frequently engage in behaviors typical of leaders.

Studies pertaining to leadership and gender in youth have indicated some differences. Given that society holds different expectations for boys and girls, boys and girls learn to lead differently (Murphy & Reichard, 2011). Young boys interact with same-sex peers in an enabling style, involving assertiveness, competition, and disagreement, while girls develop constricting habits of interaction including turn taking and providing support. Additionally, different behavior leads to effective leadership for young boys and girls. For example, girls who have strong social skills and social intelligence and whose classmates liked them are more likely to be seen as leaders, whereas these factors do not predict leadership for young boys. Day and Antonakis (2012) reported that, for girls, the gap between the behaviors that predict leadership success at a young age are not the same as those that define leader success in later years. For example, when adult women are overly communal, they can be perceived as un-leader-like, but when they are overly independent and lack communal behavior, they can be perceived as un-woman-like. In either case, the outcome is detrimental to perceptions of female leaders' effectiveness. This inconsistency can cause girls to lose the motivation and confidence to lead.

Nemerowicz and Rosi (2013) found that both fourth- and fifth-grade boys and girls preferred to depict their own gender as the leader; however, boys did so 95% of the time as compared to 53% for girls. In a study of students in grades 6–11, Karnes and D'Ilio (1989) found that the girls in both groups perceived most leadership roles to be suitable for either gender, whereas the boys held more traditional stereotypical views. Karnes and D'Ilio (1989) also found significant differences favoring girls on emotional stability, dominance, and the secondary factor of independence using the High School Personality Questionnaire (HSPQ;

Cattell, Cattell, & Johns, 1984) with gifted students in grades 6–11. Karnes and Riley (2005) found that, when asked, "Who are the three greatest leaders of this century?", 29.1% of the 6th- through 11th-grade girls participating in the Leadership Gifted Studies Program listed their mother, while 2.9% of the boys in the program listed their father. The most frequent response made by boys in the Leadership Studies Program sample was Martin Luther King, Jr. Aside from mothers and teachers, female leaders were not frequently mentioned, which indicates more traditional views of leadership were reflected in this study.

Studies have shown that psychological type can be a good predictor of leadership style and behavior (Barr & Barr, 1989; Campbell & Velsor, 1985; Lawrence, 1982; McCaulley & Staff of the Center for Applications of Psychological Type, 1990; Myers & Myers, 1980). Alvino (1989) reviewed data collected using the Myers-Briggs Type Indicator with gifted students and young adults. He found that high school student leaders who were not necessarily identified as gifted fell predominantly into a group described as analytical managers of facts and details, practical organizers, imaginative harmonizers of people, and warmly enthusiastic planners of change. Leaders in student government activities fell predominantly into a group described as independent, enthusiastic, intuitive, aggressive, and innovative.

Several studies have indicated that participation in extracurricular and community activities provides unique opportunities for students to belong and contribute to a group, as well as to experience success (Bass, 1981; Bennett, 1986; McNamara, Haensly, Lupkowski, & Edlind, 1985; Stogdill, 1974). Using the Leadership Strengths Indicator (Ellis, 1990) with disadvantaged youth ages 10–15, Riley and Karnes (1994a) found that students' scores fell within the normal range. A significant difference favoring boys was found in the scale High Level Participator in Group Activities. Slight nonsignificant differences were found among the Enjoys Group Activities, Journalistic, and Courageous scales. The same measure was administered to intellectually gifted students in grades 4–6, and significant differences were found favoring girls on two scales, Sympathetic and Conscientious, and the total score (Riley & Karnes, 1994b). Intellectually gifted students in grades 6–12 in suburban and rural settings also were administered the same instrument, and no significant differences were found (Abel & Karnes, 1993). Wade and Putnam (1995) found that the willingness of gifted high school sophomores and juniors to participate in extracurricular and community activities would be increased by providing them opportunities for input, choice, responsibility, and meaningful influence. These studies emphasized the importance of extracurricular activities and group work in the development of leadership potential.

Leadership and Giftedness

Unique parallels exist between the concepts of giftedness and leadership. Definitions in both areas are expanding, becoming more inclusive, and considering cultural and situational factors. Identification and assessment procedures for both giftedness and leadership also have developed to reflect the complexity and multidimensionality of the concepts.

Of all of the types of giftedness set forth in the various state and federal definitions, leadership is one of the least recognized areas. The Marland report (1972) gave the first formal federal definition of giftedness, which included "leadership ability" as one of six domains of giftedness. The more recent federal definition of gifted and talented students (Javits Act, 1988) states:

> The term "gifted and talented students" means children and youth who give evidence of high performance capability in such areas as intellectual, creative, artistic, or leadership capacity, or in specific academic fields; and who require services or activities not ordinarily provided by the schools in order to develop such capabilities fully. (P.L.100–297, Sec. 4103. Definitions)

Although most states accept this federal definition in their legislation and in their written program plans, the majority of special programs focus primarily on intellectual, academic, creative, and artistic capabilities. Stephens and Karnes (2000) found that only 18 states recognize leadership as a part of the state definition. Although leadership has been included in formal definitions for more than 30 years, many agree that it remains the most neglected and least served of the areas of giftedness (Chan, 2000; Hays, 1993; Huckaby & Sperling, 1981; Karnes & Bean, 1996; Roach et al., 1999; Smith, Smith, & Barnette, 1991). This may be due to the intricate nature of the concept of leadership (Bass & Stogdill, 1990) and the lack of agreement it yields (Edmunds & Yewchuk, 1996; Simonton, 1995). Others have indicated that the inattention to leadership may be due to the lack of valid and reliable measures of leadership ability (Edmunds, 1998; Jarosewich, Pfeiffer, & Morris, 2002) or the lack of research connecting youth leadership behavior/training with adult leadership performance (Foster, 1981; Huckaby & Sperling, 1981; Roach et al., 1999).

Whatever reasons may exist, there are too few studies devoted to leadership and giftedness, too few states that identify leadership among the gifted, and too few in-school leadership development programs designed for students with strong leadership potential. Furthermore, every year, millions of dollars are spent for leadership training in business and industry, the military, government, religion, and sports, but few dollars are spent for leadership education and development of children and youth in elementary and secondary schools.

Although gifted students often are deemed the future leaders at local, state, national, and international levels, little has been or is being undertaken to identify young leaders and help them develop their leadership potential. According to Wade and Putnam (1995), all cultures need role models, and most professions depend upon people who exercise intelligence, creativity, and critical judgment in decision making. Unfortunately, leadership is the most controversial and neglected area in gifted education (Lindsay, 1988), with few gifted programs incorporating leadership into their curriculum (Florey & Dorf, 1986). Schools must go beyond educating the gifted for followship and must become involved in understanding the fundamentals of leadership and incorporating it into the school curriculum (Foster & Silverman, 1988).

Intelligence has been researched as a factor in leader emergence because smarter leaders are thought to be more effective leaders. Intelligence, as it relates to understanding people and social situations, tends to be more associated with effective leadership than cognitive ability (Murphy & Reichard, 2011). One study from the larger Fuller Longitudinal Study (Gottfried, Gottfried et al., 2011) investigated potential relationships between intelligence, childhood intrinsic motivation, adolescent intrinsic motivation, and motivation to lead in adulthood. There were no significant relationships between intelligence and any of the motivation outcomes (intrinsic or leadership motivation), however children with high academic intrinsic motivation demonstrated high levels of affective-identity and noncalculative motivation to lead as adults.

There are, however, many connections between the characteristics used to describe an effective leader and a gifted individual. Both often are highly verbal, socially sensitive, visionary, problem solvers, critical and creative thinkers, initiators, responsible, and self-sufficient (Black, 1984; Chauvin & Karnes, 1983; Plowman, 1981). Terman's (1925) classic study of the gifted revealed that gifted students often were the leaders in school. Hollingworth (1926) indicated that, among a group of children with average intelligence, the IQ of leaders was likely to fall between 115 and 130. Schakel (1984) found that, in comparison with nonintellectually gifted students, intellectually gifted students could be characterized as visionary leaders, whereas nongifted students seemed to be organizational leaders.

Individuals vary considerably in leadership ability, just as they do in intellectual, academic, creative, artistic, and other abilities; however, the following leadership skills are often observed in gifted children:

» acting responsibly in social situations;
» accurately reading the feelings of others;
» displaying good social judgment;

» projecting a confident self-image;
» motivating others;
» getting along with others;
» instilling trust and confidence in others;
» showing flexibility and comfort with divergent points of view;
» speaking well in front of others; and
» demonstrating social savvy, including respect for authority, rules, and social conventions.

Although the need for more effective leaders is clear and gifted students typically possess the characteristics to become effective leaders, the development of leadership skills in gifted youth often is neglected.

Screening and Identification of Gifted Leaders

The status of screening and identification instruments in leadership for elementary and secondary youth is limited (Karnes & Meriweather-Bean, 1991). Instruments with validity and reliability are limited in number. All vary on several aspects, including grades or ages, number of items specific to leadership, response modes, scoring procedures interpretation, and scores rendered. Current measures include:

» The Eby Gifted Behavior Index (Eby, 1989);
» The Gifted and Talented Evaluation Scales (Gilliam, Carpenter, & Christensen, 1996);
» The Gifted Education Scale–Second Edition (Henage, McCarney, & Anderson, 1998);
» The High School Personality Questionnaire (Cattell et al., 1984);
» Khatena-Morse Multitalent Perception Inventory (Khatena & Morse, 1994);
» Leadership: A Skill and Behavior Scale (Sisk & Rosselli, 1987);
» The Leadership Characteristics (Part IV) of the Scales for Rating the Behavioral Characteristics of Superior Students: Revised Edition (Renzulli et al., 2002);
» Myers-Briggs Type Indicator (Myers & McCaulley, 1985);
» Murphy-Meisgeier Type Indicator for Children (Meisgeier & Murphy, 1987);
» The Gifted Rating Scales (GRS; Pfeiffer & Jarosewich, 2003);
» Roets Rating Scale for Leadership (Roets, 1986);
» Student Leadership Practices Inventory (Kouzes & Posner, 2006); and
» Student Talent and Risk Profile (Institute for Behavioral Research in Creativity, 1990).

Resources for Leadership Development

The acquisition and application of the necessary leadership concepts and skills (based on those identified as necessary to function as an adult leader in society) are the basis for the Leadership Development Program (Karnes & Chauvin, 2000b). The Leadership Skills Inventory (LSI; Karnes & Chauvin, 2000a), a diagnostic-prescriptive instrument, has nine subscales: fundamentals of leadership, written communication, speech communication, character building, decision making, group dynamics, problem solving, personal development, and planning. Eight samples of students in grade 4 through junior college in seven states were included in the standardization. Criterion and content validity studies have been conducted. Reliability data are reported in the manual.

Upon beginning a leadership program, the students are administered the LSI, which is a self-rating and self-scoring instrument. After they complete the inventory, scores are plotted on the LSI Profile Sheet, which graphically depicts their strengths and weaknesses in leadership concepts and skills on the nine subscales. The concepts and skills that have been acquired and those in need of strengthening are immediately apparent. This information provides the teacher with the necessary data to assist the student in planning the appropriate instructional activities for every item on the LSI. One or more instructional strategies for each item are provided in the Leadership Development Program. The teacher does not have to incorporate all of the activities, only those that will provide the improvement necessary to become an effective leader based on the student's self-perceived strengths and weaknesses. Group discussions, simulations, and role-playing activities are the primary vehicle for learning, and they are student-centered rather than teacher-directed.

Crucial to the program is the application of the acquired leadership concepts and skills, which is facilitated through developing and implementing a "Plan for Leadership." After the completion of the instructional component, each student identifies an area in which he or she may initiate something new or change an already existing area of need in his or her school, community, or religious affiliation. The plan must have two major purposes: (a) to bring about desirable changes in the behavior of others and (b) to solve a major problem or work toward major improvements. Within the abilities of the students, it should be realistic, well-sequenced, and comprehensive. The student writes a plan with an overall goal with accompanying objectives, activities, resources, timelines, and methods for evaluation. Each plan developed is presented in class for peer review. An example of a completed plan and the types of plans prepared by male and female students for the school, community, and religious affiliation and the numbers of plans developed during each year of the program have been described by Karnes and Meriweather (1989).

The instrument and the materials are the foundation of the Leadership Studies Program, a one-week summer residential experience, which has been validated (Karnes, Meriweather, & D'Ilio, 1987). The statistical analysis of the data collected in the programs indicates pre- and postassessment gains to be significant ($p = .01$).

After a careful analysis of all of the program components, including the nine instructional areas necessary for being a leader and the plan for leadership, teachers, administrative decision makers, and community leaders can readily select the format of the program appropriate for their school and town. It may be an ongoing component of a resource enrichment program, conducted as a separate class at the junior or senior high school level, or the appropriate components may be included in English, speech, social studies, and other academic courses. Mentorship and internship provisions for leadership growth also should be made readily available to students after the completion of the instructional activities.

Another approach to examining leadership in youth is the Leadership Strengths Indicator (Ellis, 1990), a 40-item self-report questionnaire designed to obtain students' evaluations of their leadership traits and abilities. Eight cluster scores and an overall total leadership score are rendered on the 40-item self-report instrument. The eight clusters contain two to six items within the following areas: enjoys group activities, key individual in group activities, high-level participator in group activities, journalistic, sympathetic, confident, courageous, conscientious, and self-confident. The response choices on the rating scale are *excellent*, *very good*, *better than most*, *okay*, and *not so good*. The indicator is intended to be a discussion starter for guidance and leadership development classes designed for students in grades 6–12. The psychometric properties, including validity and reliability, are reported in the manual.

Research has been conducted using the indicator with gifted students. Disadvantaged gifted students ranging in age from 10–15 had scores within the normal range. A significant difference on Cluster Scale III, high-level participator in group activities, was found favoring boys (Riley & Karnes, 1994a). Rural and suburban gifted high school youth were compared with no significant differences found (Abel & Karnes, 1993).

Parker (1989) proposed a leadership model designed to serve as the foundation for gifted programs. According to the theory on which her Leadership Training Model is based, leadership potential can be developed through the strengthening of four essential components: cognition, problem solving, interpersonal communication, and decision making. In their book, *Developing Creative Leadership*, Parker and Begnaud (2003) included an overview of leadership theory and suggested strategies for developing creative leadership in gifted students, as well as a variety of leadership units designed for use with gifted students of all ages.

For almost three decades, commercially prepared instructional materials for teaching leadership have been available. As early as 1980, Magoon and Jellen designed 25 strategies for developing leadership. Designed, according to the authors, to assist students in becoming future leaders by acquiring the skills of leading, the materials offer instructional assistance such as a checklist for committee work, a group observation scale, and a listing of references.

One of the more recent contribution to resources for leadership development is *Changing Tomorrow: Leadership Curriculum for High-Ability High School Students*, by Avery and VanTassel-Baska (2013). The curriculum includes 10 lessons in leadership skill development focusing on biographical studies, generalizations about the concept of leadership, and ideas and exercises adapted from contemporary leadership literature. Complete with pre- and postassessment rubrics, this resource is aligned with 21st-century skills, the Common Core State Standards for English Language Arts, and the NAGC Pre-K–Grade 12 Gifted Education Programming Standards. It is available at three grade levels.

The Leadership Series, which contains six instructional units in analyzing leadership, group skills, self-esteem, communication skills, values and goal setting, and social responsibility, was designed by House (1980). Based on Bloom's (1956) Taxonomy of Educational Objectives, each unit contains 30 instructional activities with reproducible worksheets. Objectives with emphasis on the high thinking levels of analysis, synthesis, and evaluation are the basis of the program.

A curricular unit on leadership for upper elementary and junior high school gifted youth was developed by Gallagher (1982). Content specialists and teachers of the gifted worked to construct the instructional lessons, which had three specific objectives: to illustrate a particular leadership concept, to provide opportunities for the students to understand and internalize the concepts, and to develop the students' higher level thinking skills. Three types of leaders were highlighted in the lesson plans: traditional, legal-rational, and charismatic. The activities in each lesson are grouped at three levels: awareness, instructional, and extension. Reproducibles for student use are included in the materials. An annotated bibliography on leadership and evaluation forms for students and parents are provided for the teacher.

Leadership: A Skills Training Program (Roets, 1997) is an instructional program for students ages 8–18. The instructional activities are based on four themes: people of achievement, language of leadership, project planning, and debate and discussion. Suggested readings for young people, both fiction and nonfiction, and a list of readings for adults are provided.

Several books directed to elementary and secondary school youth and teachers are available, and each contains many instructional activities for leadership training. The goals of the leadership materials presented in *Leadership Education: Developing Skills for Youth* (Richardson & Feldhusen, 1987), which had previously been developed by Feldhusen, Hynes, and Richardson (1977) with a grant in vocational-technical education, are to develop the social skills of leadership and an understanding on the part of the student as a potential leader. The 11 chapters include an introduction to leadership, outcomes of leadership education, personal characteristics of effective leaders, skills of a group leader, communication skills for leaders, leadership skills for group members, group goals development, group activity plans, committee organization, parliamentary procedure skills, and leadership and special abilities. Feldhusen and Kennedy (1986) reported evaluation results on the use of the materials in a summer leadership program with secondary gifted youth.

Sisk and Shallcross (1986) developed a guide, *Leadership: Making Things Happen*, to help clarify the meaning of leaders and leadership. The book is divided into 10 chapters: What Is Leadership, Self-Understanding, Intuitive Powers, Visual Imagery, Communication, Motivation, Creative Problem-Solving Process, Futuristics, Women in Leadership Positions, and Learning Styles. Activities presented in each chapter may be used in a wide variety of instructional situations within schools. References for each topic are presented at the end of each chapter.

Sisk and Roselli (1987) coauthored *Leadership: A Special Kind of Giftedness* to assist in the understanding of the concepts of leadership and in applying current theories to personal lives and teaching. The book includes a definition of leadership, the theories, a model for planning and developing leadership training activities, a succinct summary of teaching/learning models, and a discussion on issues and trends in leadership. The four elements of the model developed by Sisk are characteristics of gifted leadership, selected teaching strategies, teaching/learning models, and key concepts. Twenty lessons are provided.

Lead On (Hagemann & Newman, 1999) helps educators and students address leadership problems more effectively. The book offers strategies for students and teachers to work together as they develop interpersonal and intrapersonal skills. Objectives, procedures, and extended activities provide cross-curricular connections, best practices, and real-life leadership applications for the 21st century.

The outstanding leadership stories of girls are highlighted in *Girls and Young Women Leading the Way* (Karnes & Bean, 1993). Twenty biographies of girls from elementary school through college are provided as role models for leadership. Each story contains personal information followed by a detailed overview of leadership accomplishment. There are questions to challenge the reader to leadership and a listing of appropriate agencies/organizations from which to gain more information. Quotations from nationally known female leaders are included to provide motivation and inspiration. Suggestions for actions to record in a leadership notebook and an extensive reading list on female leaders from kindergarten to the young adult level are provided.

The second edition of *Leadership for Students: A Guide for Young Leaders* (Karnes & Bean, 2010), a book for young leaders ages 8–18, contains guidance and advice about moving into leadership positions in the home, school, and community. The book contains chapters on leadership definitions, self-assessment of leadership, opportunities and training for leadership, influence and encouragement from others, great leaders, and advice to others. Figures 16.2 through 16.5 are examples of activities from the book that help extend students' views of leadership and assist them in planning for leadership. The book was designed to be interactive through the use of the Leadership Action Journal, which allows students to record their thoughts and actions pertaining to leaders and leadership. Stories of young leaders offer examples of peers and explain how they became leaders.

Incorporating Leadership Into the Curriculum for Gifted Students

The goal of cultivating young leaders is of such critical importance to the individual and to society that it should be made an integral part of school and community programs for youth. Without more purposeful and intentional approaches to developing young leaders, only a few students are likely to emerge as effective adult leaders, and the world will continue to be in need of more. Given the parallels between characteristics of effective leaders and gifted individuals, leadership education is a natural fit. And, with the flexibility that often exists in the curriculum for gifted learners, programs and services for the gifted present environments that are most conducive to leadership development.

Toward this end, the concept of leadership must be a more direct part of the curriculum. It also must be broadened from the narrow view of leadership as elected or appointed positions in politics, government, business, or industry, to an expanded view of leadership permeating all dimensions of life, across all disciplines, ages, cultures, and levels of society. Leadership can and should be infused into the broad-based concepts, themes, and issues of the curriculum for gifted students. Leadership should be explored as it connects to power, symbols, culture, patterns, relationships, and values. The conceptual frameworks for thinking about leadership are valuable parts of one's leadership development.

There are many approaches that could prepare gifted learners for leadership roles. Instructional units on leadership should be taught in programs for the gifted. These units could include the study of the history of leadership, great leaders, ethical dimensions of leadership, theories and styles of leadership, leadership across cultures, leadership and futurism, and so on.

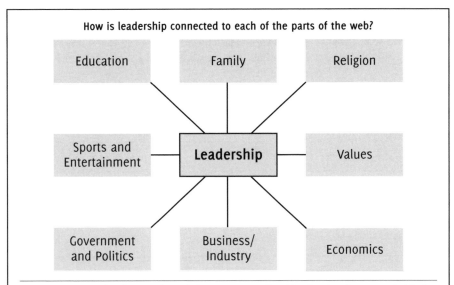

How is leadership connected to each of the parts of the web?

Figure 16.2. Leadership web activity. From *Leadership for Students: A Guide for Young Leaders* (2nd ed., p. 123), by F. A. Karnes and S. M. Bean, 2010, Waco, TX: Prufrock Press. Copyright 2010 by Prufrock Press. Reprinted with permission.

Using books, journals, and online resources to gather information about great leaders of the past and present, complete the Leadership Matrix by writing names in the blanks. Be sure to include female and male leaders, as well as those from different ethnic and religious backgrounds.

Leaders in . . .	International	National	State	Community/ Regional
Business/Industry				
Education				
Government				
Humanities				
Mathematics				
Medicine				
Performing Arts				
Politics				
Religion				
Science/ Technology				
Sports				

Figure 16.3. Great leaders matrix. From *Leadership for Students: A Guide for Young Leaders* (2nd ed., p. 169), by F. A. Karnes and S. M. Bean, 2010, Waco, TX: Prufrock Press. Copyright 2010 by Prufrock Press. Reprinted with permission.

Research how leadership has been demonstrated throughout history. Make brief notes about how leaders worked with people in each historical situation. Then compare these notes to how leaders in today's society work. How are they the same? Different?

Tribal Leadership_____
_____
_____

Leadership in Royalty _____
_____
_____

Democratic Leadership _____
_____
_____

Cooperative or Shared Leadership_____
_____
_____

Leadership in Today's Society_____
_____
_____

Figure 16.4. Changes in leadership over time activity. From *Leadership for Students: A Guide for Young Leaders* (2nd ed., p. 126), by F. A. Karnes and S. M. Bean, 2010, Waco, TX: Prufrock Press. Copyright 2010 by Prufrock Press. Reprinted with permission.

My goal: _____
_____
_____

Objectives: _____
_____
_____

Activities: _____
_____
_____

Resources/People: _____
_____
_____

Timeline:_____
_____
_____

Other: _____
_____
_____

Figure 16.5. Leadership development plan activity. From *Leadership for Students: A Guide for Young Leaders* (2nd ed., p. 183), by F. A. Karnes and S. M. Bean, 2010, Waco, TX: Prufrock Press. Copyright 2010 by Prufrock Press. Reprinted with permission.

Education about leadership is important, but it is not enough. Even those individuals with extensive knowledge about leadership may be poor leaders. Knowing what to do is not the same as knowing when, where, and how to do it. The skills of leadership are significant, too. Leadership through experience begins with the development of intrapersonal and interpersonal skills. Gifted students need guidance in self-understanding and access to their own feelings and emotions, examining individual strengths and limitations, accepting those that cannot be changed, and setting goals to develop areas needed for personal growth and human relations. Also critical to leadership skills is the ability to see events from the perspective of another, understand and relate to others, and perceive human needs and motivations. Gardner (1990) referred to these skills as the crowning capacity of the human condition, which supersedes and presides over other forms of intelligence. Teachers may use journaling, bibliotherapy, and other strategies for self-reflection and analysis. For interpersonal skills to flourish, teachers should intentionally plan group discussions and collaborative work. Problem-solving skills, conflict resolution, role-playing, and creative drama all are strategies that can be used to develop the seeds of early leadership development.

Schools should offer structured courses on leadership for which credit is granted. Within these courses, students may assess their own leadership potential and develop plans of leadership to be implemented in schools, communities, and religious organizations. Students need the opportunity to examine areas of interest to which leadership experiences could be applied.

Mentorships and internships offer real-life experiences for adult leaders to collaborate with schools for the purpose of developing young leaders. Pairing adult leaders with students interested in developing their leadership potential can be a positive practice for student and adult leaders, as well as the school and community.

Riley and Karnes (1996; Karnes & Riley, 2005, 2013) recommended competitions as a vehicle for incorporating leadership in the curriculum and for recognizing and inspiring young leaders. Competitions such as the "I Dare You!" Scholarship, the Kohl's Cares scholarship, and the "Prudential Spirit of Community Awards" recognize those who have achieved in the area of leadership and service. Many such programs reward promising young leaders with scholarships to attend an international leadership conference. These and other such competitions not only can help inspire and recognize young leaders, but can promote goal setting and a sense of autonomy and provide the opportunity for students to meet other young leaders with similar interests and abilities.

Teachers also must be prepared to expose gifted learners to the array of choices for leadership opportunities outside the school. Youth leadership conferences, seminars, and weekend and summer programs are offered through colleges and universities, civic organizations, and business and industries across the nation.

Such services and programs often serve as a spark to ignite the desire for becoming a leader and a boost in self-confidence, which is critical to effective leadership.

Educators must seek every opportunity to identify potential leaders at an early age and infuse leadership concepts and skills into the learning environment for gifted students. The ultimate goal is for each gifted student to understand the importance of leadership, realize his or her potential for leadership, gain the knowledge and skills necessary to be an effective leader, and be exposed to all avenues of leadership development within and outside the school environment. A few ideas include:

» Books, television, and film afford wonderful opportunities for reading about and discussing examples of leaders. Lessons can be learned from biographies and documentaries of the lives people who have influenced others. Many fictional characters also provide good examples of effective and ineffective leadership.

» Volunteer work offers gifted youth the opportunity to observe, model, and practice leadership skills in real-life settings. Volunteering in all types of school, community, and religious organizations can help students appreciate how different groups function in the real world.

» Mentoring relationships with community leaders also introduce gifted youth to real-world leadership experiences. Principals, ministers, rabbis, government officials, police and fire department officers, and heads of nonprofit community agencies are often willing to mentor responsible adolescents.

» Summer leadership courses designed for gifted students, such as those offered by universities and other precollege programs, are intensive, residential programs intended for youth committed to rigorous classroom and service-learning experiences.

Summary

Researchers are still struggling to generate appropriate definitions and theories of leadership. These conceptual frameworks for thinking about leadership bring meaning and relevance to one's leadership development. Although the majority of research on leadership centers on adults, studies focusing on leadership development of children and youth have emerged over the last decade. In particular, the similarities of characteristics and behaviors of effective leaders and gifted learners have been recognized. Leadership screening and identification instruments have been identified, and strategies for incorporating leadership into the curriculum for gifted learners have been discussed.

The primary goal is to heighten students' interest in the concept of leadership and help them to become more reflective and active in their individual pursuits of leadership potential. This goal requires support and commitment from all educators and other interested adults. Purposeful and creative approaches to leadership development must be pursued vigorously by those interested in the challenge.

Teacher Statement

Leaders of any age and type typically have strong intrapersonal and interpersonal skills, and these are, perhaps, the most important skills we should be developing in emerging leaders. As a teacher of gifted learners, one of my primary goals has been to help these bright young people learn skills of leadership, as well as the value of developing themselves as leaders. I have used the information in this chapter to guide me as I help students discover what their own personal strengths and limitations are and how to develop themselves as both followers and leaders. I have found that some of my students may be able to tell others what to do, but they have tremendous difficulty in the role of follower. In my unit on leadership, we discuss the importance of good leaders being good followers, too. Through various group activities, my students engage in leading and following others, team building and problem solving, and collaboration, and with all of these, the debriefing, reflection, and self-assessment sessions are critical.

In addition to the skills of leadership, I have used the resources in this chapter to help me know how to infuse some aspect of leadership into all of the units I teach. For instance, in our study of Europe, the students explored the influence of European leaders in many areas, such as artists, inventors, mathematicians, and politicians. Learning about leaders themselves is of great value. At the conclusion of our units, we reflect on what new understandings we have about leadership and how it changes in different times, with different types of people, and in different lands.

—Beverly Alexander

DISCUSSION QUESTIONS

1. Why is it important to incorporate leadership development into programs and services for gifted children and youth?

2. Why do you think leadership has been one of the most neglected types of giftedness?

3. How has society's concept of leadership changed over time and how do these changes affect the ways educators should approach leadership development with children and youth?

4. How are the qualities, characteristics, and behaviors of gifted learners similar to those of strong leaders?

5. Examine the screening and identification instruments for young gifted leaders. Which one(s) are most appropriate for your needs?

6. Compare and contrast various strategies for incorporating leadership into the curriculum for gifted students. Which strategies would work best for your program and your population of gifted learners?

7. Analyze the materials available for leadership development. Which materials match your students' needs?

8. What are the most important concepts and skills of leadership you want your gifted learners to gain?

Teacher Resources

Annotated Bibliography of Books to Use With Students

Avery, L. D., & VanTassel-Baska, J. (2013). *Changing tomorrow 3: Leadership curriculum for high-ability high school students.* Waco, TX: Prufrock Press

This curriculum unit includes 10 lessons in leadership skill development focusing on biographical studies, generalizations about the concept of leadership, and ideas and exercises adapted from contemporary leadership literature. Complete with pre-and postassessment rubrics, this resource is aligned with 21st-century skills, Common Core State Standards for English Language Arts, and the NAGC Pre-K–Grade 12 Gifted Education Programming Standards. Volumes for elementary and middle school students are also available.

Boccia, J. A. (Ed.). (1997). *Students taking the lead: The challenges and rewards of empowering youth in schools.* San Francisco, CA: Jossey-Bass.

Contributors to this volume suggest that broader integration of leadership training and opportunities into school programs will allow educators to tap into the rich networks of peer influence that exist among adolescents and reach the goal of citizenship education. As a student educational goal, leadership development encompasses lessons from civics, communications, critical thinking, history, and a host of other disciplines. As an institutional value, student leadership reflects the practice of democratic principles that underlie U.S. public education. And, as an administrative structure, student leadership provides a dynamic, renewable resource for feedback and ideas about teaching, learning, and living in a school.

Delisle, D., & Delisle, J. (1996). *Growing good kids: 28 activities to enhance self-awareness, compassion, and leadership.* Minneapolis, MN: Free Spirit.

Created by teachers and classroom-tested, these fun and meaningful enrichment activities build children's skills in problem solving, decision making, cooperative learning, divergent thinking, and communication while promoting self-awareness, tolerance, character development, and service. Many activities include extensions and variations for use at school, at home, and in the community. The book includes 33 reproducible handout and transparency masters.

Ellis, J., Small-McGinley, J., & DeFabrizio, L. (2002). *Caring for kids in communities: Using mentorship, peer support, and student leadership programs in schools.* New York, NY: Peter Lang.

Caring for Kids in Communities invites schools to consider the use of mentorship, peer support, and student leadership programs to support the growth and learning of all students. It presents research on successful programs spanning kindergarten through grade 12 and includes a wealth of case studies of individual programs, as well as individual pairs of mentors and mentees. Thus, this book provides insight into the experiences of students, mentors, teachers, and coordinators from these programs, as well as descriptive, practical material for implementing similar programs.

Karnes, F. A., & Bean, S. M. (2010). *Leadership for students: A guide for young leaders* (2nd ed.). Waco, TX: Prufrock Press.

This book includes positive ideas and activities that will help students discover their leadership abilities. The activities throughout this book stimulate the exploration of ideas and encourage critical thinking about leadership. Students will find guidance and advice that emphasize leadership skills in a variety of settings, including leadership in the classroom, school activities, and the community. The book includes real-life stories on how students took on leadership positions and journaling activities for students to complete.

MacGregor, M. G. (1997). *Leadership 101: Developing leadership skills for resilient youth* (Facilitator's guide). Denver, CO: Youthleadership.com.

    Leadership 101 is a foundational curricular guide for adolescent and young adult leaders. The facilitator's guide consists of eighteen 90-minute lessons and more than thirty 50-minute lessons. Topics include defining leadership, qualities of leaders/ leadership, self-assessment, power/influence/authority, communication and listening, consensus building, ethical leadership, team building, gender and leadership, tolerance and diversity, motivation, risk-taking, decision making, and creative thinking. Other topics are addressed in the debriefing and application of each activity/ lesson. An accompanying student workbook also is available.

MacGregor, M. G. (1999). *Designing student leadership programs: Transforming the leadership potential of youth.* Denver, CO: Youthleadership.com.

    Designing Student Leadership Programs arose as a result of an ongoing effort to prepare adults who work with educating youth leaders. It is set up as a "guidebook" to be used within staff members or as part of focus groups or discussions as a program/ school evaluates or establishes their youth leadership program. As a guidebook, there are pages that consist of lists of ideas and/or statements that have been gathered and tested in various youth leadership programs. There are also pages with questions to consider when establishing a program or evaluating existing efforts.

Marx, J. (1999). *How to win a high school election.* New York, NY: Jeff Marx Books.

    This book contains advice and ideas from more than 1,000 high school seniors about how to win a high school election. Via e-mail, the seniors contributed input for this book about things they observed that worked or didn't work; things that were memorable or funny, mistakes they made or watched someone else make; ideas for platforms, issues, promises, posters, and campaign speeches; advice on how to speak in front of peers without appearing nervous; and having the right attitude.

Project Adventure. (1994). *Youth leadership in action: A guide to cooperative games and group activities.* Dubuque, IA: Kendall/Hunt.

    This is a how-to guide that prepares young people to lead experiential programs that teach team and leadership skills to other youth and adult groups. It includes directions to 52 activities, sample programs, and comprehensive overviews of critical facilitation skills.

van Linden, J. A., Fertman, C. I., & Long, J. A. (1998). *Youth leadership: A guide to understanding leadership development in adolescents.* San Francisco, CA: Jossey-Bass.

    Based on 15 years of work with teens and the adults in their lives, the authors of *Youth Leadership* identify the three major stages of adolescent leadership development. It outlines practical tactics for developing leadership skills through experiences at home, school, community, and work and, most importantly, it shows how adults in these settings can have a positive impact. The authors provide flexible strategies that can be used with adolescents in any program and in varied settings and offer diagrams, tables, and charts to clarify recommendations and processes.

Publications About Leadership and Students

Alford, B. (1997). Leadership for increasing the participation and success of students in high school advanced courses: Implications for rural educational settings. *The many faces of rural education: Proceedings of the Annual NREA Convention, USA, 89.*

Abel, T., & Karnes, F. (1993). Self-perceived strengths in leadership abilities between suburban and rural gifted students. *Psychological Reports, 73,* 687–690.

Addison, L. (1985). Leadership skills among the gifted and talented. *ERIC Digest.* Retrieved from ERIC database. (ERIC Document Reproduction Service No. ED262511)

Avery, L. D., & VanTassel-Baska, J. (2013). *Changing tomorrow 3: Leadership curriculum for high-ability high school students.* Waco, TX: Prufrock Press.

Bean, S. (2010). *Developing leadership potential in gifted students.* Waco, TX: Prufrock Press.

Biggs, D., & Colesante, R. (2000). The Albany approach to urban youth development. *The School Community Journal, 10*(2), 21–35.

Bisland, A. (2004). Developing leadership skills in young gifted students. *Gifted Child Today, 27*(1), 24–27.

Bisland, A., Karnes, F., & Cobb, Y. (2004). Leadership education: Resources and web sites for teachers of gifted students. *Gifted Child Today, 27*(1), 50–56.

Black, J. D. (1984). *Leadership: A new model particularly applicable to gifted youth.* Retrieved from ERIC database. (ERIC Document Reproduction Service No. ED253990)

Bonner II, F. A., Jennings, M. E., Marbley, A. F., & Brown, L. (2008). Capitalizing on leadership capacity: Gifted African-American males in high school. *Roeper Review, 30,* 93–103.

Bonner, F. A., & Jennings, M. (2007). Never too young to lead: Gifted African American males in elementary school. *Gifted Child Today, 30*(2), 30–36.

Chan, D. (2003). Leadership skills training for Chinese secondary students in Hong Kong: Does training make a difference? *Journal of Secondary Gifted Education, 14,* 166–174.

Chan, D. (2007). Components of leadership giftedness and multiple intelligences among Chinese gifted students in Hong Kong. *High Ability Studies, 18,* 155–172.

Chan, D. (2007). Leadership and intelligence. *Roeper Review, 29,* 183–189.

College of William and Mary Center for Gifted Education. (1998). *Gifted education/ School-to-work models: Best practices and unique approaches.* Washington, DC: National School-to-Work Opportunities Office.

Gonsoulin Jr., W., Ward, R., & Figg, C. (2006). Learning by leading: Using best practices to develop leadership skills in at-risk and gifted populations. *Education, 126,* 690–701.

Karnes, F., & Bean, S. (1996). Leadership and the gifted. *Focus on Exceptional Children, 29*(1), 1–12.

Lee, S., & Olszewski-Kubilius, P. (2006). The emotional intelligence, moral judgment, and leadership of academically gifted adolescents. *Journal for the Education of the Gifted, 30*(1), 29–67.

Loh, G., & Chang, A. S. C. (1996). *Political leadership qualities of bright adolescents and their willingness to lead.* Retrieved from ERIC database. (ERIC Document Reproduction Service No. ED424720)

Manning, S. (2005). Young leaders: Growing through mentoring. *Gifted Child Today, 28*(1), 14–20.

Matthews, M. S. (2004). Leadership education for gifted and talented youth: A review of the literature. *Journal for the Education of the Gifted, 28*(1), 77–113.

Milligan, J. (2004). Leadership skills of gifted students in a rural setting: Promising programs for leadership development. *Rural Special Education Quarterly, 23*(1), 16–21.

Morris, G. (1992). Adolescent leaders: rational thinking, future benefits, temporal perspective, and other correlates. *Adolescence, 27,* 173–81.

Newsom, T. (2010). Developing African-American leaders in today's schools: Gifted leadership, the unfamiliar dimension in gifted education. *Black History Bulletin, 73*(1), 18–23.

Pleasants, R., Stephens, K. R., Selph, H., & Pfeiffer, S. (2004). Incorporating service learning into leadership education: Duke TIP's leadership institute. *Gifted Child Today, 27*(1), 16–21.

Riley, T., & Karnes, F. (1994). Intellectually gifted elementary students' perceptions of leadership. *Perceptual & Motor Skills, 79*(1), 47–50.

Rudnitski, R. (1994). A generation of leaders for gifted education. *Roeper Review, 16,* 265–270.

Scharf, M., & Mayseless, O. (2009). Socioemotional characteristics of elementary school children identified as exhibiting social leadership qualities. *Journal of Genetic Psychology, 170*(1), 73–96.

Seon-Young, L., Olszewski-Kubilius, P., Donahue, R., & Weimholt, K. (2008). The Civic Leadership Institute: A service learning program for academically gifted youth. *Journal of Advanced Academics, 19,* 272–308.

Shaunessey, E., & Karnes, F. (2004). Instruments for measuring leadership in children and youth. *A Gifted Child Today, 27*(1), 42–47.

Smyth, E., & Ross, J. A. (1999). Developing leadership skills of pre-adolescent gifted learners in small group settings. *Gifted Child Quarterly, 43,* 204–211.

VanTassel-Baska, J., & Avery, L. D. (2013). *Changing tomorrow 1: Leadership curriculum for high-ability high school students.* Waco, TX: Prufrock Press.

VanTassel-Baska, J., & Avery, L. D. (2013). *Changing tomorrow 2: Leadership curriculum for high-ability high school students.* Waco, TX: Prufrock Press.

Wade, R., & Putnam, K. (1995). Tomorrow's leaders? Gifted students' opinions of leadership and service activities. *Roeper Review, 18,* 150–151.

Websites

Buzzle—http://www.buzzle.com/articles/leadership
    This website contains leadership activities and games for leaders of all ages.

Do Something—http://www.dosomething.org
    Do Something is an organization that encourages children and teenagers to take an active role in public affairs.

Envision Experience—http://www.envisionexperience.com
    Envision Experience is a career and leadership development program.

Free the Children—http://www.freethechildren.org
>   This organization is dedicated to empowering children with the skills necessary to become effective leaders who make a global impact.

GenerationOn—http://www.generationon.org/orgs/join/go-lead
>   Empowering youth leaders through service, goLEAD (generationOn Leadership, Education, and Development program) is generationOn's signature youth leadership training program.

Hugh O'Brian Youth Leadership—http://www.hoby.org
>   The mission of this foundation is to seek out, recognize, and develop leadership potential commencing with high school sophomores.

National Alliance for Secondary Education and Transition (NASET)—http://www.naset alliance.org/youthdev
>   NASET offers resources for positive youth leadership development for schools, families, and communities.

National Council on Youth Leadership—http://www.ncyl.org
>   This organization recognizes and fosters high ideals of leadership and integrity among the youth of America.

National Resource Center for Youth Development (NRCYD)—http://www.nrcyd.ou.edu/youth-engagement/youth-leadership-development
>   The NRCYD is a service of the Children's Bureau dedicated to promoting life skills learning and providing resources for youth leadership development.

National Young Leaders Conference—http://www.cylc.org
>   This is an organization that offers conferences on educational leadership for youth from the United States and abroad.

National Youth Leadership Council—http://www.nylc.org
>   The National Youth Leadership Council's mission is to build vital, just communities with young people through service learning.

The Student Leadership Challenge—http://www.studentleadershipchallenge.com/
>   The Student Leadership Challenge offers resources to develop student leaders.

Youth Leadership Institute (YLI)—http://www.yli.org
>   The YLI works with young people and the adults and systems that impact them to build communities that invest in youth.

Youth Leadership Support Network—http://www.worldyouth.org
>   The Youth Leadership Support Network is a violence prevention, arts, education, media, and training network based in Washington, DC. Its mission is to empower youth to express themselves and to have a voice in society through intergenerational and diverse leadership opportunities and civic engagement.

References

Aarons, G. (2006). Transformational and transactional leadership: Associations with attitudes toward evidence-based practice. *Psychiatric Services, 57,* 1162–1169.

Abel, T., & Karnes, F. A. (1993). Self-perceived strengths in leadership abilities between suburban and rural gifted students using the Leadership Strength Indicator. *Psychological Reports, 73,* 687–690.

Alvino, J. (1989). Psychological type: Implications for gifted. *Gifted Children Monthly, 10*(4), 1–2, 23.

Avery, L. D., & VanTassel-Baska, J. (2013). *Changing tomorrow 3: Leadership curriculum for high-ability high school students.* Waco, TX: Prufrock Press

Avolio, B., Bass B., & Jung, D. (1999). Re-examining the components of transformational and transactional leadership using the Multifactor Leadership. *Journal of Occupational and Organizational Psychology, 72,* 441–462.

Avolio, B., Rotundo, M., & Walumbwa, F. (2009). Early life experiences as determinants of leadership role occupancy: The importance of parental influence and rule breaking behavior. *The Leadership Quarterly, 20,* 329–342.

Bar-On, R. (1997). *BarOn Emotional Quotient Inventory: Technical manual.* Toronto, Ontario, Canada: Multi-Health Systems.

Barr, L., & Barr, N. (1989). *The leadership equation.* Austin, TX: Eakin Press.

Bass, B. M. (1981). *Stogdill's handbook of leadership: A survey of theory and research.* New York, NY: Free Press.

Bass, B. M., & Bass, R. (2008). *The Bass handbook of leadership: Theory, research, and managerial applications* (4th ed.). New York, NY: Free Press.

Bass, B. M., & Riggio, R. E. (2006). *Transformational leadership.* Mahwah, NJ: Lawrence Erlbaum.

Bass, B. M., & Stogdill, R. M. (1990). *Bass and Stogdill's handbook of leadership: Theory, research, and managerial applications* (3rd ed.). Riverside, NJ: Simon & Schuster.

Bennett, W. J. (1986). *What works: Research about teaching and learning.* Washington, DC: U.S. Department of Education.

Bennis, W. G., & Nanus, B. (1985). *Leaders: The strategies for taking charge.* New York, NY: Harper & Row.

Bennis, W. G., & Thomas, R. J. (2002). *Geeks and geezers: How era, values, and defining moments shape leaders.* Boston, MA: Harvard Business School Press.

Black, J. D. (1984). *Leadership: A new model particularly applicable to gifted youth* (Report No. EC171399). Retrieved from ERIC database. (ERIC Document Reproduction Service No. ED253990)

Blake, R. R., & Mouton, J. S. (1985). *The managerial grid III.* Houston, TX: Gulf.

Bloom, B. (Ed.). (1956). *Taxonomy of educational objectives. Handbook I: Cognitive domain.* New York, NY: McKay.

Bono, J., & Judge, T., (2004). Personality and transformational and transactional leadership: A meta-analysis. *Journal of Applied Psychology, 89,* 901–910.

Bradberry, T. R., & Su, L. D. (2006). Ability-versus skill based assessment of emotional intelligence. *Psichothema, 18,* 65.

Campbell, D., & Velsor, E. V. (1985). *The use of personality measures in the leadership development program.* Greensboro, NC: Center for Creative Leadership.

Caspi, A., Harrington, H., Milne B., Amell, J., Theodore, R., & Moffitt, T. (2003). Children's behavioral styles at age 3 are linked to their adult personality traits at age 26. *Journal of Personality, 71,* 495–514.

Caspi, A., & Silva, P. (1995). Temperamental qualities at age three predict personality traits in young adulthood: Longitudinal evidence from a birth cohort. *Child Development, 66,* 486–498.

Cattell, R. B., Cattell, M. D., & Johns, E. F. (1984). *Manual and norms for the High School Personality Questionnaire.* Champaign, IL: Institute for Personality & Ability Testing.

Chan, D. W. (2000). Assessing leadership among Chinese secondary students in Hong Kong: The use of the Roets Rating Scale for Leadership. *Gifted Child Quarterly, 44,* 115–122.

Chauvin, J. C., & Karnes, F. A. (1983). A leadership profile of secondary gifted students. *Psychological Reports, 53,* 1259–1262.

Clark, K. E., & Clark, M. B. (1994). *Choosing to lead.* Charlotte, NC: Iron Gate Press.

Criswell, C., & Martin, A. (2007). *10 trends: A study of senior executives' views on the future.* Greensboro, NC: Center for Creative Leadership.

Day, D. (2011). Integrative perspectives on longitudinal investigations of leader development: From childhood through adulthood. *The Leadership Quarterly, 22,* 561–571.

Day, D., & Antonakis, J. (2012). *The nature of leadership.* Los Angeles, CA: Sage.

Dhuey, E., & Lipscomb, S. (2008). What makes a leader? Relative age and high school leadership. *Economics of Education Review, 27,* 173–183.

Eby, J. W. (1989). *Eby gifted behavior index (Administration manual).* East Aurora, NY: D.O.K.

Edmunds, A. L. (1998). Content, concurrent, and construct validity of the Leadership Skills Inventory. *Roeper Review, 20,* 281–284.

Edmunds, A. L., & Yewchuk, C. R. (1996). Indicators of leadership in gifted grade twelve students. *Journal of Secondary Gifted Education, 7,* 345–355.

Ellis, J. L. (1990). *Leadership strengths indicator: A self-report leadership analysis instrument for adolescents.* New York, NY: Trillium Press.

Elmore, T. E. (2001). *Nurturing the leader within your child: What every parent needs to know.* Nashville, TN: Thomas Nelson.

Feldhusen, J. F., Hynes, K., & Richardson, W. B. (1977). Curriculum materials for vocational youth organizations. *Clearinghouse, 50,* 224–226.

Feldhusen, J. F., & Kennedy, D. (1986). Leadership training for gifted and talented youth. *Leadership Network Newsletter, 1*(2), 1–2.

Fisch, K. (2012). SOAR study skills. *We are currently preparing students for jobs that don't yet exist.* Retrieved from http://studyskills.com/parents/career-preparation/we-are-currently-preparing-students-for-jobs-that-don%E2%80%99t-yet-exist%E2%80%A6/

Florey, J. E., & Dorf, J. H. (1986). *Leadership skills for gifted middle school students.* Retrieved from ERIC database. (ERIC Document Reproduction No. ED273404)

Foster, W. (1981). Leadership: A conceptual framework for recognizing and educating. *Gifted Child Quarterly, 25,* 17–25.

Foster, W. H., & Silverman, L. (1988). Leadership curriculum for the gifted. In J. VanTassel-Baska, J. Feldhusen, K. Seeley, G. Wheatley, L. Silverman, & W. Foster (Eds.), *Comprehensive curriculum for gifted learners* (pp. 356–360). Boston, MA: Allyn & Bacon.

Gallagher, J. J. (1982). *A leadership unit.* New York, NY: Trillium Press.

Galton, F. (1869). *Hereditary genius: An inquiry into its laws and consequences.* London, England: Macmillan.

Gardner, J. W. (1990). *On leadership.* New York, NY: Free Press.

George, B. (2010). *True north: Discover your authentic leadership.* Hoboken, NJ: Jossey Bass.

Gilliam, J. E., Carpenter, B. O., & Christensen, J. R. (1996). *Gifted and Talented Evaluation Scales.* Austin, TX: PRO-ED.

Gladwell, M. (2008). *Outliers: The story of success.* Boston, MA: Little, Brown.

Gordon, E. (2013). *Future jobs: Solving the employment and skills crisis.* Santa Barbara, CA: ABC-CLIO, LLC.

Gottfried, A. E., Gottfried, A. W., Reichard, R. J., Guerin, D. W., Oliver, P. H., & Riggio, R. E. (2011). Motivational roots of leadership: A longitudinal study from childhood through adulthood. *The Leadership Quarterly, 22,* 510–519.

Guerin, D., Oliver, P., Gottfried, A. W., Gottfried, A. E., Reichard, R., & Riggio, R. (2011). Childhood and adolescent antecedents of social skills and leadership potential in adulthood: Temperamental approach/withdrawal and extraversion. *The Leadership Quarterly, 22,* 482–494.

Hagemann, B., & Newman, C. (1999). *Lead on.* Marion, IL: Pieces of Learning.

Hays, T. S. (1993). An historical content analysis of publications in gifted education journals. *Roeper Review, 16,* 41–43.

Henage, D., McCarney, S. B., & Anderson, P. D. (1998). *Gifted Evaluation Scale* (2nd ed.). Columbia, MO: Hawthorne Educational Services.

Hersey, P., & Blanchard, K. H. (1982). Leadership style: Attitudes and behaviors. *Training and Development Journal, 36*(5), 50–52.

Hollander, E. P., & Offerman, L. (1990). Power and leadership in organizations: Relationships in transition. In K. E. Clark & M. B. Clark (Eds.), *Measures of leadership* (pp. 83–97). West Orange, NJ: Leadership Library of America.

Hollingworth, L. S. (1926). *Gifted children: Their nature and nurture.* New York, NY: Macmillan.

House, C. (1980). *The leadership series.* Coeur D'Alene, ID: Listos.

Howe, N., & Strauss, W. (2000). *Millennials rising.* New York, NY: Vintage Books.

Huckaby, W. O., & Sperling, H. B. (1981). Leadership giftedness: An idea whose time has not yet come. *Roeper Review, 3*(3), 19–22.

Institute for Behavioral Research in Creativity. (1990). *Student talent and risk profile.* Salt Lake City, UT: Author.

Jacob K. Javits Gifted and Talented Students Education Act (Javits Act). P. L. 100-297, Title IV, Part B, Sec. 1101. (1988).

Jarosewich, T., Pfeiffer, S. I., & Morris, J. (2002). Identifying gifted students using teacher rating scales: A review of existing instruments. *Journal of Psychoeducational Assessment, 20,* 322–336.

Judge, T., Bono, J., Ilies, R., & Gerhardt, M. (2002). Personality and leadership: A qualitative and quantitative review. *Journal of Applied Psychology, 87,* 765–780.

Judge, T., Colbert, A., & Ilies, R. (2004). Intelligence and leadership: A quantitative review and test of theoretical. *Journal of Applied Psychology, 89,* 542–552.

Karnes, F. A., & Bean, S. M. (1993). *Girls and young women leading the way.* Minneapolis, MN: Free Spirit.

Karnes, F. A., & Bean, S. M. (1996). Leadership and the gifted. *Focus on Exceptional Children, 29*(1), 1–12.

Karnes, F. A., & Bean, S. M. (2010). *Leadership for students: A guide for young leaders* (2nd ed.). Waco, TX: Prufrock Press.

Karnes, F. A., & Chauvin, J. C. (2000a). *Leadership skills inventory.* Scottsdale, AZ: Gifted Psychology Press.

Karnes, F. A., & Chauvin, J. C. (2000b). *The leadership development program.* Scottsdale, AZ: Gifted Psychology Press.

Karnes, F. A., & D'Ilio, V. (1989). Leadership positions and sex role stereotyping among gifted children. *Gifted Child Quarterly, 33,* 76–78.

Karnes, F. A., & Meriweather, S. (1989). Developing and implementing a plan for leadership: An integral component for success as a leader. *Roeper Review, 11,* 214–217.

Karnes, F. A., Meriweather, S., & D'Ilio, V. (1987). The effectiveness of the Leadership Studies Program. *Roeper Review, 9,* 238–241.

Karnes, F. A., & Meriweather-Bean, S. (1991). Leadership and gifted adolescents. In M. Bireley & J. Genshaft (Eds.), *Understanding the gifted adolescent: Educational, developmental, and multicultural issues* (pp. 122–138). New York, NY: Teachers College Press.

Karnes, F. A., & Riley, T. L. (2005). *Competitions for talented kids.* Waco, TX: Prufrock Press.

Karnes, F. A., & Riley, T. L. (2013). *The best competitions for talented kids: Win scholarships, big prize money, and recognition.* Waco, TX: Prufrock Press.

Khatena, J., & Morse, D. T. (1994). *Khatena-Morse multitalent perception inventory.* Bensonville, IL: Scholastic Testing Service.

Kouzes, J., & Posner, B. (2006). *The student leadership practices inventory.* San Francisco, CA: Jossey-Bass.

Kruse, K. (2013). What is leadership? *Forbes.* Retrieved from http://www.forbes.com/sites/kevinkruse/2013/04/09/what-is-leadership/

Lawrence, G. (1982). *People types and tiger stripes: A practical guide to learning styles.* Gainesville, FL: Center for the Applications of Psychological Type.

Lee, R. J., & King, S. N. (2001). *Discovering the leader in you: A guide to realizing your personal leadership potential.* Greensboro, NC: Center for Creative Leadership and Jossey-Bass.

Leslie, J. (2003). *Leadership skills and emotional intelligence.* Greensboro, NC: Center for Creative Leadership.

Lindsay, B. (1988). A lamp for Diogenes: Leadership, giftedness, and moral education. *Roeper Review, 11,* 8–11.

Magoon, R. A., & Jellen, H. G. (1980). *Leadership development: Democracy in action.* Poquoson, VA: Human Development Press.

Marland, Jr., S. P. (1972). *Education of the gifted and talented: Report to the Congress of the United States by the U.S. Commissioner of Education and background papers submitted to the U.S. Office of Education,* 2 vols. Washington, DC: U.S. Government Printing Office. (Government Documents, Y4.L 11/2: G36)

Martin, A. (2007). *The changing nature of leadership.* Greensboro, NC: Center for Creative Leadership.

McCaulley, M. H., & Staff of the Center for Applications of Psychological Type. (1990). The Myers-Briggs Type Indicator and leadership. In K. E. Clark & M. B. Clark (Eds.), *Measures of leadership* (pp. 381–418). New York, NY: Center for Creative Leadership.

McNamara, J. F., Haensly, P. A., Lupkowski, A. E., & Edlind, E. P. (1985, November). *The role of extracurricular activities in high school education.* Paper presented at the annual convention of the National Association for Gifted Children, Denver, CO.

Media Literacy Clearinghouse. (n.d.). *Resources on media habits of children.* Retrieved from http://www.frankwbaker.com/mediause.htm

Meisgeier, C., & Murphy, E. (1987). *Murphy-Meisgeier Type Indicator for Children.* Palo Alto, CA: Consulting Psychologists Press.

Murphy, S., & Johnson, S. (2011). The benefits of a long-lens approach to leader development: Understanding the seeds of leadership. *The Leadership Quarterly, 22,* 459–470.

Murphy, S. & Reichard, R. (2011). *Early development and leadership: Building the next generation of leaders.* New York, NY: Taylor and Francis.

Myers, I. B., & McCaulley, M. (1985). *Manual: A guide to the development and use of the Myers-Briggs Type Indicator.* Palo Alto, CA: Consulting Psychologists Press.

Myers, I. B., & Myers, P. B. (1980). *Gifted differing.* Palo Alto, CA: Consulting Psychologists Press.

Nemerowicz, G., & Rosi, E. (2013). *Education for leadership and social responsibility.* New York, NY: Routledge.

Northouse, P. (2014). *Introduction to leadership: Concepts and practices.* Thousand Oaks, CA. Sage Publications.

Parker, J. P. (1989). *Instructional strategies for teaching the gifted.* Boston, MA: Allyn & Bacon.

Parker, J. P., & Begnaud, L. G. (2003). *Developing creative leadership.* Englewood, CO: Teacher Ideas Press.

Partnership for 21st Century Skills. (2009). *P21 framework definitions.* Retrieved from http://www.p21.org/storage/documents/P21_Framework_Definitions.pdf

Pfeiffer, S. I., & Jarosewich, T. (2003). *Gifted Rating Scales.* San Antonio, TX: The Psychological Corporation.

Plowman, P. D. (1981). Training extraordinary leaders. *Roeper Review, 3,* 13–16.

Popper, M., & Mayseless, O. (2007). The building blocks of leader development: A psychological conceptual framework. *Leadership & Organization Development Journal, 28,* 664–684.

Reeves, B., Malone, T., & O'Driscoll. T. (2008, May). Leadership's online labs. *Harvard Business Review,* 1–10.

Renzulli, J. S., Smith, L. H., White, A. J., Callahan, C. M., Hartman, R. K., & Westberg, K. L. (2002). *Scales for rating the behavioral characteristics of superior students: Revised edition.* Waco, TX: Prufrock Press.

Richardson, W. B., & Feldhusen, J. F. (1987). *Leadership education: Developing skills for youth.* New York, NY: Trillium.

Riley, T. L., & Karnes, F. A. (1994a). Intellectually gifted elementary students' perceptions of leadership. *Perceptual and Motor Skills, 79,* 47–50.

Riley, T. L., & Karnes, F. A. (1994b). A leadership profile of disadvantaged youth based on Leadership Strengths Indicator. *Psychological Reports, 74,* 815–818.

Riley, T. L., & Karnes, F. A. (1996). *Competitions as an avenue for inspiring and recognizing young leaders.* Unpublished manuscript, The University of Southern Mississippi, Hattiesburg.

Roach, A. A., Wyman, L. T., Brookes, H., Chavez, C., Heath, S. B., & Valdes, G. (1999). Leadership giftedness: Models revisited. *Gifted Child Quarterly, 43,* 13–24.

Roets, L. (1986). *Roets Rating Scale for Leadership.* Des Moines, IA: Leadership Publishers.

Roets, L. S. (1997). *Leadership: A skills training program* (8th ed.). New Sharon, IA: Leadership Publishers.

Sandmann, L. R., & Vandenberg, L. (1995). A framework for 21st century leadership. *Journal of Extension* [Online], *33*(6) Article 6FEA1. Retrieved from http://www.joe.org/joe/1995december/a1.php

Schakel, L. (1984). *Investigation of the leadership abilities of intellectually gifted students* (Unpublished doctoral dissertation). University of South Florida, Tampa, FL.

Simonton, D. K. (1995). Personality and intellectual predictors of leadership. In D. H. Saklofske & M. Zeidner (Eds.), *International handbook of personality and intelligence* (pp. 739–757). New York, NY: Plenum Press.

Sisk, D. A., & Rosselli, H. C. (1987). *Leadership: A special kind of giftedness.* New York, NY: Trillium.

Sisk, D. A., & Shallcross, D. J. (1986). *Leadership: Making things happen.* Buffalo, NY: Bearly Limited.

Smith, D. L., Smith, L., & Barnette, J. (1991). Exploring the development of leadership giftedness. *Roeper Review, 14,* 7–12.

Stephens, K. R., & Karnes, F. A. (2000). State definitions for the gifted and talented revisited. *Exceptional Children, 66,* 219–238.

Stogdill, R. M. (1974). *Handbook of leadership.* New York, NY: Free Press.

Terman, L. M. (1925). *Genetic studies of genius: Vol. 1. Mental and physical traits of a thousand gifted children.* Stanford, CA: Stanford University Press.

Wade, R. C., & Putnam, K. (1995). Tomorrow's leaders? Gifted students' opinions of leadership and service activities. *Roeper Review, 18,* 150–151.

Wiseman, L., & McKeown, G. (2010). *Multipliers: How the best leaders make everyone smarter.* New York, NY: Harper Collins.

Yammarino, F. J., & Bass, B. M. (1990). Long-term forecasting of transformational leadership and its effect among naval officers: Some preliminary findings. In K. E. Clark & M. B. Clark (Eds.), *Measures of leadership* (pp. 151–169). West Orange, NJ: Leadership Library of America.

17
Chapter

EXTENDING LEARNING THROUGH MENTORSHIPS

BY DEL SIEGLE, D. BETSY MCCOACH, AND CINDY M. GILSON

A mentor is someone who allows you to see the hope inside yourself.

—Oprah Winfrey

How often does a high school student have an opportunity to study the diet of hummingbirds in the far reaches of Chile? Search a local archeological site for native artifacts? Shadow a photojournalist? Use advanced research skills to collect and analyze data on gender bias?

High school students in Connecticut experienced these opportunities because university mentors were willing to share their time, passion, and resources during a summer mentoring program at their state university (Palmer, 2002; Purcell, Renzulli, McCoach, & Spottiswoode, 2001; Wray, 2002). Not all gifted children need or want such mentoring experiences, nor should all adults serve as mentors; however, when both parties are ready, willing, and able, mentoring opportunities such as these can be extraordinary experiences for all.

Parents, classroom teachers, and teachers of the gifted cannot be all things to the young people in their charge. The nature and diversity of gifted students' interests may demand resources beyond the confines of the school and demonstrate the need for mentors and other resource people. Mentors provide content sophistication that normally would not be accessible from traditional resources (Siegle, 2001).

Mentoring, unlike other programs for the gifted, is essential when students have skills and interests that are "so advanced or divergent from the typical school resources that they need to be placed in situations where those resources are available" (Coleman & Cross, 2001, p. 325). Gifted students who have interests that their peers are not yet ready to explore need this special contact with others who are interested in their ideas (Roberts & Inman, 2001). For instance, college students studying American Sign Language (ASL) would be prime candidates for mentoring elementary gifted students interested in ASL, as it is not typically taught in the traditional curriculum (Buisson & Salgo, 2012a, 2012b). In addition, when students are paired with a mentor, it is possible to focus intensely on an emerging interest in a ceilingless learning environment (Purcell et al., 2001). Mentoring can provide the benefits of both enrichment (Nash, 2001) and acceleration (Nash, 2001; Rogers & Kimpston, 1992).

Gifted students demonstrate career awareness at an earlier age than their peers and benefit from exposure to a variety of careers (Silverman, 2000). Mentors who are involved in the work world can provide special details on the demands and preparation required of future jobs. In addition to providing information about their careers, mentors serve as role models for students who wish to enter a career field (VanTassel-Baska & Baska, 2000). Mentoring may be the most fertile form of career education for the gifted, as prominent adults often attribute their successes to the influence of mentors (Merriam, 1983).

A mentorship usually involves a one-on-one relationship between someone younger and an older expert or someone with knowledge or passion in a field (Roberts & Inman, 2001). One-on-one relationships can be one of the best educational approaches for meeting the needs of gifted and talented children, as they often master content and skills faster than their peers. Mentoring is one of the three most popular one-on-one approaches to learning besides independent study and tutoring (Coleman & Cross, 2001).

Definition of a Mentorship

Mentoring that typically involves a relationship between a gifted student and a knowledgeable older individual is a viable alternative option to traditional schooling (Bisland, 2001). Mentoring can be a formal arrangement that is care-

fully planned and executed (Nash, 2001; Tomlinson, 2001). It also can be a serendipitous meeting of like-minded souls who have a common interest (Nash, 2001;
Tomlinson, 2001). Finally, it can be an informal attempt by someone with more
experience to reach out to someone less experienced (Tomlinson, 2001).

The union between a student and mentor should be carefully planned
(Reilly, 1992b). The mentoring relationship differs from the typical teacher-
student relationship in that mentors and mentees form a partnership to explore
their passion, interest, or career (Roberts & Inman, 2001). A mentorship also differs from an internship in that it is not limited to specific tasks or jobs (Swassing
& Fichter, 1991). "The quality of the relationship between teachers, mentors, and
coaches is the cornerstone of the transformation of abilities into fulfilled potential" (Calderon, Subotnik, Knotek, Rayhack, & Gorgia, 2007, p. 358). This may
occur as mentor and mentees explore multiple interests over several years or even
a lifetime.

Being a mentor goes beyond being a role model (Rimm, 2003). In addition
to providing skills, mentors help students develop a vision for their future, while
offering a combination of support and challenge to help students in their quest for
that vision (Kaufmann, 2003). Mentors also serve as friends who help to advance
students' knowledge of a particular field (Silverman, 2000). Mentoring generally
involves development of in-depth academic projects, exploration of strong personal interests and hobbies, or examination of career opportunities (Nash, 2001).
Mentoring is necessary when a student's interest in a particular area cannot be met
at school (Bisland, 2001).

The Effectiveness of Mentoring

Torrance (1984) documented that mentors make a difference in the creative
achievement and educational attainment of mentees. Individuals with mentors
complete more education than those without, and having a mentor is significantly
related to adult achievement. Study and program evaluation reports consistently
show positive results for mentoring (Beck, 1989; Ellingson, Haeger, & Feldhusen,
1986; Hamilton & Hamilton, 1992; Prillaman & Richardson, 1989; Schatz,
1999; Swassing & Fichter, 1991; Wright & Borland, 1992).

Research has demonstrated that mentoring can support special populations
of gifted students. In case studies conducted by Hébert and Olenchak (2000), the
influence of a significant adult improved achievement in underachieving gifted
males. Hébert and Olenchak believed the mentoring worked because the mentors demonstrated open-minded and nonjudgmental characteristics that helped
sustain an ongoing relationship. Shevitz, Weinfeld, Jeweler, and Barnes-Robinson
(2003) found mentoring benefits for twice-exceptional students. Mentoring pro-

vided the students with opportunities to produce alternative products in their strength areas, which increased their self-confidence.

The benefits of a mentorship may also include increased self-confidence, self-awareness (Nash, 2001), self-concept of job skills (Little, Kearney, & Britner, 2010), commitment, self-trust, empathy (Tomlinson, 2001), responsibility, future-mindedness (Purcell et al., 2001), exceptional production (Nash, 2001), work and study skills, organizational skills, time management, and responsibility (Davalos & Haensly, 1997). Students in telementoring programs also report improved technology and telecommunication skills and increased school attendance (International Telementor Program, n.d.).

"Powerful mentorships help prepare young people to live with greater purpose, focus, and appreciation at a younger age by drawing not only on the knowledge of the past, but on its wisdom as well" (Tomlinson, 2001, p. 27). For example, as a high school student, Eleanor Roosevelt attended Allenswood, a boarding school in England at which she met an inspiring mentor:

> The founder and headmistress of Allenswood was Mlle. Marie Souvestre, a passionate humanist committed to human justice. . . . Eleanor was one of her favorite students, chosen to sit beside her at dinner and to travel with her during several vacations. These were the happiest years of Eleanor's life. For the rest of her life she kept Marie Souvestre's portrait on her desk. Her life reflected Souvestre's influence and spirit. (Geiger, 2001, p. 347)

It naturally followed that Eleanor would later become an activist for human rights. Likewise, Charles Darwin reported that his mentor, John Stevens Henslow, influenced his career more than any other circumstance (McGreevy, 1990). Dr. Terence Tao, an eminent mathematician who participated in the Study of Mathematically Precocious Youth, reflected on the influence of his mentors growing up:

> . . . my parents found a number of very good mentors (retired or active math professors, mainly) whom I could visit every weekend or so and talk with on a very informal level (say, over tea and cookies) concerning mathematics. I think that was very important for me, in getting a glimpse of how professional mathematicians view the subject and why they enjoy it (which is quite different from how I perceived mathematics at the high school and college levels, where it felt more like an abstract game). (Muratori et al., 2006, p. 310)

Of course, there can be roadblocks to successful mentoring as well. Simonton (2000) warned that mentors who are past their prime and not receptive to new ideas may stifle gifted students' creativity. Mentors may not be aware that gifted students need to develop their social skills, self-confidence, and risk-taking abilities, which may lead mentors to assume that their mentees are defiant or uncommitted to a project (Calderon et al., 2007). In addition, a disadvantage of mentoring, and a sign of the times, includes the need for careful supervision of individual mentor to mentee relationships (Olszewski-Kubilius, 2010).

Benefits to Mentors

There are benefits to the mentor, as well as to the mentee. Corporation employees who volunteer as mentors have better teamwork skills, improved morale and self-worth, and higher retention rates. Mentors in Hébert and Olenchak's (2000) descriptive case studies experienced personal and professional growth as a result of a mentorship process. In another study, 75% of the Allstate Insurance Company's employees who served as mentors said participation in the mentorship improved their attitudes at work (National Mentoring Partnership, n.d.). Roberts and Inman (2001) described one mentor's reflection on mentoring:

> The joy in mentoring is that it doesn't feel at all like real work. Gifted kids learn independently, usually acquire an interest in ideas for their own sake, and are nourished more by the mentor's enthusiasm than by smoothness in the mentor's teaching technique. (p. 10)

Mentoring can add satisfaction to mentors' lives as well as renewed enthusiasm for their own career when they have the opportunity to share it with a mentee (Bisland, 2001). The process helps perpetuate interest and knowledge in mentors' passion areas, develops the pleasure of knowing and working with a young person on a personal basis (Roberts & Inman, 2001), helps mentors better understand themselves and their own past experiences, and increases mentors' skills (Philip & Hendry, 2000).

Mentoring at Different Ages

Mentoring is particularly effective in the later elementary, middle, and high school years (Roberts & Inman, 2001), although young children benefit from it as well (Moon & Callahan, 2001). Early mentoring can help young students recognize, explore, and validate their creativity, develop respect for their own uniqueness, grow in self-esteem, and interact with adults in a manner that gains their respect (Bennetts, 2001). Participating in mentorship experiences at an early age provides the emotional support and encouragement that children need to pursue their talents. Many creative young people suffer and actually delay or stop their skill development because they do not have access to a mentor (Torrance, 1984).

Adolescents also benefit from opportunities for collaboration and personal achievement, assistance with the transitions from youth to adulthood and from high school to college, and exposure to esoteric resources and inspiration to feed creativity (Bennetts, 2001). Later, as mentees reach adulthood, mentors take their mentees' creative work seriously, provide a critical review of their work, listen to their ideas and give feedback (Bennetts, 2001), and open doors of opportunity.

Mentoring Underserved Populations

Three groups of gifted and talented students are in greatest need of mentorships: the highly gifted, disadvantaged, and underachieving. The highly gifted require challenges well beyond the school's capability; the disadvantaged benefit from successful role models, college and career guidance, and possible summer employment and scholarship opportunities; and the underachieving benefit from meaningful learning experiences, individual attention, and a change from the status quo (VanTassel-Baska, 2000).

In addition to the needs presented by these groups of gifted students, other populations benefit from mentoring opportunities. In the next section, the mentoring of gifted females, culturally diverse students, and economically disadvantaged populations will be discussed.

Gifted Females

Providing gifted females with mentors is an effective strategy for helping gifted females succeed (Reis, 1998). A study of the Gaining Options: Girls Investigate Real Life (GO-GIRL) Program, in which college females mentored potentially talented at-risk seventh-grade girls who were interested in mathematics and science, indicated increases in the young females' confidence and skills in mathematics. The seventh-grade females also reported greater appreciation for and knowledge of college life (Reid & Roberts, 2006).

Several special issues confront women who are interested in finding mentors. First, men tend to avoid female mentees. Second, women who have worked their way up in male-dominated fields often are reluctant to serve as mentors for other women. Third, social pressure and concern about appearances limit older men from serving as mentors for younger women. Fourth, limited numbers of female mentors exist because many young women fail to find mentors, causing them to be less likely to later serve as mentors (Shaughnessy & Neely, 1991).

Females tend to express stronger support for mentoring than males (Shaughnessy & Neely, 1991). Females may be better role models for other females, but the limited number of female mentors often results in males serving as mentors for females. Females tend to be less satisfied with their mentors than men (Torrance, 1984), which may be due to the limited number of available female mentors and their need for more personal and friendship relations; however, when they do encounter significant teachers, their lives are greatly influenced (List & Renzulli, 1991).

College students as mentors. To address the challenge of finding enough mentors for adolescent gifted girls, female college students may be potential candidates, especially those who have an interest in mentoring youths as part of a community service initiative (Leyton-Armakan, Lawrence, Deutsch, Williams, & Henneberger, 2012). This may be a potentially viable option as female college students are more likely to volunteer than males; furthermore, mentoring youth was reported as one of the top three ways both male and female college students spent their time volunteering (Kirby, Marcelo, & Kawashima-Ginsberg, 2009).

Certain characteristics of college students should be considered when matching mentors with early adolescent girls. Leyton-Armakan et al. (2012) investigated the characteristics of female college mentors participating in the Young Women Leaders Program. In this program, mentors took two courses emphasizing best practices of mentoring and issues experienced by adolescent girls. Mentors also met on a weekly basis with mentees as a group and individually on a monthly basis. The authors found ". . . it may be especially important for college women to feel competent academically, value their own parental relationships, and not be overly autonomous or depressed if they are to forge quality mentoring relationships" (p. 915). One implication to consider is that college student mentors who have high levels of autonomy may possibly experience conflict with adolescent girls, especially if the mentors do not share decision making with their mentees.

In addition to teaching college students the best practices of mentoring, they should also understand the characteristics and needs of gifted students (Buisson & Salgo, 2012a). If possible, the college students' interests should be considered when matching them with mentees, especially if the mentors work with gifted students during school time.

Mentoring in the STEM areas. Mentoring gifted girls in the areas of science, technology, engineering, and mathematics (STEM) is especially crucial given that women are inconsistently represented across STEM areas and careers. Although more than 50% of the bachelor's degrees were awarded to women in psychology, social sciences, agricultural sciences, and biology in 2010, only about 43% were in mathematics, 18% in computer science and engineering, and 41% in physical sciences (National Science Foundation, 2011). In addition, about 60% of master's degrees and 50% of the doctoral degrees awarded to women in 2010 were in the science and engineering fields, where the majority focused on psychology. Translated into the workforce, however, females are underrepresented in certain STEM careers. For example, in 2008, females represented about only 27% of the workforce in science and engineering (National Science Foundation, 2011).

The Institute of Education Sciences (IES), as part of a set of guidelines for increasing girls' interest and achievement in the STEM areas, recommended that teachers "Expose girls to female role models who have succeeded in math and science" (Halpern et al., 2007, p. 19). Although IES cautioned that this recommendation was based primarily on research studies of college students and not K–12 girls, it posited that exposure to role models can help to negate inaccurate and debilitating stereotypes about women's abilities in the STEM areas. IES also suggested that role models, women or even older students, could be invited to the classroom as guest speakers or tutors. In addition, mentoring programs could provide gifted girls with beneficial opportunities to meet successful females in STEM careers. Through their interactions, gifted girls may be inspired to persevere through challenges and recognize that struggle and self-doubts are normal components of the process of becoming an expert.

Culturally Diverse Students

Mentors can be positive role models and encourage protégés who face alienation, exclusion, and disenfranchisement caused by societal stereotypes. For this reason, mentors must be willing to take risks and acquire a broad knowledge of human differences and similarities. It is possible that more students from underrepresented populations might qualify for gifted and talented programs if they were exposed to mentoring because mentors act as talent scouts who recognize, acknowledge, and develop students' strengths. They use students' potential to build success, skills, and abilities, rather than focus on their deficits.

Gifted African American males represent one group of underrepresented students in gifted programs. To address this issue, cultivation of nontraditional types of giftedness, such as leadership potential, could be facilitated through mentoring experiences with elementary and high school African American males (Bonner & Jennings, 2007; Bonner, Jennings, Marbley, & Brown, 2008). Mentorships may open the door to exposing African American students to the expectations and roles of leaders and to supporting the development of students' identity as well as resiliency in facing road blocks to their success.

As for race, the research findings suggest that race by itself does not play a significant role in determining whether or not a mentor and mentee form a strong relationship and the extent to which it leads to positive changes for the youth. In one study, there were a few differences in outcomes when the same-race and cross-race groups were further differentiated by gender, but those differences did not seem to suggest a pattern (Jucovy, 2002). In fact, the findings suggest that the effects of race on relationships are subtle and act in combination with other factors, such as gender and the mentor's interpersonal style, to shape the ultimate influence of mentoring. Sánchez and Colón's (2005) review of racial similarity or dissimilarity found that "naturally occurring mentoring relationships among urban, Latino, and African youth report mentors of the same race/ethnicity" (p. 195). Many programs are committed to same-race mentoring, which can be problematic because 15%–20% of adult volunteers are members of a racial minority, while approximately 50% of the students who apply for programs are from a racial minority. For programs committed to same-race matches, the result is that minority youth may spend a long time on a waiting list until a mentor becomes available (Rhodes, 2002). A study sponsored by the AOL Time Warner Foundation (2002) found that people of color are as likely, or more likely, than Whites to report being mentors. The discrepancy between this finding and the Rhodes finding may be that people of color may function more often as natural rather than formal mentors (Sánchez & Colón, 2005).

One way to increase the number of culturally diverse mentors is simply to invite them to serve as mentors. The majority of mentors serve because they are asked, and 75% join through an affiliate organization (AOL Time Warner Foundation, 2002). Additionally, asking older minority students to mentor gifted youth should also be considered as an older student might be viewed as "a role model for success" (Bisland, 2001, p. 3).

Jucovy (2002) suggested that mentors adhere to three recommendations when mentoring diverse students:

1. Mentors are the experienced one in the relationship.
2. Mentors should be themselves.
3. Mentors should learn about the mentee's culture, lifestyle, and age group, but they never will be from that group, so they should avoid trying to overidentify with it.

Mentors should honestly examine their own prejudices and stereotypes, make a personal commitment to be culturally sensitive, see the mentee first and foremost as a valuable and unique person, and approach cultural differences as an opportunity to expand their own understanding. All mentors, regardless of whether they are matched with youth of the same race, can benefit from training in cultural understanding.

Economically Disadvantaged Students

Mentorships are highly recommended for gifted students from economically disadvantaged backgrounds (Burney & Beilke, 2008; Hébert & Olenchak,

2000; Olszewski-Kubilius & Scott, 1992; Wright & Borland, 1992). College and career guidance is a valuable mentoring outcome for underserved populations. Gifted economically disadvantaged students are as motivated to attend college as their middle-class peers, and they receive similar support; however, they report being less prepared to go to college (Olszewski-Kubilius & Scott, 1992). The mentoring process can facilitate that preparation. The University of Winnipeg has experienced success at implementing mentorship programs for at-risk gifted individuals. Its mentoring program, which was infused with Creative Problem Solving strategies, increased at-risk participants' independence and motivation (McCluskey, Baker, & McCluskey, 2005). Higher Achievement is another program for middle school students that incorporates academic mentoring within its afterschool and summer programs (see http://www.higherachievement.org). Located in four different states, the purpose of the program is to reduce the academic gap for at-risk students and help students enter into top high schools and colleges. Mentors volunteer their time to work with the students for 2 hours once a week from September to May. Students benefit from working closely with role models from different backgrounds and receive academic and personal support.

Economically disadvantaged students also can serve as mentors for younger students (Bisland, 2001). Using older students to mentor younger ones can have a positive effect on both parties in the relationship. Moon and Callahan (2001) were interested in understanding the effect of different combinations of curriculum modifications, family outreach, and mentoring on high-risk, high-potential primary students' academic achievement and the rate at which the students were identified for a gifted and talented program compared to a control group. All students, regardless of intervention group, demonstrated achievement gains and were at grade level by the end of the study. In other words, no one specific intervention had an effect on student achievement; however, students who had participated in the treatment groups were referred to and placed in gifted programs at a higher percentage than those in the control groups.

Telementoring

Not all mentoring occurs in person. Mentoring experiences can occur over the Internet or through books and other resource materials. One of the fastest growing areas of mentoring is telementoring, also known as virtual mentoring, e-mentoring (Nash, 2001), or iMentoring. "The general goal of most telementoring programs is to provide individualized academic, motivational, and emotional support by using technology to bring adults into children's school experiences" (Siegle, 2003, p. 3). The National Mentoring Partnership (http://www.mentoring.org) features an extensive website on all aspects of organizing and running mentorship programs, including information about telementoring and links to telementoring organizations such as the International Telementor Program (http://www.telementor.org).

By developing interesting classroom projects centered on the use of e-mail and the Internet, telementoring helps bridge the digital divide separating those who regularly use new information technologies from those who do not. It also allows mentor volunteers to use their limited time effectively and efficiently.

Telementoring can be divided into three types of programs: mentor experts who agree to respond to questions, mentors who are paired with a single learner, and mentors who work in partnerships (Riel, n.d.). First, mentor experts usually have short interactions with students. This often involves topical focus websites that are sponsored by corporations or organizations. Students e-mail their questions to the organization and an expert on the topic e-mails a reply. One of the more well-known mentor expert sites is the MadSci Network (http://www.mad-sci.org). The plethora of Ask an Expert sites online provide unlimited indexes of experts' in a variety of subject areas. The most successful telementoring programs usually are partnerships that include a three-component design that involves students, their teachers, and mentors. Students in these programs may not participate unless a teacher sponsors them; however, some programs allow parents to sponsor their children. The teacher works with the student to design a mentoring proposal. Together they submit the student's proposal to an online mentoring organization that posts it for consideration by potential mentors (Dahle, 1998). Once a mentor match is made, the teacher usually monitors the student's participation. E-mail is the most common communication format for the mentor and mentee to use.

Telementoring has some unique advantages over traditional mentoring, including that it (International Telementor Program, n.d.):

» provides a means of connecting thousands of professionals with students on a scale that is impractical in traditional face-to-face mentoring;
» matches students with appropriate mentors without geographic limitation;
» allows convenient, consistent, weekly communication between students and mentors and creates an archive of all communication;
» eliminates scheduling problems between mentors and students because an e-mail or text communication can be sent any time; and
» provides the opportunity for students to work on long-term projects with their mentors and allows mentors to see the impact they are having on students.

Telementoring provides four major benefits for teachers (International Telementor Program, n.d.):

» With telementoring projects, students become fully engaged in them, which make teachers' jobs much easier. Teachers then can act to facilitate learning, rather than trying to convince students that they need to learn.

» Students are responsible for developing their own special projects based on their interests.

» Telementoring utilizes the skills and knowledge of adult professionals.

» The value of students interacting with people outside the classroom includes learning about different careers, lifestyles, and cultures.

Mentoring Partnerships in the STEM Areas

Specialized schools emphasizing the study of STEM content areas are one option for gifted students interested in these areas. These open the door for unique opportunities—such as mentoring with a prominent scholar or a teacher who has a Ph.D. in a STEM content area—that students might not otherwise experience in their regular school (Olszewski-Kubilius, 2010).

Mentorships in a STEM area might focus on participating in authentic research. An implicit benefit includes the development of tacit knowledge about the realities of having a career in a STEM field. For example, students might learn "what kinds of experiences and education it takes to be a scientist or mathematician, the real nature of the process of scientific research, the purpose and nature of graduate training, and how to get noticed as a rising star" (Olszewski-Kubilius, 2010, p. 68).

Having a mentorship opportunity with a professional in a STEM area may be especially beneficial for low-income, minority students who wish to pursue a STEM career at a college but are not prepared for the rigors of the program and lack support from their families (Church, 2010). A student at the Academy for Math, Engineering, and Science (AMES) STEM high school participating in a National Science Foundation-funded mentoring program between students at the University of Utah and Salt Lake City high schools, shared his perspective: "Learning from real scientists and college students allowed me to be less afraid of asking questions, making mistakes, and trying new ideas about science and me" (Church, 2010, p. 13).

If students are not able to attend a specialized STEM school, they could still arrange to find a mentor to collaborate with on a research project at a local university, research center, or industrial facility. These types of authentic opportunities will better prepare students for careers in the STEM field (Olszewski-Kubilius, 2010). STEM mentor programs can also be in the form of afterschool activities. For instance, the national ACE Mentor Program inspires students to explore careers and mentorships in architecture, construction, and engineering as they meet twice weekly with teachers and industry professionals (Abdul-alim, 2011). A commonality between the ACE and AMES mentoring programs is the recognition of the importance of relationships that develop between mentors and mentees.

Establishing a Mentorship Program

Mentoring programs usually are organized and conducted by schools, universities, parent groups, service organizations, businesses and corporations, or spiritual groups. The suggestions presented in this chapter are applicable to all of these, although an emphasis is placed on programs organized by schools.

Programs must be able to recruit, screen, and train mentors; match them with youth; monitor the matches; and identify and help resolve problems as they arise. Prior to planning a mentoring program, visit the National Mentoring Partnership's extensive website (http://www.mentoring.org), which includes a myriad of information ranging from developing plans, to training mentors, to evaluating program outcomes. Veterans and neophytes alike will gain valuable information from the hundreds of screens of useful information and free material posted there.

A successful program requires a coordinated effort from planning through evaluation. The following sections describe a detailed, six-step plan for planning, operating, and evaluating a mentorship program.

Step 1. Developing a Plan

A planning committee usually is formed to develop and implement a mentoring program. Aside from the program coordinator, the committee should include teachers, a school administrator, the school psychologist or counselor, parents, students, and community members. The teachers build support for the program within the school. The administrator offers insight into program operations and school budgets. The school psychologist is helpful when evaluating students and mentors. Student input is invaluable when selecting the type of program to offer. Parents and community members can assist in building community support and gaining access to potential mentors.

The first priority of the planning committee is determining what type of mentoring program to establish. Although mentoring can be a combination of the following, mentoring usually falls into one of three categories based on its purpose (Milam, 2001):

1. Interest area mentoring is a way of expanding or enriching the curriculum to enable students with special skills, knowledge, and interests to work with others who have expertise in those areas.

2. Career investigation mentoring provides opportunities for career exploration.

3. Affective development mentoring focuses on issues of self-esteem, values, and emotional support and seeks to provide role models for students. (p. 527)

One or a combination of these purposes can be achieved through academic tutoring, job shadowing, career exploration, job and life skills development, or participation in internships (National Mentoring Center, n.d.).

Mentors who assist students on a regular basis with classwork or special projects fall into the academic tutoring category. They may work with students at school or at the mentor's workplace. This type of mentoring may abate as soon as a special project is completed or may continue throughout the student's school career.

Job shadowing is usually a short-term option where the student spends from 1–2 days to several weeks at the mentor's workplace learning about a given career. Job shadowing can develop into a career exploration mentorship. Under this option, the student spends a substantial amount of in-depth time on location with the mentor. For example, one student spent a semester job shadowing a veterinarian at an animal clinic, where she assisted with several animal surgeries.

Mentors also can assist young people in developing job and life skills that will help them gain employment and be successful in the workplace. In one study of high school students participating in a 3-week summer mentoring program with university professors, Little et al. (2010) found that students' perceived their research skills and self-concept of their job skills to have increased over the course of the program. Finally, students may participate in paid internships where they provide assistance and develop their talents simultaneously. Kim (2010) surveyed high-achieving high school students from International Baccalaureate programs and a Governor's School Program about their top choices for career-related programs. These included Advanced Placement courses, dual enrollment, career guidance, and mentoring opportunities from high school. Although job shadowing and internships were on the students' top choices list, more students preferred mentoring. Students also mentioned mentorships as one of the most influential school experiences in selecting their future career.

In addition to the type of program, the scope of the program also must be considered. Typical programs match mentors and mentees for 6 months to a year (National Mentoring Partnership, n.d.), although many young people can benefit from longer relationships. The frequency of meetings between mentors and mentees also should be considered. Finally, the depth to which the organization wishes to develop mentoring should be discussed.

Ultimately, the mentoring program that is established should be based on the needs of the students and the resources of the school and community. These will drive the program goals. Unfortunately, planners often take shortcuts when establishing program goals. Many program handbooks contain lofty program goals that have little to do with what actually happens in the program. The time needed to discuss student needs and the available resources of the program is time well spent. Once clearly defined goals are established, selection of mentors, mentees, program activities, and program evaluation methods and tools is much easier.

Student needs. Students at schools with a variety of accelerated classes and extensive honors and Advanced Placement programs have different needs than those students being serviced with a resource enrichment program or those with no program at all.

Available resources. Planners should ask how current resources can be used and what additional resources are necessary. Mentorship programs sometimes appear to be an attractive alternative for schools because they seem to cost less than other services for gifted students (Coleman & Cross, 2001).

Three questions to ask about available resources are (National Mentoring Partnership, n.d.).:

1. Is there already a sufficient, trained staff to plan and implement the program without significantly restructuring or adding new staff?
2. What type of administrative support and overhead is available for space and administrative support?
3. What are the program costs and how will they be funded?

Liability. Liability must be well thought out during the planning phase. The safety and well-being of the students is the first priority, and it must be discussed with parents, mentors, and mentees at orientation meetings.

Schools should conduct criminal checks on mentor volunteers (Roberts & Inman, 2001). The National Mentoring Partnership (2008) also recommends writing a "Volunteer's Code of Conduct" to address appropriate activities for mentors, explicit rules about drug and alcohol use, and boundaries of mentor/mentee relationships, and this document should be written and shared with anyone involved in the program. An organization's insurance company should be consulted regarding how the current liability coverage specifically applies to mentoring efforts. The coverage should shield mentors from claims by participants, as well as shield the organization from claims by mentors and mentees. The Nebraska Work-Based Project (Nebraska Department of Education, 2000) suggested the following insurance considerations for parents, school administrators, and employers: health and life insurance, automobile accident insurance, accident and liability insurance, worker's compensation, and medical treatment waivers.

Step 2. Recruiting Mentors

Any recruitment of participants should portray accurate expectations and benefits (National Mentoring Partnership, n.d.). Presentations to local organizations and businesses, articles in the local school newspapers, radio and television news coverage, websites, school newsletters, and brochures are effective ways to promote the program. Promotional material should include (Nash & Treffinger, 1993):

- » history of the program,
- » program philosophy,
- » program components,
- » student selection process,
- » mentor role,
- » student role,
- » parent role, and
- » coordinator role.

It may take some creativity to locate mentors, but they can be found in a variety of places including service groups and community organizations; research institutions; cultural institutes; government agencies; area businesses; area libraries; sports organizations; outdoor/environmental associations; and senior citizen centers (Nash & Treffinger, 1993).

Beyond the traditional pool of mentors from community resources and service clubs, there may be willing volunteers within the school (VanTassel-Baska & Baska, 2000). The value of teachers serving as mentors should not be overlooked. In reviewing her research on Presidential Scholars, Kaufmann (2003) noted that 66% of her respondents reported their most significant mentor had been a secondary or graduate school teacher.

Recruiting mentors from the community can be time consuming and expensive. Initially, it may be easier to recruit mentors from a single source, such as a particular service organization. It also may be easier to recruit mentors who work or live in close geographic proximity to the program. Once the program begins, existing mentors can make the best recruiters for future mentors (National Mentoring Partnership, n.d.).

Having skill in an area is not a sufficient reason for someone to be a mentor. The mentor must have the desire and the ability to establish a nurturing relationship (Roberts & Inman, 2001; Schatz, 1999). In order to appreciate and perceive the artistry of the traditional mentor relationship, it is essential to perceive and sense the whole. "Mentors do not so much teach as live the process . . . and in so doing, provide for others a foundation for learning and living throughout the lifespan" (Bennetts, 2001, p. 260).

Dr. Lenhard Ng, a highly successful mathematician and professor, reflected upon his appreciation for his mentors, "I've had the good luck that my mentors and advisors were all patient and gracious with their time, and their encouragement gave me the confidence I needed to progress" (Muratori et al., 2006, p. 318). The responsibilities of mentors also include being open to sharing their knowledge, being patient and understanding of gifted students' curiosity and high levels of energy, and being willing to listen to and motivate mentees (Bisland, 2001).

Other characteristics of a quality mentor almost always include:

» understands and appreciates the general and specific giftedness of the mentee;
» is caring;
» is respectful of the mentee's right to make his or her own choices;
» holds the mentee to high standards;
» extends the mentee's experiences;
» can provide constructive, rather than critical, feedback; and
» is comfortable being a role model for the mentee.

Mentors frequently seek out mentees, cultivate friendship, share their lives, and offer advice and support (Geiger, 2001). Mentees could also seek out mentors (Hess, 2008), although, the student should receive some guidance in how to actively find a mentor on their own.

Questions to consider about potential mentors include (Berger, 1990):

1. Does the mentor like working with gifted young people?
2. Is the mentor's teaching style compatible with the student's learning style?
3. Is the mentor willing to be a role model by sharing his or her excitement and joy of learning?
4. Is the mentor optimistic and positive about the future?

Step 3. Selecting Mentees

Not all students want or need mentors. The following four questions should guide the decision to find a mentor for a student (Berger, 1990):

» Does the mentee want a mentor, or simply some exposure to a particular subject or career field?
» What type of mentor does the student need?
» Is the student willing to invest a significant amount of time with the mentor?
» Does the student fully understand the purpose, benefits, and limitations of a mentoring relationship?

Does the mentee want a mentor, or simply some exposure to a particular subject or career field? A mentorship is appropriate for a student who has a clear goal, such as an in-depth investigation of an issue. It may not be appropriate if the student simply wants some advice on a school project (Kaufmann, 2003) or if the student is only seeking quick answers to his or her questions. Prior to considering a mentorship, students should reflect on the following questions (Rimm, 2003):

» What do I hope to get from this relationship?
» What type of adult would I get along with best?
» Are there any special skills or interests that I want my mentor to have?
» What can I do to help my mentor bring out the best in me?
» How can I help my mentor in return? (p. 91)

Students who are disenfranchised within their educational program sometimes indicate that they wish to work on their own with a mentor. However, just because students indicate that they want to work on their own does not necessarily mean a mentorship is the best arrangement. Reilly (1992b) cautioned that, because schools have the primary responsibility to educate children, they should investigate a variety of available resources within the school before asking others for a long-term mentoring commitment.

An authentic mentorship is more than a student receiving supplemental information. Because of the demanding level of interaction between a mentee and mentor, other sources of information or other types of interaction between the student and a knowledgeable adult may be more appropriate. For example, the telementoring option of asking an expert (discussed earlier in this chapter) may be more appropriate. Perhaps one or two meetings with a knowledgeable adult who is willing to share resources with the student would suffice.

What type of mentor does the student need? A mentor can serve five different roles (Shaughnessy & Neely, 1991):

» Mentors serve as models for their mentees. Mentees may seek to emulate the talents, skills, or personality characteristics of their mentors.
» Mentors provide a knowledge base for mentees.
» Mentors help students formulate future plans and ways to achieve them.
» Mentors help students think about the world differently and look at the world through new eyes.
» Mentors help students better understand themselves. (p. 131)

Selecting the right mentor is a difficult task. Torrance's (1984) research indicated that females mention the following top three positive characteristics of mentors: (a) encouraging, praising; (b) skilled, expert; and (c) a friend. Men mention (a) skilled, expert; (b) a friend; and (c) encouraging, prodding. In a more recent study, Little et al. (2010) found that high school students attending a summer mentoring program valued their relationships with mentors and wished they had additional time with them. The mentees described their mentors as "nice, friendly, cool, easy to talk with, awesome, and having good ideas" (p. 193).

The mentor's personality and teaching style should be compatible with the student's personality and learning style (Berger, 1990; Kaufmann, 2003). Potential mentors and mentees may wish to complete a learning style inventory to assess their compatibility. The mentee also must identify with the mentor. Identification with a role model is based on three variables: "(1) nurturance, or the warmth of the relationship between the child and a particular adult; (2) similarities that children see between themselves and an adult; and (3) the power of the adult as perceived by the child" (Rimm, 2001, p. 27).

Selecting a mentor for students is not simply finding the most knowledgeable person in a student's area of interest and considering compatible learning styles. An appraisal of the student's expertise or performance level is warranted. Bloom (1985) and his colleagues discovered that experts in different fields progressed through three distinct phases of learning and that the length of these phases, the type of interaction involved at each phase, and the sequence of the phases were instrumental in talent development.

Based on this work, Bloom (1985) identified three different types of mentors/instructors. Students who are new to a topic or talent field require mentors who help them develop a passion for the field of study. These mentors are less concerned with right and wrong and measurable objectives than they are with sharing the field and having fun with it. Students who have already fallen in love with a discipline require a different type of mentor. These mentors are selected for their expertise in the talent area. Mentoring at this level focuses on technical skill development and perfecting the small details of the talent field. Most students will never reach or require the third type of mentor. Mentors at this phase are masters who help their mentees transition from technical precision to personal expression.

Building on Bloom's (1985) work and others, Calderon et al. (2007) described a new talent development model that recognizes the important role of teachers, coaches, parents, and mentors in facilitating the transformation of gifted students' competencies into expertise and then expertise to scholarly productivity or artistry (SP/A). These roles include guiding students in problem solving, sharing their tacit knowledge, and supporting students' career development. Pinnacle is a program that primarily focuses on developing gifted adolescents' expertise into SP/A by matching them with eminent scholars who share their expertise and creativity. The relationships between mentors and mentees through Pinnacle are maintained throughout the year and participants have the opportunity to reunite at an annual summit reunion.

Is the student willing to invest a significant amount of time with the mentor? Effective mentoring demands passionate commitments from mentees whether the experience is short-term or longer. The Mentee Selection Scale shown in Figure 17.1 features characteristics for students who are likely to invest the time and energy necessary for successful mentoring.

Students who have exhausted their available resources are likely candidates for mentoring because this indicates they have the necessary interest and motivation. Coordinators should screen students to ensure successful experiences. This includes a review of the students' intent, expectations, and motivation; depth of background on the topic; ability to learn as evidenced by previous grades; and school attendance. Likely candidates have a clear understanding of their interest area and have demonstrated past initiative in independently expanding their knowledge of it (Reilly, 1992a).

Does the student fully understand the purpose, benefits, and limitations of a mentoring relationship? A successful mentorship provides benefits for both the mentor and the mentee, evidenced by the fact that those who have been recipients of mentoring relationships often become mentors (Bennetts, 2001). The mentor and mentee work together as a team to develop objectives and goals for the mentoring experience. An end product or final goal then guides the mentoring relationship (Roberts & Inman, 2001). The mentor and mentee must be flexible and willing to modify or even change these goals as their investigation develops. Mentoring fails when the pace is too slow or too fast (likely too fast); the mentor demonstrates too much personal sacrifice in his or her career; the mentor has a limited perspective; gender and race barriers exist; or the mentor doesn't approve of the mentee's behavior (Torrance, 1984).

Rimm (2003) suggested that mentees show their appreciation to their mentors by being respectful, prompt, and providing assistance to the mentor. She also warned young people that even role models have their weaknesses.

> Role models can help you identify the traits you admire, but even people you look up to exhibit some qualities you'd rather not have. . . . You can still learn from these people. The trick is to take the best from each person. (p. 94)

Step 4. Matching Mentors and Mentees

The match between mentor and mentee is crucial. These matches are particularly important because one of the roles of mentors is the transmission of values and attitudes (Kaufmann, 2003). As one of Kaufmann's Presidential Scholars noted,

> He [The mentor] had an absolute passion for teaching! Nothing seemed to excite him like having a student suddenly grasp something. It is that

As related to the potential mentoring topic, the student . . .

	Never	Rarely	Occasionally	Frequently	Always
1. Is not being challenged by traditional educational methods and activities	☐	☐	☐	☐	☐
2. Possesses extensive vocabulary on the topic	☐	☐	☐	☐	☐
3. Asks questions that are not being answered by classes or the present curriculum	☐	☐	☐	☐	☐
4. Shows evidence of previous and current active involvement with the topic	☐	☐	☐	☐	☐
5. Focuses and exerts extended effort on tasks related to the topic	☐	☐	☐	☐	☐
6. Maintains curiosity and interest in the topic	☐	☐	☐	☐	☐
7. Displays a personal sense of responsibility and autonomy	☐	☐	☐	☐	☐
8. Knows or is willing to learn process or methodology skills related to the topic	☐	☐	☐	☐	☐
9. Is open to guidance and suggestions	☐	☐	☐	☐	☐
10. Easily interacts with adults	☐	☐	☐	☐	☐
Add Column Total:	_____	_____	_____	_____	_____
Multiply by Weight:	X 1	X 2	X 3	X 4	X 5
Add Weighted Column Totals:	_____ +	_____ +	_____ +	_____ +	_____

Scale Total: _____ / 50

Figure 17.1. Mentee Selection Scale for evaluating students who are likely candidates for mentorship experiences *Note.* From *Developing Mentorship Programs for Gifted Students* (p. 21), by D. Siegle, 2005, Waco, TX: Prufrock Press. Copyright ©2005 by Del Siegle. Reprinted with permission. This form may be reproduced for educational purposes.

excitement, rather than the specific subjects he taught, that has stayed with me and emerged as the most significant contribution of his mentorship. (Kaufmann, 2003, p. 5)

Mentors, mentees, and parents ought to be interviewed prior to making a match. A committee of at least three members ought to participate in interviews. The special skills and insight of school psychologists may be useful in matching potential mentors and mentees (VanTassel-Baska & Baska, 2000). Interviews can be time-consuming, and it may be difficult to coordinate the interview and interviewee's schedules, but the benefits may outweigh the disadvantages. Hess (2008), a former science research mentee, advised other mentees to

Treat this as a job interview, dressing and acting professionally. The potential mentor will interview you to make sure you can do the work, but it is just as important for you to ask questions to be certain the lab will be a good match for *you*. Send a thank you note after the meeting. (p. 15)

Aside from considering the ability levels of the mentor and mentee, the following areas also are worth exploring during the interviews (Forster, 1994):

» *Level of interest in the program*: This involves all parties: student, parents, teacher, and school.
» *Reason for involvement*: What does each party hope to achieve?
» *Level of interest in the area*: What has the student/mentor already done in this area?
» *Standards of work*: What is the quality of previous work in the area of interest?
» *Learning style*: Is the mentee comfortable working with adults? What characteristics would the mentee like in a mentor and vice versa? Is humor important? Gender? Ethnicity?
» *Recommendation*: What have others said about the mentor/mentee?

The following points of compatibility should be considered when making a match (National Mentoring Partnership, n.d.):

» *Personal preferences*: Mentors and youth may request someone of the same gender, a certain age range, or other characteristic. These requests should be honored whenever possible.
» *Temperament*: Try to ensure that personality and behavior styles mesh. Does the mentor have a nurturing, familial approach or a more businesslike, impersonal one? Match each mentor with a young person who responds best to his or her particular style.
» *Life experiences and interests*: Do the potential mentor and mentee share hobbies, lifestyles, or family makeup?

Mentors and mentees should have an opportunity to express a preference regarding a match, understand how matching decisions are made, and be given an opportunity to request a different match if their original match is not satisfactory after reasonable effort.

Step 5. Training and Orientation Meetings

Mentor training. A primary reasons mentors drop out is a lack of training and inadequate screening. Generally, interested mentors attend an orientation meeting that covers an overview of the program. If they are interested and selected as mentors, they usually attend a 2- to 3-hour follow-up training session. Most organizations hold separate initial training for mentors and mentees. For advanced training, however, they may conduct combined events. Some of the topics (e.g., career development and cross-difference mentoring) actually may be more stimulating and beneficial if both groups attend (Phillips-Jones, n.d.).

The first mentor training includes an explanation of the purpose, benefits, and limitations of mentoring and an explanation of the mentee's rights and responsibilities. This 2- to 3-hour training session provides volunteer mentors with the skills they'll need to start and maintain a successful mentoring relationship. During this session, mentors can address their concerns and expectations, explore boundary issues, discuss communication styles, and learn about the stages of the mentoring relationship through a combination of role-playing, interactive exercises, and lecture. The goals of the training are to (Hamilton Fish Institute, 2007):

» help participants understand the scope and limits of their role as mentors;
» help them develop the skills and attitudes they need to perform well in their role;
» introduce them to the concept of positive youth development;
» provide information about the strengths and vulnerabilities of the children or youth who are in the program;
» provide information about program requirements and supports for mentors;
» answer questions they may have about the mentoring experience; and
» build their confidence as they prepare to start working with their mentee. (pp. 1–2)

At a minimum, the following topics should be covered during mentor training:
» steps of the formal mentoring process (a more detailed discussion of the process appears in the next section);
» how to negotiate various aspects of a mentoring partnership;
» how to assist mentees in developing goals and planning activities;

» key mentor and mentee process skills (listening actively, building trust, being encouraging, identifying goals and current reality, instructing/developing capabilities, inspiring, opening doors, managing risks, providing corrective feedback, acquiring additional mentors, learning quickly, showing initiative, following through, managing the relationship, career awareness);

» how to conduct some basic evaluation of the mentee's progress and the relationship;

» unexpected challenges and solutions (Phillips-Jones, n.d.); and

» an understanding of diversity and cultural awareness.

Upon completion of their training, mentors should exhibit a clear understanding of their role in the areas listed below. These guidelines are meant to help mentors avoid situations that might negatively reflect on themselves or the organization that they serve in the community.

1. *Preparedness*: Mentors are prepared to be a friend to a young person and demonstrate consistent, dependable, trustworthy, accepting, honest, and respectful behaviors.

2. *Integrity*: Mentors consistently act in ways that are ethical, earning the respect and trust of their mentees and supporting community partners.

3. *Commitment*: Mentors are steadfast in their commitment to the policies and procedures of the guiding organization.

4. *Knowledge builder*: Mentors actively seek out shared opportunities that enhance the knowledge, skills, and abilities of their mentees.

5. *Inclusive attitude*: Mentors value the diverse racial, economic, cultural, and religious traits of their mentees.

6. *Maintain confidentiality*: Mentors act in the best interest of the mentoring organization and ensure confidentiality, taking care to protect against inadvertent disclosure.

7. *Accountability*: Mentors make regular contact with the mentoring organization to ensure effective mentoring practices.

8. *Appropriate behavior*: Mentors refrain from profanity, criticism of school faculty or staff, inappropriate physical contacts, and violations of laws or school codes of conduct.

9. *Eligibility*: Mentors authorize the completion of required background checks to cover criminal history, driving records, personal interviews, and other forms of screening as deemed appropriate.

10. *Service to community*: Mentors maintain a steady presence in the lives of youth and in community efforts that strive to encourage others toward participation in volunteer efforts (Letting Education Achieve Dreams [LEAD], n.d.).

Mentee training. Mentees also require an introduction to the mentoring process. Their training should prepare them to understand the purpose of and their responsibilities in the relationship. This should include a discussion of the following topics:

» setting important goals,
» evaluating their progress,
» appropriate mentor/mentee relations,
» providing feedback to mentors,
» showing appreciation to mentors, and
» options for an unsuccessful match.

Step 6. Monitoring and Evaluating the Mentorship

Mentoring goes through three stages. An understanding of these stages and clear communication during them is essential for a successful mentoring relationship. In the first stage, mentors and mentees become acquainted and identify their common interests and goals. Communication tends to be awkward because neither party has developed trust. Trust begin to develop at this stage. Predictability and consistency are the foundation for this trust. Keeping appointments, arriving on time, and following up on promises are essential component to building this trust. Establishing confidentiality will also further develop trust. During the first stage, the pair begins to explore achievable goals together as they transition to the second stage. During the second stage, mentors and mentees begin confiding in each other as they start working on the goals they set in the first stage. As confidence develops, the two partners begin to accomplish their goals during the second stage. New goals may develop as old ones are met and new challenges emerge. The final stage involves the closure of the mentorship. The relationship may be redefined. This also may include defining next steps (Workforce Board, n.d.). Callahan and Kyburg (2005) warned that this final stage can be problematic for gifted and talented children. "Highly developed emotional sensitivities and ability of gifted youth may lead to a tendency to form especially strong empathetic bonds with mentors and can make transitions to new mentors and/or terminations of mentoring arrangements especially challenging" (p. 435).

After the mentorship coordinator initially links the mentor and mentee and sets a time for their first meeting, further meeting arrangements should be made by the mentor, mentee, and parents. The next location and time should be firmly set following each meeting between the mentor and mentee. All parties should understand who will be making the next contact. The coordinator should check to ensure that contact is made. E-mail is efficient when contacting mentors and mentees. All parties should feel free to contact the coordinator if problems arise (Forster, 1994).

The coordinator also should periodically contact mentors and mentees regarding their progress and whether they are satisfied with the match. Students and mentors may be asked to evaluate the experience at the end of the first month to make sure that both parties are interested in continuing their relationship. The coordinator also should monitor whether the mentee is identifying with the mentor, how well his or her self-esteem and confidence are developing, and whether any unrealistic expectations have risen (Berger, 1990).

Evaluations of mentoring programs are necessary and need not be expensive. They can be as simple as asking mentors and mentees about their experiences. Three initial program concerns that warrant early evaluation are the effectiveness of the match, the mentor's willingness to recognize and develop the mentee's talent, and the mentee's satisfaction with the experience. Evaluations also can be included as part of a follow-up activity in which students write or talk about their experiences.

More formal evaluations cover the processes and the outcomes of a program. Process information pertains to the number of mentor/mentee matches, types of activities that were held, length of the mentorship relations, frequency and duration of meetings, and perceptions of the relationship. Outcome information includes data such as the mentee's grades, behaviors, and attitudes; the teacher's reports of the mentee's classroom behaviors; the mentor's reflections on his or her experiences; the mentee's optimism about the future; parent-child relationships; and graduation rates (National Mentoring Partnership, n.d.).

If the program goals were clearly articulated at the start of the program, evaluating them is an easier task. Without clearly defined goals, deciding how to define program success can be difficult.

Conclusion

Torrance (1984) stated it best:

The Most Important Things Mentors Can Do for Creatively Gifted Youth Help them to:
  » Be unafraid of "falling in love with something" and pursue it with intensity and in-depth. [People are] motivated most to do the things they love and can do best.
  » Know, understand, take pride in, practice, use, exploit, and enjoy their greatest strengths.
  » Learn to free themselves from the expectations of others and to walk away from the games that others try to impose upon them.

» Free themselves to play their own game in such a way as to make the best use of their strengths and follow their dreams.

» Find some great teachers and attach themselves to these teachers.

» Avoid wasting a lot of expensive, unproductive energy in trying to be well-rounded.

» Learn the skills of interdependence and give freely of the infinity of their greatest strength. (pp. 56–57)

"Often the gifted do not fail intellectually, but emotionally. Obstacles or circumstances become so overwhelming that even the best consider giving up" (McGreevy, 1990, p. 8). Because they have years of experience, mentors know the roadblocks talented students face. They also know the incremental nature of talent development and are able to advance students along it (Purcell et al., 2001). To accomplish this, they transform students from reactive to proactive learners (Nash, 2001).

Mentoring works. It works at all age levels. It works under a variety of conditions. It works because mentors recognize young people's talents and interests and provide them with opportunities to explore and develop them. Each year, hundreds of thousands of young people benefit from the wisdom and dedication of adult mentors. Mentoring makes a difference in lives. In their simplest form, mentoring programs can begin with one child working with one adult. From that simple beginning, the possibilities are limitless.

Student Statement: Mentoring in Action

Austin Costello is currently a puppetry major at the University of Connecticut. He reflected on his passion for puppets and the role mentoring has played in pursuing his interest in this piece he wrote for Johns Hopkins Center for Talented Youth's Imagine *magazine.*

My junior year was also when I started thinking seriously about college. One day, as I was freaking out about what activities I would include on my college applications, I received an e-mail from one of my friends. The timing was so perfect that it was like a scene from a movie. "You should TOTALLY check out this program," my friend wrote. "It's called UConn Mentor Connection. It will be the best four weeks of your life." She had attended the program the year before and thought it would be great for me. When I saw where it was and what it entailed, I knew she was right.

UConn Mentor Connection is a program for rising juniors and seniors, who apply to different "[mentorship] sites," or learning groups, that focus on topics including puppet arts, archaeology, chemistry, math, biology, and more. I was thrilled and a little nervous when I was accepted into the month-long program. While I looked forward to bringing newfound puppetry and acting knowledge to school in the fall, I'd never stayed away from home that long.

The puppetry program was led by UConn professor of puppetry Bart Roccoberton, who has been working in puppetry for more than 20 years. He has performed with many international puppetry groups and has worked on television in the U.S. and overseas. Also in charge was Joe Therrien, then a student in the puppetry department. The puppetry [mentoring] program had just six students, including me. Some kids were interested in acting in general, and some just wanted to know more about puppetry, but I was the only one interested in puppetry as a career. Despite our different reasons for [selecting the mentorship site], we quickly became a tight-knit group that worked really well together.

On our first day, we started by discussing some basic questions about drama in general and puppetry in particular: What makes a good story? Where and how are puppets used? How would we make our own puppets? We also discussed very early on what our final project would be. At the end of the program, each Mentor Connection site would present their research to all the students and faculty to demonstrate what they had learned. We decided that we would perform a short play, which we would write, featuring puppets that we would build.

Our group met at the university's Puppet Arts Complex (also known as the Puppet Lab). We had a whole workshop full of materials to use—furs, felt, foam, metals, woods, and anything else you could think of to build a puppet—so our creativity was in full flow as we each designed our own puppets. As a group, we considered character types, settings, scenarios, and elements of plot that we could use to make an enjoyable and entertaining show. Every day, we came up with more and more storyline based on characters we were creating. . . .

When we performed the play at the end of the program, the audience enjoyed the show, and we performers were overjoyed to know that the project we had made from scratch was such a hit. I got a lot of positive feedback after the show, and even now, every so often, people compliment me on the puppets I made for it.

When I returned to high school in the fall, my drama teacher and director gave me many opportunities to use puppetry in class and in our drama productions. My senior year was filled with puppetry. I built puppets and directed a series of puppet-based sketches for a theater variety night at my high school. . . . But the most challenging work I did was for the spring production of Little Shop of Horrors, in which the plant, Audrey II (a cross between a shark and a Venus fly-trap), "grows" larger throughout the course of the musical through the use of four increasingly larger puppets. This part is notoriously difficult to perform because the puppets range from a small, lightweight hand puppet to a massive, heavy beast of a puppet (approximately the size of a Volkswagen Beetle), with a complex system of beams and counterweights within to perform it.

To better learn how to manipulate these puppets, I called Martin Robinson, whom I'd met on the Sesame Street set back in middle school. Marty performed Audrey II in Little Shop's original Off-Broadway run in New York City and in the revival of the show on Broadway. He had become a mentor to me over the years, and he taught me how to move these puppets in a way that would both look realistic and be safe for me, as I was strapped into the 150-pound plant puppet for the hour-long second act of the musical.

Outside of school, I found opportunities to learn more about puppetry. I have taken workshops with Steve Whitmire, who has performed Kermit the Frog since Jim Henson's death, and with John Tartaglia, of Avenue Q and Sesame Street fame. I've been incredibly fortunate to learn from puppeteers whose work I admire. All of these amazing teachers have taught me not only the art and craft of puppetry, but also that if you stay faithful to what you do and keep your chin up, you can do whatever you put your mind to. For the past two years, I have tried to pass that message on as I've taught sock puppet construction and performance at a local summer camp.

Jim Henson, creator of the Muppets and one of my puppetry heroes, once said, "My ambition was to be one of the people who made a difference in this world. My hope is to leave the world a little better for having been there." This is a goal of mine, too. I hope that, like Jim, I can make the world a better place by entertaining through puppetry.

Reprinted from "My Life in Felt and Foam" by A. Costello, 2012, *Imagine: Big Ideas for Bright Minds, 19*(4), 25–27. Copyright 2012 Austin Costello. Reprinted with permission.

DISCUSSION QUESTIONS

1. What makes a good mentor?

2. Why do gifted students need mentors? Which types of gifted students are especially likely to need mentors?

3. What is the difference between a mentorship and an internship?

4. How is a mentor relationship beneficial for the mentor?

5. What are the advantages and disadvantages of telementoring programs?

6. What are the three main categories of mentorship programs? How would your approach to setting up a mentorship program differ depending on the category of mentorship you envision using?

7. What are the steps to creating a successful mentorship program?

8. How can you tell whether a student will benefit from a mentorship experience? What are the qualities that make someone a good mentee?

9. What legal and ethical considerations should you address when starting a mentorship program?

10. What kind of training should you provide for mentors, mentees, or both?

Teacher Resources

Publications

DuBois, D. L., & Karcher, M. J. (Eds.). (2005). *Handbook of youth mentoring*. Thousand Oaks, CA: Sage.

Miller, A. (2002). *Mentoring students and young people: A handbook of effective practice*. London, England: Taylor & Francis.

Miller, C. (2006). *Mentoring teens: A resource guide*. Charleston, SC: BookSurge.

Probst, K. (2006). *Mentoring for meaningful results: Asset-building tips, tools, and activities for youth and adults*. Minneapolis, MN: Search Institute.

Reilly, J. (1992). *Mentorships: The essential guide for schools and business*. Dayton: Ohio Psychology Press.

Siegle, D. (2005). *Developing mentorship programs for gifted students*. Waco, TX: Prufrock Press.

Torrance, E. P. (1984). *Mentor relationships: How they aid creative achievement, endure, change, and die*. Buffalo, NY: Bearly Limited.

Websites

Center for Talented Youth SET Peer Network and Mentor Form—http://cty.jhu.edu/set/pcnet.html

> The Study of Exceptional Talent (SET) Mentor Program facilitates relationships between older and younger SET members. Mentors advise SET members on their academic concerns and career interests, as well as the challenges of being an exceptional student.

International Telementor Program—http://www.telementor.org

> The International Telementor Program is a leader in telementoring. Students and potential mentors can register at this site, which also includes valuable information on the telementor process.

MadSci Network—http://www.madsci.org

> MadSci Network is an interactive site where students can post questions related to science that are answered by a pool of scientists.

National Mentoring Partnership—http://www.mentoring.org

> The National Mentoring Partnership is probably the most extensive mentorship-related site on the Internet. It contains step-by-step instructions for developing and running a mentoring program, as well as links to established mentoring programs.

National Mentoring Center Resource Collections—http://educationnorthwest.org/nmc/resourcecollections

> This site features publications and web resources on mentoring.

The Mentoring Center—http://www.mentor.org

This is a 501(c)(3) tax-exempt private nonprofit organization in the San Francisco Bay area. This site contains information on mentoring and links to mentoring programs.

U.S. Department of Education Mentoring Resource Center—http://www.edmentoring.org

This site offers resources for organizations developing mentoring programs. Fact sheets provide information on a variety of topics including avoiding poor matches and higher education partnerships. In addition, this site provides information about U.S. Department of Education Mentoring grants for educational agencies and nonprofit organizations.

Volunteer Match—http://www.volunteermatch.org

This national networking site matches volunteers to community-based programs.

References

Abdul-alim, J. (2011). Mentor program provides STEM options. *Education Week, 30*(17), 10–11.

AOL Time Warner Foundation. (2002). *Mentoring in America*. New York, NY: Author.

Beck, L. (1989). Mentorships: Benefits and effects on career development. *Gifted Child Quarterly, 33*, 22–28.

Bennetts, C. (2001). Fanning the aesthetic flame: Learning for life. *Gifted Education International, 15*, 252–261.

Berger, S. L. (1990). *Mentor relationships and gifted learners* (Digest No. E486). Reston, VA: ERIC Clearinghouse on Handicapped and Gifted Children. (ERIC Document Reproduction Service No. ED321491)

Bisland, A. (2001). Mentoring: An educational alternative for gifted students. *Gifted Child Today, 24*(4), 22–25.

Bloom, B. S. (Ed.). (1985). *Developing talent in young people*. New York, NY: Ballantine Books.

Bonner, F. A., II, & Jennings, M. (2007). Never too young to lead: Gifted African American males in elementary school. *Gifted Child Today, 30*(2), 30–36.

Bonner, F. A., II, Jennings, M. E., Marbley, A. F., & Brown, L.-A. (2008). Capitalizing on leadership capacity: Gifted African American males in high school. *Roeper Review, 30*, 93–103.

Buisson, G. J., & Salgo, J. (2012a). Mentorship: Mutual benefits for ASL students and gifted students (Part 1). *American Annals of the Deaf, 157*, 81–86.

Buisson, G. J., & Salgo, J. (2012b). College collaboration with gifted programs: Deaf studies unit (Part 2). *American Annals of the Deaf, 157*, 87–91.

Burney, V. H., & Beilke, J. R. (2008). The constraints of poverty on high achievement. *Journal for the Education of the Gifted, 31*, 171–197.

Calderon, J., Subotnik, R., Knotek, S., Rayhack, K., & Gorgia, J. (2007). Focus on the psychosocial dimensions of talent development: An important potential role for consultee-centered consultants. *Journal of Educational and Psychological Consultation, 17*, 347–367.

Callahan, C. M., & Kyburg, R. M. (2005). Talented and gifted youth. In D. L. DuBois & M. J. Karcher (Eds.), *Handbook of youth mentoring* (pp. 424–439). Thousand Oaks, CA: Sage.

Church, A. (2010, Fall). STEM mentoring—Aspiration to achievement. *NCSSSMST Journal, 16*, 13–14.

Coleman, L. J., & Cross, T. L. (2001). *Being gifted in school: An introduction to development, guidance, and teaching*. Waco, TX: Prufrock Press.

Costello, A. (2012). My life in felt and foam. *Imagine: Big Ideas for Bright Minds, 19*(4), 25–27.

Dahle, C. (1998). *HP's mentor connection*. Retrieved from http://www.fastcompany.com/35698/hps-mentor-connection

Davalos, R. A., & Haensly, P. A. (1997). After the dust has settled: Youth reflect on their high school mentored research experience. *Roeper Review, 19*, 204–207.

Ellingson, M. K., Haeger, W. M., & Feldhusen, J. F. (1986). The Purdue mentor program: A university-based mentorship experience for G/C/T children. *G/C/T, 9*(2), 2–5.

Forster, J. (1994). Mentor links program. *Gifted Education International, 10*, 24–30.

Geiger, R. (2001). Nurturing for wisdom and compassion: Influencing those who influence. In N. Colangelo & S. Assouline (Eds.), *Talent development IV: Proceedings from the 1998 Henry B. and Jocelyn Wallace National Research Symposium* (pp. 345–349). Scottsdale, AZ: Great Potential Press.

Halpern, D., Aronson, J., Reimer, N., Simpkins, S., Star, J., & Wentzel, K. (2007). *Encouraging girls in math and science* (NCER 2007-2003). Washington, DC: National Center for Education Research, Institute of Education Sciences, U.S. Department of Education. Retrieved from http://ies.ed.gov/ncee/wwc/PracticeGuide.aspx?sid=5

Hamilton Fish Institute. (2007). *Training new mentors: Effective strategies for providing quality youth mentoring in schools and communities.* Retrieved from http://education-northwest.org/webfm_send/164

Hamilton, S. F., & Hamilton, M. A. (1992). Mentoring programs: Promise and paradox. *Phi Delta Kappan, 73,* 546–550.

Hébert, T. P., & Olenchak, F. R. (2000). Mentors for gifted underachieving males: Developing potential and realizing promise. *Gifted Child Quarterly, 44,* 196–207.

Hess, A. (2008, Fall). Finding a mentor for high school independent scientific research. *Understanding our Gifted, 21*(1), 13–15.

International Telementor Program. (n.d.). *Telementor.* Retrieved from http://www.telementor.org

Jucovy, L. (2002). *Same-race and cross-race matching* (Technical Assistance Packet #7). Retrieved from https://www.nationalserviceresources.gov/files/m2344-same-race-and-cross-race-matching.pdf

Kaufmann, F. (2003, Winter). Mentorships for gifted students: What parents and teachers need to know. *PAGE Update, 1,* 5, 11.

Kim, M. (2010). Preferences of high achieving high school students in their career development. *Gifted and Talented International, 25,* 65–75.

Kirby, E. H., Marcelo, K. B., & Kawashima-Ginsberg, K. (2009). *Volunteering and college experience* (Fact sheet). Retrieved from http://www.civicyouth.org/PopUps/FactSheets/College_Volunteering.pdf

Letting Education Achieve Dreams. (n.d.). *Mentoring.* Retrieved from http://www.uhv.edu/lead/mentoring.htm

Leyton-Armakan, J., Lawrence, E., Deutsch, N., Williams, J. L., & Henneberger, A. (2012). Effective youth mentors: The relationship between initial characteristics of college women mentors and mentee satisfaction and outcome. *Journal of Community Psychology, 40,* 906–920.

List, K., & Renzulli, J. S. (1991). Creative women's developmental patterns through age thirty-five. *Gifted Education International, 7,* 114–122.

Little, C. A., Kearney, K. L., & Britner, P. A. (2010). Students' self-concept and perceptions of mentoring relationships in a summer mentorship program for talented adolescents. *Roeper Review, 32,* 189–199.

McCluskey, K. W., Baker, P. A., & McCluskey, A. L. A. (2005). Creative Problem Solving with marginalized populations: Reclaiming lost prizes through in-the-trenches interventions. *Gifted Child Quarterly, 49,* 330–341.

McGreevy, A. (1990). Darwin and teacher: An analysis of the mentorship between Charles Darwin and professor John Henslow. *Gifted Child Quarterly, 34,* 5–9.

Merriam, S. (1983). Mentors and protégés: A critical review of the literature. *Adult Education Quarterly, 33,* 161–173.

Milam, C. P. (2001). Extending learning through mentorships. In F. A. Karnes & S. M. Bean (Eds.), *Methods and materials for teaching the gifted* (pp. 523–558). Waco, TX: Prufrock Press.

Moon, T. R., & Callahan, C. M. (2001). Curricular modifications, family outreach, and a mentoring program: Impacts on achievement and gifted identification in high-risk primary students. *Journal for the Education of the Gifted, 24,* 305–321.

Muratori, M. C., Stanley, J. C., Ng, L., Ng, J., Gross, M. U. M., Tao, T., & Tao, B. (2006). Insights from SMPY's greatest former child prodigies: Drs. Terence ("Terry") Tao and Lenhard (Lenny") Ng reflect on their talent development. *Gifted Child Quarterly, 50,* 307–324.

Nash, D. (2001, December). Enter the mentor. *Parenting for High Potential,* 18–21.

Nash, D., & Treffinger, D. (1993). *The mentor kit: A step-by-step guide to creating an effective mentor program in your school.* Waco, TX: Prufrock Press.

National Mentoring Center. (n.d.). *Mentor recruitment postcards.* Retrieved from http://educationnorthwest.org/webfm_send/239

National Mentoring Partnership. (2008). *Mentor guidelines and code of conduct.* Retrieved from www.mentoring.org/downloads/mentoring_561.doc

National Mentoring Partnership. (n.d.). *About MENTOR.* Retrieved from http://www.mentoring.org/about_mentor

National Science Foundation. (2011). *Women, minorities, and persons with disabilities in science and engineering.* Retrieved from http://www.nsf.gov/statistics/wmpd/2013/tables.cfm

Nebraska Department of Education. (2000). *Nebraska work-based learning manual.* Retrieved from http://nlcs1.nlc.state.ne.us/epubs/E2400/H038-2000.pdf

Olszewski-Kubilius, P. (2010). Special schools and other options for gifted STEM students. *Roeper Review, 32,* 61–70.

Olszewski-Kubilius, P., & Scott, J. M. (1992). An investigation of the college and career counseling needs of economically disadvantaged minority gifted students. *Roeper Review, 14,* 141–148.

Palmer, J. (2002, February 4). Mentoring program helps teen make research connection. *UConn Advance.* Retrieved from http://www.advance.uconn.edu/2002/020204/02020412.htm

Philip, K., & Hendry, L. B. (2000). Making sense of mentoring or mentoring making sense? Reflections on the mentoring process by adult mentors with young people. *Journal of Community & Applied Social Psychology, 10,* 211–223.

Phillips-Jones, L. (n.d.). *Ideas about mentoring.* Retrieved from http://www.mentoringgroup.com/advancedtrng.html

Prillaman, D., & Richardson, R. (1989). The William and Mary mentorship model: College students as a resource for the gifted. *Roeper Review, 12,* 114–118.

Purcell, J. H., Renzulli, J. S., McCoach, D. B., & Spottiswoode, H. (2001, December). The magic of mentorships. *Parenting for High Potential,* 22–26.

Reid, P. T., & Roberts, S. K. (2006). Gaining options: A mathematics program for potentially talented at-risk adolescent girls. *Merrill-Palmer Quarterly, 52,* 288–304.

Reilly, J. (1992a). *Mentorships: The essential guide for schools and business.* Dayton: Ohio Psychology Press.

Reilly, J. (1992b). When does a student really need a professional mentor? *Gifted Child Today, 15*(3), 2–8.

Reis, S. M. (1998). *Work left undone: Choices & compromises of talented females*. Mansfield Center, CT: Creative Learning Press.

Rhodes, J. E. (2002). *Stand by me: The risks and rewards of mentoring today's youth*. Cambridge, MA: Harvard University Press.

Riel, M. (n.d.). *Tele-mentoring over the net*. Retrieved from http://www.iearn.org/circles/mentors.html

Rimm, S. (2001, December). Parents as role models and mentors. *Parenting for High Potential*, 14–15, 27.

Rimm, S. (2003). *See Jane win for girls: A smart girl's guide to success*. Minneapolis, MN: Free Spirit.

Roberts, J., & Inman, T. (2001, December). Mentoring and your child: Developing a successful relationship. *Parenting for High Potential*, 8–10.

Rogers, K. B., & Kimpston, R. D. (1992). Acceleration: What we do vs. what we know. *Educational Leadership, 50*(2), 58–61.

Sánchez, B., & Colón, Y. (2005). Race, ethnicity, and culture in mentoring relationships. In D. L. DuBois & M. J. Karcher (Eds.), *Handbook of youth mentoring* (pp. 191–204). Thousand Oaks, CA: Sage.

Schatz. E. (1999). Mentors: Matchmaking for young people. *Journal of Secondary Gifted Education, 11,* 67.

Shaughnessy, M. F., & Neely, R. (1991). Mentoring gifted children and prodigies: Personological concerns. *Gifted Education International, 7,* 129–132.

Shevitz, B., Weinfeld, R., Jeweler, S., & Barnes-Robinson, L. (2003). Mentoring empowers gifted/learning disabled students to soar! *Roeper Review, 26,* 37–40.

Siegle, D. (2001, December). "One size fits all" doesn't work when selecting a mentor. *Parenting for High Potential,* 7, 11.

Siegle, D. (2003). Technology: Mentors on the net: Extending learning through telementoring. *Gifted Child Today, 26,* 51–54.

Siegle, D. (2005). *Developing mentorship programs for gifted students*. Waco, TX: Prufrock Press.

Silverman, L. K. (2000). Career counseling. In L. K. Silverman (Ed.), *Counseling the gifted and talented* (pp. 215–238). Denver, CO: Love.

Simonton, D. K. (2000). Genius and giftedness: Same or different? In K. A. Heller, F. J. Mönks, R. J. Sternberg, & R. F. Subotnik (Eds.), *International handbook of giftedness and talent* (pp. 111–122). Amsterdam, The Netherlands: Elsevier.

Swassing, R. H., & Fichter, G. R. (1991). University and community-based programs for the gifted adolescent. In M. Bireley & J. Genshaft (Eds.), *Understanding the gifted adolescent: Educational, developmental, and multicultural issues* (pp. 176–185). New York, NY: Teachers College Press.

Tomlinson, C. A. (2001, December). President's column. *Parenting for High Potential, 5,* 27.

Torrance, E. P. (1984). *Mentor relationships: How they aid creative achievement, endure, change, and die*. Buffalo, NY: Bearly Limited.

VanTassel-Baska, J. (2000). Academic counseling for the gifted. In L. K. Silverman (Ed.), *Counseling the gifted and talented* (pp. 201–214). Denver, CO: Love.

VanTassel-Baska, J., & Baska, L. (2000). The roles of educational personnel in counseling the gifted. In L. K. Silverman (Ed.), *Counseling the gifted and talented* (pp. 181–200). Denver, CO: Love.

Workforce Board. (n.d.). *Stages of a mentoring relationship*. Retrieved from http://www.wtb.wa.gov/Documents/mentoringstages_000.doc

Wray, J. (2002, April 1). Where are they now? Success stories from UConn Mentor Connection students. *UConn Advance,* 5.

Wright, L., & Borland, J. H. (1992). A special friend: Adolescent mentors for young, economically disadvantaged, potentially gifted students. *Roeper Review, 14,* 124–129.

TEACHING THROUGH SIMULATION AND GAMING FOR THE GIFTED

18
Chapter

BY DOROTHY A. SISK

Game-based learning represents new territory for most schools, yet many students invest a great deal of their free time and energy in the virtual online world, becoming enthusiastic "gamers." Parents report they often have to pry their children away from video games for dinner and bedtime. The challenge for educators, particularly in gifted education, is how to craft a force that can be equally as captivating in schools.

Orson Scott Card, an innovator in education, made predictions on the importance of simulation saying, "Educational games should be more like the school corridors, where kids experiment, interact, create, and share what they create with others" (Squire & Jenkins, 2003, p. 8). In his science fiction novel *Ender's Game* (1985), written in the age of Pac-Man and the Defenders with simple graphics, confined playing fields, and limited chances for customization, Card predicted games would become the open-ended, highly-responsive environments represented in current simulations and games. In *Ender's Game*, the Earth is facing a life-and-death struggle with invading aliens. The best and brightest young minds, the gifted, gather together and train through a curriculum consisting of games, both electrical and physical. Card's school was a "constructive utopia" in which students were left on their own to experiment and solve problems, learning strategies and tactics they could then apply to saving the Earth.

Teachers and administrators want to accelerate and extend the ability of gifted students to become critical thinkers and to solve problems in a variety of situations, and simulation and gaming is an important teaching tool to help accomplish this objective. This chapter will suggest guidance on when it is the right tool to use, and more importantly, it will provide action steps to design ways to use simulation and gaming in the classroom.

Background and Definitions

Simulation as a teaching tool is not new by any means; instructional simulation games game have roots dating back 5,000 years ago. It is thought that board games, like chess and draughts, were initially devised or simulated to teach the art of war (Drummer, 2002). The Chinese board game Wei Hai and the Hindu game of Chaturanga are early examples of simulation. In these games, the military strategy of Sun-Tzu was used and dice were employed to provide chance elements. Playing pieces included miniaturized foot soldiers, light cavalry, elephants, and chariots, and in the 17th and 18th centuries, other war games were introduced. The modern era of simulation gaming began in the late 1950s (Crookhall & Oxford, 1991).

Simulation is a natural activity in which most young children engage as they pretend and role-play. They simulate interaction with other people, animals, and objects, and build an understanding of the world around them. Teachers use mental simulations when they ask, "What would have happened if South America had been colonized by the British and North America colonized by the Spanish?" Computers, video, and online simulation games are woven into the fabric of life of today's "Games Generation" or "Generation.com" students (Prensky, 2001). This difference can be conveyed more explicitly with the terms *digital immigrants* versus *digital natives* (Prensky, 2004).

There is little consensus on the terms used in the literature to define simulation, and a few of the terms are used interchangeably including: *simulation, game, role-play, simulation game, computer simulation, online gaming,* and *role-play simulation*. Simulation is a much broader concept than role-playing. Simulation is more complex, lengthy, and relatively inflexible, while role-playing usually is quite simple, brief, and flexible. In simulations, participants simulate real-life situations, and in role-playing, participants represent and experience a character or type known to them in everyday life, although simulations do include elements of role-playing.

Simulation Is Real-World Experience

Simulation simplifies reality to highlight certain key ideas (Renzulli, Leppien, & Hays, 2000). Simulation is useful in work, education, and play. In the work environment, simulation provides an important role in research and development (Romme, 2003). Professional simulations are used daily in most professions. City planners simulate factors that enable a metropolis to thrive or die. The United States Department of Defense simulates conditions, battles, and equipment. Physicians and medical students learn and practice new techniques using simulation. On-the-job flight simulations train pilots, and training simulations for the corporate world present strategies on how to change behavior and obtain results.

Playing for Keeps With Game-Based Learning

Katie Salen of the Institute of Play, a nonprofit with a focus on game-based learning, said that gaming is making inroads in the K–12 school environment despite the fears that many educators have that simulation and gaming will take the place of a full curriculum and/or textbooks (McCrea, 2013). In many classrooms, students relate what they learn in gaming experiences at home or in after-school activities to classroom lectures. In some cases, teachers and students design games to use in their classes. One teacher, John Rudman, has been using games in his classes for more than 8 years, and 3 years ago, he expanded his use of gaming to include student design. His students make their own games and play each others' games. Rudman completed a dissertation on gaming, and found student retention of learning markedly increased when students design their own games, rather than simply playing a commercial game (McCrea, 2013).

Support From the National Educational Technology Plan (NETP)

The U.S. Department of Education's (2010) NETP, *Transforming American Education: Learning Powered by Technology*, has objectives of dramatically improving teaching and learning, personalizing instruction, and ensuring that the educational environments offered to all students keep pace with the 21st century. Much of the plan emphasizes 21st-century learning and competencies including critical thinking, complex problem solving, collaboration, and multimedia communication. The NETP argues that technology can be leveraged to provide personalized learning and move away from a one-size-fits-all approach. One recommendation includes research and development into the use of gaming, simulations, and virtual worlds for instruction and assessment The plan includes case studies of the ideas and activities that are underway including the online cultural history project at Winona Middle School ("Winona Middle School's Cultural History Project," n.d.), the School of One (Rubenstein, 2010), and research into the science of learning at Carnegie Mellon University (n.d.).

Growing Importance of Distance Learning

Higher education uses a model whose costs over the last 30 years has steadily increased, and these costs have reached a point where students, parents and government are beginning to question if the product is worth the price (Anderson & Dron, 2011). Consequently, higher education is attempting to create new models to provide high educational value with less cost per student. One new model, online and blended learning, is playing a major role in enabling more students to be taught without increasing instructional costs.

Melton (2002), in *Planning and Developing Open and Distance Learning: A Quality Assurance Approach*, predicted that a majority of higher education students will take at least 80% of their classes online or in a blended format by 2020. Tablets will be the dominant learning platform and will contain the course content. Students will engage in online study groups with access to libraries with endless numbers of volumes. Bogdanovic (2012) reported that distance education is very effective with the use of instructional materials with multimedia content, including visual, auditory, and audiovisual. Visual content includes text, drawings, pictures, graphs, and models; auditory includes oral presentations or a speech and musical accompaniment; and multimedia combines text, images, sound animation, and video. Using multimedia effectively engages students in online education and computerized simulations.

Computers and Science

A major restriction for distance learning in science was the difficulty of providing laboratory activities; however, this difficulty is overcome with the use of simulation programs running on a web browser instead of requiring face-to-face lab experiences. Physics simulations are effective tools for enhancing learning and understanding complex subject matters (Kim, Park, Lee, Yuk, & Lee, 2001). At National University in Korea, students use simulation programs running on a web browser instead of hands-on laboratory experiences. This virtual reality (VR) world circumvents the physical, safety, and cost constraints that limit schools in the type of environment they can provide for "learning by doing." In a controlled study, Kim et al. (2001) found the VR group of students had greater content knowledge than students taught in traditional labs and lectures. They defined VR as a highly interactive, computer-based multimedia environment in which the student becomes a participant in a computer-generated world.

In another connection with science, the University of Waterloo in Ontario, Canada, is using computer simulations and animation to show stepwise sequences of diagrams, numbers, or images to illustrate complicated concepts or theories. In these simulations, the student enters or alters certain parameters, and the computer then reveals the consequences or changes. With a java applet, Chieh and Newman (2000) used equations to simulate a system for students to explore the differences of how real gas differs from ideal gas. Students were asked to identify conditions in which van der Waals' ideal gas law gives results within a set error limit.

Computer Simulation Games

Computer games evoke mixed response and reactions in educators. Some are troubled and concerned with the violent themes in certain casual computer games, while others are concerned with the intensity of involvement and amount of time young people devote to playing them. On a positive note, games such as the *SimCity*™ series are instructive and enlightening. In *SimCity*, the player sees each element of a city grow or decline, depending on the decisions the player makes. Buildings, roads, utilities, and other objects are built by dragging icons, and these icons or "tiles" change dynamically depending on the variables of the game. Roads fill up with traffic, factories flourish or shut down, and disasters strike when firemen or police are insufficient in numbers. *The Sims*™, a successor of *SimCity*, incorporates a variety of ways of modeling reality including linear equations, a spreadsheet, and cellular automata in which the behaviors of certain objects come from their known properties and rules for how these properties interact with neighbors. Creating a world piece-by-piece and watching each piece grow or decline is part of the game language and vocabulary of the Games Generation (Prensky, 2001).

Computer simulations in "casual" games are widely used for entertainment and play, and "serious" games are designed with the intention of improving some specific aspect of learning and players come to serious games with that expectation. Serious games can be found at every level of education, at all types of schools and universities throughout the world. Game genre, complexity, and platforms are as varied as those found in casual games. Play is an important contributor to human development and maturation, and learning is a mandatory ingredient of serious games (Day, 2001).

Numerous highly popular computer games are available such as the World of Warcraft™ series. Students can learn how to manage a small business, command troops in a Civil War battle, conduct a series of chemistry experiments, and travel to Jupiter by using computer simulation programs. Students also can interact with the web and move beyond the classroom walls to visit the White House, see the latest expedition of NASA, view current Smithsonian exhibits, check the status of the stock market, and interact with other students in classrooms throughout the world (Lewis & Doorlag, 2003).

Reporter Project™ is a computer simulation to encourage students to be writers using a simulated newspaper format. The student reporter is placed in a situation in which choices are made concerning the sections of the paper that will target a story. The student role-plays a reporter and searches for pertinent facts and writes the story. Later, the student role-plays a writer, writing and submitting the story to the editor (the computer) that checks key words in the story, and the editor then provides feedback about the logic of the facts. Real news footage is used in this simulation. The software also provides opportunities for students to print their stories.

Simulation in the Classroom

Thiagarajan (2006), known as Thiagi, said in *100 Favorite Games* that he made the important connection between playing and learning as a high school physics teacher. His students were not excited about learning about the four-stroke cycle of the internal combustion engine, so he asked them to bring carburetors to class, which they secured from abandoned cars, a repair shop, and a mysterious source. He designed a game that involved taking the carburetor apart, identifying each part, and putting everything back together again. Players earned score points for their physical skill and cognitive talents. Thiagi kept simplifying the scoring system, and rewarding student players for higher order thinking skills. Today he conducts public and in-house workshops on designing training games, including online games and e-learning courses integrated with games and simulations.

Brozo and Simpson (2003) reported on a secondary history teacher providing opportunities for students to participate in a simulation activity called *Government Experiment*. In this activity, students are divided into two groups, the Oros and Bindus, and each group is given a set of directions for electing representatives to make laws or rules. The Bindus can only make rules that apply to themselves, whereas the Oros can impose rules on the Bindus if they choose. Each group is then given a lump sum of $100 play money for its treasury.

The teacher, as a leader of the Oros, immediately began imposing laws on the Bindus that roughly paralleled the Stamp Act and the Tea Act. He levied the Paper-and-Pencil Rule, which taxed every Bindu $5 for every pencil, pen, and piece of paper used, and the Pop Rule, which taxed the Bindus $10 for having a soda. Soon the Bindus challenged the authority of the Oros by drinking soda without paying taxes and using the materials without paying. In a debriefing session, the students began to analyze the situation. The Bindus argued that it was extremely unfair for a separate group of people to tell them what to do. They said they wanted and were able to take care of themselves. One student said, "What gives you the right to tax us?" The students listed the rules imposed by the Oros and the Bindus' reactions to those rules. As they discussed the list, they began to see the similarity between their view and the colonial American view during the Revolutionary War.

Max Fischer, a middle school teacher of social studies and history, said when students are provided an affective outlet in which feelings are aroused, deep learning is stimulated. He developed the *King's M&M's* simulation to help students realize how American colonists felt about King George's Stamp Act and the subsequent Intolerable Acts that taxed various imported goods. Fischer described simulation as a staged replication of an event or concept through the manipulation of the classroom to enhance the students' understanding of the nature of a given concept or event (Hopkins, 2002).

Whyville: A Virtual Reality

Whyville™ is a web-based virtual world to provide inquiry-based education for middle school students. Jim Bower, a professor at the University of Texas and founder of CalTech's Pre-College Science Initiative designed *Whyville*. Students think of *Whyville* as a game, but teachers who use it in Waco, TX, in their eighth-grade career-exploration classes describe *Whyville* as a tool for delivering lessons in a comprehensive package. In the game, when the Whypox, a plague that causes people to break out in red spots hits *Whyville*, the residents have to go to the Center for Disease Control to learn about the epidemic. When the WhyFlu infects the people, those able to be vaccinated are protected. But as new viruses escape from a biotechnology project, the residents must scramble to develop new vaccines. Add a deadly red tide to the challenges in the game, with citizens needing to gather water samples to send to the Oceanographic Institution to find solutions. Then Hurricane Alice lands, and the residents take a crash course on the impact of global climate change.

Waco teacher Johnbelle Line and several of her students from George Washington Carver Academy were involved in a virtual airplane factory at *Whyville* PlaneWorks. The students used computers to manipulate personal avatars and interacted in an animated online environment. Line said her students were able to drag images of matching plane parts together and build the largest number of airplanes in the shortest period of time. Each student tried the timed game alone, then worked in a group team effort to find strategies to increase their team's efficiency. NASA, the Woods Hole Oceanographic Institution, the Getty Museum, and the School Nutrition Association are sponsors of projects in *Whyville*. Students access the simulation through a web browser, it uses simple graphics, and most students report it easy to learn.

The National Education Association (NEA, 2014) policy brief, *Global Competencies in a 21st Century*, identified student acquisition of higher order thinking skills as a national goal and stressed that in a world in which technology is changing rapidly, workers need to think creatively and solve problems to keep the United States economically competitive. Consequently, a primary objective for teachers is to prepare students for the world of tomorrow.

Definition of Simulation Games

Simulation represents an operating imitation of a real process, and a game is defined as any contest (play) among adversaries (players) operating under constraints (rules) for an objective (winning, victory, or consensus building). The term *game* is applied to a simulation that works wholly or partly on the basis of decisions made by players because the environment and activities of participants have the characteristics of games. Players have goals, sets of activities to perform, constraints on what can be done, and payoffs (good and bad) as consequences of action.

> Simulation represents an operating limitation of a real process. A game includes:
> - play,
> - players, and
> - rules.

Adventure games are quite similar to simulations, except the situations portrayed are selected primarily for entertainment value rather than educational value. In adventure games, participants engage in role-playing, and decisions made by the players alter the course of the adventure. Adventure games are found in arcade-type computer games. Players earn points by skillful maneuvering and careful aim as they battle with an opponent, make their way through a maze or labyrinth, or play an electronic version of a sport or conventional arcade game.

Simulations contribute to the richness of the learning environment for gifted students in numerous ways. Some of these have been described, and others can be found in magazines such as *Technology & Learning*. The website for *Technology & Learning* reprints articles from the magazine and has searchable databases for technology products, grants related to technology, and technology conferences and events.

There are many exciting simulation games available; however, the examples provided in this chapter were primarily selected as examples of simulations successfully used by the author in gifted programs and in the training of teachers of the gifted: *Star Power*™, *Tag Game*™, *Barnga*™, *Land of the Sphinx and Land of the Rainbow*™, *BaFá BaFá*™, *Parlé*™, and *Infotactics*™. Several publishing companies have numerous simulation materials available, notably Broderbund, Interact, and Prufrock Press. A number of these simulations are listed under the Teacher Resources section at the end of the chapter.

Why Is Simulation Effective for Gifted Students?

Teaching at its most fundamental level is task-focused on the creation of an environment in which students interact and learn how to learn (Beesley & Apthorp, 2010; Dewey, 1916; Joyce, Weil, & Calhoun, 2000; Moore, 2011). Simulation games create an environment in which gifted students learn because they see a useful reason to learn—to succeed and win. Playing to win a simulation game taps into the competitive nature of many gifted students, and the gaming aspect provides opportunities to develop and enhance their higher level thinking and problem-solving skills. Social values are enhanced through simulation as gifted students compete and come to realize cooperation is necessary to reach the goal of winning the game. Gifted students build empathy for real-life situations in simulations, particularly as they make difficult decisions in games. In addition, simulation helps build a cohesive classroom community, which is increasingly being recognized as the foundation for successful learning (Tompkins, 2014).

Simulations call for teachers to be flexible and willing to take the time to process the simulation activity with skill and patience. With the current emphasis on experiential learning and developing decision-making and cooperative learning skills, simulation is a timely strategy (May, 1997; Moore, 2011). In addition, simulation activities provide qualitatively differentiated learning opportunities for gifted students, and they meet the program standards of the Council for Exceptional Children (CEC) and the National Association for Gifted Children (NAGC; NAGC, 2010; NAGC & CEC-TAG, 2006).

Csikszentmihalyi (1990) said flow is the state in which one becomes so involved in an activity that nothing else seems to matter. Flow is an optimal state of performance in a task with a sense of enjoyment and control, in which skills are matched to the challenges being faced. The concept of flow provides a clear window of understanding to the feelings of enjoyment and engagement game players experience in a simulation (Garris, Ahlers, & Driskell, 2002).

Crookhall and Oxford (1991) endorsed the use of simulation to learn the highly developed language skills that gifted students need, including the ability to express agreement and disagreement, to persuade, to defend a point of view, to elicit cooperation, to analyze data, and to make judgments. For example, *Island Game*™, developed by Crookhall and Oxford (1991), illustrates the collective decision making and engagement that simulation can provide for gifted students. In *Island Game*, a group of individuals are stranded on an island, and a volcano is going to erupt in 30–60 minutes. The group must devise an escape plan to be implemented quickly. There are lifeboats to carry all of the group to safety on neighboring islands, but an overall group consensus must be reached on who will go where and with whom. The students complete an individual profile with information on their sex, age, nationality, background, and practical skills and then identify their top three preferred islands. In debriefing the simulation, students identify and rank order the five main factors that influenced their decision making in forming groups and choosing islands and escape boats. These factors are discussed in the debriefing session to provide opportunities for gifted students to experience different points of view, to build individual tolerance, and to gain a level of acceptance for differing points of view.

Other communication skills enhanced through the use of simulation include listening, understanding directions, initiating, speaking, writing, and reading. Simulations of political and societal situations encourage gifted students to use authentic tools and concepts within content study and to build cross-cultural understanding. Another popular simulation is *The Oregon Trail*™ in which students simulate the journey of the pioneers across the United States.

Simulation provides information about a situation that students will encounter and then asks them to make decisions. In a simulation on space, student travelers, for example, would need to select provisions for their journey and to chart the route they will follow. When a simulation begins, events unfold and more choices must be made. Many simulations have an element of chance so that students may be unsuccessful despite careful planning and prudent decisions. Simulations, unlike tutorials and drills, represent discovery learning as students learn through experience by perceiving the consequences of their decisions.

In *All Around Frippletown*™, students use a set of devices with which to manufacture cookies that match the model presented by the program. The order in which the devices are used affects the outcome, so students need to experiment to come up with the right product. In this computer-based program, students are presented with a problem and allowed to gather information about the program, suggest alternative solutions, and evaluate their effectiveness.

Simulation experiences provide rich content and opportunities for gifted students to build a more realistic paradigm of the world by exploring issues and examining the multiple perspectives and experiences of specific events or situations. Several Interact simulations provide this type of learning experience including *Kid Town: A Thematic Simulation about Community Life* and *Lost Tribe of Tocowans*.

In the nonjudgmental environment of simulation, gifted students can practice new behaviors and experiment with new attitudes and points of view. They act and interact and become involved in the facts, the processes, and the key concepts to be learned in the game; this interaction becomes a legitimate vehicle for learning. Powerful and deep learning takes place as gifted students engage in exciting and satisfying play (Gregory, 2000).

> Simulation is effective for gifted students because it:
> ▸ provides for collective decision making;
> ▸ develops language skills;
> ▸ builds cross-cultural understanding;
> ▸ develops decision-making skills;
> ▸ builds a realistic paradigm of the world; and
> ▸ provides opportunities for experimenting with ideas.

Multilevel Learning Derived From Simulation Games

Gifted students learn on three levels as they participate in simulation games: (a) learning facts and information embodied in the context and dynamics of the game; (b) learning processes simulated in the game; and (c) learning the relative costs, benefits, risks, and potential rewards of using alternative strategies for decision making. This interaction of information, processes, and strategies provides gifted students the experience of simultaneously operating on all three levels and reinforces that decision making is not a simple process (Lewis & Doorlag, 2003). Many gifted students operate on several levels simultaneously, and they enjoy the engaging nature of simulation.

Major Benefits of Simulation and Gaming for Gifted Students

They provide opportunities for:
▸ building critical thinking,
▸ questioning of assumptions and exploring diverse opinions,
▸ integrating higher order thinking,
▸ building personal responsibility,
▸ understanding the role of chance,
▸ enhancing knowledge and skills,
▸ understanding social systems,
▸ developing leadership skills,
▸ encouraging independence in action and thought,
▸ building group dynamics, and
▸ understanding complex situations.

Critical Thinking

Simulation games motivate and reward the critical thinking of gifted students as they analyze possible decisions, reflect on the probable consequences of decisions, and then plan and think through countermoves and strategies. Simulation games also encourage and develop the intuitive thinking of gifted students as they engage in spontaneous decision making. Critical thinking empowers gifted students to take charge of their learning and life (Paul & Elder, 2001). Logical students become more spontaneous, and spontaneous students become more logical as they use critical thinking in simulations.

Questioning of Assumptions and Exploration of Diverse Opinions

Simulation games provide opportunities for gifted students to encounter different points of view and to explore the social values of cooperation, empathy, and compassion.

Integrating Higher Order Thinking Processes and Building Personal Responsibility

Players make choices and receive rapid feedback from other players in simulations, and in lively interchange, students realize the consequences of their decisions. They learn their actions affect others, as well as themselves, both in the present and in the future.

Understanding the Role of Chance

Simulation games demonstrate that life is not always predictable, nor is it guided by logical plans; gifted students learn that most individuals are rarely, if ever, completely in control of their lives. As a result, they learn the importance of flexibility in life decisions and action. Most designers of simulations include "chance variables" for the players to adapt to chance and change.

Enhancing Knowledge and Skills

Simulation games build upon the knowledge and skills gifted students bring to the simulation. In the intense interaction of the games, the students learn from one another. Simulations also increase the gifted students' knowledge of specific terms, concepts, facts, structures, and relationships.

Understanding of Social Systems

Teachers can assist gifted students in developing social skills in simulation as they guide them through the process of examining individual and group opinions and attitudes. Simulation games provide opportunities for students to think and to ask the kinds of questions that expand their understanding of social systems in a global situation.

Leadership Skills

Simulation games provide a safe and structured situation for gifted students to experiment, to try new ideas and new behaviors, and to develop leadership skills to persuade others to listen to their point of view and to initiate actions.

Independence in Action and Thought

In simulations, learning is turned over to the students, and gifted students thrive on this aspect of simulation. They enjoy the intellectual freedom in the gaming process, for in simulation games, the teacher acts as a facilitator. Rules of the game direct the students; consequently, the teacher is not viewed as a judge or jury. This role encourages the students to focus attention on what is happening in the game and relinquish the "push-pull" for control that sometimes exists between gifted students and their teachers. As a result, simulation games build and reinforce a close teacher-student working relationship.

Group Dynamics

Simulation creates a sense of community among student participants. In the low-risk environment of simulation, gifted students build greater self-awareness, and learning continues beyond the game as they continue to experience insight. Active group interaction builds a sense of trust and community and develops a high degree of motivation because the students enjoy their group roles.

Understanding Complex Issues

In complicated computer-based model simulations, complex behaviors are modeled to provide somewhat simple inputs. Students learn complicated things such as the parts of an airplane, a system (the weather) or behavior management without risk, and they make a wide variety of assumptions and changes and see the results.

Simulations Aid International Study

Simulation games are used at the highest levels of international policy study. One example is Project IDEELS, an interdisciplinary international collaborative of diverse groups of educators and researchers from five tertiary institutions in four European countries. Its goal is to provide Europeans with an effective means of harnessing the power, creativity, and richness of cultural diversity to address challenges facing Europe. IDEELS owes much of its operating procedure to Project IDEALS, a United States based National Science Foundation funded telematics simulation directed by David Crookhall at the University of Alabama, and from ICONS, a telematics simulation program with an international relations focus directed by Jonathan Wilkenfeld at the University of Maryland.

A Teacher's Checklist for Effective Simulations

Powerful and deep learning takes place as gifted students engage in exciting and satisfying simulations. Effective simulations:

- ▸ motivate and reward creative thinking,
- ▸ provide opportunities to encourage different points of view,
- ▸ demonstrate that life is not always predictable,
- ▸ provide experiences to deal constructively and effectively with the environment,
- ▸ build on students' knowledge and skills,
- ▸ provide a safe and structured opportunity to experiment,
- ▸ build and reinforce close teacher-student working relationships, and
- ▸ create a sense of community.

Description of the Method

To better understand what a simulation game actually is, each individual part will be examined: (a) the activity, (b) the simulation, and (c) the game. Most teachers are familiar with small-group activities in which teachers and students discuss or "process" a completed exercise or activity that provides opportunities to learn by doing. For example, a well-known activity is the puzzle activity. The leader asks a small group to put a puzzle together and then gives each student a few of the pieces, and they set about completing the task. After about 5 minutes, the leader is instructed to stop the activity and ask the students what they have learned from the activity. Students are usually frustrated because everyone doesn't share their pieces, and there were no specific directions given; for example, there are no directions saying, "You can share." Concepts identified in this type of activity and discussion include cooperation, power, and the need for strategic planning and leadership.

This activity can be converted into a simulation by asking the students, "What workplace roles would be appropriate for putting the puzzle together?" The students might suggest "puzzle assemblers," "assembly managers," "timekeepers," and "group leaders." Following this interchange, the teacher can ask for volunteers to play each of the identified roles and give each student an appropriate identification badge. Then they can continue to put the puzzle together, but with designated ways of relating to each other to complete the task. This activity now represents a simulation.

To turn this simulation into a simulation game, you add game-like elements and rules. You could give some of the puzzle assemblers specific constraints such as blindfolds or impose a rule that they can only touch inside pieces, not edges. You could give chips to the assembly managers to be used as rewards or give chips to the timekeepers to reward fast assembly and then take away chips when the students make errors. You could give the student group leader the puzzle box with the picture of what the completed puzzle looks like or give the student group leader a separate puzzle to complete. Payoff chips could be distributed for each puzzle that is correctly put together. This activity is now considered a "simulation game" because of the addition of game-like elements and rules. At the completion of the simulation game, the teacher would then engage in debriefing, and these discussions are usually quite revealing. Comments made by a group of middle school gifted students on completion of a simulation game included: "Even though you said the student group leader could see the puzzle picture, our group leader didn't share that information," "Every time someone received chips for finishing a puzzle, I became so frustrated, I couldn't think, it's like knowing who the best kid in the class is," "The timekeeper bothered me; I don't work well under pressure," and "This activity was more exciting with the roles and rules, I liked it, and can we do another?"

Examples of Simulation Games

To better understand simulation games, several different games will be briefly examined with differing key concepts, props, number of participants, and time involvement. All of the games have been used with gifted students at the elementary, middle, and high school levels, not only in the United States, but throughout the world in training seminars with teachers and their gifted students in collaboration with the World Council for Gifted and Talented Children.

BaFá BaFá™

In *BaFá BaFá*, developed by Shirts (1974), players are divided into two cultures: Alpha and Beta. Separately, each group learns the rules specific to its own culture. Alpha is an in-group/out-group and a touching culture, and Beta is a foreign language-speaking, task-oriented culture. Once players learn and practice the rules of their own culture, observers and visitors are exchanged. After each exchange, the players return to their culture and try to describe their experiences in observing and interacting with the other culture. *BaFá BaFá* teaches that what seems irrational, contradictory, or unimportant in one culture may seem rational, consistent, and very important to a person from another culture. Shirts developed *BaFá BaFá* for the Navy to help military personnel successfully coexist within different cultures.

Barnga™

Bargna™ was created by Thiagarajan (1989) and the big idea in the simulation is that cultural differences exist in subtle forms, and often are covered up by obvious similarities. Players in groups of four are taught to play a quick card game. Each group thinks the groups are all learning the same game, but each game is slightly different. After 5 minutes, the players are asked to play the games silently and to settle any disagreements by communicating through gestures. After 5 additional minutes, two players from each table are moved to the next table under the guise of a tournament. Because there are two sets of rules now in operation, there is heated discussion expressed through gestures. After 5 minutes of play at this table, the players shift once more to the next table. The game is terminated after 5 minutes at this final table. MacGregor (2008) provided a full description of the game with samples of rules that can be implemented and follow-up questions for teachers.

Infotactics™

This game was developed by Sisk (1999) and focuses on the problem of information overload that many people experience in the Information Age. In *Infotactics*, students participate in one of four leadership teams designated as Azul, Verde, Roja, and Amarillo. Each team follows a brief scenario to role-play and interact with the other teams. An "Infotactic" is given to each team to use in communicating with the other teams, and the other teams do not know this piece of information. The goal of the simulation game is to communicate as a team and to convince the other teams of each individual team's leadership and point of view. The four infotactics used are Vapor Tactic, Double Channel Tactic, Need to Know Tactic, and Generalizing Tactic.

Land of the Sphinx and Land of the Rainbow™

This game was developed by Sisk (1983) to assist a group of psychologists in experiencing cerebral differences and learning preferences. The setting for the game is the year 2050, and a minimum of four travelers are selected to visit two different lands, the *Land of the Sphinx* and the *Land of the Rainbow*. Each land has been asked to develop three projects to shape its future: (a) education, (b) research, and (c) environment. In small groups, the participants identify and develop their three projects, and then they receive the travelers. The scenario for the *Land of the Sphinx* describes the land as being inhabited by people who trust logic, objectivity, and implicit action. Order is very important to them, particularly schedules and routine. The *Land of the Rainbow* is described as being inhabited by people who are interested in a deeper, larger, all-embracing reality, and they follow their hunches. People in one land do not have the description or scenario of the people in the other land.

In the simulation game, the travelers generate questions to ask the citizens of the two lands, and they experience many different reactions to these questions. The travelers are instructed to ask their questions with enthusiasm and curiosity; to be bold, open, and courageous; and to seek as much information about each land as possible. In the debriefing, the participants discuss whether or not they felt welcome or comfortable in their assigned land and are asked to select the land they would choose to remain in as a citizen. This game can be played with as many as 100 players. Large numbers require the creation of several Lands of the Sphinx and Lands of the Rainbow to provide at least five citizens in each land and to provide a sufficient number of travelers to visit all of the lands.

In the debriefing, discussion centers around which environment is more conducive to individual aspiration, curiosity, and goal attainment. People from different cultures quickly identify the similarities between the simulated lands and their own country. This simulation game has been used as an opening exercise in the annual residential Texas Governor's School to build a sense of community. Secondary gifted students quickly identify the similarity of the characteristics of the travelers with the characteristics of gifted students (Sisk, 2012).

Parlé™

This simulation game was developed by Sisk (1976) to provide gifted students an opportunity to experience leadership as they simulate different roles in 10 imaginary countries (Shima, Myna, Ila, Usa, Pam, Bonay, Shivey, Lani, Ranu, and Bili). Each country has three key elements to be considered: defense, resources, and demography. The major theme or big idea of *Parlé* is the importance of negotiation and interdependence between and among countries. Several chance crisis incidents are introduced such as a revolution in Ranu and a famine in Bili. The teacher/leader can vary the point of time to reflect the past or present, or the game can be projected into the future. The only way a country can win in this simulation is through cooperation and sharing of resources.

Tag Game™

Tag Game™ was developed by Shirts (1985) at Simulation Training Systems. It is a short, highly participative game to encourage players to focus on similarities and differences and openly discuss these in debriefing. Players wear tags of different shapes and colors, walk around silently, observe each other, and without any talking, the teacher/leader asks the students to group themselves. After a couple of rounds, the players hand in their tags and receive new unique tags. Again they are asked to observe one another, but not to talk before they decide on how to group themselves. Debriefing plus game time usually takes less than one hour. Gifted students quickly list the obvious similarities and differences among people, and soon begin to identify deeper, more abstract similarities and differences.

Elements of Simulation Games

A comparison of the selected simulation games across a range of gaming characteristics including time, props, number of participants, and debriefing issues can be helpful in building greater understanding of simulation as a teaching strategy.

Time

Simulation games can take a short period of time. Some like *Tag Game*, *Parlé*, and *Barnga* can be accomplished in an hour, or they can take a longer period of time as in the *Land of the Sphinx* and *Land of the Rainbow*. *BaFá BaFá* can take several hours to a half day for completion.

Props

Some games use simple props or artifacts such as the paper clips and construction paper used in *Tag Game* or more sophisticated props like those used in *BaFá BaFá*, and others use only the instructions (*Land of the Sphinx and Land of the Rainbow*). In addition, simulation games can simulate whole cultures or only specific aspects of a culture as in *Parlé* and *BaFá BaFá*.

Number of Participants

Parlé can be played with 40–80 participants, or it can be played with as few as 14 individuals, although much of the rich interaction and involvement of the game is lost with a small number of participants. *Tag Game* can be played with nine people, but it is more effective with 16–20. It also can be played in a large area using tables and chairs with 100–200 people. Most games have an optimum number for playing, but with ingenuity by the teacher, games can be reduced or expanded to accommodate varying numbers of participants. One simple way to expand a game is to run several simultaneous games.

Debriefing Issues

Parlé is a nonthreatening simulation game that can be used as an introduction to gaming for gifted students to help them learn how to discuss sensitive issues. When the game ends, the teacher can debrief the simulation and encourage the students to draw analogies to real life. For example, a group of gifted high school students identified biased perception as a communication problem, and they listed a number of misconceptions they experienced because of viewing another culture from the lens of their own culture.

In debriefing simulation games that focus on multicultural issues, teachers will need to encourage gifted students to identify and to discuss specific real-life situations that are simulated in the games. For example, after playing *Land of the Sphinx and Land of the Rainbow*, the teacher can ask students to address what might be done when someone is placed in a situation of not knowing the rules in a new culture, but thinking they do. "Processing" is the heart of simulation games, and debriefing focuses on what happened in the game, what the consequences of the actions were, how misperception can lead to mistakes, and how certain strategies are more effective. Brozo and Simpson (2003) stressed the importance of teachers observing and debriefing stereotyping and dealing with content issues such as cultural biases, values, and the need for adaptation and accommodation.

Using Simulation Effectively

It is important for the teacher to motivate students by using warm-ups that include a brief introduction to the game and a simple explanation of the rules and patterns of play. This presentation needs to be clear, and the teacher/leader needs to move on to accommodate the eagerness gifted students exhibit in wanting to get started in the gaming process. Clarity of expectations is essential for the game to progress. When students begin to play the game, the role of the teacher is to be observant, alert, and unobtrusive. In calling for the game to halt for debriefing, a simple bridge from the game to debriefing can be, "Let's talk about what happened during the past half-hour or so . . ." Flexibility and imagination are essential in organizing gifted students for a successful experience in simulation games. The high degree of student-to-student communication in simulations requires an atmosphere that encourages physical and intellectual mobility. To facilitate this environment, the teacher/leader needs to develop a sense of timing, and to know or sense when it is appropriate to offer aid and support, and when to interrupt the simulation to process or debrief the action.

Debriefing or processing encourages gifted students to analyze their experiences and capitalize on the full learning potential of the strategy. The importance of processing is reflected in the Brozo and Simpson (2003) assertion that until students reflect, total learning has not taken place. Students learn and remember best when they fully participate in the debriefing. As gifted students inductively arrive at a consensus of ideas, the role of the teacher/leader is to direct their critical attention to the concepts and processes simulated in the game.

Initially, they may need to simply describe what happened; however, it is helpful for them to hear the experiences of others, as well as to share their own experiences. As students discuss the beliefs and feelings they experience during a simulation game, the teacher/leader can encourage them to analyze why certain things happened and ask them to identify the basis for their decisions. Samuel Johnson said more than 200 years ago, "The seeds of knowledge may be planted in solitude, but they must be cultivated in public" (Boswell, 1979). With teacher guidance and encouragement, debriefing sessions will naturally move toward summarizing, generalizing and identifying the big idea or key concept of the simulation game. Another effective debriefing technique is to ask the students to list and to share specific ideas generated during their discussion and to draw further inferences and generalizations based on these ideas. This process enables the students to draw more meaningful conclusions and to make broader generalizations.

Clark (2012) cautioned teachers to be aware that the sensitivity and empathy gifted students develop in simulation games may cause them to lose their critical sense. Games can trigger intense feelings, and occasionally arguments may lead to expressions of personal hostility. A skillful and sensitive teacher can help prevent outbursts by closely observing the group during the simulation and resolving ill feelings as they emerge during the debriefing. In discussing disagreements, the teacher can ask the students to identify which rules were being ignored and why, and then encourage them to analyze their behavior during the game. This self-reflection will build on the interpersonal and intrapersonal behaviors of giftedness as described by Gardner (1983).

Teachers need to ensure that simulation games are culturally appropriate because participative learning is not traditional in all cultures. Unfortunately, there is no set rule for making decisions on whether or not to use a simulation game. The factors correlated with successful use of simulation include the comfort level of the teacher with the method, the degree of trust developed between the teacher and the students, and the effectiveness of the teacher to frame the game in meaningful and relevant terms to the maturity level of the students. When these factors are considered, simulation games have been used successfully in cross-cultural training when there appeared to be little or no chance for their success.

Designing a Simulation Game

A simulation game takes a real-life situation as a model and draws out the key features, struggles, roles, and dilemmas. Simulation games imitate reality, and the players experience "walking in the shoes of others." Rules, symbols, the goals to be achieved, and the timeframe motivate gifted students to become quickly involved from the beginning of a simulation game.

Designing a simulation game is a complicated procedure and not to be taken lightly. The following six steps are helpful in designing a game: (a) identify the key concepts or big ideas on which the game will focus and then select the real-life situation the game will simulate; (b) identify the structure of the game and the roles or characters to be involved; (c) decide on a point in time for the simulation; (d) establish the goals to be accomplished; (e) identify resources or props needed; and (f) decide on the sequence of events. Are there external factors that need to be considered? Will there be score sheets, tables, graphs, chance cards, spinners, dice, board tokens, and similar devices to add to the structure of the game?

Once these six steps are addressed, then the rules can be written. What is the order of play? What do the players do? How does the game end? In designing a game, test, retest, and revise the game. Adjust the game to reality, comprehensiveness, playability, and validity. Trying out a game with participants is one way to troubleshoot the game. The International Simulation and Gaming Association (ISAGA) encourages members and participants to field-test new games in association meetings with veteran gamers. *Infotactics* was introduced at an ISAGA meeting in Kyoto, Japan, and many new ideas and suggestions for revising the game were gained. Gifted students enjoy assisting in the revision and in the design of games, and this involvement provides a sense of ownership in the emerging game.

A format for designing games developed by Reid (1987) can be quite helpful (see Figure 18.1). Reid suggested starting with a problem and deciding on a concise statement of the problem such as, "A communicable disease virus has broken out in a community." Then you decide on the objectives of the simulation game such as, "The students will (a) experience group dynamics in reaching consensus, (b) develop insight into their personal value system and the value system of others, and (c) experience a variety of decision-making methods."

Name of the Game

▸ **Statement of the problem:** Be brief and precise.
▸ **Objective:** Be specific. What do you plan to achieve?
▸ **Scenario:** Include past events, background information, the present time, setting, and conditions that may affect the game.
▸ **Characters:** Give a brief description of the physical characteristics, personality, and goals of the players in the game.
▸ **Point in Time:** The exact place and time the game begins.
▸ **Resources:** Props for the game—physical, social, economical, political, or personal.
▸ **Rules:** Rules that govern the players, the game pattern, scoring, and implementation.
▸ **Debriefing and Evaluation:** What did you experience in the process? What did you learn? Were the objectives reached and how can the game be improved?

Figure 18.1. Design your own simulation. *Note.* From "Turn to page 84," by Avis Reid, in *Creative Teaching of the Gifted* (p. 114), by D. Sisk, 1987, New York: McGraw-Hill. Copyright©1987 by McGraw-Hill. Reprinted with permission.

After you identify the objectives, you then write the scenes or scenario including past events, background information, the point in time, setting, and any conditions that will affect the game such as, "The community is culturally diverse, including citizens who are White, Hispanic, Asian, and African American, and the community is comparatively isolated; it is midwinter and the decision concerning what to do about the communicable disease must be made in 24 hours."

Characters and their roles are then identified ("Doctors, nurses, parents, teachers, principals, students, community members, and citizens") who will be involved in the decision-making process. Brief descriptions can be written concerning the physical characteristics and personality characteristics of the characters. Keeping these descriptions brief will encourage students to use their creativity in role-playing the characters. Descriptions can be as brief as the following: "The doctor is the only one who knows how the cure or antidote must be used; he or she is to be assisted by an Advisory Panel of citizens, parents, teachers, principals, and students including two nurses who are adamantly against using the antidote or serum." Roles can be more specific, leaving little leeway for improvisation, or they can leave considerable leeway for gifted .

Resources (e.g., physical, social, economical, political, or personal) may need to be added because resources add greater complexity to simulations, and they heighten the interest of the students. Rules and rules administration including rules to govern the student players, the game pattern, the scoring, and the implementation are the last to be added. In the case of the *Communicable Disease* simulation game, the rules are, "Several people (15) have been exposed to a communicable disease, and there is serum for only eight people. How can a decision be made to save eight people and to sacrifice the lives of seven others?" Each person is given a role on the Advisory Panel and a certain number of points. A consensus is required for a decision to be made, and there is a time constraint of one hour.

The last step in devising a simulation game is the debriefing or processing stage. In the debriefing, students reflect on how their decisions were made and how they feel about the process and their decision making. They can be encouraged to ask more complex questions, to analyze the situation thoroughly, and to search for more knowledge. For many gifted students, empathy developed in simulations may lead to a profound commitment to social justice and global concerns. During debriefing, the teacher can reinforce the positive social attitudes observed and arrange follow-up experiences for the students to gather information to extend greater understanding of the issues involved in their decision making. Analogies can be drawn to present and past situations and from observations the gifted students share with one another. The time allotment for debriefing usually is one fourth of the total time allotted to a game. In the case of the game *Communicable Disease*, one hour is allotted to the simulation, so the debriefing time would be 15 minutes.

Situations in Which Simulation Games Are Useful

Simulation games have proved useful with international graduate students in preparation for reentry to their home countries. At the Center for Creativity, Innovation and Leadership at Lamar University, simulation games were used in the United States Agency for International Development training programs for international graduate students studying at major universities and colleges throughout the United States. The students from mostly underdeveloped countries readily responded to the simulation *Land of the Sphinx and Land of the Rainbow*. They identified areas of misunderstanding they anticipated encountering on return to their countries. In open discussions, they discussed expected problems including overgeneralizations from families and friends concerning work and family relations. Most of the students had spent 2–4 years in the United States, learning and accepting many aspects of Western culture. They realized how difficult it was going to be to return home and to "re-experience" the culture of their countries. Simulations provided opportunities to step outside the real dilemma of reentry and to analyze in the safety of a simulation. *BaFá BaFá* was particularly helpful in stimulating a healthy exchange of ideas and generating positive strategies for successful reentry.

Simulations have been useful in preparing secondary students for exchange programs in which the students will experience different cultures. *BaFá BaFá* builds an understanding of the importance of keen observation and flexibility in interacting and responding appropriately with people from different cultures.

Simulation games are useful with a broad age span of students, and most games require little alteration or change in their operating format to accommodate age differences. For example, *Parlé* can be played with middle school students studying environmental science to learn the importance of the interrelationship between the environment and humans and how humans alter the environment. Secondary students can play *Parlé* to focus on problems and issues dealing with foreign policy and the importance of personal diplomacy and individual responsibility in transforming sensitive international relationships. Recently, a group of secondary students playing *Parlé* identified similarities to the Middle East controversy, and elementary gifted children successfully played *Parlé* to develop an understanding of the importance of leadership and the interaction of resources and demography in countries. The intensity of simulation games motivates gifted students to quickly learn content, and if the game is played for a period of a time, followed by periodic breaks, the students often ask for extended time to research answers to questions that emerge during the game. Then they can apply this new information when the game commences.

Simulation has been used by schools or school districts to gather information and identify attitudes toward proposals or proposed action that affects the total system. For example, *Land of the Sphinx and Land of the Rainbow* assisted a school district in planning and hosting an international educational seminar. The simulation helped the district personnel understand and appreciate the complexities of different cultures and the many different ways that people respond and behave. The organizers of the conference gained many useful insights from playing the simulation game, particularly in how to organize the seminar to be more meaningful and successful. They incorporated different aspects of the cultures of the participating countries as a resource including specific customs of greeting, food, music, art, and dance.

Simulation games are great tools to assist gifted students facing new experiences and challenges such as leaving elementary school to attend middle school. By playing *Tag Game*, students learn how to interact more effectively and how to become contributing members of a new and older group of students. In simulation games, gifted students develop an awareness of their strengths and weaknesses and the strengths and weaknesses of others, and they experience the power of being able to help others reach common group goals. Leu and Kinzer (2003) defined meaningful simulations as ones in which students role-play and put themselves in the place of others to truly experience "walking in the shoes of others."

Manipulation of time and space is one of the more meaningful and motivating aspects of simulations. In simulations, gifted students eliminate the interval between learning concepts, skills, and their application. Students bind the present and the future, skills, values, and knowledge together to experience relevant and useful learning. Simulations provide gifted students opportunities to practice leadership and creative behavior in the context of a safe classroom environment under the guidance of their teachers (Lewis & Doorlag, 2003).

There are many situations in which simulation is useful as a method of instruction in conjunction with computers, particularly in science and social studies. In many cases, the skills that need to be taught in science are both complex and dangerous, and the computer becomes a way to safely engage students. In the classroom, students cannot actually view a volcano erupting or peer through an electron microscope; however, the Internet can provide teachers and students opportunities to observe eruptions and to experience how it feels to use sophisticated and expensive research tools. Montgomery and Palmer (2006) found students of teachers using technology and manipulative activities in the classroom including the Internet performed better on the National Assessment of Educational Progress science assessment than students in traditional classes in which teachers did not use these strategies. They found students more easily mastered subject matter when they were able to view "reality" and engage in scientific reasoning as they grappled with how the natural world works. Using the Internet to bring reality into the classroom, coupled with simulations in which students simulate reality, adds both rigor and relevance to their studies.

The State of Simulation and Gaming in Schools

Iuppa and Borst (2010) called today's students the "Next generation" and emphasized they have been immersed in interactive media since childhood. They described these "millennials" as visually intuitive and responsive to experiential and collaborative learning methodologies. With current emphasis on preparation for standardized testing and "skill and drill" approaches, these students are frustrated. Jonas-Dwyer & Pospisil (2004) described the "millennials" as having grasshopper minds and they said the old ways of training and persuading are going to be even less successful for them when they gain employment. Yet, there is growing evidence that applying entertainment videogame mechanics and techniques to learning and communication objectives pays dividends. In an interview with the website *Gamezone,* James Paul Gee (2007) said, "It has dawned on me that good games were learning machines. Built into their very designs were good learning principles, principles supported, in fact, by cutting edge research of cognitive science" (p. 2).

Aldrich (2009) advocated learning "how to do" or "how to be" rather than "how to know." He said there is a divide between the gaming community and educators, with gamers dismissing educational simulations as boring and irrelevant, and educators dismissing gaming as trivial. Yet, Aldrich and Sandler, a member of Texas Governor Rick Perry's 21st Century Commission on Higher Education, said serious games and simulations can change the world of education. Sandler (2009) stated:

> Today's classrooms, curricula, term papers, corporate training programs, business plans, and linear analysis should be banished to the intellectual slums and backwaters because I have seen the future first hand, or at least a glimpse of it. As a pilot, I've experienced how the most sophisticated flight simulators instill the skills, judgment and coolness under pressure needed to safely land a crippled Airbus on the Hudson River. As a parent, I've watched my six, seven and twelve year old children have fun playing *Zoo Tycoon* and *Sim City*, while absorbing sophisticated business pattern recognition that took me years to learn at Harvard Business School. (p. xxi)

Recently at a state gifted conference I attended, when the 1,000 or more participants were asked how many were using simulations or gaming with their gifted students, less than 20 teachers raised their hands. Over the course of the conference, the teachers shared they had no funds to buy simulations and that time was too limited. They also said they did not have the needed technology, and a remarkable number said they had never experienced simulation as learners and questioned its usefulness.

Eliminating the Barriers

Many simulations are free and they are available on the Internet. To address the lack of time, teachers can think about ways a simulation can replace a lecture and many of the online simulations can be assigned to students for work at home or in afterschool programs. Where technology is limited or unavailable, teachers can use noncomputer simulations such as those described in this chapter. And most importantly, teachers can educate themselves concerning the use and benefits of simulation and gaming by using Google and the links listed in this chapter. One such resource is http://Games2train.com.

Comparison With Other Teaching Methods

Using the selected variables of responsiveness and variety of input modes to compare simulation with other teaching methods including lectures, workbooks, textbooks, written materials, and computer-assisted presentations, it can be noted that simulation games require an active response from individual students, and each student responds to the actions of other students. This interaction cycle is dynamic and synergistic, and the pace of learning is more accelerated than learning in other methods. Surveys conducted at a school for gifted students found that the students overwhelmingly preferred collaborative experiences in the group work of simulation games to more individual experiences (Christensen, 1994; Sisk, 2007). Simulation games incorporate a wide variety of input methods and ways information can be presented including speeches, prints, pictures, charts, maps, and diagrams. This variety broadens the appeal and positive learning for teachers and students. The use of a number of props depends on the players and the teachers. A group of middle school gifted students in the *Land of the Sphinx and Land of the Rainbow* created songs, wrote histories of their land, devised unique greetings for the visitors, and created a constitution that was dramatically presented to the travelers.

Some simulations present information by the physical position of tokens on a board, furniture in the room, or even the students themselves. Simulation games may take a longer period of time than more didactic methods, but the learning in simulations is quick, and often more insightful and meaningful to gifted students because the games are more active and intense than other teaching methods. Figure 18.2 lists advantages and disadvantages that will be helpful for teachers to use in deciding if a simulation is an appropriate tool for a given lesson or area of study and in deciding if the advantages outweigh the disadvantages.

Conclusion

Simulations have been used for decades in businesses, in the military, and in higher education. Their potential use in K–12 programs is immense, and that potential is growing daily as witnessed by the increase in the number of simulation games and computer-based programs available. Simulation meets all five of the essential factors that VanTassel-Baska and Little (2011) suggested educators keep in mind in assessing curriculum for gifted students: complexity, depth, challenge, creativity, and acceleration.

The highly motivating nature of simulation makes it a complementary teaching tool for gifted programs, and the intellectual "jolt" it provides gifted students in learning how to learn can be amazing. In debriefing sessions with their teachers and other students, gifted students reflect on the content, skills, and values they learn and relearn in simulation games. Gifted students learn how to make more intelligent decisions about life as they experience the variety of processes employed in simulation games including interactive negotiation, persuasive communication, decision making, and creative problem solving. One of the more effective outcomes of simulation for gifted students is the positive effect it has on the study of issues.

Advantages	Disadvantages
‣ Active involvement ‣ Fun and challenging ‣ Encourages risk-taking and creativity in a safe environment ‣ Promotes change of learning pace ‣ Builds cohesive classroom community ‣ Promotes problem-solving skills and analytical and critical thinking skills ‣ Provides opportunities for practice ‣ Provides immediate feedback ‣ Employs social construction of knowledge ‣ Simplifies complicated issues or concepts ‣ Encourages empathy ‣ Uses prior knowledge ‣ Blends theory and strategy in realistic experience ‣ Promotes student-student interaction ‣ Encourages students to expand relationships ‣ Enables students to make/act on their own choices ‣ Practices communication skills	‣ Time consuming ‣ May require special space or equipment requirements ‣ Expense of commercial games ‣ Not considered legitimate training ‣ Students may act and react immaturely ‣ Cultural issues may arise with multicultural groups ‣ Unsophisticated learners may not monitor their actions ‣ Intense enthusiasm for active learning may cause student resistance to more traditional learning ‣ Can oversimplify complex issues and concepts ‣ Not all students are metacognitively aware ‣ Momentum of game may mask objective ‣ Students may have trouble with or refuse to relinquish game roles ‣ All students may not have the same experience ‣ Some students may monopolize ‣ Demands a great deal of imagination on the part of students and teachers

Figure 18.2. Advantages and disadvantages of simulation games. *Note.* Compiled from Brozo and Simpson (2003); Heward (2012); Leu and Kinzer (2003); Lewis and Doorlag (2003); Moore (2011); Sapon-Shevin (2010); Turnbull, Turnbull, Shank, Smith, and Leal (2003).

Building a strong, cohesive classroom community is increasingly recognized as the foundation for successful classrooms (Tompkins, 2014). Simulations provide opportunities for students to feel safe, respected, and valued, as well as to learn new skills. In simulations, students have opportunities to take risks, and they are challenged to be open to new possibilities. Simulations provide students structure within the safe environment of a game to act boldly and take individual and collective responsibility for making things different and better in the gaming situation. When teachers use simulations to help students see ways to shape society, they are teaching for change in the students, in the world, and in themselves as teachers.

Teachers can learn using games as well as their students. A classroom simulation for teachers called *simSchool*™ provides practice in using teacher skills on virtual students and teachers receive feedback on how the strategies they select affect the learning of the students. University students can compete in a contest called *Hidden Agenda* in which they design a "genius game for a middle school crowd" using "stealth education." A winning entry called *Refuse of Space* teaches physics and aeronautics via players steering a pirate ship through space. Another promising development is reported by Rajagopalan and Schwartz (2005) in the increasing numbers of universities developing interdisciplinary degree courses of study in games design and development. As "digital natives" who are gifted use their innate desire to create, they can become involved in becoming producers of games as well as consumers. These new literacies that students are developing at home and in school will continue to present a challenge to the cultures of our schools to adapt and embrace gaming technologies in education. The payoff is evident, as Johnson, Hornik, and Salas (2008) reported early studies show that gamers perceive the world more clearly, are more creative problem solvers, are more confident, and are more social. As Scherer (2013) said, "It's time to stop playing catch up with the kids and start leading the way with learning rich technology" (p. 7). Her statement represents a beautiful segue for simulation and gaming.

Teacher Statement

Simulation is a form of interactive learning that engages and excites my students. In the simulation *Cells: The True Story*, students act as a cell organelle to build an understanding of the job and location of each organelle. They role play a series of cell processes, and they need to cooperate to perform the basic cell functions. In another simulation *Dancing With the Cells,* the students pair up to form duplicated chromosomes and attach themselves to spindle fibers represented by long strings of yarn. The objective is to construct a human model of cell division by acting out each stage of mitosis. In *Quick Frozen Critters,* another simulation that the students enjoy, they are assigned roles of predator or prey in order to understand how adaptations and limiting factors affect wildlife populations. Predators must each capture two prey in order to survive. Prey must obtain three food tokens and reach permanent shelter to survive, and they can avoid capture by freezing or seeking temporary shelter in a hula hoop. After participating in simulations, the students better understand difficult concepts in science and tend to perform well on both written and verbal assessments. They look forward to using simulation games in my classes, and so do I! The enthusiasm of the students for learning more about science is highly motivating for me and my students. My students all use video games and free simulations at home. As Dr. Sisk says, "Serious games and engaging simulations can change the world of education." In simulation games, students learn the "big" skills that count: leadership, negotiation, and stewardship.

—Laura Pitre, St. Anne Catholic School

DISCUSSION QUESTIONS

1. One consequence of an interdependent world is people in any one country have to learn to think in intercultural terms. There are few opportunities for such learning in today's schools. What are ways that simulations like *Parlé* can be used in a school's efforts to encourage students to be more aware of our growing multicultural society? In social studies? In language arts?

2. There are times when simulation games can become charged with heightened emotion. When students are debriefing, they may be quite candid with one another and make statements like, "That was just plain stupid." At that point, the teacher needs to intervene and make sure that hurt feelings are handled. Discuss how humor might be used to ease the tension.

3. Climate setting for simulation is essential, and teachers need to be cautious in attempting to hurry the game by skipping this aspect. The teacher can talk briefly about the value of simulation, of trying on new roles, and "walking in someone else's shoes." Discuss the importance of climate setting, particularly the importance of legitimizing feelings and individual perceptions.

4. Processing is a key aspect of simulation, and the teacher needs to avoid close-ended questions that limit discussion. Discuss processing one of the games and list several open-ended questions that might be used. Remember to maintain a sense of "play" and that simulations can be fun. Then, discuss what occurred even though the learning may be substantial and serious. Think of a situation that could be made into a simulation. Using the guidelines included in Figure 18.1, outline the beginning of a simulation.

5. There are cultural differences in interacting with others, and some students may be reluctant or unwilling to enter into a simulation game. Discuss how you would handle this situation. What are some roles the student or students might play such as observer, timekeeper, and so forth?

6. Computer games tend to evoke mixed responses and reactions in education circles. What are some advantages and disadvantages of the use of computer games?

7. What do we do when the web, which has upended just about every other traditional institution, sets its sights squarely on schooling?

8. Teachers report that they don't use simulation and gaming because of the high cost of games, lack of time, and lack of knowledge concerning simulation and gaming. If you heard teachers making these statements, what might you tell them, having read this chapter?

9. How does simulation and gaming fit in with the Department of Education's Technology Plan? Do you think there will be an increase in the use of K–12 simulation and gaming as a result of this plan?

Teacher Resources

Top Free Educational Video Games

1. **Revolution™:** *Learning Objective*: Experience historical incentives for the American Revolution from the grassroots level. *Host URL*: http://education.mit. edu/projects/revolution

2. **Re-Mission 2™:** *Learning Objective*: Understand cancer better and develop a positive attitude toward defeating it. *Host URL*: http://www.re-mission.net/

3. **River City™:** *Learning Objective*: Develop an understanding of the scientific method through inquiry and teamwork, as well as an appreciation for history and environmental issues. *Host URL*: http://muve.gse.harvard.edu/muvees2003/ index.html

4. **America's Army™:** *Learning Objectives*: Teamwork, and a greater understanding of U.S. military expectations for recruits. *Host URL*: http://www.americasarmy. com

5. **Food Force™:** *Learning Objectives*: Understand world hunger and efforts to alleviate it. *Host URL*: http://www.educational-freeware.com/freeware/food-force. aspx

6. **Whyville™:** *Learning Objectives*: Provide a student-centered, hands-on environment for exploring various school subjects. *Host URL*: http://www.whyville.net/ smmk/nice

7. **SimCity™:** *Learning Objectives*: Understand variable manipulations for urban management while having fun building a simulated city. *Host URL*: http://www. simcity.com/en_US/product/simcity-classic

Nobel Prize Organization Education Games

The educational section of http://Nobelprize.org consists of 46 productions. Of these, 29 are interactive learning games of various sorts and degrees of difficulties.

Language Arts Publications

Jaffe, C. (1991). *Enchanted castle*. Fort Atkinson, WI: Interact.
> A simulated journey through a fantasy world of fairy tales. Students receive a Story Guide Map and Travel Tickets to plan a journey to an enchanted castle. Appropriate for grades 2–4.

Jaffe, C. (1991). *Missing persons*. Fort Atkinson, WI: Interact.
> In this simulation, each student secretly chooses a literary figure to bring to life. Through the research of the literature in which the character appears and other references materialize, students fill out a Missing Person's report. The report includes the author's purpose, point of view, cause and effect, story mood, story summary, and character delineations. On the lineup day, the students pair up and read character profiles and often wear appropriate costumes. Appropriate for grades 3–8.

Jaffe, C., & Liberman, M. (1989). *Odyssey.* Fort Atkinson, WI: Interact.

> A simulated journey through the world of classic Greek mythology where student teams meet heroes, heroines, gods, and goddess. Students read at least eight classical myths in teams. They work to climb Mt. Olympus to work through each level, and team members analyze the myths cooperatively. Appropriate for grades 3–7.

Math Publications

Bippert, J., & Steigar, J. (1989). *Lost tribe of Tocowans.* Fort Atkinson, WI: Interact.

> Using a scenario of searching for the imaginary lost tribe of Tocowans, students reinforce and master their multiplication skills. The adventure involves taking a jeep across a desert. Students purchase water, fuel, food, and camping gear to stay at least 15 days in this remote area. Each jeep full of students is responsible for successfully completing multiplication and division speed drills and making decisions about purchases. Appropriate for grades 4–7.

Bippert, J., & Steiger, J. (1989). *Shopping spree.* Fort Atkinson, WI: Interact.

> This is a game show simulation to teach students calculator and estimation skills. As contestants on a game show, students reinforce their calculator skills, make purchasing decisions, and spend game show money in six different shops. Appropriate for grades 3–8.

Draze, D. (2005). *The stock market game: A simulation of stock market trading.* Waco, TX: Prufrock Press.

> This is a stock market simulation game that provides the framework for students to learn about economics and the psychology of the stock market. Using exercises and information on company ownership, students prepare for the long-term project of tracking and participating in the stock market over several months. Appropriate for students in grades 5–8.

Rink, R., & Heath, J. (2004). *Mastering math.* Fort Atkinson, WI: Interact.

> This simulation blends math, music, and mystery. A distressed Sherlock Holmes loudly protests that he can never learn math, but with the help of other players in the simulation, he is soon a "singing success." The simulation has many math problem-solving techniques including guess and check, make a table or chart, work backward, act it out, draw a picture, and find a pattern. Appropriate for grades 2–6.

Persson, M., & Bergensten, J. (2009). *Minecraft.* Stockholm, Sweden: Mojang.

> *Minecraft* allows players to build constructions out of textured cubes in a 3D procedurally generated world. Other activities include exploration, gathering resources, survival, crafting, and combat.

Bippert, J., & Vandling, L. (2006). *Game factory: A simulation exploring the connection between games and probability.* Culver City, CA: Interact

> Cheatum Swindle is running the Goodwin's game factory into the ground by producing unfair games. Students use their arithmetic skills to save the company. Students work in pairs performing hands-on experiments with spinners, dice, coins, and cards to test the probabilities of Cheatum's games. Students examine games and

make modifications and record reasons for their decisions. Appropriate for grades 3–7.

Science Publications

Arner, B. (1994). *Invent.* Fort Atkinson, WI: Interact.

In this simulation, students gain insight into the creative process of inventing as they research inventors and discover how their ideas have changed our lives. The students practice brainstorming, tinkering, and actually create their own inventions. They learn how to patent, advertise, and market their products. A Consumer Advocacy Group questions their inventions, and a culminating activity is a Thomas Edison Day to share their inventions. Appropriate for grades 6–8.

Barnes, D., Lawson, J., & Wheetley, J. (2010). *Surf tsunami.* Culver City, CA: Interact.

This simulation CD combines geography, math, and science skills as student "surfers"'" research the world's best beaches. Students plan simulated trips to the leading surf spots using geography skills to find the locations and math skills to budget their travel expenses. Appropriate for grades 4–8.

Bippert, J., & Vanding, L. (1995). *Project Polaris.* Fort Atkinson, WI: Interact.

In this simulation, students build a space station using estimation and measurement skills. In cooperative learning space pods, students use estimation and hands-on measurements at each of 10 constellation stopping points in space. The mission is to build a space station where everyone can convene in a united effort to ensure galactic peace. Appropriate for grades 3–6.

Bohland, M. (2005). *Mystery disease.* Waco, TX: Prufrock Press.

Students work in teams to track down the source of a mystery illness. Using science, math, social sciences, and critical thinking skills, students become public health workers as they get to the root of the spreading disease. Appropriate for students grades 5–8.

Bohland, M. (2008). *Mystery river: A problem-based ecology unit.* Waco, TX: Prufrock Press.

Students investigate the disappearance of freshwater mussels in the fictional town of Hopewell. Using observation charts, newspapers, maps, and ecological research, students learn research and critical thinking skills as they develop presentations to show their results. Appropriate for students in grades 5–8.

Carnegie Mellon and Stanford University scientists (2010). *EteRNA.* Washington, DC: National Science Foundation.

In *EteRNA*, players solve puzzles related to the folding of RNA molecules. Players are presented with a given target shape into which an RNA strand must fold. A player can change the sequence by placing any of the four RNA nucleotides (adenine, cytosine, guanosine and uracil) at various positions; this can alter the free energy of the system and dramatically affect the RNA strand's folding dynamics. Once players have completed a sufficient number of RNA puzzles, they unlock the chance to generate puzzles for other players. Appropriate for grades 10–12 and university students.

Flindt, M. (1990). *Zoo*. Fort Atkinson, WI: Interact.

> The mayor and city council members plan to close Zooland because it is outdated, the animals are poorly treated, and attendance is declining. Students take action to work to save Zooland. Appropriate for grades 2–5.

Libetzky, J., & Hildebrand, J. (1993). *Adapt*. Fort Atkinson, WI: Interact.

> Students become geographers examining the importance of the physical environment to the lives of past and present human beings living in hunting and gathering societies. Appropriate for grades 6–9.

Schulz, K. (2005). *Crime scene detective: Using science and critical thinking to solve crimes*. Waco, TX: Prufrock Press.

> This simulation combines criminal investigation, forensic science, and critical thinking. The culminating project is a school-wide arson investigation, during which students learn how to interrogate suspects and critically analyze evidence to discover the true criminal. Appropriate for students in grades 5–8.

Schulz, K. (2007). *Crime scene detective: Theft*. Waco, TX: Prufrock Press.

> Students to become detectives as they investigate the theft of an expensive digital camera. As part of a crime scene investigation, the students analyze evidence and participate in real-life forensic labs. Appropriate for grades 5–8.

Social Studies Publications

Muzzy Lane Software. (2007). *Making history*. Newburyport, MA: Author.

> *Making History* is a multiplayer simulation game in which students take on the roles of European leaders, before, during, and after World War II.

Simpson, A. (1997). *Kid town*. Culver City, CA: Interact

> Students play workers and consumers as they learn the key social studies concept of what makes a community. Players name their town and work in cooperative learning groups to set up stores and services. Students practice reading, speaking, math, and art skills; go on study trips in their community; and elect a mayor. Appropriate for grades K–3.

Blumenthal, H., Calderwood, D., & Curley, D. (2012). *Where in the world is Carmen San Diego?* San Francisco, CA. Broderbund.

> Students learn facts and skills in geography while tracking Carmen across the globe. The 2012 version is a downloadable version of the game. A classic version of the game (first introduced in the 1980s) is also available with online searches. Appropriate for grades 5–12.

Calls, J. M. (1983). *Amigos*. Fort Atkinson, WI: Interact.

> Students work in teams to map their way through the West Indies, Mexico, Central America, and South America. They race from El Paso, TX, to the tip of Latin America, Tierra del Fuego. Teams write reports and complete projects to earn points that move them along the map. Each team prepares an activity for a culminating fiesta. Appropriate for grades 5–9.

Lacey, B. (1998). *Great American confrontations: Calhoun vs. Garrison*. Fort Atkinson, WI: Interact.

    This simulation uses a confrontational talk show format to facilitate a conversation between John C. Calhoun, Southern advocate, and William Lloyd Garrison, an abolitionist. They debate whether or not Americans should allow slavery to remain in the nation. Appropriate for grades 7–12.

Plantz, C., & Callis, J. M. (1995). *Pacific Rim*. Fort Atkinson, WI: Interact.

    Pacific Rim helps students understand the growing importance of Pacific Rim countries, lands, people, and cultures. Students complete research projects and written reports. They simulate travel on a ship from Japan to New Zealand. Appropriate for grades 5–9.

Chan, T. (2001). *Capitalism II*. Montreuil, France: UBISOFT

    Players create and control a business empire. This in-depth strategy game covers almost every aspect of business that could be encountered in the real world, including marketing, manufacturing, purchasing, importing and retailing. Appropriate for grades 10–12 and university students.

Sweeny, T., Brown, E., & Burak, A. (2007). *Peace maker*. Los Angeles, CA: Impact Games.

    Peace Maker simulates the Israeli-Palestinian conflict. Players choose to play the leader of Israel or the Palestinian Authority. They deal with events presented using real-world pictures and footage, react and make social, political and military decisions that their position entails within a game-play system. The goal of the game is to solve the conflict with a two-state solution. Appropriate for grades 9–12.

Addresses and Websites

Broderbund
c/o Riverdeep, Inc.
71 Stevenson Street, 4th Floor
San Francisco, CA 94105
(800) 395-0277
http://www.broderbund.com

Electronic Arts
209 Redwood Shores Pkwy.
Redwood City, CA 94065
(650) 801-0520
http://www.ea.com

Impact
4470 West Sunset Boulevard #126 Los Angeles, CA 90027
(818) 841-8862
http://www.highimpactgames.com

Interact
10200 Jefferson Blvd., Box 802
Culver City, CA 90232
(800) 421-4246
http://www.interact-simulations.com

North American Simulation and Gaming Association
P.O. Box 78636
Indianapolis, IN 46278
(888) 432-GAME
http://www.nasaga.org

Prufrock Press
P.O. Box 8813
Waco, TX 76714-8813
(800) 998-2208
http://www.prufrock.com

Simulation Training Systems
P.O. Box 910
Del Mar, CA 92014
(800) 942-2900
http://www.stsintl.com

The Thiagi Group—Sivasailam Thiagarajan
4423 E. Trailridge Rd.
Bloomington, IN 47408
(812) 332-1478
http://www.thiagi.com

Association for Business Simulations and Experimental Learning—http://www.absel.org
International Simulation and Gaming Association—http://www.isaga.info

References

Aldrich, C. (2009). *Simulations and serious games.* San Francisco, CA: John Wiley & Sons.

Anderson, T., & Dron, J. (2011). Three generations of distance education pedagogy. *International Review of Research on Distance and Open Learning, 12*(3), 80–92.

Beesley, A. D., & Apthorp, H. S. (2010). *Classroom instruction that works: Research report* (2nd ed.). Denver, CO: Mid-continent Research for Education and Learning.

Bogdanovic, M. (2012). Growing importance of distance education. *Modern Education and Computer Science, 3,* 35–41.

Boswell, J. (1979). *The life of Samuel Johnson.* New York, NY: Viking Press.

Brozo, W., & Simpson, M. (2003). *Readers, teachers, learners.* Columbus, OH: Merrill Prentice Hall.

Card, O. S. (1985). *Ender's game.* New York, NY: Tor Books.

Carnegie Mellon University. (n.d.). *Learn more about OLI.* Retrieved from http://oli.cmu.edu/get-to-know-oli/learn-more-about-oli/

Chieh, C., & Newman, K. (2000, June). *Computer animation and simulations in general chemistry.* Paper presented at the International Science conference, Seoul, Korea.

Christensen, P. (1994). An investigation of gifted students' perceptions involving competitive and noncompetitive learning situations. In N. Colangelo, S. G. Assouline, & D. L. Ambrose (Eds.), *Talent development* (Vol. 2, pp. 505–507). Dayton, OH: Psychology Press.

Clark, B. (2012). *Growing up gifted* (8th ed.). Columbus, OH: Merrill/Prentice Hall.

Crookhall, D., & Oxford, R. (1991). *Simulation, gaming, and language learning.* New York, NY: Newbury House.

Csikszentmihalyi, M. (1990). *Flow: The psychology of optimal performance.* New York, NY: Cambridge University Press.

Day, D. (2001). Leadership development: A review in content. *Leadership Quarterly, 11,* 58l–613.

Dewey, J. (1916). *Democracy and education.* New York, NY: Macmillan.

Drummer, P. (2002). *Computer simulation in education.* Springfield, IL: University of Illinois.

Gardner, H. (1983). *Frames of mind: The theory of basic intelligences.* New York, NY: Basic Books.

Garris, R., Ahlers, R., & Driskell, J. (2002). Games, motivation, and learning: A research and practice model. *Simulation Gaming, 33,* 441–467.

Gee, J. P. (2007). *Good video games and good learning: Collected essays on video games, learning and literacy.* NY: Peer Lang Publishing.

Gregory, T. (2000). *Social studies curricula for gifted learners in elementary and middle school.* (Unpublished master's thesis). College of William and Mary, Williamsburg, VA.

Heward, W. (2012). *Exceptional children: An introduction to special education.* Columbus, OH: Merrill/Prentice Hall.

Hopkins, G. (2002). *Introduction to special education.* Columbus, OH: Merrill/Prentice Hall.

Iuppa, N., & Borst, T. (2010). *End-to-end game development.* Burlington, MA: Focal Press.

Johnson, R. D., Hornik, K. S., & Salas, E. (2008). An empirical examination of factors contributing to the creation of successful e-learning environments. *International Journal of Computer Studies, 66,* 356–369.

Jonas-Dwyer, D., & Pospisil, R. (2004). *The millennial effect: Implications for academic development.* Retrieved from http://citeseerx.ist.psu.edu/viewdoc/download?doi=10.1.1.216.2538&rep=rep1&type=pdf

Joyce, B., Weil, B., & Calhoun, E. (2000). *Models of teaching.* Boston, MA: Allyn & Bacon.

Kim, J., Park, S., Lee, H., Yuk, K., & Lee, H. (2001). Virtual reality simulations in physics education (Korea Research Foundation Report 99-005-D000076). *Interactive Multimedia Electronic Journal of Computer-Enhanced Learning, 3*(2).

Leu, D., & Kinzer, C. (2003). *Effective literacy instruction.* Columbus, OH: Merrill/Prentice Hall.

Lewis, R., & Doorlag, D. (2003). *Teaching special students.* Columbus, OH: Merrill/Prentice Hall.

MacGregor, A. (2008). *Barnga: A game about inter-cultural awareness.* Retrieved from http://socrates.acadiau.ca/courses/educ/reid/games/Game_descriptions/Barnga1.htm

May, D. (1997). Simulations: Active learning for gifted students. *Gifted Child Today, 20*(2), 28–34.

McCrea, B. (2013). Game-based learning is playing for keeps. *THE Journal: FETC.*

Melton, R. F. (2002). *Planning and developing open and distance learning: A quality assurance approach.* London, England. Routledge Falmer.

Montgomery, H., & Palmer, J. (2006). Improving understanding and exam scores: Five minutes at a time: Manipulative activities in class. *The Texas Science Teacher, 35,* 19–23.

Moore, K. (2011). *Effective instructional strategies: From theory to practice* (4th ed.). Thousand Oaks, CA: Sage.

National Association for Gifted Children. (2010). *NAGC Pre-K–Grade 12 Gifted Programming Standards: A blueprint for quality gifted education programs.* Washington, DC: Author.

National Association for Gifted Children, & The Association for the Gifted, Council for Exceptional Children. (2006). *NAGC-CEC teacher knowledge and skill standards for gifted and talented education.* Retrieved from http://www.nagc.org/uploadedFiles/Information_and_Resources/NCATE_standards/final%20standards%20(2006).pdf

National Education Association. (2014). *Global competencies in a 21st century* (NEA Policy Brief). Washington, DC: Author.

Paul R., & Elder, L. (2001). *Critical thinking: Tools for taking charge of your learning and your life.* Upper Saddle River, NJ: Prentice Hall.

Prensky, M. (2001). *Digital game-based learning.* New York, NY: McGraw Hill.

Prensky, M. (2004). Our brains extended. *Educational Leadership, 70*(6), 22–27.

Rajagopalan, M., & Schwartz, D. (2005). Gamer design and game development education. *Phi Kappa Phi Forum, 85*(2), 29–32.

Reid, A. (1987). Turn to page 84. In D. Sisk (Ed.), *Creative teaching of the gifted* (pp. 116–117). New York, NY: McGraw-Hill.

Renzulli, J., Leppien, J., & Hays, T. (2000). *The multiple menu model: A practical guide for developing differentiated curriculum.* Waco, TX: Prufrock Press.

Romme, G. (2003). *Microworlds for management education and learning.* Tilburg, The Netherlands: Tilburg University.

Rubenstein, G. (2010, June 11). Personalized learning and the school of one [Web log post]. Retrieved from http://www.edutopia.org/blog/personalized-learning-school-of-one

Sandler, J. (2009). Foreword. In C. Aldrich, *Simulations & serious games* (p. xxii). San Francisco, CA: John Wiley & Sons.

Sapon-Shevin, M. (2010). *Because we can change the world* (2nd ed.). Boston, MA: Allyn & Bacon.

Scherer, M. (2013). Playing catch up with kids. *Educational Leadership, 70*(6), 7.

Shirts, R. (1985). *Tag game.* Del Mar, CA: Simulation Training Systems.

Shirts, R. G. (1974). *BaFá BaFá.* Del Mar, CA: Simulation Training Systems.

Sisk, D. (1976). *Parlé: A simulation game:* Washington, DC: Department of Health Education & Welfare.

Sisk, D. (1983). *Land of the sphinx and land of the rainbow.* Tampa: University of South Florida Center for Creativity, Innovation, and Leadership.

Sisk, D. (1999). *Infotactics.* Beaumont, TX: Lamar University, Center for Creativity, Innovation, and Leadership.

Sisk, D. (2007). *Making great students greater: Easing the burden of being gifted.* Thousand Oaks, CA: Corwin Press.

Sisk, D. (2012). *Texas Governor's School final report.* Beaumont, TX: Lamar University.

Squire, K., & Jenkins, H. (2003). Harnessing the power of games in education. *Insight, 3,* 7–29.

Thiagarajan, S. (1989). *Barnga: A simulation game on cultural clashes.* Yarmouth, ME: Intercultural Press.

Thiagarajan, S. (2006). *100 favorite games.* San Francisco, CA: John Wiley & Sons.

Tompkins, G. (2014). *Literacy for the 21st century: A balanced approach.* New York, NY: Pearson.

Turnbull, R., Turnbull, A., Shank, M., Smith, S., & Leal, D. (2003). *Exceptional lives: Special education in today's schools* (4th ed.) Columbus, OH: Merrill Prentice Hall.

U.S. Department of Education. (2010). *Transforming American education: Learning powered by technology.* Washington, DC: Office of Educational Technology.

VanTassel-Baska, J., & Little, C. (2011). *Content-based curriculum for high-ability learners* (2nd ed.). Waco, TX: Prufrock Press.

Winona Middle School's Cultural History Project. (n.d.). Retrieved from http://www.ed.gov/technology/draft-netp-2010/winona-middle-school

19
Chapter

CREATING A SUSTAINABLE DIGITAL ECOSYSTEM FOR THE GIFTED EDUCATION CLASSROOM

BY KEVIN D. BESNOY

Six years ago, Joshua R. Goodman began redesigning his gifted education classroom. Inspired by his then 6-year-old son and students in his classroom, he learned how to use blogs and podcasts to create an engaging learning environment. Over the past few years, his classroom has transformed from a place where students created dioramas in old shoeboxes and presented their science fair project findings on a trifold board, to one where students engaged with video editing software to create book trailers, social networks to connect with content experts across the globe, and microblogging sites to broadcast their research findings. Before his classroom transformation began, one would describe Mr. Goodman as a reluctant technology adopter; however, he quickly noticed the impact technology had on his classroom and realized that his gifted students' motivation levels were piqued by his integration of technology into the classroom. As his technology proficiency and comfort levels grew, Mr. Goodman observed that his students tended to solely focus on the products they produce with the technology tools. Rather than using technology to develop his students' critical thinking skills, he recognized that he was substituting a current technology for an outdated one. In the past, Mr. Goodman was able to use the library, reference books, and guest speakers to develop students' critical thinking skills. As a result, 2 years ago Mr. Goodman began his journey toward creating a learning environment that uses technology to develop his students' creative-productive abilities. What emerged was a sustainable digital ecosystem.

Information, Communication, and Technology

During the last decade, researchers (Besnoy, Dantzler, & Siders, 2012; Clarke & Besnoy, 2010; Housand & Housand, 2012; O'Brien, Friedman-Nimz, Lacey, & Denson, 2005; Palak & Walls, 2009; Siegle & Mitchell, 2011) have articulated the need to integrate technology into the gifted education classroom, yet teachers of the gifted no longer need convincing to integrate technology into their classrooms. Instead, the current challenge is to chronicle best practices that allow gifted and talented students to develop their abilities into marketable skills. To accomplish this task, it is important that the field moves beyond integrating technology simply because digital natives have grown up with these tools. Just as book trailers replaced shoebox dioramas, technology best practices must be redesigned to reflect the building of critical thinking and marketable skills. By approaching technology integration solely from a product-driven approach, the powerful influence technology can have on developing critical thinking skills in the gifted education classroom is neglected.

Why Is "How We Integrate Technology" Important?

Although much of this chapter describes how to integrate technology into the gifted education classroom, one cannot lose sight of the perspective that technology should be integrated with a process-oriented, future-needs purpose in mind. As the field develops a deeper research base describing appropriate practices for integrating technology into the gifted education classroom, it must do so through a future-needs lens and a keen eye on developing critical skills and components that help develop students for the future marketplace. Furthermore, thinking about technology integration through this future-needs lens allows teachers of the gifted to design classroom digital ecosystems that produce young people competent in using technology, but more importantly, it allows teachers to produce students who are capable of engaging with technology to develop innovative products and processes.

Chapter Goals

This chapter provides teachers of the gifted with the necessary theoretical knowledge and practical resources to design sustainable classroom digital ecosystems. Keep in mind that it will be another 12 years before current kindergarteners enter postsecondary settings. Although current middle and high school students will transition out of K–12 environments much sooner, rapidly changing workplace demands require that they too must be equipped with a process-oriented skill set. Thus, one goal of this chapter is to help establish a mindset that quality technology integration prepares current K–12 students for workplace conditions that have yet to be defined. It is important for the reader to be forward thinking and approach this chapter with the mindset that technology is forever progressing; however, teaching gifted students the mechanics of the critical thinking and learning process is paramount.

A second goal is to provide teachers of the gifted with practical resources that will help them sustain content rich, robust digital ecosystems. You will see these items highlighted in the text as "Teacher's Corner" discussion boxes. Rather than detailing a technology integration blueprint focusing on specific technology tools, this chapter describes technology integration through a future-needs, process-oriented lens (see Table 19.1).

Future Digital Marketplaces

Future digital marketplaces require a workforce capable of producing and distributing innovative digital goods and services. Gifted students' precocious abilities for advanced information retention, knowledge recall, abstract thought, and creative-productivity (Reis & Sullivan, 2009) means they have the unique potential to satisfy marketplace demands. One common myth held by many outside the field of gifted education is that gifted students neither need specialized programs nor require targeted services aimed at developing their unique gifts (Gallagher, 1991; Neihart, Reis, Robinson, & Moon, 2002). As such, it is critical that we do not apply this myth to technology integration into gifted education settings. Just as gifted students have unique social/emotional and academic needs that require specialized programming, targeted instruction must also be developed to promote innovation through technology.

According to Greenhalgh and Rogers (2010), economists generally recognize two types of innovation: (a) product and (b) process. Product innovation is "the introduction of a new product or a significant qualitative change in an existing product. Process innovation is a new way of making or delivering goods and services" (Greenhalgh & Rogers, 2010, p. 3). Gifted students will only fill these

TABLE 19.1
Teacher's Corner: Hierarchy of Process-Oriented Technology Skills

Progression from basic to advanced skills ↑	Engage with social media to promote digital goods, services, and ideas.
	Use digital relationships to collaboratively produce digital goods, services, and ideas.
	Communicate ideas to others in a socially responsible manner.
	Establish and maintain digital social relationships.
	Authenticate the veracity of information.
	Gather and disseminate information through digital media.

demands if their learning environments are designed with future needs in mind. Rather than focusing on specific technology tools, this chapter describes a process-oriented approach to technology integration through which gifted students gain experience developing innovative processes and products (see Table 19.2).

In describing the jobs of the current and future economies, Casey (2012) asserted that many professions are seeking process-oriented individuals who are capable of developing innovative processes and/or products. Successful persons in these economies are able to demonstrate critical thought, reflective judgment, and creative imagination while simultaneously exhibiting cross-cultural competence. Deardorff (2006) defined cross-cultural competence as the "ability to communicate effectively and appropriately in intercultural situations based on one's intercultural knowledge, skills, and attitudes" (p. 253). As a result of technology's role in expanding the globalization of modern economies, this skill set must be valued and developed in gifted education classrooms.

To become workplace ready, gifted students require learning environments that prepare them for a digital marketplace (Burger, 2007; Chin, Chang, & Atkinson, 2008). In addition to managing and manipulating techno-science knowledge, 21st-century marketplaces are seeking workers who have cross-cultural, collaborative abilities to create, express, market, and disseminate innovative products and ideas (Casey, 2012; Greenhalgh & Rogers, 2010). To satisfy this need, Besnoy et al. (2012) suggested that teachers of the gifted create effective digital ecosystems or learning environments that liberate gifted learners to freely associate their innate talent with technology. It is critical to recognize that technology is a channel through which young people can develop innovative skills and market their precocious talents (see Table 19.3 for ideas of career readiness skills).

Gifted Education and Technology Integration

Although this chapter will not focus on describing the principles of gifted education pedagogy, it is important to take a moment and establish a perspective

TABLE 19.2
Teacher's Corner: Exploring Innovative Products and Processes

Process	Products
3D Printing (http://shapeways.com/): The process of creating a solid three-dimensional object from a digital design. During the past 10 years, there has been a large growth in the production and sales of 3D printers. In the coming years, people and schools will have 3D personal computers that allow students to design and print a variety of personally engineered products.	**3D Printer (http://3dprinter.net/):** 3D printing is achieved using an additive process, where successive layers of material are laid down in different shapes. Examples of products that can be printed include prosthetic limbs, engineering prototype models, and statues. In the near future, students will be able to enter in the 3D Rocket Engine Design Challenge from their own classrooms.
Crowdsourcing (http://dailycrowdsource.com): Crowdsourcing is a type of participative online activity in which an individual or group seeks the public's help in accomplishing a task. The task can be something monumental or locally focused.	**Katrina PeopleFinder Project (http://en.wikipedia.org/wiki/Katrina_PeopleFinder_Project):** This project used crowdsourcing to collect data from those displaced by the storm. More than 90,000 entries were made. **Galaxy Zoo (http://galaxyzoo.org/):** This is an online astronomy project that invites people to assist in the morphological classification of large numbers of galaxies.
Massive Open Online Classes (MOOC; http://mooc-list.com): This originated from the open educational resources movement and is a process of creating, or participating, in free distance education courses. Typically, participation is free of charge, yet offers no academic credit for course completion.	**Peer 2 Peer University (http://p2pu.org/en/):** This is a grassroots, open-education project that organizes learning outside of institutional walls and gives learners recognition for their achievements. P2PU creates a model for lifelong learning alongside traditional formal higher education. Leveraging the Internet and educational materials openly available online, P2PU enables high-quality low-cost education opportunities.

TABLE 19.3
Teacher's Corner: Developing Career Readiness Skills That Prepare Students to Create and Distribute Digital Goods and Services

Task	Description
Advertise student created products through social media.	Teach students to leverage social media by requiring them to upload, share, and promote their final products. Through this process, students will explore how to digitally distribute goods and services.
Create a charitable fund drive.	Use crowdsourcing to promote awareness and seek assistance for a local nonprofit organization. Through this process, students learn how to develop a digital charitable campaign drive.
Develop a series of public service announcements (PSAs).	Teach students to identify issues of public health and safety and disseminate multimedia information that addresses those issues. Through this process, students learn how to raise the public's awareness to current critical issues.

around which technology integration can be described. Technology is only one, albeit important, of the resources that can be used to meet gifted students' social/emotional and academic needs. At the same time, it is a critical, dynamic resource that can be integrated across populations, disciplines, and settings.

Technology Frame Theory

The Technology Frame Theory (TFT) is a conceptual framework that was formed from a digital immigrant's perspective as a user, teacher, instructional technology specialist, and researcher (see Figure 19.1). The theory was developed as a result of exploring technology for personal purposes, integrating technology into classrooms, empowering other teachers to use technology as pedagogy tool, and designing experimental research studies to investigate the impact that technology has on the teaching and learning relationship. Some of these endeavors were more successful than others, yet these collective experiences have led to the conclusion that sustainable digital ecosystems result from a combination of two principle dynamics: (a) teachers/students need supportive school and home environments and (b) teachers/students need digital interaction with discipline-specific pedagogy and content.

Contemporary school environments are natural digital ecosystems, although some are more ecologically sound than others. Even schools with limited technology resources have a digital ecosystem; they simply have fewer assets with which to sustain an environmentally sound system. The TFT can be applied to any setting and contextualizes technology integration as a process-oriented experience that melds pedagogy, curriculum, and technology with teacher and student readiness. One goal of developing this theory is to provide a conceptual framework around which educators of the gifted can discuss the factors that contribute to a sustainable classroom digital ecosystem. A second goal is to establish a set of variables to use when evaluating a digital ecosystem's quality. Although the first goal is important for future empirical studies, the second enables teachers of the gifted to develop ecologically sound practices.

The organizing principle of the TFT is the digital ecosystem, which defines the sources of energy around which the TFT is structured. To successfully integrate technology into their classrooms, teachers of the gifted must recognize the various sources of energy that flow in and out of the ecological system (see Table 19.4).

More importantly, teachers of the gifted need to know how to harness those sources and channel them in proper directions. Harnessing the sources of energy requires teachers of the gifted to combine gifted education pedagogy with the elements of the classroom digital ecosystem. The catalyst for this process is Technological Pedagogical Content and Knowledge (TPACK; Mishra & Koehler,

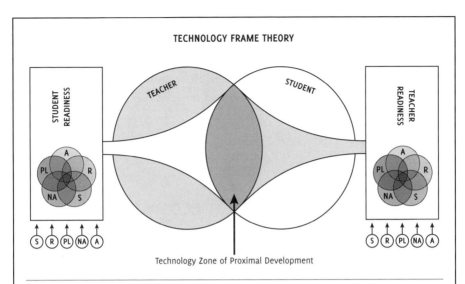

Figure 19.1. Technology Frame Theory. *Note.* S = Support; R = Resources; PL = Prior Learning; NA = Natural Ability; A = Attitude. For a full description of these factors, see Table 19.8.

TABLE 19.4
Teacher's Corner: Tips to Identifying Elements
of Your Classroom Digital Ecosystem

Tip	Considerations
How does your school climate contribute to classroom technology integration?	▸ Does your administration (school/district) expect and support your efforts to teach with technology? ▸ Are there technology-focused professional development opportunities offered at your school? ▸ Are your students encouraged to bring their own technology devices to school? ▸ Does your school/district encourage you to use technology?
How do you use technology for teaching and learning?	▸ Do you take the time to learn new technology tools on your personal time? ▸ Have you participated in technology-focused professional developments? ▸ How do you use technology to develop students' autonomous learner skills? ▸ Do you use technology to connect with experts from outside your school/district?
How do your students use technology for teaching and learning?	▸ What type of technology devices do your students use when they are not in school? ▸ How do your students use technology to research answers to questions about non-class-related information? ▸ Do your students use technology to connect with content experts in their areas of interests?

2006). TPACK is the practice of interweaving technology, pedagogy, and content for purposeful teaching and learning (Wilson, Wright, & Inman, 2010). Hsu (2010) wrote, "integrating technology into teaching means considering the needs of students, the curriculum, and available technology, as well as the lesson planning and media design issues, and somehow combining them into practices that will enhance students' learning" (p. 310). The TFT combines the ecological principles of the digital ecosystem and the pedagogical foundations of TPACK to produce a technology integration framework.

Classroom Digital Ecosystems

Like other ecosystems found in nature, a classroom digital ecosystem's sustainability is determined by its flexible environment, which allows energy to flow in and out. These energy forces are dynamic variables that morph depending on a variety of teacher, student, school climate, cultural, and social variables. In order to sustain a content rich, pedagogically sound digital classroom ecosystem, teachers of the gifted must appreciate this delicate balance and take the necessary steps to allow for a harmonious flow of energy in and out of the environment (see Table 19.5).

A healthy classroom digital ecosystem combines content-specific pedagogy strategies with purposeful technology applications and involves students in meaningful instruction (Zambo, 2009). These ecosystems are an amalgamation of equipment, expectations, and experiences that allow students and teachers to redefine traditional processes, test novel hypotheses, and report innovative findings (Besnoy, Housand, & Clarke, 2009; Besnoy et al., 2012; Burger, 2007; Chin et al., 2008; de Bono, 1970; Zhao & Frank, 2003). Figure 19.2 illustrates the small "window" of overlapping constructs needed to create a sustainable digital ecosystem.

How Do I Evaluate the Quality of My Classroom's Digital Ecosystem?

Gone are the days when having state of the art technology was the strongest indicator of a quality, ecologically sound classroom. Perhaps, when availed of these resources, teachers might be more likely to create a sustainable classroom digital ecosystem; however, the quality of a digital ecosystem must be measured on the type of creative-productive users it produces (Besnoy et al., 2012; see Table 19.6). Gifted students immersed in robust digital ecosystems will mature into

TABLE 19.5
Teacher's Corner: Tips to Harness the Sources of Energy That
Flow In and Out of the Digital Classroom Digital Ecosystem

Tip	Consideration
Keep an open mind.	Teachers must be willing to adapt proven process-oriented pedagogies to new technology tools.
Appreciate the delicate balance between teacher and learning partner.	Teachers need to embrace the notion that they are learning new pedagogies and technologies alongside their students.
Expect students to use technology tools in and out of the classroom.	Gifted students need to be taught how to be autonomous learners.
Create opportunities for students to apply their precocious talents to authentic learning situations.	Teachers can hone students' autonomy by exposing them to a variety of digital experiences.

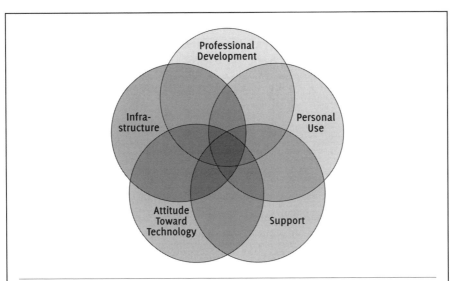

Figure 19.2. A model supporting and evaluating a sustainable classroom digital ecosystem. Adapted from "Creating a Digital Ecosystem for the Gifted Education Classroom" by K. D. Besnoy, J. A. Dantzler, and J. A. Siders, 2012, *Journal of Advanced Academics*, 23, 305–325.

TABLE 19.6

Teacher's Corner: Evaluating the Quality of My Classroom's Digital Ecosystem

Teachers' Behaviors	Students' Behaviors
To what extent am I using available school-based technology resources to engage my students with digital content?	To what extent are my students using available school-based technology resources to engage with digital content?
How frequently do I learn about new technologies and pedagogical strategies?	How frequently do my students engage with technology to complete process-oriented tasks?
How frequently do I use technology in my personal life?	How frequently are my students using technology in their personal lives?
To what extent do my school administrators encourage me to integrate technology into my instruction?	To what extent do my students' parents encourage their children to use technology for learning purposes?
How confident am I in my ability to learn new technologies and to integrate them into the teaching/learning process?	How confident are my students in their ability to learn new technologies and to use them for learning purposes?

a generation of inventors, entrepreneurs, and innovators. The value of such an environment reaps benefits from the synergy invested into these dynamic settings.

Technological Pedagogical Content and Knowledge

Purposeful technology integration only occurs when teachers of the gifted coalesce their knowledge of technology, pedagogy, and content. Teachers of the gifted can embrace the TPACK framework by designing purposeful, thoughtful, and process-oriented technology integration. Figure 19.3 illustrates the interconnectedness of content, pedagogical, and technological knowledge. Consider your expertise in each of these three areas and how this framework can be used to develop gifted students' marketplace readiness.

TPACK should be used by teachers of the gifted as they begin to mesh content, pedagogy, and technology. A promising feature of TPACK is that it encourages teachers of the gifted to leverage technology to differentiate instruction for high-ability learners. As a result, technology tools are integrated into content-based curriculum models through similar means as described in the Integrated Curriculum Model (VanTassel-Baska, 2011). Documenting the impact of integrating technology in a process-oriented approach, as opposed to a tool simply to create products, is critical.

Mobile technology is creating a more democratic, globally connected society. Many of the common barriers to using technology (e.g., affordability, access, and

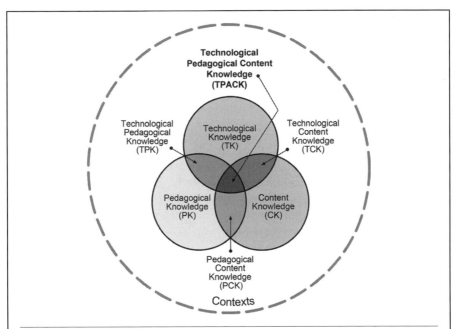

Figure 19.3. The TPACK Model describing the knowledge teachers require to teach effectively with technology. Reproduced by permission of the publisher, © 2012 by http://tpack.org.

user-friendliness) are dissipating, therefore enhancing the dynamic potential with which everyone can participate in the digital age. In fact, the term *upward mobility* (i.e., one's access to higher levels of the socioeconomic class structure) begins to take on an added layer of meaning. The digital divide is decreasing as more students and teachers own affordable mobile devices and have greater access to free online resources. When framed within the TFT, TPACK is a philosophical approach that enables teachers of the gifted to provide access and opportunity to gifted students of all backgrounds.

Effective teachers of the gifted are able to design instruction to meet discipline-specific standards, while emphasizing advanced content and developing autonomous learner skills. Digital ecosystems and TPACK have a symbiotic relationship that brings together teachers and gifted students and allows for the creation of novel processes and products. Although the TFT connects these two concepts, the core of the theory hinges on the relationship between teacher and learner.

Technology Zone of Proximal Development

An individual's readiness to engage with technology is determined by the confluence of several factors. The influence that each factor has on an individual's readiness to engage with technology for process-oriented purposes in a process-oriented environment that yields creative productivity varies depending on the convergence of the factors in Figure 19.1.

Teacher readiness to integrate technology into the gifted education class-room is essential to sustaining a digital ecosystem (Zambo, 2009). For example, a teacher with unlimited technology resources who lacks the pedagogical knowl-edge, technical proficiency, administrative support, and/or teacher disposition to meaningfully integrate them into the curriculum will not be able to sustain the digital ecosystem. Given this specific context, a lack of teacher readiness hinders the digital ecosystem's sustainability and limits gifted students' potential to utilize technology for creative-productive purposes.

At the same time, student readiness to utilize technology is also crucial to the teaching and learning process (Zambo, 2009; see Table 19.7). Consider for a moment a teacher who has unlimited technology resources, strong TPACK skills, and a positive disposition toward technology integration. If this teacher's students lack technology resources at home, experience learning problems with technology, and/or have a low interest in using technology for creative-productive purposes, then their readiness to learn with technology is low. Within this specific context, without student readiness the teacher will not be able to fully integrate technology in ways that yields creative productivity.

To gain a deeper understanding of the TFT, one can also explore Vygotsky's (1978) ideas about the Zone of Proximal Development. A central tenant of both the TFT and Zone of Proximal Development is that successful learning environ-ments require both teacher and student readiness. Vygotsky described the Zone of Proximal Development as the distance between what learners can perform with-out assistance and what learners can only perform with the assistance of others. In Vygotsky's theory, the learner traditionally refers to children and the person providing assistance refers to the teacher. Although "the zone of proximal devel-opment is created by the teacher and student in the context of specific academic tasks through mutual participation" (Subramaniam, 2007, p. 1,058), the inferen-tial nature of the social contract is that the learner (child) evolves along a devel-opmental path with the assistance of the teacher (adult). According to the TFT, teachers and students experience technology advancement together.

Siegle and Mitchell (2011) asserted that, "teachers' use of technology affects how students use technology" (p. 350). Although accurate, teachers of the gifted must also consider the degree to which students influence their own use of tech-nology. A digital ecosystem is a synergistic environment that draws strength from

TABLE 19.7

Teacher's Corner: How Can Teachers and Students Learn Technology Together?

Idea	Outcome
Teachers should invite students to bring technology tools into the classroom.	Because teachers are not always more technology savvy or proficient than their students, this empowers students to share new technologies or applications.
Students should help plan learning activities that demonstrate how they use technology for learning purposes.	Because everyone is encouraged to think about new ways to apply technology tools to the teaching and learning process, this will encourage a fresh approach to using these tools for process-oriented purposes.
Teachers should collaborate with their students in the research process.	Because students are not as proficient in conducting research, this will enable teachers to demonstrate how to use technology to engage in the learning process.
Teachers and students should create a classroom technology improvement plan that seeks to increase the frequency and efficiency of using technology for teaching and learning purposes.	Because sustainable digital ecosystems require a harmonious relationship, this empowers teachers and students to identify ways to improve classroom technology integration.

the ebb and flow between student-centered and teacher-led instruction. The optimal Technology Zone of Proximal Development is achieved when readiness to teach and learn with technology blurs the line between the traditional teacher and student relationship. The result is an ecologically sound digital ecosystem where the learner is not inherently the child. Rather, the child and adult simultaneously use technology to develop their content knowledge through pedagogically sound experiences (Zambo, 2009).

Teacher and Student Readiness

Technology integration that yields gifted students who are capable of creative productivity requires a strategic approach that goes beyond simply putting computers in the classroom. It requires that teachers and students are ready to use technology in ways that allow for the production of novel products and processes. The concept of readiness to use technology for these purposes means that teachers of the gifted understand how to properly use technology (pedagogy) in their disciplinary content areas (content knowledge). At the same time, it requires that students are ready to participate in the teaching and learning process that meets the demands of current and future marketplaces. The environmental variables defined in Table 19.8 illustrate that "readiness" is a multicontextual construct that

TABLE 19.8

Teacher's Corner: Factors Contributing to Technology Readiness

Teacher	Student
(S)upport The level of support received from district/school administrators, colleagues, and technology coordinators refers to a school's technology climate. This can be in the form of encouragement and expectations that technology is part of the teacher's instructional and recreational practices.	**(S)upport** The level of support received from parents and peers refers to a student's home technology climate. This can be in the form of encouragement and expectations that technology is part of the student's academic and recreational life.
(R)esources This factor is determined by the quantity and quality of technology resources available to the teacher. It is measured by access to hardware/software resources that a teacher has at home and school for teaching and personal purposes.	**(R)esources** This factor is determined by the quantity and quality of technology resources accessible to the student at home and at school. It is measured by the student's availability to engage with hardware/software resources for learning and recreational purposes.
(P)rior (L)earning Amount of technology-focused experiences and professional development completed by the teacher. This also refers to the amount of informal learning a teacher participates in to improve technology integration.	**(P)rior (L)earning** Amount of technology-focused experiences and learning completed by the students. This can refer to in-class formal learning and out-of-class informal learning in which the student engages.
(N)atural (A)bility An individual's proficiency to use technology for professional and personal purposes impacts a teacher's comfort level. Furthermore, it refers to a teacher's ability to learn new technology skills in a way that allows for technology integration into the classroom and personal life.	**(N)atural (A)bility** This refers to a student's proficiency to use technology for scholarly and personal purposes. Furthermore, it refers to a student's ability to learn new technology skills in a way that allows for technology integration in academic and personal lives.
(A)ttitude A teacher's attitude refers to the degree a teacher is willing to learn how to integrate technology into the curriculum and willing to learn new technology integration strategies. Attitude also refers to the teacher's willingness to integrate technology for process-oriented outcomes versus technology tool-focused activities.	**(A)ttitude** A student's attitude refers to the degree to which the student desires to use technology as a learning tool. It also reflects a student's desire to use technology to demonstrate learning. Attitude also refers to a student's willingness to use technology for process-oriented outcomes versus technology tool-focused activities.

determines the Technology Zone of Proximal Development and influences the way technology is integrated into the gifted education classroom.

(S)upport

The idea of support has been discussed in literature and generally refers to the degree to which teachers feel their efforts are encouraged and reinforced. According to researchers (Besnoy & Clarke, 2010; Siegle & Mitchell, 2011; Staples, Pugach, & Himes, 2005), there are three types of support: (a) administrative, (b) technical, and (c) collegial. These researchers conclude that a classroom is conducive to nurturing a digital ecosystem when a school climate possesses these three elements.

Technical support is usually addressed in school systems by technology coordinators; however, parental support is also critical to developing a child's technology readiness. As teachers of the gifted foster a symbiotic relationship with the digital ecosystem, students also require an appropriate level of support as they develop process-oriented technology skills. A student's ability to learn and produce innovative ideas with technology is also determined by factors outside the classroom. These supports can be in the form of parental encouragement and expectations that technology is part of their child's academic and recreational life (Davies, 2011). Additional supports can be found in their extracurricular activities. Students can engage with digital materials, produce digital artifacts documenting what they do outside of school, and establish pen pal relationships through digital media. By offering this level of parental assistance, families can build sustainable home digital ecosystems.

(R)esources

In some respects, the technology resources variable is the most difficult to describe for a variety of reasons. Currently, there is no consensus as to what constitutes appropriate resources. Not only do questions persist (Besnoy, 2007; Siegle & Mitchell, 2011; Zhao & Frank, 2003) about how much new technology to introduce into the digital ecosystem at any given time, but there are also questions about how frequently to update hardware and software. These questions continue to persist even in today's Web 2.0 world. More read/write collaborative tools are available online than ever before, therefore questioning the need for expensive software packages, but continuing the need for connectivity.

As the ownership of mobile devices (such as smartphones and tablets) and availability of Wi-Fi networks continues to grow, concerns for technology availability in K–12 classrooms will be lessened. With more researchers claiming that the gap has "narrowed considerably" (Guadagno, Muscanell, & Pollio, 2013, p. 86), concerns remain about the digital divide; the gap between those who have and do not have access to information technologies. Reinhart, Thomas, and Toriskie (2011) challenged educators to consider the Second-Level Digital Divide, which refers to how technology is used as opposed to who has access to the technology and who does not. The researchers found that those students who used technology at home for schoolwork, and those schools who had technology advisors to help teachers design technology use had academic advantages over those who did not. Reinhart et al. (2011) further noted that the Second-Level Digital Divide could be preventable through teachers' professional development in technologies that can support pedagogical practice. Families can also implement easy activities to use technology at home (see Table 19.9).

(P)rior (L)earning

Although it is difficult to identify one factor as the keystone to successful technology integration, research has demonstrated that it cannot be accomplished without sustained professional development. Research describing successful technology integration makes clear the critical role that professional development has on the process; however, implementing technology tools to foster and enhance higher order thinking skills cannot be attempted in a haphazard manner. In fact, if teachers have not received appropriate training on how to integrate IT tools into the classroom, these technologies will go unused and the support unappreciated, or even resented. Thus, without continuous IT focused training that demonstrates how to integrate these tools in ways that promote the more complex levels of the Depth of Knowledge model (Webb, 1997), even teachers of the gifted might fall victim to a technology integration paradox. Professional development that aligns with teachers' values is important and includes those technologies that customize specific learning needs, allow for communication and collaboration, and engage and motivate students (Ottenbreit-Leftwich, Glazewski, Newby, & Ertmer, 2010) Sustained professional development has been proven to improve attitudes toward computers and increases teachers' abilities to utilize the computer as an effective instructional tool to promote higher order thinking skills (Kanaya, Light, & Culp, 2005; Matzen & Edmunds, 2007; Shaunessy, 2005; Staples et al., 2005).

(N)atural (A)bilities

Natural technology ability is a concept that has yet to be fully explored in the gifted literature. On the surface, it appears that some individuals (e.g., teachers and students) have a natural affinity for integrating technology devices in their personal and professional/academic lives. At the same time, regardless of ability, it appears as though some individuals are more inclined and willing to integrate technology into their daily personal/professional lives. In order to understand

TABLE 19.9
Teacher's Corner: Tips for Parents to Enhance Student Technology Readiness

Tip	Description
Family Smartphone Day	Pick one day a week/month and allow child to document the day's activities with a smartphone. Children can upload photos to social media, blog about the day's events, or create QR codes about items of interest.
Family Video Pen Pal	Register for a Skype in the Classroom account and locate a video pen pal. This will allow the family to explore other cultures and to develop their telecommunications skills.
Family Newspaper Mornings	Weekend mornings are great times to read online newspapers. Additionally, most online articles allow for readers to post comments. As a family, pick one article each weekend and post your opinions about the article in the comments box.

Natural Abilities further, research should investigate (a) how natural technology ability impacts the teaching/learning process and (b) how nontechnology natural abilities impact the use of technology for teaching/learning purposes.

By their very definition, gifted students have precocious abilities. The field of gifted education has not investigated how, or if, identified gifted students (across all domains) are utilizing technology in combination with their precocious abilities. Furthermore, determining if gifted students learn with technology differently from nongifted peers is unknown. A line of inquiry that addresses this gap in the research might allow the field of gifted education to better prepare gifted students to compete in the global marketplace. According to researchers (Besnoy et al., 2012; Palak & Walls, 2009), documenting the hybridization of gifted abilities and technology might yield theoretical models (e.g., TFT or Technology Zone of Proximal Development) that enable teachers of the gifted to create and sustain student-centered, digital ecosystems.

Some researchers (O'Brien et al., 2005; Siegle, 2004, 2007) have reported that new technology-gifted constructs are emerging. Preliminary findings from those studies suggest the presence of measurable technology-giftedness characteristics such as (a) an early acquisition of technology skills, (b) a keen interest in engaging with technology, (c) an ability to mentor others in technology use, (d) a capacity to transfer technology skills across platforms, and (e) an innate talent to produce complex products with technology. Given the promise and potential impact of these studies, researchers interested in promoting this particular area should continue to explore questions that refine the characteristics of the technology-giftedness construct. Those findings, however, do not include technology use by gifted students whose precocious abilities fall outside the technology-gifted domain.

(A)ttitudes

According to Shaunessy (2007), a teacher's attitude toward technology integration, coupled with computer-focused professional development, were strong predictors of technology integration. Although this particular study measured attitude toward technology, and not the impact that other conditions had on technology integration, the conclusions drawn from the study indicated that professional development and access to sufficient resources had a positive influence on a teacher's attitude towards technology.

Technology-focused professional development has a significant impact on a teacher's attitude toward it. Typically, teachers will not integrate technology into their classrooms unless they are equipped with (a) a theoretical knowledge of why technology is an important educational tool and (b) practical skills to successfully integrate technology into their specific classroom (Shaunessy, 2007). Furthermore, teachers of the gifted who hold a more positive view of integrating digital technologies into the classroom are more likely to utilize them as an instructional tool. Students' attitudes toward technology are also influenced positively by those activities that construct learning (Davies, 2011) and allow them to create and contribute content (Valenza, 2013).

Creating a Process-Oriented Digital Ecosystem

Technology integration is not a one-size-fits-all solution to preparing gifted learners to meet future challenges. When designing technology-rich learning experiences, remember that it's not the technology that engages the learner, it's the design of the experiences. Having access to technology resources is only one variable in the integration equation, the other parts (content, pedagogy, and skill set) are critical components. As the facilitator of learning, it is critical to view the Technology Zone of Proximal Development as a harmonious area where teachers and students learn together. Although you might be the pedagogy expert, in a robust digital ecosystem, you might not be the content or technology expert. Just as mentioned before, use the expertise around you to create a robust, thought-provoking learning environment. As teachers plan for process-oriented digital ecosystems, the types of technology tools to integrate and the purposes of the learning activity should be considered.

Implementing Technology Tools

As with any new instructional endeavor, teachers of the gifted should implement new technology tools in slow, methodical steps. According to Besnoy et al. (2009), although novices must be patient when attempting to integrate new technology tools, they must also be willing to experiment with new approaches that engage their students in meaningful instruction. Integrating technology in a random manner will not lead to a sustainable digital ecosystem. A good way to structure new strategies into an existing curriculum and to develop an ecologically sound classroom is to follow the Revised 5-Step Integration Plan listed below. Originally conceived as the 5-Step Integration Plan (Besnoy et al., 2009), this updated plan was designed with TFT and TPACK in mind. Rather than only describing technology from a teacher's perspective, the Revised 5-Step Integration Plan considers the symbiotic relationship between teachers of the gifted and their students.

Step 1: Identify a technology tool. Before integrating a new technology tool into the gifted education classroom, a teacher of the gifted must research the advantages and disadvantages. Several sites where teachers can begin researching which tools they want to integrate into their classrooms can be found later in the chapter (see Teacher Resources section). It is important to experiment with a few tools and determine which ones best meet the needs of the gifted students. First-time users should plan extra time to experiment with the functionality of the selected technology tool.

The TFT describes a harmonious situation where teachers and students share in the teaching and learning of technology tools. As such, teachers of the gifted must invite their students to introduce new tools into the classroom digital eco-system. One avenue through which to accomplish this is for students to explore resources (see Teacher Resources) and to create a "technology integration wish list." A second way to meet this same goal is to have a technology show-and-tell day where students share technology tools they are using in their personal lives.

Once a pool of technology tools have been identified, teachers and students together should begin exploring curriculum entry points where they can integrate new tools and technology-focused pedagogies. Exploring these points together accomplishes two goals: (a) it establishes where these tools and pedagogies can be integrated into the gifted education classroom, and (b) it allows students to share in the learning process by demonstrating ways they learn with technology.

Step 2: Establish content-specific, process-oriented outcomes. Next, teachers of the gifted need to design an instructional unit that engages gifted students in process-oriented activities. When designing this unit, it is important to do so in a manner where students can apply higher order and metacognitive thinking skills. It is critical that technology be integrated in a way where students experience producing innovative products and processes through exploration and development of their areas of interests. Furthermore, teachers of the gifted must develop assessment materials that measure process skills. When establishing content specific, process-oriented outcomes, it is important to consider the Technology Zone of Proximal Development and the symbiotic relationship between teacher and student readiness.

To initiate this step, teachers and students should identify a product(s) to create; however, it is essential that product creation is not the sole outcome of the instructional unit. As such, teachers and students need to identify specific process skills on which they will focus while creating the product. Although each core discipline has specific technology skills that students should be able to demonstrate, the International Society for Technology in Education has produced National Education Technology Standards for Students and National Education Technology Standards for Teachers that teachers of the gifted use as a guide when integrating technology into their classrooms. The advantage of these standards is that they are not technology tool specific; rather, they detail process-oriented goals that expect students to use technology to analyze, learn, and explore content. Many of the collaborative instructional ideas already describe in this chapter will help teachers of the gifted and their students focus on developing content specific, critical thinking skills.

Step 3: Reflect on initial efforts and revise strategies. Although one may be equipped with new technology tools and pedagogy, developing the skills and expertise necessary to combine them for teaching and learning purposes will take time. In order to develop content specific skills, teachers and students need to reflect on the successes and failures of the pedagogical strategy and instructional tool's effectiveness. Implementing a new technology tool and pedagogical approach requires an initial investment of planning time, but also additional reflective efforts that will culminate in revised approaches. These continuous efforts strengthen teacher/student readiness and support an ecologically sound classroom.

There are a couple of reasons for this initial reflection and revisions step. First, teacher and student readiness are typically imbalanced, thus resulting in a wide spread in the Technology Zone of Proximal Development. Second, teachers of the gifted and their students need to become more skilled at learning with technology for content specific, process-oriented purposes. As such, it is important for the teacher and students to collectively reflect on the teaching learning process and engage in an open discussion as to how to improve upon the initial plans.

This collaborative reflection will facilitate oscillation between student-centered and teacher-led instruction. Not only will the teacher of the gifted be able to verify the effectiveness of the new tools and strategies, but also gifted students will have the opportunity to describe their learning process. This metacognitive element, by both the teacher and students, is critical because it helps teachers of the gifted to more effectively use the TPACK model. The teacher and students can use the results of the collaborative reflection to modify how everyone demonstrates their content, process-skill, and technical knowledge.

Step 4: Reflect on revised efforts and invite outside observers. As teachers of the gifted and their students' technology readiness evolve, they must continue to reflect on and refine the classroom digital ecosystem. Although it is important that the teacher of the gifted closely monitor the content of the project to ensure that accurate knowledge is being constructed, it is equally essential to ensure that these revised efforts concentrate on developing more advanced process-oriented skills. As the digital ecosystem becomes more robust and sustainable, gifted students will be more motivated to collaborate with peers and develop 21st-century marketable skills.

By this step, gifted students should be prepared to present their information to an authentic audience. One easy way to accomplish this expectation is to seek out colleagues, administrators, and community leaders to serve as observers in the process. This will establish that the work students are completing is important and will add authenticity to the digital ecosystem. Additionally, it will serve as a public relations activity to demonstrate the advanced work being completed in your classroom. Although local populations make for a great audience, their presence alone does not address the need for students to learn how to distribute digital goods and services. To remedy this, students should publish and promote their work on the Internet and through social media. This added element is a characteristic of a sustainable digital ecosystem.

Step 5: Receive public feedback and refine the digital ecosystem. A defining characteristic of the current digital age is the ease with which people can provide feedback to items posted online. You will know that you have successfully created a robust, sustainable digital ecosystem if your students' digital work is posted in a public forum and receiving comments. Once you have achieved this level of technology integration, it is important to work with your gifted students to read the public comments, evaluate them for accuracy, and refine your collaborative efforts.

Tools to Embrace the Technology Shift

As stated earlier, one goal for this chapter is to present technologies as tools that can be used for process-oriented purposes. Thinking about technology integration through this lens will help the reader connect this chapter to others in the textbook. To help explain this, it is best to illustrate how process-oriented tasks are used to complete goals (see Table 19.10).

This section focuses on pedagogical practices that can be sustained by the teacher and/or the student, depending on the goals and the needs for classroom teaching and learning. In presenting these practices, the tools and resources assist the teacher of the gifted to weave together technology, pedagogy, and content.

TABLE 19.10

Teacher's Corner: Meeting Goals Through Process-Oriented Tasks

Goal	Process-Oriented Tasks to Complete Goal
Students create a book trailer.	‣ Read the book. ‣ Conduct research about the book. ‣ Complete a character analysis. ‣ Write a script. ‣ Produce or find pictures that tell your story. ‣ Create music to enhance the book trailer. ‣ Produce book trailer. ‣ Publish and share book trailer. ‣ Evaluate book trailer.
Students and teacher create a classroom technology improvement plan.	‣ Inventory classroom's hardware and software resources. ‣ Inventory teachers' and students' current technology resources found in the home. ‣ Conduct a technology skills assessment. ‣ Establish technology hardware and software acquisition goals. ‣ Establish technology skills goals. ‣ Identify teaching strategies to incorporate into the classroom.
Students participate in a classroom public service announcement (PSA) contest.	‣ Identify a local issue of public interest around which students can raise awareness. ‣ Conduct research about the issue and gather data to support the need for a PSA. ‣ Complete research polls to determine how behaviors need to be changed. ‣ Create scenarios demonstrating the need for change. ‣ Write scripts for actions and dialogue. ‣ Video or audiorecord the actors reading the script. ‣ Edit the video or audio recording. ‣ Publish the PSA to a video or audio sharing site. ‣ Use social medial to promote the PSA.

This web of resources further enables gifted students to experience, create, and transform knowledge. Embrace the paradigm shift of larger concepts of technology integration discussed earlier in the chapter and do not view technology as a piece of hardware and/or a software package. Remember, no single tool should be viewed separate to teaching and learning but rather as a part of the larger digital ecosystem.

Although studies have consistently shown over the last decade that technology can engage the student and help in the acquisition of knowledge, the pedagogical practices of how that engagement can occur has drastically shifted. In the past, it was reasonable, and even exemplary, for teachers to expect students to follow a lecture, then sit in front of a personal computer, open a program that requires licensing by the school, and create a document or presentation that was later printed and turned in for evaluation. Today, technology offers a very different dynamic for the classroom and often converges many different resources toward a common goal.

The goal of creating a 21st-century learning environment has been extensively discussed in the literature (Besnoy, 2007; Besnoy et al., 2009; Besnoy et al., 2012; Clarke & Besnoy, 2010; Housand & Housand, 2012; Palak & Walls, 2009; Siegle & Mitchell, 2011). The conclusions are that technology integration requires students to engage with content and colleagues in ways that allow them to create, and disseminate, novel solutions. One exciting aspect of current technologies is the ease with which students can collaborate with their global community.

The 20th-century constructivist notion that knowledge is independently processed in an individual's mind was appropriate during a time void of social media, text messaging, the Internet, and smartphone technologies. Viewing the learning process as a phenomenon that occurs solely through an individual's experiences and perceptions is limiting given the proliferation of collaborative digital media into contemporary life. Researchers (Besnoy et al., 2012; Eshet-Alkali & Chajut, 2010) have pointed to the interactive nature and collaborative potential that digital content offers, and they have suggested that adhering to traditional, constructivist theories about how students learn are not congruent with future workplace demands. Quay (2003) maintained that new pedagogical approaches must be developed to enhance the digital literacies. In the current digital society, learning and developing new knowledge is a collaborative process that requires students to socialize with one another.

One of the most popular examples of this concept is the flipped classroom model, described in detail below. For example, today, students can receive the lecture at home through the flipped classroom model. Then, in class the next day, students bring various mobile devices (as a result of a BYOD—Bring Your Own Device—initiative), and students and teachers interact through various read/write Web 2.0 tools to further engage in the content. After the in-class experience, communication and collaboration can continue and be extended past the brick and mortar of our classroom walls through use of social networking tools.

Next, in providing an overview of each of these concepts, keep in mind that each concept should not be viewed as a stand-alone pedagogical practice but rather as practices that can be concurrently implemented. Current K–12 students (as well as our future students) must be equipped with a ubiquitous, process-oriented, technology focused skill set. These overarching categories (a) leveraging mobility, (b) promoting a flipped classroom, (c) integrating Web 2.0 tools, and (d) using social networking resources will help ensure technology and marketplace readiness.

Leveraging Mobility

Ownership of mobile devices (e.g., smartphones, tablets like the iPad and Kindle) has now surpassed laptop ownership, which surpassed desktop computer use in the late 1990s. Teachers of the gifted must leverage the power of mobility and seek ways to encourage it in our classroom. No longer does the burden of fully providing the technology (both hardware and software) fall on the schools' administration. This shift can potentially open up more spaces (i.e., computer labs and Maker Spaces) and provide funding for other creative activities. The changing landscape of computing device ownership has prompted many school districts and individual schools to encourage and promote BYOD events. Using mobile devices can be leveraged to encourage students' ownership of their learning, enabling the classroom to go beyond the concrete walls of a computer lab where each student (and teacher) is held captive to a particular computer and a set assignment.

Flipped Classroom

A flipped classroom essentially takes lectures and repurposes them using videos, presentations, and other online resources to move the lecture space from the classroom to the home, where the content can be available online, 24 hours a day, 7 days (24/7) a week. Additionally, in this model, the content can be watched and reviewed several times. A flipped classroom helps free valuable classroom time to dig deeper into the content, encourage additional exploration, and include more discussion, collaboration, problem-solving activities, and application of the content. It is for these reasons that the concept of the flipped classroom is quickly gaining in popularity. Of course, increased access to technologies (both at home and via mobile devices) also contributes to the success of flipping the class and allows for students to move at their own pace. There are other benefits of a flipped classroom, including teachers creating curriculum to replace expensive and aging textbooks (Fulton, 2012), as well as students' creating content that, in turn, can validate their work (Valenza, 2013) and improve their attitudes toward learning. Table 19.11 includes some tips for creating a flipped classroom.

Teachers of the gifted can approach the flipped classroom in multiple ways. First, the teacher can choose to create customized content as a video or a presentation. To create videos, tools such as MovieMaker or iMovie can be used and then saved for web delivery on venues such as a private YouTube channel, TeacherTube, or a school/classroom website; however, there many educational videos on the web (such as Ted-ed); once vetted, many teachers may choose to provide students with links to the videos. Ted-ed (http://ed.ted.com/) also offers an easy-to-use flipping tool that allows a teacher to quickly create a flipped lesson, using existing online content. Another option for creating flipped classroom

TABLE 19.11

Teacher's Corner: Tips to Creating a Flipped Classroom

Tip	Resources
Identify short, existing classroom presentations (5–10 minutes in length) that can be posted online.	**Knowmia (http://knowmia.com):** This website is a destination for learning that features short video lessons. You can also upload your videos to this site.
Allow students the opportunity to apply the knowledge they gain through multimedia presentation.	**Putting Students at the Center (http://techsmith.com/flipped-classroom-aaron-sams.html):** This short video describes how one teacher engages students with the flipped classroom.
Design in-class lessons that require students to collaboratively engage in a problem-based approach with the content from the flipped multimedia lessons.	**Flipped Classroom Model (http://youtube.com/watch?v=ojiebVw8Oog):** This instructional video illustrates how to engage students within the flipped classroom.
Require that students create flipped lessons rather than in-class presentations. This will change the nature of their class project from simple presentation to meaningful learning activities.	**June Harless Center Flipped Classroom Project (http://vimeo.com/62436357):** This informational video describes the benefits of the flipped classroom for student learning.

content is to create online presentations for students to view and study at home. Some outstanding, free online tools include SlideRocket (http://www.sliderocket.com/) and Prezi (http://prezi.com/). Teachers and students can also create content using PowerPoint, add narration, and save as a video file. Lastly, content can be captured from one's computer using screen capturing or screencasting tools such as Jing (http://www.techsmith.com/jing.html) and Screenr (http://www.screenr.com). The flipped classroom concept is gaining momentum as teachers around the world develop networks to build content (Bergmann & Sams, 2012). For more information and advice from teachers who have flipped classroom learning, see http://flippedclassroom.org.

Keep in mind that creating the content and assigning students to view the information alone does not meet the definition of the flipped classroom nor does it develop students' process-oriented skills. The novelty of the flipped classroom idea is that the teacher-centered portion of the class is transferred outside of the classroom and on to the Internet to allow students to access the content as often as is needed. Although educators often criticize the notion of the teacher being a "sage on the stage," there is a place for a teacher-led potion of the class. Developing new technology and pedagogical knowledge by flipping the classroom allows teachers to still deliver important content knowledge.

A robust digital ecosystem is not solely a teacher-led ecological environment. Thinking about the flipped classroom through the TFT lens, teachers of the gifted should require students to create their own flipped lessons, or class presentations, to share with their classmates. Rather than being consumers of the knowledge, gifted students must learn to be innovators of both process and product. By requiring students to create flipped classroom presentations, teachers can harness the synergistic sources of energy that define a sustainable digital ecosystem.

Web 2.0 Tools

Web 2.0 is a term coined to describe the current nature of read and write—collaborative—tools of the Internet. Web 1.0 refers to a flat environment that does not allow for collaborative, real time content additions and change. Web 2.0 tools allow for synchronous and asynchronous information sharing, multiple authorship, and interaction. One of the best examples of the difference between Web 1.0 and Web 2.0 is the creation of a website. Before Web 2.0 availability, a teacher would create a website using a hypertext markup language tool (HTML), save the files, and upload to a server. If a change needed to be made, the file was downloaded back to a local drive, changed with the HTML editor, and then transferred back to the server. Today, users can quickly create, change, and save content to the web through read/write services, eliminating multiple steps and saving valuable time. Some user-friendly resources include Weebly (http://www.weebly.com/), GoogleSites (http://sites.google.com/), and wikis (PBWorks [http://pbworks.com] or Wikispaces [https://www.wikispaces.com]). These resources, as is the case for so many Web 2.0 tools, offer free options for educators.

There are many Web 2.0 tools online that teachers and students can use; however, researchers have found that teachers who leverage Web 2.0 tools to encourage "always on learning communities" through "careful instructional planning" helped to "create sustained, meaningful communication" for their students (Light, 2011, p. 11). These tools, if used consistently to develop process-oriented processes, will successfully impact gifted students' attainment of 21st-century marketplace skills. Again, the tool should not be the focus, but rather how it is being used to enhance teaching and learning. Wikis are a great place to start. Both PBWorks and Wikispaces offer easy-to-use educator spaces. Students can collaborate and provide content, building reports and projects that have an ongoing life and are not purposed for a one-time grade. Some teachers have actually worked with students to build curricula for future classes.

To illustrate the many offerings of Web 2.0 tools, Price and Wright (2012) used Creswell's research process cycle to demonstrate the versatile affordances of 10 tools. For example, they outlined how Cacoo (http://cacoo.com) can visually present a research problem. Delicious (https://delicious.com/), a social bookmarking tool can be used to organize the literature review; then a GoogleDoc (http://docs.google.com) can provide the space for researchers to collaborate on the research as it develops and as data are collected via tools such as Survey Monkey (https://www.surveymonkey.com). Lastly, the authors discussed how various social networking tools (i.e., blogs) are used to help disseminate the findings and research results. The read/write, dynamic potential of Web 2.0 allows for students to be content providers, while learning how to better collaborate and communicate ideas, give feedback, and to reflect on learning. These are essential characteristics for students to develop as they work toward meeting the challenges of tomorrow's workplace.

By designing learning environments that take advantage of Web 2.0 tools, teachers of the gifted allow students to develop advanced process-oriented technology skills (see Table 19.1). As with other tools described in this chapter, teachers must involve gifted students in the design and implementation process.

Social Networking

Inherent in the challenges to prepare gifted learners for jobs of tomorrow is to ensure their ability to interact with others in a creative-productive manner. The idea of being *social* is now "ubiquitous in educational scholarship" (Dawson, 2010, p. 737), however, the challenge in using social networks in teaching and learning is to develop a learning community that encourages and sustains engagement. It has never been easier for teachers of the gifted to use instructional technologies in the classroom with students having access to mobile devices and user-friendly Web 2.0 tools. The new "literacies of the digital age—immediacy, community, interactivity, and transparency" (Mills & Chandra, 2011, p. 35) are especially prevalent in social networking tools, such as Twitter, Facebook, blogging, and platforms with an educational focus like Edmodo.

These resources allow for much more than simple chat and routine status updates. They can be leveraged in the learning environment to promote electronic news reporting, threaded discussions on a new topic, professional development learning communities, the sharing of digital media, and participatory writing exercises. With Edmodo (http://edmodo.com), teachers of the gifted can develop a secure, social network for each class, allowing for posting of content, files, and media (even grades may be posted in a secure manner). Mills and Chandra (2011) noted that the use of social networking, specifically microblogging: (a) blurs the distinction between authors and readers, (b) transforms elements of the writing process, (c) creates a supportive virtual community of learners, and (d) promotes self-initiated literacy practice.

Conclusion

As the field of gifted education continues to describe ways to use technology for instructional purposes, it must do so with a future-needs focus in mind. In order to successfully meet the demands of the digital marketplace, teachers of the gifted must begin to consider not only their own readiness to teach and learn with technology but also that of their students. The principles described in the TFT can bring the field of gifted education to a place where students of all precocious talents can develop process-oriented skills that enable them to produce and distribute innovative goods and services. Establishing the reliability of this model, or subsequent versions, will help teachers to create classroom digital ecosystems. Technology-rich, digital ecosystems must materialize in order to prepare gifted students to compete for their place in evolving business and industrial occupations. The current and future marketplaces require a workforce equipped with the ability to use technology for innovative, novel purposes. Digital ecosystems may foster such a skill set and potentially amplify the precocious abilities of advanced learners to redefine the workplace.

Teacher Statement

I have been a teacher of the gifted for the past 4 years. During that time, I have learned to integrate technology into my classroom in purposeful ways. My experiences have taught me that technology integration is most successful when there is an equal partnership between my students and myself. Not only must I be ready to teach with technology by having the necessary resources and training but my students must also have equal access so that they are ready to learn with technology. The result is a shared responsibility to create a sustainable digital ecosystem.

This chapter opened my eyes to a much-needed shift in the use of technology within gifted education. To make students marketable for the 21st century, technology must be integrated into all we do in the classroom so that it becomes as natural to the students as any other means of communication and production. For that to happen, technology must also become natural to me. After reading this chapter, I can see now how important the role of the teacher is in a sustainable classroom digital ecosystem.

My students and I have created a balanced digital ecosystem by utilizing available technology resources to become prepared for a future focused workplace. Although many of my students are already quite adept with using technology, they do not always use the technology as the means to a different end. In my first year as a teacher of the gifted, my students saw using technology to create a product as the goal or objective. Now I have shifted my instruction so that my students view the product as catalyst for innovation.

—Jessica Thomas

DISCUSSION QUESTIONS

1. Identify three end-of-unit products for students to produce with technology and describe five process skills that students need in order create those products.

2. Summarize why it is important for classroom technology integration to focus on process skill development.

3. Describe your current classroom digital ecosystem and detail five steps you can take to create a more sustainable classroom digital ecosystem.

4. Explain how the Technology Frame Theory combines content-specific skills and technology integration principles to produce a sustainable digital ecosystem.

5. Describe how student readiness to use technology can help teachers become more proficient with integrating technology into classroom instruction.

6. Explain how teacher readiness to use technology can help students develop the required skills to meet future marketplace demands.

Teacher Resources

Around the World With 80 Schools—http://aroundtheworldwith80schools.net
> This website is an ongoing project that aims to connect a school with 80 other schools around the world using Skype. It also allows each classroom to create a blog to journal about the connections and to record how it impacts the students' learning.

Bubbl.us—https://bubbl.us/
> Users can use web-based application to create their own mindmap.

ClassTools.net—http://www.classtools.net/
> This website allows users to design activities, games, and diagrams.

Draw Anywhere—http://www.drawanywhere.com/
> With this interactive website, users can create diagrams, share content, and store content in the cloud.

Exploratree—http://www.exploratree.org.uk/
> Students and teachers can access ready-made interactive thinking guides or customize them for a particular lesson.

Funnel Brain—http://www.funnelbrain.com/
> This website is an academic question and answer resource that encourages collaborative, team based learning. Users can easily create flashcards by inserting video, photos, or text.

Glogster EDU—http://edu.glogster.com/
> This tool provides users an avenue for creative digital expression. By creating GLOGS, students can demonstrate and share photos, graphics, videos, and thoughts.

LibriVox—https://librivox.org
> This website is a warehouse of public domain books that have been converted into audio books.

LiveBinders—http://www.livebinders.com
> Users can organize their information, notes, and digital work in the cloud and access that content from anywhere.

Lovely Charts—http://www.lovelycharts.com
> This web-based diagramming program enables users to produce professional quality flowcharts, sitemaps, and organizational charts.

LucidChart—https://www.lucidchart.com
> This website assists users by creating crisp, attractive flow charts that can be reproduced and disseminated.

TheBrain—http://thebrain.com
> This is dynamic mindmapping tool that allows users to link together any variety of ides by simply dragging and dropping files and web pages into the program.

Vye Music—http://vyemusic.com/
> This is a web-based music player that allows the users listen to and share music.

References

Bergmann, J., & Sams, A. (2012). Before you flip, consider this: Leaders of the flipped classroom movement say each teacher will have a different experience, but securing school leadership support, time, and IT resources will be important to every effort. *Phi Delta Kappan, 94*(2), 25.

Besnoy, K. D. (2007). Creating a personal technology improvement plan. *Gifted Child Today, 30*(4), 44–49.

Besnoy, K. D., & Clarke, L. W. (Eds.). (2010). *High-tech teaching success: A step-by-step guide to using innovative technology in your classroom.* Waco, TX: Prufrock Press, Inc.

Besnoy, K. D., Dantzler, J., & Siders, J. A. (2012). Creating a digital ecosystem for the gifted education classroom. *Journal for Advanced Academics, 23,* 305–325.

Besnoy, K. D., Housand, B. C., & Clarke, L. W. (2009). Changing nature of technology and the promise of educational technology for gifted education. In F. A. Karnes & S. Bean (Eds.), *Methods and materials for teaching the gifted* (3rd ed., pp. 783–802). Waco, TX: Prufrock Press.

Burger, J. (2007). Protective sustainability of ecosystems using department of energy buffer lands as a case study. *Journal of Toxicology and Environmental Health: Part A, 70,* 1815–1823.

Casey, C. (2012). *Economy, work, and education.* New York, NY: Routledge.

Chin, K. L., Chang, E., & Atkinson, D. (2008). A digital ecosystem for ICT educators, ICT Industries, and ICT students. In *2nd International Conference on Digital Ecosystems and Technology (DEST 2008), Feb 26, 2008.* Phitsanulok, Thailand: IEEE. Retrieved from http://ieeexplore.ieee.org/stamp/stamp.jsp?arnumber=04635225

Clarke, L. W., & Besnoy, K. D. (2010). Connecting the old to the new: What technology-crazed adolescents tell us about teaching content area literacy. *Journal of Media Literacy Education, 2*(1), 47–56.

Davies, C. (2011). Digitally strategic: How young people respond to parental views about the use of technology for learning in the home. *Journal of Computer Assisted Learning, 27,* 324–335.

Dawson, S. (2010). 'Seeing' the learning community: An exploration of the development of a resource for monitoring online student networking. *British Journal of Educational Technology, 41,* 736–752.

de Bono, E. (1970). *Lateral thinking: Creativity step by step.* New York, NY: Harper & Row.

Deardorff, D. K. (2006). Identification and assessment of intercultural competence as a student outcome of internationalization. *Journal Studies in International Education, 10,* 241–266.

Eshet-Alkalai, Y., & Chajut, E. (2010). You can teach old dogs new tricks: The factors that affect changes over time in digital literacy. *Journal of Information Technology in Education, 9,* 173–181.

Fulton, K. (2012). 10 reasons to flip: A southern Minnesota school district flipped its math classrooms and raised achievement and student engagement. *Phi Delta Kappan, 94*(2), 20.

Gallagher, J. J. (1991). Programs for gifted students: Enlightened self-interest. *Gifted Child Quarterly, 35,* 177–178.

Greenhalgh, C., & Rogers, M. (2010). *Innovation, intellectual property, and economic growth.* Princeton, NJ: Princeton University Press.

Guadagno, R., Muscanell, N., & Pollio, D. (2013). The homeless use Facebook?! Similarities of social network use between college students and homeless young adults. *Computers in Human Behavior, 29,* 86–89.

Housand, B. C., & Housand A. M. (2012). The role of technology in gifted students' motivation. *Psychology in the Schools, 49,* 706–715.

Hsu, S. (2010). The relationship between teachers' technology integration ability and usage. *Journal of Educational Computing Research, 43,* 309–325.

Kanaya, T., Light, D., & Culp, K. M. (2005). Factors influencing outcomes from a technology-focused professional development program. *Journal of Research on Technology in Education, 37,* 313–329.

Light, D. (2011). Doing Web 2.0 right. *Learning and Leading With Technology, 38*(5), 11–15.

Matzen, N., & Edmunds, J. (2007). Technology as a catalyst for change: The Role of professional development. *Journal of Research on Technology in Education, 39,* 417–430.

Mills, K., & Chandra, V. (2011). Microblogging as a literacy practice for educational communities. *Journal of Adolescent & Adult Literacy, 55*(1), 35–45.

Mishra, P., & Koehler, M. J. (2006). Technological pedagogical content knowledge: A new framework for teacher knowledge. *Teachers College Record, 108,* 1017–1054.

Neihart, M., Reis, S. M., Robinson, N. M., & Moon, S. M. (Eds.). (2002). *The social and emotional development of gifted children: What do we know?* Waco, TX: Prufrock Press.

O'Brien, B., Friedman-Nimz, R., Lacey, J., & Denson, D. (2005). From bits and bytes to C++ and Web sites: What is computer talent made of? *Gifted Child Today, 28*(3), 56–63.

Ottenbreit-Leftwich, A. T., Glazewski, K. D., Newby, T. J., & Ertmer, P. A. (2010). Teacher value beliefs associated with using technology: Addressing professional and student needs. *Computers & Education, 55,* 1321–1335.

Palak, D., & Walls, R. T. (2009). Teachers' beliefs and technology practices: A mixed-methods approach. *Journal of Research on Technology in Education, 41,* 417–441.

Price, G., & Wright, V. (2012). Aligning web-based tools to the research process cycle: A resource for collaborative research projects. *The Journal of Interactive Learning, 11,* 121–127. Retrieved from http://www.ncolr.org/issues/jiol/v11/n3

Quay, J. (2003). Experience and participation: Relating theories of learning. *Journal of Experiential Education, 26,* 105–112.

Reinhart, J., Thomas, E., & Toriskie, J. (2011). K–12 teachers: Technology use and the second level digital divide. *Journal of Instructional Psychology, 38,* 181–193.

Reis, S. M., & Sullivan, E. E. (2009). Characteristics of gifted learners: Consistently varied; refreshingly diverse. In F. A. Karnes & S. Bean (Eds.), *Methods and materials for teaching the gifted* (3rd ed., pp. 3–36). Waco, TX: Prufrock Press.

Shaunessy, S. E. (2005). Teachers' attitudes toward information technology in the gifted classroom. *Gifted Child Today, 28*(3), 45–53.

Shaunessy, S. E. (2007). Attitudes toward information technology of teachers of the gifted: Implications for gifted education. *Gifted Child Quarterly, 51,* 119–135.

Siegle, D. (2004). Identifying students with gifts and talents in technology. *Gifted Child Today, 27*(4), 30–33, 64.

Siegle, D. (2007). Identifying and developing technological giftedness: Exploring another way to be gifted in the 21st century. *Gifted Education Communicator, 38*(1), 18–21.

Siegle, D., & Mitchell, M. S. (2011). Learning from and learning with technology. In J. VanTassel-Baska & C. A. Little (Eds.), *Content-based curriculum for high-ability learners* (2nd ed., pp. 347–374). Waco, TX: Prufrock Press.

Staples, A., Pugach, M. C., & Himes, D. (2005). Rethinking the technology integration challenge: Cases from three urban elementary schools. *Journal of Research on Technology in Education, 37,* 285–311.

Subramaniam, K. (2007). Teachers' mindsets and the integration of computer technology. *British Journal of Educational Technology, 38,* 1056–1071.

VanTassel-Baska, J. (2011). An introduction to the integrated curriculum model. In J. VanTassel-Baska & C. A. Little (Eds.). *Content-based curriculum for high-ability learners* (2nd ed., pp. 9–32). Waco, TX: Prufrock Press.

Valenza, J. (2013). The flipping librarian. *Teacher Librarian, 40*(2), 22–25.

Vygotsky, L. S. (1978). *Mind in society.* Cambridge, MA: Harvard University Press.

Webb, N. (1997). *Research Monograph No. 6: Criteria for alignment of expectations and assessment on mathematics and science education.* Washington, DC: CCSSO.

Wilson, E., Wright, V., & Inman, C. (2010). Images over time: The intersection of social studies through technology, content, and pedagogy. *Contemporary Issues in Technology and Teacher Education, 10,* 220–233. Retrieved from http://www.citejournal.org/vol10/iss2/socialstudies/article1.cfm

Zambo, D. (2009). Gifted students in the 21st century: Using Vygotsky's theory to meet their literacy and content area needs. *Gifted Education International, 25,* 270–280.

Zhao, Y., & Frank, K. A. (2003). Factors affecting technology used in schools: An ecological perspective. *American Educational Research Journal, 40,* 807–840.

SECTION

SUPPORTING AND ENHANCING GIFTED PROGRAMS

PUBLIC RELATIONS AND ADVOCACY FOR THE GIFTED

20
Chapter

BY JOAN D. LEWIS AND FRANCES A. KARNES

You are a fifth-grade teacher of gifted learners who wants to acquaint the community with your students' accomplishments. Recently, they participated in a service-learning project with the Keep America Beautiful campaign to clean the local river. Your reasons for sharing your students' accomplishments might include the following: (a) they made significant contributions beyond what might be expected for their ages; (b) they developed an extensive knowledge of the environment, local industrial processes, and public relations strategies; (c) you want to see children and youth receive positive recognition; and (d) you want to see gifted students and their instruction featured in the news so people will recognize that there are practical reasons for supporting their education.

Another scenario might be that you are the enrichment specialist in your school, teaching elementary gifted students in resource classes and collaborating with teachers for their cluster groups in the regular classroom. Parents have come to you about extending the gifted program beyond the elementary school level. This has been a concern of yours for some time. You would like for your district to provide a comprehensive array of services for gifted learners at all grade levels. Your reasons might include the following: (a) program options are limited in your district; (b) research supports qualitatively and quantitatively differentiated instruction for gifted learners; (c) gifted students are a heterogeneous group that cannot be served adequately with only one program option; and (d) traditionally underserved gifted students are more likely to receive services with expanded educational options.

Definition of Terms

The terms *advocacy*, *lobbying*, and *public relations* (PR) are at times used synonymously, yet their meanings differ. Consider the following definitions of the terms from http://dictionary.reference.com:

> *advocacy:* The act of pleading or arguing in favor of something, such as a cause, idea, or policy; active support.
> *lobby:* 1. To try to influence public officials on behalf of or against (proposed legislation, for example): *lobbied the bill through Congress; lobbied the bill to a negative vote.* 2. To try to influence (an official) to take a desired action.
> *public relations:* 1. *(used with a sing. verb)* The art or science of establishing and promoting a favorable relationship with the public. 2. *(used with a pl. verb)* The methods and activities employed to establish and promote a favorable relationship with the public.

West (1985, as cited in Kowalski, 1996) described PR in education in a comprehensive manner that identifies some of the key concepts that will be employed throughout this chapter:

> *Educational PR:* a systematically and continuously planned, executed, and evaluated program of interactive communication and human relations that employs paper, electronic, and people media to attain internal, as well as external support for an educational institution. (as cited in Kowalski, 1996, p. 7)

The more recent National School Public Relations Association (NSPRA, n.d.) professional definition is:

> Educational public relations is a planned and systematic management function to help improve the programs and services of an educational

organization. It relies on a comprehensive two-way communications process involving both internal and external publics, with a goal of stimulating a better understanding of the role, objectives, accomplishments and needs of the organization. Educational public relations programs assist in interpreting public attitudes, identifying and helping shape policies and procedures in the public interest, and carrying on involvement and information activities which earn public understanding and support. (para.1)

Rationale for PR in Gifted Education

Professionals in gifted education have voiced their concerns regarding the lack of PR and advocacy for several decades. A search of educational databases and Google will demonstrate a number of recent articles describing advocacy (e.g., Duquette, Orders, Fullarton, & Robertson-Grewal, 2011; Kaplan, 2012; Leggett, Shea, & Wilson, 2010; McGee, 2012; Willis, 2012; Wiskow, Fowler, & Christopher, 2011), with more publications on advocacy strategies (e.g., Besnoy, 2005; Bisland, 2003; Center for Talent Development, n.d.; Duke University Talent Identification Program, 2013; Gilman, 2008; Grantham, Fraiser, Roberts, & Bridges, 2005; Lewis, 2008; Matthews, Georgiades, & Smith, 2011; Ohio Association of Gifted Children, n.d.; Roberts, 2010, 2014; Roberts & Siegle, 2012). Very few emphasize public relations as a necessary tool for advocacy. Resistance to gifted education has existed for decades (Clark, 2012). Gifted children and youth often are misunderstood and are victims of myths and stereotyping that not only affect their educational opportunities but also their social and emotional well-being (National Association for Gifted Children [NAGC], n.d.a).

When money is tight, as it has been recently, services for gifted learners are often reduced as a way to save money (Bisland, 2003). In 2011, Congress withdrew funding for the Jacob K. Javits Gifted and Talented Students Education Act, the only federally funded support for gifted education. Funding was reinstated for 2014 at $5 million, equal to the funding in 1997 for an Act that was originally funded at $7.9 million in 1989. The only lower funding was 1996 ($3 million) and 1995 ($4.7 million; NAGC, n.d.b). Public relations and advocacy are needed from the local to the national and international levels to build an accurate understanding of gifted learners and their education; otherwise, the myths prevail.

Advocates for gifted learners need to give teachers and their administrators clear, concise reasons why it is not only appropriate, but equitable to teach *all* students to the highest level of which they are capable. The issue is frequently seen as a conflict between equity and excellence, yet these two philosophies need not be mutually exclusive. When all students receive an education that meets their cognitive and affective needs, both equity and excellence will be achieved.

Roberts and Inman (2009) pointed out that differentiation methods used to provide gifted learners increased challenge and rigor can also improve learning for all students. Unfortunately, few, if any, teachers differentiate for gifted learners. When Westberg and Daoust (2003) reproduced the "The Classroom Practices Observation Study" from 10 years earlier, results were similar; teachers provided little, if any, differentiation.

There is evidence that many teachers recognize highly capable students need attention in school and should not be left to languish. The Thomas B. Fordham Institute published results from the recent National Teacher Survey demonstrating that "most teachers believe that academically advanced students are not a high priority at their schools. They think that these students are bored, underserved, and unlikely to get the curriculum enrichment and resources that high achievers need" (Loveless, Farkas, & Duffett, 2008, p. 51). Teachers and administrators have been unsure about how to educate these children and have not seen the need to gather progress data on them. Furthermore, elective classes that would be suitable for high-ability learners have decreased (Loveless et al., 2008). Professional development on how to teach gifted children and monitor their progress is sorely needed. The benefits of quality elective class options for all students and differentiated and suitably challenging education for every student needs to be a focus of PR: providing critical information to educators, the general public, and legislators. To be effective, advocacy needs a better informed populace.

Although schools have become increasingly more diverse, gifted programs have not achieved a similar diversity. Finding and serving these underrepresented populations is all the more important since the No Child Left Behind Act (NCLB, 2002) does not encourage quality teaching or provide an education for a diverse student body (Gentry, 2006). Gathering information on current services and needed improvements is an essential first step (Grantham et al., 2005) in developing accurate PR for advocacy. Gifted learners are in those underserved populations.

The U.S. Department of Education's (1993) report *National Excellence: A Case for Developing America's Talent* is as true today as it was when first published.

> To accomplish the goal of identifying and serving students with outstanding talent so that they reach their full potential, we must elicit the help of the entire community. Policymakers, educators, business leaders, civic organizations, and parents can all play important roles in improving education for America's most talented students. . . . Only a challenging educational environment that elevates standards for everyone can create the schools our students need to take their places in tomorrow's world. (p. 14)

It is important to speak out for the needs of gifted learners and educate ourselves with the necessary skills to employ a variety of PR strategies in order to make the dream of high-quality education a reality. "In today's media-saturated culture, effective PR is a crucial part of any public undertaking. Image and public opinion mean everything, especially in the increasingly influential realm of social media" (Roos, 2007, para. 1). Contrary to popular belief, gifted learners need teachers and a quality education; they aren't going to "make it on their own."

Targeting Your Audience

The general population is comprised of many subgroups based on interests. When planning PR, it is important to target the specific population(s) that will benefit the most. The details of the message itself and the manner in which it is delivered may vary depending on the interests of these groups, even though the basic message remains the same.

PR may be viewed as planned and unplanned. Part of the planning will include identifying the target audiences and devising strategies that will best explain the selected goal and supporting purposes. *Every person working on PR activities must speak the same message to avoid confusing the audience.* Unplanned interactions with people throughout the school and community also need to perpetuate a central message; otherwise problems and complaints tend to be what is heard, not the positive aspects of gifted children and their education.

Without a focus on local support, changes in policy at any other level are not likely to be quickly or completely enacted, because data verifying student achievement is what matters in this age of educational accountability (Kaplan, 2004b). Principals hire teachers, arrange for staff development, grant leave for further professional development, and oversee data gathering for school improvement, among their many responsibilities. If principals are not supportive or are unaware of the value of gifted education for this segment of their student body, few gifted learners will receive the level of education they need (Lewis, Cruzeiro, & Hall, 2007).

The quality of students' learning is a powerful tool for ongoing PR for advocacy (Hunsaker, 2000; Kaplan, 2004b). The value of gifted education shared with the community through *continuous* PR cannot be overstated. When local programs are strong and the community is well-informed and supportive, documentation of the benefits of gifted education is available for advocacy at local, state, and national levels.

Audiences Internal to the Educational System

Audiences with a background or special interest in education (public, private, parochial) will likely be more informed about general educational issues than individuals whose primary interests lie elsewhere; however, even within this group, expertise will vary widely from school board members to administrators, teachers, counselors, media specialists, parents/guardians, and students. Although these audience members have a strong interest in the education of young people in common, their beliefs about how children should be taught can be very different. Analyze who is supportive already, which educators have little or no knowledge about gifted education, and finally, who may be actively opposed to giving gifted learners a different education from other students, despite their reduced academic progress. Solicit the help of the first group to broaden the support base.

The second group, those who have little or no knowledge about gifted education, will be the focus of the bulk of PR strategies. Individuals who are opposed to gifted education will require special attention. Learning about their concerns and misconceptions often can be a useful tool for designing a message (Yale, 1995). Refrain from directly disagreeing with an opponent; this only calls attention to her or his views. It usually is more effective to counter the misinformation obliquely. That is, write or speak accurate information about gifted children and their education. The errors espoused by opponents will be countered in the process of spreading the main message.

When targeting parents or guardians and other family members, keep in mind their concern for providing what they believe is best for their children; however, the amount of time and energy they have to contribute may be limited. Remember that family members are both an audience and a potentially powerful force for advocacy. The students themselves also are an audience and can be excellent advocates. Who better to speak to the benefits of quality services than the students themselves? Include all students and parents, not only those with ties to gifted education. PR planners would be wise to take into consideration the needs and feelings of these diverse groups.

The manner in which various groups are approached may need to be different. To parents and guardians, the individual student is paramount. The challenges of meeting the needs of a heterogeneous population often are not recognized. Most educators have focused their primary attention on the large majority; however, with accountability has come increased focus on low-achieving students in an effort to close the achievement gap (Loveless et al., 2008). Relative to the needs of the majority and the evident needs of students with disabilities and other low achievers, the needs of gifted learners may not seem very pressing.

Audiences External to the Educational System

The broadest of all audiences is the general public, which includes both people inside the educational system and those who are not overtly connected to the schools. Neighbors, friends, and relatives are people who are seen every day and often are not thought of in terms of PR. Similarly, informal dealings with various organizations, religious affiliation members, and others within the community can have a powerful impact on perceptions of gifted children and their education. The general public also may be thought of in terms of people in the arts, business and industry, the media, political organizations, the government, and other professions. The way the message is packaged and delivered to the arts community may need to be a little different from the way it is presented to businesses or the media.

PR Strategies

A wide variety of strategies is available for bringing a message to the attention of the targeted audience(s). An extensive shopping list of strategies with a brief description of each is provided in Figures 20.1, 20.2, and 20.3 grouped under the headings nonprint, print, and other media. Regardless of the methods chosen, be sure the information is correct, brief, and timely. Use of old standbys or the newest social media will depend on how technologically savvy your target audience is.

Some methods are free while others range in cost. When selecting the strategies, consider the overall cost, the effectiveness for reaching the targeted audience(s), and the ease of use. Be sure to get the most "bang for your buck," which does not always equate with free or inexpensive. It is worth the time to consider carefully a suitable mix of strategies. Grika (1986) described an extensive and creative media campaign conducted by the Wisconsin state gifted organization. Many of these strategies could be used locally by scaling them down in size; even "gift wrapping" the capitol building with ribbon signed by gifted children from all over the state could be adapted to the local level by wrapping the district administration building or city hall with ribbon signed by students from the local school district(s).

Print media will be an important strategy, and there are several formats that can be effective (see Figure 20.2). For specific suggestions on writing techniques, media relations, and application of practical strategies, see Besnoy (2005), Bisland (2003), Courtright (2010a, 2010b), Duke University Talent Identification Program (2013), Lewis (2008), NAGC (n.d.c), Ohio Association of Gifted Children (n.d.), and Roberts (2010, 2014). Parents, teachers, and other professionals need to write articles for the mass media based on their knowledge and

Closed Circuit Television—Adult/student generated (Lewis, 2008)

_____Demonstration
_____Morning announcements
_____School news

Computer Graphics—Amateur/professional/student generated

_____Part of a multimedia presentation
_____Use on school, program, district webpage
_____Other_____

Podcast—Professional/amateur; Adult/student generated (Lewis, 2008)

_____Classes
_____Interviews
_____Meetings
_____Staff development

Radio

_____Community calendar
_____Editorials
_____Hard news
_____Human interest stories
_____Interviews
_____Public service announcements
_____Talk shows

Teleconferencing

_____Classes
_____Interviews
_____Meetings
_____Staff development

Telephone

_____Advertised hotlines
_____Planned networks to spread news rapidly

Television

_____Community calendar
_____Community channels
_____Editorials
_____Hard news
_____Human interest stories
_____Interviews
_____Public service announcements
_____Talk shows (national experts, local professionals, gifted students)

Video—Professional/amateur/student generated

_____Displays (at meetings, malls, fairs, conferences)
_____News releases for TV
_____Public interest segments on TV and ETV
_____QuickTime/streamed video (in web-based class/staff development, on webpage)
_____Staff development

Webcam—Continually running, activated at set times

_____Class activities
_____Special events

YouTube—Professional/amateur/student generated (Lewis, 2008)

_____Professional development
_____Special events
_____Student activities

Figure 20.1. Nonprint media.

Advertising—Donated/paid; display/classified

_____ Journals
_____ Magazines
_____ Newspapers
_____ Television
_____ Web-based

Advertising Slug—Specialized imprint that accompanies stamp on postage meter for bulk mailing

_____ Logo
_____ Slogan (short phrase)

Articles—Single/series, electronic/paper

_____ Journals
_____ Listservs (electronic mailing lists)
_____ Magazines
_____ Newsletters
_____ Newspapers
_____ Web-based (established websites, own website)

Bibliographies—Electronic/paper (book listings on variety of topics)

_____ General list
_____ Specific list

Billboards—Unused space available rent-free for nonprofit groups

_____ General information
_____ Specific information

Blogs—Individual/multiple individuals (electronic postings on selected websites; type of social media)

_____ Personal "journaling"
_____ Sharing of experiences, observations, opinions, on specific topic
_____ Marketing tool to obtain feedback on products and services

Bookmarks

_____ Key information about gifted students, class, program, organization
_____ Logo of program, organization, special project
_____ Slogan

Brochures/Fliers

_____ General information about gifted children
_____ Information about organizations (local, state)
_____ Program information (school, Saturday, summer)
_____ Specific topics

Bumper Stickers

_____ Program information
_____ Recognition
_____ Slogan

Bus Placards—Side panels donated on space-available basis

_____ General information
_____ Specific information

Direct Mail—Packets of selected information mailed to targeted groups

_____ Specific audience external to school _____
_____ Specific audience internal to school _____

Editorials—Guest/invited, electronic/paper

_____ Journals
_____ Magazines
_____ Newsletters
_____ Newspapers
_____ Web (established websites, own web-site)

Electronic Bulletin Boards

_____ Newsgroups
_____ Private (you belong to sponsoring organization)
_____ Public

Electronic Signs—External message boards for short public service information

_____ Banks
_____ Businesses
_____ Schools
_____ Other

E-mail

_____ Individual and group mailings
_____ Listservs (electronic mailing lists)

Figure 20.2. Print media.

Fact Sheets—Single/series, electronic/paper

_____ Specific audience external to school
_____

_____ Specific audience internal to school
_____

Faxes—Single/series sent to legislators, state board of education members, state commissioner/superintendent of education, other officials

_____ Fact sheets
_____ Letters

Handbook—Electronic/paper (compiled by local, state, national organizations; Lewis, 2008)

_____ Advocacy methods
_____ Characteristics and needs of gifted students (primarily for parents)
_____ Identification procedures
_____ Instructional strategies
_____ Program development

Journals—Electronic/paper (professional publications; send for publication guidelines)

_____ State _____
_____ National _____
_____ International _____

Letters—To individuals/groups, electronic/paper

_____ Educator written
_____ Parent written
_____ Student written

Letters to the Editor—Fact, opinion, advice, solicit information, change attitudes, express gratitude, build coalitions

_____ Educator written
_____ Parent written
_____ Student written

Magazines—General/specific topic publications, electronic/paper (send for publication guidelines)

_____ State _____
_____ National _____
_____ International _____
_____ News releases
_____ Advertising (paid or donated)

_____ Articles (single or feature series)
_____ Calendars of upcoming events
_____ Editorials
_____ Letters to the editor

Newsletters—Electronic/paper (in-house publications for employees/members)

_____ Businesses _____
_____ Organizations _____
_____ Schools _____

Newspapers—Electronic/paper

_____ Advertising (paid/donated; display/classified)
_____ Articles (single/feature series)
_____ Community calendars
_____ Editorials
_____ Letters to the editor
_____ News releases
_____ Op-ed (commentary published opposite editorial page; check guidelines)
_____ Public service announcements

News Releases—Immediate/continuing news coverage

_____ Brief summary of special events
_____ Feature stories
_____ Opinion pieces
_____ Other items of interest

Novelty Items—Print with logo/slogan

_____ Buttons
_____ Dry erase boards
_____ Magnets
_____ Mugs
_____ Pencils
_____ Pens
_____ Other school items
_____ Sticky notes
_____ Hats
_____ Visors

Piggyback Mailing—Information included in another group's mailing

_____ Brochure
_____ Fact sheet
_____ Other _____

Figure 20.2. Continued.

Position Papers—Key topics

_____ Local _____
_____ State _____
_____ National _____

Position Papers—Electronic/paper, share with other educational groups/organizations

_____ Local
_____ State
_____ National
_____ International

Postcards

_____ Calendar of special events
_____ Invitations
_____ Meeting reminder
_____ Special messages

Posters—Various sizes, colors, messages

_____ In buses
_____ In business windows
_____ In libraries
_____ In store windows
_____ On school bulletin boards

Rubber Stamp—Use with bright-colored ink on all outgoing material

_____ Program logo
_____ Program slogan

School Bulletin Board

_____ Special event notice/after event display
_____ Student work

Scrapbooks—Record of program benefits and opportunities for display

_____ PTA/PTO meetings
_____ School district office
_____ School open houses
_____ Other _____

Social Networking Websites (e.g., Facebook, Twitter; Lewis, 2008)

_____ Characteristics and needs of gifted individuals
_____ Connect with others having similar interests
_____ Program opportunities and benefits

Stickers—Various sizes and colors

_____ Program logo
_____ Program slogan
_____ Small stickers (make envelopes and papers stand out)
_____ Large stickers (attract attention on car bumpers)

T-Shirts—Special events, trips, gifts

_____ Program logo
_____ Program slogan

Text Messaging—Quick notices

_____ Educator written
_____ Parent written
_____ Student written

Thank You Letters—Sent by individuals/organizations

_____ Continuing support
_____ Expected favorable vote
_____ Favorable vote

Webpages—Teacher/school/organization/business/social media (link numerous resources within own site or to other sites, access to relevant documents, may contain internal search tool)

_____ Advertising
_____ Announcements
_____ Calendars
_____ General articles (single/series)
_____ Specific articles (single/series)
_____ News releases
_____ Link internally
_____ Link externally (articles, ERIC documents, school homepages, organization homepages, search engines)

WebQuests—Instructional units developed on the Web, usually containing specific components; teacher or student made

_____ Advocacy instruction
_____ Content instruction for other teachers' use
_____ Public relations information for professional or business groups
_____ Staff development for educators and counselors

Figure 20.2. Continued.

White Papers—Long position paper; electronic or paper, share with other educational groups/organizations

_____ Local
_____ State
_____ National
_____ International

Wikipedia—Free Web-based encyclopedia; correct or add information (Lewis, 2008)

_____ Advocacy definition and methods
_____ Assessment
_____ Characteristics of gifted children
_____ Cognitive development

_____ Debunking myths
_____ Educational strategies
_____ Identification
_____ Program development and evaluation
_____ Social and emotional needs
_____ Staff development
_____ Support organizations
_____ Teacher qualification

Wire Service—Forward quality news articles for broader coverage and listing in news databases

_____ Specific article _____
_____ Specific wire service _____

Figure 20.2. Continued.

Displays—Instructional materials, student work, scrapbook, competition trophies, video on endless loop

_____ Business and industry lobbies
_____ Conferences
_____ Libraries
_____ School or district office lobby
_____ Store windows

Recognition Ceremonies for Supporters—With or without a meal, present certificates, gifts, plaques

_____ Recognition of student/class contributions to the community
_____ Seminars
_____ Sponsorships
_____ Staff development
_____ Workshops

Special Events

_____ Booths at conferences/malls
_____ Contests
_____ Conferences

_____ Panel discussions
_____ Proclamations (governor - state gifted month; mayor - local gifted week)
_____ Ribbon cutting/wrapping

Speeches—Local, state, national, international (present at conferences, events, meetings)

_____ Business
_____ Civic
_____ Education
_____ Social groups

Student Performances—Local, state, national, international (present at various events)

_____ Conferences
_____ Fairs
_____ Mall events
_____ Meetings
_____ Other _____

Figure 20.3. Other media.

experiences to broaden the general public's understanding of gifted children using current technological tools and more traditional methods. Consider reaching out beyond the local newspaper, even for a local program or school issue. Newspapers with regional or state coverage can spread the message and possibly gather support from other communities that are working on similar problems. Newsletters for various community or even state organizations and businesses have broad audiences. Increase the support base for PR by involving others in reciprocal or collaborative projects. Many people now use smartphones and social media, so try using one or more of these strategies to spread the message and elicit support: (a) send mass mailings via e-mail, a local or national listserv, or bulletin board; (b) use group texting instead of a phone tree for quick response; (c) share ideas on blogs (Ohio Association of Gifted Children, n.d.), Facebook, Twitter, and YouTube (search for local, state, and national organizations); and (4) create a teacher or class webpage linked to the school or district website.

Some former PR activities can be recycled (Horowitz, 1996; Yale, 1995), a strategy that is practical for any size PR plan. Horowitz suggested collecting news articles in a file for future use on bulletin boards, in scrapbooks, or in media publicity packets. Teachers can use classroom and library bulletin boards, or even the school entry to display articles and photographs chronicling their students' participation in various activities (e.g., academic competitions, special programs, community service, student contributions to the newspaper, special events, and newspaper articles or blogs about the gifted program). This can be a source of pride for the students and the school, as well. These same types of materials can be kept in a "brag book" (scrapbook) and displayed in the school lobby, the library, at PTA/PTO meetings, and open houses (Bisland, 2003). These ideas are so commonplace that one tends to overlook their value for building an understanding about the students and the program. Several articles published on the same topic, such as the Keep America Beautiful example in the first scenario, show it is newsworthy. Leverage these articles to bring the news to a local radio, cable, or public access television station for additional coverage.

Pictures of events as well as print, blog, video, or web notices can be recycled through one or more social media. Facebook, for example, is a powerful modern equivalent of a scrapbook and reaches far more people. Video of your students describing their Keep America Beautiful project can be uploaded to YouTube or still pictures linked up through Pinterest. A link can be included on a teacher or school webpage, Facebook, added to newsletters, and e-mailed to newspapers for their electronic editions. The power of social media (e.g., Facebook, Twitter, Pinterest, Tumblr, Instagram, YouTube) has surpassed virtually all other methods for quick responses and sharing events.

Basic Planning for Effective PR

PR activities need to be approached with careful planning to maximize their effectiveness. Individual strategies in isolation do not work as well as a coordinated, systematic plan for the year. If time and resources are limited, start small with one or two activities. New strategies can be added each year. Publicize class activities in print or on social media. It is easier and more efficient to share the load with others, so consider working with colleagues from the school or district, teachers from other districts, and parents of students. Whether working as a member of a small group or for a large organization, it is important to develop a basic plan. It will save more time and energy than it consumes and will enhance effectiveness. Local parent support groups and state, national, and international gifted organizations need to appoint a standing committee charged with the development of a PR plan for the organization. Be sure to make use of the social media strategies now available. For example, set up a school or district Facebook page. This is a popular way to share successes and update information.

Roberts (2010) shared 11 lessons from her experience advocating for a state residential math and science high school that can also be applied to smaller public relations for advocacy ventures that support and add on to those that follow:

1. Establish the point of coordination for the advocacy plan.
2. Identify your goal and plan your message.
3. Establish relationships with key decision makers.
4. Educate individuals about the need.
5. Solicit position statements from key stakeholders and policy makers and make them known.
6. Find new friends and supporters.
7. Use expertise to build support.
8. Link with groups that may influence decisions.
9. Use advisory groups for ideas and contacts.
10. Stay up to date with research and recommendations.
11. Keep public relations plans ongoing.

Another important aspect of planning is familiarizing oneself with district policies that regulate publicity. Check with a school official about district guidelines. People in small schools need to follow the chain of administrative command, which usually starts with the principal or superintendent, while large school systems usually have a person designated for PR. Work closely with this individual to increase the effectiveness of PR efforts. Written parental permission usually is needed for using photographs of children and youth. Remember, too, that you are always under obligation to disseminate information in a clear and accurate manner so as not to misrepresent your position.

Be Clear About What You Want to Achieve and Why

Before selecting the PR strategies to be used, it is critical to be clear about the goals and rationale for these goals. Is the goal primarily to inform the community of the students' activities and accomplishments, or is the goal to make something occur or prevent an action? Write down goals and related rationale in clear, concise language. Note supporting reasons to explain why this action is being taken.

Agree on the Goal and Develop a Goal Statement

Everyone working on the publicity activities needs to come to an agreement on a specific goal. A goal statement is then developed to help provide direction. Activities that do not effectively further this goal should be carefully reviewed, and decisions should be made on an individual basis.

Know the Subject Before Working to Convince Others

This basic requirement is so obvious that it can be overlooked. All participants in PR activities should have an adequate knowledge of the needs of gifted learners and be able to explain clearly how what one wants to accomplish will further the goal of meeting these needs. Preparing a fact sheet will save time and reduce the chances of someone making a costly error. Confusion or misstatements can hinder reaching the goal. An added bonus of this fact sheet, whether digital or paper, is that it can double as one of the PR strategies.

For accurate supporting information, organizers can visit the websites for the Council for Exceptional Children, NAGC, and the National Research Center on the Gifted and Talented (NRCGT). NAGC has gathered together and developed many resources for educators and parents (e.g., Information & Resources and Advocacy & Legislation). Search the site for "digests" and "fact sheets" for a variety of resources in this form. NAGC's 15 networks specializing in critical areas of gifted education offer more specific supporting facts. Abstracts of research reports, as well as other useful materials, are available at the NRCGT Website (http://www.gifted.uconn.edu/NRCGT). Finally, websites that provide a wealth of information on specific areas of gifted education and other support materials are included in Lewis (2008).

Successful advocacy does not only depend on being knowledgeable about gifted education. Advocates also need to be familiar with local and state policies that govern gifted education, the processes whereby these policies were created, and how they can be changed (Robinson & Moon, 2003a, 2003b). Even if current PR efforts are focused on educating various constituencies and not on policy change, becoming familiar with relevant policies and the people who have power over them will help target efforts and prepare for the future.

Determine the Target Audience(s)

Selecting who comprises the primary audience(s) can save time, money, and energy. The audience will be chosen based on what is to be accomplished. Ongoing PR can increase collective understanding of the characteristics and educational needs of gifted learners by targeting the general public or specific individual groups.

Selecting a specific audience is not enough. Kaplan (2004a) reminded advocates that the timing of their efforts needs to be considered too. Tax dollars for education fund a wide range of educational services. Gifted education is only one program and is habitually underfunded. Advocates for gifted learners should be sensitive to the needs of other educational groups when planning the unveiling of specific PR activities.

Dealing with crisis management or implementing program change is somewhat different. Each requires separate strategies, but they can work in tandem. To meet a crisis or implement changes in policy requires that one identifies those who wield the power and their advisors. Target people who can accomplish what is needed, rather than the general public. In the first scenario at the beginning of the chapter, the goal can be accomplished by targeting the general public. This is an example of ongoing PR.

The second scenario is more complicated, and both general and specific audiences would need to be targeted. The main audience to change district policy will be those individuals internal to the school, such as the superintendent, director of gifted programs or special education, curriculum developers, building principals, and teachers (gifted, regular, content area, and special education). Target others who are likely to be affected. Disseminating *all* of your information to everyone in the community may not be very efficient; however, including the general public when publicizing the unique characteristics and educational needs of gifted students would help raise general awareness in your community for future use. In addition, it can enhance economic development by building partnerships with key members of the business community. A strong educational system is an asset when attempting to attract new business and industry to an area. Targeting the media usually is worthwhile regardless of the intended outcome because the media can help share the message with a wider audience.

Decide on the Basic Message

What basic message is to be disseminated? Be sure it is focused and free of educational jargon to avoid confusion. Once that decision is made, all members of the PR committee, regardless of size, need to practice the message so that everyone speaks with the same voice. It is particularly important to be clear about the goal and rationale for the goal; otherwise, your message might be lost.

Establish a Realistic Timeline and Evaluation

A reasonable timeline needs to be developed based on the nature of the plan. Allowing either too little or too much time can lead to failure. Each individual activity should be placed on the calendar in logical order and have a specific time limit, with the person/people responsible noted. Then, adjust the number of activities to make sure the overall schedule can be kept. In the community scenario, the timeline would be short; otherwise the news will be old. Expanding educational program options for gifted children may need several years, with shorter timelines for the various components necessary for achieving such a broad goal. Consider having a standard plan in place for fast-breaking stories so they can be dealt with in a timely manner.

Establish evaluation criteria so success can be documented. Ask yourself what you will need to see to know that the PR strategies have been successful. These criteria will vary depending on the goals. Writing letters to key people, publishing articles in the newspaper, or talking to school officials does not mean your goal was accomplished. These are the means, not the ends you are trying to achieve. In the first scenario, a news article with a picture in the local paper and television coverage may be the criteria. In the second scenario, a preliminary criterion might be the formation of a committee to investigate possible educational options for gifted students. Later criteria might include implementation of a specific number of differentiated options.

Get Others Involved

Organizations need to appoint a committee to coordinate their PR activities. Individual teachers and parents who want to contribute to improving the public's view of gifted education should locate at least one or two others with whom they can work. They might even begin a special interest group or work within another organization. PR can be carried out by one person, but it is more effective to involve others. Once the nucleus of a committee has completed the basic planning, find as many volunteers as possible to broaden the support base and increase good will. Be certain these volunteers are clear about the goal and the message.

The Message

After deciding on the goal(s) and rationale, specific strategies should be selected. Figure 20.4 lists questions that will help in the selection of one or more topics for articles, speeches, or discussions on radio or television to help reach the goal(s). Figure 20.5 presents an array of additional publication sources and suggested formats available to share the message. The message to the general public

There are numerous topics from which you can choose as subjects for writing blogs; fact sheets; newspaper, newsletter, magazine, and web-based articles; as well as for speeches at meetings and conferences, and for discussions on radio and television. These questions will help determine the topic.

1. How are gifted learners different from high-ability learners cognitively and affectively?
2. How does your program meet these unique needs of gifted learners?
3. What are your program's special/unique features?
4. What are some of the activities, projects, and individuals you would like to spotlight?
5. What educational opportunities are available to gifted learners around the country, via technology, and on the Internet?
6. How have your students contributed to the local community?
7. How will society benefit from providing an appropriately challenging education for gifted learners?
8. Why is developmentally appropriate academic rigor important for all students and particularly for those who are gifted?
9. How are gifted students being left behind in the educational environment of No Child Left Behind?
10. How can schools use RtI (Response to Intervention) to better serve gifted learners?

Figure 20.4. Determining topics for advocacy.

Information can be disseminated in different formats. Consider the options below and select one or more that will meet your particular needs. You may wish to prioritize them for current and future use.

Format for publication choices:

_____ **Advertisements**—Paid/donated	_____ **Fact sheets**
_____ **Article(s)**—Single/feature series/ position paper/white paper	_____ **Letters**—Educators (principal, superintendent, school board);
_____ **Blogs**	legislators; newspaper editor
_____ **Brochures**	_____ **News releases**
_____ **Editorials or op-ed pieces**	

Consider your target audience(s) and decide on the breadth of your advocacy and/or public relations plans. Select one or more of the following publication choices. Younger generations are more likely to access social or electronic rather than traditional media.

Publication sources for articles and news:

_____ **Blogs**	_____ **National wire services**
_____ **Bulletin Boards**—Electronic/school/ supermarket	_____ **Newsletters**—Electronic/paper; Business/industry/organization/
_____ **E-mail**	school district
_____ **Facebook**	_____ **Newspapers**—Electronic/paper;
_____ **Faxes**	Local/state/national
_____ **Letters**—Personal/piggyback mail-ing	_____ **Postcards**
_____ **Listservs**—Electronic mailing lists	_____ **Twitter**—Quick updates
_____ **Magazines**—Electronic/paper; Local/state/national/professional	_____ **Webpages**—District/program/ school/other_____

Figure 20.5. Information dissemination.

in the first scenario will include information generated by answering Questions 1, 4, 6, and 7 in Figure 20.4. For scenario two, responses to Question 1 will be formatted in a considerably different manner when targeting the general public and school officials. Target the latter group with Question 7, descriptions of exemplary classes and programs from around the country (a variation of Question 5), and use the answers to Questions 8 and 9 to call for more accountability.

Certain words and terms carry more power than others in the current social climate. Kaplan (2004b) wrote, "We can build our advocacy efforts on the common language used by policymakers in general education to the advantage of gifted education" (p. 59). "Social justice," "the achievement gap," "the democratic classroom," "accountability," and "academic rigor" are concepts that have the power to broaden discussions of education (Kaplan, 2004b, pp. 59–60). Kaplan indicated different perspectives for these terms: Where is the social justice of meeting the educational needs of some students while denying those of others? Several studies (e.g., Clark, 2005; Jolly & Makel, 2010; Mendoza, 2006; Reis, 2007) have demonstrated that gifted learners are not making annual yearly progress under NCLB (2002). Large national reports have recently shown that high-achieving students (usually the 90th percentile and above) are only making minimal progress (e.g., Loveless et al., 2008; Thomas B. Fordham Institute, 2008; Xiang, Dahlin, Cronin, Theaker, & Durant, 2011). Some learners who are gifted experience an achievement gap for the same reason as some general education students—they may be from diverse populations or have a disability (e.g., Plucker, Burroughs, & Song, 2010; Plucker, Hardesty, & Burroughs, 2012).

Another achievement gap exists between gifted learners who enjoy quality programs that meet their needs and students who are not so fortunate. It is popular to talk about and model democracy in the classroom, but is it democratic when "the unique and differential needs, interests, and abilities of all students, and this includes the needs, interests, and abilities of gifted students" (Kaplan, 2004b, p. 65) are overlooked or ignored? Should policy makers and educators not be held accountable for the decisions they make that lead to inequities for gifted learners as much as for other students? Kaplan (2004b) referred to "provocative questions that ask why and how decisions are made concerning the education of the gifted" as a form of "moral accountability" (p. 65). Finally, Kaplan (2004a, 2004b) encouraged advocates to explain the why and how of providing academic rigor in general education, as well as gifted education. Although the "excellence gaps remain large and, in many cases, continue to grow" (Plucker et al., 2012, p. 23), there may be hope on the horizon. All states now have "K–12 college- and career ready (CCR) standards" although less than half the states require all students to meet them (Achieve, 2013, p. 5). These higher expectations should benefit gifted learners particularly if time on task is individualized, another potential area for advocacy.

All educators, including counselors and administrators, need to work together on shared goals to reduce the achievement gaps and raise U.S. students' performance with respect to the rest of the developed world (National Center for Education Statistics, n.d.). Parents too need to be included in this effort. Several articles provide guidance for parents of intellectually gifted learners who are twice-exceptional or from a different culture that teachers can share with their students' parents/guardians (e.g., Duquette et al., 2011; Grantham et al., 2005).

"Student performance data" is yet another popular phrase used to describe how policy makers hold all educators accountable. Hunsaker (2000) described three different levels of data that are needed to verify student achievement for those who make educational decisions. Level 1 demonstrates that students have received "a sound basic education" and experience no harm from gifted programs (p. 81). These data, he says, can be used to advocate for more challenging learning opportunities. Level 2 reveals that despite "an excellent education" with its current emphasis on standards, gifted students' progress often is limited because the challenge level is not high enough (p. 81). Level 3 addresses the gifted component of the students' education intended to document their attainment of both program and individual goals. (See Hunsaker 2000, p. 81, for suggested assessment strategies at each level.)

Talent Identification

In the earlier sections of this chapter, a variety of PR strategies were discussed. Now it is time to identify Points of Personal Power (see Figure 20.6). Individuals have more power than they realize and know many others who will help once they know they are needed. People's lives are comprised of many overlapping areas of influence. Friends, colleagues, and acquaintances in each of these areas are not only an audience, but they are also part of the support. Use Figure 20.7 to document those many connections.

The purpose of PR is to convert members of the audience to supporters. Consider first those people with whom you come in contact because of your career. These include not only coworkers, but also support people, supervisors, business associates, and members of professional organizations, to name just a few. For teachers, there will be considerable overlap of career and school. The school sphere includes people internal and external to the school.

Who are contacts to consult when managing money? Bankers, tellers, and loan officers are a few of the most common. Some people have financial advisors, stockbrokers, or investment counselors. One may also belong to a club or organization focusing on financial issues.

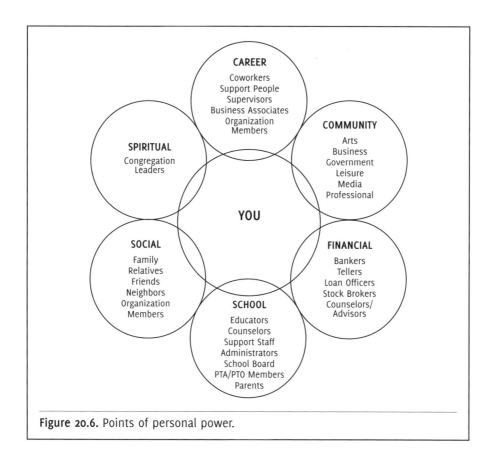

Figure 20.6. Points of personal power.

Family, friends, and acquaintances can be recruited to help during a public relations campaign. Record names of people with whom you interact in your various spheres of influence. These are your personal power connections. Make use of them as you plan your public relations. Valuable advocacy efforts can range from a onetime small contribution of time to ongoing participation at any level.

Career _____
Community _____
- ▸ Arts _____
- ▸ Business _____
- ▸ Governmental_____
- ▸ Leisure_____
- ▸ Media _____
- ▸ Professional _____

Financial_____
School_____
Social _____
Spiritual _____

Figure 20.7. Personal power connections.

Socially, there are many possibilities. Family and neighbors are important contacts. With whom do you spend time? This can be in person, on the phone, or even online. Include acquaintances, as well as closest friends. One may also know these contacts from organizations, leisure activities, or work. Who do you know because of your religious affiliation? This can include spiritual and lay leaders and members of the congregation.

Community is an amorphous whole that can be subdivided into various groups. The arts includes the fine arts of painting and sculpture, photography, dance, theater, places that house the arts, and museums. There are many businesses in any town, such as supermarkets, drug stores, and specialty shops. Include large and small industries in this category, too. Government encompasses local, county, state, and national leaders and their supporters. Leisure can include sports, entertainment, exercise, crafts, reading, and much more. Newspapers, radio, and television comprise the media. And, finally, the category of professionals includes doctors, nurses, dentists, lawyers, architects, and the people who work for them. Using Figure 20.7 as a guide, note in each of these areas people who might be supportive or have skills that can help. Remember to gather job and special interest information from the parents of students. Each of these contacts can be included in a resource file for future use.

The people known in each of these dimensions are Points of Personal Power. Now it is time to begin identifying your own and others' talents (see Figure 20.8). To produce continuous PR, gather committee members with creative, developmental (obtaining money), interpersonal, organizational, speaking, and writing skills or those who have connections to people with expertise in these areas. The task can sound daunting until one considers the contacts that can be assembled together.

What are your unique talents? Place initials beside each of the skills on Figure 20.8 that you consider your strengths, adding examples as needed. Do the same for collaborators, then include names from your resource file to fill holes in critical areas. Each unique skill need not be filled, particularly if the present plans are for a small publicity effort. More comprehensive PR plans will utilize a larger number of talents.

For example, to inform the community of students' excellent work with the Keep America Beautiful committee in the first scenario, you might write a news release for the local newspaper. That is a good beginning, but consider additional options. A parent, another adult, or the students themselves could develop a videotape about their work that could be used to raise awareness of community conservation efforts while increasing public understanding of gifted students' capabilities. Depending on the content, the tape then could be used as a community interest feature on television; at meetings of Keep America Beautiful, Rotary, Kiwanis, PTO/PTA, and other organizations; as a display in the mall; as

You and your supporters have many useful skills between you. Initial by your strengths, such as "Creative Skills," or single out specific skills, like "Graphics" or "Advertising." Repeat with supporters or potential supporters. All skills need not be covered, only those important to your plan. Actively recruit people to fill critical vacancies. Even the process of filling needed positions is a form of advocacy.

Creative Skills _____
- ▸ Advertising_____
- ▸ Displays _____
- ▸ Graphics _____
- ▸ Slogans _____
- ▸ Videos _____
- ▸ Webpages _____

Development Skills_____
- ▸ Annual Giving _____
- ▸ Goods and Services _____
- ▸ Grant Proposals_____
- ▸ Scholarships _____

Interpersonal Skills_____
- ▸ Build Alliances_____
- ▸ Facebook _____
- ▸ Facilitate Collaboration _____

Organizational Skills_____
- ▸ Committees _____
- ▸ Governmental _____
- ▸ Plan Projects _____
- ▸ Power Brokers_____
- ▸ Special Events_____

Speaking Skills _____
- ▸ Presentations _____
- ▸ Radio Interviews_____
- ▸ Talk Shows_____
- ▸ Telephone Calls_____
- ▸ Television Interviews _____

Technology Skills_____
- ▸ Blogs _____
- ▸ Facebook _____
- ▸ Other Social Media _____
- ▸ Texting _____
- ▸ Twitter _____
- ▸ YouTube _____
- ▸ Websites_____

Writing Skills _____
- ▸ Advertisements_____
- ▸ Brochures_____
- ▸ Fact Sheets _____
- ▸ Letters to Educators _____
- ▸ Letters to Legislators _____
- ▸ Letters to Organizations _____
- ▸ Letters to the Editor_____
- ▸ News Articles_____
- ▸ Newsletter Articles _____
- ▸ Position or White Papers_____
- ▸ Surveys_____

Figure 20.8. Talent identifier of unique skills.

an educational tool to share with other children in the school and district; and as staff development for district teachers. The children could create a before-and-after display at the library or in a store window. Students could conduct a survey of their classmates and members of the community about environmental issues. Results could be shared by writing letters to their legislators, letters to the editor, and a news article for national newspapers. Students also could share what they learned from their projects by making presentations to various organizations, at conferences, and on local radio and television talk shows. Legislators could be invited into the classroom or taken on a tour of the site while the students explain the conservation issues. The media usually are willing to cover the activities of public figures, and, by association, the students and the educational program would receive excellent news coverage. Meanwhile, students learn useful interpersonal skills.

Involving Others

Everyday interactions with other teachers can influence their thinking about gifted education. Remaining positive even amid challenges is necessary. Collaborating with fellow educators can help dispel notions of elitism, discredit myths, and augment education for all students.

Kaplan (2004a) suggested enlisting the help of other educators to harness the "spill-over effect" of multiple educators working toward mutual goals (p. 48). Although the educational needs of gifted learners frequently differ from other students, there are instances when the goal might be the same, even though the reasons may differ. An example might be working for a challenging and engaging curriculum for all students. Regardless of educational ability, all students would benefit with more developmentally appropriate subject matter. The challenge level may still be less demanding than most gifted learners need; nevertheless, as Renzulli (1998) reminds us, "a rising tide lifts all ships."

Visitors who have been invited to a classroom and citizens met while on field trips or other school outings are both an audience and potential new advocates for gifted education. The way teachers and students present themselves to the outside world influences the attitudes people form regarding gifted learners and their talents. Preparing visitors and people you expect to meet on field trips for the kinds of questions gifted learners ask can help prepare them for the level of knowledge and curiosity from these students. People who are not accustomed to little children asking big questions can come away baffled by such an encounter; however, when they know what to expect, they are more likely to appreciate the children's advanced thinking.

Students can be empowered to advocate for themselves in many ways. "Becoming politically savvy," as Kaplan (2012, p. 150) recommends, can furnish students the intellectual and affective tools to buttress their self-advocacy efforts. Bisland (2003) emphasized teaching gifted students oral and written communication and other process skills in the context of a unit on PR. The students could help develop their own strategies for publicizing their program, ranging from developing PR goals, to evaluating the effectiveness of their plan and its individual strategies. These are authentic learning opportunities that can build skills students will need as adults. Examples of possible strategies include participating in and conducting interviews, creating displays of their projects, giving performances of personal or group creations (e.g., songs, plays, poetry), writing press releases, producing a class newsletter, and creating a digital or paper scrapbook. Another practical idea for student-led PR is having gifted learners conduct tours of the school for business, industry, and community leaders and government representatives. The students would need to be trained to use the appropriate personal and interpersonal skills as they identify key educational opportunities, accomplishments, and perhaps the history of the school ("VIP Tour," 1991, as cited in Bisland, 2003).

The school principal and other administrators should not be forgotten. As the instructional leader of the school, the principal sets the tone for interactions between and among students and school personnel. Although the principal may only have an indirect effect on student achievement, he or she plays a vital role in the evaluation of student data, including determining which data will be evaluated and how programs will be strengthened. For these reasons alone, the principal should be a target for PR efforts (Lewis et al., 2007), with the intent of creating an ally. Other school administrators make decisions about the nature of the education gifted learners receive. Consequently, Besnoy's (2005) advice about inviting administrators to the classroom to observe or participate in selected activities with gifted students appears to be a critical one. Such targeted opportunities to build understanding of gifted students' capabilities are essential strategies for increasing the quality of education and could be used to reveal the need to expand service to additional grade levels as in scenario two.

Robinson (2003) described benefits accrued from collaborating with school principals and other school administrators within the district and through state administrators' associations. Gifted specialists in schools are encouraged to give themselves credit for doing administrative tasks such as budgets even if they wear a teacher hat as well. By viewing themselves as administrators, they could start finding ways they could collaborate with local administrators, thus being part of the decision-making process. Sharing the needs of gifted learners in this venue has the potential to be very effective. Robinson also pointed out advantages of gifted education administrators forming a statewide organization and joining the state school administrators' association.

Teachers of the gifted can coordinate with colleagues, parents, and students when organizing special displays and activities for the school or community. The various holidays provide opportunities for students to display their creativity in the form of plays, music, art, and creative writing. Performances can be given at a PTA/PTO meeting, a civic or business group's meeting, or a locally held convention. Creative writing or artwork can be displayed in the local library or store windows. These PR activities are much easier to arrange when teachers include others in the planning.

When legislators are in town, invite them to a class to see for themselves what gifted students are learning. This would be a good opportunity to thank them for past support with a plaque, certificate, or some other memento. Invite the local media to take pictures and write an article for the newspaper, or you do the news coverage and give it to the newspaper. Invite local artists, business leaders, and professionals to the class to discuss careers, help provide instruction in a specialty area, or judge products and performances. Remember, this is a learning experience for the guests as well as for students. A parent support group's PR committee or a few parents and teachers can make the arrangements.

Yet another way to involve others is to hold a contest to create a slogan for bringing more attention to a particular program or for a full-fledged PR campaign. The competition could be as small as the gifted classes in the school or expanded to the district, community, state, or even national level, depending on the purpose. Even a competition just within one school can be an event with local celebrities judging the entries (Roberts & Inman, 2003), thus involving people from the community.

Parents have a great deal of power. Individually they can accomplish a lot; as an organized support group, their power is increased. Not only can they advocate for students and the program in ways a teacher cannot, such as talking with administrators about specific needs and concerns, they too can gain information and support. It is worth the time it takes to organize parents and other stakeholders. Matthews et al. (2011) described the process they used.

Parents can help with publicity by writing news releases and newsletters—the latter can be electronically distributed to all parents, school personnel, community leaders, and legislators. Additional writing projects might include a letter to the editor congratulating the school district on its gifted and talented program and letters to legislators thanking them for their support. Parents can advertise coming events with e-mail, posters, telephone trees, texting, or Twitter and take photographs and videos for publicity. Use the talent identifier (see Figure 20.8) to find the unique skills of students' parents and invite them to help build a strong, positive image for gifted learners. Remember that the members of a support group need to be shown appreciation for their work and be provided with support themselves (Sheard, n.d.).

Staff development focused on gifted education is sorely needed in nearly every school. Few general educators have sufficient knowledge of gifted students' cognitive and social-emotional characteristics to work with them effectively, and new research on the identification of underserved populations and more effective instructional methods is being conducted. When experts in the field are not available to give the training, DVDs can deliver needed information (Lewis, 2008). NAGC provides a wide range of professional development topics as webinars (see http://www.nagc.org/WOW.aspx#what_are_wow) and in other formats (see http://nagc.sclivelearningcenter.com/index.aspx?).

Working within an organization can be a practical method for increasing public awareness regarding the need for gifted education. Whether helping to start a parent/teacher support group or working with an established organization, many people are available to help circulate the message. In either case, a PR committee needs to be formed that will plan and coordinate all activities. One person can be the catalyst that motivates the group to extend its informational reach beyond its current level. If the organization already has an active PR program, suggest some of the strategies provided in this chapter.

A valuable strategy for any organization, local, state, or national, is getting to know new legislators and other officials by visiting or talking with them on a regular basis (Robinson & Moon, 2003a). The contacts can be invaluable when it comes to advocating for or against specific legislation. Locally, individuals and members of parent support organizations can begin building relationships with key school board members, district administrators, and school principals in case their help is needed to protect, modify, or expand gifted programming. An invitation to serve on committees or task forces may help make the decisions.

Use of Organizers

The worksheets provided in this chapter will help in planning for ongoing PR and advocacy. Whether sharing information about gifted students in your class or initiating a large state campaign, using an organizer will improve efficiency. Use Figures 20.1, 20.2, and 20.3 to select strategies that will help reach the goal. Chances of success can be increased with only a little more work if several strategies are coordinated and others are involved.

Expand the base of supporters with the organizers in Figures 20.7 and 20.8. Distribute them to groups such as those at staff development, educational and community meetings, conferences, and parent meetings to identify strengths of potential new volunteers. People often are motivated to help with a project or join a committee when they see their strengths are valued. People may also know others who would like to join the effort. Everyone has points of personal power (Figure 20.6), contacts they have made over the years in a wide variety of venues who might be tapped to become active supporters for gifted education. Figure 20.7 provides a place to record those personal power connections. Small and large organizations can use the Talent Identifier of Unique Skills (Figure 20.8) to survey members for strengths and interests. Teachers can use these organizers to collect information from the parents of their students. A rich supply of talent for class activities can be found among the family members and their friends, as well as for PR and advocacy. Both individual teachers and organizations benefit from a group of supporters who can share responsibilities for regular, ongoing PR.

If one article or activity can increase public awareness of gifted learners and their unique needs, how much more effective is a year of coordinated strategies? The annual plan is a way to categorize and coordinate PR, whether for the class-room; school or district gifted program; local, state, national, or international gifted organization; or other supporters of gifted education (see Figure 20.9). Even if a group can only fill in a few activities, it's a beginning. Next year, or even next month, another strategy can be added. By keeping track of who is responsible and how effective the technique is, planning can be used more efficiently. In addition, it will aid in knowing who is being reached and who still needs targeting.

Most schools have an open house in the early fall and holiday programs near the end of the year; these are excellent PR opportunities. Decide how to make use of them and record them on a calendar. Plan to write about some of the students' special accomplishments and submit them to a local newspaper several times during the year and include them on your webpage. Educators frequently neglect to follow this simple step, yet how else is the community to become aware of what transpires in the classroom? Stories about children and their accomplish-ments provide a necessary counterbalance to the usual news, serving as reminders that the next generation is hard at work preparing to become productive citizens and future leaders. For examples of PR activities aimed at increasing educator and community awareness, see Figure 20.10.

Organizations might include membership drives, fundraising plans, and con-ventions or special programs as key activities on their annual plan. Writing news articles, a brochure, a fact sheet, and webpage text and seeing that this informa-tion is disseminated appropriately might come next. These are generic ideas for PR with no specific plan behind them. Effectiveness can be increased by coordi-nating activities around a particular goal. Organizations need to continually build a strong base of support among the general public, the educational community, business and industry leaders, government officials, and the media in order to be prepared to protect or increase services to gifted students when necessary.

Month	Objectives	Strategies/ Activities	Person Responsible	Due Date	Expected Outcome
August					
September					
October					
November					
December					
January					
February					
March					
April					
May					
June					
July					

Figure 20.9. Public relations annual plan.

Involving Other Constituencies

Teachers and other advocates in gifted education may wish to join together with educational groups and associations (e.g., state reading or science groups, administrators) at local, state, and national levels to identify PR and advocacy opportunities. By networking with other organizations, greater results are possible through collaboration and partnerships than when working alone.

Recommendations for reaching out to other constituencies include, but are not limited to, the following suggestions:

» Encourage gifted teachers and other gifted specialists to publish in the newsletters and journals of organizations outside gifted education (e.g., those of other education and counseling organizations, community organizations, business and industry, and the popular press; see NAGC, n.d.c., for sample newspaper articles).

» Submit proposals to conferences and volunteer to speak at meetings of different organizations in order to broaden the audience that hears accurate information about gifted learners.

» Finally, organizations supporting gifted education should include key legislators, business leaders, and representatives from other organizations on their advisory boards and encourage their own members to serve on other boards.

The contacts and understandings gained from working together this way can have far-reaching results.

LEWIS AND KARNES

Month	Objectives	Strategies/Activities	Person Responsible	Due Date	Expected Outcome
August	Build supportive atmosphere	Welcome letters/e-mails to students and parents. Older students might prefer text messages.	Teacher	Week 1 of school	Students/parents appear at ease talking with G/T teacher.
September	Parents, educators, others understand G/T program	Open house, students share selected activities and learning goals. Student planned/directed as part of student-led PR. Invite administrators, school board, legislators, business leaders, media.	Teacher/student leaders (part of student-led PR)	School open house	Parents/educators/others can explain what students do in G/T and why.
October	Develop rapport with other teachers	Put short fact sheet about gifted learners, tic-tac-toe activity, simple differentiated lesson, or similar materials in teachers' mailboxes each week.	Teacher	Mon., Week 1–4	One or more teacher(s) differentiate some lessons; students report less busy work.
November	Increase community awareness of G/T	Students work with Salvation Army to gather food, toys for needy as part of service learning unit. Publicize in newspaper, local TV station, school website.	Teacher/student leaders (part of student-led PR)	Publicity: Dec. 1 Project end: Dec. 20	Awareness of student contributions to community increases.
December	Increase parent/educator awareness of G/T students	Publish first semester newsletter to parents/district personnel; students write articles on activities, upcoming events, book list.	Teacher with HS newspaper sponsor	Wed., Week 2	Parents/educators speak positively about program benefits.
January	Build understanding and cooperation with classroom teachers	Begin lunch bunch for teachers. Rotate bringing treats and responsibility. Discuss diversity (learning style, culture, SES, ability) and how to build student success.	School counselor (hide own role to increase success)	Every Friday	Teachers share examples of G/T students related to areas of diversity.

Figure 20.10. Sample public relations annual plan.

February	Demonstration of talent to local community	Performance of student written, acted, directed play for PTO; publish news article with pictures in local paper, school/program website.	Teacher/student leaders (part of student-led PR)	Monthly meeting	Increased awareness of student talent, G/T contributions.
March	Demonstration of talent to state G/T teachers/educators	Performance of play as lunch entertainment at state gifted convention; article and picture in state newsletter.	Teacher and parent volunteer	Annual convention	Statewide recognition through program and newsletter.
April	Build legislator recognition of G/T education	State/local legislators speak to class; students share their learning; newspaper pictures. Follow up with student-written thank you notes.	Teacher/student leaders (part of student-led PR)	Week 3	Legislators can talk knowledgeably about G/T learners.
May	Increase parent/educator awareness of G/T students	Publish second semester newsletter; summarize accomplishments and share summer activity options.	Teacher with HS newspaper sponsor	Wed., Week 2	Parents/educators speak positively about program benefits.
June	Build differentiation skills	Staff development on differentiation for all teachers; state G/T speaker.	Teacher	Immediately after school ends	Teachers create one differentiated lesson each, share.
July	Build differentiation skills	Work session(s) with willing teachers on differentiation; share work.	Teacher	July 31	Teachers create differentiated lessons, express greater comfort teaching G/T.

Figure 20.10. Continued.

Summary

PR is a continuous need in gifted education. It provides the background knowledge for advocacy. Selecting the appropriate target audience(s) for PR efforts is an important initial decision. In addition, be sure that all participants understand the main message and speak with one voice. To make this critical component easier to accomplish, it is recommended that a basic plan be clearly written. A wide variety of PR strategies are available, and it is crucial to select the appropriate tactics for each target audience. Objective evaluation criteria are needed to find out if the PR plan has been effective. Joining with other interested individuals and organizations has the potential to expand one's ability to reach the selected audiences. The goal of conveying accurate information about gifted learners and their education is never-ending, yet worthwhile. How else will people outside the classroom learn of gifted students' contributions to their communities or why a differentiated education is so important for them to realize their considerable potential? Everyone who cares about gifted education needs to make a lifelong commitment to become PR specialists for gifted children and youth.

Teacher Statement

Being given the position of district coordinator for the high-ability learners (gifted students) in our district, I was faced with many new challenges and concerns. The first obstacles were revising and utilizing our district plan, coordinating a team of educators with whom to collaborate, and beginning a program of public awareness for our new gifted program.

To understand the importance of public relations and to have another look at what steps I might need to take in implementing public awareness, I reviewed material that I had used in college. This chapter was one of my primary sources for help. It explained the need for voicing support and advocacy for the gifted, how to develop an effective plan so you can move in the right direction, the use of a variety of strategies and ideas to present information with a new approach or style, and how to deliver that message to your audience in a clear, complete way.

Overall, what ended up being the most useful information in the chapter was how to broaden the existing support base of my gifted program to include a variety of groups, businesses, and organizations that allow for involvement and awareness. Many public relation activities are listed in the chapter that provide ideas and participation not only for educators, but for parents and community members as well. My favorite activities were those that allowed for student involvement. Having your students write press releases and create public displays not only opens up creative approaches to learning, but allows opportunity for parental involvement.

—Valerie Vincent

DISCUSSION QUESTIONS

1. Discuss why it is necessary to formulate a plan of action for your proposed public relations campaign, whether it is a small parent- or teacher-run activity or a statewide campaign developed by the state's gifted association.

2. How would you decide who would make effective members of your planning committee? Consider such variables as committee size, the support you would gain, and the unique skills members might bring.

3. Discuss the pros and cons of the following strategies:
   * writing a letter to the editor about something that pleases you about the gifted program and a letter expressing your displeasure that the district does not provide a service you want;
   * writing an article for the local newspaper describing your students' work with Keep America Beautiful (first scenario);
   * submitting an article to another organization's newsletter;
   * developing a newsletter for your gifted program;
   * inviting school board members and legislators to speak to your students; and
   * developing a fact sheet to distribute to your fellow educators.

4. Discuss how your students could enhance the public's understanding of their gifted education opportunities. Consider also how your students could learn from these experiences. Could you build some of these opportunities into your curriculum?

5. Explain how you have personal power within your career, financial, school, social, and spiritual contacts.

6. Explain how you have personal power within the following groups from your community: the arts, business and industry, government, leisure, the media, and the various professions.

7. Using the Public Relations Annual Plan Organizer (see Figure 20.9), develop four activities you could use to let more people know what your students are doing during one school year. Support your reasons for selecting each activity.

8. If you were the chairperson of the public relations committee for your state organization, what resources would you select for a yearlong campaign? Are free methods better choices than those for which you must spend some money? Explain your reasoning for your choices.

9. If you were the chairperson of the public relations committee for your state organization, what resources would you select for a yearlong campaign? Are free methods better choices than those for which you must spend some money? Explain your reasoning for your choices.

References

Achieve. (2013). *Closing the expectations gap: 2013 annual report on the alignment of state K–12 policies and practice with the demands of college and careers.* Mountain View, CA: Author.

Besnoy, K. (2005). Using public relations strategies to advocate for gifted programming in your school. *Gifted Child Today, 28*(1), 32–37.

Bisland, A. (2003). Student-created public relations for gifted education. *Gifted Child Today, 26*(2), 60–64.

Center for Talent Development. (n.d.). *Becoming an advocate for your gifted student: An interview with Carol Morreale.* Retrieved from http://www.ctd.northwestern.edu/resources/displayArticle/?id=41

Clark, B. (2012). *Growing up gifted: Developing the potential of children at home and at school* (8th ed.). Upper Saddle River, NJ: Pearson.

Clark, L. (2005). Gifted and growing. *Educational Leadership, 63*(3), 56–60.

Courtright, R. (2010a, January). Administrators of gifted programs: Paying attention to the "man behind the curtain." *Digest of Gifted Research.* Durham, NC: Duke University Talent Identification Program. Retrieved from https://tip.duke.edu/node/932

Courtright, R. (2010b, April). Advocacy: From micro to macro. *Digest of Gifted Research. Durham, NC:* Duke University Talent Identification Program. Retrieved from https://tip.duke.edu/node/939

Duke University Talent Identification Program. (2013, July). Advocating for your gifted child with autism. *Digest of Gifted Research. Durham, NC:* Duke University Talent Identification Program. Retrieved from https://tip.duke.edu/node/1512

Duquette, C., Orders, S., Fullerton, S., & Robertson-Grewal, K. (2011). Fighting for their rights: Advocacy experiences of parents of children identified with intellectual giftedness. *Journal for the Education of the Gifted, 34,* 488–512.

Gentry, M. (2006). No Child Left Behind: Neglecting excellence. *Roeper Review, 29*(1), 24–27.

Gilman, B. J. (2008). *Academic advocacy for gifted children: A parent's complete guide.* Scottsdale, AZ: Great Potential Press.

Grantham, T. C., Frasier, M. M., Roberts, A. C., & Bridges, E. M. (2005). Parent advocacy for culturally diverse gifted students. *Theory Into Practice, 44,* 138–147.

Grika, J. T. (1986). Gifted children—Waste not, want not: The how-to's of a statewide g/c/t awareness campaign. *Gifted Child Today, 9*(1), 25–29.

Horowitz, S. (1996). What to do after your story gets covered by the media. *Trust for Educational Leadership, 25*(4), 22–23.

Hunsaker, S. L. (2000). Documenting gifted program results for key decision-makers. *Roeper Review, 23,* 80–82.

Jolly, J. L., & Makel, M. C. (2010). No Child Left Behind: The inadvertent costs for high-achieving and gifted students. *Childhood Education, 87*(1), 35–40. doi:10.1080/00094056.2010.10521436

Kaplan, S. N. (2004a). The spill-over effect: An advocacy strategy. *Gifted Child Today, 27*(1), 48–49.

Kaplan, S. N. (2004b). Using their words to support our advocacy efforts. *Gifted Child Today, 27*(3), 59, 65.

Kaplan, S. N. (2012). Becoming politically savvy—Being gifted in the current educational climate. *Gifted Child Today, 35*(2), 150–151. doi:10.1177/1076217511436088

Kowalski, T. J. (1996). *Public relations in educational organizations.* Englewood Cliffs, NJ: Merrill.

Leggett, D. G., Shea, I., & Wilson, J. A. (2010). Advocating for twice-exceptional students: An ethical obligation. *Research in the Schools, 17*(2), 1–10.

Lewis, J. D. (2008). *Advocacy for gifted children and gifted programs.* Waco, TX: Prufrock Press.

Lewis, J. D., Cruzeiro, P. A., & Hall, C. A. (2007). Impact of two elementary principals' leadership on gifted education in their buildings. *Gifted Child Today, 3*(2), 56–62.

Loveless, T., Farkas, S., & Duffett, A. (2008). *High-achieving students in the era of NCLB.* Washington, D.C.: Thomas B. Fordham Institute.

Matthews, M. S., Georgiades, S. D., & Smith, L. F. (2011). How we formed a parent advocacy group and what we've learned in the process. *Gifted Child Today, 34*(4), 28–34.

McGee, C. D. (2012). Time to face the need for advocacy. *Parenting for High Potential, 1*(8), 14–15.

Mendoza, C. (2006). Inside today's classrooms: Teacher voices on No Child Left Behind and the education of gifted children. *Roeper Review, 29*(1), 28–31.

National Association for Gifted Children. (NAGC, n.d.a). *Dispelling myths, serving students.* Retrieved from http://www.nagc.org/myths.aspx

National Association for Gifted Children. (NAGC, n.d.b). *Jacob Javits Gifted and Talented Students Education Act.* Retrieved from http://www.nagc.org/index.aspx?id=1006

National Association for Gifted Children. (NAGC, n.d.c). *Working with the media.* Retrieved from http://www.nagc.org/index2.aspx?id=1004

National Center for Education Statistics. (n.d.). *Program for International Student Assessment (PISA).* Washington, DC: Institute of Education Sciences, National Center for Education Statistics. Retrieved from http://nces.ed.gov/surveys/pisa/pisa2012/pisa2012highlights_1.asp

National School Public Relations Association. (n.d.). *Getting started.* Retrieved from http://www.nspra.org/getting_started

No Child Left Behind (NCLB) Act of 2001, Pub. L. No. 107–110, § 115, Stat. 1425 (2002).

Ohio Association of Gifted Children. (n.d.). *Advocacy for gifted students.* Retrieved from http://highability.wordpress.com/advocacy-for-gifted-students/

Plucker, J. A., Burroughs, N., & Song, R. (2010). *Mind the (other) gap! The growing excellence gap in K-12 education.* Bloomington: University of Indiana, Center for Evaluation and Education Policy.

Plucker, J. A., Hardesty, J., & Burroughs, N. (2012). *Talent on the sidelines: Excellence gaps and America's persistent talent underclass.* Storrs: University of Connecticut, Center for Education Policy Analysis at the Neag School of Education.

Reis, S. M. (2007). No child left bored. *School Administrator, 64*(2), 22.

Renzulli, J. S. (1998). *A rising tide lifts all ships: Developing the gifts and talents of all students.* Retrieved from http://www.gifted.uconn.edu/sem/semart03.html

Roberts, J. L. (2010). Lessons learned: Advocating for a specialized school of mathematics and science. *Roeper Review, 32,* 42–47. doi:10.1080/02783190903386876

SUPPORTING AND ENHANCING GIFTED PROGRAMS

Roberts, J. L. (2014). Advocacy. In C. M. Callahan & J. A. Plucker (Eds), *Critical issues and practices in gifted education: What the research say*s (2nd ed., pp. 65–76). Waco, TX: Prufrock Press.

Roberts, J., & Inman, T. (2003, March). Building advocacy with a public relations campaign. *Parenting for High Potential*, 24–27.

Roberts, J. L., & Inman, T. F. (2009). *Strategies for differentiating instruction: Best practices for the classroom* (2nd ed.). Waco, TX: Prufrock Press.

Roberts, J. L., & Siegle, D. (2012). Teachers as advocates: If not you—who? *Gifted Child Today, 35*(1), 58–61.

Robinson, A. (2003). Collaborating and advocating with administrators: The Arkansas gifted education administrators' story. *Gifted Child Today, 26*(4), 20–25.

Robinson, A., & Moon, S. M. (2003a, March). Advocating for talented youth: Lessons learned from the national study of local and state advocacy in gifted education. *Parenting for High Potential*, 8–13.

Robinson, A., & Moon, S. M. (2003b). National study of local and state advocacy in gifted education. *Gifted Child Quarterly, 47*, 8–25.

Roos, D. (2007). *How public relations works*. Retrieved from http://money.howstuffworks.com/business-communications/how-public-relations-works.htm

Sheard, W. (n.d.). *The care and feeding of gifted parent groups: A guide for gifted coordinators, teachers, and parent advocates.* Retrieved from http://www.nsgt.org/wp-content/uploads/2013/01/article_sheard_parent_groups.pdf

Thomas B. Fordham Institute. (2008). *In a nutshell: High-achieving students in the era of NCLB.* Washington, DC: Author.

U.S. Department of Education, Office of Educational Research and Improvement. (1993). *National excellence: A case for developing America's talent.* Washington, DC: U.S. Government Printing Office.

Westberg, K., & Daoust, M. (2003, Fall). The results of the replication of the class-room practices survey replication in two states. *The National Research Center on the Gifted and Talented Newsletter*, 3–8.

Willis, M. (2012). Be proactive with parent advocacy groups. *Parenting for High Potential, 2*(1), 14–15.

Wiskow, K., Fowler, V. D., & Christopher, M. M. (2011). Active advocacy: Working together for appropriate services for gifted learners. *Gifted Child Today, 34*(2), 20–25.

Xiang, Y., Dahlin, D., Cronin, J., Theaker, R., & Durant, S. (2011). *Do high flyers maintain their altitude? Performance trends of high performers.* Washington, DC: The Thomas B. Fordham Institute.

Yale, D. R. (1995). *Publicity and media relations check lists.* Lincolnwood, IL: NTC Business Books.

GETTING WHAT YOU NEED

Locating and Obtaining Money and Other Resources

BY KRISTEN R. STEPHENS AND FRANCES A. KARNES

A teacher of the gifted in a rural school district has worked diligently for several years to receive more than $600,000 in grants. A staff development day for teachers of the gifted at a local university offered her an overview of researching funding sources and procedures for writing grant proposals. With a 1-hour seminar as her introduction to the fund-development processes, she successfully perfected her skills and now makes presentations on the topic to groups of teachers.

With the limited amount of money available in school districts for classroom materials and projects, finding external funding opportunities has become necessary for many teachers of the gifted. This chapter provides an overview of the types of funding agencies that exist and how to locate them, as well as how to develop an idea and write a grant proposal. Information on other sources of funding also is given, as well as procedures for determining policies at the district level.

Status of Federal Funding for Gifted Education

The only federal legislation that has exclusively designated funds for gifted and talented education is the Jacob K. Javits Gifted and Talented Students Education Act (1990). This act directed the Secretary of Education to make grants and contracts for programs and projects to meet the educational needs of gifted and talented students. Between 2002–2005, $11 million was allocated for the Javits Program. These funds supported

» the National Research Center on the Gifted and Talented;

» demonstration grants, awarded on a competitive basis, to examine ways to identify and serve underserved gifted students; and

» statewide grants, awarded on a competitive basis, to support programs and services.

In 2006 and 2007, Javits was funded at $9.6 million and from fiscal years 2008 through 2010, $7.46 million was allocated for the program. From 2011–2013, the Javits program received $0, and for the fiscal year 2014, the program received $5 million. Due to the constant struggle to obtain funding, advocates for the Javits Act have put their support behind a new piece of legislation—the TALENT Act.

The TALENT Act provides a way for the needs of gifted and talented students to be addressed as an amendment to the Elementary and Secondary Education Act. The TALENT Act introduced to the 113th Congress as S.512 by Senators Grassley (IA), Casey (PA), and Mikulski (MD) focuses on four areas: (a) changes to assessment and accountability systems to ensure that students make learning gains, (b) emphasis on classroom practice by expanding professional development opportunities for teachers in gifted education pedagogy, (c) focus on underserved populations to ensure that all students regardless of circumstance have adequate support to achieve their full potential, and (d) emphasis on research and dissemination so that schools have access to the latest developments in gifted education.

In particular, the TALENT Act proposes that states be required to do the following (Stephens, 2011):

» Report the learning growth for the most advanced students on their state report cards.

» Describe within their application for funds under Title II, Part A Grants the comprehensive strategy the state will use to improve educators' teaching skills for students who are gifted and talented.

» Include in their Title I plans steps the state will take to assist local school districts in supporting gifted students, including high-ability students who have not been formally identified.

It is important to note that there is no funding tied to the TALENT Act at this time. At a time when financial resources are scarce and there is a continued reluctance to fund new programs in Washington, advocates feel the current focus should be on accountability of addressing the needs of these students in schools. Once the funding climate improves, funding to support the research components of the act may be requested.

Types of Funding

There are essentially two types of funding: public and private. Some projects will be appropriate for both types of funding, while others may be best suited for one or the other. Private sources often will not support projects for which there are already substantial amounts of public funding available, such as in the area of children with disabilities. Furthermore, the purpose of public funds is set by legislation, whereas private funds focus on emerging needs and issues pertaining to special interest populations. Funding within the school district and at the state department of education also should be explored. Some states have monies for instructional aids, technological equipment, and other materials.

There are several other differences between public and private funding sources. For example, public funding sources generally have the most money to award and are more likely to pay all project costs. In contrast, private funders may be more restrictive in what expenses are covered, and, with the exception of the major foundations, most offer smaller amounts of money. The proposal format is another area in which the two funding types differ. Public sources use prescribed formats for proposals, which can be lengthy and complex, whereas proposals for private sources often are less formal.

Public funding can be located through federal, state, and local agencies. Some examples of federal agencies include the U.S. Department of Education, the National Institutes of Health, and the National Science Foundation. State and local agencies may be more geographic in scope, limiting their funds to specific regions in which they are involved.

Private funding sources include foundations, corporations, and professional and trade associations. Examples of foundations are The Carnegie Foundation, the W. K. Kellogg Foundation, and the Spencer Foundation. Corporations that provide grant monies include AT&T, Toyota, and Whirlpool. Some examples of associations providing grant monies are the American Association of University Women (AAUW), the National Education Association (NEA), and the Council for Exceptional Children (CEC).

Once the project idea has been determined, the search for the funding source that best fits the need can begin. The funding agency's priorities must match project goals. The size of the awards offered, geographic focus, eligibility requirements, restrictions, and deadlines for submitting a proposal all need to be considered. Thorough research into these key areas can assist the grant-searching process.

Developing an Idea

Developing and refining a project idea should be the first step in the grant-searching process. Taking the initial time to outline ideas and goals can assist in locating the most relevant funding source. Keep in mind that goals and priorities must match those of the selected funding agency.

The first step in cultivating an idea is assessing needs. What areas in the classroom, school, or community need to be initiated, need improvement, or need to be adequately addressed? A needs statement can give purpose to the project and will inform a potential funder of the importance of the proposed project. It also is necessary at this point to research any previous work that has been undertaken in the needs area to establish that the problem exists statewide and nationally. The further one can broaden the potential scope and impact of the idea, the more likely funding is assured. Also, the more innovative the idea, the better the chances of finding support for the project (see Figure 21.1).

After the area of need has been identified, compile a list of goals, objectives, and activities for the proposed project; this is the plan of action. It will help identify the population the project intends to address, the staffing areas that will be needed, and the time frame in which one will be operating. Ask colleagues for advice and assistance in the development of this phase of the plan. In some schools, teams of teachers work on schoolwide projects.

Determining a working budget also will be beneficial at this point. Because many funding sources have limited funds, establishing whether one needs $100,000 or $1,000 to execute a proposed project will have a substantial impact on identifying a funding source. In developing a budget, be sure to consider all expenses related to equipment and supplies, personnel, facilities, travel, communications, general operating expenses, and overhead, which includes light, heat, and so forth. There may be individuals within a school's finance department or development office who can be of assistance when determining budget expenses. Having a preestablished budget figure will assist in eliminating many funding agencies, making the information sifting easier.

Locating a Funding Source

Once the need has been identified, a plan of action has been created to address it, and a general idea of the amount of money being requested has been

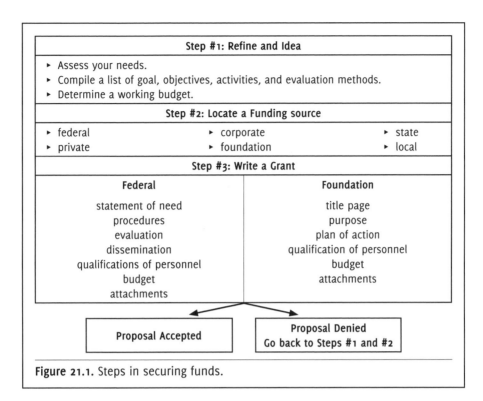

Figure 21.1. Steps in securing funds.

determined, it is time to research potential funders. Several resources can assist during this endeavor, including databases, libraries, and publications. Thorough research to locate a funding source whose priorities match project goals can be a challenging, yet potentially rewarding, experience.

Centers

The Foundation Center (http://www.foundationcenter.org) is a good place to begin research. The center offers a collection of fund-finding publications and resources, including an online subscription service that is updated continuously and lists approximately 120,000 grantmakers. Information also can be accessed at the center's libraries in Washington, DC, New York, Atlanta, Cleveland, and San Francisco. To accommodate people who do not live near these locations, Cooperating Collections exist across the United States. In each state, there is at least one library designated to maintain extensive holdings from the Foundation Center. To find a Cooperating Collection in your state, visit http://foundation-center.org. Additional information on contacting the Foundation Center about its work is found at the end of this chapter.

If one lives near a college or university, many institutions of higher learning have an Office of Research and Sponsored Programs. These offices assist university faculty in developing proposals and finding grant sources. Although they may not provide direct assistance, they may be helpful in locating sources of funding information within the community.

Publications

The Catalog of Federal Domestic Assistance (CFDA) describes all of the federal government's programs that give money. This source is published annually by the Office of Management and Budget (OMB), and it is available online (https://www.cfda.gov). The most current information relating to eligibility, application and award processes, addresses, and contacts are given.

The Chronicle of Philanthropy is a newspaper that includes articles on fundraising and philanthropy. Lists of recent grants and profiles of foundations and corporations are given. The newspaper is published biweekly and is available through The Chronicle of Higher Education, Inc. It can be found online (http://www.philanthropy.com) and in most college and university libraries.

The Federal Register, which is published every weekday except on legal holidays, provides public regulations and legal notices issued by federal agencies. *The Federal Register* is published in paper and is available at most major libraries. An online database of *The Federal Register* also is available at https://www.federalregister.gov.

The Congressional Record is a daily record of the activities within the U.S. Congress; it includes information on bills that are introduced and debated. Because legislation is directly tied to funding availability for many programs, it is essential to stay abreast of the latest information from Washington. Copies of the Congressional Record can be found at most libraries and online through the Library of Congress (http://loc.gov).

SchoolGrants *Bimonthly Newsletter* is e-mailed at no charge to subscribers and provides practical grant-writing tips, online grant-writing resources, upcoming deadlines, grant opportunities for K–12 schools and teachers, and more. SchoolGrants *Biweekly Newsletter* is sent to subscribers twice each month. Visit its website (http://www.k12grants.org/newsletter.htm) for more information.

Additional information on how to contact or subscribe to the above publications is listed at the conclusion of this chapter. The above list is not comprehensive, so check local or college and university libraries for additional sources.

Analyzing Sources

Once information has been assessed on funding agencies, there are several things to identify:

» *What are the priorities of the agency, and do they match the proposed goals and objectives?* For example, the agency may focus its efforts in urban areas, but the proposed project may be in a rural area.

» *What are past projects that this agency has funded?* Request an annual report from the funding agency and look at what projects are currently being funded or have been funded in the past. Patterns may be present. For example, even though a foundation may say it funds projects nationally, 80% of the projects funded in the past may be located in the same state or geographic region.

» *What are the limitations and restrictions?* Many agencies do not fund individuals, for-profit organizations, or political or religious associations. There also may be geographic restrictions. For example, many corporations and companies may restrict giving to areas in which there is a company presence. In addition, there may be restrictions on how the money can be used. Equipment, salaries, and overhead may not be covered.

» *Is a letter of inquiry required?* Many agencies—foundations in particular—want a brief letter explaining the organization, the goals and objectives of the project, and the proposed budget prior to submitting a formal proposal. If the proposed idea matches the agency's priorities, a more detailed proposal will be requested.

» *Are there necessary application forms?* Many agencies have standard application and cover forms that will need to be requested. Some agencies have these available to download from their websites. Check to make sure that all of the proposal guidelines are addressed so the agency is provided with all of the information requested.

» *What is the deadline?* Most deadlines follow an annual pattern, meaning they are on the same date from year to year; however, because government programs depend on legislation for funding, many programs may be changed or cut. Furthermore, some government programs do not award grants annually. Many foundations accept applications at any time with no established deadlines. Board members may meet periodically throughout the year to review proposals.

» *What is the average grant size?* It is important to find out what the average award is for each agency. For example, a specified project may need approximately $100,000 of support, but a particular agency may only make an award of up to $5,000. Find an agency that can financially support the proposed idea.

» *What is the length of support?* Many federal grants will support projects for approximately 3 years. Continued support may be available if the project proves to have made an impact. Furthermore, many agencies want to know in the proposal how the program will be supported once funding is terminated. The potential sustainability of the program is paramount to funding agencies when making the decision to provide financial support to a project.

By addressing these questions and thoroughly researching potential agencies, a lot of time can be saved and frustration avoided. Nothing can be more disappointing than spending long hours developing a proposal and sending it to the wrong agency based on an overlooked detail. Research the funding agency inside and out. If there are legitimate questions, contact the agency or foundation before writing the proposal.

Major Components of a Grant Proposal

The major components and guidelines of a grant proposal differ slightly according to each funding agency. When applying to foundations and corporations, the following components are usually requested: title page, purpose, approach, qualifications, budget, and attachments. In addition to those components, state and federal agencies usually require information on the statement of need, procedures, evaluation, and dissemination.

Foundations and Corporations

The title page of a proposal to a foundation or corporation should have the title of the project; legal name of the submitting agency; address, name, and phone number of the contact person; a short summary; amount of money requested; signatures of approval; and other assurances, such as a nondiscrimination clause.

The purpose section should set forth the goals and objectives; a description of those to be served, including geographic location and number; needs and significance of the project; and relevance to the donor's purposes.

The approach or the plan of action contains specific outcomes, staff responsibilities and training, and the evaluation design. Project dissemination activities usually are described as well. Donor recognition should be mentioned.

The qualifications of the key project staff should be given along with names of any consultants and all cooperating agencies. If special facilities, equipment, and so forth are needed and available, mention them to demonstrate capability of conducting the project.

A detailed budget usually is required, and all items essential to the project must be included. A request for additional funds after the project has been approved typically will be denied. Components of the budget may include, but are not limited to, personnel, travel, supplies and materials, data processing, printing/postage, facilities, equipment (if allowable), and indirect costs. It is important to list indirect costs such as office space, lights, heat, equipment usage, and the like. Other items to be included would be monies from other agencies, often referred to as matching funds, if any; a description of how the project will be supported after the requested funding period expires; and plans for additional fundraising, if appropriate. Consult the financial officer of your district or institution about matching funds and indirect costs.

The attachments requested from the potential donor may include the names of the members of the board of directors and their affiliations; a copy of the IRS determination; the organization's last annual report; information describing the organization; and letters of support.

Always be thorough in reviewing the requirements of the foundation or corporation because more or less information may be necessary. Only submit what has been requested, as these two groups usually are not interested in lengthy proposals.

State and Federal Agencies

The proposals forwarded to state and federal agencies usually require more detail and specificity. Components, again, differ somewhat from those required by foundations and corporations, and only those necessary components will be reviewed.

Following the title page, the abstract of approximately 200–500 words, the purpose, and the proposal to a state or federal agency should emphasize the statement of need. In this section, a thorough description should be given of the problem that is to be addressed and reasons why it is important. The emphasis should be on significance, timelines, and broad application of the solution. Recent local, state, and national statistics about the problem should set forth the need in a clear and concise manner.

The procedure section varies somewhat as to a research- or nonresearch-based project. In the latter, a general description should be offered, followed by details on the method, the participants, organization, and timelines. In the former, the data instruments should be described, as well as how the information is to be collected, analyzed, and reported.

The evaluation section of the grant proposal should include evidence that the purposes of the project have been accomplished. Information should include data collection, analysis, and evaluation; selection or development of instruments to be utilized; and the reporting procedures.

In the dissemination portion of the proposal, specifics should be given on how the findings or products of the project will be distributed (e.g., newspaper releases, presentations at conferences, journal articles). Reporting procedures to the funding agency, if and when required, also should be described.

Although the qualifications component has been briefly described in the above section on corporations and foundations, a few other points need to be considered when submitting to state and federal agencies. Résumés, along with a listing of publications, should be included for the key personnel and consultants. The amount of time each of the key personnel will give to the project and his or her responsibilities usually is required. A staff-loading chart, which depicts who will be responsible for selected activities, often is necessary.

A detailed budget with indirect costs and any matching funds is critical. Again, be sure to consult with the financial officer or grant writer in your district or institution.

Brock (2009) offered some helpful tips in securing federal grant dollars specifically for technology, while Rikard (2008) offered practical suggestions for writing smaller grant proposals to support physical education programs. The advice provided by both Brock (2009) and Rikard (2008) is also applicable to educators who are interested in writing grants for other purposes.

Sources of Funding in Your Community

There are many other sources of funding available in addition to foundations, corporations, and state/federal agencies. Sources of private-sector funding include denominational groups; neighborhood and fraternal charities; retail merchants; volunteer and business/professional associations; the United Way; the Chamber of Commerce; small and large businesses; local franchises of regional, state, and national companies; postsecondary institutions including community colleges and 4-year colleges and universities; civic groups; and arts councils. Local philanthropists, celebrities, professional athletes, and agency directors may have discretionary funds. Some local private funding sources may have guidelines for requesting monies, so call or write to determine the procedure for requesting support. A one-page summary with the purpose, goals, activities, and budget may be all that is necessary. Making an appointment with the person to discuss the request is sometimes the best procedure, while some associations or people prefer to receive the information via mail or e-mail.

At the local level, people funding requests may wish to be personally involved in the funded program, or they may wish to remain anonymous. Ask for preferences so as not to cause any embarrassment.

Creative Fundraising

For years, schools have developed fundraising strategies for various projects. Walsh (1990) suggested the following activities:

» *Balloon blast-off*: Students, teachers, parents, and community members sponsor, for a specific fee, a balloon with their name, address, and phone number attached. The person with the balloon traveling the farthest receives a prize.
» *Auctions*: These are great events. With items donated, the profits can be substantial.
» *Breakfast, lunch, or dinner with a special person*: Everyone likes to have a meal with a celebrity such as a famous athlete, TV personality, or local celebrity.

Palent (1985) advocated the following fundraising activities: a marathon (e.g., running, walking, biking), a sale of goods (e.g., antique, baked goods), and a sale of services (e.g., babysitting, car wash, house cleaning, yardwork). Swan (1990) suggested contests (e.g., fishing, golf, tractor pulls) and sales of items (e.g., candy, cards, lightbulbs) and services (e.g., handyman, house sitting, window washing, lawn care).

Additional ideas include a Quarter Rally, where double-stick tape is placed from one end of the mall to another and shoppers are asked to put down a quarter in support of the cause; a wish list that can be published in a local newspaper or sent to area businesses, organizations, or past donors; advertising by asking a local supermarket to print a message on its shopping bags for a month (this is not a direct fundraising activity, but it does generate a lot of publicity); and Rock-a-Thons, where supporters get pledges to rock in rocking chairs for a day (ARCH, 1992).

Gensheimer (1993) directed ideas on fundraising to both teachers and parents. Ideas included a used goods sale, clothesline sales, knowledge-a-thon, and a school carnival. Two unique ideas were a birthday party and a penny war. The former can be held for local children at a school with a fee charged to cover all expenses. The latter idea is based on the fact that people don't like to carry extra pennies with them. Students decorate coffee cans and place them at various local locations for the public to dispose of extra pennies.

Spencer (2009) offered fundraising ideas from A to Z including an Adoption Program (much like the one zoos have for animals) where individuals can adopt a library bookshelf to fill with books or instruments in the school orchestra. Donors can also adopt a room, a wall, or even an event to support the needs of the school. Another idea proposed by Spencer is Art Cars. In this fundraiser, the school gets a local car dealership or individual to donate an old junk car. Individuals are then charged for the opportunity to decorate the car. The resulting art car is then auctioned off to the highest bidder.

Recycling items such as ink cartridges, cell phones, mp3 players, laptops, digital cameras, and other small electronic devices can also help raise money for a school or classroom. Schools can work on their own or with local businesses to collect, ship, and earn rewards ("Trash to Cash," 2011). Funding Factory (http://www.fundingfactory.com) is one such recycling program that is completely free to schools and nonprofit organizations.

Principals can also play a critical role in helping raise funds. Graham (n.d.) profiled principals who have dressed as a rooster and danced like a chicken, kissed a goat, eaten a chocolate-covered cockroach, spent the night on the school roof, and shaved their heads to raise funds. Such endeavors not only raise school spirit but can also raise considerable funds. For example, the principal who spent the night on the school roof raised $22,000 in pledges (Graham, n.d.). These crazy stunts can also be connected to other fundraising efforts going on in the school. For example, a principal can challenge students to raise a certain amount of money from their traditional fundraiser. If students meet the challenge, the principal will have to engage in whatever crazy antic is proposed (kissing a pig, etc.).

How to Get Money for Your Classroom and School (Karnes & Stephens, 2005) offered more than 100 ideas for creative fundraising activities. When planning for activities, Karnes and Stephens (2005) suggested the following steps:

» *Get permission*: Determine the local school board policies and local, state, and federal laws and regulations regarding fundraising. Many schools do not allow students to conduct door-to-door sales and require parental permission for students to participate. Legal matters such as tort liability, taxes, insurance needs, and so forth also should be explored.

» *Form a committee and name a chairperson*: It takes many hardworking individuals to conduct a successful fundraiser. Committees should meet regularly and evaluate progress toward established goals.

» *Set goals*: It is important to have a clear purpose for the fundraiser and clearly communicate why the money is needed, how much is needed, and who will benefit from the monies raised.

» *Select an idea that will work*: Determine what has been successful in the past, is most feasible, and will be most likely to generate the amount needed.

» *Determine time and place*: Find out when other events in the community are scheduled and avoid planning additional events around the same dates. Keep in mind that some events may be better suited for certain times of year (e.g., flower sales at Valentine's or Mother's Day).

» *Make a plan*: The fundraising committee should develop a plan that details the materials and number of volunteers needed. It also is helpful to begin designating tasks, developing a master schedule of important dates and deadlines, and establishing rules and procedures that should be followed by all those involved. Ideas for promotional materials, kick-off activities, and volunteer appreciation should be considered in the planning phase.

» *Recruit and organize volunteers*: Volunteers are vital to the success of any fundraiser. Recruit individuals who have the skills to perform the tasks associated with their specific responsibility and who have a sincere interest in the project. Make certain that all volunteers are communicating the same message to potential donors regarding the purpose of the money and who will benefit from the collected revenue.

» *Target potential donors and sponsors*: The key to successful fundraising is participation. Determine which individuals within the community would be most interested in contributing to the particular cause. For example, a retired librarian might be especially interested in a fundraiser for new books for the media center.

» *Promote the event*: Publicize the fundraiser with banners, bulletin boards, flyers, radio announcements, newsletters, newspaper stories, local media, and social media (Facebook, Twitter, etc.). Don't forget to include marketing expenses in the budget.

» *Wrap things up*: A comprehensive evaluation should be conducted at the conclusion of the event. Consideration should be given to areas that may need improvement next time, as well as providing some sort of recognition to those individuals who donated their time to help meet the project's goals.

Using the Internet

DonorsChoose.org (http://www.donorschoose.org) is a website where teachers can submit project proposals for materials or experiences their students need in order to learn. Citizens choose which projects they want to support. Once the project is completed, the donor receives feedback regarding the outcome (e.g., student photos, thank you letters). Sample projects/items that teachers have requested funding for at DonorsChoose.org include library books, learning kits, digital cameras, binders, math games, magazine subscriptions, art supplies, and more. During the 2011–2012 academic year, DonorsChoose generated $80 million for schools nationwide (Bock, 2012). Other, similar sites include Adopt a Classroom.org (http://www.adoptaclassroom.org), Supply Our Schools (http://www.supplyourschools.org), Digital Wish (http://www.digitalwish.com), Schoola (http://www.schoola.com), ClassWish (http://classwish.org), and Teacher Wish Lists (http://www.teacherwishlists.com).

Online auctions also are becoming another method for securing funds for schools. For example, a high school in Massachusetts raised more than $30,000 in one month through cMarket (now called Bidding for Good; http://www.bidding forgood.com), an online auction platform for nonprofit organizations ("School fundraising," 2007). Items that were donated by individuals were auctioned off, including vacation packages, event tickets, and jewelry. Online fundraising allows schools to expand their reach to potential donors outside of the immediate community. Another similar auction site is Auction Frogs (http://www.auctionfrogs. org).

Old Strategies/New Practices

Over the last decade, public elementary and secondary school districts and programs have successfully employed fundraising strategies that had previously been associated primarily with postsecondary institutions: annual giving, endowments, commemorative planned giving, and unrestricted and restricted gifts. Local, state, and national associations also are engaging in fund development.

Annual giving usually is conducted through a wide spectrum of groups. The most obvious are students, their families, and alumni. Others to be included within the school would be the board members, teachers, administrators, and staff. In the community, those targeted for annual giving should include vendors, service groups, professional organizations, small businesses, local corporations, foundations, and the general public. Giving may be requested through personal visits, telephone calls, and letters. Gifts may be monetary (cash, checks, money orders, and charges to approved credit cards) and nonmonetary (bonds and securities, goods and services, real estate and personal property, royalties, copyrights and trademark rights, and insurance policies stating the school district or program as a beneficiary). Wereley (1992) suggested writing a clever "want ad" for a community partner. Publish the ad in the local newspaper or create a flyer to distribute to area businesses and organizations.

Commemorative gifts are becoming more popular within education. The gift is given "in memory of" or "in honor of" either a deceased or living person, and it may be restricted or unrestricted. A donor may wish to leave, either through a will or another instrument, an insurance policy for general or specific purposes. Large amounts of money may be given for endowments with the interest spent as designated by the donor (Karnes, Stephens, & Samel, 1999).

Personal property that can be donated includes art, equipment, and cars. Examples of real property include a residence, business, building, or undeveloped land. Real and personal properties must be assessed by a certified professional appraiser, and they are only helpful to districts if they can be used or sold. School districts engaged in fund development should have board-approved policies written within state and federal guidelines under the advisement of a tax attorney.

They also should have developed policies on strategies to be used, such as methods of acknowledgment/recognition and confidentiality.

Conclusion

With the limited amount of money allotted to gifted education, it is imperative that teachers and administrators become knowledgeable in grant writing and in locating additional sources of funding. Through careful research and innovation, an idea can be turned into a reality with the discovery and acquisition of a funding source. In addition, fundraising can be a philanthropic learning experience for students. Students can help select fundraising ideas, estimate gross revenue, and learn how to keep accurate records of progress toward goals to ensure fundraising efforts are both fun and financially successful. Although the process of fundraising requires a lot of work, the rewards will be well worth the efforts.

Teacher Statement

Innovative teachers know that tight budgets lead to little or no funding for their gifted classroom students, and because of this fact, grant writing has become a necessity, not an option. The advice given in this chapter is dead-on. We can either gripe about not having materials to offer unique units of study or we can do something about it. Teachers must seize the opportunity to learn how to write successful grants. Find a professional development seminar and attend with the positive attitude that you *can* do this. Look for these opportunities at universities or contact your state department of education. The time, effort, and money (if you have to pay) are well worth the results.

Learn to persevere! Rejection should be taken in stride. Just because your grant was not funded by one source doesn't mean it isn't a good project. Learn to match your grant idea with the grant source's "pet" projects. Some prefer fine art projects, while others want science or math. Be sure to read and follow the grant directions and find out what areas get preference in funding by the source. Following the directions carefully is crucial; an organization will eliminate your grant if it is two words over the limit—that is one less grant for them to read and indicates a willingness on your part to play loose with the rules.

Now, to get started: Think about that unit of study that needs something extra. Be innovative. You have to set your grant apart from all of the other grant applicants. Offer some sort of culminating activity that includes publicity for the grant. Grant sources like to see involvement by parents and the community, and it never hurts to give them credit in the media and in your final products. I have actually sent videotapes of the activities to the grant providers with my final report. Don't give up on having the classroom of your dreams. Read this chapter again and get started.

—Lia Landrum

DISCUSSION QUESTIONS

1. Make a list of five items that your school or classroom needs. Where might you start looking for necessary funding in order to meet each of the listed needs?

2. Determine what your school or district's policy is with regard to fundraising. Are there necessary signatures and approvals? How much planning time is needed to obtain these approvals? Create a timeline detailing the steps that need to be taken to secure necessary funding.

3. Discuss the pros and cons of securing funds from a federal agency, private foundation, and a corporate agency.

4. You have just been asked to chair a committee at your school to write a grant for money for new materials for the enrichment classroom. What individuals within and outside of the school will you recruit to participate in the committee's activities? Develop an agenda for the committee's first meeting.

5. Navigate the Department of Education's Web site at http://www.ed.gov. What are this agency's priorities? How have these priorities changed over the years? What legislation influences these priorities? Make some predictions about forthcoming priorities.

6. Who are the major stakeholders within your community with regard to gifted and talented education? What methods would be most advantageous in informing these individuals about your school or district's needs?

7. What current school/community partnerships does your school have? How can these be strengthened and focused around meeting the needs of gifted and talented students?

Teacher Resources

Books

Bauer, D. G. (1998). *Educator's Internet funding guide: Classroom Connect's reference guide to technology funding.* El Segundo, CA: Classroom Connect.

Bauer, D. G. (1999). *The teacher's guide to winning grants.* San Francisco, CA: Jossey-Bass.

Bauer, D. G. (2000). *Technology funding for schools.* San Francisco, CA: Jossey-Bass.

Bauer, D. G. (2011). *The "how to" grants manual: Successful grantseeking techniques for obtaining public and private grants.* Lanham, MD: Rowman & Littlefield.

Brewer, E. W., Achilles, C. M., & Fuhriman, F. R. (1995). *Finding funding: Grantwriting and project management from start to finish.* Thousand Oaks, CA: Corwin Press.

Ferguson, J., & Ward, D. (2001). *Grants for K–12 schools.* Gaithersburg, MD: Aspen.

Gensheimer, C. F. (1993). *Raising funds for your child's school.* New York, NY: Walker.

Graham, C. (2001). *Keep the money coming: A step-by-step strategic guide to annual fundraising.* Sarasota, FL: Pineapple Press.

Joachim, J. C. (2003). *Beyond the bake sale: The ultimate school fund-raising book.* New York, NY: St. Martin's Griffin.

Karges-Bone, L., & Krueger, B. (2011). *The educator's guide to grants: Grant-writing tips and techniques for schools and non-profits.* Dayton, OH: Lorenz Educational Press.

Levenson, S. (2007). *Big time fundraising for today's schools.* Thousand Oaks, CA: Corwin.

Morris, P. (2000). *A practical guide to fund-raising in schools.* London, England: Routledge.

Rowson, P. (2005). *The easy step by step guide to fundraising for your school.* Hampshire, England: Rowmark.

Ruskin, K. B., & Achilles, C. M. (1995). *Grantwriting, fund raising, and partnerships: Strategies that work.* Thousand Oaks, CA: Corwin Press.

Periodicals

Catalog of Federal Domestic Assistance—https://www.cfda.gov

The Chronicle of Philanthropy—http://philanthropy.com

Congressional Record—http://thomas.loc.gov/home/thomas.php

The Federal Register—https://www.federalregister.gov

Websites

The Foundation Center—http://www.fdncenter.org

    Provides the most current information on more than 120,000 private and corporate foundations.

Free Cycle—http://www.freecycle.org

    An online place to give what you have and don't need or to receive what you need and don't have with the goal of keeping useful items out of landfills.

Fundsnet Services—http://www.fundsnetservices.com

    Offers information and links to many funders by category.

Grantmaking at ED—http://www.ed.gov/fund/grant/about/grantmaking
> This site provides detailed information regarding the discretionary grants process at the U.S. Department of Education.

Grants.gov—http://www.grants.gov
> Details information on more than 1,000 grant programs.

Grant Wrangler—http://www.grantwrangler.com
> A biweekly bulletin update on the latest K–12 teacher and school grants.

SchoolGrants—http://k12grants.org
> Provides online and print publication regarding granting agencies. Also provides a tutorial CD on the grant writing process.

References

ARCH. (1992). *Creative fund-raising activities.* Chapel Hill, NC: ARCH National Resources Center for Crisis Nurseries and Respite Care Services.

Bock, M. (2012). Schools tap into online fundraising to expand budgets. *Education Week, 32*(5), 9.

Brock, D. H. (2009). Show us the money! Planning and preparation can help you get ed tech stimulus funding. *Learning & Leading With Technology, 37*(1), 22–25.

Gensheimer, C. F. (1993). *Raising funds for your child's school.* New York, NY: Walker.

Graham, E. (n.d.). Principals do the darndest things. *PTO Today.* Retrieved from http://www.ptotoday.com/pto-today-articles/article/614-principals-do-the-darndest-things

Jacob K. Javits Gifted and Talented Students Education Act, H.R. 637, 106 Cong. (1990).

Karnes, F. A., & Stephens, K. R. (2005). *How to get money for your classroom and school* (Rev. ed.). Waco, TX: Prufrock Press.

Karnes, F. A., Stephens, K. R., & Samel, B. (1999). Fund development in gifted education: An untapped resource. *Gifted Child Today, 22*(5), 30–33, 52.

Palent, S. A. (1985). *Fund raising for park, recreation, and conservation agencies.* Washington, DC: National Park Service.

Rikard, G. (2008, August). Money for the asking: Writing small grants for physical education. *JOPERD: The Journal of Physical Education, Recreation & Dance,* 3–15.

School fundraising auctions go online. (2007, May). *District Administration, 43*(5), 17.

Spencer, G. (2009). *Fundraising ideas from A to Z.* Monmouth, OR: Cosmic Raccoon Press.

Stephens, K. R. (2011). Federal and state response to the gifted and talented. *Journal of Applied School Psychology, 27,* 306–318.

Swan, J. (1990). *Fund raising for the small public library.* New York, NY: Neal-Schuman.

Trash to cash: Making money for your school. (2011). *Curriculum Review, 51*(3), 6.

Walsh, E. (1990). Fund raising made easy. *Parks and Recreation, 25*(10), 60–63, 78.

Wereley, J. (1992). Developing and maintaining a school partnership. In C. S. Hyman (Ed.), *The school-community cookbook: Recipes for successful projects in the schools: A "how-to" manual for teachers, parents, and community* (pp. 88–93). Baltimore: Jewish Community Federation of Baltimore, Children of Harvey and Lyn Meyerhoff Philanthropic Fund, Fund for Educational Excellence.

ABOUT THE EDITORS

Frances A. Karnes, Ph.D., served as Distinguished Professor and Director of the Frances A. Karnes Center for Gifted Studies at the University of Southern Mississippi before retiring. She also directed the Leadership Studies Program and is widely known for her research, innovative programs, and leadership training. She is author or coauthor of more than 200 published papers and is coauthor or coeditor of 74 books. Her work is often cited as the authority on gifted children and the law. She is extensively involved in university activities and civic and professional organizations in the community. Her honors include: Faculty Research Award, Honorary Doctorate from Quincy University, Mississippi Legislature Award for Academic Excellence in Higher Education, USM Professional Service Award, USM Basic Research Award, Rotary International Jean Harris Award, Woman of Achievement Award from the Hattiesburg Women's Forum, Distinguished Alumni Award from the University of Illinois, Lifetime Innovation Award from the University of Southern Mississippi and University Distinguished Professor from the University of Southern

Mississippi, and TeachTechTopia's Top 10 Most Influential Special Education Professors. The Board of Trustees of Mississippi Institutions of Higher Learning honored her by naming the research, instructional, and service center she founded at USM the Frances A. Karnes Center for Gifted Studies.

Suzanne M. Bean, Ph.D., Professor Emeritus of Mississippi University for Women (MUW), is now serving as an education and leadership consultant working with schools, colleges and universities, nonprofit community agencies, and businesses across the south. She is the author of the first congressional request that established the Roger F. Wicker Center for Creative Learning at MUW. She served as the founding director through 2010 and under her leadership, the Center received more than $13 million of grant funding for projects which have improved communities and schools across Mississippi. She serves as President of the board of directors for Mississippi Association for Partners in Education. Dr. Bean was awarded three of the highest honors MUW offers, Outstanding Faculty Member, the Kossen Award of Excellence, and the MUW Medal of Excellence. She was also awarded Educator of the Year by the Columbus-Lowndes Development LINK and the Town and Tower Award of Service by the university and community organization. Dr. Bean was also recognized by the Mississippi Legislature and Mississippi Institutions of Higher Learning as Outstanding Faculty Member at the Higher Education Appreciation Day. She has coauthored seven books and had numerous publications in professional journals. She is a member of Leadership Mississippi and has served as President of the Mississippi Association of Gifted Children and Director of the Mississippi Governor's School.

ABOUT THE AUTHORS

Dong Gun An is a doctoral candidate of gifted and creative education in the Department of Educational Psychology at the University of Georgia (UGA). She has taught Korean and has been named the Outstanding Teaching Assistant at UGA. She has received an American Association of University Women (AAUW) International Fellowship. Her research interests are in creative cognition and creativity assessment. She earned her M.S. in Culture Technology from the Korean Advanced Institute of Science and Technology (KAIST) in Korea. Prior to her work in gifted and creative education, she worked as a researcher in the Digital Storytelling & Cognition Laboratory and the Semantic Web Research Center in KAIST. She authored the book, *Educational Robot: An Educational Revolution*.

Kevin D. Besnoy, Ph.D., earned his doctorate in Curriculum, Instruction, and Special Education with an emphasis in gifted education and instructional technology in 2006 from The University of Southern Mississippi. From 2006–2011, Dr. Besnoy worked at Northern Kentucky University, where he specialized in integrating technology in elementary and gifted educations curriculum. In addition, he cofounded the Institute for Talent Development and Gifted Studies at Northern Kentucky. Today, Dr. Besnoy is an assistant professor at The University of Alabama. His research interests focus on developing a theoretical model for creating a sustainable classroom digital ecosystem, documenting advocacy experiences of parents of twice-exceptional children, and identifying giftedness among culturally diverse populations. Dr. Besnoy has more than a decade's experience developing, implementing, and evaluating K–12 curricula for gifted and talented children. He is currently conducting research investigating teacher and student readiness to teach and learn with technology. In particular, Dr. Besnoy is interested in the nature of the various factors that determine readiness and how they impact technology integration in the gifted education classroom.

Elissa Brown, Ph.D., is a Distinguished Lecturer and Director of the Hunter College Center for Gifted Studies and Education. Previously, she was the Director of Teacher and Leader Education Programs and Gifted Education at the North Carolina Department of Public Instruction. From 2002–2007, she was the Director of the Center for Gifted Education at the College of William and Mary in Williamsburg, VA. She has served as a state director of gifted programs, a USED grant manager, a district program coordinator, a principal of a specialized high school, and a teacher of gifted students. As a professor, Elissa coordinates and teaches the advanced certificate program in gifted and talented and has served as an adjunct professor at several universities, including Rutgers and Duke University. She is a published author in the field of gifted education and presents widely. She was the recipient of the 2012 Distinguished Service Award from the N.C. Association for Gifted & Talented, the 2007 Dean's award at the College of William and Mary, and the 2004 Early Leader award from the National Association for Gifted Children. She has three grown children and lives in East Harlem.

Kate Brown, Ph.D., is the director of outreach and innovation at Mississippi University for Women and a past director of the Mississippi Governor's School. A former teacher of the gifted, Dr. Brown served more than 10 years on the board of the Mississippi Association for Gifted Children, holding the position of president from 2004–2006. Her major areas of interest include the development of emotional intelligence and leadership in youth and adults. From 2002–2006, Dr. Brown was the project director and principal investigator for the CHAMPS Project, the only Javits grant for gifted education ever awarded in the state of Mississippi. In 2008, she was awarded the Frances A. Karnes Award for Excellence in Gifted Education for significant contributions toward the improvement and advancement of gifted education. A frequent presenter at state and national conferences, Dr. Brown developed the IMPACT Leadership Model and provides training in leadership and personal development to corporate, educational, and nonprofit entities. Since 2007, Dr. Brown has been engaged in community development work in Kenya.

Carolyn M. Callahan, Ph.D., is currently Commonwealth Professor of Education at the University of Virginia. In addition to developing and overseeing the master's and doctoral programs in gifted education and teaching classes in gifted education, Dr. Callahan developed the Summer and Saturday Enrichment Programs at UVA and has been the principal investigator on projects of the National Research Center on the Gifted and Talented for more than 20 years and principal investigator on four Javits grants. She has been recognized as Outstanding Professor of the Commonwealth of Virginia and Distinguished Scholar of the National Association for Gifted Children (NAGC) and has served as President of the National Association for Gifted Children and the Association for the Gifted and as editor of *Gifted Child Quarterly*. She currently serves as Association Editor for NAGC. Dr. Callahan has published more than 200 articles and 50 book chapters on the topics of evaluation of gifted programs, gifted females, curriculum, and the identification of gifted students. She is the coeditor of the recently published books, *Fundamentals of Gifted Education: Considering Multiple Perspectives* and *Critical Issues in Gifted Education* (2nd ed.).

Sarah Marie Catalana is a doctoral student in educational psychology at the University of Georgia in the Gifted and Creative Education program. She has taught high school biology, undergraduate educational psychology courses, and creative science classes for gifted children. She recently accepted a position as an independent contractor for the Center for Childhood Creativity in California. She is a member of the National Association for Gifted Children and the American Psychological Association. Her research interests include unique career pressures of gifted children and the importance of creative transformation in viewing personal problems as opportunities for growth. She holds a bachelor's degree in biology, as well as certification in secondary education from Wofford College, and has spent time studying and teaching abroad in Ecuador.

Bonnie Cramond, Ph.D., is the Director of the Torrance Center for Creativity and Talent Development at the University of Georgia and a professor of Educational Psychology there. She has been a member of the Board of Directors of the National Association for Gifted Children, editor of the *Journal of Secondary Gifted Education*, and is on several editorial and advisory boards. An international speaker and consultant who has been to 33 countries, she has also been a speaker at several national, regional, and local conferences. She has published numerous articles and chapters, a book on creativity research, and teaches classes on giftedness and creativity. In fact, she is a survivor of parenting two gifted and creative people (so far). She is particularly interested in the identification and nurturance of creativity, especially among individuals considered at risk because of their different way of thinking, such as those misdiagnosed with ADHD, emotional problems, or those who drop out.

Laurie J. Ecke is a teacher and the Assistant Director for Innovative and Advanced Programs for Hall County Schools in Gainesville, GA. She began her teaching career as a teacher of the gifted in middle and high school math and literature after earning a B.A. in English Literature from the University of Georgia and an M.Ed. in Math Education from the University of North Georgia. She is a Ph.D. candidate in Gifted and Creative Education at UGA. Currently, she teaches the gifted endorsement courses for Pioneer RESA in northeast Georgia and is an International Baccalaureate Examiner and past IB Coordinator. Mrs. Ecke is a member of NAGC and a Region Representative for the Georgia Association for Gifted Children.

Stephanie Ferguson, Ph.D., is Executive Director of Early College and Director of the Program for the Exceptionally Gifted (PEG) at Mary Baldwin College in Staunton, VA. Her professional experience includes 10 years of middle and secondary teaching in Louisiana in general and gifted education as well as academic counseling; education faculty positions at various universities and colleges across the country, including being a Certified Advanced Facilitator for the School of Advanced Studies at the University of Phoenix; and numerous presentations and publications at the state, regional, national, and international levels. She is the author of *Social and Emotional Teaching Strategies* published by Prufrock Press. Dr. Ferguson's research interests include single-gender educational settings, advocacy for the gifted, integrating the affective domain in curricula, radical acceleration/early college entrance, arts integration across the curricula, uses of bibliotherapy/cinematherapy, and developing teacher leaders. She may be contacted at sakfergusonphd@gmail.com.

Shelagh A. Gallagher, Ph.D., spent 13 years leading the gifted education program at the University of North Carolina at Charlotte prior to her current role as consultant and author. She also spent 3 years working at the Illinois Mathematics and Science Academy, one of the nation's premiere high schools for gifted students, where she began her work in Problem-Based Learning (PBL). While at the Center for Gifted Education at the College of William and Mary, she was the first manager of the Javits grant that produced the William and Mary PBL science units. She then went on to direct two Javits grants, each of which produced PBL curricula. She has received the National Association for Gifted Children (NAGC) Curriculum Division award five times for her PBL units. Dr. Gallagher has conducted research, made presentations, and published articles on topics including personality attributes associated with giftedness, gender differences in mathematics performance, questioning for higher order thinking, developmental and academic needs of gifted adolescents, and twice-exceptional students. She served two terms on the NAGC Board of Directors and continues to serve in leadership roles for NAGC. She is also a Senior Fellow at Yunasa, a program for highly gifted youth offered through the Institute for Educational Advancement. She has received the Distinguished Service Award and the James J. Gallagher Award for Advocacy from the North Carolina Association for Gifted and Talented, the Provost's Award for Teaching Excellence from UNC Charlotte, and the Article of the Year Award from NAGC.

Cindy M. Gilson, Ph.D., is an Assistant Professor of Gifted Education at University of North Carolina at Charlotte. Her research interests include differentiated curriculum and instruction for gifted and talented students, teachers' questioning and listening behaviors within the context of classroom discourse, and professional development.

Krystal K. Goree, Ph.D., is the director of clinical practice in the School of Education at Baylor University in Waco, TX, and teaches classes in gifted and talented education at Baylor University. She has worked in the field of gifted education for more than 20 years in the roles of parent, teacher, consultant, presenter, and program administrator. She serves as chair of the Texas Education Agency Commissioner's Advisory Council on the Education of Gifted and Talented Students and provides consultation and program evaluation for school districts. In addition to presenting at state and national conferences, she has authored or coauthored articles and book chapters. She is past president of the Texas Association for the Gifted and Talented and serves as editor of its journal, *Tempo*, and as senior editor and product reviewer for *Gifted Child Today*.

Susan K. Johnsen, Ph.D., is a professor in the Department of Educational Psychology at Baylor University in Waco, TX, where she directs the Ph.D. program and programs related to gifted and talented education. She is editor of *Gifted Child Today* and coauthor of *Identifying Gifted Students: A Practical Guide*, the *Independent Study Program*, *RtI for Gifted Students*, *Using the National Gifted Education Standards for University Teacher Preparation Programs*, *Using the National Gifted Education Standards for PreK–12 Professional Development*, and more than 200 articles, monographs, technical reports, and other books related to gifted education. She has written three tests used in identifying gifted students: Test of Mathematical Abilities for Gifted Students (TOMAGS), Test of Nonverbal Intelligence (TONI-4), and Screening Assessment for Gifted Elementary and Middle School Students (SAGES-2). She serves on the Board of Examiners of the National Council for Accreditation of Teacher Education and is a reviewer and auditor of programs in gifted education. She is past president of The Association for the Gifted (TAG), Council for Exceptional Children and past president of the Texas Association for Gifted and Talented (TAGT). She has received awards for her work in the field of education, including NAGC's President's Award, TAG's Leadership Award, TAGT's President's Award, and Baylor University's Investigator Award, Teaching Award, and Contributions to the Academic Community award. She may be reached at Susan_Johnsen@baylor.edu.

Joan D. Lewis, Ph.D., is a professor emeritus in the department of teacher education at the University of Nebraska at Kearney. Until her retirement, she directed the graduate program in gifted and talented education for the University of Nebraska system, developing all of its six endorsement classes, including for distance transmission, later converting to interactive online delivery. She has published widely and speaks frequently at local, state, regional, national, and international conferences in the areas of alternative assessment, gifted girls, public relations and advocacy, use of RtI for identifying and serving gifted and talented learners, rural issues, social and emotional needs of gifted learners, and uses of technology in education. The most recent focus of Dr. Lewis' research is on the role of school principals in supporting quality education for gifted learners. Prufrock Press published her books, *Advocacy for the Gifted* (2008) and *The Challenge of Educating the Gifted in Rural Areas* (2009), as part of its Practical Strategies Series in Gifted Education. Her work with local and state associations in gifted education has spanned more than 30 years. Upon retirement, the Nebraska Association for Gifted presented her with a plaque for "lifelong work in gifted education."

D. Betsy McCoach, Ph.D., is a professor in the educational psychology department at the University of Connecticut. Betsy has published more than 75 journal articles, book chapters, and books. Betsy served as the founding coeditor for the *Journal of Advanced Academics*, and she is the current coeditor of *Gifted Child Quarterly*. Betsy serves as a Co-Principal Investigator and research methodologist on several federally funded research grants, and she has served as the Research Methodologist for the National Research Center on the Gifted and Talented for the last 7 years.

Suehyeon Paek is a doctoral student in the Department of Educational Psychology at the University of Georgia. She has empirically researched creativity, divergent thinking, and problem finding. Mrs. Paek is a graduate assistant in the

Torrance Center for Creativity and Talent Development and has assisted with the Torrance Tests of Creative Thinking scoring certificate program, Duke TIP program, and taught elementary school students for 7 years in Korea.

Hyeri Park is a doctoral student in the Gifted and Creative Education (GCE) Program at the University of Georgia (UGA). She holds an M.A. in curriculum and instruction from Kyungnam University in Korea. Before joining the GCE program at UGA, she served for $3\frac{1}{2}$ years as a research fellow in the Institute of Gifted Education in Science (IGES) at Kyungnam University. With support from several national grants, she had various opportunities to conduct numerous studies for the nation in the gifted education field. Currently, she serves as a teaching assistant for graduate courses on gifted education and creativity at UGA; her research interests center around identification of the gifted and creativity studies.

Sandra Parks has served as a curriculum and staff development consultant on teaching thinking since 1978. Since 1983, she has presented professional development institutes for the Association for Supervision and Curriculum Development and at national and regional conferences. She conducted research on teaching critical thinking at the Indiana State University Laboratory School and was founding president of the Indiana Association for the Gifted. She taught gifted education courses at the University of North Florida and the University of Miami. With Robert Schwartz, Parks founded the National Center for Teaching Thinking.

Sally M. Reis, Ph.D., is the Vice Provost of Academic Affairs and a Board of Trustees Distinguished Professor at the University of Connecticut. She holds the Letitia Neag Morgan Endowed Chair in Educational Psychology. She was a public school teacher for 15 years, 11 of which were spent working with academically talented students on the elementary, junior high, and high school levels. She is a well-known scholar and has authored or coauthored more than 250 articles, books, book chapters, monographs, and technical reports. Her research interests are related to academic talent development, differentiation of instruction, enrichment programs, and diverse groups of talented students. She is also interested in extensions of the Schoolwide Enrichment Model for academically talented students and as a way to expand offerings and provide general enrichment to identify talents and potentials in all students. Dr. Reis is a past President of the National Association for Gifted Children, has earned multiple awards for scholarship, including awards for distinguished scholarship, and is a fellow of the American Psychological Association.

Sara J. Renzulli, Ph.D., is an academic advisor in the College of Liberal Arts and also serves as an adjunct faculty member in the Department of Educational

Psychology at the University of Connecticut. She graduated with her Ph.D. in counseling psychology and counselor education in May of 2013 from the University of Connecticut. Sara's research interests include academic counseling strategies to enhance academic success and the effectiveness of learning strategy instruction at the postsecondary level. Sara is also interested in twice-exceptional students and the compensation strategies they use to succeed in school.

Tracy Riley, Ph.D., specializes in gifted and talented education as an associate professor at Massey University in New Zealand. She teaches undergraduate and postgraduate courses in the field in addition to supervising postgraduate research. She is the coeditor of *APEX: The New Zealand Journal of Gifted Education* and is on the editorial board of *Gifted Child Today*. An active advocate for gifted and talented students, Dr. Riley has served on numerous Ministry of Education advisory groups and has coauthored the Ministry handbook, *Gifted and Talented Students: Meeting Their Needs in New Zealand Schools* (2000, 2012). She publishes and presents widely at both national and international levels. In 2007, Dr. Riley was awarded the Vice-Chancellor's Award for Sustained Excellence in Teaching and was the recipient of a national Tertiary Teaching Excellence Award. She is a past member of the executive committee of the Ako Aoteoroa Academy of Tertiary Teaching Excellence and is chairperson of the board for giftEDnz: The Professional Association for Gifted Education.

Julia Link Roberts, Ed.D., is the Mahurin Professor of Gifted Studies at Western Kentucky University. She is Executive Director of The Center for Gifted Studies and the Carol Martin Gatton Academy of Mathematics and Science in Kentucky. Dr. Roberts is a member of the Executive Committee of the World Council for Gifted and Talented Children, the president of The Association for the Gifted, and a member of the board of the Kentucky Association for Gifted Education. She has authored or coauthored seven books, numerous chapters, articles, and columns on advocacy, differentiation, products, innovation, and gifted education. Dr. Roberts has been honored with the NAGC Distinguished Service Award, the Acorn Award (outstanding professor at a Kentucky 4-year college or university), the Kentucky Association of School Administrator's Award for Visionary Leadership, and the WKU Spirit Award. She directs summer and Saturday programming for elementary, middle, and high school young people. She also teaches graduate courses in gifted education and provides professional development across the country.

Richard A. Roberts is a professor of teacher education in the School of Teacher Education at Western Kentucky University. Dr. Roberts has been a leading developer of the Kentucky Teacher Internship Program, and he directs the internship program at Western Kentucky University. He has been actively involved in providing various types of support for programs for children and young people who are gifted and talented, educators, and parents that are offered by The Center for Gifted Studies.

Noparat Sricharoen is a Ph.D. Candidate in the Gifted and Creative Education program at the University of Georgia. Her doctoral work at UGA is supported by the Institute for the Promotion of Teaching Science and Technology (IPST) in Thailand. Upon graduation, Mrs. Sricharoen will return to IPST as a researcher. Her interests include developing creativity tests and curricula in the sciences. Noparat is currently researching the use of creativity tests as a tool for identifying and assessing gifted students in the sciences and in order to help science students effectively master content, skills, and creative thinking abilities.

Dana E. Seymour is the Director of the Teacher Education for Rural Middle Schools (TERMS) project at Mississippi State University, where she is also a doctoral student in educational psychology. Professional areas of interest are middle level education, alternate route teacher preparation, and models for virtual teacher mentoring and support. Current research includes critical thinking dispositions and need for cognition, and the traits and beliefs of alternate route teacher candidates. A member of the second graduating class of Louisiana's only public residential high school for gifted students some 25 years ago, she knows firsthand how appropriate gifted education can change lives and improve futures.

Del Siegle, Ph.D., is a professor in gifted and talented education and Head of the Department of Educational Psychology at the University of Connecticut. He is a past president of the Montana Association of Gifted and Talented Education (Montana AGATE), past president of the National Association for Gifted Children (NAGC), and chair of the Research on Giftedness, Creativity, and Talent SIG of the American Educational Research Association (AERA). Along with D. Betsy McCoach, he is coeditor of *Gifted Child Quarterly*. He writes a technology column for *Gifted Child Today*. Dr. Siegle is coauthor with Gary Davis and Sylvia Rimm of the popular textbook, *Education of the Gifted and Talented*. He is also author of a new book, *The Underachieving Gifted Child: Recognizing, Understanding, and Reversing Underachievement*. Prior to becoming a professor, Del worked with gifted and talented students in Montana.

Dorothy A. Sisk, Ph.D., holds an endowed chair in education of gifted students at Lamar University in Beaumont, TX. Dr. Sisk is an international consultant focusing on leadership and creativity development. She was a professor at the University of South Florida, coordinating programs for training teachers of the gifted, and the former director of the U.S. Office of Gifted and Talented in Washington, DC. She currently directs the C.W. Conn Gifted Child Center at Lamar University and teaches the courses for the endorsement in gifted education. She received the Distinguished Leaders Award from the Creative Education Foundation (CEF) in 1989; the Distinguished Service Award from the National Association for Gifted Children (NAGC) in 1983 and 1994; the Creative Lifetime Achievement Award from CEF in 1994; and she was selected for the Hall of Fame Award of CEF in 2005. Dr. Sisk served as one of the founders and first president of the American Creativity Association and president of The Association for Gifted and Talented (TAG), the Florida Association for Gifted, and the World Council for Gifted and Talented Children (WCGTC), where she was executive administrator, and editor of *Gifted International* from 1980–1990. She has conducted training sessions throughout the United States and internationally. Dr. Sisk is author of *Creative Teaching of the Gifted* and *Making Great Kids Greater;* coauthor with Doris Shallcross of *Leadership: Making Things Happen, The Growing Person,* and *Intuition: An Inner Way of Knowing;* coauthor with E. Paul Torrance of *Gifted Children in the Regular Classroom* and *Spiritual Intelligence: Developing Higher Level Consciousness;* coauthor with Susan Israel and Cathy Block of *Collaborative Literacy: Using Gifted Strategies to Enrich Learning for Every Student;* and coauthor with Hava Vidergor of *Enhancing the Gift of Leadership: Innovative Programs for all Grade Levels.* In addition, she has contributed numerous articles and chapters in books on gifted education.

Kristen R. Stephens, Ph.D., is an associate professor of the practice in the Program in Education at Duke University, where she directs the Academically/ Intellectually Gifted Licensure Program for teachers. Prior to this appointment, Dr. Stephens served as the gifted education research specialist for the Duke University Talent Identification Program. She is the coauthor of numerous books and coeditor of the Practical Strategies Series in Gifted Education (Prufrock Press), a series comprised of more than 30 books on issues pertinent to gifted child education. Dr. Stephens has served on the board of directors for the National Association for Gifted Children and is past president of the North Carolina Association for Gifted and Talented. She also serves on the board of directors for the American Association for Gifted Children.

Erin E. Sullivan is a school psychologist in Mansfield, CT, and will complete her doctorate at the University of Connecticut in 2014 in school psychology and gifted education. Erin's research interests are in the area of underachievement of gifted and talented students and nonverbal learning disabilities.

Sarah E. Sumners, Ph.D., is an assistant research scientist and the assistant director of the E. Paul Torrance Center for Creativity and Talent Development at the University of Georgia. She is on the review board for several peer-reviewed journals, is a member of the National Association for Gifted Children, has taught graduate courses on teacher education and creativity, and has written several grants to fund creativity research at the Torrance Center. Before joining the Torrance Center, Dr. Sumners served as the principal investigator for the CHAMPS Mathematics and Science Partnership and Project Citizen grants for the state of Mississippi. In this capacity, she designed and orchestrated considerable professional development opportunities for teachers in the state. Prior to working for the Center for Creative Learning at Mississippi University for Women, Dr. Sumners served as the project manager for the Jacob K. Javits grant for gifted and talented education at the Mississippi School for Mathematics and Science, where she also taught high school social studies. Dr. Sumners has a wide range of experience in grant writing, teaching, and professional development. She holds an M.Ed. in gifted studies from Mississippi University for Women and a Ph.D. in Curriculum and Instruction from Mississippi State University.

Royal Toy, Ed.D., is an assistant professor of gifted studies in the department of education at Mississippi University for Women (MUW) in Columbus, MS, where he is also the director of the Mississippi Governor's School, a summer residential program for gifted youth. Toy also coordinates the Summer Discovery program for elementary school youth at MUW, and has coordinated the Leadership Enrichment Program at the University of Northern Colorado since 2005. Toy is president-elect of the National Conference of Governor's Schools (NCoGS). He has presented at national and international conferences on the Autonomous Learner Model (ALM), and his professional interests include young gifted children, characteristics of individuals who are gifted, twice-exceptionality and underachievement, and the ALM.

Burak Türkman is a doctoral student in the Gifted and Creative Education program at the University of Georgia. Originally from Turkey, he received a bachelor's degree in gifted education from Istanbul University and then worked at Eyuboglu Educational Institutions with gifted students. Upon receiving a prestigious scholarship given by the Turkish Ministry of Education, he pursued his graduate studies at Purdue University, obtaining a master's degree in education. His research interests include divergent thinking, dreams and creativity, curriculum differentiation for gifted students, cognitive abilities, task motivation, emotional issues, and guidance.

Sonya Türkman is a doctoral student in the art education program at the University of Georgia. Sonya studied at the Savannah College of Art and Design, and her work reflects her persistent interest in child art and the influence of the urban landscape on the art made by children and adults. She holds a Master of Arts from SCAD and Bachelor of Business Administration from the Terry College at UGA.

Joyce VanTassel-Baska, Ed.D., is the Smith Professor Emerita at The College of William and Mary in Virginia, where she developed a graduate program and a research and development center in gifted education. Formerly, she initiated and directed the Center for Talent Development at Northwestern University. She has also served as the state director of gifted programs for Illinois, as a regional director of a gifted service center in the Chicago area, as coordinator of gifted programs for the Toledo, OH, public school system, and as a teacher of gifted high school students in English and Latin. Dr. VanTassel-Baska has published widely, including 27 books and more than 500 refereed journal articles, book chapters, and scholarly reports. Her major research interests are on the talent development process and effective curricular interventions with the gifted.

INDEX